THE BOOK OF KINGS

VOLUME TWO

THE BOOK OF KINGS

A Royal Genealogy

COMPILED BY
ARNOLD McNAUGHTON

VOLUME TWO
THE FAMILIES

QUADRANGLE/THE NEW YORK TIMES BOOK COMPANY

THE BOOK OF KINGS

A Royal Genealogy

Library of Congress Catalog Card Number: 72–77538
International Standard Book Number: 0–8129–0280–7
Published simultaneously in the United States and Canada.

Printed in Great Britain.

Set in 14 point Monotype Bembo, leaded 2 points, and printed by Butler & Tanner Limited, Frome, Somerset, on Dalmore Antique Laid paper supplied by Frank Grunfeld Limited.

CONTENTS

XVII

THE FAMILIES OF GREAT BRITAIN

XVII. ABEL SMITH 1, from page 230

Sir Henry Abel Smith
March 8, 1900, London —
m. October 24, 1931, Balcombe

* **May,** Lady Cambridge, born Princess of Teck, daughter of the Earl of Athlone, born Prince Alexander of Teck, and of his wife, Princess Alice of Great Britain and Ireland, Princess of Albany.
January 23, 1906, Claremont, Esher, England —

Issue: 1. Anne Abel Smith (1932–)
m. David Liddell-Grainger (1930–)
see: *Liddell-Grainger* XVII, page 529

2. Richard Abel Smith (1933–)
m. Marcia Kendrew (1940–)
see: *Abel Smith* XVII 2, below

3. Elizabeth Abel Smith (1936–)
m. Peter Wise (1936–)
see: *Wise* XVII, page 536

XVII. Abel Smith 2, from above

* **Richard Abel Smith,** only son of Sir Henry Abel Smith.
October 11, 1933, Kensington Palace —
m. April 28, 1960, London

Marcia Kendrew, daughter of Douglas Kendrew and of his wife,
March 27, 1940, Gerrards Cross —

Issue: 1. Katherine Emma Abel Smith
March 11, 1961, Windsor —

XVII. ALLEN 1, from page 329

Anthony Bryan Allen, M.D.
May 6, 1931, Connah's Quay, Wales —
m. December 20, 1952, London
* **Nadeshda (Nadajda) Dimitrievna,** Princess Romanova, daughter of Prince Dimitrii Aleksandrovich of Russia and of his first wife, Countess Marina Sergeievna Golenistcheva-Koutouzova.
July 4, 1933, Boulogne-sur-Seine, France —

Issue: 1. Penelope Allen
February 27, 1953, London —

2. Marina Allen
July 10, 1955, London —

3. Alexandra Allen
December 10, 1958, Redruth, Cornwall, England —

XVII. AMBLER 1, from page 502

John Kenneth Ambler
June 6, 1924, London —
m. June 30, 1964, Oeland, Sweden
* **Margaretha,** Princess of Sweden, daughter of Prince Gustaf Adolf of Sweden, Duke of Västerbotten, and of his wife, Princess Sibylle of Saxe-Coburg and Gotha.
October 31, 1934, Haga Castle, Sweden —

Issue: 1. Sibylla Louise Ambler
April 14, 1965, London —

2. Charles Edward Ambler
July 14, 1966, London —

3. James Patrick Ambler
June 10, 1967, Oxford —

XVII. ARMSTRONG-JONES (Snowdon) 1, from page 15

Antony Armstrong-Jones, created First Earl of Snowdon, October 3, 1961.
March 7, 1930, London —
m. May 6, 1960, Westminster Abbey
★ **Margaret,** Princess of Great Britain and Ireland, daughter of King George VI of Great Britain and Ireland and of his wife, Lady Elizabeth Bowes-Lyon.
August 21, 1930, Glamis Castle, Scotland —

Issue: 1. David Armstrong-Jones, Viscount Linley
November 3, 1961, Clarence House, London —

2. Sarah Armstrong-Jones
May 1, 1964, Kensington Palace —

XVII. BALFOUR 1, from page 631

Neil Balfour
, 1934, —
m. September , 1969, London
★ **Elizabeth,** Princess of Yugoslavia, daughter of Prince Paul of Yugoslavia and of his wife, Princess Olga of Greece and Denmark.
April 7, 1936, Belgrade, Yugoslavia —
(She m. 1: and divorced: Howard Oxenburg – see: *Oxenburg* XXIV, page 1022.)

Issue: 1. Nicholas Balfour
, 1970, London —

XVII. BRANDRAM 1, from page 194

Richard Campbell Andrew Brandram
August 5, 1911, Bexhill-on-Sea, England —
m. April 21, 1947, The Royal Palace, Athens, Greece
★ **Ekaterini (Catherine),** Princess of Greece and Denmark, daughter of King Konstantinos I of the Hellenes and of his wife, Princess Sophie of Prussia.
May 14, 1913, Athens —

Issue: 1. Paul Brandram
April 1, 1948, Baghdad, Iraq —

XVII. BUTTER 1, from page 534

David Henry Butter
March 18, 1924, London —
m. November 5, 1946,
* **Myra Alice Wernher,** daughter of Major General Sir Harold Wernher, 3rd Baronet, and of his wife, Countess Anastasia Mikhailovna de Torby.
March 8, 1925, Edinburgh, Scotland —

Issue: 1. Sandra Elizabeth Zia Butter
July 26, 1948, London —

2. Maralyn Davina Butter
March 22, 1950, London —

3. Rohays Georgina Butter
April 9, 1952, London —

4. Georgina Marguerite Butter
July 9, 1956, London —

5. Charles Harold Alexander Butter
April 10, 1960, London —

XVII. CAMPBELL (Argyll) 1, from page 11

John Campbell, Marquess of Lorne, 9th Duke of Argyll. (Governor-General of Canada 1878–1883.)
August 6, 1845, London — May 2, 1914, Kent House, Isle of Wight
m. March 21, 1871, Windsor Castle
* **Louise,** Princess of Great Britain and Ireland, daughter of Queen Victoria of Great Britain and Ireland, and of her husband, Prince Albert of Saxe-Coburg and Gotha, Duke of Saxony.
March 18, 1848, Buckingham Palace — December 3, 1939, London

No Issue.

XVII. CARNEGIE (Southesk) 1, from page 518

Charles Carnegie, 11th Earl of Southesk.
September 23, 1893, Edinburgh, Scotland —
m. 1: November 12, 1924, London
* **Maud,** Princess of Great Britain and Ireland, born Lady Duff, daughter of Sir Alexander Duff, First Duke of Fife and of his wife, Princess Louise of Great Britain and Ireland.
She was created Princess of Great Britain and Ireland by her maternal grandfather, King Edward VII, in November 1905.
April 3, 1893, East Sheen Lodge — December 14, 1945, London
m. 2: May 16, 1952, London
Evelyn Williams-Freeman, formerly Mrs. Campbell (widow), daughter of

Issue of first marriage:
1. The Honourable James Carnegie, Duke of Fife (1929–)
m. and divorced: The Honourable Caroline Cecily Dewar (1934–)
see: *Carnegie* XVII, 2, below

XVII. Carnegie 2, from above

* **James Carnegie,** Duke of Fife, only son of the 11th Earl of Southesk. Succeeded as Duke of Fife on the death of his maternal aunt in 1956.
September 23, 1929, London —
m. September 11, 1956, Perth. Divorced: December , 1966, Edinburgh, Scotland
Caroline Cecily Dewar, daughter of Sir Henry Dewar, 3rd Baron Forteviot, and of his wife, Cynthia Monica Starkie.
February 10, 1934, Bardowie Castle —

Issue: 1. Lady Alexandra Carnegie
June 20, 1959, London —

2. Charles, Lord Carnegie, Earl of Macduff
March 3, 1961, London —

XVII. COLEMAN

1, from page 340

Peter Coleman, the Reverend
August 28, 1928, London —
m. May 14, 1960, Vienna

* **Elisabeth,** Princess Reuss zu Köstritz, daughter of Prince Heinrich XXXIX Reuss zu Köstritz and of his wife, Countess Antonia zu Castell-Castell.
June 8, 1932, Vienna —

Issue: 1. Antonia Coleman
August 22, 1961, London —

2. Basil Henry Coleman
May 1, 1963, London —

3. Benedict Coleman
September 17, 1965, Taunton, Somerset —

XVII. DUFF (Fife)

1, from page 12

Alexander Duff, First Duke of Fife, created Duke on the day of his marriage by Queen Victoria.
November 10, 1849, London — January 29, 1912, Aswan, Egypt
m. July 27, 1889, Buckingham Palace

* **Louise,** Princess Royal of Great Britain and Ireland, daughter of King Edward VII of Great Britain and Ireland and of his wife, Princess Alexandra of Denmark.
February 20, 1867, Marlborough House — January 4, 1931, London

Issue: 1. Alexandra, Lady Duff, Duchess of Fife (1891–1956)
m. Arthur, Prince of Great Britain and Ireland, Prince of Connaught (1883–1938)
see: *Great Britain* (*Windsor*) I i–2, page 21

2. Maud, Lady Duff (1893–1945)
m. Sir Charles Carnegie, 11th Earl of Southesk (1893–)
see: *Carnegie* XVII, page 517

NOTE: Lady Alexandra and Lady Maud Duff were created Princesses of Great Britain and Ireland by their maternal grandfather, King Edward VII, in November 1905. Lady Alexandra succeeded her father, in her own right, to the Dukedom of Fife as Duchess of Fife on his death in 1912.

XVII. EARLE 1, from page 34

Sir George Foster Earle
February 8, 1890, Cottingham — December 11, 1965, Baggrave Hall, Leicester
m. December 8, 1915, London. Divorced: November 8, 1926, London
* **George Daphne FitzGeorge,** daughter of George FitzGeorge and of his wife, Rosa Frederica Baring.
February 23, 1889, London — June 1, 1954, Castiglione della Pescaia, Italy

No Issue.

XVII. FITZGEORGE-BALFOUR 1, from page 34

Robert Shekelton Balfour
March 7, 1869, Stirling — November 1, 1942, London
m. December 12, 1912, London
* **Mabel Iris FitzGeorge,** daughter of George FitzGeorge and of his wife, Rosa Frederica Baring.
September 23, 1886, London —
(She m. 2: Vladimir Emanuelovich, Prince Galitzine – see: *Galitzine* XXIII, page 981.)

Issue: 1. Victor FitzGeorge-Balfour (1913–)
m. Mary Diana Christian (1914–)
see: *FitzGeorge-Balfour* XVII, 2, below

XVII. FitzGeorge-Balfour 2, from above

* **General Sir Victor FitzGeorge-Balfour,** only son of Robert Shekelton Balfour.
September 15, 1913, London —
m. December 4, 1943, London
Mary Diana Christian, daughter of Arthur Christian and of his wife,
October 12, 1914, London —

Issue: 1. Diana Mary Christian FitzGeorge-Balfour
March 8, 1946, London —

2. Robin FitzGeorge-Balfour
June 5, 1951, London —

XVII. FITZGEORGE-HAMILTON 1, from page 35

Archibald Hamilton, 5th Baronet
December 10, 1876, London — March 18, 1939, Selsey, Hampshire
m. December 18, 1897, London. Divorced: , 1902,
* **Olga FitzGeorge,** daughter of Sir Adolphus FitzGeorge and of his second wife, Margarita Beatrice Daisy Watson.
June 11, 1878, — October 15, 1928, Rouen, France
(She m. 2: Robert Charlton Lane – see: *Lane* XVII, page 527.)

Issue: 1. George FitzGeorge-Hamilton (Flight Lieutenant R.A.F.)
December 30, 1898, London — May 18, 1918, , killed in action in World War I.

2. A daughter born and died May 5, 1902

XVII. GEDDES 1, from page 794

Alexander Campbell Geddes
September 24, 1911, Dublin, Ireland —
m. July 27, 1964, London
* **Maria Anna,** Altgräfin zu Salm-Reifferscheidt, Krautheim und Dyck, daughter of Fürst Franz Josef zu Salm-Reifferscheidt, Krautheim und Dyck, and of his wife, Princess Cäcilie zu Salm-Salm.
August 18, 1933, Alfter —

Issue: 1. Camilla Joanna Campbell Geddes
December 10, 1966, London —

2. Stephen George Campbell Geddes
June 28, 1969, London —

NOTE: The Hon. Alexander Campbell Geddes is a brother of The Honourable Margaret Campbell Geddes, widow of the late Prince Ludwig of Hesse and the Rhine – see: *Hesse and the Rhine* IV z–1, page 150.

XVII. GIBBS 1, from page 230

John Evelyn Gibbs (Colonel)
December 22, 1879, London — October 11, 1932, Tetbury
m. September 2, 1919, Windsor
* **Helena,** Lady Cambridge, born Princess of Teck, daughter of Prince Adolphus of Teck, Marquess of Cambridge, and of his wife, Lady Margaret Grosvenor
October 23, 1899, Grosvenor House, London — December 22, 1969, London

No Issue.

XVII. GOODMAN 1, from page 987

Philip Goodman
June 17, 1931, London —
m. March 7, 1957, London
* **Sophie Vladimirovna,** Countess Kleinmichel, daughter of Count Vladimir Petrovich Kleinmichel and of his wife, Countess Marie (Mariya) von Carlow.
March 27, 1930, London —

Issue: 1. Mary Goodman
October 20, 1959, Montreal, Canada —

2. Catherine Goodman
April 22, 1961, London —

3. Elizabeth Goodman
January 21, 1964, London —

4. Sophia Goodman
September 11, 1965, Richmond, Surrey —

XVII. GUINESS 1, from page 239

Desmond Guiness, The Honourable
September 8, 1932, London —
m. July 3, 1954, Oxford
* **Marie Gabriele,** Countess of Württemberg, daughter of Count Albrecht Eberhard of Württemberg and of his wife, Rosemary Blackadder.
September 21, 1933, London —

Issue: 1. Patrick Guiness
August 1, 1956, Dublin, Ireland —

2. Marina Guiness
August 16, 1957, Dublin —

XVII. HAMILTON 1, from page 532

James Hamilton, Marquess of Hamilton.
July 4, 1934, —
m. October 20, 1966, Westminster Abbey, London
* **Alexandra (Sascha) Anastasia Phillips,** daughter of Harold Pedro Phillips and of his wife, Georgina Wernher.
February 27, 1946, Tuscon, Arizona, USA —

Issue: 1. James Hamilton, Viscount Strabane
August 19, 1969, —

XVII. HENLEY 1, from page 917

Robert Anthony Henley
May 17, 1921, Sheffield —
m. February 18, 1947, Trieste
* **Leontine,** Princess Windisch-Graetz, daughter of Prince Eduard Windisch-Graetz and of his wife, Princess Alexandra (Alix) zu Ysenburg-Birstein.
July 11, 1925, Birstein, Germany —

Issue: 1. Alix Henley
October 6, 1950, Ipswich —

2. Marcus Henley
December 28, 1954, Singapore —

XVII. HESSELTINE I, from page 981

Nigel Hesseltine, son of Philip Hesseltine.
July 3, 1916, London —
m. August 14, 1938, Budapest, Hungary
* **Nataliya Borisovna,** Princess Galitzine, daughter of Prince Boris Dimitrievich Galitzine and of his wife, Countess Marie (Mariya) von Carlow.
January 15, 1920, Yalta, Crimea —

Issue: 1. Elizabeth Hesseltine (1939–)
m. Graham Nesbitt (1936–)
see: *Nesbitt* XVII, page 530

XVII. HICKS I, from page 154

David Nightingale Hicks
March 25, 1929, Little Coggeshall, Essex —
m. January 13, 1960, Romsey Abbey, Hampshire
* **Lady Pamela Mountbatten,** second daughter of The Earl Mountbatten of Burma and of his wife, The Honourable Edwina Ashley.
April 19, 1929, Barcelona, Spain —

Issue: 1. Edwina Hicks
December 24, 1961, London —

2. Ashley Hicks
July 18, 1963, London —

3. India Hicks
September 5, 1967, London —

XVII. HOHLER 1, from page 527

Edward Christopher Hohler
January 22, 1917, London —
m. November 14, 1939, Warblington. Divorced: July , 1961, London
* **Jane Lane,** daughter of Robert Charlton Lane and of his wife, Olga FitzGeorge.
June 4, 1919, London —
(She m. 2: Ronald Stratford Scrivener – see: *Scrivener* XVII, page 533.)

Issue: 1. Olga Hohler
October 11, 1940, Windsor —
(m. July 5, 1969, London, Godfrey Bland
1. A son, born February 27, 1972, London)

2. Philippa Hohler
January 13, 1942, Harrogate —
(m. February 5, 1966, London, William Sanders
1. Algernon William Robert Sanders, born March 18, 1967
2. Laline Marion Jane Sanders, born February 18, 1969
3. Marietta Sanders, born February 25, 1971)

3. Frederick Hohler
August 30, 1943, Windsor —
(m. September 7, 1968, Midhurst, Sussex, Sarah Gilbert
1. Alice Hohler, born August 28, 1970
2. Emily Hohler, born December 5, 1971)

4. Robert Hohler
October 2, 1947, Windsor —

XVII. HOPE-JOHNSTONE 1, from page 492

George Granville Hope-Johnstone
November 28, 1880, London — 1950s, somewhere in South Africa
m. December 4, 1913, Vierfontein, near Kronstadt, Germany. Separated:
* **Luise,** Princess of Hohenlohe-Oehringen, daughter of Prince Felix of Hohenlohe-Oehringen and of his wife, Princess Alexandrine von Hanau, Countess von Schaumburg.
January 26, 1867, Heidelberg — July 23, 1945, Gauting, near Munich
(She m. 1: Albrecht, Prince zu Waldeck und Pyrmont – see: *zu Waldeck und Pyrmont* XXI, page 898.)

XVII. Hope-Johnstone

1 continued

Issue: 1. Victor Hope-Johnstone (1914–)
m. and divorced: Pamela Maude Cobbald (1920–)
see: *Hope-Johnstone* XVII, 2, below

XVII. Hope-Johnstone

2, from above

* **Victor Hope-Johnstone,** son of George Hope-Johnstone.
June 2, 1914, Vierfontein, Germany —
m. March 23, 1943, London. Divorced: 1950
Pamela Maude Cobbald, daughter of Colonel John Murray Cobbald and of his wife, Lady Blanche Cavendish.
March 1, 1920, Sutton Hoo, Woodbridge, Suffolk —
(She m. 2: Ambrose Alec Patrick George Cadogan.)

Issue: 1. Philip Hope-Johnstone
December 26, 1943, Glenham Hall, Woodbridge —

2. Charles Hope-Johnstone
January 26, 1948, Wassenaar, The Netherlands —

XVII. HUNTINGTON-WHITELEY

1, from page 677

John Miles Huntington-Whiteley, maternal grandson of the late Sir Stanley Baldwin, late Prime Minister of Great Britain.
July 18, 1929, Fareham, Hampshire —
m. June 20, 1960, London
* **Viktoria,** Countess zu Castell-Rüdenhausen, daughter of Count Friedrich Wolfgang zu Castell-Rüdenhausen and of his wife, Princess Caroline Mathilde of Saxe-Coburg and Gotha.
February 26, 1935, Coburg, Germany —

Issue: 1. Alice Huntington-Whiteley
July 22, 1961, London —

2. Beatrice Huntington-Whiteley
September 6, 1962, London —

3. Leopold Huntington-Whiteley
July 15, 1965, London —

XVII. JOHNSTON

1, from page 974

Charles Hepburn Johnston (KCMG in 1959)
March 11, 1912, London —
m. April 22, 1944, London
* **Nataliya Konstantinovna,** Princess Bagration-Moukhranskya of Georgia, daughter of Prince Konstantin Aleksandrovich Bagration-Moukhransky and of his wife, Princess Tatyana Konstantinovna of Russia.
April 6, 1914, Kitchrene, Crimea, Russia —

No Issue.

XVII. KNATCHBULL (Brabourne)

1, from page 154

Sir John Knatchbull, 14th Baronet, 7th Baron Brabourne.
November 9, 1924, London —
m. October 26, 1946, Romsey Abbey, Hampshire
* **Lady Patricia Mountbatten,** eldest daughter of The Earl Mountbatten of Burma and of his wife, The Honourable Edwina Ashley. Heiress to the Earldom of Mountbatten of Burma.
February 14, 1924, London —

Issue: 1. Norton Knatchbull. Heir to the titles of the Baron Brabourne and the Earl Mountbatten of Burma, the latter directly after his mother.
October 8, 1950, London —

2. Michael John Knatchbull, May 24, 1950, London —

3. Joanna Knatchbull, March 5, 1955, London —

4. Amanda Knatchbull, June 26, 1957, London —

5. Philip Knatchbull, December 2, 1961, London —

6. Nicholas Knatchbull (twin), November 18, 1964, London —

7. Timothy Knatchbull (twin), November 18, 1964, London —

XVII. LANE

1, from page 35

Robert Charlton Lane

January 26, 1873, London — May 23, 1943, Havant, Hampshire
m. January 5, 1905, London

* **Olga FitzGeorge,** daughter of Adolphus FitzGeorge and of his second wife, Margarita Beatrice Daisy Watson.

June 11, 1878, — October 15, 1928, Rouen, France
(She m. 1: Sir Archibald Hamilton, 5th Baronet – see: *FitzGeorge-Hamilton* XVII, page 520.)

Issue: 1. Jane Lane (1919–)
m. 1: and divorced: Edward Christopher Hohler (1917–)
see: *Hohler* XVII, page 524
m. 2: Ronald Stratford Scrivener (1919–)
see: *Scrivener* XVII, page 533

XVII. LASCELLES (Harewood)

1, from page 13

Henry Lascelles, 6th Earl of Harewood.

September 9, 1882, London — May 24, 1947, Harewood House, Leeds
m. February 28, 1922, Westminster Abbey, London

* **Mary,** Princess Royal of Great Britain and Ireland, daughter of King George V of Great Britain and Ireland and of his wife, Princess Mary (May) of Teck.

April 25, 1897, Sandringham — March 28, 1965, Harewood House

Issue: 1. The Honourable George Lascelles, 7th Earl of Harewood (1923–)
m. 1: and divorced: Marion Stein (1926–)
m. 2: Patricia Tuckwell (1926–)
see: *Lascelles* XVII, 2, page 528

2. The Honourable Gerald Lascelles (1924–)
m. Angela Dowding (1919–)
see: *Lascelles* XVII, 3, page 528

XVII. Lascelles 2, from page 527

* **George Lascelles,** 7th Earl of Harewood.
February 7, 1923, London —
m. 1: September 29, 1949, St. Margaret's, Westminster. Divorced: April 6, 1967, London
Marion Stein, daughter of Erwein Stein and of his wife, Sophie.
October 18, 1926, Vienna, Austria —
m. 2: July 31, 1967, New Canaan, Connecticut, USA
Patricia Tuckwell, daughter of Charles Tuckwell and of his wife, Elizabeth Jane.
November 24, 1926, Melbourne, Australia —
(She m. 1: July 7, 1948, Melbourne, divorced: 1957, Athol Shmith.)

Issue of first marriage:
1. The Honourable David Lascelles, Viscount Lascelles
October 21, 1950, London —

2. The Honourable James Lascelles
October 5, 1953, London —

3. The Honourable Jeremy Lascelles
February 14, 1955, London —

Issue of second marriage:
4. The Honourable Mark Hubert Lascelles
July 4, 1965, London —

XVII. Lascelles 3, from page 527

* **Gerald Lascelles,** second son of the 6th Earl of Harewood.
August 21, 1924, London —
m. July 15, 1952, London
Angela Dowding, daughter of Charles Stanley Dowding and of his wife,
April 20, 1919, London —

Issue: 1. Henry Ulick Lascelles
May 19, 1953, London —

XVII. LEWIS 1, from page 845

Neville Lewis

October 8, 1895, Cape Town, South Africa —

m. November 3, 1955, Stellenbach, South Africa

* **Rose,** Countess zu Solms-Baruth, daughter of Count Friedrich, 3rd Fürst zu Solms-Baruth, and of his wife, Princess Adelheid of Schleswig-Holstein-Sonderburg-Glücksburg.

May 15, 1925, Baruth —

Issue: 1. Caroline Lewis
August 31, 1954, Pineland, Cape Province, South Africa —

2. Frederick Lewis
November 23, 1961, London —

XVII. LIDDELL-GRAINGER 1, from page 513

David Liddell-Grainger

January 26, 1930, Park Lane, London —

m. December 14, 1957, Windsor Castle

* **Anne Abel Smith,** daughter of Sir Henry Abel Smith and of his wife, The Lady May Cambridge, born Princess of Teck.

July 28, 1932, Kensington Palace —

Issue: 1. Ian Richard Liddell-Grainger
February 23, 1959, Edinburgh, Scotland —

2. Charles Montague Liddell-Grainger
July 28, 1960, Edinburgh —

3. Simon Robert Liddell-Grainger
December 27, 1963, London —

4. Alice Mary Liddell-Grainger
March 2, 1965, Edinburgh —

5. Malcolm Henry Liddell-Grainger
December 16, 1967, Edinburgh —

XVII. McEACHERN 1, from page 704

Neil McEachern

December 28, 1885, — April 18, 1964, Verbania, Italy

m. July 1, 1940, London. Divorced: 1947,

* **Imma,** Princess of Erbach-Schönberg, daughter of Prince Alexander, 2nd Fürst zu Erbach-Schönberg, and of his wife, Princess Elisabeth zu Waldeck und Pyrmont.

May 11, 1901, König — March 14, 1947, London

(She m. 1: Hans Karl, Baron von Dörnberg – see: *von Dörnberg* XXI, page 686.)

No Issue.

XVII. McEWEN 1, from page 483

Alexander D. McEwen

May 16, 1935, Marchmont, Scotland —

m. June 30, 1960, London

* **Cäcilia,** Countess von Weikersheim, daughter of Fürst Franz von Weikersheim and of his wife, Princess Irma Windisch-Graetz.

October 28, 1937, London —

Issue: 1. Sophie McEwen
April 8, 1961, Edinburgh, Scotland —

2. Alexander McEwen
June 12, 1962, Edinburgh —

3. Hugo Gabriel McEwen
February 28, 1965, Duns, Scotland —

XVII. NESBITT 1, from page 523

Graham Nesbitt

September 25, 1936, Montreal, Canada —

m. July 30, 1962, London

* **Elizabeth Hesseltine,** daughter of Nigel Hesseltine and of his wife, Princess Nataliya Borisovna Galitzine.

May 27, 1939, London —

No Issue.

XVII. OGILVY 1, from page 18

Angus Ogilvy, second son of 12th Earl of Airlie.
September 14, 1928, London —
m. April 24, 1963, Westminster Abbey, London
* **Alexandra,** Princess of Great Britain and Ireland, Princess of Kent, daughter of Prince George of Great Britain and Ireland, Duke of Kent, and of his wife, Princess Marina of Greece and Denmark.
December 25, 1936, London —

Issue: 1. James Ogilvy
February 29, 1964, 'Thatched House Lodge', Richmond —

2. Marina Ogilvy
July 31, 1966, 'Thatched House Lodge' —

XVII. O'MALLEY 1, from page 156

Hamilton Keyes O'Malley
October 19, 1910, Dublin, Ireland —
m. February 15, 1941, Haywards Heath, Sussex. Divorced: 1946, New York City
* **Iris,** Lady Mountbatten, daughter of the Marquess of Carisbrooke, born Prince Alexander of Battenberg, and of his wife, Lady Irene Denison.
January 13, 1920, London —
(She m. 2: and divorced: Michael Kelly Bryan – see: *Bryan* XXIV, page 1016.)
(She m. 3: and divorced: William Kemp – see: *Kemp* XXIV, page 1020.)

No Issue.

XVII. PHILLIPS 1, from page 534

Harold Pedro Phillips
November 6, 1909, London —
m. October 10, 1944, London
* **Georgina Wernher,** daughter of Sir Harold Wernher, 11th Baronet, and of his wife, Countess Anastasia (Zia) de Torby.
October 17, 1919, Edinburgh, Scotland —

XVII. Phillips 1 continued

Issue: 1. Alexandra Anastasia (Sascha) Phillips (1946–)
m. The Honourable James Hamilton, Marquess of Hamilton (1934–)
see: *Hamilton* XVII, page 522

2. Nicholas Harold Phillips
August 23, 1947, London —

3. Fiona Mercedes Phillips
March 30, 1951, London —

4. Marita Georgina Phillips
May 28, 1954, London —

5. Natalia Ayesha Phillips
May 8, 1959, London —

XVII. RAMSAY 1, from page 20

Sir Alexander Ramsay, son of 13th Earl of Dalhousie.
May 29, 1881, London —
m. February 27, 1919, Westminster Abbey, London
* **Patricia,** Princess of Great Britain and Ireland, Princess of Connaught, daughter of Prince Arthur of Great Britain and Ireland, Duke of Connaught and Strathearn and of his wife, Princess Luise Margarete of Prussia.
March 11, 1886, Buckingham Palace —

Issue: 1. Alexander Ramsay (1919–)
m. The Honourable Flora Fraser (1930–)
see: *Ramsay* XVII, 2, below

XVII. Ramsay 2, from above

* **Alexander Ramsay,** only son of Admiral The Honourable Sir Alexander Ramsay.
December 21, 1919, London —
October 16, 1956, Fraserburgh, Scotland
Flora Fraser, only child of Alexander Arthur Fraser, 19th Earl of Saltoun and of his wife, Dorothy Geraldine Welby.
October 18, 1930, Edinburgh —

XVII. Ramsay 2 continued

Issue: 1. Katharine Ramsay
October 11, 1957, Edinburgh, Scotland —

2. Alice Ramsay
July 8, 1961, Edinburgh, Scotland —

3. Elizabeth Ramsay
April 15, 1963, Inverness, Scotland —

XVII. SCRIVENER 1, from page 527

Ronald Stratford Scrivener
December 29, 1919, London —
m. May 14, 1962, London
* **Jane Lane,** daughter of Robert Charlton Lane and of his wife, Olga FitzGeorge.
June 4, 1919, London —
(She m. 1: and divorced: Edward Christopher Hohler – see: *Hohler* XVII, page 524.)

No Issue.

XVII. SOMERSET (Beaufort) 1, from page 229

Henry Somerset, 10th Duke of Beaufort.
April 4, 1900, Hamilton —
m. June 14, 1923, London
* **Mary,** Lady Cambridge, born Princess of Teck, daughter of Prince Adolphus of Teck, Duke of Teck, First Marquess of Cambridge, and of his wife, Lady Margaret Grosvenor.
June 12, 1897, White Lodge, Richmond —

No Issue.

XVII. TOOTH

1, from page 325

Geoffrey Tooth, M.D.

September 1, 1908, London —

m. 2: April 7, 1958, Teheran, Iran and April 27, 1958, London

* **Kseniya (Xenia) Andreievna,** Princess Romanova, daughter of Prince Andrei Aleksandrovich of Russia and of his first wife, Donna Elisabeth Sasso-Ruffo.

March 10, 1919, Paris —

(She m. 1: and divorced: Calhoun Ancrum – see: *Ancrum* XXIV, page 1014.)

No Issue.

NOTE: Dr. Tooth, married first Princess Olga Aleksandrovna Galitzine, sister of Princess Nataliya who married Princess Kseniya's uncle, Prince Vassili Aleksandrovich of Russia, see: *Russia* VIII page 330.

XVII. WERNHER

1, from page 322

Harold Wernher, 3rd Baronet

January 16, 1893, London —

m. July 20, 1917, London

* **Anastasiya (Zia) Mikhailovna,** Countess de Torby, daughter of Grand Duke Mikhail Mikhailovich of Russia and of his wife, Countess Sophie von Merenberg, created Countess de Torby.

September 9, 1892, Wiesbaden, Germany —

Issue: 1. George Michael Alexander Wernher, Captain 17th/21st Lancers
August 22, 1918, Edinburgh, Scotland — December 4, 1942, Beja, North Africa, killed in action in World War II

2. Georgina Wernher (1919–)
m. Harold Pedro Phillips (1909–)
see: *Phillips* XVII, page 531

3. Myra Alice Wernher (1925–)
m. David Butter (1924–)
see: *Butter* XVII, page 516

XVII. WESTON-BAKER 1, from page 917

Cecil Thomas Weston-Baker
February 26, 1919, London —
m. May 10, 1950, Johannesburg, South Africa
* **Friederike Marie,** Princess Windisch-Graetz, daughter of Prince Eduard Windisch-Graetz and of his wife, Princess Alexandra (Alix) zu Ysenburg-Birstein.
March 13, 1924, Birstein —

Issue: 1. Christiane Weston-Baker
December 31, 1951, Johannesburg —

2. Charles Weston-Baker
April 27, 1954, Johannesburg —

3. Cecilia Weston-Baker
January 11, 1957, Johannesburg —

XVII. WHITLEY 1, from page 230

Peter Whitley
October 22, 1923, Singapore —
m. November 9, 1951, Kirtling, Newmarket, Suffolk
* **Lady Mary Cambridge,** only child of the 2nd Marquess of Cambridge, born Prince George of Teck, and of his wife, Dorothy Isabel Hastings.
September 24, 1924, London —

Issue: 1. Sarah Elizabeth Whitley
November 30, 1954, London —

2. Charles Frederick Peter Whitley
September 10, 1961, Brighton —

XVII. WILDE (Truro) 1, from page 32

Thomas Wilde, First Baron Truro of Bowes.
July 7, 1782, Castle Street, London — November 11, 1858, Eaton Square, London
m. 1: April 13, 1813, London
Mary Wileman Devaynes, daughter of William Wileman and the widow of William Devaynes.
— June 13, 1840, Guildford Street, London

XVII. Wilde (Truro) 1 continued

m. 2: August 13, 1845, London
★ **Emma D'Este,** daughter of Prince Augustus Frederick of Great Britain and Ireland, Duke of Sussex and of his wife, Lady Augusta Murray.
August 11, 1801, Grosvenor Square, London — May 21, 1866, London

Issue of first marriage: Not descendants of King George I
1. A son born and died in 1814

2. Charles Wilde, 2nd Baron Truro of Bowes (1816–1891)
m. Lucy Ray (–1879)

3. Hon. Thomas Wilde (1819–1878)
m. Emily Chapman (–   )

XVII. WISE 1, from page 513

Peter Wise
December 29, 1929, Kensington, London —
m. April 29, 1965, London
★ **Elizabeth Abel Smith,** daughter of Sir Henry Abel Smith and of his wife, Lady May Cambridge, born Princess of Teck.
September 5, 1936, Kensington Palace —

No Issue.

XVIII

THE FAMILIES OF SPAIN, PORTUGAL, FRANCE AND ITALY

XVIII. AGLIOTI 1, from page 596

Antonello Aglioti

—

m. September , 1966, Venice

⋆ **Nobile Olga Nicolis,** dei Conti di Robilant e Cereaglio, daughter of Conte Carlo Nicolis di Robilant e Cereaglio and of his wife, Caroline Kent.

November 3, 1934, Venice —

Issue:

XVIII. d'ALCANTARA di QUERRIEU 1, from page 919

Peter, Count d'Alcantara di Querrieu

November 2, 1907, Oydonek Castle, Poland — October 14, 1944, Oranienburg, near Leningrad, killed in action in World War II.

m. July 22, 1933, Brussels, Belgium

⋆ **Stephanie,** Princess Windisch-Graetz, daughter of Prince Otto Windisch-Graetz and of his wife, Archduchess Elisabeth of Austria.

July 9, 1909, Ploshwitz —

(She m. 2: Karl Axel Björklund – see: *Björklund* XIX, page 614.)

Issue: 1. Alvar Etienne (Stephen), Count d'Alcantara di Querrieu (1935–)
m. Anita Damsten (1936–)
see: *d'Alcantara di Querrieu* XVIII, 2, below

XVIII. d'Alcantara di Querrieu 2, from above

⋆ **Alvar Etienne,** Count d'Alcantara di Querrieu, only son of Count Peter.

July 30, 1935, Brussels —

m. July 19, 1956, Helsinki, Finland

Anita Damsten, daughter of

December 15, 1936, Helsinki —

Issue: 1. Patricia, Countess d'Alcantara di Querrieu
January 19, 1957, Brussels —

XVIII. d'Alcantara di Querrieu

2 continued

2. Fréderic, Count d'Alcantara di Querrieu
April 9, 1958, Brussels —

3. Véronique, Countess d'Alcantara di Querrieu
May 27, 1960, Brussels —

XVIII. d'ALMONT

1, from page 1006

Jean Albert, Baron d'Almont
September 27, 1909, Ivoy-le-Pré, France —
m. March 14, 1951, Paris
* **Kseniya (Xenia) Nikolaievna,** Princess Orlova, daughter of Prince Nikolai Vladimirovich Orlov and of his wife, Princess Nadeshda Petrovna of Russia.
March 27, 1921, — August 17, 1963,
(She m. 1: Paul de Montaignac – see: *de Montaignac* XVIII, page 580.)

Issue: 1. Nadejda, Baroness d'Almont
March 20, 1952, St. Germain-en-Laye —

XVIII. ALOISI

1, from page 937

Domenico Aloisi, M.D.
July 21, 1867, San Sebastian, Spain — May 15, 1945, Pisignano, Italy
m. June 23, 1910, Wächtersbach, Germany
* **Maria,** Princess zu Ysenburg und Büdingen in Wächtersbach, daughter of Prince Friedrich Wilhelm, 2nd Fürst zu Ysenburg und Büdingen in Wächtersbach, and of his wife, Countess Anna Dobrzensky von Dobrzenicz.
November 13, 1881, Wächtersbach — November 13, 1958, Lausanne, Switzerland

Issue: 1. Mariangela Aloisi (1911–)
m. Ludwig, Count zu Ysenburg-Philippseich (1893–)
see: *zu Ysenburg-Philippseich* XXI, page 935

2. Mario Aloisi, M.D.
September 27, 1912, Pisignano, Italy —

XVIII. Aloisi 1 continued

3. Anna Aloisi (1916–)
m. Gabriele, Conte Ginanni Fantuzzi (1905–)
see: *Ginanni Fantuzzi* XVIII, page 563

4. Carlo Aloisi (1918–)
m. Donna Adriana dei Principi Ginori Conti (1928–)
see: *Aloisi* XVIII, 2, below

5. Raimonda Aloisi (1921–)
m. Neri, Conte Revedin di San Martino (–)
see: *Revedin di San Martino* XVIII, page 594

6. Franca (Francesca) Aloisi (1923–)
m. Angelo Rossi, M.D. (1911–)
see: *Rossi* XVIII, page 599

XVIII. Aloisi 2, from above

* **Carlo Aloisi,** second son of Domenico Aloisi.
June 2, 1918, Pisignano, Italy —
m. June 2, 1955, Florence

Donna Adriana dei Principi Ginori Conti, daughter of Conte Giovanni dei Principi Ginori Conti and of his wife, Lucia Colonna di Paliano dei Principi di Summonti.
October 25, 1929, Florence —

Issue: 1. Gian-Domenico Aloisi
August 28, 1956, São Paulo, Brazil —

2. Maria Frederica Aloisi
September 26, 1957, São Paulo —

3. Andrea Aloisi
September 18, 1958, Florence —

4. Raimonda Aloisi
January 4, 1961, Florence —

XVIII. ALTIERI

1, from page 236

Don Paolo Altieri, Principe di Viano
November 17, 1849, Rome — January 4, 1901, Rome
m. February 2, 1874, Monaco
* **Mathilde Auguste,** Countess of Württemberg, Princess von Urach, daughter of Count Wilhelm of Württemberg, 1st Duke of Urach, and of his wife, Princess Theodelinde de Beauharnais.
January 14, 1854, Stuttgart — July 13, 1907, Modena, Italy

Issue: 1. Donna Theodolinda Altieri (1876–1947)
m. Don Francesco di Napoli-Rampolla (1871–1938)
see: *di Napoli-Rampolla* XVIII, page 583

2. Don Clemente Altieri
December 9, 1877, Rome — January 21, 1886, Rome

3. Don Ludovico Altieri, Principe di Viano (1878–1955)
m. Emilia Belestra (1888–)
see: *Altieri* XVIII, 2, page 542

4. Donna Maria Augusta Altieri (1880–)
m. Roberto, Marchese Pallovicino (1870–1937)
see: *Pallovicino* XVIII, page 590

5. Don Guglielmo (William) Carlo Altieri
April 5, 1884, Rome — June 8, 1894, Strada Arezzo

6. Don Marc'Antonio Altieri
October 5, 1886, Oriolo Romano — December 10, 1886, Civitavecchio

7. Donna Camilla Altieri (1889–)
m. Pasolino, Conte Pasolini dall'Onda (1876–1933)
see: *Pasolini dall'Onda* XVIII, page 590

8. Don Marc'Antonio Altieri (1891–1919)
m. Donna Frida Gallotti (–)
see: *Altieri* XVIII, 3, page 542

XVIII. Altieri 2, from page 541

* **Don Ludovico Pio Altieri,** Principe di Viano, second son of Don Paolo.
December 27, 1878, Rome — June 6, 1955, Rome
m. September 18, 1916, Rome
Emilia Belestra, daughter of
October 7, 1888, Rome —

No Issue.

XVIII. Altieri 3, from page 541

Don Marc'Antonio Altieri, fifth son of Don Paolo.
May 2, 1891, Rome — , 1919,
m.
Donna Frida Gallotti, daughter of
—

No Issue.

XVIII. ALVARES PEREIRA di MELLO 1, from page 595

Don Antonio Alvares Pereira di Mello, Marchesi di Cadaval
September 26, 1894, St. Jean de Luz — February 17, 1939, Leysin
m. July 5, 1926, Venice
* **Olga Nicolis,** Contessa di Robilant e Cereaglio, daughter of Nobile Edmondo Nicolis, Conte di Robilant e Cereaglio, and of his wife, Contessa Valentina Mocenigo.
January 17, 1900, Turin —

Issue: 1. Donna Olga Alvares Pereira di Mello
October 15, 1928, San Sebastian, Spain — September 26, 1951, Sintra, Portugal

2. Donna Graziella Alvares Pereira di Mello (1929–)
m. Friedrich Karl, Count von Schönborn-Wiesentheid (1916–)
see: *von Schönborn-Wiesentheid* XXI, page 830

XVIII. ALVAREZ de TOLEDO 1, from page 578

Don José Carlos Alvarez de Toledo y Gross
, 1930, Malaga, Spain —
m. January 13, 1961, Geneva, Switzerland
* **Donna Vittoria Marone Cinzano,** daughter of Count Enrico Marone Cinzano and of his wife, Dona Maria Cristina de Borbon y Battenberg, Infanta of Spain.
March 5, 1941, Turin, Italy —

Issue: 1. Dona Vittoria Eugenia Alvarez de Toledo y Marone
October 8, 1961, Malaga —

2. Don Borja Alvarez de Toledo y Marone
March 26, 1963, Malaga —

3. Don Marco Alfonso Alvarez de Toledo y Marone
January 23, 1965, Malaga —

XVIII. ARIAS 1, from page 957

Don Luis Arias
— February , 1970, killed in an air crash.
m. October 2, 1965, El Paular, Spain
* **Dorota,** Countess Potocka, daughter of Count Jozef Potocki and of his wife, Princess Krystyna Radziwill.
April 13, 1934, Warsaw, Poland —

Issue:

XVIII. BATAILLE 1, from page 988

Georges Bataille
—
m. , 1945,
* **Diana Eugenia Evgeniievna,** Princess Kotchoubey de Beauharnais, daughter of Prince Eugene Leontievich Kotchoubey de Beauharnais and of his wife, Helen Geraldine Pearce.
June 4, 1918, Victoria, British Columbia, Canada —
(She m. 1: and divorced: Georges Snopko – see: *Snopko* XVIII, page 605.)

Issue: 1. Julie Bataille
December 1, 1949, —

XVIII. de BATAILLE-FURÉ 1, from page 591

Vincent de Bataille-Furé
November 1, 1914, — February 21, 1960,
m. October 8, 1955, Bonneé, Loiret, France
* **Marguerite de Pasquier de Franclieu,** daughter of Antoine de Pasquier, Marquis de Franclieu, and of his wife, Elisabeth Desrousseaux de Vandières.
November 3, 1927, —

Issue: 1. Anne de Bataille-Furé, October 1, 1956 —

2. Marie-France de Bataille-Furé, May 5, 1958 —

3. Emmanuelle de Bataille-Furé, July 11, 1960 —

XVIII. de BEAUMONT 1, from page 557

Alain, Comte de Beaumont
October 19, 1938, Fontainbleau —
m. September 5, 1964, Vandières, France
* **Marcelle Desrousseaux de Vandières,** daughter of Edouard Desrousseaux de Vandières, Comte Desrousseaux, Duc de Vandières, and of his wife, Marie-France d'Illiers.
July 13, 1938, Olivet, Loiret —

Issue:

XVIII. BERGERON 1, from page 591

Gérard Bergeron
April 5, 1940, Perpignan —
m. August 6, 1962, Trébons, Alpes Pyrénées
* **Marie Thérèse de Pasquier de Franclieu,** daughter of Antoine de Pasquier, Marquis de Franclieu, and of his wife, Elisabeth Desrousseaux de Vandières.
September 21, 1941, Tarbes, Alpes Pyrénées —

Issue: 1. Christian Bergeron, November 29, 1963 —

2. Elisabeth Bergeron, April 8, 1965 —

3. Marie-Alix Bergeron, April 21, 1966 —

XVIII. BLANCO de BRIONES 1, from page 973

Don José Luis Blanco de Briones

—

m. October 24, 1968, Madrid

* **Maria de la Paz,** Princess Bagration-Moukhranskya, daughter of Prince Irakli (Heraclius) Bagration-Moukhransky and of his wife, Dona Maria de las Mercedes de Borbon y Habsburgo, Infanta of Spain.

June 27, 1947, Madrid —

Issue: 1. Dona Mercedes Blanco de Briones y Bagration-Moukhransky
October , 1969, Madrid —

XVIII. du BOIS d'AISCHE 1, from page 967

Philippe du Bois d'Aische

September 7, 1930, Brussels —

m. August 30, 1958, Warsaw

* **Izabela,** Princess Swiatopelk-Czetwertynska, daughter of Prince Stanislaw Swiatopelk-Czetwertynski and of his wife, Baronness Ewa Buxhoeveden.

July 14, 1934, Warsaw —

Issue: 1. Christine du Bois d'Aische
July 18, 1959, Louvain, Belgium —

2. Véronique du Bois d'Aische
September 20, 1960, Louvain —

3. Louis du Bois d'Aische
February 5, 1962, Louvain —

4. Gilles du Bois d'Aische
May 29, 1963, Brussels —

XVIII. BONAPARTE 1, from page 223

Jérôme Bonaparte, King of Westphalia, August 8, 1807 — October 26, 1813, youngest brother of Napoleon I, Emperor of the French.
November 15, 1784, Ajaccio — June 24, 1860, Villegenis, Seine-et-Oise
m. 1: December 24, 1803, Baltimore, USA. Annulled by order of Napoleon, March 11, 1805
Elizabeth Patterson (known as 'Mme Bonaparte'), daughter of William Patterson and of his wife,
February 6, 1785, Baltimore — April 4, 1879, Baltimore
m. 2: August 12 and 23, 1807, Paris
* **Katharina,** Princess of Württemberg, daughter of King Friedrich I of Württemberg and of his wife, Princess Auguste of Brunswick-Wolfenbüttel.
February 21, 1783, — November 28, 1835,

Issue of first marriage: Not a descendant of George I:
1. Jérôme Napoléon Bonaparte (1805–1870)

Issue of second marriage:
2. Jérôme, Prince Bonaparte
August 24, 1814, Trieste — May 12, 1847, Florence

3. Mathilde, Princess Bonaparte (1820–1904)
m. Anatole, Prince Demidov, 1st Prince of San Donato (1813–1870)
see: *Demidov* XXIII, page 979

4. Napoléon Louis, Prince Bonaparte (1822–1891)
m. Marie Clothilde, Princess of Savoy (1843–1911)
see: *Bonaparte* XVIII, 2, below

XVIII. Bonaparte 2, from above

* **Napoléon Louis** ('Plon-Plon'), Prince Bonaparte, son of Prince Jérôme.
September 9, 1822, Trieste — March 18, 1891, Rome
m. January 30, 1859, Turin, Italy
Marie Clothilde, Princess of Savoy, daughter of King Vittorio Emanuele II of Italy and of his first wife, Archduchess Adelheid of Austria.
March 2, 1843, Turin — June 25, 1911, Moncalieri Castle

Issue: 1. Napoléon Victor, Prince Bonaparte (1862–1926)
m. Clementine, Princess of Belgium (1872–1955)
see: *Bonaparte* XVIII, 3, page 547

XVIII. Bonaparte

2 continued

2. Napoléon Louis, Prince Bonaparte
   July 16, 1864, Paris — October 14, 1932, Prangins, Switzerland

3. Marie Laetitia, Princess Bonaparte (1866–1926)
   m. Amadeo, Prince of Savoy, Duke of Aosta, King of Spain (1845–1890)
   see: *Savoy (Italy)* XVIII, page 601

XVIII. Bonaparte

3, from pages 546, 286

* **Napoléon Victor,** Prince Bonaparte, eldest son of Prince Napoléon Louis.
July 18, 1862, Paris — May 3, 1926, Brussels
m. November 14, 1910, Moncalieri, near Turin

* **Clementine,** Princess of Belgium, daughter of King Leopold II of the Belgians and of his wife, Archduchess Henrietta of Austria.
July 30, 1872, Laeken Castle — March 8, 1955, Nice

Issue: 1. Marie Clothilde, Princess Bonaparte (1912–)
   m. Sergei, Count de Witt (1891–)
   see: *de Witt* XXIII, page 1010

2. Napoléon Louis, Prince Bonaparte (1914–)
   m. Alix, Comtesse de Foresta (1926–)
   see: *Bonaparte* XVIII, 4, below

XVIII. Bonaparte

4, from above

* **Napoléon Louis,** Prince Bonaparte, son of Prince Napoléon Victor. Bonapartist claimant to the Throne of France.
January 23, 1914, Brussels —
m. August 16, 1949, Linières, Dept. Maine-et-Loire, France

Alix, Comtesse de Foresta, daughter of Comte Alberic de Foresta and of his wife, Geneviève Fredet.
April 4, 1926, Marseilles —

Issue: 1. Charles, Prince Bonaparte (twin)
   October 19, 1950, Boulogne-Billancourt —

XVIII. Bonaparte 4 continued

2. Catherine, Princess Bonaparte (twin)
October 19, 1950, Boulogne-Billancourt —

3. Clémentine, Princess Bonaparte
October 8, 1952, Paris —

4. Jérôme, Prince Bonaparte
January 14, 1957, Paris —

XVIII. BOSDARI 1, from page 915

Girolamo, Conte di Bosdari
March 4, 1907, Bologna, Italy —
m. June 7, 1941, Rome
* **Maria Antoinette,** Princess Windisch-Graetz, daughter of Prince Hugo Windisch-Graetz and of his wife, Princess Christine von Auersperg-Breunner.
June 6, 1911, Gonobitz —

No Issue.

XVIII. BOULAY de la MEURTHE 1, from page 566

Alfred, Comte Boulay de la Meurthe
July 26, 1925, Paris —
m. July 3, 1948, Paris
* **Monique d'Harcourt,** daughter of Comte Bruno d'Harcourt and of his wife, Princess Isabelle of France.
January 7, 1929, Paris —

Issue: 1. Gilone, Comtesse Boulay de la Meurthe
April 25, 1949, Neuilly-sur-Seine —

2. Laure, Comtesse de la Meurthe
April 27, 1951, Rabat, Morocco —

3. Iseult, Comte Boulay de la Meurthe
April 19, 1956, Rabat, Morocco —

XVIII. de BOURDONCLE de SAINT-SALVY 1, from page 556

Olivier, Comte de Bourdoncle de Saint-Salvy
February 14, 1905, Brest, Fuisière —
m. August 8, 1827, Bonnée, Loiret

* **Anne-Marie Desrousseaux de Vandières,** daughter of Edouard, Comte Desrousseaux, Duc de Vandières, and of his wife, Princess Elisabeth zu Ysenburg und Büdingen in Wächtersbach.
June 16, 1904, Vandières —

Issue: 1. Monique de Bourdoncle de Saint-Salvy (1929–)
m. Noël Segonne (1923–)
see: *Segonne* XVIII, page 604

2. Jacques de Bourdoncle de Saint-Salvy (1930–)
m. Jeanne de Cardevac d'Havrincourt (–)
see: *de Bourdoncle de Saint-Salvy* XVIII, 2, below

3. Alain de Bourdoncle de Saint-Salvy (1934–)
m. Françoise de la Rocque de Severac (1930–)
see: *de Bourdoncle de Saint-Salvy* XVIII, 3, page 550

4. Nicole de Bourdoncle de Saint-Salvy (1938–)
m. Antoine Serre (1932–)
see: *Serre* XVIII, page 605

5. Jean-Christian de Bourdoncle de Saint-Salvy (1944–)
m. Aminta Garros (1943–)
see: *de Bourdoncle de Saint-Salvy* XVIII, 4, page 551

XVIII. de Bourdoncle de Saint-Salvy 2, from above

* **Jacques de Bourdoncle de Saint-Salvy,** eldest son of Comte Olivier.
November 30, 1930, Montauban —
m. September 9, 1953, Paris

Jeanne de Cardevac d'Havrincourt, daughter of Comte Guy de Cardevac d'Havrincourt and of his wife, Marie de Pierre de Bernes-Calvières.
September 9, 1930, —

Issue: 1. Anne-Françoise de Bourdoncle de Saint-Salvy
August 31, 1954, Paris —

XVIII. de Bourdoncle de Saint-Salvy 2 continued

2. Bruno de Bourdoncle de Saint-Salvy
   August 8, 1955, Paris —

3. Myriam de Bourdoncle de Saint-Salvy
   June 17, 1958, Paris —

4. Ludovic de Bourdoncle de Saint-Salvy
   March 18, 1963, Paris —

XVIII. de Bourdoncle de Saint-Salvy 3, from page 549

* **Alain de Bourdoncle de Saint-Salvy,** second son of Comte Olivier.
June 6, 1934, Montauban —
m. August 9, 1956, Laroquebrou, Cantal
Françoise de la Rocque de Severac, daughter of Comte Pierre de la Rocque de Severac and of his wife, Geneviève Schneider.
June 5, 1934, Versailles —

Issue: 1. Christine de Bourdoncle de Saint-Salvy
   June 1, 1957, Laroquebrou —

2. Béatrice de Bourdoncle de Saint-Salvy
   March 27, 1959, Ravensburg, Germany —

3. Anne de Bourdoncle de Saint-Salvy
   July 16, 1960, Ravensburg —

4. Catherine de Bourdoncle de Saint-Salvy
   September 21, 1962, Saumur, Maine-et-Loire —

5. Olivier de Bourdoncle de Saint-Salvy
   April 5, 1964, Saumur —

6. Eric de Bourdoncle de Saint-Salvy
   May 14, 1966, Metz —

XVIII. de Bourdoncle de Saint-Salvy

4, from page 549

* **Jean-Christian de Bourdoncle de Saint-Salvy,** third son of Comte Olivier.
January 27, 1944, Bonnée, Loiret —
m. January 27, 1967, Le Bouscat, Gironde
Aminta Garros, daughter of Maximilian Garros and of his wife, Dora Morel.
November 11, 1943, Bordeaux, Gironde —

Issue: 1. Pierre de Bourdoncle de Saint-Salvy
April 7, 1968, Bordeaux —

2. Stéphanie de Bourdoncle de Saint-Salvy
November 30, 1969, Bordeaux —

XVIII. de BROGLIE

1, from page 576

Guy, Prince de Broglie
March 11, 1924, Paris —
m. September 24, 1949, Châteauneuf-sur-Cher. Divorced: , 1955,
* **Jeanne Marie de Maillé de la Tour-Landry,** daughter of Gilles de Maillé de la Tour-Landry, 5th Duc de Maillé, and of his wife, Princess Anna Maria Radziwill.
March 28, 1929, Paris —

Issue: 1. Antoine, Prince de Broglie
March 13, 1951, Boulogne-sur-Seine —

2. Laure, Princess de Broglie
February 11, 1952, Boulogne-sur-Seine —

XVIII. BRUNETTI

1, from page 470

Tito Tomasso Brunetti
December 18, 1905, Florence — July 13, 1954, near Piacenza, Italy
m. November 12, 1946, Milan
* **Editha,** Princess of Bavaria, daughter of Crown Prince Rupprecht of Bavaria and of his wife, Princess Antonia of Luxemburg.
September 16, 1924, Hohenberg Castle —
(She m. 2: Professor Gustav Christian Schimert – see: *Schimert* XXI, page 824.)

XVIII. Brunetti 1 continued

Issue: 1. Serena Brunetti, December 22, 1947, Milan —

2. Carlotta Brunetti, June 10, 1949, Milan —

3. Antonia Brunetti, June 10, 1952, Viareggio —

XVIII. di CASTELBARCO 1, from page 554

Don Alessandro, Conte di Castelbarco, Visconti Simonetta
May 20, 1917, Turin —
m. October 5, 1952, Trento
* **Elisabeth,** Countess Ceschi a Santa Croce, daughter of Count Giovanni Ceschi a Santa Croce and of his wife, Princess Luise Windisch-Graetz.
October 6, 1924, Trento —

Issue: 1. Donna Emilia di Castelbarco, January 26, 1955 Rovereto —

2. Donna Alexandra di Castelbarco, July 20, 1956, Rovereto —

3. Don Giovanni di Castelbarco, October 2, 1962, Rovereto —

XVIII. de CENO CLEMARES 1, from page 852

Adolfo de Ceno Clemares
—
m. December 27, 1955, Valencia, Spain
* **Hertha Margarete,** Baroness von Stengal, daughter of Baron Rudolf von Stengal and of his wife, Princess Marie Luise of Schleswig-Holstein-Sonderburg-Augustenburg, born Princess of Schleswig-Holstein-Sonderburg-Glücksburg.
January 10, 1935, Berlin —

Issue: 1. Maria Teresa de Ceno Clemares y Stengal
October 1, 1956, —

2. Adolfo de Ceno Clemares y Stengal
November 14, 1957, —

XVIII. de Ceno Clemares 1 continued

3. Enrique de Ceno Clamares y Stengal
January 30, 1959, —

XVIII. CESCHI a SANTA CROCE 1, from page 937

Franz, Count Ceschi a Santa Croce, son of Count Aloys.
June 10, 1872, Trient — April 6, 1952, Povo, Italy
m. June 3, 1912, Wächtersbach
* **Therese,** Princess zu Ysenburg und Büdingen in Wächtersbach, daughter of Prince Friedrich Wilhelm zu Ysenburg und Büdingen in Wächtersbach and of his wife, Countess Anna Dobrzensky von Dobrzenicz.
June 19, 1887, Wächtersbach —

Issue: 1. Anna Leopoldine, Countess Ceschi a Santa Croce (1914–)
m. Felix Theobald, Count Czernin von und zu Chudenitz (1902–)
see: *Czernin von und zu Chudenitz* XXI, page 682

XVIII. Ceschi a Santa Croce 2, from page 913

Giovanni, Count Ceschi a Santa Croce, son of Count Aloys.
January 3, 1871, Klägenfurt, Austria — September 20, 1936, Konjice Castle
m. November 30, 1911, Haasberg Castle
* **Luise,** Princess Windisch-Graetz, daughter of Prince Hugo Windisch-Graetz and of his wife, Princess Christine von Auersperg-Breunner.
July 13, 1886, St. Veit, near Vienna —

Issue: 1. Aloys Hugo, Count Ceschi a Santa Croce
October 12, 1912, Haasberg Castle —
(m. July 5, 1958, Villa Lagarina, Marie Therese, Contessa Marzani von Stainhof und Neuhaus, born August 3, 1922
1. Marie Antoinette, April 23, 1960
2. Eleonora, February 11, 1962)

2. Christiane, Countess Ceschi a Santa Croce (1914–)
m. Nikolaus, Baron von Maasberg (1913–)
see: *von Maasberg* XXI, page 765

XVIII. Ceschi a Santa Croce 2 continued

3. Hugo Vinzenz, Count Ceschi a Santa Croce (1915–)
m. Elisabeth Anna Wenzel, Baroness von Sternbach (1923–)
see: *Ceschi a Santa Croce* XVIII, 3, below

4. Ernst Anton, Count Ceschi a Santa Croce (1917–)
m. Nicoletta Tosini (1917–)
see: *Ceschi a Santa Croce* XVIII, 4, page 555

5. Leonidas Leopold, Count Ceschi a Santa Croce (1918–)
m. Maria Theresa Nobile Roi (1922–)
see: *Ceschi a Santa Croce* XVIII, 5, page 555

6. Eduard Franz, Count Ceschi a Santa Croce
August 26, 1920, Klobenstein —
(m. May 6, 1961, Polly Wenzel, Baroness von Sternbach, born November 1, 1929
1. Philipp, Count Ceschi a Santa Croce, February 21, 1962
2. Alix, Countess Ceschi a Santa Croce, October 3, 1963)

7. Elisabeth, Countess Ceschi a Santa Croce (1924–)
m. Don Alessandro, Conte di Castelbarco, Visconti Simonetta (1917–)
see: *di Castelbarco* XVIII, page 552

XVIII. Ceschi a Santa Croce 3, from above

* **Hugo Vinzenz,** Count Ceschi a Santa Croce, second son of Count Giovanni.
November 18, 1915, Haasberg Castle —
m. July 5, 1948, Sterzing-Vitipeno

Elisabeth Anna Wenzel, Baroness von Sternbach, daughter of Baron Leopold Wenzel von Sternbach.
July 25, 1923, Iglau —

Issue: 1. Isabelle Christiane, Countess Ceschi a Santa Croce
May 8, 1949, Trento —

2. Andreas Christof, Count Ceschi a Santa Croce
December 18, 1951, Trento —

3. Marie Elisabeth, Countess Ceschi a Santa Croce
November 14, 1955, Rovereto —

XVIII. Ceschi a Santa Croce 4, from page 554

* **Ernst Anton,** Count Ceschi a Santa Croce, third son of Count Giovanni.
October 12, 1917, Trento —
m. February 14, 1945, Florence
Nicoletta Tosini, daughter of
September 18, 1917, Florence —

Issue: 1. Robert, Count Ceschi a Santa Croce, , 1951 —

2. Franz, Count Ceschi a Santa Croce, July 19, 1948, Malveno —

3. Marina, Countess Ceschi a Santa Croce, October 20, 1953, Villazzano

XVIII. Ceschi a Sant a Croce 5, from page 554

* **Leonidas Leopold**, Count Ceschi a Santa Croce, fourth son of Count Giovanni.
October 27, 1918, Haasberg Castle —
m. October 4, 1950, Montegalda
Maria Theresa Nobile Roi, daughter of Nobile Gino, Marchesse Roi, and of his wife,
June 23, 1922, Venice —

Issue: 1. Friedrich Anton, Count Ceschi a Santa Croce, September 4, 1951, Venice —

2. Alexander Veriand, Count Ceschi a Santa Croce, March 4, 1953, Milan —

3. Giovanni, Count Ceschi a Santa Croce, September 27, 1954 —

4. Barbara, Countess Ceschi a Santa Croce, February 12, 1958 —

5. Gian Clemente, Count Ceschi a Santa Croce, November 22, 1959 —

6. Maria Ludovica, Countess Ceschi a Santa Croce, October 13, 1963 —

XVIII. CHIAS 1, from page 440

Carlos Chias
February 26, 1925, Barcelona —
m. December 29, 1950, Seville, Spain
* **Dolores,** Princess of Bourbon-Sicily, Infanta of Spain, daughter of Prince Carlos of Bourbon-Sicily, Infante of Spain, and of his wife, Princess Louise of France.
November 15, 1909, Madrid —
(She m. 1: Prince August Czartoryski – see: *Czartoryski* XXII, page 944.)

No Issue.

XVIII. de COMMARQUE 1, from page 1011

Godefroi, Marquis de Commarque
December 18, 1938, Urval —
m. April 11, 1966, Cendrieux, France
* **Vera,** Countess de Witt, daughter of Count Sergei de Witt and of his wife, Princess Marie Clothilde Bonaparte.
November 7, 1945, Tunis —

Issue: 1. Grégoire de Commarque

XVIII. DESROUSSEAUX de VANDIÈRES 1, from page 937

Edouard, Comte Desrousseaux, Duc de Vandières
May 31, 1866, Vandières — May 29, 1935, Paris
m. May 21, 1901, Lugano, Switzerland
* **Elisabeth,** Princess zu Ysenburg und Büdingen in Wächtersbach, daughter of Fürst Friedrich Wilhelm zu Ysenburg und Büdingen in Wächtersbach and of his wife, Countess Anna Dobrzensky von Dobrzenicz.
November 12, 1883, Wächtersbach —

Issue: 1. Elisabeth Desrousseaux de Vandières (1902–)
m. Antoine de Pasquier, Marquis de Franclieu (1897–)
see: *de Pasquier de Franclieu* XVIII, page 590

2. Anne-Marie Desrousseaux de Vandières (1904–)
m. Olivier, Comte de Bourdoncle de Saint-Salvy (1905–)
see: *de Bourdoncle de Saint-Salvy* XVIII, page 549

3. Edouard Desrousseaux de Vandières, Comte Desrousseaux, Duc de Vandières (1909–)
m. Marie-France d'Illiers (1917–1957)
see: *Desrousseaux de Vandières* XVIII, 2, below

XVIII. Desrousseaux de Vandières 2, from above

* **Edouard Desrousseaux de Vandières,** Comte Desrousseaux, Duc de Vandières, only son of Comte Edouard.
February 13, 1909, Viareggio, Italy —
m. July 21, 1937, Olivet, Loiret, France

XVIII. Desrousseaux de Vandières 2 continued

Marie-France d'Illiers, daughter of
August 30, 1917, Paris — September 12, 1957, Paris

Issue: 1. Marcelle Desrousseaux de Vandières (1938–)
m. Alain, Comte de Beaumont (1938–)
see: *de Beaumont* XVIII, page 544

2. Françoise Desrousseaux de Vandières (1939–)
m. Andrea, Conte di Gropello (–)
see: *di Gropello* XVIII, page 565

3. Elisabeth Desrousseaux de Vandières
November 26, 1940, Olivet, Loiret —

4. Edouard Desrousseaux de Vandières (1942–)
m. Waltraud Scharnagl (–)
see: *Desrousseaux de Vandières* XVIII, 3, below

5. Michelle Desrousseaux de Vandières
August 4, 1943, Olivet —

6. Nicole Desrousseaux de Vandières (1946–)
m. Alain de Tournemire (–)
see: *de Tournemire* XVIII, page 610

7. Marie-Christine Desrousseaux de Vandières
May 18, 1948, Rambouillet —

8. Jean-Francois Desrousseaux de Vandières
March 7, 1954, Olivet —

XVIII. Desrousseaux de Vandières 3, from above

* **Edouard Desrousseaux de Vandières,** son of Comte Edouard.
January 28, 1942, Limoges —
m. January 28, 1967, St. Benoit, Loiret, France
Waltraud Scharnagl, daughter of
—

Issue:

XVIII. de DREUX-BRÉZÉ 1, from page 566

Antoine de Dreux-Brézé
August 22, 1928, Cany, Seine Maritime, France —
m. September 9, 1950, Cany
* **Gilone d'Harcourt,** daughter of Comte Bruno d'Harcourt and of his wife, Princess Isabelle of France.
January 1, 1927, Larache, Morocco —

Issue: 1. Laure de Dreux-Brézé
April 23, 1951, Cany —

2. Diane de Dreux-Brézé
February 5, 1954, Neuilly-sur-Seine —

XVIII. ECONOMO di SAN SERFF 1, from page 914

Leonidas, Baron Economo di San Serff
December 27, 1874, Trieste — July 19, 1952, Trieste
m. August 24, 1916, Haasberg Castle
* **Wilhelmine,** Princess Windisch-Graetz, daughter of Prince Hugo Windisch-Graetz and of his wife, Princess Christine von Auersperg-Breunner.
April 23, 1895, Gonobitz —

Issue: 1. Johannes Hugo, Baron Economo di San Serff (1917–)
m. 1: and annulled: Ladislaja, Countess von Meran (1926–)
m. 2: Polyxene Afenduli (1916–)
see: *Economo di San Serff* XVIII, 2, page 559

2. Christiane, Baroness Economo di San Serff (1920–)
m. Friedrich, Count zu Seilern und Aspang (1924–)
see: *zu Seilern und Aspang* XXI, page 839

3. Karoline, Baroness Economo di San Serff
February 22, 1922, Trieste —

4. Gabriele Maria, Baroness Economo di San Serff
February 22, 1928, Vienna —

XVIII. Economo di San Serff 2, from page 558

★ **Johannes Hugo,** Baron Economo di San Serff, son of Baron Leonidas.
July 15, 1917, Vienna —
m. 1: February 23, 1957, Stainz, Austria. Annulled: July 20, 1962, Turin, Italy
Ladislaja, Countess von Meran, daughter of Count Franz von Meran and of his wife, Princess Wilhelmine von Auersperg.
January 3, 1926, Graz —
(She m. 2: October 24, 1965, Seewiessen, Karl Albrecht, Hereditary Prince of Hohenlohe-Schillingsfürst, born April 30, 1926, Vienna.)
m. 2: December 3, 1962, Graz
Polyxene Afenduli, daughter of Alexander Afenduli and of his wife,
May 18, 1916, Trieste —

Issue (by adoption):
1. Helene Marie, Baroness Economo di San Serff
April 28, 1962, Milan —

XVIII. FARACE 1, from page 316

Nobile Ruggero, Marquis Farace di Villaforesta
August 4, 1909, London — September 14, 1970, Rome
m. September 15, 1937, Rome. Separated legally: 1947, Rome
★ **Ekaterina (Catherine) Ivanovna,** Princess of Russia, daughter of Prince Ivan Konstantinovich of Russia and of his wife, Princess Elena of Serbia.
July 12/25, 1915, Pavlovsk, Russia —

Issue: 1. Donna Nicoletta Farace (1938–)
m. Alberto Grundland (1931–)
see: *Grundland* XXIV, page 1019

2. Donna Fiammetta Farace (1940–)
m. Victor Arcelus (1935–)
see: *Arcelus* XXIV, page 1014

3. Don Ivan Farace (1943–)
m. Marie Claude Tillier Debesse (1944–)
see: *Farace* XVIII, 2, page 560

XVIII. Farace

2, from page 559

* **Don Ivan Farace,** only son of Nobile Ruggero, Marquis di Villaforesta.
October 20, 1943, Rome —
m. February 14, 1968, Montevideo, Uruguay
Marie Claude Tillier Debesse, daughter of
April 24, 1944, Paris —

Issue: 1. Don Alessandro Farace
August 29, 1971, Paris —

XVIII. FARINI

1, from page 465

Tomasso, Conte Farini
September 16, 1938, Turin —
m. April 25, 1964,
* **Donna Beatriz de Orleans-Borbon y Parodi di Delfino,** daughter of Don Alvaro de Orleans y Borbon, Infante of Spain, and of his wife, Carla Parodi de Delfino.
April 27, 1943, Seville, Spain —

Issue: 1. Gerardo, Conte Farini
November 22, 1967, Bologna —

2. Elena, Contessa Farini
October 27, 1969, Rome —

XVIII. FORMENTINI di TOLMINO e BIGLIA

1, from page 607

Michele, Conte Formentini di Tolmino e Biglia, M.D.
January 3, 1929, San Floriano, Gorizia, Italy —
m. January 7, 1956, Villazzano, Trento
* **Dona Alice Tasso de Saxe-Coburgo e Braganca,** daughter of Baron Lamoral Tasso di Bordogna e Valnigra and of his wife, Princess Therese of Saxe-Coburg and Gotha.
June 7, 1936, Schladming Castle, Austria —

Issue: 1. Leonardo, Conte Formentini di Tolmino e Biglia
October 28, 1956, Gorizia —

2. Isabella, Contessa Formentini di Tolmino e Biglia
January 3, 1958, Gorizia —

3. Filippo, Conte Formentini di Tolmino e Biglia
January 5, 1964, Gorizia —

XVIII. FORNI 1, from page 869

Cajetan, Conte Forni
August 3, 1856, Modena, Austria — October 28, 1921, Modena, Italy
m. February 8, 1906, Innsbruck
* **Maria,** Countess von Thun und Hohenstein, daughter of Count Franz von Thun und Hohenstein and of his wife, Princess Auguste Eugenie von Urach, Countess of Württemberg.
October 24, 1879, Innsbruck — , 1958, Modena

Issue: 1. Augusta, Contessa Forni, December 17, 1906, Greis, near Bozen —

2. Josef, Conte Forni (1908–)
m. Maria, Contessa Savelli della Porta (1917–)
see: *Forni* XVIII, 2, below

3. Maria, Contessa Forni, June 8, 1909, Greis —

4. Peter, Conte Forni, December 9, 1911 — March, 1941

5. Anton, Conte Forni, June 18, 1912 —

6. Paul, Conte Forni, December 5, 1916 —

XVIII. Forni 2, from above

* **Josef,** Conte Farini, only son of Conte Cajetan.
January 9, 1908, Greis —
m. June 15, 1940, Gubbio, Province of Perugia, Italy
Maria, Contessa Savelli della Porta, daughter of Conte Ardicino Savelli della Porta and of his wife, Princess Maddalena Rospigliosi.
March 25, 1917, Gubbio —

Issue: 1. Carlo, Conte Forni, March 19, 1941, Modena —

2. Anna, Contessa Forni, April 2, 1942, Modena —

3. Theodolinda, Contessa Forni, August 16, 1943, Modena —

4. Cristina, Contessa Forni
September 12, 1944, Bomporto, near Modena —
(m. January 5, 1966, Modena, Pietro Gennari, born September 24, 1937
1. Maddalena Gennari, October 29, 1966 —)

XVIII. Forni 2 continued

5. Julius, Conte Forni
April 27, 1946, Modena —

6. Elena, Contessa Forni
October 15, 1949, Modena —

XVIII. de FROIDCOURT 1, from page 410

Roger de Froidcourt
January 13, 1931, Louviers, France —
m. November 16, 1959, Paris
* **Eleonora,** Princess Radziwill, daughter of Prince Jerome Radziwill and of his wife, Archduchess Renata Maria of Austria.
August 2, 1918, Balice, Poland —
(She m. 1: Benoit Wladyslaw, Count Tyszkiewicz – see: *Tyszkiewicz* XXII, page 970.)

Issue: 1. Remy de Froidcourt
May 5, 1960, Paris —

XVIII. FRUCHAUD 1, from page 410

Jean Henri Fruchaud, M.D.
April 1, 1937, Paris —
m. March 24, 1966 (civil), Athens, and March 26, 1966 (religious), The Royal Palace, Athens, Greece
* **Tatiana,** Princess Radziwill, daughter of Prince Dominik Radziwill and of his wife, Princess Eugenia of Greece and Denmark.
August 28, 1939, Rouen, France —

Issue: 1. Fabiola Fruchaud
February 7, 1967, Paris —

2. Alexis Fruchaud
, 1969, Paris —

XVIII. GALOBART 1, from page 578

Don Jaime Galobart y Satrustequi
, 1935, Madrid —
m. July 24, 1967, Rapello, Italy
* **Donna Maria Theresa Marone Cinzano,** daughter of Conte Enrico Marone Cinzano and of his wife, Dona Maria Cristina de Borbon y Battenberg, Infanta of Spain.
January 4, 1945, Lausanne, Switzerland —

Issue: 1. Don Alfonso Galobart y Marone
April 12, 1969, Madrid —

XVIII. GILLIÈRON 1, from page 593

Jean-Louis Gillièron
April 24, 1916, Geneva, Switzerland —
m. January 20, 1965, Ollon-sur-Aigle, Switzerland
* **Marguerite de Plan de Sièyes,** daughter of Henri de Plan, Comte de Sièyes, and of his wife, Elisabeth de MacMahon.
February 22, 1926, Paris —

Issue: 1. Irene Gillièron
February 5, 1957, Paris —

2. Arnaud Gillièron
May 5, 1958, Paris —

XVIII. GINANNI FANTUZZI 1, from page 540

Gabriele, Conte Ginanni Fantuzzi
May 15, 1905, Florence —
m. April 25, 1906, Pisignano
* **Anna Aloisi,** daughter of Domenico Aloisi, M.D., and of his wife, Princess Maria zu Ysenburg und Büdingen in Wächtersbach.
June 2, 1918, Pisignano —

Issue: 1. Maria Ginerva, Contessa Ginanni Fantuzzi (1943–
m. Carlo Mocenni (–)
see: *Mocenni* XVIII, page 579

XVIII. GNOGNONI 1, from page 336

Ferdinand, Baron von Gnognoni
September 6, 1878, Altmünster — July 8, 1955, Klagenfurt
m. February 4, 1904, Greiz
* **Marie,** Princess Reuss zu Greiz, daughter of Prince Heinrich XXII Reuss zu Greiz and of his wife, Princess Ida of Schaumburg-Lippe.
March 26, 1882, Greiz — November 1, 1942, Klagenfurt

No Issue.

XVIII. GOMEZ-ACEBO 1, from page 433

Don Luis Gomez-Acebo y de Estrada, son of Don Jaime Gomez-Acebo y Modet, Marchesi de la Deleitosa, and of his wife, Dona Isabel de Estrada y Vereterra, Martinez de Morentin y Armada, 9th Marchesa de la Deleitosa. (Don Luis Gomez-Acebo y de Estrada is a first cousin of Queen Margarita of Bulgaria, wife of King Simeon II – she was born Dona Margarita Gomez-Acebo y Cejuala.) Don Luis is styled the Duke of Badajos.
December 23, 1934, Madrid —
m. May 6, 1967, Church of San Geronimo, Estoril, Portugal
* **Dona Maria del Pilar de Borbon y de Borbon,** Infanta of Spain, daughter of Don Juan de Borbon y Battenberg, Infante of Spain, Count of Barcelona, and of his wife, Princess Marie Mercedes of Bourbon-Sicily, Infanta of Spain.
July 30, 1936, Rome —

Issue: 1. Dona Simonetta Gomez-Acebo y de Borbon
October 31, 1968, Madrid —

2. Don Juan Filiberto Gomez-Acebo y de Borbon
December 6, 1969, Madrid —

3. Bruno Alexander Gomez-Acebo y de Borbon
June 15, 1971, Madrid —

XVIII. GRAND d'ESNON 1, from page 339

Henri Grand d'Esnon
January 24, 1918, Paris —
m. September 30, 1950 (civil), Versailles, France, and October 14, 1950 (religious), Castell, Germany

* **Gertrud,** Princess Reuss zu Köstritz, daughter of Prince Heinrich XXXIX Reuss zu Köstritz and of his wife, Countess Antonia zu Castell-Castell.
November 5, 1924, Vienna —

Issue: 1. Gasparine Amadea Grand d'Esnon
July 11, 1951, Boulogne-sur-Seine —

2. Henri-Ferdinand Grand d'Esnon
January 10, 1953, Tunis —

3. Jérôme Grand d'Esnon (twin)
May 7, 1959, Paris —

4. Vincent Grand d'Esnon (twin)
May 7, 1959, Paris —

5. Marc Grand d'Esnon
September 8, 1961, Paris —

XVIII. di GROPELLO 1, from page 557

Andrea (Andrew), Conte di Gropello
—
m. September 25, 1965, Vandières, France

* **Françoise Desrousseaux de Vandières,** daughter of Edouard Desrousseaux de Vandières and of his wife, Marie France d'Illiers.
October 4, 1939, Olivet, Loiret, France —

Issue:

XVIII. HALM-NICOLAI 1, from page 708

Carlo Halm-Nicolai

August 6, 1876, — February 23, 1951, Baldham, Munich

m. August 26, 1896, Göttlieben

* **Ilma,** Baroness von Fabrice, daughter of Baron Maximilian von Fabrice and of his wife, Countess Ilma Almásy von Zsadány und Török-Szent-Miklós.

March 28, 1877, Ziegelhaus, near Lindau, Austria — February 23, 1951, Baldham

(She was born only eight months after her sister, Luigina.)

Issue: 1. Ilma Halm-Nicolai, June 29, 1897 —

2. Ellinka Halm-Nicolai, October 26, 1900 —

3. Ilka Halm-Nicolai (1902–1965)
m. Ludwig von Bürkel (1877–1946)
see: *von Bürkel*, Addendum, page 1052

XVIII. d'HARCOURT 1, from page 457

Bruno, Comte d'Harcourt

September 20, 1899, Vevey, Switzerland — April 19, 1930, Casablanca, Morocco

m. September 15, 1923, Chesnay, near Versailles

* **Isabelle,** Princess of France, daughter of Prince Jean, Comte de Guise, and of his wife, Princess Isabelle of France.

November 27, 1900, Paris —

(She m. 2: Pierre, Prince Murat – see: *Murat* XVIII, page 582.)

Issue: 1. Bernard, Comte d'Harcourt (1925–1958)
m. Yvonne de Contades (1928–)
see: *d'Harcourt* XVIII, 2, page 567

2. Gilone d'Harcourt (1927–) (twin)
m. Antoine, Comte de Dreux-Brézé (1928–)
see: *de Dreux-Brézé* XVIII, page 558

3. Isabelle d'Harcourt (1927–) (twin)
m. Louis, Prince Murat (1920–)
see: *Murat* XVIII, 2, page 583

4. Monique d'Harcourt (1929–)
m. Alfred, Comte Boulay de la Meurthe (1925–)
see: *Boulay de la Meurthe* XVIII, page 548

XVIII. d'Harcourt 2, from page 566

★ **Bernard,** Comte d'Harcourt, eldest son of Comte Bruno.
January 1, 1925, Larache, Morocco — September 4, 1958, Larache
m. January 27, 1951, Paris
Yvonne de Contades, daughter of Jean, Viscomte de Contades, and of his wife, Jacqueline de la Begassière.
April 22, 1928, Paris —

Issue: 1. Bruno, Comte d'Harcourt
October 26, 1951, Paris —

2. François d'Harcourt
June 21, 1953, Paris —

XVIII. JAMATEL 1, from page 424

George, Count Jamatel
—
m. June 22, 1899, White Lodge, Richmond, England
★ **Marie,** Duchess of Mecklenburg-Strelitz, daughter of Grand Duke Adolf Friedrich V of Mecklenburg-Strelitz and of his wife, Princess Augusta of Great Britain and Ireland, Princess of Cambridge.
May 8, 1878, Neustrelitz — October 14, 1918, Obercassel
(She m. 2: Julius, Prince zur Lippe-Biesterfeld – see: *zur Lippe-Biesterfeld* XXI, page 754.)

Issue: 1. George, Count Jamatel (1904–)
m. Lise Barbet (–)
see: *Jamatel* XVIII, 2, below

2. Marie Auguste, Countess Jamatel (1905–)
m. Karl Barton genannt von Stedman (–1933)
see: *Barton genannt von Stedman* XXI, page 651

XVIII. Jamatel 2, from above

★ **George,** Count Jamatel, only son of Count George.
February 3, 1904, —
m. , 1948,
Lise Barbet, daughter of
—

No Issue.

XVIII. LAGUERRE 1, from page 988

André Laguerre

—

m. June 13, 1955,

★ **Nataliya Aleksandra Evgeniievna,** Princess Kotchoubey de Beauharnais, daughter of Prince Evgenii Leontievich Kotchoubey de Beauharnais and of his wife, Helen Geraldine Pearce.

May 19, 1923, Eltham, Kent, England —

Issue: 1. Michele Laguerre
June 1, 1956, —

2. Claudine Josephine Laguerre
July 13, 1964, Maine, USA —

XVIII. DE LAU d'ALLEMANS 1, from page 1010

Henri, Comte de Lau d'Allemans

July , 1927, —

m. October 17, 1959, Paris

★ **Helene,** Countess de Witt, daughter of Count Sergei de Witt and of his wife, Princess Marie Clothilde Bonaparte.

November 22, 1941, Tunis —

Issue: 1. Jean, Comte de Lau d'Allemans
December 19, 1960, Périgreux, France —

2. Alexandre, Comte de Lau d'Allemans
May 12, 1962, Périgreux —

3. Astrid, Comtesse de Lau d'Allemans
September 16, 1964, Périgreux —

XVIII. LAUR 1, from page 884

Louis Laur, M.D.

January 1, 1904, Mortain — May 10, 1957, Marseilles

m. September 19, 1923, Caen, France

★ **Karoline Mathilde,** Princess Vlangali-Handjeri, daughter of Prince Karl Vlangali-Handjeri and of his wife, Princess Amelie von Noer.

October 6, 1900, Noer, Holstein, Germany —

XVIII. Laur 1 continued

Issue: 1. Christian Louis Laur (1927–)
m. Camille de Bret (–)
see: *Laur* XVIII, 2, below

XVIII. Laur 2, from above

* **Christian Louis Laur,** only son of Dr. Louis Laur.
March 9, 1927, Paris —
m. March 10, 1948, Paris
Camille de Bret, daughter of Henri de Bret and of his wife,
—

Issue: 1. Bernard Louis Laur
December 18, 1949, Paris —

2. Eric Laur
December 12, 1953, Paris —

XVIII. LELONG 1, from page 310

Lucien Lelong
October 11, 1889, Paris — , 1959, Biarritz
m. August 10, 1927, Paris. Divorced: , 1937,
* **Nataliya Pavlovna,** Princess Paleya, daughter of Grand Duke Pavel Aleksandrovich of Russia and of his second wife, Olga Valerianovna Karnovitch, created Princess Paleya.
November 22/December 5, 1905, Paris —
(She m. 2: John C. Wilson – see: *Wilson* XXIV, page 1025.)

No Issue.

XVIII. LEQUIO 1, from page 608

Clemente Lequio
December 9, 1926, Paris —
m. June 18, 1958, Trieste
* **Donna Alessandra Torlonia,** daughter of Don Alessandro, Principe di Civitelli-Cesi, and of his wife, Dona Beatriz de Borbon y Battenberg, Infanta of Spain.
February 14, 1936, Rome —

XVIII. Lequio 1 continued

Issue: 1. Alessandro Lequio
June 17, 1960, Lausanne, Switzerland —

2. Desideria Lequio
September 19, 1962, Lausanne —

XVIII. DE LIGNE 1, from page 108

Antoine, Prince de Ligne, second son of Prince Eugene.
March 8, 1925, Brussels, Belgium —
m. August 17, 1950, Luxemburg
* **Alix,** Princess of Luxemburg, daughter of Grand Duchess Charlotte of Luxemburg and of her husband, Prince Felix of Bourbon-Parma.
August 24, 1929, Berg Castle —

Issue: 1. Michel, Prince de Ligne
May 26, 1951, Beloeil —

2. Wauthier, Prince de Ligne
July 10, 1952, Beloeil —

3. Anne, Princess de Ligne
April 3, 1954, Beloeil —

4. Christine, Princess de Ligne
August 11, 1955, Beloeil —

5. Sophie, Princess de Ligne
April 23, 1957, Beloeil —

6. Antoine, Prince de Ligne
December 28, 1959, Beloeil —

XVIII. LOMBARD DE BUFFIÈRES DE RAMBUTEAU 1, from page 574

Almeric Lombard de Buffières de Rambuteau
August 29, 1890, Geneva — December 14, 1944, Buchenwald concentration camp
m. February 5, 1921, Paris
* **Amélie de MacMahon,** daughter of Patrice de MacMahon, 2nd Duke de Magenta, and of his wife, Princess Marguerite of France.
September 11, 1900, Lunéville —

XVIII. Lombard de Buffières de Rambuteau 1 continued

Issue: 1. Françoise Lombard de Buffières de Rambuteau (1922–)
m. Philippe, Comte de Rodez-Bénavent (1913–)
see: *de Rodez-Bénavent* XVIII, page 599

2. Philibert Lombard de Buffières de Rambuteau
September 14, 1923, Paris —

3. Henri Lombard de Buffières de Rambuteau (1925–)
m. Irmeline de Fleurien (1935–)
see: *Lombard de Buffières de Rambuteau* XVIII, 2, below

4. Maurice Lombard de Buffières de Rambuteau (1927–)
m. Yolande de Mitry (1929–)
see: *Lombard de Buffières de Rambuteau* XVIII, page 572

XVIII. Lombard de Buffières de Rambuteau 2, from above

* **Henri Lombard de Buffières de Rambuteau,** second son of Almeric.
September 20, 1925, Rambuteau, Ozolles, Saône-et-Loire, France —
m. July 21, 1956, St. Georges de Reneius, Rhône
Irmeline de Fleurien, daughter of
October 17, 1935, Stockholm, Sweden —

Issue: 1. Jean Lombard de Buffières de Rambuteau
June 20, 1957, Villefranche-sur-Saône —

2. Marie-Edla Lombard de Buffières de Rambuteau
December 9, 1958, Villefranche —

3. Claude Lombard de Buffières de Rambuteau
December 13, 1959, Villefranche —

4. Philibert Lombard de Buffières de Rambuteau
March 25, 1966, Villefranche —

XVIII. Lombard de Buffières de Rambuteau 3, from page 571

* **Maurice Lombard de Buffières de Rambuteau,** third son of Almeric.
February 5, 1927, Paris —
m. July 4, 1954, Paris
Yolande de Mitry, daughter of
May 5, 1929, Paris —

Issue: 1. Emanuel Lombard de Buffières de Rambuteau
December 12, 1954, Paris —

2. François Lombard de Buffières de Rambuteau
June 19, 1956, Paris —

3. Aymar Lombard de Buffières de Rambuteau
December 13, 1959, Paris —

4. Patrice Lombard de Buffières de Rambuteau
August 21, 1960, Paris —

5. Lorraine Lombard de Buffières de Rambuteau
March 18, 1964, Paris —

6. Laurent Lombard de Buffières de Rambuteau
October 7, 1965, Paris —

XVIII. LOURIÉ 1, from page 307

Arthur Lourié
— November 13, 1966, in the USA
m. July , 1939
* **Elizabeta Alekseievna,** Countess Belevskya-Zhukovskya, daughter of Count Aleksei Alekseievich Belevsky-Zhukovsky and of his first wife, Princess Mariya Petrovna Troubetskoya.
September 8, 1896, Moscow —
(She m. 1: Petr Dimitrievich Perevostchikov – see: *Perevostchikov* XXIII, page 1007.)

No Issue.

XVIII. LUCCHESI-PALLI (dei Principi di Campofranco) 1, from page 447

Don Pietro, Conte Lucchesi-Palli
February 7, 1870, Rome — December 5, 1939, Brunnsee, Austria
m. August 12, 1906, Schwarzau am Steinfelde, Austria
* **Beatrix,** Princess of Bourbon-Parma, daughter of Duke Robert I of Parma and of his first wife, Princess Maria Pia of Bourbon-Sicily.
January 9, 1879, Biarritz — March 11, 1946, Brunnsee

Issue: 1. Don Antonio, Conte Lucchesi-Palli
June 1, 1907, Pianore — January 4, 1911, Graz

2. Don Roberto, Conte Lucchesi-Palli (1908–)
m. Donna Stefania Ruffo di Calabria (1909–)
see: *Lucchesi-Palli* XVIII, 2, below

3. Don Adinolfo, Conte Lucchesi-Palli (1911–)
m. Sarolta (Charlotte), Countess Teleki von Szek (1923–)
see: *Lucchesi-Palli* XVIII, 3, page 574

XVIII. Lucchesi-Palli (dei Principi di Campofranco) 2, from above

* **Don Roberto,** Conte Lucchesi-Palli, eldest son of Don Pietro.
July 7, 1908, Venedig —
m. June 7, 1941, Florence
Donna Stefania Ruffo di Calabria, daughter of Don Umberto Ruffo di Calabria and of his wife, Donna Isabella dei Marchesa Torrigiani.
August 25, 1909, Florence —

Issue: 1. Don Pietro, Conte Lucchesi-Palli
January 4, 1943, Rome —

2. Don Antonio, Conte Lucchesi-Palli
October 5, 1944, San Gimignano —

3. Don Roberto, Conte Lucchesi-Palli
July 20, 1946, San Gimignano —

4. Don Emanuele, Conte Lucchesi-Palli
January 11, 1952, San Gimignano —

XVIII. Lucchesi-Palli (dei Principi di Campofranco) 3, from page 573

* **Don Adinolfo,** Conte Lucchesi-Palli, second son of Don Pietro.
June 18, 1911, Brunnsee —
m. June 2, 1946, Brunnsee
Sarolta (Charlotte), Countess Teleki von Szek, daughter of Count Miklos (Michael) Telek von Szek and of his wife, Countess Pauline de Szirma-Bessenyö, Csernek und Tarkö.
March 29, 1923, Budapest, Hungary —

Issue: 1. Donna Maria, Contessa Lucchesi-Palli
April 25, 1947, Brunnsee —

2. Don Michele, Conte Lucchesi-Palli
February 5, 1949, Weinburg —

3. Donna Eva Maria, Contessa Lucchesi-Palli
September 18, 1951, Weinburg —

4. Don Pio, Conte Lucchesi-Palli
March 17, 1955, Graz, Austria —

5. Donna Maria Bernadetta, Contessa Lucchesi-Palli
May 27, 1957, Graz —

XVIII. DE MACMAHON (Magenta) 1, from page 456

Patrice de MacMahon, 2nd Duke of Magenta, 7th Marquis de MacMahon.
June 10, 1855, Outreau — May 23, 1927, Paris
m. April 22, 1896 (civil), and April 23, 1896 (religious), Chantilly, France
* **Marguerite,** Princess of France, daughter of Prince Robert, Duc de Chartres, and of his wife, Princess Françoise of France.
January 25, 1869, Ham, England — January 31, 1940, Le Fôret, Montcresson, France

Issue: 1. Elisabeth de MacMahon (1899–1951)
m. Henri de Plan, Comte de Sièyes (1883–1953)
see: *de Plan* XVIII, page 593

2. Amélie de MacMahon (1900–)
m. Almeric Lombard de Buffières de Rambuteau (1890–1944)
see: *Lombard de Buffières de Rambuteau* XVIII, page 570

XVIII. de MacMahon (Magenta) 1 continued

3. Maurice de MacMahon (1903–1954)
m. Marguerite de Riquet, Comtesse de Caramen-Chimay (1913–)
see: *de MacMahon* XVIII, 2, below

XVIII. de MacMahon (Magenta) 2, from above

* **Maurice de MacMahon,** 3rd Duc de Magenta, 8th Marquis de MacMahon, only son of Patrice de MacMahon.
November 13, 1903, Lunéville — October 27, 1954, Eureux
m. August 25, 1937, Château de Sully

Marguerite de Riquet, Comtesse de Chimay et de Caraman, daughter of Philippe de Riquet, Comte de Chimay et de Caraman, and of his wife, Jeanne de Boisgelin.
December 29, 1913, Paris —

Issue: 1. Philippe de MacMahon, 4th Duc de Magenta, 9th Marquis de MacMahon
May 15, 1938, Paris —

2. Nathalie de MacMahon
April 11, 1939, Paris —

3. Anne de MacMahon (1941–)
m. Arnould, Baron Thénard (1940–)
see: *Thénard* XVIII, page 608

4. Patrice de MacMahon (1943–)
m. Beatrix de Chayla (1945–)
see: *de MacMahon* XVIII, 3, page 576

5. Véronique de MacMahon
June 5, 1948, Château de Sully —

XVIII. de MacMahon (Magenta) 3, from page 575

* **Patrice de MacMahon,** second son of Maurice.
September 11, 1943, Lausanne, Switzerland —
m. June 11, 1966, Beaumont de Roger
Beatrix de Chayla, daughter of Bernard du Chayla and of his wife, Hélène de Lasteyrie du Saillant.
March 27, 1945, Tain l'Hérmitage (Drôme) —

Issue: 1. Diane de MacMahon
September 18, 1968, Paris —

XVIII. MAILLÉ DE LA TOUR-LANDRY 1, from page 401

Gilles de Maillé de la Tour-Landry, 5th Duc de Maillé.
September 2, 1893, Osfrasière Castle, Indre-sur-Loire, France —
m. June 16, 1928, Paris
* **Anna Maria,** Princess Radziwill, daughter of Prince Stanislaw Radziwill and of his wife, Princess Dolores Radziwill.
October 2, 1907, Balice, Poland —

Issue: 1. Jeanne Marie de Maillé de la Tour-Landry (1929–)
m. and divorced: Guy, Prince de Broglie (1924–)
see: *de Broglie* XVIII, page 551

2. Jacquelin de Maillé de la Tour-Landry, Marquis de Maillé
July 9, 1931, Paris — March 21, 1955, Paris

3. Stanislaus de Maillé de la Tour-Landry, Comte de Maillé
April 3, 1946, Paris —

XVIII. MALDONADO 1, from page 444

Don Luiz Gonzaga Maldonado y Gordon of Wardhouse
November 17, 1932, Madrid —
m. June 11, 1962, Jerez, Spain
* **Marie Marguerite,** Princess of Bourbon-Sicily, daughter of Prince Gabriel of Bourbon-Sicily and of his second wife, Princess Cecilia Lubomirska.
November 16, 1934, Warsaw, Poland —

XVIII. Maldonado 1 continued

Issue: 1. Dona Maria Margarida Maldonado y de Borbon
September 24, 1963, Madrid —

2. Dona Claudia Maldonado y de Borbon
March 30, 1965, Madrid —

3. Dona Maria Cecilia Maldonado y de Borbon
September 25, 1967, Madrid —

XVIII. MANNO 1, from page 367

Vittorio, Baron Manno, son of Baron Antonio.
—
m. May 7, 1970, Salzburg, Austria
* **Alice,** Archduchess of Austria, daughter of Archduke Gottfried of Austria and of his wife, Princess Dorothea of Bavaria.
April 29, 1941, Leutstetten Castle —

Issue:

XVIII. MANZOLINI 1, from page 963

Ettore (Hector) Manzolini, Conte di Campoleone
July 29, 1879, —
m.
* **Octavia,** Countess Rzyszczewska, daughter of Count Antoni Rzyszczewski and of his wife, Ernestine Dentler.
April 22, 1907, —

Issue: 1. Donna Eleanora Manzolini
November 6, 1944, —

2. Donna Sonia Manzolini
June 6, 1946, —

3. Donna Letitia Manzolini
September 17, 1947, —

XVIII. MARONE CINZANO

1, from page 431

Enrico Marone Cinzano, (created Count Marone, May 13, 1940, by King Vittorio Emanuele III of Italy).

March 15, 1895, Turin — October 22, 1968, Turin
m. June 10, 1940, Rome

* **Dona Maria Cristina de Borbon y Battenberg,** Infanta of Spain, daughter of King Alfonso XIII of Spain and of his wife, Princess Victoria Eugenie of Battenberg.

December 12, 1911, San Ildefonsa, Spain —

Issue: 1. Donna Vittoria Marone Cinzano (1941–)
m. Don José Carlos Alvarez de Toledo y Gross (1930–)
see: *Alvarez de Toledo* XVIII, page 543

2. Donna Giovanna Marone Cinzano (1943–)
m. Don José Maria Ruiz de Arana, Marques de Brenes (1934–)
see: *Ruiz de Arana* XVIII, page 600

3. Donna Maria Theresa Marone Cinzano (1945–)
m. Don Jaime Galobart y Satrustequi (1933–)
see: *Galobart* XVIII, page 563

4. Donna Anna Sandra Marone Cinzano (1948–)
m. Gian Carlo Stavro Santarosa (1944–)
see: *Stavro Santarosa* XVIII, page 606

XVIII. MASSETTI ZANNINI

1, from page 584

Gian Ludovico Massetti Zannini

February 2, 1929, Brescia —
m. July 6, 1963, Rome

* **Donna Eleanora di Napoli-Rampolla,** daughter of Don Vincenzo di Napoli-Rampolla, 13th Principe di Resutano, and of his wife, Contessa Teresa di Bulgarini d'Elci.

November 16, 1927, Rome —

Issue: 1. Alessandro Vincenzo Massetti Zannini
November 22, 1965, Rome —

XVIII. MOCENIGO 1, from page 913

Andrea (Andrew), Conte Mocenigo
August 3, 1850, Venice — June 26, 1878, Salzburg
m. October 7, 1876, Haasberg Castle
* **Olga,** Princess Windisch-Graetz, daughter of Prince Hugo Windisch-Graetz and of his wife, Duchess Luise of Mecklenburg-Schwerin.
March 17, 1853, Florence — December 27, 1934, Gonobitz

Issue: 1. Valentina, Contessa Mocenigo (1878–1950)
m. Edmondo Nicolis, Conte di Robilant e Cereaglio (1871–1941)
see: *Robilant e Cereaglio (Nicolis)* XVIII, page 594

XVIII. MOCENNI 1, from page 563

Carlo Mocenni
—
m. September 6, 1969, Brisighella
* **Maria-Ginerva,** Contessa Ginanni Fantuzzi, daughter of Conte Gabriele Ginanni Fantuzzi and of his wife, Anna Aloisi.
November 12, 1943, Brisighella —

Issue:

XVIII. DE MONBRISON 1, from page 309

Hubert, Comte de Monbrison
August 15, 1892, St. Avertin, France —
m. April 11, 1950, Biarritz
* **Irina Pavlovna,** Princess Paleya, daughter of Grand Duke Pavel (Paul) Aleksandrovich of Russia and of his second wife, Olga Valerianovna Karnovitch, created Princess Paleya.
December 8/21, 1903, Paris —
(She m. 1: and divorced: Feodor Aleksandrovich, Prince of Russia – see: *Russia* VIII w–1, page 327.)

No Issue.

XVIII. DE MONTAIGNAC 1, from page 1006

Paul de Montaignac

—

m. April 1, 1943, . Divorced: February , 1951,

* **Kseniya (Xenia) Nikolaievna,** Princess Orlova, daughter of Prince Nikolai Vladimirovich Orlov and of his wife, Princess Nadeshda Petrovna of Russia.

March 27, 1921, Paris — August 17, 1963,

(She m. 2: Jean Albert, Baron d'Almont – see: *d'Almont* XVIII, page 539.)

Issue: 1. Calixte August de Montaignac
September 24, 1944, —

XVIII. MORALES 1, from page 441

Don Luis Morales y Aguado

October 8, 1933, Granada, Spain —

m. January 21, 1965, Madrid

* **Ines,** Princess of Bourbon-Sicily, Infanta of Spain, daughter of Prince Alfonso of Bourbon-Sicily, Infante of Spain, and of his wife, Princess Alice of Bourbon-Parma.

February 18, 1940, Ouchy, near Lausanne, Switzerland —

Issue: 1. Dona Isabel Morales y de Borbon
April 10, 1966, Madrid —

2. Dona Eugenia Morales y de Borbon
December 14, 1967, Madrid —

XVIII. MORELL 1, from page 588

Don Fausto Morell y Rovira

September 12, 1916, Palma de Mallorca, Balearic Islands, Spain —

m. January 8, 1954, Palma de Mallorca

* **Dona Isabel Orlandis y Habsburgo,** daughter of Don Ramon Orlandis y Villalonga and of his wife, Archduchess Maria Antonia of Austria.

March 12, 1931, Palma de Mallorca —

XVIII. Morell 1 continued

Issue: 1. Don Fausto Morell y Orlandis
December 18, 1954, Palma de Mallorca —

2. Don Francisco Javier Morell y Orlandis
December 5, 1955, Palma de Mallorca —

3. Don Carlos Morell y Orlandis
January 24, 1957, Palma de Mallorca —

4. Dona Maria Immaculada Morell y Orlandis
May 14, 1958, Palma de Mallorca —

5. Dona Maria Gabriela Morell y Orlandis
March 20, 1961, Palma de Mallorca —

6. Don Miguel Morell y Orlandis
October 6, 1963, Palma de Mallorca —

XVIII. MORENO 1, from page 441

Don Inigo Moreno y Arteaga, Marques de Laula
April 18, 1934, Madrid —
m. April 16, 1961, Madrid
* **Theresa,** Princess of Bourbon-Sicily, Infanta of Spain, daughter of Prince Alfonso of Bourbon Sicily, Infante of Spain, and of his wife, Princess Alice of Bourbon-Parma.
February 6, 1937, Lausanne, Switzerland —

Issue: 1. Don Rodrigo Moreno y de Borbon
February 1, 1962, Madrid —

2. Dona Alicia Moreno y de Borbon
June 6, 1964, Jerez de la Frondern, Spain —

3. Don Alfonso Moreno y de Borbon
October 19, 1965, Madrid —

4. Dona Beatriz Moreno y de Borbon
May 10, 1967, Madrid —

XVIII. MORETTI 1, from page 964

Paul Moretti
January 20, 1908, Cervione, France —
m. November 11, 1954, Cervione
* **Maria,** Countess Skorzewska, daughter of Count Zygmund (Sigismund) Skorzewski and of his wife, Princess Leontyna Radziwill.
August 13, 1908, Czerniejew, Poland —

Issue: 1. Henriette Moretti
March 2, 1955, Cervione —

2. Jean Charles Moretti
September 24, 1959, Cervione —

3. Louis-Constantin Moretti
October 12, 1964, Cervione —

XVIII. MOZOYER 1, from page 605

Marcel Mozoyer
—
m. , 1967,
* **Catherine Snopko,** daughter of Georges Snopko and of his wife, Princess Diana Eugenie Evgenievna Kotchoubey de Beauharnais.
April 28, 1941, —

Issue:

XVIII. MURAT 1, from page 457

Pierre, Prince Murat
April 6, 1900, Paris — June 30, 1948, Rabat, Morocco
m. July 12, 1934, Jouey-en-Josas
* **Isabelle,** Princess of France, daughter of Prince Jean, Duc de Guise and of his wife, Princess Isabelle of France.
November 27, 1900, Paris —
(She m. 1: Bruno, Comte d'Harcourt – see: *d'Harcourt* XVIII, page 566.)

No Issue.

XVIII. Murat 2, from page 566

Louis, Prince Murat
September 4, 1920, Paris —
m. October 20, 1948, Paris

* **Isabelle d'Harcourt,** daughter of Comte Bruno d'Harcourt and of his wife, Princess Isabelle of France.
January 1, 1927, Larache, Morocco —

Issue: 1. Pierre, Prince Murat
October 17, 1949, Neuilly-sur-Seine —

2. Xavier, Prince Murat
July 16, 1951, Casablanca — September 30, 1951, Fedala, Morocco

3. Leila, Princess Murat
March 17, 1953, Boulogne-Billancourt —

4. Laura, Princess Murat
September 20, 1954, Boulogne-Billancourt —

5. Bernard, Prince Murat
January 20, 1959, Neuilly-sur-Seine —

6. Jérôme, Prince Murat
April 2, 1966, Neuilly-sur-Seine —

XVIII. DI NAPOLI-RAMPOLLA 1, from page 541

Don Francesco di Napoli-Rampolla, 12th Duke di Bonfornello, 7th Principe di Monteleone, 5th Principe de Condro, 12th Principe di Resuttano.
October 24, 1871, Palermo — November 6, 1938, Polizzi Generosa
m. June 20, 1897, Rome

* **Theodolinda Altieri,** daughter of Paolo Altieri, Principe di Viano, and of his wife, Countess Mathilde Auguste of Württemberg.
November 5, 1876, Rome — September 21, 1947, Rome

Issue: 1. Don Vincenzo di Napoli-Rampolla, 13th Duke di Bonfornello, 8th Principe di Monteleone, 6th Principe di Condro, 13th Principe di Resuttano (1898–1965)
m. Teresa, Contessa di Bulgarini d'Elci (1900–)
see: *di Napoli-Rampolla* XVIII, 2, page 584

XVIII. di Napoli-Rampolla 1 continued

2. Don Federico di Napoli (1900–)
m. Elsa Dragoni (–)
see: *di Napoli* XVIII, 6, page 586

XVIII. di Napoli-Rampolla 2, from page 583

* **Don Vincenzo di Napoli-Rampolla,** 13th Duke di Bonfornello, 8th Principe di Monteleone, 6th Principe di Condro, 13th Principe di Resuttano, eldest son of Don Francesco.
April 19, 1898, Rome — February 5, 1965, Rome
m. September 23, 1920, Siena
Teresa, Contessa di Bulgarini d'Elci, daughter of Conte Ferdinando di Bulgarini d'Elci and of his wife, Josephine Barel dei Marchese di Lucinge.
April 8, 1900, Rome —

Issue: 1. Donna Paola di Napoli-Rampolla, Sister Teresa of the Order of Assunzione.
October 26, 1921, Siena —

2. Don Francesco di Napoli-Rampolla (1923–)
m. Clara de Marsanich (1922–)
see: *di Napoli-Rampolla* XVIII, 3, page 585

3. Don Alceo di Napoli-Rampolla (1925–)
m. Livia Borgia (1914–)
see: *di Napoli-Rampolla* XVIII, 4, page 585

4. Donna Eleanora di Napoli-Rampolla (1927–)
m. Gian Ludovico Massetti Zannini (1929–)
see: *Massetti Zannini* XVIII, page 578

5. Don Fernando di Napoli-Rampolla (1931–)
m. Wanda Piscitelli (1929–)
see: *di Napoli-Rampolla* XVIII, 5, page 586

XVIII. di Napoli-Rampolla 3, from page 584

★ **Don Francesco di Napoli-Rampolla,** 14th Duke di Bonfornello, 9th Principe di Monteleone, 7th Principe di Condro, 14th Principe di Resuttano, eldest son of Don Vincenzo.
July 3, 1923, Rome —
m. December 2, 1950, Rome
Clara, Contessa di Marsanich, daughter of Conte Alberto di Marsanich and of his wife, Maria, dei Marchesi Bisleti.
August 1, 1922, Nancy, France —

Issue: 1. Don Ludovico di Napoli-Rampolla
November 21, 1951, Rome —

2. Donna Federica di Napoli-Rampolla
July 3, 1954, Rome —

3. Donna Theodolinda di Napoli-Rampolla
May 1, 1925, Rome —

4. Don Vincenzo di Napoli-Rampolla
June 25, 1965, Rome —

XVIII. di Napoli-Rampolla 4, from page 584

★ **Don Alceo di Napoli-Rampolla,** second son of Don Vincenzo.
August 24, 1925, Rome —
m. August 20, 1950, Pentolina
Livia Borgia, daughter of Nobile Alberto Borgia and of his wife, Mathilde Bruno.
September 21, 1914, Ferrara —

Issue: 1. Don Matteo di Napoli-Rampolla
June 15, 1951, São Paulo, Brazil —

2. Don Marco di Napoli-Rampolla
October 24, 1952, Assis, Brazil —

3. Donna Paola di Napoli-Rampolla
February 5, 1954, Assis — November 16, 1954, Assis

4. Don Luca di Napoli-Rampolla
April 28, 1955, Buenos Aires, Argentina —

XVIII. di Napoli-Rampolla 4 continued

5. Donna Maurizia di Napoli-Rampolla
September 1, 1957, Florence —

XVIII. di Napoli-Rampolla 5, from page 584

* **Don Fernando di Napoli-Rampolla,** youngest son of Don Vincenzo.
January 15, 1931, Rome —
m. June 1, 1964, Naples
Wanda Piscitelli, daughter of
February 5, 1929, Naples —

No Issue.

XVIII. di Napoli 6, from page 584

* **Don Federico di Napoli,** second son of Don Francesco di Napoli-Rampolla.
September 6, 1900, Rome —
m. April 30, 1930, Milan
Elsa Dragoni, daughter of Emilio Dragoni and of his wife,
—

Issue: 1. Don Emilio di Napoli (1931–)
m. no information available
see: *di Napoli* XVIII, 7, below

XVIII. di Napoli 7, from above

* **Don Emilio di Napoli,** only son of Don Federico.
June 17, 1931, Milan —
m. no information available
—

Issue: 1. Don Marc'Antonio di Napoli
—

XVIII. de NICOLAY 1, from page 462

René, Comte de Nicolay
January 17, 1910, Le Lude, Sarthe, France —
m. August 12, 1948, Paris
* **Pia Maria,** Princess de Orleans e Braganca, daughter of Dom Luiz de Orleans e Braganca and of his wife, Princess Maria Pia of Bourbon-Sicily.
March 4, 1913, Boulogne-sur-Seine —

Issue: 1. Louis Jean, Comte de Nicolay
September 18, 1949, Le Mans, Sarthe —

2. Robert, Comte de Nicolay
February 17, 1952, Neuilly-sur-Seine —

XVIII. ODESCALCHI (di Monteleone) 1, from page 391

Alexander Erba Odescalchi, Principe di Monteleone
March 23, 1914, Budapest, Hungary —
m. August 17, 1943, Tihany, Hungary
* **Margarethe (Margit),** Archduchess of Austria, daughter of Archduke Joseph of Austria and of his wife, Princess Anna of Saxony.
August 17, 1925, Budapest —

Issue: 1. Sibylla Odescalchi, Principessa di Monteleone
April 7, 1945, Stockholm, Sweden —

XVIII. OLIVETTI 1, from page 143

Jacques Olivetti
—
m. August 6, 1949, Paris. Divorced:
* **Elisabeth,** Princess of Hesse (-Philippsthal-Barchfeld), daughter of Prince Christian of Hesse (-Philippsthal-Barchfeld) and of his first wife, Elizabeth Reid Rodgers.
November 2, 1915, Berlin —

No Issue.

XVIII. ORLANDIS 1, from page 370

Don Ramon Orlandis y Villalonga
December 24, 1896, Palma de Mallorca, Spain —
m. November 10, 1936, Palma de Mallorca
* **Maria Antonia,** Archduchess of Austria, daughter of Archduke Leopold Salvator of Austria and of his wife, Princess Blanka of Bourbon, Princess of Castile.
July 13, 1899, Agram —
(She m. 2: Luis Perez Sucre – see: *Sucre* XXIV, page 1024.)

Issue: 1. Dona Blanca Maria de las Nieves Orlandis y Habsburgo (1926–1969)
m. Don Juan Ereñú y Ferreira (1908–1969)
see: *Ereñú* XXIV, page 1017

2. Don Juan Orlandis y Habsburgo (1928–)
m. Dona Hildegarda Bragagnolo y Daiqui Chevalier (1932–)
see: *Orlandis* XVIII, 2, below

3. Dona Maria Antonia Orlandis y Habsburgo
November 28, 1929, Palma de Mallorca —

4. Dona Isabel Orlandis y Habsburgo (1931–)
m. Don Fausto Morell y Rovira (1916–)
see: *Morell* XVIII, page 580

5. Dona Maria Alfonsa Orlandis y Habsburgo
February 16, 1936, Palma de Mallorca —

XVIII. Orlandis 2, from above

* **Don Juan Orlandis y Habsburgo,** Baron de Pinopar, only son of Don Ramon.
January 2, 1928, Palma de Mallorca —
m. March , 1951, Buenos Aires, Argentina
Dona Hildegarda Bragagnolo y Daiqui Chevalier, daughter of Efrain Bragagnolo and of his wife, Carmen.
July 25, 1932, Buenos Aires, Argentina —

XVIII. Orlandis 2 continued

Issue: 1. Dona Maria del Carmen Orlandis y Bragagnolo
February 2, 1952, Barcelona, Spain —

2. Don Ramon Orlandis y Bragagnolo
April 28, 1953, Viareggio, Italy —

3. Don Luis Orlandis y Bragagnolo
June 13, 1954, Viareggio —

4. Dona Maria del Pilar Orlandis y Bragagnolo (twin)
May 28, 1955, Viareggio —

5. Dona Hildegarda Orlandis y Bragagnolo (twin)
May 28, 1955, Viareggio —

6. Dona Marta Orlandis y Bragagnolo
January 6, 1957, La Amettla del Valles —

7. Dona Cristina Orlandis y Bragagnolo
, 1964, Barcelona —

8. Don Juan Orlandis y Bragagnolo
, 1965, Barcelona —

XVIII. PALLAVICINI 1, from page 244

Frederico, Marchese Pallavicini
December 23, 1924, Budapest, Hungary —
m. August 23, 1961, Friedrichshafen, Germany
* **Helene,** Duchess of Württemberg, daughter of Duke Philipp of Württemberg and of his wife, Archduchess Rosa of Austria.
June 29, 1929, Stuttgart —

Issue: 1. Donna Maria Cristina Pallavicini
January 4, 1963, Salzburg, Austria —

2. Donna Antoinetta Pallavicini
January 9, 1964, Ravensburg, Germany —

XVIII. Pallavicini 1 continued

3. Donna Gabriela Pallavicini
April 23, 1965, Ravensburg —

4. Don Gian-Garlo Pallavicini
April 8, 1967, Ravensburg —

XVIII. PALLOVICINO 1, from page 541

Roberto, Marchese Pallovicino
August 14, 1870, Florence — September 10, 1937, Arenzano
m. January 10, 1916, Rome
* **Maria Augusta Altieri,** daughter of Paolo Altieri, Principe di Viano, and of his wife, Countess Mathilde Auguste of Württemberg.
October 31, 1880, Rome —

Issue: 1. Andrea Pallovicino
November 8, 1916, Bologna —

XVIII. PASOLINI dall'ONDA 1, from page 541

Pasolino, Conte Pasolini dall'Onda
January 11, 1876, Ravenina — December 2, 1933, Ravenina
m. February 2, 1917, Rome
* **Camilla Maria Altieri,** daughter of Paolo Altieri, Principe di Viano, and of his wife, Countess Mathilde Auguste of Württemberg.
December 3, 1889, Rome —

No Issue.

XVIII. de PASQUIER de FRANCLIEU 1, from page 556

Antoine de Pasquier de Franclieu, Marquis de Franclieu
March 24, 1897, Epernay —
m. September 11, 1925, Bonnée, Loiret, France —
* **Elisabeth Desrousseaux de Vandières,** daughter of Edouard, Comte Desrousseaux, Duc de Vandières, and of his wife, Princess Elisabeth zu Ysenburg und Büdingen in Wächtersbach.
August 2, 1902, Vandières —

XVIII. de Pasquier de Franclieu 1 continued

Issue: 1. Jean de Pasquier de Franclieu (1926–)
m. Christiane de Pasquier de Franclieu (1925–)
see: *de Pasquier de Franclieu* XVIII, 2, below

2. Marguerite de Pasquier de Franclieu (1927–)
m. Vincent de Bataille-Furé (1914–)
see: *de Bataille-Furé* XVIII, page 544

3. Robert de Pasquier de Franclieu (1932–)
m. Claude Le Boulanger de Chapelle (1931–)
see: *de Pasquier de Franclieu* XVIII, 3, below

4. Marie-Thérèse de Pasquier de Franclieu (1941–)
m. Gérard Bergeron (1940–)
see: *Bergeron* XVIII, page 544

XVIII. de Pasquier de Franclieu 2, from above

* **Jean de Pasquier de Franclieu,** eldest son of Antoine.
June 16, 1926, Lascazeres —
m. August 6, 1947, Puymaurin, Haute-Garonne, France
Christiane de Pasquier de Franclieu, daughter of Comte Camille de Pasquier de Franclieu.
—

Issue: 1. Georges de Pasquier de Franclieu, May 25, 1948 —

2. Edith de Pasquier de Franclieu, May 30, 1949 —

3. Robert de Pasquier de Franclieu, November 27, 1950 —

4. Véronique de Pasquier de Franclieu, December 23, 1957 —

5. Jacques de Pasquier de Franclieu, June 16, 1960 —

XVIII. de Pasquier de Franclieu 3, from above

* **Robert de Pasquier de Franclieu,** second son of Antoine.
July 21, 1932, Bonnée, Loiret —
m. July 2, 1955,
Claude Le Boulanger de Chapelle, daughter of Georges Le Boulanger de Chapelle and of his wife,
May 31, 1931, Paris —

XVIII. de Pasquier de Franclieu 3 continued

Issue: 1. Philippe de Pasquier de Franclieu
October 23, 1955, Paris —

2. Bruno de Pasquier de Franclieu
October 15, 1956, Paris —

3. Thibaut de Pasquier de Franclieu
July 13, 1959, Nancy —

XVIII. PATINO 1, from page 477

Don Alfonso Patino, Marquez Patino, Marquez de Castro des Duques de Grimaldi
August 7, 1936, San Sebastian, Spain —
m. November 23, 1963, Madrid

* **Dona Maria Theresia de Baviera y de Mesia,** daughter of Prince Joseph Eugen of Bavaria, Infante of Spain, Count Odiel, and of his wife, Dona Maria Solange de Mesia y Lesseps.
January 11, 1941, Madrid —

Issue: 1. Dona Myrta Sofia Patino y de Baviera
October 27, 1965, Madrid —

2. Dona Sonia Victoria Patino y de Baviera
June 7, 1969, Madrid —

XVIII. PELLEGRINO 1, from page 988

Pierre Pellegrino
—
m. December 2, 1947,

* **Helen Josephine Evgeniievna,** Princess Kotchoubey de Beauharnais, daughter of Prince Evgenii Leontievich Kotchoubey de Beauharnais and of his wife, Helen Geraldine Pearce.
April 5, 1928, Paris —

Issue: 1. Elisabeth Pellegrino, July 18, 1948, —

2. Eugenie Pellegrino, April 27, 1955, —

3. Alexandra Pellegrino, April 29, 1958, Paris — April 30, 1958, Paris

XVIII. PESCATORE 1, from page 930

Dominik Pescatore

April 12, 1879, Berlin — May 8, 1957, Hohenkirchen, near Munich

m. September 1, 1913, Hohenthurm Castle

* **Gisela von Wuthenau-Hohenthurm,** daughter of Carl Hans Fedor von Wuthenau-Hohenthurm and of his wife, Wilma von Wuthenau-Hohenthurm.

November 2, 1893, Geuz — January 26, 1937, Grosshesselohe

Issue: 1. Bonaventura Pescatore (1921–)
m. Traute Christel Plep (1921–), see: *Pescatore*, Addendum, page 1069

2. Wilfried Pescatore, August 7, 1923, Hohenkirchen — August 8, 1943, Nikolskoye, Russia

XVIII. de PLAN de SIÈYES 1, from page 574

Henri de Plan, Comte de Sièyes

November 6, 1883, Aix-en-Provence — June 20, 1953, La Fôret, Montcresson

m. September 22, 1924, Paris

* **Elisabeth de MacMahon,** daughter of Patrice de MacMahon, 2nd Duke de Magenta, 7th Marquis de MacMahon, and of his wife, Princess Marguerite of France.

June 19, 1899, Lunéville — September 28, 1951, Voreppe, Isère

Issue: 1. Marguerite de Plan de Sièyes (1926–)
m. Jean-Louis Gillièron (1916–), see: *Gillièron* XVIII, page 563

2. Isabelle de Plan de Sièyes
November 8, 1927, Paris — April 27, 1951, Montcresson

3. François de Plan, Comte de Sièyes, July 16, 1929, Paris —

XVIII. de RAMOS-BANDIERA 1, from page 246

Antonio de Ramos-Bandiera (Portuguese Diplomat)

August 2, 1937, Lisbon, Portugal —

m. February 18, 1969, Altshausen Castle

* **Sophie,** Duchess of Württemberg, daughter of Duke Albrecht of Württemberg and of his wife, Princess Nadeshda of Bulgaria.

February 16, 1937, Stuttgart —

XVIII. REVEDIN di SAN MARTINO 1, from page 540

Neri, Conte Revedin di San Martino
—
m. June , 1951, Pisignano, Italy
* **Raimonda Aloisi,** daughter of Dr. Domenico Aloisi and of his wife, Princess Maria zu Ysenburg und Büdingen in Wächtersbach.
November 3, 1921, Florence —

Issue: 1. Alvise, Conte Revedin di San Martino
April 21, 1952, Florence —

2. Anna, Contessa Revedin di San Martino
February , 1954, Florence —

XVIII. RIERA y de LEYVA 1, from page 374

Don Jose Riera y de Leyva
November 13, 1934, Almeria, Spain —
m. February 1, 1960, Barcelona
* **Alejandra Habsburg,** daughter of Archduke Karl of Austria and of his wife, Crista Satzger de Baloanyos.
January 20, 1941, Viareggio, Italy —

Issue: 1. Dona Alejandra Riera y Habsburgo
November 4, 1960, Lima, Peru —

XVIII. ROBILANT e CEREAGLIO (Nicolis) 1, from page 579

Edmondo Nicolis, Conte di Robilant e Cereaglio
August 4, 1871, Vienna — March 14, 1941, Rome
m. November 3, 1896, Venice
* **Valentina,** Contessa Mocenigo, daughter of Conte Andrea (Andrew) Mocenigo and of his wife, Princess Olga Windisch-Graetz.
July 5, 1878, Salzburg — May 1, 1950, Sintra, Portugal

XVIII. Robilant e Cereaglio (Nicolis) 1 continued

Issue: 1. Carlo Nicolis, Conte di Robilant e Cereaglio (1897–)
m. Caroline Kent (1905–)
see: *Robilant e Cereaglio* XVIII, 2, below

2. Nobile Andrea (Andrew) Nicolis, dei Conti di Robilant e Cereaglio (1899–)
m. 1: and divorced: Gabriella, Contessa di Bosdari (1900–)
m. 2: Alice Allen (1901–)
see: *Robilant e Cereaglio* XVIII, 4, page 596

3. Nobile Olga Nicolis, dei Conti de Robilant e Cereaglio (1900–)
m. Don Antonio Alvares Pereira di Mello (1894–1939)
see: *Alvares Pereira di Mello* XVIII, page 542

4. Nobile Edmondo Nicolis, dei Conti di Robilant e Cereaglio (1901–)
m. Helen Tompkins-Westerveld (–)
see: *Robilant e Cereaglio* XVIII, 7, page 598

5. Nobile Giovanni Nicolis, dei Conti di Robilant e Cereaglio (1905–)
m. Lina Biondi (1907–)
see: *Robilant e Cereaglio* XVIII, 8, page 598

XVIII. Robilant e Cereaglio (Nicolis) 2, from above

* **Nobile Carlo Nicolis,** Conte di Robilant e Cereaglio, eldest son of Conte Edmondo.
July 3, 1897, Kalksberg —
m. October 1, 1929, Venice
Caroline Kent, daughter of Frederick Kent and of his wife, Louise Bolton.
July 15, 1905, Ashville, North Carolina, USA —

Issue: 1. Nobile Frederico Nicolis, dei Conti di Robilant e Cereaglio (1930–)
m. Giovanna Stringher (1934–)
see: *Robilant e Cereaglio* XVIII, 3, page 596

XVIII. Robilant e Cereaglio (Nicolis) 2 continued

2. Nobile Olga Nicolis, dei Conti di Robilant e Cereaglio (1934–)
m. Antonello Aglioti (–)
see: *Aglioti* XVIII, page 538

XVIII. Robilant e Cereaglio (Nicolis) 3, from page 595

* **Nobile Frederico Nicolis,** dei Conti di Robilant e Cereaglio, son of Nobile Carlo Nicolis, Conte di Robilant e Cereaglio.
August 29, 1930, Rome —
m. April 21, 1958, Rome
Giovanna Stringher, daughter of Bonaldo Stringher and of his wife, Magda Thompson.
September 24, 1934, Rome —

Issue: 1. Nobile Alberto Nicolis, dei Conti di Robilant e Cereaglio
September 21, 1958, Rome —

2. Nobile Massimiliano Nicolis, dei Conti di Robilant e Cereaglio
September 8, 1960, Rome —

3. Nobile Ludovico Nicolis, dei Conti di Robilant e Cereaglio
September 9, 1962, Udine, Italy —

XVIII. Robilant e Cereaglio (Nicolis) 4, from page 595

* **Nobile Andrea Nicolis,** dei Conti di Robilant e Cereaglio, second son of Nobile Edmondo, Conte di Robilant e Cereaglio.
January 13, 1899, Venice —
m. 1: July 10, 1920, Bologna, Italy. Divorced: 1937, in Switzerland
Gabriella, Contessa di Bosdari, daughter of Conte Filippo di Bosdari and of his wife, Beatrice di Rossi.
March 1, 1900, Bologna —
(She m. 2: Francesco Starrabba, Principe di Giardinelli.)

XVIII. Robilant e Cereaglio (Nicolis) 4 continued

m. 2: July 22, 1937, London, England
Alice Allen, daughter of George Allen and of his wife, Zoe Saunders.
July 11, 1901, Riga, Latvia —

Issue of first marriage:
1. Nobile Alvise Nicolis, dei Conti di Robilant e Cereaglio (1925–)
m. Elizabeth Stokes (1931–)
see: *Robilant e Cereaglio* XVIII, 5, below

2. Nobile Carlo Nicolis, dei Conti di Robilant e Cereaglio (1927–)
m. Marie Amelie von Heller (1926–)
see: *Robilant e Cereaglio* XVIII, 6, page 598

XVIII. Robilant e Cereaglio (Nicolis) 5, from above

* **Nobile Alvise Nicolis,** dei Conti di Robilant e Cereaglio, eldest son of Nobile Andrea (Andrew).
February 19, 1925, Venice —
m. April 30, 1956, Rome
Elizabeth Stokes, daughter of William Miles Stokes and of his wife, Lily Banks Clark.
August 21, 1931, Lynchburg, Virginia, USA —

Issue: 1. Nobile Andrea (Andrew) Nicolis, dei Conti di Robilant e Cereaglio
February 3, 1957, Rome —

2. Nobile Filippo Nicolis, dei Conti di Robilant e Cereaglio
April 3, 1959, Rome —

3. Nobile Tristano Nicolis, dei Conti di Robilant e Cereaglio
September 11, 1964, London —

XVIII. Robilant e Cereaglio (Nicolis) 6, from pages 597, 720

* **Nobile Carlo Nicolis,** dei Conti di Robilant e Cereaglio, second son of Nobile Andrea (Andrew).
July 11, 1927, Venice —
m. December 19, 1949, Lausanne, Switzerland
* **Marie Amelie von Heller,** daughter of Eduard von Heller and of his wife, Princess Clementine of Saxe-Coburg and Gotha.
August 9, 1926, Aubonne, Switzerland —

Issue: 1. Nobile Maurizio Nicolis, dei Conti di Robilant e Cereaglio
April 2, 1951, Rome —

2. Nobile Alessandro Nicolis, dei Conti di Robilant e Cereaglio
October 23, 1953, Lausanne, Switzerland —

3. Nobile Edmondo Nicolis, dei Conti di Robilant e Cereaglio
April 30, 1958, Milan —

XVIII. Robilant e Cereaglio (Nicolis) 7, from page 595

* **Nobile Edmondo Nicolis,** dei Conti di Robilant e Cereaglio, third son of Nobile Edmondo, Conte di Robilant e Cereaglio.
January 13, 1901, Turin —
m. September 28, 1931, New York City
Helen Tompkins-Westerveld, daughter of
— deceased

No Issue.

XVIII. Robilant e Cereaglio (Nicolis) 8, from page 595

* **Nobile Giovanni Nicolis,** dei Conti di Robilant e Cereaglio, fourth son of Nobile Edmondo, Conte di Robilant e Cereaglio.
March 7, 1905, Turin —
m. August 3, 1946, Rome
Lina Biondi, daughter of Biondo Biondi and of his wife, Marina Gentile.
November 24, 1907, Florence —

No Issue.

XVIII. de RODEZ-BÉNAVENT 1, from page 571

Philippe, Comte de Rodez-Bénavent
January 2, 1913, Auch, Gers, France
m. September 2, 1946, Rambuteau, Ozolles, Saône-et-Saône
* **Françoise Lombard de Buffières de Rambuteau,** daughter of Almeric Lombard de Buffières, Comte de Rambuteau, and of his wife, Amélie de MacMahon.
May 21, 1922, Paris —

Issue: 1. Marc-Antoine, Comte de Rodez-Bénavent
July 20, 1947, Macon, Saône-et-Loire —

2. Hughes, Comte de Rodez-Bénavent
July 13, 1951, Montpellier, Hérault —

3. Marie-Amélie, Comtesse de Rodez-Bénavent
August 30, 1952, Montpellier —

XVIII. ROSA 1, from page 914

Leone Rosa
October 23, 1884, Salerno, Italy —
m. July 27, 1961, Florence
* **Elisabeth,** Princess Windisch-Graetz, daughter of Prince Hugo Windisch-Graetz and of his wife, Princess Christine von Auersperg-Breunner.
February 19, 1889, Vienna —

No Issue.

XVIII. ROSSI 1, from page 540

Angelo Rossi
July 29, 1911, Pisa, Italy —
m. October 8, 1956, Pisignano, Italy
* **Franca (Francesca) Aloisi,** daughter of Dr. Domenico Aloisi and of his wife, Princess Maria zu Ysenburg und Büdingen in Wächtersbach.
April 14, 1923, Pisignano —

XVIII. Rossi 1 continued

Issue: 1. Francesco Rossi, August 12, 1957, Forte dei Marmi —

2. Guilia Rossi, June 8, 1959, Florence —

3. Maria Rossi, March 8, 1961, Florence —

XVIII. ROUSSEL 1, from page 964

Jean-Claude Roussel
August 14, 1923, Koblenz —
m. July 4, 1955, Versailles
* **Jadwiga (Hedwig),** Countess Skorzewska, daughter of Count Zygmund (Sigismund) Skorzewski and of his wife, Princess Leontyna Radziwill.
October 4, 1930, Czerniejew, Poland —

Issue: 1. Michel Roussel
December 3, 1956, Neuilly-sur-Seine —

2. Henri Roussel
June 7, 1959, St. Germain-en-Laye —

3. Fréderic Roussel
June 10, 1960, St. Germain-en-Laye —

4. Marie Noël Roussel
September 5, 1962, St. Germain-en-Laye —

XVIII. RUIZ 1, from page 578

Don José Maria Ruiz de Arana, Marques de Brenes
March , 1933, Madrid —
m. April 22, 1967, Geneva, Switzerland
* **Donna Giovanna Marone Cinzano,** daughter of Conte Enrico Marone Cinzano and of his wife, Dona Maria Cristina de Borbon y Battenberg, Infanta of Spain.
January 31, 1943, Lausanne —

Issue: 1. Dona Cristina Ruiz de Arana y Marone
March 25, 1968, Madrid —

XVIII. SAGRAMOSO 1, from page 929

Alvise, Conte Sagramoso
October 2, 1924, Milan —
m. December 28, 1962, Montevideo, Uruguay
* **Marie Antoinette von Wuthenau-Hohenthurm,** daughter of Franz Ferdinand von Wuthenau-Hohenthurm and of his wife, Elinor Bromberg.
August 7, 1932, Buenos Aires, Argentina —

Issue: 1. Lionello, Conte Sagramoso
November 6, 1963, Buenos Aires —

2. Domitilla, Contessa Sagramoso
December , 1964, Buenos Aires —

XVIII. SALDIVAR 1, from page 928

Antonio Saldivar y Fernandez de Valle
October 4, 1933, Mexico City —
m. January 19, 1963, San Angelo, Mexico
* **Franzesca-Fernanda von Wuthenau-Hohenthurm,** daughter of Alexander von Wuthenau-Hohenthurm and of his first wife, Rachelle di Catinelli Edle von Obradich-Bevilaqua.
September 10, 1940, Taxco de Alarcon, Mexico —

Issue: 1. Don Alejandro Francisco Saldivar y Wuthenau-Hohenthurm
May 29, 1965, Mexico City —

2. Don Juan Saldivar y Wuthenau-Hohenthurm
April 11, 1966, Mexico City —

XVIII. SAVOY (Italy) 1, from page 547

Amadeo, Prince of Savoy, Duke of Aosta, son of King Vittorio Emanuele II of Italy. Became King of Spain December 4, 1870; abdicated February 11, 1873.
May 30, 1845, Turin — January 18, 1890, Turin
m. 1: May 30, 1867, Turin
Maria Vittoria, Principessa dal Pazzo della Cisterna, daughter of Emanuele dal Pazzo, Principe della Cisterna, and of his wife, Ludovica Ghislaine, Comtesse de Merode.
August 9, 1847, Paris — November 8, 1876, San Remo, Italy
m. 2: September 11, 1888, Turin
* **Marie Lätitia,** Princess Bonaparte, daughter of Prince Napoléon Victor Bonaparte and of his wife, Princess Clothilde of Savoy.
December 20, 1866, Paris — October 25, 1926, Moncalieri Castle

XVIII. Savoy (Italy) 1 continued

Issue of first marriage: Not descendants of King George I

1. Emanuele Filiberto, Prince of Savoy, Duke of Aosta (1869–1931)
   m. * Hélène, Princess of France (1871–1951)
   see: *Savoy (Italy)* XVIII, 2, below

2. Vittorio Emanuele, Prince of Savoy
   November 24, 1870, Turin — October 16, 1946, Brussels

3. Luigi, Prince of Savoy
   January 29, 1873, Madrid — March 18, 1933, Mogadishu, Somaliland

Issue of second marriage: A descendant of King George I

4. Umberto, Prince of Savoy, Conte di Salemi
   June 23, 1889, Turin — October 19, 1918, killed in action in World War I at the Battle of Grappenberg.

XVIII. Savoy (Italy) 2, from above and page 455

Emanuele Filiberto, Prince of Savoy, Duke of Aosta, son of Prince Amadeo, Duke of Aosta.
January 13, 1869, Genoa — July 4, 1931, Turin
m. June 25, 1895, Kingston-upon-Thames, England
* **Hélène,** Princess of France, daughter of Prince Philippe, Comte de Paris, and of his wife, Princess Isabelle of France, Princess of Orleans.
June 13, 1871, Twickenham, England — January 20, 1951, Naples

Issue: 1. Amadeo, Prince of Savoy, Duke of Aosta (1898–1942)
   m. Anne, Princess of France (1906–)
   see: *Savoy (Italy)* XVIII, 3, page 603

2. Aimone, Prince of Savoy, Duke of Spoleto, Duke of Aosta (1900–1948)
   m. Iriny (Irene), Princess of Greece and Denmark (1904–)
   see: *Savoy (Italy)* XVIII, 4, page 603

XVIII. Savoy (Italy) 3, from pages 602, 457

* **Amadeo,** Prince of Savoy, Duke of Aosta, eldest son of Prince Emanuele of Savoy, Duke of Aosta. He was Italian Viceroy of Abyssinia (Ethiopia) 1936–1942.

October 21, 1898, Turin — March 3, 1942, in an Allied concentration camp at Nairobi, East Africa

m. November 5, 1927, Naples

* **Anne,** Princess of France, daughter of Prince Jean, Duc de Guise, and of his wife, Princess Isabelle of France.

August 5, 1906, Château-en-Thierache, France —

Issue: 1. Margherita, Princess of Savoy (1930–)
m. Robert, Archduke of Austria (1915–)
see: *Austria (Habsburg)* X h–1, page 362

2. Maria Cristina, Princess of Savoy (1933–)
m. Casimir, Prince of Bourbon-Sicily (1938–)
see: *Bourbon-Sicily* XIII j–3, page 445

XVIII. Savoy (Italy) 4, from pages 602, 194

* **Aimone,** Prince of Savoy, Duke of Spoleto from September 22, 1904; Duke of Aosta from March 3, 1942; second son of Prince Emanuele Filiberto, Duke of Aosta. He was created King of Croatia as Tomislav II by Benito Mussolini in 1941. He vacated this throne, without ever having seen his new country, upon the Allied defeat of the Fascist régime in 1943.

March 9, 1900, Turin — January 30, 1948, Buenos Aires, Argentina

m. July 1, 1939, Florence

* **Iriny (Irene),** Princess of Greece and Denmark, daughter of King Constantine I of the Hellenes and of his wife, Princess Sophie of Prussia.

February 13, 1904, Athens —

Issue: 1. Amadeo, Prince of Savoy, Duke of Aosta (1943–)
m. Claude, Princess of France (1943–)
see: *Savoy (Italy)* XVIII, 5, page 604

XVIII. Savoy (Italy) 5, from pages 603, 459

* **Amadeo,** Prince of Savoy, Duke of Aosta, Duke of Spoleto, Principe della Cisterna e di Belriguardo, Marchese di Voghera, Conte di Ponderano, son of Prince Aimone, Duke of Aosta.
September 27, 1943, Florence —
m. July 22, 1964, Sintra, Portugal
* **Claude,** Princess of France, daughter of Prince Henri, Comte de Paris, and of his wife, Princess Isabella of Orleans e Bragança.
December 11, 1943, Larache, Morocco —

Issue: 1. Bianca, Princess of Savoy
April 2, 1966, Florence —

2. Aimone, Prince of Savoy
October 13, 1967, Florence —

3. Mafalda, Princess of Savoy
September 20, 1969, Florence —

XVIII. Savoy (Italy) 6, from page 439

Eugenio, Prince of Savoy-Genoa, Duke of Ancona, son of King Vittorio Emanuele II of Italy who, on March 17, 1861, became the first King of Italy.
March 13, 1906, Turin —
m. October 29, 1938, Nymphenburg Castle, Munich
* **Lucia,** Princess of Bourbon-Sicily, daughter of Prince Ferdinand of Bourbon-Sicily and of his wife, Princess Maria of Bavaria.
July 9, 1908, Munich —

Issue: 1. Isabella, Princess of Savoy-Genoa
June 23, 1943, Rome —

XVIII. SEGONNE 1, from page 549

Noël Segonne
November 5, 1923, St. Cyril —
m. May 7, 1962, Bonnée, Loiret
* **Monique de Bourdoncle de Saint-Salvy,** daughter of Comte Olivier de Pasquier, Marquis de Franclieu, and of his wife, Anne-Marie Desrousseaux de Vandières.
October 11, 1929, Bonnée, Loiret

No Issue.

XVIII. SERNERI 1, from page 370

Nobile Igino Neri Serneri
July 22, 1891, Rome — May 1, 1950, Viareggio
m. July 14, 1932, Rome
* **Maria Immakulata,** Archduchess of Austria, daughter of Archduke Leopold Salvator of Austria and of his wife, Princess Blanka of Bourbon, Princess of Castile.
September 9, 1892, Lemberg —

No Issue.

XVIII. SERRE 1, from page 549

Antoine Serre
February 8, 1932, Paris —
m. May 19, 1962, Bonnée, Loiret
* **Nicole de Bourdoncle de Saint-Salvy,** daughter of Olivier, Comte de Bourdoncle de Saint-Salvy, and of his wife, Anne-Marie Desrousseaux de Vandières.
April 22, 1938, Reims —

Issue: 1. Patrice Serre
February 25, 1962, Paris —

2. François Serre
December 16, 1964, Paris —

3. Benoit Serre
November 23, 1967, Paris —

XVIII. SNOPKO 1, from page 988

Georges Snopko
, 1894, —
m. May 13, 1939,
* **Diana Eugenia Evgeniievna,** Princess Kotchoubey de Beauharnais, daughter of Prince Eugene (Evgenii) Leontievich Kotchoubey de Beauharnais and of his wife, Helen Geraldine Pearce.
June 4, 1918, Victoria, British Columbia, Canada —
(She m. 2: Georges Bataille – see: *Bataille* XVIII, page 543.)

Issue: 1. Catherine Snopko (1941–)
m. Marcel Mozoyer (–)
see: *Mozoyer* XVIII, page 582

XVII. STAVRO SANTAROSA

1, from page 578

Gian Carlo Stavro Santarosa
May , 1944, Trieste —
m. December 7, 1968, Turin
* **Donna Anna Sandra Marone Cinzano,** daughter of Conte Enrico Marone Cinzano and of his wife, Dona Maria Cristina de Borbon y Battenberg, Infanta of Spain.
December 21, 1948, Turin —

Issue:

XVIII. TALIANI DI MARCHIO

1, from page 370

Francesco Maria, Marchese Taliani di Marchio
October 22, 1887, Ascoli Piceno, Italy —
m. November 27, 1937, Sonnberg Castle, Austria
* **Margarita,** Archduchess of Austria, daughter of Archduke Leopold Salvator of Austria and of his wife, Princess Blanka of Bourbon, Princess of Castille.
May 8, 1894, Lemberg —

No Issue.

XVIII. TASSO DE SAXE-COBURGO E BRAGANCA

1, from pages 607, 368

* **Dom Carlos Tasso de Saxe-Coburgo e Braganca,** eldest son of Baron Lamoral Taxis di Bordogna e Valnigra – see that title, page 607.
July 16, 1931, Gmunden, Austria —
m. 1: December 15, 1956, São Paulo, Brazil. Divorced by Civil Law: March 30, 1967, São Paulo; annulled by the Church, November 14, 1967, Munich
Denyse Paes de Almeida, daughter of Sebastian Paes de Almeida and of his wife, Diva Maria Morse.
April 27, 1936, São Paulo —
m. 2: January 30, 1969, Trento, Italy
* **Walburga,** Archduchess of Austria, daughter of Archduke Georg of Austria and of his wife, Countess Marie Valerie von Waldburg-Zeil.
July 23, 1942, Muri, Aargau, Switzerland —

Issue of second marriage:

1. Dom Alfonso-Carlos Tasso de Saxe-Coburgo e Braganca
January 30, 1970, Frankfurt-am-Main —

XVIII. TAXIS DI BORDOGNA E VALNIGRA 1, from page 279

Lamoral, Baron Taxis di Bordogna e Valnigra
December 7, 1900, Unter-Mais — January 28, 1966, Trento
m. October 6, 1930, Salzburg
* **Theresia,** Princess of Saxe-Coburg and Gotha, daughter of Prince August Leopold of Saxe-Coburg and Gotha and of his wife, Archduchess Karoline of Austria.
August 23, 1902, Walterkirchen —

NOTE: By Brazilian Court Law, as of October 25, 1951, the family of Taxis di Bordogna e Valnigra became the family of Tasso de Saxe-Coburgo e Braganca.

Issue: 1. Dom Carlos Tasso de Saxe-Coburgo e Braganca (1931–)
m. 1: and divorced: Denyse Paes de Almeida (1936–)
m. 2: Walburga, Archduchess of Austria (1942–)
see: *Tasso de Saxe-Coburgo e Braganca* XVIII, 1, page 606

2. Dona Alice Tasso de Saxe-Coburgo e Braganca (1936–)
m. Michele, Conte Formentini di Tolmino e Biglia (1929–)
see: *Formentini di Tolmino e Biglia* XVIII, page 560

3. Dom Philippe Tasso de Saxe-Coburgo e Braganca
January 3, 1939, Gmunden, Austria —

4. Dona Maria Cristina Tasso de Saxe-Coburgo e Braganca
January 31, 1945, Pergine, Trento, Italy —

XVIII. TEISSIER 1, from page 1007

Lucien Teissier
—
m. May , 1944, Paris. Divorced: , Versailles
* **Mariya Petrovna Perevostchikova,** daughter of Peter Dimitrievich Perevostchikov and of his wife, Countess Elizabeta Alekseievna Belevskya-Zhukovskya.
December 27, 1917, Odessa, Ukraine —

XVIII. Teissier 1 continued

Issue: 1. Alexis Teissier
August 27, 1946, Paris —

2. Marie Beatrice Teissier
March 10, 1950, Paris —

XVIII. THÉNARD 1, from page 575

Arnould, Baron Thénard
March 4, 1940, Versailles —
m. October 5, 1963, Château de Sully
* **Anne de MacMahon,** daughter of Maurice de MacMahon, 3rd Duke de Magenta, 8th Marquis de MacMahon, and of his wife, Marguerite de Riquet, Comtesse de Caramen-Chimay.
August 9, 1941, Château de Sully —

Issue: 1. Jacques, Baron Thénard
January 23, 1965, Paris —

2. Stanislas, Baron Thénard
April 21, 1966, Paris —

3. Henri, Baron Thénard
April 21, 1968, Paris —

XVIII. TORLONIA 1, from page 431

Don Alessandro Torlonia, Principe Torlonia, Principe di Civitelli-Cesi.
December 7, 1911, Rome —
m. January 14, 1935, Rome
* **Dona Beatriz de Borbon y Battenberg,** Infanta of Spain, daughter of King Alfonso XIII of Spain and of his wife, Princess Victoria Eugenie of Battenberg.
June 22, 1909, San Sebastian, Spain —

Issue: 1. Donna Alessandra (Sandra) Torlonia (1936–)
m. Clemente Lequio (1926–)
see: *Lequio* XVIII, page 569

XVIII. Torlonia 1 continued

2. Don Marco Torlonia (1937–)
m. Donna Orsetta Caracciolo di Castegneto (1940–1966)
see: *Torlonia* XVIII, 2, below

3. Don Marino Torlonia
December 13, 1941, Rome —

4. Donna Olympia Torlonia (1943–)
m. Paul Annik Weiller (1933–)
see: *Weiller* XVIII, page 611

XVIII. Torlonia 2, from above

* **Don Marco Torlonia,** eldest son of Don Alessandro.
July 2, 1937, Rome —
m. September 6, 1960, Rome
Donna Orsetta Caracciolo di Castegneto, daughter of Don Adolfo Caracciolo di Castegneto and of his wife, Donna Anna Visconti di Madrone.
May 17, 1940, Rome — , 1966, Rome
(Don Marco m. 2: April , 1968, Rome, Phillipa from Australia, who was formerly married to a French Count – no further information available.)

Issue: 1. Don Giovanni Torlonia
September 19, 1962, Lausanne, Switzerland —
By his second marriage Don Marco has a daughter:
2. Donna Victoria Eugenia Torlonia, born July 1971, Rome

XVIII. TORRE e TASSO 1, from page 197

Don Raymond, Principe della Torre e Tasso, 2nd Duke di Castel Duino.
March 16, 1907, Duino Castle, Trieste —
m. November 28, 1949, Athens, Greece
* **Eugenie,** Princess of Greece and Denmark, daughter of Prince George of Greece and Denmark and of his wife, Princess Marie Bonaparte.
February 10, 1910, Paris —
(She m. 1: and divorced: Dominik, Prince Radziwill – see: *Radziwill* XI l–2, page 410.)

Issue: 1. Carlos Alessandro, Principe della Torre e Tasso
February 10, 1952, —

XVIII. DE TOURNEMIRE 1, from page 557

Alain de Tournemire, son of Comte de Tournemire.

—

m. June , 1968, Vandières, Marne

* **Nicole Desrousseaux de Vandières,** daughter of Eduard, Comte Desrousseaux, Duc de Vandières, and of his wife, Marie-France d'Illiers.

May , 1946, —

Issue:

XVIII. DE URQUIJO 1, from page 477

Don Juan Manoel de Urquijo y de Morales

—

m. July 12, 1967, Madrid

* **Dona Maria Cristina de Baviera y de Mesia,** Condessa de Odiel, daughter of Prince Josef Eugen of Bavaria, Infante of Spain, and of his wife, Dona Maria Solange de Mesia y Lesseps, Condessa de Odiel.

February 6, 1935, Paris —

No Issue.

XVIII. VÉROLA 1, from page 215

Paul Vérola

July 13, 1863, Nice — April 11, 1931, Cavalaire, Var, France

m. June 8, 1885, Funchal, Madeira

* **Alexandra,** Countess von Ostenburg, daughter of Duke Nikolaus of Oldenburg and of his wife, Maria Bulatzelly, created Countess von Ostenburg.

June 7, 1864, Geneva — July 23, 1952, Paris

Issue: 1. Marie Claire Vérola (1886–1943)
m. Aleksandr, Count Mordvinov (1887–1950)
see: *Mordvinov* XXIII, page 1004

2. Raymond Vérola
May 3, 1888, Paris — March 23, 1895, Paris

XVIII. WEILLER 1, from page 609

Paul Annik Weiller
July 28, 1933, —
m. June 26, 1965, Rome
★ **Donna Olympia Torlonia,** daughter of Don Alessandro Torlonia, Principe di Cevitelli-Cesi, and of his wife, Dona Beatriz de Borbon y Battenberg, Infanta of Spain.
December 27, 1943, Lausanne —

Issue: 1. Beatrice Aliki Victoria Weiller
March 23, 1967, Paris —

2. Sibilla Weiller
June , 1969, Paris

3. Paul Alexander Weiller
January , 1971, Paris —

XVIII. DE ZULUETA 1, from page 386

Eduardo de Zulueta y Dato
December 4, 1923, Paris —
m. June 26, 1957, Stockholm, Sweden
★ **Renata Habsburg von Altenburg,** created Princess von Altenburg on December 15, 1949, daughter of Archduke Karl Albrecht of Austria and of his wife, Alice Ankarcrona.
April 13, 1931, Zywiec, Poland —

Issue: 1. Carlos Eduardo de Zulueta y Habsburgo-Lorena
October 19, 1958, New York City —

2. Ernesto Maria de Zulueta y Habsburgo-Lorena
July 7, 1961, New York City —

3. Isabel de Zulueta y Habsburgo-Lorena
March 7, 1965, Madrid —

XIX

THE FAMILIES OF THE LOW COUNTRIES AND SCANDINAVIA

XIX. VON ARBIN

1, from page 507

Nils Magnus von Arbin
August 17, 1910, Störkinge, Sweden —
m. October 16, 1936, Frötuna, Sweden
⋆ **Dagmar,** Countess Bernadotte, daughter of Count Carl Oskar Bernadotte and of his wife, Baroness Marianne de Geer af Leufsta.
April 10, 1916, Stockholm —

Issue: 1. Marianne von Arbin (1937–)
m. Miles Carl Flach (1934–)
see: *Flach* XIX, page 618

2. Lovisa von Arbin (1940–)
m. Per-Erik Bergstrom (1936–
see: *Bergstrom* XIX, page 614

3. Cathrine von Arbin
June 26, 1946, Stockholm —

4. Jeanette von Arbin
May 19, 1951, Stockholm —

5. Madeleine von Arbin
January 27, 1955, Stockholm —

XIX. BAENKLER

1, from page 505

Hans Jörg Baenkler
September 24, 1939, —
m. March 31, 1967, Mainau Castle, Lake Konstanz
⋆ **Cecilia (Cia),** Countess Bernadotte, daughter of Count Lennart Bernadotte af Wisborg, born Prince of Sweden, and of his wife, Karin Nissvandt.
April 9, 1944, Stockholm —

Issue:

XIX. BERGSTROM 1, from page 613

Per-Erik Bergstrom
October 22, 1936, Stockholm —
m. July 29, 1961, Kimstad
* **Lovisa von Arbin,** daughter of Colonel Nils Magnus von Arbin and of his wife, Countess Birgitta Bernadotte.
May 27, 1940, Stockholm —

Issue: 1. Therese Marianne Bergstrom
September 10, 1963, Stockholm —

2. Dick Michael Bergstrom
December 10, 1965, Stockholm —

XIX. BITSCH 1, from page 616

Poul Bitsch
October 5, 1930, Balle, Denmark —
m. April 4, 1950, Norbek, Denmark
* **Dagmar Castenskiold,** daughter of Jörgen Castenskiold and of his wife, Princess Dagmar of Denmark.
September 11, 1931, 'Kongstedlund', near Copenhagen —

Issue: 1. Erik Bitsch
August 9, 1950, Aarhus, Denmark —

2. Hans Jörgen Bitsch
January 14, 1954, Brönshöj, Denmark —

3. Christian Bitsch
August 18, 1959, Brönshöj —

XIX. BJÖRKLUND 1, from page 919

Karl Axel Björklund
December 21, 1906, Hogsjo, Sweden —
m. November 14, 1945, Boitsfort-Brussels, Belgium
* **Stephanie,** Princess Windisch-Graetz, daughter of Prince Otto Windisch-Graetz and of his wife, Archduchess Elisabeth of Austria.
July 9, 1909, Ploshkowitz —
(She m. 1: Peter, Count d'Alcantara de Querrieu – see: *d'Alcantara di Querrieu* XVIII, page 538.)

XIX. Björklund 1 continued

Issue: 1. Björn-Axel Björklund (1944-)
m. Marianne Vellut (1943-)
see: *Björklund* XIX, 2, below

XIX. Björklund 2, from above

* **Björn-Axel Björklund,** only son of Karl Axel.
October 20, 1944, Brussels —
m. December 17, 1965, Brussels
Marianne Vellut, daughter of
February 15, 1943, Brussels —

Issue:

XIX. CEDERGREN 1, from page 506

Carl Axel Cedergren
July 26, 1891, Hälsingborg —
m. September 18, 1929, Stockholm
* **Elsa Victoria,** Countess Bernadotte, daughter of Prince Oskar Bernadotte, Count af Wisborg, born Prince of Sweden, and of his wife, Ebba Henrietta Munk af Filkila.
August 3, 1893, Stockholm —

No Issue.

XIX. CASTENSKIOLD 1, from page 181

Jörgen Castenskiold
November 30, 1893, Copenhagen —
m. November 23, 1922, Fredensborg Castle
* **Dagmar,** Princess of Denmark, daughter of King Frederik VIII of Denmark and of his wife, Princess Lovisa of Sweden and Norway.
May 23, 1890, Charlottenlund — October 11, 1961, 'Kongstedlund', near Copenhagen

Issue: 1. Carl Frederik Castenskiold (1923-)
m. and divorced: Bente Grevenkop-Castenskiold (1927-)
see: *Castenskiold* XIX, 2, page 616

XIX. Castenskiold 1 continued

2. Christian Castenskiold (1926–)
m. Cecily Abbots (1927–)
see: *Castenskiold* XIX, 3, below

3. Jörgen Castenskiold (1928–1964)
m. 1: and divorced: Kirsten Schlichtkrull (1934–)
m. 2: Birgit Tingstedt (1932–)
see: *Castenskiold* XIX, 4, page 617

4. Dagmar Castenskiold (1931–)
m. Poul Bitsch (1930–)
see: *Bitsch* XIX, page 614

XIX. Castenskiold 2, from page 615

* **Carl Frederik Castenskiold,** eldest son of Jörgen Castenskiold.
November 13, 1923, 'Kongstedlund', Denmark —
m. October 23, 1948, Copenhagen. Divorced: May 8, 1963, Aarhus

Bente Grevenkop-Castenskiold, daughter of Helmuth Grevenkop-Castenskiold and of his wife, Tilita Bryndum.
April 5, 1927, Hörsholm, Denmark —

Issue: 1. Helmuth Castenskiold
August 9, 1949, Copenhagen —

2. Jörgen Castenskiold
December 16, 1951, Copenhagen —

3. Dagmar Birgitte Castenskiold
January 26, 1956, Copenhagen —

XIX. Castenskiold 3, from above

* **Christian Castenskiold,** second son of Jörgen Castenskiold.
July 10, 1926, 'Kongstedlund' —
m. November 11, 1952, New York City

Cecily Abbots, daughter of Richard Abbots and of his wife, Kirsten Schiödt.
August 10, 1927, Lyons, France —

XIX. Castenskiold

3 continued

Issue: 1. Alexandra Castenskiold
June 11, 1965, Los Angeles, California, USA —

XIX. Castenskiold

4, from page 616

* **Jörgen Castenskiold,** third son of Jörgen Castenskiold.
March 16, 1928, 'Kongstedlund', Denmark — May 4, 1964, Naestved
m. 1: July 14, 1956, Copenhagen. Divorced: , 1958, Naestved
Kirsten Schlichtkrull, daughter of Captain Christian O. Schlichtkrull and of his wife, Helene Hoffmeyer.
March 24, 1934, —
(She m. 2: P. G. Olsen.)
m. 2: October 17, 1959, Vordingborg
Birgit Tingstedt, daughter of E. Tingstedt and of his wife, Johanne Jörgensen.
September 3, 1932, Vordingborg, Denmark —

Issue of first marriage:
1. Susanne Castenskiold
April 13, 1957, Naestved —
(Adopted by her step-father, P. G. Olsen, in 1958.)

Issue of second marriage:
2. Maria-Lovisa Castenskiold
November 10, 1960, Holbok, Denmark —

XIX. VAN EYCK

1, from page 129

Robert Floris van Eyck
May , 1916, The Hague, The Netherlands —
m. December 3, 1962, London
* **Christine,** Princess of Hesse, daughter of Prince Christoph of Hesse and of his wife, Princess Sophia of Greece and Denmark.
January 10, 1933, Friedrichshof Castle —
(She m. 1: and divorced: Andrea, Prince of Yugoslavia – see: *Yugoslavia* XX, page 629.)

XIX. van Eyck 1 continued

Issue: 1. Helen Sophie van Eyck
October 25, 1963, London —

2. Mark Nicholas van Eyck
February 16, 1966, London —

XIX. FERNER 1, from page 190

Johan Martin Ferner
July 22, 1927, Oslo —
m. January 13, 1961, Asker, Norway.
* **Astrid,** Princess of Norway, daughter of King Olav V of Norway and of his wife, Princess Märtha of Sweden and Norway.
February 12, 1932, Oslo —

Issue: 1. Cathrine Ferner
July 22, 1962, Oslo —

2. Benedikte Ferner
September 27, 1963, Oslo —

3. Alexander Ferner
March 15, 1965, Oslo —

4. Elisabeth Ferner
March 30, 1969, Oslo —

(Mr. J. M. Ferner was formerly married to and divorced from Bette Hesselberg-Meyer.)

XIX. FLACH 1, from page 613

Miles Carl Flach
August 10, 1934, Stockholm —
m. September 5, 1958, Stockholm. Divorced:
* **Dagmar von Arbin,** daughter of Colonel Nils Magnus von Arbin and of his wife, Countess Dagmar Bernadotte.
August 2, 1937, Stockholm —

Issue: 1. Jana Camilla Gabrielle Flach
December 22, 1960, Stockholm —

XIX. FLEETWOOD (Märten)

1, from page 506

Carl Märten, Baron Fleetwood
September 19, 1885, Göteborg —
m. May 14, 1917, Stockholm
* **Ebba Sophia,** Countess Bernadotte, daughter of Prince Oskar Bernadotte, Count af Wisborg, born Prince of Sweden, and of his wife, Ebba Henrietta Munk af Filkila.
May 17, 1892, Karlskrona — June 21, 1936, Stockholm

No Issue.

XIX. HOLSTEIN-LEDREBORG

1, from page 108

Knud, Count of Holstein-Ledreborg
October 2, 1919, Ledreborg, Denmark —
m. November 6, 1951, Kolmar, Berg Castle
* **Marie Gabrielle,** Princess of Luxemburg, Princess of Nassau-Weilburg, Princess of Bourbon-Parma, daughter of Grand Duchess Charlotte of Luxemburg and of her husband, Prince Felix of Bourbon-Parma.
August 2, 1925, Berg Castle —

Issue: 1. Monica, Countess of Holstein-Ledreborg
July 29, 1952, Ledreborg —

2. Lydia, Countess of Holstein-Ledreborg
February 22, 1955, Ledreborg —

3. Veronica, Countess of Holstein-Ledreborg
January 29, 1956, Ledreborg —

4. Sylvia, Countess of Holstein-Ledreborg
January 1, 1958, Ledreborg —

5. Camilla, Countess of Holstein-Ledreborg
February 26, 1959, Ledreborg —

6. Tatiana, Countess of Holstein-Ledreborg
April 4, 1961, Ledreborg —

7. Antonia, Countess of Holstein-Ledreborg
June 19, 1962, Ledreborg —

XIX. LORENTZEN 1, from page 190

Erling Sven Lorentzen
January 28, 1923, Oslo —
m. May 15, 1953, Asker, Norway
* **Ragnhild,** Princess of Norway, daughter of King Olav V of Norway and of his wife, Princess Märtha of Sweden and Norway.
June 9, 1930, Oslo —

Issue: 1. Haakon Lorentzen
August 23, 1954, Oslo —

2. Ingeborg Lorentzen
February 27, 1957, Oslo —

XIX. MOES 1, from page 674

Karl Moes
October 17, 1937, Copenhagen —
m. November 3, 1961, Copenhagen
* **Thyra,** Countess zu Castell-Castell, daughter of Count Luitpold zu Castell-Castell and of his wife, Princess Alexandrine-Lovisa of Denmark.
September 14, 1939, Berlin —

Issue: 1. Marie-Lovisa Moes
July 7, 1966, Copenhagen —

2. Benedikte Moes
November 11, 1968, Copenhagen —

XIX. NILERT 1, from page 507

Tore Henrik Nilert
February 9, 1915, Stockholm —
m. October 9, 1948, Osmo, Sweden
* **Marta Elsa,** Countess Bernadotte, daughter of Count Oskar Bernadotte and of his wife, Baroness Marianne de Geer af Leufsta.
April 14, 1926, Stockholm —

Issue: 1. Jan Nilert
March 11, 1950, New York City —

XIX. Nilert

1 continued

2. Charlotte Nilert
   May 20, 1952, New York City —

3. Anne Marie Nilert
   March 1, 1954, New York City —

4. Fredrik Nilert
   February 10, 1959, New York City —

XIX. REUTERSVÄRD

1, from page 508

Pontus Reutersvärd
May 28, 1943, —
m. March 14, 1970, Frötuna, Sweden
★ **Ebba,** Countess Bernadotte, daughter of Count Oskar Bernadotte and of his first wife, Baroness Ebba-Anna Gyllenkrok.
March 2, 1945, Stockholm —

Issue:

XIX. SILFVERSCHIÖLD

1, from page 503

Nils August, Baron Silfverschiöld
May 31, 1934, Koberg Castle, Sweden —
m. June 5, 1964, Stockholm
★ **Desirée,** Princess of Sweden, daughter of Prince Gustaf Adolf of Sweden and of his wife, Princess Sibylle of Saxe-Coburg and Gotha.
June 2, 1938, Haga Castle —

Issue: 1. Carl Edmund, Baron Silfverschiöld
   March 22, 1965, Göteborg —

2. Kristina Lovisa, Baroness Silfverschiöld
   September 29, 1966, Göteborg —

3. Helene Sibylle, Baroness Silfverschiöld
   September 20, 1968, Göteborg —

XIX. DE SPIRLET 1, from page 861

Jack de Spirlet
April 3, 1930, Woluwe St. Pierre, near Brussels —
m. October 9, 1954, Hall, Tyrol
* **Anna Regina,** Countess zu Stolberg-Stolberg, daughter of Count Bernhard zu Stolberg-Stolberg and of his wife, Archduchess Hedwig of Austria.
December 20, 1927, Bad Ischl, Austria —

Issue: 1. Beatrice Marie de Spirlet
February 21, 1955, —

2. Isabell de Spirlet
June 26, 1957, Brussels —

3. Marie Elisabeth de Spirlet
April 30, 1960, Brussels —

4. Guy de Spirlet
May 13, 1962, Brussels —

5. Nicholas de Spirlet
October 9, 1964, Brussels —

XIX. STRAEHL 1, from page 505

Friedrich Otto Straehl
November 22, 1922, —
m. June 11, 1955, Mainau Castle, Lake Konstanz
* **Birgitta,** Countess Bernadotte, daughter of Count Lennart Bernadotte af Wisborg, born Prince of Sweden, and of his wife, Karin Nissvandt.
May 3, 1933, Stockholm —

Issue: 1. Friedrich Lennart Straehl
April 10, 1956, Kreuzlingen —

2. Andreas Straehl
July 16, 1957, Kreuzlingen —

3. Maria Kristina Straehl
April 23, 1960, Kreuzlingen —

XIX. Straehl 1 continued

4. Desirée Elisabeth Straehl
October 20, 1961, Kreuzlingen —

5. Stephen Straehl
July 13, 1964, Kreuzlingen —

XIX. ULLENS DE SCHOOTEN 1, from page 511

Albert Ullens de Schooten
November 11, 1927, Cairo, Egypt —
m. October 6, 1962, Stockholm
* **Madeleine,** Countess Bernadotte, daughter of Prince Carl of Sweden and Norway, Duke of Ostergötland, Prince Bernadotte after 1937, and of his first wife, Countess Elsa von Rosen.
October 8, 1938, Stockholm —

Issue: 1. Marie-Christine Ullens de Schooten
March 24, 1964, Brussels —

2. Jean Charles Ullens de Schooten
October 6, 1965, Brussels —

XIX. VAREKAMP 1, from page 266

Axel Varekamp
January 21, 1937, Amsterdam, The Netherlands —
m. August 25, 1962, Cuxhaven
* **Heike,** Baroness von Saalfeld, daughter of Baron Hans von Saalfeld and of his wife, Elisabeth Faust.
June 8, 1941, Lenggries —

Issue: 1. Maj Varekamp
July 21, 1963, Blaricum, The Netherlands —

2. Nanon Varekamp
July 5, 1965, Blaricum —

XIX. VIND 1, from page 188

Ivar Emil Vind

January 5, 1921, —

m. May 2, 1951, Copenhagen

* **Alexandra,** Countess of Rosenberg, daughter of Prince Erik of Denmark, Count of Rosenborg, and of his wife, Lois Booth.

February 5, 1927, Arcadia, California, USA —

Issue: 1. Marie Lovisa Vind
February 7, 1952, Hellerup, Denmark —

2. Erik Vind
May 5, 1954, Hellerup —

3. Georg Vind
August 5, 1958, Hellerup —

XIX. VAN VOLLENHOVEN 1, from page 99

Pieter van Vollenhoven

April 30, 1939, Schiedam, near Rotterdam, The Netherlands —

m. January 10, 1967, The Hague

* **Margriet,** Princess of the Netherlands, daughter of Queen Juliana of the Netherlands and of her husband, Prince Bernhard zur Lippe-Biesterfeld, Prince of the Netherlands.

January 19, 1943, Ottawa, Canada —

Issue: 1. Mauritz van Vollenhoven
April 17, 1968, Utrecht —

2. Bernhard van Vollenhoven
December 25, 1969, Utrecht —

3. Pieter van Vollenhoven
March 22, 1972, Nijmegen —

XX

THE FAMILIES OF THE BALKANS AND THE MIDDLE EAST

XX. BUNEA

1, from page 911

Jon Bunea

November 13, 1899, Bucharest —

m. February 5, 1948, Bucharest, Romania

* **Marie Eleonore,** Princess of Wied, daughter of Prince Wilhelm zu Wied, former King of Albania, and of his wife, Princess Sophie of Schönburg-Waldenburg.

February 19, 1909, Potsdam — September 29, 1956, Romania, in a concentration camp.

(She m. 1: Alfred, Prince of Schönburg-Waldenburg – see: *Schönburg-Waldenburg* XXI, page 833.)

No Issue.

XX. BYRON-PATRIKIADES

1, from page 1009

Charles Byron-Patrikiades

December 15, 1919, Constantinople, Turkey —

m. May 9, 1965, New York City

* **Elizabeta Vladimirovna Sverbeeva,** daughter of Vladimir Sergeievich Sverbeev and of his wife, Countess Mariya Alekseievna Belevskya-Zhukovskya.

August 28, 1923, Berlin —

(She m. 1: and divorced: Aleksandr Georgeievich Tarsaidze – see: *Tarsaidze* XXIII, page 1009.)

No Issue.

XX. ISSARESCU

1, from page 88

Stefan Issarescu

October 5, 1906, Turnu-Severin, Romania —

m. June 20, 1954, Boston, Massachusetts, USA

* **Ileana,** Princess of Romania, daughter of King Ferdinand I of Romania and of his wife, Princess Marie of Great Britain and Ireland.

January 5, 1909, Bucharest, Romania —

(She m. 1: and divorced: Anton, Archduke of Austria – see: *Austria* (*Habsburg*) X r–1, page 372.)

(In May 1962 Princess Ileana entered the Russian Orthodox Order of Sisters at Bussy-sur-Othe, France. She is now Abbess Alexandra of the Orthodox Abbey of the Transfiguration, Ellwood City, Pennsylvania.)

No Issue.

XX. JOANNIDES

1, from page 192

Pericles Joannides, Admiral, Greek Navy.
November 1, 1881 — February 7, 1965, Athens, Greece
m. December 16, 1921, Wiesbaden, Germany, and January 22, 1922, Munich
* **Marie,** Princess of Greece and Denmark, daughter of King George I of the Hellenes and of his wife, Grand Duchess Olga Konstantinovna of Russia.
March 3, 1876, Athens — December 14, 1940, Athens
(She m. 1: Georgii Mikhailovich, Grand Duke of Russia - see: *Russia* VIII t-1, page 322.)

No Issue.

XX. MONTENEGRO (Petrovich-Niegosh)

1, from page 424

Danilo I, King of Montenegro, son of King Michael. Succeeded as King on the death of his father, March 1, 1921, and abdicated in favour of his nephew, King Michael II, six days later on March 7, 1921.
June 17, 1871, Cettigne — September 24, 1939, Vienna
m. July 15, 1899, Cettigne
* **Jutta,** Duchess of Mecklenburg-Strelitz, daughter of Grand Duke Georg Adolf Friedrich V of Mecklenburg-Strelitz and of his wife, Princess Elisabeth of Anhalt-Dessau.
January 24, 1880, Neustrelitz — February 17, 1946, Rome
(She changed her name to Militza at the time of her marriage.)

No Issue.

XX. SAAD

1, from page 844

Salim Farid Saad
September 9, 1922, Kaferakka, Lebanon —
m. December 20, 1957, Beirut, Lebanon
* **Jutta,** Countess zu Solms-Wildenfels, daughter of Count Friedrich Magnus (V) zu Solms-Wildenfels and of his wife, Princess Marie Antoinette of Schwarzburg.
February 12, 1928, Wildenfels, Germany —

Issue:

XX. SFIRIS 1, from page 978

Elia Sfiris

August 20, 1932, Athens, Greece —

m. June 20, 1965, Athens

* **Kseniya (Xenia) Nikolaievna,** Countess Cheremeteva, daughter of Count Nikolai Dimitrievich Cheremetev and of his wife, Princess Irina Felixovna Yousoupova, Countess Soumarakova-Elston.

March 1, 1942, Rome —

Issue: 1. Tatiana Sfiris

August 28, 1968, Athens —

XX. YUGOSLAVIA (Karadjorgevic) (Karageorgevitch) 1, from page 88

Aleksandăr I, King of Serbia, Croatia and Slovenia, King of Yugoslavia in 1929, eldest son of King Petar I whom he succeeded as King upon the latter's death, August 16, 1921. He became First King of Yugoslavia on October 3, 1929.

December 17, 1891, Cettigne — assassinated October 9, 1934, Marseilles, France

m. June 8, 1922, Belgrade

* **Marie,** Princess of Romania, daughter of King Ferdinand I of Romania and of his wife, Princess Marie of Great Britain and Ireland, Princess of Edinburgh.

January 9, 1900, Gotha — June 22, 1961, London, England

Issue: 1. Peter II (Petar), Last King of Yugoslavia (1923–1970)

m. Alexandra, Princess of Greece and Denmark (1921–)

see: *Yugoslavia* XX, 2, page 629

2. Tomislav, Prince of Yugoslavia (1928–)

m. Margarita, Princess of Baden (1932–)

see: *Yugoslavia* XX, 3, page 629

3. Andrea (Andrew), Prince of Yugoslavia (1929–

m. 1: and divorced: Christine, Princess of Hesse (1933–)

m. 2: Kira, Princess of Leiningen (1930–)

see: *Yugoslavia* XX, 4, page 629

XX. Yugoslavia (Karadjorgević) 2, from pages 628, 195

* **Petar II (Peter),** Last King of Yugoslavia, eldest son of King Aleksandar I. Succeeded as King on the assassination of his father, October 9, 1934, under the Regency of his late father's first cousin, Prince Pavle (Paul) of Yugoslavia. He assumed full powers of Kingship on March 27, 1941, and was deposed by Marshal Josip Broz Tito on November 29, 1945.

September 6, 1923, Belgrade — November 3, 1970, Denver, Colorado

m. March 20, 1944, London

* **Alexandra,** Princess of Greece and Denmark, daughter of King Alexander I of the Hellenes and of his wife, Aspasia Manos.

March 25, 1921, Athens (posthumous) —

Issue: 1. Alexandar, Crown Prince of Yugoslavia
July 17, 1945, London —
(m. July 1, 1972, Seville, Spain, Princess Maria da Gloria of Orleans e Braganca – see: *Bourbon* (*Orleans e Braganca*) *Brazil*, XIII u–1, page 461.)

XX. Yugoslavia (Karadjorgević) 3, from pages 628, 649

* **Tomislav,** Prince of Yugoslavia, second son of King Aleksandar I

January 19, 1928, Belgrade —

m. June 6, 1957, Salem Castle, Baden, Germany

* **Margarita,** Princess of Baden, daughter of Margrave Berthold Friedrich of Baden and of his wife, Princess Theodora of Greece and Denmark.

July 14, 1932, Salem Castle —

Issue: 1. Nikola (Nicholas), Prince of Yugoslavia
March 15, 1958, London —

2. Katarina, Princess of Yugoslavia
November 26, 1959, London —

XX. Yugoslavia (Karadjorgević) 4, from pages 628, 129, 744

* **Andrea (Andrew),** Prince of Yugoslavia, third son of King Aleksandar I.

June 28, 1929, Bled, Yugoslavia —

m. 1: August 2, 1956, Friedrichshof Castle. Divorced: February , 1962, London

* **Christine,** Princess of Hesse, daughter of Prince Christoph of Hesse and of his wife, Princess Sophia of Greece and Denmark.

January 10, 1933, Friedrichshof Castle —

(She m. 2: Robert Floris van Eyck – see: *van Eyck* XIX, page 617.)

XX. Yugoslavia (Karadjorgević) 4 continued

m. 2: September 18, 1963, London
★ **Kira,** Princess of Leiningen, daughter of Prince Karl, 6th Fürst zu Leiningen, and of his wife, Princess/Grand Duchess Mariya Kirillovna of Russia.
July 18, 1930, Coburg, Germany —

Issue of first marriage:
1. Marija Tatiana, Princess of Yugoslavia
July 18, 1957, London —

2. Krsta (Christopher), Prince of Yugoslavia
February 4, 1960, London —

Issue of second marriage:
3. Karlo Vladimir, Prince of Yugoslavia
March 11, 1964, London —

4. Dimitrije (Dimitri), Prince of Yugoslavia
April 21, 1965, London —

5. Lavinia Marie, Princess of Yugoslavia (by adoption)
March 22, 1967, London —

XX. Yugoslavia (Karadjorgević) 5, from page 197

Pavle (Paul), Prince of Yugoslavia, only son of Prince Arsen and first cousin of King Aleksandar I of Yugoslavia. He became Prince Regent of Yugoslavia upon the assassination of King Aleksandar I, October 9, 1934, for the latter's eldest son, King Petar II. He relinquished the Regency, March 10, 1941, when King Petar II assumed full powers.
April 15, 1893, St. Petersburg, Russia —
m. October 22, 1923, Belgrade
★ **Olga,** Princess of Greece and Denmark, daughter of Prince Nicholaos of Greece and Denmark and of his wife, Grand Duchess Elena (Helen) Vladimirovna of Russia.
June 11, 1903, Tatoi, Greece —

XX. Yugoslavia (Karadjorgević) 5 continued

Issue: 1. Aleksandar, Prince of Yugoslavia (1924–)
m. and divorced: Maria Pia, Princess of Savoy (1934–)
see: *Yugoslavia* XX, 6, below

2. Nikola (Nicholas), Prince of Yugoslavia
June 29, 1928, London — April 12, 1954, near Datchet, Buckinghamshire, England, killed in a road accident

3. Jelisaveta (Elisabeth), Princess of Yugoslavia (1936–)
m. 1: and divorced: Howard Oxenburg (1919–)
see: *Oxenburg* XXIV, page 1022
m. 2: Neil Balfour (–)
see: *Balfour* XVII, page 515

XX. Yugoslavia (Karageorgevich) 6, from above

* **Aleksandar,** Prince of Yugoslavia, eldest son of Prince Pavle (Paul).
August 13, 1924, Richmond, England —
m. February 12, 1955, Estoril, Portugal. Divorced: 1966

Maria Pia, Princess of Savoy, daughter of King Umberto II of Italy and of his wife, Princess Marie José of Belgium.
September 24, 1934, Naples —

Issue: 1. Dimitrije (Dimitri), Prince of Yugoslavia (twin)
June 18, 1958, Paris —

2. Marko (Michael), Prince of Yugoslavia (twin)
June 18, 1958, Paris —

3. Sergije (Serge), Prince of Yugoslavia (twin)
March 11, 1963, Paris —

4. Jelena (Elena), Princess of Yugoslavia (twin)
March 11, 1963, Paris —

XXI

THE FAMILIES OF CENTRAL EUROPE

GERMANY; AUSTRIA; HUNGARY; BOHEMIA

XXI. AEBI 1, from page 960

Marc Aebi

August 10, 1928, Montreux, Switzerland —
m. October 6, 1962, Lagos, Nigeria

★ **Joanna,** Countess Potocka, daughter of Count Ignacz Potocki and of his wife, Jadwiga Dembinska.

July 17, 1933, Sieniszny, Poland —

No Issue.

XXI. DE AFIF-GESSAPH 1, from page 289

Robert de Afif-Gessaph

November 30, 1916, Mexico City —
m. May 1, 1953, Paris

★ **Anna,** Princess of Saxony, daughter of Prince Friedrich Christian of Saxony, Margraf von Meissen, and of his wife, Princess Elisabeth von Thurn und Taxis.

December 13, 1929, Bad Worishofen —

Issue: 1. Alexander de Afif-Gessaph
February 12, 1953, Munich —

2. Friedrich Wilhelm de Afif-Gessaph
October 5, 1955, Mexico City —

3. Karl August de Afif-Gessaph
January 1, 1958, Mexico City —

XXI. VON AMMON 1, from page 485

Eberhard von Ammon

September 11, 1885, Magdeburg-Sudenburg — January 29, 1950, Berlin-Charlottenburg
m. January 27, 1915, Berlin. Divorced: July 6, 1933, Berlin

★ **Erika,** Princess of Hohenlohe-Oehringen, daughter of Prince Friedrich of Hohenlohe-Oehringen and of his wife, Countess Marie von Hatzfeldt.

December 1, 1893, Sommerberg —
(She m. 2: Hans Jost – see: *Jost* XXI, page 729.)

XXI. von Ammon 1 continued

Issue: 1. Friedrich-Karl von Ammon (1916–)
m. Charlotte Vitenne (1909–)
see: *von Ammon*, 2, below

2. Margarethe von Ammon
October 9, 1903, Potsdam —

XXI. von Ammon 2, from above

Friedrich-Karl von Ammon, son of Eberhard.
August 26, 1916, Berlin —
m. December 8, 1939, Munich
Charlotte Vitenne, daughter of Otto Vitenne and of his wife,
May 30, 1909, Görlitz —

Issue: 1. Dieter Friedrich von Ammon
April 27, 1941, Munich —

2. Uwe Eberhard von Ammon
May 1, 1945, Bad Wiessee —

XXI. ANDREE 1, from page 22

Karl Otto (Jim) Andree
February 10, 1912, Düsseldorf —
m. December 21, 1948, Coburg. Divorced: December 27, 1949,
* **Caroline Mathilde,** Princess of Saxe-Coburg and Gotha, daughter of Duke Carl Eduard of Saxe-Coburg and Gotha and of his wife, Princess Viktoria Adelheid of Schleswig-Holstein-Sonderburg-Glücksburg.
June 22, 1912, Callenberg Castle —
(She m. 1: and divorced: Friedrich-Wolfgang, Count zu Castell-Rüdenhausen – see: *Castell-Rüdenhausen* XXI, page 677.)
(She m. 2: Max Schnirring – see: *Schnirring* XXI, page 827.)

No Issue.

THE HOUSE OF ANHALT

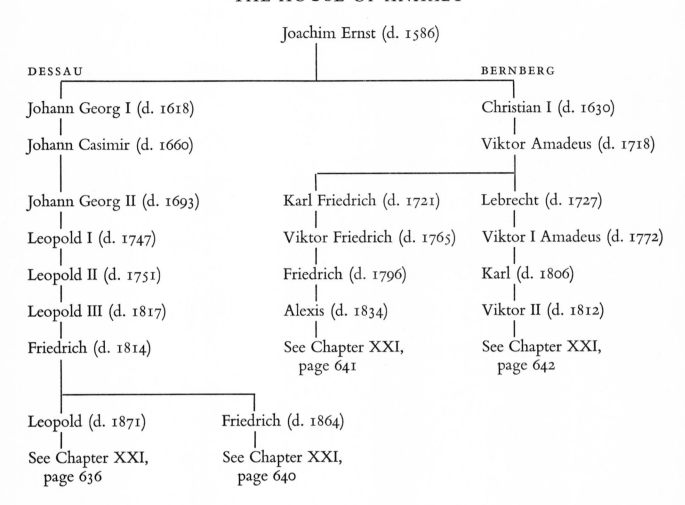

- Joachim Ernst (d. 1586)
  - DESSAU
    - Johann Georg I (d. 1618)
      - Johann Casimir (d. 1660)
        - Johann Georg II (d. 1693)
          - Leopold I (d. 1747)
            - Leopold II (d. 1751)
              - Leopold III (d. 1817)
                - Friedrich (d. 1814)
                  - Leopold (d. 1871)
                    - See Chapter XXI, page 636
                  - Friedrich (d. 1864)
                    - See Chapter XXI, page 640
  - BERNBERG
    - Christian I (d. 1630)
      - Viktor Amadeus (d. 1718)
        - Karl Friedrich (d. 1721)
          - Viktor Friedrich (d. 1765)
            - Friedrich (d. 1796)
              - Alexis (d. 1834)
                - See Chapter XXI, page 641
        - Lebrecht (d. 1727)
          - Viktor I Amadeus (d. 1772)
            - Karl (d. 1806)
              - Viktor II (d. 1812)
                - See Chapter XXI, page 642

XXI. ANHALT-DESSAU 1, from page 72

Leopold IV Friedrich, Reigning Duke of Anhalt-Dessau, eldest son of Prince Friedrich.
October 1, 1794, — May 22, 1871, Dessau
m. April 18, 1818, Berlin

* **Friederike,** Princess of Prussia, daughter of Prince Friedrich Ludwig of Prussia and of his wife, Duchess Friederike Karoline of Mecklenburg-Strelitz.
October 30, 1796, Berlin — January 1, 1850, Dessau

Issue: 1. Auguste, Princess of Anhalt-Dessau
November 28, 1819, — December 11, 1828,

2. Agnes, Princess of Anhalt-Dessau (1824–1897)
m. Ernst I, Reigning Duke of Saxe-Altenburg (1826–1908)
see: *Saxe-Altenburg* VII q–2, page 274

3. Friedrich I, Reigning Duke of Anhalt-Dessau (1831–1904)
m. Antoinette, Princess of Saxe-Altenburg (1838–1908)
see: *Anhalt-Dessau* XXI, 2, below

4. Marie Anne, Princess of Anhalt-Dessau (1837–1906)
m. Friedrich Karl, Prince of Prussia (1828–1885)
see: *Prussia* (*Hohenzollern*) II r–2, page 66

XXI. Anhalt-Dessau 2, from above and page 272

* **Friedrich I,** Reigning Duke of Anhalt-Dessau, only son of Duke Leopold Friedrich.
April 29, 1831, Dessau — January 24, 1904, Ballenstedt
m. April 22, 1854, Altenburg

Antoinette, Princess of Saxe-Altenburg, daughter of Prince Eduard of Saxe-Altenburg and of his wife, Princess Amalie of Hohenzollern-Sigmaringen.
April 17, 1838, Bamberg — October 13, 1908, Berchtesgaden

Issue: 1. Leopold, Hereditary Prince of Anhalt-Dessau (1855–1886)
m. Elisabeth, Princess of Hesse(-Cassel) (1861–1955)
see: *Anhalt-Dessau* XXI, 3, page 637

XXI. Anhalt-Dessau 2 continued

2. Friedrich II, Reigning Duke of Anhalt-Dessau (1856–1918)
m. Marie, Princess of Baden (1865–)
see: *Anhalt-Dessau* XXI, 4, page 638

3. Elisabeth, Princess of Anhalt-Dessau (1857–1877)
m. Adolf Friedrich, Reigning Grand Duke of Mecklenburg-Strelitz (1848–1914)
see: *Mecklenburg-Strelitz* XII g–3, page 424

4. Eduard, Reigning Duke of Anhalt-Dessau (1861–1918)
m. and divorced: Luise, Princess of Saxe-Altenburg (1873–1953)
see: *Anhalt-Dessau* XXI, 5, page 638

5. Aribert, Prince of Anhalt-Dessau (1864–1933)
m. and divorced: Marie Louise, Princess of Schleswig-Holstein-Sonderburg-Augustenburg (1872–1956)
see: *Anhalt-Dessau* XXI, 8, page 640

6. Alexandra, Princess of Anhalt-Dessau (1868–1958)
m. Sizzo, Fürst zu Schwarzburg (1860–1926)
see: *Schwarzburg* XXI, page 837

XXI. Anhalt-Dessau 3, from pages 636, 125

* **Leopold,** Hereditary Prince of Anhalt-Dessau, eldest son of Duke Friedrich I.
July 18, 1855, Dessau — February 2, 1886, Cannes, France
m. May 26, 1884, Philippsruhe Castle

* **Elisabeth,** Princess of Hesse(-Cassel), daughter of Landgrave Friedrich Wilhelm of Hesse (-Cassel) and of his wife, Princess Anne of Prussia.
June 13, 1861, Copenhagen — January 1, 1955, Dessau, East Germany

Issue: 1. Antoinette, Princess of Anhalt-Dessau (1885–1963)
m. Friedrich, Prince of Schaumburg-Lippe (1868–1945)
see: *Schaumburg-Lippe* XXI, page 819

XXI. Anhalt-Dessau 4, from pages 637, 648

* **Friedrich II,** Reigning Duke of Anhalt-Dessau, second son of Duke Friedrich I.
August 19, 1856, Dessau — April 21, 1918, Ballenstedt Castle
m. July 2, 1889, Karlsruhe
* **Marie,** Princess of Baden, daughter of Prince Wilhelm of Baden and of his wife, Princess Mariya Maksimilianovna Romanovskya de Beauharnais, Duchess of Leuchtenberg.
July 26, 1865, Baden —

No Issue.

XXI. Anhalt-Dessau 5, from pages 637, 275

* **Eduard,** Reigning Duke of Anhalt-Dessau, third son of Duke Friedrich I.
April 18, 1861, Dessau — September 13, 1918, Berchtesgaden
m. February 6, 1895, Altenburg. Divorced: January 1, 1918,
* **Luise,** Princess of Saxe-Altenburg, daughter of Prince Moritz of Saxe-Altenburg and of his wife, Princess Auguste of Saxe-Meiningen.
August 11, 1873, Altenburg — April 14, 1953, Altenburg

Issue: 1. Marie Auguste, Princess of Anhalt-Dessau (1898–)
m. 1: Joachim, Prince of Prussia (1890–1920)
see: *Prussia (Hohenzollern)* II 0–1, page 62
m. 2: and divorced: Johannes Michael, Baron von Loën (1902–)
see: *von Loën* XXI, page 759

2. Joachim Ernst, Last Reigning Duke of Anhalt-Dessau (1901–1947)
m. 1: and divorced: Elisabeth Strickrodt (1903–)
m. 2: Editha Marwitz (1905–)
see: *Anhalt-Dessau* XXI, 6, page 639

3. Eugen, Prince of Anhalt-Dessau (1903–)
m. Anastasia Jungmeier (1901–1970)
see: *Anhalt-Dessau* XXI, 7, page 640

4. Wolfgang, Prince of Anhalt-Dessau
July 12, 1912, — April 10, 1936,

XXI. Anhalt-Dessau 6, from page 638

***Joachim Ernst,** Last Reigning Duke of Anhalt-Dessau, eldest son of Duke Eduard. Abdicated on November 12, 1918.

January 11, 1901, Dessau — February 18, 1947, Buchenwald, Germany

m. 1: March 3, 1927, Ballenstedt Castle. Divorced: June 17, 1929,

Elisabeth Strickrodt, daughter of

September 3, 1903, Plauen —

(She was created Countess von Askanien on marriage.)

m. 2: October 15, 1929, Dessau

Editha von Marwitz, daughter of

August 20, 1905, Düsseldorf —

(She was adopted in 1920 by Bertha von Stephani.)

(She m. 1: November 18, 1926, Berlin; divorced: March 4, 1927, Berlin, Maximilian Ritter und Edler von Rogister.)

Issue of second marriage:

1. Marie Antoinette, Princess of Anhalt-Dessau (1930–)
   m. Karl-Heinz Guttmann (1911–)
   see: *Guttmann* XXI, page 717

2. Anna Luise, Princess of Anhalt-Dessau
   March 26, 1933, Ballenstedt Castle —

3. Friedrich, Hereditary Prince of Anhalt-Dessau
   April 11, 1938, Ballenstedt Castle — , 1966, killed in a road accident

4. Edda, Princess of Anhalt-Dessau
   January 30, 1940, Ballenstedt Castle —

5. Eduard, Hereditary Prince of Anhalt-Dessau
   December 3, 1941, Ballenstedt Castle —
   (m. , 1971, Astrid, Countess von Deym, born August 17, 1952, Munich.)

XXI. Anhalt-Dessau 7, from page 638

* **Eugen,** Prince of Anhalt-Dessau, second son of Duke Eduard.
April 17, 1903, Dessau —
m. October 2, 1935, Munich
Anastasia Jungmeier, daughter of Max Jungmeier and of his wife, Anastasia Steiner.
July 25, 1901, Straubing — February 20, 1970, Vevey, Switzerland

Issue: 1. Anastasia, Princess of Anhalt-Dessau (1940–)
m. Maria Emanuel, Prince of Saxony, Margraf von Meissen (1926–)
see: *Saxony* VII dd–1, page 290

XXI. Anhalt-Dessau 8, from pages 637, 169

* **Aribert,** Prince of Anhalt-Dessau, fourth son of Duke Eduard.
June 6, 1864, Wörlitz — December 24, 1933, Munich
m. July 6, 1891, Windsor Castle. Divorced: December 13, 1900,
* **Marie Louise,** Princess of Schleswig-Holstein-Sonderburg-Augustenburg, daughter of Prince Christian of Schleswig-Holstein-Sonderburg-Augustenburg and of his wife, Princess Helena of Great Britain and Ireland.
August 12, 1872, Cumberland House, Windsor — December 8, 1956, London

No Issue.

XXI. Anhalt-Dessau 9, from page 123

Friedrich, Prince of Anhalt-Dessau, third son of Prince Friedrich.
September 23, 1799, Dessau — December 4, 1864, Dessau
m. September 11, 1832, Rumpenheim Castle
* **Marie,** Princess of Hesse-Cassel, daughter of Prince Wilhelm of Hesse-Cassel and of his wife, Princess Charlotte of Denmark.
May 9, 1814, Copenhagen, Denmark — July 28, 1895, Hohenberg Castle, Bavaria

XXI. Anhalt-Dessau 9 continued

Issue: 1. Adelheid, Princess of Anhalt-Dessau (1833–1916)
m. Adolf, Grand Duke of Luxemburg (1817–1905)
see: *Luxemburg* (*Nassau-Weilburg*) III d–4, page 106

2. Bathildis, Princess of Anhalt-Dessau (1837–1902)
m. Wilhelm, Prince of Schaumburg-Lippe (1834–1906)
see: *Schaumburg-Lippe* XXI, page 818

3. Hilda, Princess of Anhalt-Dessau
December 13, 1839, Dessau — December 22, 1926, Dessau

XXI. ANHALT-BERNBERG 1, from page 116

Alexis, Prince of Anhalt-Bernberg, son of Prince Friedrich.
June 12, 1767, Ballenstedt — March 24, 1834, Ballenstedt
m. 1: November 29, 1794, Cassel. Divorced:
* **Friederike,** Princess of Hesse-Cassel, daughter of Landgrave Wilhelm IX of Hesse-Cassel (later Elector Wilhelm I of Hesse) and of his wife, Princess Caroline of Denmark.
September 14, 1768, Hanau — April 17, 1839, Hanau
m. 2: January 11, 1818,
Dorothea von Sonnenberg, daughter of Johann Friedrich von Sonnenberg and of his wife,

January 23, 1781, — May 23, 1818,
(She was given the surname 'von Hoym'.)
m. 3: May 2, 1819,
Ernestine von Sonnenberg, daughter of Johann Friedrich von Sonnenberg and of his wife,

February 19, 1789, — September 28, 1845,
(She was given the surname 'von Hoym'.)

Issue of first marriage:
1. Katharine, Princess of Anhalt-Bernberg
January 1, 1796, — February 24, 1796,

2. Luise, Princess of Anhalt-Bernberg (1799–1882)
m. Friedrich, Prince of Prussia (1794–1863)
see: *Prussia* (*Hohenzollern*) II u–2, page 72

XXI. Anhalt-Bernberg 1 continued

3. Friedrich, Prince of Anhalt-Bernberg
April 19, 1801, — May 24, 1801,

4. Alexander Karl, Prince of Anhalt-Bernberg (1805–1863)
m. Friederike, Princess of Schleswig-Holstein-Sonderburg-Glücksburg (1811–1902)
see: *Anhalt-Bernberg* XXI, 2, below

XXI. Anhalt-Bernberg 2, from above and page 171

* **Alexander Karl,** Prince of Anhalt-Bernberg, son of Prince Alexis. The last of the male line.
March 2, 1805, Ballenstedt — August 19, 1863,
m. October 30, 1834, Luisenlund Castle
* **Friederike,** Princess of Schleswig-Holstein-Sonderburg-Glücksburg, daughter of Duke Wilhelm of Schleswig-Holstein-Sonderburg-Glücksburg and of his wife, Princess Luise of Hesse-Cassel.
October 9, 1811, Gottorp —July 10, 1902, Alexisbad

No Issue.

XXI. ANHALT-BERNBERG-SCHAUMBURG-HOYM 1, from page 103

Viktor II, Fürst zu Anhalt-Bernberg-Schaumburg-Hoym, son of Fürst Karl.
November 2, 1767, Schaumburg — April 22, 1812,
m. October 29, 1793,
* **Amelie,** Princess of Nassau-Weilburg, daughter of Prince Karl Christian of Nassau-Weilburg and of his wife, Princess Caroline of Orange-Nassau.
August 7, 1776, Kirchheimbolanden — February 19, 1841, Schaumburg
(She m. 2: Friedrich von Stein-Liebenstein – see: *von Stein-Liebenstein* XXI, page 851.)

Issue: 1. Hermine, Princess of Anhalt-Bernberg-Schaumburg-Hoym (1797–1817)
m. Josef, Archduke of Austria (1776–1847)
see: *Austria (Habsburg)* X ee–1, page 388

XXI. Anhalt-Bernberg-Schaumburg-Hoym 1 continued

2. Adelheid, Princess of Anhalt-Bernberg-Schaumburg-Hoym (1783–1853)
m. August, Reigning Grand Duke of Oldenburg (1783–1853)
see: *Oldenburg* V bb–2, page 205

3. Emma, Princess of Anhalt-Bernberg-Schaumburg-Hoym (1802–1858)
m. Georg Friedrich, Fürst zu Waldeck und Pyrmont (1789–1845)
see: *zu Waldeck und Pyrmont* XXI, page 892

4. Ida, Princess of Anhalt-Bernberg-Schaumburg-Hoym (1804–1828)
m. August, Reigning Grand Duke of Oldenburg (1783–1853)
see: *Oldenburg* V bb–2, page 205

XXI. VON ARCO-ZINNEBURG 1, from page 787

Ludwig, Count von Arco-Zinneburg
November 25, 1913, Munich — February 18, 1942, near Projawno, Russia, killed in action in World War II
m. January 25, 1940, Moos, Bavaria
* **Maria Theresia,** Countess von Preysing-Lichtenegg-Moos, daughter of Count Johann Georg von Preysing-Lichtenegg-Moos and of his wife, Princess Gundelinde of Bavaria.
March 23, 1922, Moos, Bavaria —
(She m. 2: Ulrich Philipp, Count von Arco-Zinneburg – see: *von Arco-Zinneburg*, below.)

Issue: 1. Rupprecht-Maximilian, Count von Arco-Zinneburg
January 14, 1941, Pähl —
(m. July 11, 1968, Rottach-Egern, Katharina, Countess Henkel, Baroness von Donnersmarck, born June 17, 1943, Tegernsee, Bavaria.)

XXI. von Arco-Zinneburg 2, from above and page 787

Ulrich Philipp, Count von Arco-Zinneburg, brother of Count Ludwig.
December 12, 1917, Maxhrain —
m. September 26, 1943, Niederaltaich, near Deggendorf
* **Maria Theresia,** Countess von Preysing-Lichtenegg-Moos, daughter of Count Johann Georg von Preysing-Lichtenegg-Moos and of his wife, Princess Gundelinde of Bavaria.
March 23, 1922, Moos, Bavaria —

XXI. von Arco-Zinneburg 2 continued

(She m. 1: Ludwig, Count von Arco-Zinneburg – see *von Arco-Zinneburg* XXI, page 643.)

Issue: 1. Ludwig, Count von Arco-Zinneburg
June 20, 1944, Moos — August 14, 1944, Moos

2. Riprand, Count von Arco-Zinneburg
July 25, 1955, Munich —

XXI. VON ARENBERG 1, from page 471

Johann Engelbert, Prince and Duke von Arenberg
July 14, 1921, The Hague, The Netherlands —
m. January 18 and 20, 1955, Berchtesgaden, Bavaria
* **Sophie,** Princess of Bavaria, daughter of Crown Prince Rupprecht of Bavaria and of his second wife, Princess Antonia of Luxemburg.
January 20, 1935, Starnberg, Bavaria —

Issue: 1. Leopold-Engelbert, Prince and Duke von Arenberg
February 20, 1956, Tervüren —

2. Karl-Ludwig, Prince and Duke von Arenberg
March 13, 1957, Tervüren —

3. Marie Gabrielle, Princess and Duchess von Arenberg
June 2, 1958, Tervüren —

4. Heinrich, Prince and Duke von Arenberg
May 20, 1961, Tervüren —

XXI. ARONT 1, from page 663

Thomas Edward Aront
October , 1918, , Georgia, USA —
m. December 8, 1947, Munich, Germany
* **Marie Caroline,** Countess von Blankenstein, daughter of Count Karl von Blankenstein and of his wife, Countess Eugenie von Enzenberg zum Freyen und Jöchelsthurn.
August 16, 1924, Battelau —

Issue: 1. Joann Aront
July 2, 1948, Munich —

XXI. Aront 1 continued

2. Charlotte Aront
   March 20, 1950, Munich —

3. Alexandra Aront
   October 21, 1958, Warner Robins, Georgia, USA —

4. Edward Aront
   November 1, 1960, Warner Robins —

5. Robert Ernst Aront
   March 8, 1963, Warner Robins —

6. Richard Paul Aront
   January 12, 1965, Warner Robins —

7. Christa Aront
   April 5, 1967, Warner Robins —

XXI. VON AUERSPERG-BREUNNER 1, from page 376

Heinrich, Prince von Auersperg-Breunner, son of Prince Karl, first cousin of Karl Adolf, 10th Fürst von Auersperg.
May 21, 1931, Ainödt —
m. July 6, 1959, Persenbeug Castle, Austria
* **Elisabeth,** Archduchess of Austria, daughter of Archduke Hubert Salvator of Austria and of his wife, Princess Rosemary zu Salm-Salm.
March 18, 1935, Persenbeug Castle —

Issue: 1. Weikhard, Prince von Auersperg-Breunner
   October 23, 1961, Buenos Aires, Argentina —

2. Isabel, Princess von Auersperg-Breunner
   December 31, 1962, Vienna —

3. Maximilian, Prince von Auersperg-Breunner
   August 8, 1964, Vienna —

4. Dominica, Princess von Auersperg-Breunner
   February 28, 1970, Buenos Aires —

XXI. BABOTAI 1, from page 266

Istvan Babotai
August 17, 1939, Budapest, Hungary —
m. July 27, 1961, Zürich, Switzerland. Divorced: September 9, 1965,
* **Maleen,** Baroness von Saalfeld, daughter of Baron Hans von Saalfeld and of his wife, Elisabeth Faust.
May 21, 1927, Munich —
(She m. 2: Hans Wolfgang Müller – see: *Müller* XXI, page 774.)

No Issue.

XXI. BADEN (Zähringen) 1, from page 202

Leopold I, Reigning Grand Duke of Baden, fifth son of Grand Duke Karl Friedrich. Succeeded as Grand Duke on the death of his brother, Grand Duke Ludwig I, on March 30, 1830.
August 29, 1790, Karlsruhe — April 24, 1852, Karlsruhe
m. July 25, 1819, Karlsruhe
* **Sophie,** Princess of Sweden, daughter of King Gustaf IV Adolf of Sweden and of his wife, Princess Friederike of Baden.
May 21, 1801, Stockholm — July 6, 1865, Karlsruhe

NOTE: Grand Duke Leopold I's wife, Princess Sophie, was the daughter of his half-brother Prince Karl of Baden's daughter – thus Princess Sophie was actually a half-great-niece of her own husband.

Issue: 1. Alexandrine, Princess of Baden (1820–1904)
m. Ernst II, Reigning Duke of Saxe-Coburg and Gotha (1818–1893)
see: *Saxe-Coburg and Gotha* VII s–2, page 277

2. Ludwig, Prince of Baden
October 26, 1822, Karlsruhe — November 16, 1822, Karlsruhe

3. Ludwig II, Reigning Grand Duke of Baden. Succeeded as Grand Duke on the death of his father, April 24, 1852.
August 15, 1824, Karlsruhe — January 22, 1858, Karlsruhe

4. Friedrich I, Reigning Grand Duke of Baden (1826–1907)
m. Luise, Princess of Prussia (1838–1923)
see: *Baden (Zähringen)* XXI, 2, page 647

XXI. Baden (Zähringen) 1 continued

5. Wilhelm, Prince of Baden (1829–1897)
m. Mariya Maksimilianovna, Princess Romanovskya, Duchess of Leuchtenberg (1841–1914)
see: *Baden (Zähringen)* XXI, 4, page 648

6. Karl, Prince of Baden
March 9, 1832, — December 3, 1906,
(m. May 17, 1871, Baroness Rosalie von Beust; June 10, 1845 — October 15, 1908. She was created Countess von Rhena
1: Friedrich, Count von Rhena
January 20, 1877 — November 19, 1908)

7. Marie, Princess of Baden (1834–1899)
m. Ernst, 4th Fürst zu Leiningen (1830–1904)
see: *Leiningen* XXI, page 743

8. Cäcilie (Olga Feodorovna), Princess of Baden (1839–1891)
m. Mikhail Nikolaievich, Grand Duke of Russia (1832–1909)
see: *Russia* VIII s–1, page 320

XXI. Baden (Zähringen) 2, from above and page 50

* **Friedrich I,** Reigning Grand Duke of Baden, third son of Grand Duke Leopold I. Succeeded as Grand Duke, January 22, 1858.
September 9, 1826, Karlsruhe — September 28, 1907, Mainau
m. September 20, 1856, Berlin
* **Luise,** Princess of Prussia, daughter of King Wilhelm I of Prussia, German Emperor, and of his wife, Princess Auguste of Saxe-Weimar-Eisenach.
December 3, 1838, Berlin — April 23, 1923, Baden-Baden

Issue: 1. Friedrich II, Last Reigning Grand Duke of Baden (1857–1928)
m. Hilda, Princess of Nassau-Weilburg (1864–1952)
see: *Baden (Zähringen)* XXI, 3, page 648

2. Viktoria, Princess of Baden (1862–1930)
m. Gustaf V, King of Sweden (1858–1950)
see: *Sweden (Bernadotte)* XVI b–2, page 500

XXI. Baden (Zähringen) 3, from pages 647, 106

★ **Friedrich II,** Last Reigning Grand Duke of Baden, only son of Grand Duke Friedrich I. Succeeded as Grand Duke on the death of his father, September 28, 1907, and abdicated November 14, 1918.

July 9, 1857, Karlsruhe — August 9, 1928, Badenweiler

m. September 20, 1885, Hohenberg Castle

★ **Hilda,** Princess of Nassau-Weilburg, daughter of Reigning Grand Duke Adolf of Luxemburg, Prince of Nassau-Weilburg, and of his wife, Princess Adelheid of Anhalt-Dessau.

November 5, 1864, Biebrich — February 8, 1952, Badenweiler

No Issue.

XXI. Baden (Zähringen) 4, from page 991

★ **Wilhelm,** Prince of Baden, fourth son of Grand Duke Leopold I.

December 18, 1829, Karlsruhe — April 27, 1897, Karlsruhe

m. February 11, 1863, St. Petersburg, Russia

★ **Mariya Maksimilianovna,** Princess Romanovskya, Duchess of Leuchtenberg, daughter of Maximilian de Beauharnais, Prince Romanovsky, Duke of Leuchtenberg, and of his wife, Grand Duchess Mariya Nikolaievna of Russia.

October 4/16, 1841, St. Petersburg — February 16, 1914, Karlsruhe

Issue: 1. Marie, Princess of Baden (1865–)

m. Friedrich II, Reigning Duke of Anhalt-Dessau (1856–1918)

see: *Anhalt-Dessau* XXI, page 638

2. Maximilian, Prince and Margrave of Baden (1867–1929)

m. Marie Luise, Princess of Hanover, Great Britain and Ireland (1879–1900)

see: *Baden* (*Zähringen*) XXI, 5, below

XXI. Baden (Zähringen) 5, from above and page 27

★ **Maximilian,** Prince and Margrave of Baden, only son of Prince Wilhelm. Last German Imperial Chancellor, October–November 1918.

July 10, 1867, Baden-Baden — November 6, 1929, Konstanz

XXI. Baden (Zähringen) 5 continued

m. July 10, 1900, Gmunden, Austria
★ **Marie Luise,** Princess of Hanover, Great Britain and Ireland, daughter of Prince Ernst August (II) of Hanover, Prince of Great Britain and Ireland, 3rd Duke of Cumberland and Teviotdale, and of his wife, Princess Thyra of Denmark.
October 11, 1879, Gmunden — January 31, 1948, Salem Castle

Issue: 1. Marie Alexandra, Princess of Baden (1902–1944)
m. Wolfgang Moritz, Prince of Hesse (1896–)
see: *Hesse* IV f–1, page 129

2. Berthold Friedrich, Prince and Margrave of Baden (1906–1963)
m. Theodora, Princess of Greece and Denmark (1906–1969)
see: *Baden (Zähringen)* XXI, 6, below

XXI. Baden (Zähringen) 6, from above and page 198

★ **Berthold Friedrich,** Prince and Margrave of Baden, only son of Prince Maximilian.
February 24, 1906, Karlsruhe — October 27, 1963, near Baden-Baden
m. August 17, 1931, Baden-Baden
★ **Theodora,** Princess of Greece and Denmark, daughter of Prince Andrew of Greece and Denmark and of his wife, Princess Alice of Battenberg.
May 30, 1906, Athens — October 16, 1969, Konstanz

Issue: 1. Margarita, Princess of Baden (1932–)
m. Tomislav, Prince of Yugoslavia (1928–)
see: *Yugoslavia (Karageorgevich)* XX, page 629

2. Maximilian, Prince and Margrave of Baden (1934–)
m. Valerie, Archduchess of Austria (1941–)
see: *Baden (Zähringen)* XXI, 7, page 650

3. Ludwig, Prince of Baden (1937–)
m. Marianne, Princess von Auersperg-Breunner (1943–)
see: *Baden (Zähringen)* XXI, 8, page 650

XXI. Baden (Zähringen) 7, from pages 649, 377

* **Maximilian,** Prince and Margrave of Baden, eldest son of Prince Berthold Friedrich.
July 3, 1934, Salem Castle —
m. September 30, 1966, Persenbeug Castle, Austria
* **Valerie,** Archduchess of Austria, daughter of Archduke Hubert Salvator of Austria and of his wife, Princess Rosemary zu Salm-Salm.
May 23, 1941, Vienna —

Issue: 1. Marie-Luise, Princess of Baden
July 3, 1969, Salem Castle —

2. Bernhard, Hereditary Prince of Baden
May 27, 1970, Salem Castle —

3. Leopold, Prince of Baden
October 7, 1971, Salem Castle —

XXI. Baden (Zähringen) 8, from page 649

* **Ludwig,** Prince of Baden, second son of Prince Berthold Friedrich.
March 16, 1937, Karlsruhe —
m. October 21, 1967, Wald Castle, Austria
Marianne, Princess von Auersperg-Breunner, daughter of Prince Karl von Auersperg-Breunner and of his wife, Countess Henriette von Meran.
December 15, 1943, Zselis, Hungary —

No Issue.

XXI. Baden (Zähringen) 9, from page 227

Wilhelm, Prince of Baden, sixth son of Grand Duke Karl Friedrich.
April 8, 1792, Karlsruhe — October 11, 1859, Karlsruhe
m. October 16, 1830, Stuttgart
* **Elisabeth,** Duchess of Württemberg, daughter of Duke Ludwig of Württemberg and of his second wife, Princess Henriette of Nassau-Weilburg.
February 27, 1802, Riga, Latvia — December 5, 1864, Karlsruhe

XXI. Baden (Zähringen) 9 continued

Issue: 1. Henriette, Princess of Baden
May 7, 1833, Karlsruhe — August 7, 1834, Karlsruhe

2. Sophie, Princess of Baden (1834–1904)
m. Waldemar, Prince zur Lippe-Detmold (1824–1895)
see: *Lippe-Detmold* XXI, page 754

3. Elisabeth, Princess of Baden
December 18, 1835, Karlsruhe — May 15, 1891, Karlsruhe

4. Leopoldine, Princess of Baden (1837–1903)
m. Hermann, 6th Fürst zu Hohenlohe-Langenburg (1832–1913)
see: *Hohenlohe-Langenburg* XVI a–1, page 480

XXI. BAIER VON EHRENBERG 1, from page 868

Ernst Baier von Ehrenberg
August 2, 1855, Frankfurt-am-Main — September 22, 1920, Baden-Baden
m. September 22, 1883, Lindau
* **Sophie,** Countess von Taubenheim, daughter of Count Wilhelm von Taubenheim and of his wife, Countess Marie of Württemberg.
October 25, 1852, Stuttgart — March 19, 1936, Baden-Baden

Issue: 1. Wilma Baier von Ehrenberg
October 5, 1884, Berlin — September 2, 1938, Aachen

XXI. BARTON GENANNT VON STEDMAN 1, from page 567

Karl Barton genannt von Stedman
September 30, 1875, Ettlingen — September 30, 1933, Neustrelitz
m. May 8, 1928, Dresden,
* **Marie Auguste,** Countess Jamatel, daughter of Count Georges Jamatel and of his wife, Duchess Marie of Mecklenburg-Strelitz.
September 11, 1905, St. Germain-en-Laye, France —

Issue: 1. Ralph Joachim Barton genannt von Stedman
February 24, 1933, Besselich —
(m. November 25, 1964, Asta Knorr, born January 13, 1948
1. Gloria Barton von Stedman, December 15, 1964 —)

XXI. BAUSCHER

1, from page 745

Karl-Anton Bauscher

August 26, 1931, Grafenwöhr —
m. November 25, 1961, Amorbach

* **Mechtilde,** Princess of Leiningen, daughter of Prince Karl, 6th Fürst zu Leiningen and of his wife, Princess/Grand Duchess Mariya Kirillovna of Russia.

January 2, 1936, Würzburg —

Issue: 1. Ulf-Stefan Bauscher
February 23, 1963, Frankfurt-am-Main —

2. Berthold Bauscher
October 30, 1965, Bamberg —

3. Johann Bauscher
, 1971, —

XXI. BECK

1, from page 771

Ortwin Beck

September 30, 1915, Karlsruhe —
m. April 15, 1953,

* **Alexandra Merton,** daughter of Richard Merton and of his wife, Princess Elisabeth zu Löwenstein-Wertheim-Freudenberg.

December 2, 1932, Rottach-Egern —

Issue: 1. Michael Otto Beck
October 16, 1956, —

2. Andreas Florian Beck
August 18, 1958, —

XXI. BECKENBAUER

1, from page 727

Klaus Beckenbauer

August 11, 1939, —
m. May 13, 1967, Weinheim

* **Luitgart Luise Hug,** daughter of Rudolf Hug and of his wife, Princess Marie Therese of Prussia.

November 25, 1943, Tübingen —

Issue:

XXI. BECKER 1, from page 713

Rolf Becker
December 15, 1936, Menden —
m. June 9, 1967, Herdringen
* **Christiane,** Baroness von Fürstenberg-Herdringen, daughter of Count Wenemar von Fürstenberg-Herdringen and of his wife, Countess Marie-Elisabeth von Matuschka, Baroness von Topolczan und Spaetgen.
May 1, 1943, Herdringen —

Issue: 1. Oliver Becker
, 1968, Neheim Hüsten —

XXI. BECKER-ELDENA 1, from page 879

Hans Becker-Eldena
January 28, 1916, Berlin —
m. April 15, 1945, Skopau
* **Huberta von Trotha,** daughter of Major-General Thilo von Trotha and of his wife, Princess Ida zu Ysenburg und Büdingen in Wächtersbach.
January 22, 1917, Skopau —
(She m. 1: and divorced: Albert Heino, Baron von Beust – see: *von Beust* XXI, page 662.)
(She m. 2: and divorced: Angus, Count von Douglas – see: *von Douglas* XXI, page 687.)

Issue: 1. Beatrice Becker-Eldena (1946–)
m. Hans Gaul (1941–)
see: *Gaul* XXI, page 714

XXI. DE BELICZEY DE BAICZA 1, from page 659

Istvan (Stephen) de Beliczey de Baicza
November 10, 1936, Budapest, Hungary —
m. December 10, 1965, Burgsteinfurt
* **Marie Adelheid,** Princess zu Bentheim und Steinfurt, daughter of Prince Viktor Adolf, 5th Fürst zu Bentheim und Steinfurt, and of his wife, Princess Helene zu Solms-Hohensolms-Lich.
April 14, 1935, Münster —

Issue: 1. Katharina Maritta Charlotte de Beliczey de Baicza
November 3, 1966, Bergisch-Gladbach —

XXI. de Beliczey de Baicza — 1 continued

2. Nikolaus de Beliczey de Baicza
   June 26, 1968, Bergisch-Gladbach —

3. Juliane de Beliczey de Baicza
   January 1, 1970, Bergisch-Gladbach —

XXI. BENTHEIM

THE HOUSE OF BENTHEIM

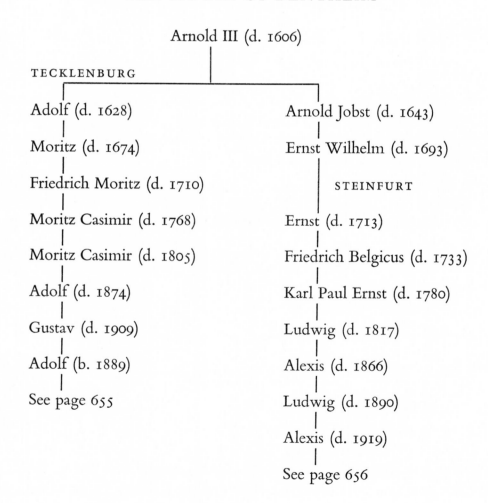

Arnold III (d. 1606)

TECKLENBURG

- Adolf (d. 1628)
- Moritz (d. 1674)
- Friedrich Moritz (d. 1710)
- Moritz Casimir (d. 1768)
- Moritz Casimir (d. 1805)
- Adolf (d. 1874)
- Gustav (d. 1909)
- Adolf (b. 1889)
- See page 655

- Arnold Jobst (d. 1643)
- Ernst Wilhelm (d. 1693)

STEINFURT

- Ernst (d. 1713)
- Friedrich Belgicus (d. 1733)
- Karl Paul Ernst (d. 1780)
- Ludwig (d. 1817)
- Alexis (d. 1866)
- Ludwig (d. 1890)
- Alexis (d. 1919)
- See page 656

XXI. BENTHEIM UND TECKLENBURG 1, from page 832

Adolf, 5th Fürst zu Bentheim und Tecklenburg, son of Prince Gustav.
June 29, 1889, Rheda —January 4, 1967, Cologne
m. July 26, 1922, Droyssig
* **Amelie,** Princess of Schönburg-Waldenburg, daughter of Prince Heinrich of Schönburg-Waldenburg and of his wife, Princess Olga zu Löwenstein-Wertheim-Freudenberg.
April 27, 1902, Langenzell —

Issue: 1. Moritz Casimir, Hereditary Prince zu Bentheim und Tecklenburg (1923–)
m. Huberta, Countess von Hardenburg (1932–)
see: *Bentheim und Tecklenburg* XXI, 2, below

2. Nikolaus, Prince zu Bentheim und Tecklenburg (1925–)
m. Franziska, Countess von Hoyos (1921–)
see: *Bentheim und Tecklenburg* XXI, 3, page 656

3. Gustava, Princess zu Bentheim und Tecklenburg (1929–)
m. Botho, Count von Hohenthal (1926–)
see: *von Hohenthal* XXI, page 724

4. Heinrich, Prince zu Bentheim und Tecklenburg
February 1, 1940, Rheda —

XXI. Bentheim und Tecklenburg 2, from above

* **Moritz Casimir,** Hereditary Prince of Bentheim und Tecklenburg, eldest son of Fürst Adolf.
October 12, 1923, Rheda —
m. July 26, 1958, Rheda
Huberta, Countess von Hardenburg, adopted daughter of Count Heinrich von Hardenburg and of his wife, Alice-Louise de Pasquier.
February 28, 1932, Divelskoof —

Issue: 1. Gustav, Prince zu Bentheim und Tecklenburg
June 6, 1960, Herford —

2. Philipp, Prince zu Bentheim und Tecklenburg
June 15, 1964, Rheda —

XXI. Bentheim und Tecklenburg 2 continued

3. Christoph, Prince zu Bentheim und Tecklenburg
May 29, 1966, Rheda —

4. Maximilian, Prince zu Bentheim und Tecklenburg
August 6, 1969, Rheda —

XXI. Bentheim und Tecklenburg 3, from pages 655, 726

* **Nikolaus,** Prince zu Bentheim und Tecklenburg, second son of Fürst Adolf.
March 12, 1925, Rheda —
m. September 15, 1951, Werenweg
* **Franziska,** Countess von Hoyos, daughter of Count Friedrich von Hoyos-Sprinzenstein and of his wife, Wilhelmine von Wuthenau-Hohenthurm.
September 28, 1921, Hohenthurm —

No Issue.

XXI. BENTHEIM UND STEINFURT 1, from page 893

Alexis, 4th Fürst zu Bentheim und Steinfurt, son of Prince Ludwig.
November 17, 1845, Burgsteinfurt — January 21, 1919, Burgsteinfurt
m. May 7, 1881, Arolsen
* **Pauline,** Princess zu Waldeck und Pyrmont, daughter of Reigning Prince Georg-Victor zu Waldeck und Pyrmont and of his wife, Princess Helene of Nassau-Weilburg.
October 19, 1855, Arolsen — July 3, 1925, Wittgenstein

Issue: 1. Eberwyn, Prince zu Bentheim und Steinfurt (1882–1949)
m. 1: and divorced: Pauline (Lily) Langenfeld (1884–)
m. 2: and divorced: Ellen Bischoff-Korthaus (1894–1936)
m. 3: Anne Luise Husser (1891–1951)
see: *Bentheim und Steinfurt* XXI, 2, page 657

2. Viktor Adolf, 5th Fürst zu Bentheim und Steinfurt (1883–1961)
m. 1: Stephanie, Princess of Schaumburg-Lippe (1899–1925)
m. 2: Rosa Helene, Princess zu Solms-Hohensolms-Lich (1901–1963)
see: *Bentheim und Steinfurt* XXI, 3, page 658

XXI. Bentheim und Steinfurt 1 continued

3. Karl Georg, Prince zu Bentheim und Steinfurt (1884–1951)
   m. Margarita, Princess of Schönaich-Carolath (1888–)
   see: *Bentheim und Steinfurt* XXI, 4, page 660

4. Elisabeth, Princess zu Bentheim und Steinfurt
   July 12, 1886, Bentheim — May 8, 1959, Burgsteinfurt

5. Viktoria, Princess zu Bentheim und Steinfurt
   August 18, 1887, Bentheim — January 30, 1961, Garmisch-Partenkirchen

6. Emma, Princess zu Bentheim und Steinfurt
   February 19, 1889, Bentheim — April 25, 1905,

7. Alexis Rainer, Prince zu Bentheim und Steinfurt
   December 16, 1891, Burgsteinfurt — June 30, 1923,

8. Friedrich, Prince zu Bentheim und Steinfurt (1894–)
   m. Luise von Gülich (1893–1949)
   see: *Bentheim und Steinfurt* XXI, 8, page 662

XXI. Bentheim und Steinfurt 2, from page 656

* **Eberwyn,** Prince zu Bentheim und Steinfurt, eldest son of Fürst Alexis. Renounced rights as a member of the family, October 1, 1906.

April 10, 1882, Potsdam — July 31, 1949, Munich

m. 1: October 26, 1906, London (marriage not recognized). Divorced: February 14, 1914, Berlin

Pauline (Lily) Langenfeld, daughter of Christian Langenfeld and of his wife, Constance Langenfeld.

February 11, 1884, Hückeswagen — December 30, 1970, Garmisch-Partenkirchen

(She m. 2: Wladyslaw, Prince Radziwill – see: *Radziwill* XI k–2, page 408.)

(She m. 3: August 14, 1924 (civil), and September 4, 1929 (religious), Munich, Count Alfred von Korff genannt Schmising-Kerssenbrock.)

m. 2: August 24, 1918, Munich (marriage not recognized). Divorced: December 13, 1919, Berlin

XXI. Bentheim und Steinfurt 2 continued

Ellen Bischoff-Korthaus, daughter of
October 6, 1894, Munich — March 27, 1936, near Zompango, Mexico, killed in an air crash with her second husband
(She m. 2: Adolf, Prince of Schaumburg-Lippe – see: *Schaumburg-Lippe* XXI, page 813.)
m. 3: August 16, 1920, Wiesbaden-Sonnenberg (marriage not recognized)
Anne-Luise Husser, daughter of
July 2, 1891, Fond du Lac, Wisconsin, USA — October 19, 1951,
(She m. 1: and divorced: a man named Fritschen.)

Issue of first marriage: (assumed the maiden name of her mother)
1. Ellen Ingeborg Langenfeld
April 24, 1911, —

XXI. Bentheim und Steinfurt 3, from pages 656, 820

* **Viktor Adolf,** 5th Fürst zu Bentheim und Steinfurt, second son of Fürst Alexis.
July 18, 1883, Potsdam — June 4, 1961, Burgsteinfurt
m. 1: September 9, 1921, Ratiboritz
* **Stephanie,** Princess of Schaumburg-Lippe, daughter of Prince Friedrich of Schaumburg-Lippe and of his wife, Princess Lovisa of Denmark.
December 19, 1899, Odenburg — May 2, 1925, Burgsteinfurt
m. 2: June 30, 1931, Lich
Rosa Helene, Princess of Solms-Hohensolms-Lich, daughter of Fürst Reinhard zu Solms-Hohensolms-Lich and of his wife, Countess Marka von Solms-Sonnenwalde.
August 14, 1901, Hohensolms — April 14, 1963, Burgsteinfurt

Issue of first marriage:
1. Alexis, Hereditary Prince of Bentheim und Steinfurt
July 30, 1922, Burgsteinfurt — December 2, 1943, over the Mediterranean, killed in action in World War II

2. Christian, 6th Fürst zu Bentheim und Steinfurt (1923–)
m. Sylvia, Countess von Pückler, Baroness von Groditz (1930–)
see: *Bentheim und Steinfurt* XXI, 4, page 659

XXI. Bentheim und Steinfurt 3 continued

Issue of second marriage:

3. Juliane, Princess zu Bentheim und Steinfurt
   December 22, 1932, Münster —

4. Reinhard, Prince zu Bentheim und Steinfurt
   March 27, 1934, Münster —

5. Marie Adelheid, Princess zu Bentheim und Steinfurt (1935–)
   m. Istvan de Beliczey de Baicza (1936–)
   see: *de Beliczey de Baicza* XXI, page 653

6. Charlotte, Princess zu Bentheim und Steinfurt (1936–)
   m. Wolfgang Paul Winkhaus (1929–)
   see: *Winkhaus* XXI, page 921

7. Ferdinand, Prince zu Bentheim und Steinfurt
   August 13, 1938, Münster —
   (m. December 29, 1970, Burgsteinfurt, Leonie Klara Luise Keller, born October 24, 1946, Esslingen.)

8. Otto Viktor, Prince zu Bentheim und Steinfurt
   July 24, 1940, Münster —

9. Oskar Arnold, Prince zu Bentheim und Steinfurt
   March 8, 1946, Burgsteinfurt —

XXI. Bentheim und Steinfurt 4, from page 658

* **Christian,** 6th Fürst zu Bentheim und Steinfurt, second son of Fürst Viktor Adolf.
December 9, 1923, Burgsteinfurt —
m. August 7, 1950, Burgsteinfurt

Sylvia, Countess von Pückler, Baroness von Groditz, daughter of Count Sylvius von Pückler, Baron von Groditz, and of his wife, Baroness Alice von Richthofen.
May 16, 1930, Burkersdorf —

No Issue.

XXI. Bentheim und Steinfurt 4, from page 657

* **Karl Georg,** Prince zu Bentheim und Steinfurt, third son of Fürst Alexis.
December 10, 1884, Bentheim — February 14, 1951, Munich
m. July 24, 1914, Haseldorf

Margarita, Princess of Schönaich-Carolath, daughter of Prince Emil of Schönaich-Carolath and of his wife, Katharina von Knorring.
June 5, 1888, Davos-Dorf, Switzerland —

Issue: 1. Georg-Viktor, Prince zu Bentheim und Steinfurt
May 26, 1915, Potsdam — May 3, 1940, Rotenburg, near Hanover, killed in action in World War II

2. Manfred, Prince zu Bentheim und Steinfurt (1918–)
m. 1: and divorced: Karin-Annabel von Grumme-Douglas (1929–)
m. 2: Irene von Sydow (1931–)
see: *Bentheim und Steinfurt* XXI, 5, below

3. Hubertus, Prince zu Bentheim und Steinfurt (1919–)
m. Eva Luise Wagner (1925–)
see: *Bentheim und Steinfurt* XXI, 6, page 661

4. Botho, Prince zu Bentheim und Steinfurt (1924–)
m. Alexandra, Princess zu Waldeck und Pyrmont (1924–)
see: *Bentheim und Steinfurt* XXI, 7, page 661

XXI. Bentheim und Steinfurt 5, from above

* **Manfred,** Prince zu Bentheim und Steinfurt, second son of Prince Karl Georg.
July 31, 1918, Burgsteinfurt —
m. 1: September 1, 1953, Stockholm, Sweden. Divorced: February 10, 1956,

Karin-Annabel von Grumme-Douglas, daughter of Wilhelm von Grumme-Douglas and of his wife, Annabel von Arnim.
July 6, 1929, Köln —

XXI. Bentheim und Steinfurt 5 continued

m. 2: October 22, 1957, Hamburg
Irene von Sydow, daughter of Kurt-Viktor von Sydow and of his wife, Irmgard Christoph.
June 2, 1931, Hamburg —

No Issue.

XXI. Bentheim und Steinfurt 6, from page 660

* **Hubertus,** Prince zu Bentheim und Steinfurt, third son of Prince Karl Georg.
October 26, 1919, Ilsenburg —
m. August 6, 1957, Haseldorf, Holstein
Eva Luise Wagner, daughter of Artur Wagner and of his wife, Elise Hühn.
October 20, 1925, Jena, Austria —

Issue: 1. Rudolf, Prince zu Bentheim und Steinfurt
April 28, 1959, Oldenburg —

2. Huberta, Princess zu Bentheim und Steinfurt
June 19, 1961, Oldenburg —

3. Nikolaus, Prince zu Bentheim und Steinfurt
October 3, 1962, Oldenburg —

XXI. Bentheim und Steinfurt 7, from pages 660, 895

* **Botho,** Prince zu Bentheim und Steinfurt, fourth son of Prince Karl Georg.
June 29, 1924, Ilsenburg —
m. June 28, 1949, Arolsen
* **Alexandra,** Princess zu Waldeck und Pyrmont, daughter of Fürst Josias zu Waldeck und Pyrmont and of his wife, Duchess Altburg of Oldenburg.
September 25, 1924, Rastede, Oldenburg —

Issue: 1. Georg-Viktor, Prince zu Bentheim und Steinfurt
March 30, 1950, Münster —

2. Wolfgang, Prince zu Bentheim und Steinfurt
February 17, 1952, Arolsen —

XXI. Bentheim und Steinfurt 8, from page 657

* **Friedrich,** Prince zu Bentheim und Steinfurt, fifth son of Fürst Alexis.
May 27, 1894, Burgsteinfurt —
m. August 7, 1934, Berlin
Luise von Gülich, daughter of
June 6, 1893, Berlin — March 3, 1949, Gütersloh

No Issue.

XXI. BEIERL 1, from page 878

Leopold Beierl
September 12, 1915, Nikolsburg, Bohemia —
m. July 10, 1951, Oberurf
* **Marielier (Lily) Treusch,** Baroness von Buttlar-Brandenfels, daughter of Baron Hans Treusch von Buttlar-Brandenfels and of his wife, Countess Marie Luise (Marielier) von Schaumburg.
April 25, 1928, Siemenstadt, near Berlin —

Issue: 1. Franz Beierl
March 31, 1953, Fritzlar —

2. Elisabeth Beierl
August 15, 1955, Fritzlar —

XXI. VON BEUST 1, from page 879

Albert Heino, Baron von Beust
July 21, 1911, Nimritz —
m. 1: July 25, 1936, Skopau
* **Huberta von Trotha,** daughter of Thilo von Trotha and of his wife, Princess Ida zu Ysenburg und Büdingen in Wächtersbach.
January 22, 1917, Skopau —
(She m. 2: and divorced: Angus, Count von Douglas – see: *von Douglas* XXI, page 687.)
(She m. 3: Hans Becker-Eldena – see: *Becker-Eldena* XXI, page 653.)
m. 2: March 27, 1948, Augsburg
Gerda Reuschel, daughter of Hermann Reuschel and of his wife, Frieda Leukert.
September 19, 1913, Cottbus —

XXI. von Beust 1 continued

(She m. 1: May 9, 1936, Gerhard Schoen, born July 7, 1910, Johannesburg, South Africa, killed in action in World War II, April 20, 1945, near Rechlin.)

Issue of first marriage:
1. Marie-Therese, Baroness von Beust
   August 21, 1937, Hall-an-der-Saale —

Issue of second marriage: Not a descendant of King George I
2. Joachim-Heino, Baron von Beust
   July 23, 1950, Augsburg —

XXI. VON BLANKENSTEIN 1, from page 695

Karl, Count von Blankenstein
June 30, 1891, Battelau — April 13, 1947, Linz, Austria
m. June 12, 1922, Innsbruck

* **Eugenie,** Countess von Enzenberg zum Freyen und Jöchelsthurn, daughter of Count Rudolf Josef von Enzenberg zum Freyen und Jöchelsthurn and of his wife, Countess Marie zu Hardegg zur Glatz und im Machlande.
March 20, 1900, Innsbruck —

Issue: 1. Johann Karl, Count von Blankenstein (1923–)
m. Viktoria, Countess von Kuefstein (1929–)
see: *von Blankenstein* XXI, 2, page 663A

2. Marie Caroline, Countess von Blankenstein (1924–)
m. Thomas Edward Aront (1918–)
see: *Aront* XXI, page 644

3. Rudolf, Count von Blankenstein (1927–)
m. Beatrice, Countess Douglas (1944–)
see: *von Blankenstein* XXI, 3, page 663A

4. Marie Therese, Countess von Blankenstein (1929–)
m. Rudolf, Count von Meran (1917–)
see: *von Meran* XXI, page 769

XXI. von Blankenstein 1 continued

5. Ernst, Count von Blankenstein (1938–)
m. Aloysia Christiane, Countess Brühl (1942–)
see: *von Blankenstein* XXI, 4, page 664

XXI. von Blankenstein 2, from page 663

* **Johann Karl,** Count von Blankenstein, eldest son of Count Karl.
May 23, 1923, Battelau —
m. June 30, 1951, Greillenstein Castle —
Viktoria, Countess von Kuefstein, daughter of Count Ferdinand von Kuefstein and of his wife, Countess Stephanie Marschal.
October 8, 1929, Vienna —

Issue: 1. Karl Ferdinand, Count von Blankenstein
June 26, 1952, Vienna —

2. Maria Chiera, Countess von Blankenstein
June 7, 1955, Vienna —

3. Albrecht, Count von Blankenstein
October 17, 1957, Vienna —

XXI. von Blankenstein 3, from page 663

* **Rudolf,** Count von Blankenstein, second son of Count Karl.
November 8, 1927, Battelau —
m. June 19, 1965,
Beatrice, Countess Douglas, daughter of Count Ludwig Douglas and of his wife, Edith Strael.
April 23, 1944, Konstanz —

Issue: 1. Stephanie, Countess von Blankenstein
July 2, 1966, Konstanz —

2. Tatjana, Countess von Blankenstein
April 16, 1968, Seville, Spain —

XXI. von Blankenstein 4, from page 663A

* **Ernst,** Count von Blankenstein, third son of Count Karl.
September 27, 1938, Battelau —
m. August 12, 1967, Münster, Westphalia
Aloysia Christiane, Countess Brühl, daughter of Count Friedrich-August Brühl and of his wife, Countess Marie Elisabeth von Korff genannt Schmising-Kerssenbrock.
December 12, 1942, Breslau, Germany —

Issue:

XXI. VON BLIXEN-FINECKE 1, from page 124

Karl Friedrich, von Baron Blixen-Finecke, Baron Nasbyholm
August 15, 1822, Dallund — January 6, 1873, Baden-Baden
m. May 28, 1854, Panker Castle, Holstein
* **Auguste,** Princess of Hesse-Cassel, daughter of Landgrave Wilhelm of Hesse-Cassel and of his wife, Princess Charlotte of Denmark.
October 23, 1823, Copenhagen — July 17, 1889, Copenhagen

Issue: see: *von Blixen-Finecke*, Addendum, page 1050

XXI. BLÜCHER VON WAHLSTATT 1, from page 401

Gebhard, 3rd Fürst Blücher von Wahlstatt
March 18, 1836, Radun — July 12, 1916, Krieblowitz
m. 1: October 2, 1860, Prague
Marie, Princess Lobkowicz, daughter of Prince Ferdinand, Fürst von Lobkowicz, and of his wife, Princess Marie of Liechtenstein.
July 18, 1841, Eisenberg, Bohemia — October 7, 1870, Rome
m. 2: July 27, 1889, Neudorf
Elisabeth, Countess von Perponcher-Sedlnitzky, daughter of Count Wilhelm von Perponcher-Sedlnitzky and of his wife, Countess Antoinette Maltzan.
September 4, 1858, — March 31, 1894, Radun
m. 3: May 6, 1895, St. Petersburg, Russia
* **Wanda,** Princess Radziwill, daughter of Prince Wilhelm Radziwill and of his wife, Countess Katarzyna Rzewuska.
January 30, 1877, Posen, Poland — August 9, 1966, Havilland Hall, Guernsey, Channel Islands

XXI. Blücher von Wahlstatt I continued

Issue of first marriage: Not descendants of King George I

1. Gebhard, 4th Fürst Blücher von Wahlstatt (1865–1931)
   m. Evelyn Stapleton-Bretherton (1876–). No Issue.

2. Gustav, 5th Fürst Blücher von Wahlstatt
   August 29, 1866, Radun – August 25, 1945, Schönberg

3. Ferdinand, Count Blücher von Wahlstatt (1868–1892)
   m. Alma Loeb (1871–). No Issue.

Issue of second marriage: Not descendants of King George I

4. Lothair, Count Blücher von Wahlstatt (1890–1928)
   m. * Ludwika, Princess Radziwill (1876–)
   see: *Blücher von Wahlstatt* XXI, 2, page 666

5. Gebhardine, Countess Blücher von Wahlstatt (1893–)
   m. Ulrich von Schimony-Schimonsky (1887–1943)

Issue of third marriage: Descendants of King George I

6. Elisabeth, Countess Blücher von Wahlstatt
   March 11, 1897, Insel Herm —June 21, 1966, Guernsey, Channel Islands

7. Wanda, Countess Blücher von Wahlstatt (1898–1945)
   m. Herbert von Schimony-Schimonsky (1887–1945)
   see: *von Schimony-Schimonsky* XXI, page 824

8. Hubert, Count Blücher von Wahlstatt (1902–1945)
   m. Ursula von Siemens (1906–)
   see: *Blücher von Wahlstatt* XXI, 3, page 666

XXI. Blücher von Wahlstatt

2, from pages 665, 401

Lothair, Count Blücher von Wahlstatt, fourth son of 3rd Fürst Gebhard.
April 20, 1890, Insel Herm in Kanal — April 3, 1928, Arosa, Switzerland
m. January 11, 1913, Vienna

* **Ludwika,** Princess Radziwill, daughter of Prince Wilhelm Radziwill and of his wife, Countess Katarzyna Rzewuska.
April 5, 1876, Berlin — June 21, 1966, Havilland Hall, Guernsey

Issue: 1. Hugo, 6th Fürst Blücher von Wahlstatt
October 12, 1913, London, England — January 6, 1948, Havilland Hall, Guernsey, Channel Islands

2. Nikolaus, Count Blücher von Wahlstatt
May 14, 1915, London — May 23, 1943, Batna, North Africa, killed in action in World War II

3. Alexander, 7th Fürst Blücher von Wahlstatt
June 16, 1916, Guernsey —
(Fürst Alexander was married in 1969 at Johannesburg, South Africa. No further information available at the time of writing.)

NOTE: Princess Ludwika Radziwill, wife of Count Lothair, above, became the step-daughter of her own sister, Princess Wanda, who married Lothair's father, as the latter's third wife – see: *Blücher von Wahlstatt* XXI, 1, page 665.

XXI. Blücher von Wahlstatt

3, from page 665

* **Hubert,** Count Blücher von Wahlstatt, fifth son of 3rd Fürst Gebhard.
September 19, 1902, Radun — May 13, 1945, Troppau
m. August 19, 1931, Berlin

Ursula Margarete von Siemens, daughter of Carl Friedrich von Siemens and of his wife, Auguste Bötzow.
August 25, 1906, Kingston-upon-Thames, England —

XXI. Blücher von Wahlstatt 3 continued

Issue: 1. Nikolaus, Count Blücher von Wahlstatt (1932–)
m. Ursula Gromann (1929–)
see: *Blücher von Wahlstatt* XXI, 4, below

2. Irene, Countess Blücher von Wahlstatt
August 8, 1934, Guernsey — August 8, 1954, Guernsey

3. Sibylle, Countess Blücher von Wahlstatt
May 21, 1937, Munich —

XXI. Blücher von Wahlstatt 4, from above

* **Nikolaus,** Count Blücher von Wahlstatt, only son of Count Hubert.
July 25, 1932, Munich —
m. April 20, 1955, Reinscheid
Ursula Gromann, daughter of Joseph Gromann and of his wife, Helene Charlotte Decker.
November 4, 1929, Essen —

Issue: 1. Livia Irene, Countess Blücher von Wahlstatt
October 8, 1955, Kiel —

2. Lukas Friedrich, Count Blücher von Wahlstatt
May 29, 1956, Kiel —

XXI. BÖCKING 1, from page 707

Edgar Böcking
, 1861, Verviers — deceased (date unknown)
m. November 20, 1901, Göttlieben. Divorced: April 29, 1911, Zürich, Switzerland
* **Luigina,** Baroness von Fabrice, daughter of Baron Maximilian von Fabrice and of his wife, Countess Ilma Almásy von Zsadány und Török-Szent-Miklós.
July 30, 1876, Nonnenhorn, Bavaria — April 29, 1958, Augsburg
(She m. 1: Walther Sturtzkopf – see: *Sturtzkopf* XXI, page 867.)
(She m. 3: and divorced: Hans Hippolyt von Simpson – see: *von Simpson* XXI, page 839.)
(She m. 4: Dr. Edwin Tietjens – see: *Tietjens* XXIII, page 876.)

Issue:

XXI. BODEY 1, from page 342

Alexander Bodey, M.D.
December 28, 1920, Fürstenwalde/Spree —
m. March 27, 1954, Berlin. Divorced: January 13, 1956, Mannheim
* **Marie Luise,** Princess Reuss zu Köstritz, daughter of Prince Heinrich XXXIII Reuss zu Köstritz and of his wife, Princess Viktoria Margarete of Prussia.
January 9, 1915, Cassel —
(She m. 1: and divorced: Erich Theisen – see: *Theisen* XXI, page 868.)

No Issue.

XXI. VON UND ZU BODMAN 1, from page 708

Emanuel, Baron von und zu Bodman
January 23, 1874, Friedrichshafen — May 21, 1946, Göttlieben
m. 1: August 7, 1902, . Divorced: November 13, 1909, Zürich, Switzerland
* **Blanche,** Baroness von Fabrice, daughter of Baron Maximilian von Fabrice and of his wife, Countess Ilma Almásy von Zsadány und Török-Szent-Miklós.
April 5, 1880, Göttlieben — June 1, 1968, Ludwigshafen am Bodensee
(She m. 2: Wilhelm Schäfer – see: *Schäfer* XXI, page 809.)
m. 2: March 16, 1914, St. Gallen
Clara Herzog, daughter of
January 9, 1890, St. Gallen —

No Issue.

XXI. von und zu Bodman 2, from page 794

Othmar, Baron von und zu Bodman
March 22, 1925, Baden-Baden —
m. November 11, 1960, Wolfsegg
* **Isabella,** Countess Saint-Julien-Wallsee, daughter of Count Eduard Saint-Julien-Wallsee and of his wife, Countess Ottilie von Enzenberg zum Freyen und Jöchelsthurn.
July 26, 1935, Wolfsegg —

Issue: 1. Felix, Baron von und zu Bodman
March 17, 1961, Munich —

XXI. von und zu Bodman 2 continued

2. Daniela, Baroness von und zu Bodman
August 28, 1963, Munich —

XXI. VON BOLTENSTERN 1, from page 865

Hans Albrecht von Boltenstern
October 4, 1905, Tratzen — September 4, 1940, killed in action in World War II
m. November 30, 1935, Rossla
* **Karoline Christine,** Princess zu Stolberg-Rossla, daughter of Prince Christoph Martin, 3rd Fürst zu Stolberg-Rossla, and of his wife, Princess Ida Reuss zu Greiz.
December 3, 1912, Potsdam —
(She m. 2: Wilhard, Baron von Eberstein – see: *von Eberstein* XXI, page 692.)

Issue: 1. Ruth Ingrid von Boltenstern
May 6, 1937, Greifswald, Pomerania —

2. Gisela von Boltenstern
November 17, 1938, Hanover —

XXI. BOLZA 1, from page 855

Anton, Count Bolza —
June 13, 1916, Pressburg —
m. August 20, 1955, Klagenfurt, Austria —
* **Rosmarie Daublebky,** Baroness von Sterneck zu Ehrenstein, daughter of Otto Daublebky, Baron von Sterneck zu Ehrenstein, and of his wife, Marie-Hermine Kunigl, Countess zu Ehrenburg, Baroness von Warth.
August 19, 1926, Klagenfurt —

Issue: 1. Antoinette, Countess Bolza
January 2, 1958, Klagenfurt —

2. Peter, Count Bolza
October 3, 1960, Klagenfurt —

XXI. VON BOSE

1, from page 117

Karl, Count von Bose
November 7, 1814, — December 25, 1887, Baden-Baden
m. May 15, 1845,

* **Luise,** Countess von Reichenbach-Lessonitz, daughter of Elector Wilhelm II of Hesse and of his second wife, Emilie Ortlopp, created Countess von Reichenbach (1821) and Countess von Lessonitz (1824).
February 26, 1813, Berlin — October 3, 1883, Baden-Baden

No Issue.

XXI. VON BRANDENSTEIN

1, from page 879

Alexander von Brandenstein
January 15, 1909, Berlin —
m. September 3, 1938, Skopau. Divorced: April 17, 1950,

* **Alexandra von Trotha,** daughter of Major-General Thilo von Trotha and of his wife, Princess Ida zu Ysenburg und Büdingen in Wächtersbach.
February 24, 1919, Skopau —

Issue: 1. Gerd von Brandenstein
April 4, 1942, Berlin —

XXI. VON BRAUN

1, from page 367

Friedrich Hubert Edler von Braun
December 26, 1934, Regensburg —
m. April 28, 1965, Salzburg

* **Elisabeth,** Archduchess of Austria, daughter of Archduke Gottfried of Austria and of his wife, Princess Dorothea of Bavaria.
October 22, 1939, Achberg Castle —

Issue: 1. Bernadette Elde von Braun
July 21, 1966, Bad Godesberg —

2. Dominik Elder von Braun
September 21, 1967, Bonn —

XXI. VON BRAUNBEHRENS 1, from page 266

Volkmar von Braunbehrens
March 22, 1941, Freiburg —
m. March 25, 1968, West Berlin
* **Lerke,** Baroness von Saalfeld, daughter of Baron Hans von Saalfeld and of his wife, Elisabeth Faust.
September 25, 1944, Lenggries —

Issue:

XXI. BREHM 1, from page 727

Erich Brehm
July 10, 1930, Ellwangen/Jagst —
m. June 30, 1961, Lützelsachsen, Bergstrasse
* **Charlotte Hug,** daughter of Rudolf Hug and of his wife, Princess Marie Therese of Prussia.
June 25, 1935, Freiburg —

Issue: 1. Bernhard Brehm
August 1, 1962, Heidelberg —

XXI. VON BRUCH 1, from page 994

Martin von Bruch
July 10, 1911, —
m. November 18, 1958, Bonn
* **Eugenie Nikolaievna de Beauharnais,** Duchess of Leuchtenberg, daughter of Nikolai Nikolaievich de Beauharnais, Duke of Leuchtenberg, and of his second wife, Elisabeth Müller-Himmler.
May 18, 1929, Munich —

Issue: 1. Irene Alexandra von Bruch
December 17, 1959, Bonn —

THE HOUSE OF CASTELL

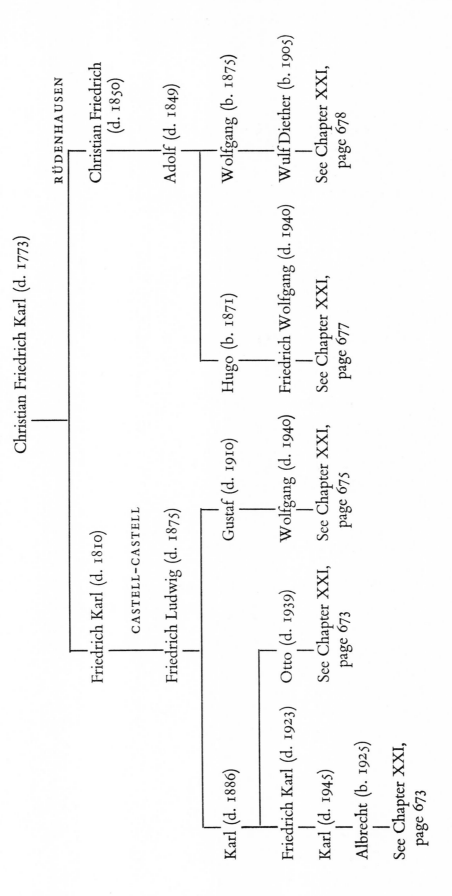

- Christian Friedrich Karl (d. 1773)
  - Friedrich Karl (d. 1810)
    - CASTELL-CASTELL
    - Friedrich Ludwig (d. 1875)
      - Karl (d. 1886)
        - Friedrich Karl (d. 1923)
          - Karl (d. 1945)
            - Albrecht (b. 1925)
              - See Chapter XXI, page 673
        - Otto (d. 1939)
          - See Chapter XXI, page 673
      - Gustaf (d. 1910)
        - Wolfgang (d. 1940)
          - See Chapter XXI, page 675
  - RÜDENHAUSEN
  - Christian Friedrich (d. 1850)
    - Adolf (d. 1849)
      - Hugo (b. 1871)
        - Friedrich Wolfgang (d. 1940)
          - See Chapter XXI, page 677
      - Wolfgang (b. 1875)
        - Wulf Diether (b. 1905)
          - See Chapter XXI, page 678

XXI. CASTELL-CASTELL 1, from page 896

Albrecht Carl, 3rd Fürst zu Castell-Castell, second son of Fürst Carl.
August 13, 1925, Castell —
m. May 23, 1951, Arolsen

* **Marie Luise,** Princess zu Waldeck und Pyrmont, daughter of Prince Maximilian zu Waldeck und Pyrmont and of his wife, Countess Gustava zu Platen-Hallermund.
November 30, 1920, Kiel —

Issue: 1. Philippa, Countess zu Castell-Castell (twin)
January 23, 1952, Castell —

2. Johanna, Countess zu Castell-Castell (twin)
January 23, 1952, Castell —

3. Maximilian, Count zu Castell-Castell
May 23, 1953, Castell —

4. Alexander, Count zu Castell-Castell
November 8, 1954, Castell —

5. Georg, Count zu Castell-Castell
November 26, 1956, Castell —

6. Christina, Countess zu Castell-Castell
March 4, 1962, Castell — November 11, 1964, Castell

7. Ferdinand, Count zu Castell-Castell
May 20, 1965, Castell —

8. Stephanie, Countess zu Castell-Castell
September 26, 1966, Castell —

XXI. Castell-Castell 2, from page 761

Otto, Count zu Castell-Castell, son of Count Friedrich Karl.
May 12, 1868, Castell — July 8, 1939, Hochburg-Ach
m. October 5, 1903, Langenzell

* **Amelie,** Princess zu Löwenstein-Wertheim-Freudenberg, daughter of Prince Alfred zu Löwenstein-Wertheim-Freudenberg and of his wife, Countess Pauline von Reichenbach-Lessonitz.
June 24, 1883, Langenzell —

XXI. Castell-Castell 2 continued

Issue: 1. Luitpold, Count zu Castell-Castell (1904–1941)
m. Alexandrine-Lovisa, Princess of Denmark (1914–1962)
see: *Castell-Castell* XXI, 3, below

2. Pauline, Countess zu Castell-Castell (1906–)
m. Georg, Prince of Schönburg-Waldenburg (1908–)
see: *Schönburg-Waldenburg* XXI, page 835

3. Gustav, Count zu Castell-Castell (1912–1941)
m. Vibeke, Baroness von Lotzbeck (1915–)
see: *Castell-Castell* XXI, 4, page 675

4. Marie Therese, Countess zu Castell-Castell (1917–)
m. Philipp Ernst, 4th Fürst zu Salm-Horstmar (1909–)
see: *zu Salm-Horstmar* XXI, page 799

XXI. Castell-Castell 3, from above and page 184

* **Luitpold,** Count zu Castell-Castell, son of Count Otto.
November 14, 1904, Langenzell — November 6, 1941, Bankta, near Sofia, Bulgaria, in a concentration camp
m. January 22, 1937, Copenhagen, Denmark

* **Alexandrine-Lovisa,** Princess of Denmark, daughter of Prince Harald of Denmark and of his wife, Princess Helene of Schleswig-Holstein-Sonderburg-Glücksburg.
December 12, 1914, Jaegersborghus — April 26, 1962, Hellerup, Denmark

Issue: 1. Amelie-Alexandrine, Countess zu Castell-Castell (1938–)
m. Oscar Heinrich Ritter von Miller zu Aichholz (1934–)
see: *Ritter von Miller zu Aichholz* XXI, page 791

2. Thyra, Countess zu Castell-Castell (1939–)
m. Karl Moes (1937–)
see: *Moes* XIX, page 620

3. Otto-Luitpold, Count zu Castell-Castell
March 13, 1942, Berlin — March 29, 1943, Berlin

XXI. Castell-Castell 4, from page 674

* **Gustav,** Count zu Castell-Castell, second son of Count Otto.
December 9, 1912, Munich —January 19, 1941, Steyning, Sussex, England, killed on a bombing raid in World War II
m. July 14, 1936, Braaby, Denmark

Vibeke, Baroness von Lotzbeck, daughter of Baron Christian von Lotzbeck and of his wife, Fanny Evers.
April 9, 1915, Copenhagen —
(She m. 2: October 23, 1958, Baron Erik Juel-Brockdorf, born November 26, 1906, at Copenhagen.)

Issue: 1. Christa, Countess zu Castell-Castell (1939–)
m. Franz, Count von Walderdorff (1930–)
see: *von Walderdorff* XXI, page 899

2. Karl, Count zu Castell-Castell
July 5, 1942, Kolberg —
(m. May 2, 1967, Ach, Austria, Adelheid, Baroness Jordis von Lohausen
1. Amelie, Countess zu Castell-Castell
February 18, 1968, Salzburg —)

XXI. Castell-Castell 5, from page 338

Wolfgang, Count zu Castell-Castell, son of Count Gustav.
May 27, 1877, Munich — February 8, 1940, Breslau
m. October 5, 1920, Ernstbrunn

* **Sibylle,** Princess Reuss zu Köstritz, daughter of Prince Heinrich XXIV Reuss zu Köstritz and of his wife, Princess Elisabeth Reuss zu Köstritz.
September 26, 1888, Köstritz —

Issue: 1. Prosper Friedrich, Count zu Castell-Castell (1922–)
m. Elisabeth, Princess zur Lippe-Weissenfeld (1940–)
see: *Castell-Castell* XXI, 6, page 676

2. Friedrich Ludwig, Count zu Castell-Castell (1927–)
m. Amelie, Countess von Pfeil und Klein-Ellguth (1930–)
see: *Castell-Castell* XXI, 7, page 676

XXI. Castell-Castell 6, from pages 675, 757

* **Prosper Friedrich,** Count zu Castell-Castell, son of Count Wolfgang.
September 4, 1922, Köstritz —
m. July 8, 1961, Bischofsheim
* **Elisabeth,** Princess zur Lippe-Weissenfeld, daughter of Prince Christian zur Lippe-Weissenfeld and of his wife, Countess Pauline von Ortenburg.
December 8, 1940, Bautzen —

Issue: 1. Johannes Friedrich, Count zu Castell-Castell
August 17, 1962, Munich —

2. Heinrich, Count zu Castell-Castell
June 25, 1966, Munich —

XXI. Castell-Castell 7, from page 675

* **Friedrich Ludwig,** Count zu Castell-Castell, son of Count Wolfgang.
October 5, 1927, Ernstbrunn —
m. April 8, 1958 (civil), Karlsruhe, and May 16, 1958 (religious), Karlsruhe
Amelie, Countess von Pfeil und Klein-Ellguth, daughter of Count Otto von Pfeil und Klein-Ellguth and of his wife, Elise von Zitzewitz.
May 26, 1930, Hermsdorf —

Issue: 1. Andreas, Count zu Castell-Castell
May 15, 1959, Würzburg —

2. Johann Philipp, Count zu Castell-Castell (twin)
September 14, 1960, Veitschöchheim —

3. Desirée, Countess zu Castell-Castell (twin)
September 14, 1960, Veitschöchheim —

4. Hubertus, Count zu Castell-Castell
September 16, 1961, Veitschöchheim —

5. Friederike-Christiane, Countess zu Castell-Castell
April 18, 1964, Wertheim —

XXI. CASTELL-RÜDENHAUSEN

1, from page 22

Friedrich-Wolfgang, Count zu Castell-Rüdenhausen, son of Count Hugo.

June 27, 1906, Berlin — July 11, 1940, over England, killed in action with the Luftwaffe in World War II

m. 1: December 14, 1931, Veste, Coburg. Divorced: May 2, 1938, Berlin

* **Caroline Mathilde,** Princess of Saxe-Coburg and Gotha, daughter of Prince Charles Edward of Great Britain and Ireland, Duke of Albany, last reigning Duke Carl Eduard of Saxe-Coburg and Gotha, and of his wife, Princess Viktoria Adelheid of Schleswig-Holstein-Sonderburg-Glücksburg.

June 22, 1912, Callenberg Castle —

(She m. 2: Captain Max Schnirring – see: *Schnirring* XXI, page 827.)

(She m. 3: and divorced: Karl Otto (Jim) Andree – see *Andree* XXI, page 634.)

m. 2: April 26, 1939, Rüdenhausen

Elisabeth, Countess zu Castell-Rüdenhausen, daughter of Count Casimir, 2nd Fürst zu Castell-Rüdenhausen, and of his wife, Countess Mechtild von Bentinck.

August 24, 1914, Rüdenhausen —

(She m. 2: January 11, 1947, Theodor Düvelius, born May 16, 1916, Wilhelmshaven.)

Issue of first marriage:

1. Bertram, Count zu Castell-Rüdenhausen (1932–)
   m. Felizitas, Countess von Auersperg (1944–)
   see: *zu Castell-Rüdenhausen* XXI, 2, page 678

2. Conradin, Count zu Castell-Rüdenhausen (1934–)
   m. Märta Lönegren (1939–)
   see: *zu Castell-Rüdenhausen* XXI, 3, page 678

3. Viktoria, Countess zu Castell-Rüdenhausen (1935-)
   m. John Miles Huntington-Whiteley (1929–)
   see: *Huntington-Whiteley* XVII, page 525

Issue of second marriage: Not descendant of King George I

4. Hesso, Count zu Castell-Rüdenhausen
   April 17, 1940, Würzburg —

XXI. Castell-Rüdenhausen 2, from page 677

* **Bertram,** Count zu Castell-Rüdenhausen, eldest son of Count Friedrich-Wolfgang.
July 12, 1932, Gölsen —
m. October 10, 1964, Vienna
Felizitas, Countess von Auersperg, daughter of Count Hanno von Auersperg and of his wife, Klothilde Ryndziak.
September 9, 1944, Vienna —

Issue: 1. Dominik, Count zu Castell-Rüdenhausen
July 20, 1965, Vienna —

2. Michael, Count zu Castell-Rüdenhausen
November 4, 1967, Vienna —

XXI. Castell-Rüdenhausen 3, from page 677

* **Conradin,** Count zu Castell-Rüdenhausen, second son of Count Friedrich-Wolfgang.
October 10, 1934, Berlin —
m. July 6, 1961, Vesta, Finland
Märta Lönegren, daughter of Bjorne Lönegren and of his wife, Göta Ingeborg Isaksson.
April 17, 1939, Helsinki, Finland —

Issue: 1. Anne Charlotte, Countess zu Castell-Rüdenhausen
April 7, 1962, Vesta —

2. Carl Eduard, Count zu Castell-Rüdenhausen
March 15, 1964, Helsinki —

XXI. Castell-Rüdenhausen 4, from page 132

Wulf Diether, Count zu Castell-Rüdenhausen, son of Count Wolfgang.
November 20, 1905, Berlin —
m. 1: June 22, 1928, Munich. Divorced: December 15, 1941, Berlin
* **Hildegard,** Princess von Hanau und Horowitz, Countess von Schaumburg, daughter of Prince Friedrich von Hanau und Horowitz, Count von Schaumburg, and of his wife, Countess Hildegard Almásy von Zsadány und Török-Szent-Miklós.
March 12, 1903, Sökking, Bavaria —
(She m. 1: and divorced: Karl Max, Count von Sandizell – see: *von Sandizell* XXI, page 799.)

XXI. Castell-Rüdenhausen 4 continued

m. 2: February 16, 1942, Berlin
Luise Ullrich, daughter of Richard Ullrich and of his wife, Aloysia Bernart.
October 31, 1912, Vienna —

Issue of second marriage: Not descendants of King George I
1. Gabriele, Countess zu Castell-Rüdenhausen
January 30, 1943, Dresden —
(m. March 11, 1963, Munich, Rolf Kröning, born June 19, 1940)

2. Michaela, Countess zu Castell-Rüdenhausen
October 4, 1945, Munich —
(m. January 5, 1968, Kempten, Bernd Rosemeyer, born November 12, 1937)

XXI. CHIZZALI 1, from page 701

Otto Horst Chizzali, Edler von Bonfadini zu Colle Lucia.
April 11, 1924, Innsbruck —
m. September 3, 1955, Schwaz
* **Wiltrud Marie,** Countess von Enzenburg zum Freyen und Jöchelsthurn, daughter of Count Karl Eugen von Enzenberg zum Freyen und Jöchelsthurn and of his wife, Carola Ossenbeck.
November 26, 1933, Innsbruck —

Issue: 1. Hemma Chizzali
December 19, 1956, Innsbruck —

2. Elisabeth Chizzali
January 18, 1958, Innsbruck —

XXI. CHRISTOFORETTI 1, from page 920

Josef Christoforetti
January 27, 1919, Kurtatch, near Bozen, Austria —
m. May 2, 1956, Mariazell
* **Stefanie,** Princess Windisch-Graetz, daughter of Prince Ernst Veriand Windisch-Graetz and of his wife, Ellen Skinner. (A great-great-granddaughter of Franz Josef I of Austria.)
January 21, 1933, Vienna —

XXI. Christoforetti 1 continued

Issue: 1. Angeline Christoforetti
November 16, 1956, Salzburg —

2. Alexander Christoforetti
January 18, 1958, Salzburg —

3. Claudia Christoforetti
June 22, 1960, Salzburg —

4. Nikolaus Christoforetti
October 27, 1963, Salzburg —

XXI. VON CLARY UND ALDRINGEN 1, from page 403

Karl, 5th Fürst von Clary und Aldringen, son of 4th Fürst Edmund.
April 3, 1844, Vienna — March 25, 1920, Teplitz-Schönau
m. June 5, 1873, Antonin, Poland
* **Felicia,** Princess Radziwill, daughter of Prince Boguslaw Radziwill and of his wife, Countess Leontine von Clary und Aldringen.
February 25, 1849, Teplitz — December 7, 1930, Teplitz

Issue: 1. Marie, Countess von Clary und Aldringen
September 19, 1874, Teplitz — April 11, 1929, Brixen

2. Johannes, 6th Fürst von Clary und Aldringen (1878–1930)
m. Eugenie Hospodar (1882–1959)
see: *von Clary und Aldringen* XXI, 2, below

XXI. von Clary und Aldringen 2, from above

* **Johannes,** 6th Fürst von Clary und Aldringen, only son of Fürst Karl.
August 11, 1878, Teplitz — March 5, 1930, Reichenhall
m. July 16, 1910, London, England, and September 12, 1911, Vienna
Eugenie Hospodar, daughter of
October 24, 1882, Smichov, Poland — March 30, 1959, Henningen

No Issue.

XXI. CROY 1, from page 471

Karl Emmanuel, Hereditary Prince of Croy, eldest son of the 13th Duke Karl Rudolf.
October 11, 1914, Düsseldorf —
m. June 18, 1953, Leutstetten
* **Gabriele,** Princess of Bavaria, daughter of Crown Prince Rupprecht of Bavaria and of his wife, Princess Antonia of Luxemburg, Princess of Nassau-Weilburg.
May 10, 1927, Berchtesgaden —

Issue: 1. Marie Therese, Princess of Croy
March 29, 1954, Dülmen, Westphalia —

2. Rudolf, Prince of Croy
July 8, 1955, Dülmen —

3. Stefan, Prince of Croy
May 17, 1959, Merfeld —

XXI. VON CURLAND 1, from page 61

Karl, Prince Biron von Curland
June 15, 1917, Wartenberg Castle —
m. August 16, 1938, Potsdam
* **Herzelaide,** Princess of Prussia, daughter of Prince Oskar of Prussia and of his wife, Countess Ina Marie von Bassewitz-Levetzow, Countess von Ruppin.
December 25, 1918, Bristow, Mecklenburg —

Issue: 1. Viktoria Benigna, Princess Biron von Curland (1939–   )
m. Johann, Baron von Twickel (1940–   )
see: *von Twickel* XXI, page 881

2. Ernst, Prince Biron von Curland (1940–   )
m. Elisabeth, Countess zu Ysenburg-Philippseich (1941–   )
see: *von Curland* XXI, 2, page 682

3. Michael, Prince Biron von Curland (1944–   )
m. Kristin von Oertzen (1944–   )
see: *von Curland* XXI, 3, page 682

XXI. von Curland 2, from pages 681, 935

* **Ernst,** Prince Biron von Curland, eldest son of Prince Karl.
August 6, 1940, Berlin —
m. August 15, 1967, Munich
* **Elisabeth,** Countess zu Ysenburg-Philippseich, daughter of Count Ludwig zu Ysenburg-Philippseich and of his wife, Mariangela Aloisi.
December 9, 1941, Rome —

No Issue.

XXI. von Curland 3, from page 681

* **Michael,** Prince Biron von Curland, second son of Prince Karl.
January 20, 1944, Wartenberg Castle —
m. July 2, 1969, Munich
Kristin von Oertzen, daughter of Joachim von Oertzen and of his wife, Gerda von Siemens.
November 4, 1944, Liessow —

Issue: 1. Veronika, Princess Biron von Curland
January 23, 1970, Munich —

XXI. CZERNIN VON UND ZU CHUDENITZ 1, from page 553

Felix Theobald, Count Czernin von und zu Chudenitz
March 7, 1902, Hluschitz —
m. 1: September 19, 1933, Meran. Divorced: 1950
* **Anna Leopoldine,** Countess Ceschi a Santa Croce, daughter of Count Franz Ceschi a Santa Croce and of his wife, Princess Therese zu Ysenburg und Büdingen in Wächtersbach.
April 8, 1914, Trient, Italy —
m. 2: January 20, 1951,
Franziska von Mayer-Gunthof, daughter of
December 18, 1926, Vienna —

Issue of first marriage:
1. Paul, Count Czernin von und zu Chudenitz
July 16, 1934, Trautenau —

XXI. Czernin von und zu Chudenitz 1 continued

Issue of second marriage: Not descendants of King George I

2. Josef, Count Czernin von und zu Chudenitz
   January 7, 1952, Vienna —

3. Reta, Countess Czernin von und zu Chudenitz
   September 25, 1953, Vienna —

4. Johannes, Count Czernin von und zu Chudenitz
   October 23, 1954, Vienna —

NOTE: Count Paul Czernin von und zu Chudenitz is married and has a daughter, Countess Maria Theresa, but at the time of writing no further information is available.

XXI. VON DECKEN 1, from page 123

Georg, Baron von Decken. He became Count von Decken in 1835.
November 23, 1787, — August 20, 1859, Rumpenheim Castle
m. April 4, 1833, Gotha

* **Luise,** Princess of Hesse-Cassel, daughter of Landgrave Friedrich of Hesse-Cassel and of his wife, Princess Caroline of Nassau-Usingen.
April 9, 1794, Maastricht — March 16, 1881, Frankfurt-am-Main

No Issue.

XXI. VON DEGENFELD-SCHÖNBURG 1, from page 918

Gottfried, Count von Degenfeld-Schönburg
April 3, 1925, Würzburg —
m. September 19, 1957, Trieste

* **Wilhelmine,** Princess Windisch-Graetz, daughter of Prince Eduard Windisch-Graetz and of his wife, Princess Alexandra (Alix) zu Ysenburg und Birstein.
June 6, 1930, Graz, Austria —

XXI. von Degenfeld-Schönburg

1 continued

Issue: 1. Ferdinand, Count von Degenfeld-Schönburg
May 16, 1960, Geislingen-an-der-Steige —

2. Alix, Countess von Degenfeld-Schönburg
July 15, 1962, Geislingen-an-der-Steige —

3. Veronica, Countess von Degenfeld-Schönburg
May 20, 1964, Geislingen-an-der-Steige —

XXI. DEYM VON STRITEZ

1, from page 849

Albrecht, Count Deym von Stritez
September 17, 1924, Mariakirchen —
m. January 2, 1965, Arnstorf
* **Monika,** Countess Matz von Spiegelfeld, daughter of Count Sigismund Matz von Spiegelfeld and of his wife, Countess Marie von Lodron-Loterano.
April 27, 1927, Tijucas, Brazil —
(She m. 1: Count Franz Deym von Stritez – see: *Deym von Stritez* XXI, 2, below.)

No Issue.

XXI. Deym von Stritez

2, from above

Franz, Count Deym von Stritez
October 12, 1925, Arnstorf — August 3, 1962, Munich
m. April 5, 1961, Innsbruck
* **Monika,** Countess Matz von Spiegelfeld, daughter of Count Sigismund Matz von Spiegelfeld and of his wife, Countess Marie von Lodron-Loterano.
April 27, 1927, Tijucas, Brazil —
(She m. 2: Albrecht, Count Deym von Stritez – see: *Deym von Stritez* XXI, 1, above.)

Issue: 1. Martin, Count von Deym
January 12, 1962, Landshut —

XXI. DIERKES 1, from page 705

Josef Dierkes

, Dahlhausen —

m. May 2, 1951, Goldschmiedin. Divorced: April 29, 1960,

* **Edda Marie,** Princess zu Erbach-Schönberg, daughter of Fürst Georg Ludwig zu Erbach-Schönberg and of his wife, Marie-Marguerite Deringer.

April 28, 1930, Schönberg —

Issue: 1. Anja Dierkes
April 11, 1952, Schönberg —

2. Petra Dierkes
July 5, 1953, Schönberg —

3. Jan-Wilm Dierkes
July 17, 1956, Darmstadt — March 9, 1959, Darmstadt

4. Tatjana Dierkes
April 29, 1960, Darmstadt —

XXI. ZU DOHNA-SCHLOBITTEN 1, from page 779

Heinrich, Burggraf and Count zu Dohna-Schlobitten [Burggraf = Lord of the castle.]

April 24, 1907, Potsdam — May 22, 1940, Maubeuge, France, killed in action in World War II

m. April 10, 1934, Bayerhof Castle

* **Amelie,** Countess zu Ortenburg, daughter of Count Friedrich von Ortenburg and of his wife, Princess Ilka zu Löwenstein-Wertheim-Freudenberg.

December 19, 1909, Langenzell —

Issue: 1. Ilka, Burggräfin and Countess zu Dohna-Schlobitten
June 10, 1937, Königsberg —
(m. May 11, 1968, at Garmisch, Alfred Lorenz, born June 21, 1925, Interlaken. No Issue.)

2. Amelie, Burggräfin and Countess zu Dohna-Schlobitten
December 10, 1939, Königsberg —
(m. May 9, 1970, Garmisch, Hermann Bürgers, born October 31, 1936,
1. Heinrich Bürgers, b. July 9, 1971, Munich)

XXI. VON DÖRNBERG

I, from pages 75, 704

Hans Karl, Baron von Dörnberg
December 23, 1875, Cassel — March 22, 1924, Darmstadt
m. 1: June 17, 1914, Risoir, Belgium. Divorced: February 7, 1923, Berlin

★ **Marie Viktoria,** Countess von Hohenau, daughter of Count Wilhelm von Hohenau and of his wife, Princess Margarethe of Hohenlohe-Oehringen.
August 30, 1889, Berlin — June 9, 1934, Slawentzitz
m. 2: May 31, 1923, Frankfurt-am-Main

★ **Imma,** Princess zu Erbach-Schönberg, daughter of Fürst Alexander zu Erbach-Schönberg and of his wife, Princess Elisabeth zu Waldeck und Pyrmont.
May 11, 1901, König — March 14, 1947, London, England
(She m. 2: and divorced: Neil McEachern – see: *McEachern* XVII, page 530.)

Issue of first marriage:

1. Viktoria Margarethe, Baroness von Dörnberg (1915–)
m. Gustav Adolf von Halem (1899–)
see: *von Halem* XXI, page 717

2. Friedrich Wilhelm, Baron von Dörnberg
November 7, 1916, Münster — August 6, 1942, near Rshew, Russia, killed in action in World War II

XXI. DOUGLAS

I, from page 81

Robert, Count Douglas
April 24, 1880, Villa Douglas, Konstanz — August 26, 1955, Langenstein
m. April 23, 1939, Langenstein Castle, Baden

★ **Auguste Viktoria,** Princess of Hohenzollern-Sigmaringen, daughter of Fürst Wilhelm zu Hohenzollern-Sigmaringen and of his wife, Princess Marie Therese of Bourbon-Sicily.
August 19, 1890, Potsdam — August 29, 1966, Münchhöf, Baden
(She m. 1: Manoel II, last King of Portugal – see: *Portugal* VII t–2, page 278.)

No Issue.

XXI. VON DOUGLAS 1, from page 879

Angus, Count von Douglas
July 30, 1913, Ralswieck auf Rügen —
m. June 23, 1939, Ralswieck. Divorced: August 11, 1943, Ralswieck

★ **Huberta von Trotha,** daughter of Thilo von Trotha and of his wife, Princess Ida zu Ysenburg und Büdingen in Wächtersbach.
January 22, 1917, Skopau —
(She m. 1: and divorced: Albert Heino, Baron von Beust – see: *von Beust* XXI, page 662.)
(She m. 3: Hans Becker-Eldena – see: *Becker-Eldena* XXI, page 653.)

Issue: 1. Angus, Count von Douglas
June 24, 1940, Ralswieck —

2. Gol, Count von Douglas
January 30, 1942, Ralswieck —

XXI. DUKEN 1, from page 263

Johann Duken, M.D.
January 12, 1889, Brake, Oldenburg — August 20, 1954, Heidelberg
m. April 25, 1917, Munich

★ **Elisabeth,** Baroness von Saalfeld, daughter of Prince Ernst of Saxe-Meiningen and of his wife, Katharina Jensen, created Baroness von Saalfeld.
February 2, 1895, Florence — June 4, 1934, Giessen

No Issue.

XXI. VON DUNGERN 1, from page 118

Wilhelm, Baron von Dungern
June 20, 1809, Weilburg — July 3, 1874, Wildbad
m. November 3, 1841,

★ **Friederike,** Countess von Reichenbach-Lessonitz, daughter of Elector Wilhelm II of Hesse and of his wife, Emilie Ortlopp, created Countess von Reichenbach (1821) and Countess von Lessonitz (1824).
December 16, 1821, Cassel — February 23, 1898, Weilburg

Issue: 1. Wilhelmine, Baroness von Dungern (1842–1924)
m. Hermann, Baron von Dungern (1836–1880)
see: *von Dungern* XXI, 2, page 688

XXI. von Dungern 2, from page 687

Hermann, Baron von Dungern
May 9, 1836, Wiesbaden — December 16, 1880, Bayerhof
m. June 16, 1861, Weilburg
* **Wilhelmine,** Baroness von Dungern, daughter of Baron Wilhelm von Dungern and of his wife, Countess Friederike von Reichenbach-Lessonitz.
July 22, 1842, Wiesbaden — May 13, 1924, Stuttgart

Issue: 1. Friederike, Baroness von Dungern (1862–1925)
m. Reinhard, Baron von Gise (1854–1913)
see: *von Gise*, Addendum, page 1058

2. Isabelle, Baroness von Dungern (1863–1896)
m. 1: Alfred, Baron Wolffskeel von Reichenberg (1851–1936)
see: *Wolffskeel von Reichenberg*, Addendum, page 1084
m. 2: Kurt, Baron Truchess von Wetzhausen (1859–1919)
see: *Truchess von Wetzhausen*, Addendum, page 1084

3. Otto Wilhelm, Baron von Dungern (1869–)
m. Elise von Schreven (1873–)
see: *von Dungern* XXI, 3, below

4. Dora, Baroness von Dungern (1871–1930)
m. Kurt Kollmann (1868–1900)
see: *Kollmann*, Addendum, page 1062

5. Hermann, Baron von Dungern (1874–1947)
m. Marie von Hesse (1874–1954)
see: *von Dungern* XXI, 4, page 689

6. Ilka, Baroness von Dungern (1880–1952)
m. Richard, Baron von Niemans (1876–1943)
see: *von Niemans* XXI, page 776

XXI. von Dungern 3, from above

Otto Wilhelm, Baron von Dungern, eldest son of Baron Hermann.
July 14, 1869, Bayerhof — deceased
m. September 22, 1892, Bayerhof
Elise von Schreven, daughter of
February 20, 1873, Batavia —

Issue: 1. Irene, Baroness von Dungern
August 6, 1893, Dehrn —
m. Wilhelm Brandt

XXI. von Dungern 3 continued

2. Vera, Baroness von Dungern
April 3, 1901, Wiesbaden —

3. Sibylle, Baroness von Dungern
June 21, 1911, Wiesbaden —

XXI. von Dungern 4, from page 688

* **Hermann,** Baron von Dungern, second son of Baron Hermann.
March 3, 1874, Freiburg im Breisgau — March 7, 1947, Schwappach
m. June 2, 1897, Auerbach

Marie von Hesse, daughter of Heinrich von Hesse and of his wife, Baroness Marie von Senarclens-Grancy.
March 3, 1874, Trier — July 22, 1954, Ober-Schwappach

Issue: 1. Hermann-Heinrich, Baron von Dungern (1898–)
m. 1: and divorced: Adelheid von Veltheim (1898–)
m. 2: Margarete Heffelmann (–)
see: *von Dungern* XXI, 5, below

2. Dorothea, Baroness von Dungern
May 9, 1901, Weilburg —

3. Helgo, Baron von Dungern (1903–)
m. Jula, Baroness von Seefried (1898–)
see: *von Dungern* XXI, 7, page 690

4. Camill, Baron von Dungern (1904–)
m. Mechtilde Semper (1910–)
see: *von Dungern* XXI, 8, page 691

5. Martin, Baron von Dungern (1906–)
m. Ulla-Brita Nordstierna (1909–)
see: *von Dungern* XXI, 9, page 692

XXI. von Dungern 5, from above

* **Hermann-Heinrich,** Baron von Dungern, eldest son of Baron Hermann.
July 23, 1898, Bayerhof —
m. 1: May 24, 1923, Putbus Castle. Divorced: July , 1951,

XXI. von Dungern 5 continued

Adelheid von Veltheim, daughter of Ludwig von Veltheim and of his wife, Countess Viktoria Wylich und Lottum.

April 19, 1898, Pasewalk —

m. 2:

Margarete Heffelmann, daughter of

—

Issue of first marriage:

1. Maximilian, Baron von Dungern (1926–)
   m. Wanja Wawrinska (–)
   see: *von Dungern* XXI, 6, below

2. Asta, Baroness von Dungern
   January 1, 1929, Waldschwind —

XXI. von Dungern 6, from above

* **Maximilian,** Baron von Dungern, only son of Baron Hermann-Heinrich.

September 12, 1926, Waldschwind —

m. September 26, 1952, Stockholm, Sweden

Wanja Wawrinska, daughter of Swen Wawrinsky and of his wife,

—

Issue: 1. Peter Maximilian, Baron von Dungern, July 19, 1953, Stockholm —

2. James, Baron von Dungern, February 1, 1955, Wiarton Ontario, Canada —

3. Friederich, Baron von Dungern, April 1, 1958, Owen Sound, Ontario —

4. Eric, Baron von Dungern, February 19, 1960, Wiarton

XXI. von Dungern 7, from page 689

* **Helgo,** Baron von Dungern, second son of Baron Hermann.

July 22, 1903, Weilburg —

m. November 28, 1929, Munich

Iula, Baroness von Seefried, daughter of Baron Philipp von Seefried and of his wife, Marie von Wendland.

December 8, 1898, Ansbach —

XXI. von Dungern 7 continued

Issue: 1. Helwig-Philipp, Baron von Dungern (1931–)
m. Adele Regnat (1939–)
see: *von Dungern* XXI, 7a, below

2. Elisabeth, Baroness von Dungern
February 18, 1934, Ober-Schwappach —

XXI. von Dungern 7a, from above

⋆ **Helwig-Philipp,** Baron von Dungern, only son of Baron Helgo.
January 17, 1931, Bad Kissingen, Bavaria —
m. April 30, 1959, Würzburg
Adele Regnat, daughter of Michael Regnat and of his wife,
—

Issue: 1. Alexander, Baron von Dungern
April 8, 1960 —

XXI. von Dungern 8, from page 689

⋆ **Camill,** Baron von Dungern, third son of Baron Hermann.
September 19, 1904, Ober-Schwappach —
m. September 28, 1937, Berneuchen
Mechtilde Semper, daughter of Hans Semper and of his wife, Auguste von Viebahn.
September 17, 1910, Eberswalde —

Issue: 1. Dorette, Baroness von Dungern (1939–)
m. Eggbrecht Kühne (1935–)
see: *Kühne* XXI, page 739

2. Cordula, Baroness von Dungern (1941–)
m. Arnulf, Baron Heyl zu Herrnsheim (–)
see: *Heyl zu Herrnsheim* XXI, page 722

3. Camill, Baron von Dungern
December 10, 1944, Landsberg —

XXI. von Dungern 9, from page 689

* **Martin,** Baron von Dungern, fourth son of Baron Hermann.
August 26, 1906, Ober-Schwappach —
m. May 20, 1937, Ober-Schwappach

Ulla-Brita Nordstierna, daughter of Otto Rudolf Nordstierna and of his wife, Emmy Maria Malmquist.
March 7, 1909, Hälsingborg, Sweden —

Issue: 1. Signe, Baroness von Dungern (1941–)
m. Dr. Friedrich von Fischer-Treuenfeld (1941–)
see: *von Fischer-Treuenfeld* XXI, page 708

2. Wilhelmina, Baroness von Dungern
February 1, 1946, Gerolzhofen —

XXI. DURST 1, from page 740

Gilbert Durst
December 6, 1912, Innsbruck, Austria —
m. May 20, 1953, Ehrenburg

* **Marie Elisabeth Künigl,** Countess zu Ehrenburg, Baroness von Warth, daughter of Karl Heinrich Künigl and of his wife, Countess Ilse Liane zu Platen-Hallermund.
July 7, 1932, Greiz —

Issue: 1. Alice Maria Durst
February 17, 1954, Brixen, Italy —

2. Evelyn Andrea Durst
July 18, 1955, Brixen —

3. Irina Michaela Durst
January 22, 1961, Brixen —

XXI. VON EBERSTEIN 1, from page 865

Wilhard, Baron von Eberstein
November 11, 1894, Hamburg — May 10, 1964, Schleiden, Eifel
m. April 12, 1944, Rossla

* **Karoline,** Princess zu Stolberg-Rossla, daughter of Prince Christoph Martin, 3rd Fürst zu Stolberg-Rossla, and of his wife, Princess Ida Reuss zu Greiz.
December 3, 1912, Potsdam —

XXI. von Eberstein 1 continued

(She m. 1: Major Hans Albrecht von Boltenstern – see: *von Boltenstern* XXI, page 669.)

No Issue.

XXI. EHLING 1, from page 853

Hans Ehling
June 13, 1916, Trier —
m. October 15, 1942, Munich-Päsing
* **Erika Benzel,** Countess von Sternau und Hohenau, daughter of Count Franz Moritz Benzel von Sternau und Hohenau and of his first wife, Elisabeth Rosenow.
November 20, 1920, Auhof, near Mörlach —

Issue: 1. Götz-Ottfried Ehling, September 28, 1943, Lüneberg —

2. Elena Ehling, July 22, 1946, Munich —

XXI. EHRHARDT 1, from page 488

Hermann Ehrhardt
November 29, 1881, Diersberg —
m. August 13, 1927, Neuruppin
* **Margarethe,** Princess of Hohenlohe-Oehringen, daughter of Prince Max of Hohenlohe-Oehringen and of his wife, Countess Helene von Hatzfeldt.
July 20, 1894, Sommerberg —

Issue: 1. Marie Elisabeth Ehrhardt
May 6, 1929, Wuthenow, near Neuruppin —

2. Hermann Georg Ehrhardt (1930–)
m. Hildegard Lore Schulz (1934–)
see: *Ehrhardt* XXI, 2, below

XXI. Ehrhardt 2, from above

* **Hermann Georg Ehrhardt**
November 15, 1930, Wuthenow —
m. May 23, 1958, Rio de Janeiro, Brazil
Hildegard Lore Schulz, daughter of
June 3, 1934, —

XXI. Ehrhardt 2 continued

Issue: 1. Christian Georg Ehrhardt
July 27, 1961, Hamburg —

2. Susanne Margarethe Ehrhardt
December 9, 1966, Munich —

XXI. EISENBACH 1, from page 864

Dr. Walther Eisenbach
August 12, 1906, Toluca, Mexico — August 20, 1944, Lukawa, near Sandomierz, Poland, killed in action in World War II
m. January 22, 1941, Michelsdorf
* **Elisabeth,** Countess zu Stolberg-Stolberg, daughter of Count Georg zu Stolberg-Stolberg and of his wife, Princess Regina Reuss zu Köstritz.
June 2, 1918, Vienna —
(She m. 2: Alexander, Baron von Warsberg – see: *von Warsberg* XXI, page 902.)

Issue: 1. Georg Michael Eisenbach
January 17, 1942, Stuttgart —

2. Franziskus Eisenbach
May 1, 1943, Gross-Stichlitz —

3. Martin Eisenbach
July 26, 1944, Gross-Stichlitz —

XXI. VON ENZENBERG ZUM FREYEN UND JÖCHELSTHURN 1, from page 236

Parzival Rudolf, Count von Enzenberg zum Freyen und Jöchelsthurn, Chamberlain at the Court of the Emperor of Austria.
August 25, 1835, Innsbruck — January 1, 1874, Schwaz
m. October 4, 1865, Lichtenstein
* **Auguste Eugenie,** Princess von Urach, Countess of Württemberg, daughter of Duke Wilhelm von Urach, Count of Württemberg, and of his wife, Theodelinde de Beauharnais, Duchess of Leuchtenberg.
December 27, 1842, Stuttgart — March 11, 1916, Schwaz
(She m. 2: Franz, Count von Thun und Hohenstein – see: *von Thun und Hohenstein* XXI, page 869.)

XXI. von Enzenberg zum Freyen und Jöchelsthurn — 1 continued

Issue: 1. Theodolinde, Countess von Enzenberg zum Freyen und Jöchelsthurn (1866–1951)
m. Rudolf, Count Vetter von der Lilie (1860–1932)
see: *Vetter von der Lilie* XXI, page 882

2. Rudolf Josef, Count von Enzenberg zum Freyen und Jöchelsthurn (1868–1932)
m. 1: Caroline Lucchesi-Palli (1872–1905)
m. 2: Maria, Countess zu Hardegg auf Glatz und im Machlande (1875–1942)
see: *von Enzenberg zum Freyen und Jöchelsthurn* XXI, 2, below

3. Eberhard, Count von Enzenberg zum Freyen und Jöchelsthurn (1872–1945)
m. Marie, Countess zu Lodron-Loterano (1873–1959)
see: *von Enzenberg zum Freyen und Jöchelsthurn* XXI, 4, page 696

XXI. von Enzenberg zum Freyen und Jöchelsthurn — 2, from above

* **Rudolf Josef,** Count von Enzenberg zum Freyen und Jöchelsthurn, eldest son of Count Parzival Rudolf.
May 19, 1868, Schwaz — December 13, 1932, Schwaz
m. 1: April 20, 1899, Venedig
Caroline, Contessa Lucchesi-Palli, daughter of Conte Adinolfo Lucchesi-Palli, Principe di Campofranco, and of his wife,
March 2, 1872, Graz — November 4, 1905, Schwaz
m. 2: July 19, 1909, Vienna
Maria, Countess zu Hardegg auf Glatz und im Machlande, daughter of Count Julius zu Hardegg auf Glatz und im Machlande and of his wife,
July 16, 1875, Schmida — June 11, 1942, Schmida

Issue of first marriage:
1. Eugenie, Countess von Enzenberg zum Freyen und Jöchelsthurn (1900–)
m. Karl, Count von Blankenstein (1891–1947)
see: *von Blankenstein* XXI, page 663

XXI. von Enzenberg zum Freyen und Jöchelsthurn 2 continued

2. Anton, Count von Enzenberg zum Freyen und Jöchelsthurn (1901–)
m. Alice, Countess von Waldstein, Herrin von Wartenberg (1909–)
see: *von Enzenberg zum Freyen und Jöchelsthurn* XXI, 3, below

3. Ottilie, Countess von Enzenberg zum Freyen und Jöchelsthurn (1902–)
m. Eduard, Count Saint-Julien-Wallsee (1895–1955)
see: *Saint-Julien-Wallsee* XXI, page 793

Issue of second marriage:

4. Josepha, Countess von Enzenberg zum Freyen und Jöchelsthurn (1913–)
m. Norbert Mayer (1906–)
see: *Mayer* XXI, page 768

XXI. von Enzenberg zum Freyen und Jöchelsthurn 3, from above

* **Anton,** Count von Enzenberg zum Freyen und Jöchelsthurn, eldest son of Count Rudolf Eugen.
June 23, 1901, Schwaz —
m. January 26, 1937, Vienna. Divorced: May 8, 1948,
Alice, Countess von Waldstein, Herrin von Wartenberg, daughter of
April 22, 1909, Leoben —

No Issue.

XXI. von Enzenberg zum Freyen und Jöchelsthurn 4, from page 695

* **Eberhard Franz,** Count von Enzenberg zum Freyen und Jöchelsthurn, second son of Count Parzival Rudolf.
May 25, 1872, Schwaz — January 16, 1945, Schwaz
m. June 6, 1898, Graz
Marie, Countess zu Lodron-Loterano, daughter of
November 14, 1873, Graz — November 12, 1959, Schwaz

XXI. von Enzenberg zum Freyen und Jöchelsthurn 4 continued

Issue: 1. Hubert, Count von Enzenberg zum Freyen und Jöchelsthurn (1899–)
m. Leonhilde, Baroness Klezl von Norburg (1899–)
see: *von Enzenberg zum Freyen und Jöchelsthurn* XXI, 5, below

2. Marie, Countess von Enzenberg zum Freyen und Jöchelsthurn (1900–)
m. Dr. Sigmund Matz, Count von Spiegelfeld (1898–)
see: *Spiegelfeld (Matz)* XXI, page 848

3. Franz Josef, Count von Enzenberg zum Freyen und Jöchelsthurn (1901–)
m. Luise Maria Eltz (1907–)
see: *von Enzenberg zum Freyen und Jöchelsthurn* XXI, 7, page 700

4. Karl Eugen, Count von Enzenberg zum Freyen und Jöchelsthurn (1903–)
m. Carola Ossenbeck (1904–)
see: *von Enzenberg zum Freyen und Jöchelsthurn* XXI, 8, page 700

XXI. von Enzenberg zum Freyen und Jöchelsthurn 5, from above

* **Hubert,** Count von Enzenberg zum Freyen und Jöchelsthurn, eldest son of Count Eberhard.
May 21, 1899, Schwaz —
m. February 10, 1923, Mödling, near Vienna
Leonhilde, Baroness Klezl von Norburg, daughter of Baron Otto Klezl von Norburg and of his wife, Marie Edle von Raab.
October 24, 1899, Hitzing, near Vienna —

Issue: 1. Alfred, Count von Enzenburg zum Freyen und Jöchelsthurn (1924–)
m. Elisabeth Junker (1924–)
see: *von Enzenberg zum Freyen und Jöchelsthurn* XXI, 6, page 698

2. Leonhard, Count von Enzenberg zum Freyen und Jöchelsthurn (1926–)
m. Sylvia von Mann, Edle von Tiechler (1940–)
see: *von Enzenberg zum Freyen und Jöchelsthurn* XXI, 6a, page 699

XXI. von Enzenberg zum Freyen und Jöchelsthurn 5 continued

3. Eugen, Count von Enzenberg zum Freyen und Jöchelsthurn (1927–)
m. 1: and divorced: Doris Ullrich (1933–)
m. 2: Inge Pregenzer (1940–)
see: *von Enzenberg zum Freyen und Jöchelsthurn* XXI, 6b, page 699

4. Leonhilde, Countess von Enzenberg zum Freyen und Jöchelsthurn (1941–)
m. Christoph von Norman und Audenhove, Count von Kuenburg (1936–)
see: *von Norman und Audenhove (von Kuenburg)* XXI, page 776

XXI. von Enzenberg zum Freyen und Jöchelsthurn 6, from page 697

* **Alfred,** Count von Enzenberg zum Freyen und Jöchelsthurn, eldest son of Count Hubert.
March 26, 1924, Schwaz —
m. November 22, 1952, Rotholz
Elisabeth Junker, daughter of Johann Junker and of his wife, Martha Knapp.
December 18, 1924, Rotholz —

Issue: 1. Ernst, Count von Enzenberg zum Freyen und Jöchelsthurn
October 18, 1953, Innsbruck —

2. Maria, Countess von Enzenberg zum Freyen und Jöchelsthurn
November 13, 1956, Innsbruck —

3. Wolfgang, Count von Enzenberg zum Freyen und Jöchelsthurn
October 19, 1960, Innsbruck —

XXI. von Enzenberg zum Freyen und Jöchelsthurn 6a, from page 697

* **Leonhard,** Count von Enzenberg zum Freyen und Jöchelsthurn, second son of Count Hubert.
August 20, 1926, Pill, near Schwaz —
m. March 10, 1962,
Sylvia von Mann, Edle von Tiechler, daughter of
November 30, 1940, Breslau —

Issue: 1. Manuela, Countess von Enzenberg zum Freyen und Jöchelsthurn
December 19, 1962, Bad Reichenhall —

2. Carina, Countess von Enzenberg zum Freyen und Jöchelsthurn
September 22, 1964, Erlangen —

3. Konstantin, Count von Enzenberg zum Freyen und Jöchelsthurn
August 14, 1969, Bad Reichenhall —

XXI. von Enzenberg zum Freyen und Jöchelsthurn 6b, from page 698

* **Eugen,** Count von Enzenberg zum Freyen und Jöchelsthurn, third son of Count Hubert.
September 5, 1927, Pill, near Schwaz —
m. 1: April 20, 1954, Pill. Divorced: July 15, 1963, Innsbruck
Doris Ullrich, daughter of Dragodin Ullrich and of his wife, Esther Szitvay.
October 30, 1933, Vucova —
m. 2: June 6, 1964, Innsbruck
Inge Pregenzer, daughter of Josef Pregenzer and of his wife, Viktoria Tollinger.
August 15, 1940, Innsbruck —

Issue of first marriage:
1. Angelika, Countess von Enzenberg zum Freyen und Jöchelsthurn
January 8, 1955, Innsbruck —

2. Pia, Countess von Enzenberg zum Freyen und Jöchelsthurn
May 8, 1956, Schwaz —

3. Esther, Countess von Enzenberg zum Freyen und Jöchelsthurn
December 15, 1957, Schwaz —

XXI. von Enzenberg zum Freyen und Jöchelsthurn 6b continued

Issue of second marriage:

4. Veronika, Countess von Enzenberg zum Freyen und Jöchelsthurn
December 2, 1965, Innsbruck —

5. Hartmann, Count von Enzenberg zum Freyen und Jöchelsthurn
March 17, 1967, Innsbruck —

XXI. von Enzenberg zum Freyen und Jöchelsthurn 7, from page 697

* **Franz Josef,** Count von Enzenberg zum Freyen und Jöchelsthurn, son of Count Eberhard Franz.
August 5, 1901, Schwaz —
m. 1: December 27, 1937, Innsbruck. Divorced
Luise Maria Eltz, daughter of
October 11, 1907, Vienna —
m. 2:
Esther von Zistray
, 1908, —

No Issue.

XXI. von Enzenberg zum Freyen und Jöchelsthurn 8, from page 697

* **Karl Eugen,** Count von Enzenberg zum Freyen und Jöchelsthurn, son of Count Eberhard Franz.
February 10, 1903, Schwaz —
m. May 28, 1930, Schwaz
Carola Ossenbeck, daughter of Anton Ossenbeck and of his wife,
August 29, 1904, Elberfeld — February 27, 1950, Schwaz

Issue: 1. Sighard, Count von Enzenberg zum Freyen und Jöchelsthurn (1931–)
m. Christine Schwarz (1937–)
see: *von Enzenberg zum Freyen und Jöchelsthurn* XXI, 9, page 701

XXI. von Enzenberg zum Freyen und Jöchelsthurn 8 continued

2. Wiltrud Marie, Countess von Enzenberg zum Freyen und Jöchelsthurn (1933–)
m. Otto Horst Chizzali (1924–)
see: *Chizzali* XXI, page 679

3. Uta Helene, Countess von Enzenberg zum Freyen und Jöchelsthurn (1937–)
m. Walter Kunz (1932–)
see: *Kunz* XXI, page 741

4. Dietlind Gabrielle, Countess von Enzenberg zum Freyen und Jöchelsthurn (1939–)
m. Karl Heinz Wackerle-Fürich (1934–)
see: *Wackerle-Fürich* XXI, page 885

5. Mechtilde, Countess von Enzenberg zum Freyen und Jöchelsthurn
January 7, 1941, St. Pölten, near Vienna —

6. Albrecht, Count von Enzenberg zum Freyen und Jöchelsthurn
May 26, 1944, St. Pölten —

XXI. von Enzenberg zum Freyen und Jöchelsthurn 9, from page 700

* **Sighard,** Count von Enzenberg zum Freyen und Jöchelsthurn, eldest son of Count Karl Eugen.
June 11, 1931, Innsbruck —
m. October 17, 1959, Vienna
Christine Schwarz, daughter of Karl Schwarz and of his wife,
June 24, 1937, Vienna —

Issue: 1. Alexander, Count von Enzenberg zum Freyen und Jöchelsthurn
November 24, 1961, Vienna —

2. Isabelle, Countess von Enzenberg zum Freyen und Jöchelsthurn
December 19, 1966, Vienna —

XXI. ZU ERBACH-ERBACH 1, from page 859

Georg-Albrecht, Count zu Erbach-Erbach
August 22, 1844, Erbach — April 19, 1915, Ober-Mossau
m. September 12, 1878, Stolberg
* **Erika,** Princess zu Stolberg-Stolberg, daughter of Fürst und Graf Alfred zu Stolberg and of his wife, Princess Auguste zu Waldeck und Pyrmont.
July 15, 1856, Stolberg — March 20, 1928, Rottleberode

Issue: 1. Erasmus, Count zu Erbach-Erbach
March 23, 1883, Erbach — February 10, 1920, Frankfurt-am-Main
(m. 1: September 1, 1905, London, Dora Fischer, born 1884
m. 2: Hellwig)

XXI. ZU ERBACH-ERBACH UND VON WARTHENBERGH-ROTH
1, from page 895

Franz August, Count zu Erbach-Erbach und von Warthenbergh-Roth
February 5, 1925, Eulbach —
m. March 26, 1952, Arolsen
* **Margarethe,** Princess zu Waldeck und Pyrmont, daughter of Hereditary Prince Josias zu Waldeck und Pyrmont and of his wife, Duchess Altburg of Oldenburg.
May 2, 1923, Munich —

Issue: 1. Alexandra, Countess zu Erbach-Erbach und von Warthenbergh-Roth
August 2, 1955, Frankfurt-am-Main —

2. Franz Eberhard, Count zu Erbach-Erbach und von Warthenbergh-Roth
June 2, 1958, Erbach —

XXI. ZU ERBACH-FÜRSTENAU 1, from page 841

Raimund, Count zu Erbach-Fürstenau, son of Count Alfred.
February 21, 1868, Fürstenau — January 2, 1926, Fürstenau
m. April 21, 1921, Hungen Castle
* **Helene,** Princess zu Solms-Braunfels, daughter of Prince Hermann zu Solms-Braunfels and of his wife, Princess Elisabeth Reuss zu Schleiz.
February 15, 1890, Berlin —

Issue: 1. Jutta, Countess zu Erbach-Fürstenau
April 3, 1922, Fürstenau —

XXI. zu Erbach-Fürstenau 1 continued

2. Eugen, Count zu Erbach-Fürstenau (1923–)
m. Elisabeth, Countess zu Erbach-Fürstenau (1929–)
see: *zu Erbach-Fürstenau* XXI, 2, below

XXI. zu Erbach-Fürstenau 2, from above

* **Eugen,** Count zu Erbach-Fürstenau, only son of Count Raimund.
May 13, 1923, Fürstenau —
m. June 17, 1950, Fürstenau
Elisabeth, Countess zu Erbach-Fürstenau, daughter of Count Alfred zu Erbach-Fürstenau and of his wife, Maria-Domina von Maltitz.

Issue: 1. Raimund, Count zu Erbach-Fürstenau
April 2, 1951, Heidelberg —

2. Lukardis, Count zu Erbach-Fürstenau
April 2, 1953, Darmstadt —

3. Kraft, Count zu Erbach-Fürstenau
March 9, 1962, —

XXI. zu Erbach-Fürstenau 3, from page 841

Joseph, Count zu Erbach-Fürstenau, son of Count Alfred.
July 10, 1874, Krähenberg —
m. April 21, 1921, Hugen Castle
* **Marie-Agnes,** Princess zu Solms-Braunfels, daughter of Prince Hermann zu Solms-Braunfels and of his wife, Princess Elisabeth Reuss zu Schleiz.
December 5, 1888, Potsdam —

Issue: 1. Adolf, Count zu Erbach-Fürstenau
January 9, 1924, Fürstenau — September 11, 1944, Darmstadt, killed in an Allied air raid during World War II

2. Kraft, Count zu Erbach-Fürstenau
November 2, 1925, Mannheim — April 21, 1945, Osten, killed in action in World War II

XXI. zu Erbach-Fürstenau 3 continued

3. Hermann-Albrecht, Count zu Erbach-Fürstenau
November 18, 1926, Mannheim —January 19, 1945, Osten, killed in action in World War II

XXI. ZU ERBACH-SCHÖNBERG 1, from page 894

Alexander, 2nd Fürst zu Erbach-Schönberg, son of Prince Gustav.
September 12, 1872, Schönberg — October 18, 1944, Bensheim
m. May 3, 1900, Arolsen
* **Elisabeth,** Princess zu Waldeck und Pyrmont, daughter of Fürst Georg Viktor zu Waldeck und Pyrmont and of his wife, Princess Helene of Nassau-Weilburg.
September 6, 1873, Arolsen — November 23, 1961, Elmshausen

Issue: 1. Imma, Princess zu Erbach-Schönberg (1901–1947)
m. 1: Hans Karl, Baron von Dörnberg (1875–1924)
see: *von Dörnberg* XXI, page 686
m. 2: and divorced: Neil McEachern (1885–)
see: *McEachern* XVII, page 530

2. Georg Ludwig, 3rd Fürst zu Erbach-Schönberg (1903–)
m. Marie-Marguerite Deringer (1903–)
see: *zu Erbach-Schönberg* XXI, 2, below

3. Wilhelm Ernst, Prince zu Erbach-Schönberg (1904–1947)
m. Alexandra, Baroness Schlitz genannt von Görtz (1910–)
see: *zu Erbach-Schönberg* XXI, 5, page 706

4. Helene, Princess zu Erbach-Schönberg
April 8, 1907, König —

XXI. zu Erbach-Schönberg 2, from above

* **Georg Ludwig,** 3rd Fürst zu Erbach-Schönberg, eldest son of Fürst Alexander.
January 1, 1903, König —
m. July 2, 1925, Schönberg
Marie-Marguerite Deringer, daughter of Alfons Deringer, Russian Imperial State Hypothecary, and of his wife, Marguerite Brehm.
December 12/25, 1903, Tsarskoye-Selo, Russia —

XXI. zu Erbach-Schönberg 2 continued

Issue: 1. Ludewig Wilhelm, 4th Fürst zu Erbach-Schönberg (1926–)
m. Rosemarie Moshage (1927–)
see: *zu Erbach-Schönberg* XXI, 3, below

2. Edda Marie, Princess zu Erbach-Schönberg (1930–)
m. and divorced: Josef Dierkes (1929–)
see: *Dierkes* XXI, page 685

3. Maynolf, Prince zu Erbach-Schönberg (1936–)
m. Marie-Katherine Markert (1921–)
see: *zu Erbach-Schönberg* XXI, 4, below

XXI. zu Erbach-Schönberg 3, from above

* **Ludewig Wilhelm,** 4th Fürst zu Erbach-Schönberg, eldest son of Fürst Georg Ludwig.
October 17, 1926, Schönberg —
m. March 9, 1946 (civil), and March 10, 1946 (religious), Schönberg
Rosemarie Moshage, daughter of Karl Moshage and of his wife, Ottilie Rasche.
September 22, 1927, Schlewecke, near Wolfenbüttel —

Issue: 1. Burckhard, Hereditary Prince zu Erbach-Schönberg
April 7, 1951, Gross-Gerau —

2. Dietrich, Prince zu Erbach-Schönberg, March 27, 1954, Gross-Gerau —

3. Uta, Princess zu Erbach-Schönberg, August 1, 1955, Gross-Gerau —

4. Patricia, Princess zu Erbach-Schönberg, December 15, 1967, Kronberg —

XXI. zu Erbach-Schönberg 4, from above

* **Maynolf,** Prince zu Erbach-Schönberg, second son of Fürst Georg Ludwig.
May 13, 1936, Darmstadt —
m. May 14, 1959, Darmstadt
Marie-Katherine Markert, daughter of
January 16, 1921, Darmstadt —

Issue: 1. Xenia, Princess zu Erbach-Schönberg
May 23, 1963, Darmstadt —

XXI. zu Erbach-Schönberg 5, from page 704

* **Wilhelm Ernst,** Prince zu Erbach-Schönberg, second son of Fürst Alexander.
January 4, 1904, König — September 27, 1947, Krassni-Lubsch, Russia, in a concentration camp
m. October 4, 1938, Schlitz
Alexandra, Baroness Schlitz genannt von Görtz, daughter of Baron Wilhelm Schlitz genannt von Görtz and of his wife, Baroness Katharina zu Eisenach.
September 24, 1910, Darmstadt —

Issue: 1. Marianne, Princess zu Erbach-Schönberg
December 15, 1939 — December 15, 1939, Darmstadt

XXI. VON ERFFA 1, from page 209

Rüdiger, Baron von Erffa
April 19, 1936, Regensburg —
m. July 8, 1967, Rastede
* **Altburg,** Duchess of Oldenburg, daughter of Hereditary Grand Duke Nikolaus of Oldenburg and of his wife, Princess Helene zu Waldeck und Pyrmont.
October 14, 1938, Lensahn —

Issue: 1. Mattias, Baron von Erffa
December 20, 1968, Lübeck —

XXI. VON ESMARCH 1, from page 166

Johann Friedrich von Esmarch
January 9, 1823, Tönning — February 23, 1908, Kiel
m. February 28, 1872, Primkenau
* **Henriette,** Princess of Schleswig-Holstein-Sonderburg-Augustenburg, daughter of Duke Christian of Schleswig-Holstein-Sonderburg-Augustenburg and of his wife, Countess Lovisa Sophia Danneskiold-Samsoe.
August 2, 1833, Augustenburg — October 18, 1917,

Issue: see: *von Esmarch*, Addendum, page 1083

XXI. VON FABRICE 1, from page 118

Oswald, Baron von Fabrice
January 8, 1820, Bonn — June 3, 1898, Munich
m. January , 1843, Dresden
* **Helene,** Countess von Reichenbach-Lessonitz, daughter of Elector Wilhelm II of Hesse and of his second wife, Emilie von Ortlopp, created Countess von Reichenbach-Lessonitz.
August 8, 1825, Cassel — March 14, 1898, Munich

Issue: 1. Maximilian, Baron von Fabrice (1845–1914)
m. Ilma Almásy von Zsadány und Török-Szent-Miklós (1842–1914)
see: *von Fabrice* XXI, 2, below

2. Helene, Baroness von Fabrice
July 28, 1846, Dresden — May 11, 1907, Florence, Italy

XXI. von Fabrice 2, from above

* **Maximilian,** Baron von Fabrice, only son of Baron Oswald.
August 30, 1845, Dresden — November 18, 1914, Munich
m. September 13, 1874, Dresden
Countess Ilma Almásy von Zsadány und Török-Szent-Miklós, daughter of Paul Almásy von Zsadány und Török-Szent-Miklós and of his wife, Countess Amelie Batthyany von Nemet-Ujar.
February 20, 1842, Budapest — January 27, 1914, Göttlieben

Issue: 1. Ellinka, Baroness von Fabrice (1875–1938)
m. 1: and divorced: Dr. Paul von Gans (1866–1915)
see: *von Gans* XXI, page 714
m. 2: Haupt, Count von Pappenheim (1869–1954)
see: *von Pappenheim* XXI, page 781

2. Luigina, Baroness von Fabrice (1876–1958)
m. 1: Walther Sturtzkopf (1871–1898)
see: *Sturtzkopf* XXI, page 867
m. 2: and divorced: Edgar Böcking (1861–)
see: *Böcking* XXI, page 667
m. 3: and divorced: Hans Hippolyt von Simpson (1885–)
see: *von Simpson* XXI, page 839
m. 4: Edwin Tietjens (1894–1944)
see: *Tietjens* XXI, page 876

XXI. von Fabrice 2 continued

3. Ilma, Baroness von Fabrice (1877–1951)
   m. Carlo Halm-Nicolai (1876–1951)
   see: *Halm-Nicolai* XXI, page 566

4. Blanche, Baroness von Fabrice (1880–)
   m. 1: and divorced: Emanuel, Baron von und zu Bodman (1874–1946)
   see: *von und zu Bodman* XXI, page 668
   m. 2: Wilhelm Schäfer (1868–1952)
   see: *Schäfer* XXI, page 809

5. Agnes, Baroness von Fabrice (1881–)
   m. Walther von Stockar-Scherer-Castell (1878–1938)
   see: *von Stockar-Scherer-Castell* XXI, page 856

XXI. VON FISCHER-TREUENFELD 1, from page 692

Friedrich von Fischer-Treuenfeld, M.D.
August 22, 1941, Oberschwappach —
m. June 1, 1969, Eichelsdorf
* **Signe,** Baroness von Dungern, daughter of Baron Martin von Dungern and of his wife, Ulla-Brita Nordstierna.
August 22, 1941, Oberschwappach —

Issue:

XXI. VON FLOTOW 1, from page 787

Andreas Friedrich von Flotow
April 16, 1913, Brussels —
m. November 3, 1941, Friedland
* **Ella,** Countess von Pückler, daughter of Count Karl Friedrich, 3rd Count von Pückler-Burghauss, Baron von Groditz, and of his wife, Princess Olga of Saxe-Altenburg.
April 8, 1914, Friedland —

Issue: 1. Adrian von Flotow (1943–)
   m. Sylvia Maria Kolck (1945–)
   see: *von Flotow* XXI, 2, page 709

XXI. von Flotow 1 continued

2. Viola Isabelle von Flotow
   March 27, 1945, Prague, Czechoslovakia —

3. Cyrill Andreas von Flotow
   December 1, 1955, Nonnenhorn, Bavaria —

XXI. von Flotow 2, from page 708

* **Adrian von Flotow,** son of Andreas Friedrich.
June 5, 1943, Friedland —
m. July 10, 1968, Siggen, Allgäu
Sylvia Maria Kolck, daughter of Werner Kolck and of his wife, Countess Gisela von Beissel-Gymmich.
March 27, 1945, Berlin —

XXI. VON FRANCKEN-SIERSTORPFF 1, from page 485

Hans-Clemens, Count von Francken-Sierstorpff
July 30, 1895, Franxdorf — December 5, 1944, Pasadena, California
m. September 29, 1920, Munich
* **Elisabeth,** Princess of Hohenlohe-Oehringen, daughter of Prince Friedrich of Hohenlohe-Oehringen and of his wife, Countess Marie von Hatzfeldt.
July 31, 1896, Sommerberg —

Issue: 1. Erwein, Count von Francken-Sierstorpff, July 3, 1921, Baden-Baden —
(m. July 4, 1960, Munich, Ina Weinert, born April 3, 1921
1. Friedrich Kraft, Count von Francken-Sierstorpff, December 29, 1961
2. Philipp, Count von Francken-Sierstorpff, February 12, 1966)

2. Constance, Countess von Francken-Sierstorpff (1923–)
m. 1: Hyacinth, Count Strachwitz von Gross-Zauche und Cammenitz – see: *Strachwitz von Gross-Zauche und Cammenitz* XXI, page 866
m. 2: William Denson – see: *Denson* XXIV, page 1016

3. Elizabeth, Countess von Francken-Sierstorpff (December 20, 1925 — December 12, 1928)

XXI. FRANK 1, from page 853

Heinz Frank
February 17, 1914, Frankfurt-am-Main —
m. January 29, 1940, Munich-Päsing
* **Elizabeth Benzel,** Countess von Sternau and Hohenau, daughter of Count Franz Moritz Benzel von Sternau und Hohenau and of his first wife, Elizabeth Rosenow.
April 14, 1919, Auhof, near Mörlach —

Issue: see: *Frank*, Addendum, page 1055

XXI. VON FRANKENSDORFF 1, from page 812

Johann, Baron Herring von Frankensdorff
September 1, 1891, Gmunden —
m. January 1, 1930, Granau, near Gmunden, Austria
* **Elisabeth,** Princess of Schaumburg-Lippe, daughter of Prince Georg of Schaumburg-Lippe and of his wife, Princess Marie of Saxe-Altenburg.
May 31, 1909, Bückeburg — February 25, 1933, Grünau

Issue: 1. Sybille, Baroness Herring von Frankensdorff
March 13, 1932, Grünau —
(m. March 13, 1955, Emil Jemail, born November 19, 1929, Newport, Rhode Island.)

2. Hans-Georg, Baron Herring von Frankensdorff (1933–)
m. Anneliese Buchholz (1941–)
see: *von Frankensdorff* XXI, 2, below

XXI. von Frankensdorff 2, from above

* **Hans-Georg,** Baron Herring von Frankensdorff, only son of Baron Johann.
February 5, 1933, Grünau —
m. June 13, 1964,
Anneliese Buchholz, daughter of Richard Buchholz and of his wife,
May 4, 1941, Prague —

Issue: 1. Elizabeth, Baroness Herring von Frankensdorff
October 2, 1964, Krems —

XXI. VON FÜRSTENBERG 1, from page 334

Karl Egon III, Fürst von Fürstenberg
March 4, 1820, Donaueschingen — March 15, 1892, Paris
m. November 4, 1844, Greiz
* **Elisabeth,** Princess Reuss zu Greiz, daughter of Prince Heinrich XIX Reuss zu Greiz and of his wife, Princess Gasparine de Rohan-Rochefort.
March 23, 1824, Greiz — May 7, 1861, Berlin

Issue: 1. Amelie, Princess of Fürstenberg
May 25, 1848, Schafthausen — March 8, 1918, Baden-Baden

2. Karl Egon IV, Fürst von Fürstenberg (1852–1896)
m. Dorothée, Princesse de Tallyrand-Périgord et Sagan (1862–1948)
see: *von Fürstenberg* XXI, 2, below

XXI. von Fürstenberg 2, from above

* **Karl Egon IV,** Fürst von Fürstenberg, only son of Fürst Karl Egon III.
August 25, 1852, Kruschwitz — November 27, 1896, Nice, France
m. July 6, 1881, Sagan, Silesia
Dorothée, Princesse de Tallyrand-Périgord et Sagan, daughter of Prince Napoléon Louis de Tallyrand-Périgord, Duc de Valencay, Duc de Sagan (1862); Duc de Tallyrand (1872), and of his second wife, Pauline de Castellane.
November 17, 1862, Valencay — June 17, 1948,
(She m. 2: June 2, 1898, Paris, Jean, Comte de Castellane.)

No Issue.

XXI. von Fürstenberg 1, from page 882

Erasmus, Baron von Fürstenberg
November 9, 1936, Landshüt, Bavaria —
m. March 3, 1962 (civil), Weihenstephan, and May 2, 1962 (religious), Singen Hohentweil
* **Maria Antonia**, Countess Vetter von der Lilie, daughter of Count Rudolf Vetter von der Lilie and of his wife, Baroness Dorothea Wenzel von Sternbach.
April 1, 1932, Innsbruck —

XXI. von Fürstenberg 1 continued

Issue: 1. Friedrich-Leopold, Baron von Fürstenberg
February 4, 1963, Landshüt —

2. Ferdinand, Baron von Fürstenberg
August 30, 1964, Landshüt —

3. Maria, Baroness von Fürstenberg
September 11, 1965, Landshüt —

XXI. VON FÜRSTENBERG-HERDRINGEN 1, from page 767

Wenemar, Count von Fürstenberg-Herdringen
August 7, 1897, Dahlhausen —
m. April 24, 1923, Gross-Neukirch
* **Marie-Elisabeth**, Countess von Matuschka, Baroness von Topolczan und Spaetgen, daughter of Count Eberhard von Matuschka, Baron von Topolczan und Spaetgan, and of his wife, Countess Elisabeth von Hohenau.
February 7, 1901, Gross-Neukirch — May 27, 1956, Herdringen

Issue: 1. Engelbert-Eberhard, Baron von Fürstenberg-Herdringen (1924–)
m. Irene Ruge (1929–)
see: *von Fürstenberg-Herdringen* XXI, 2, page 713

2. Sylvester, Baron von Fürstenberg-Herdringen (1925–)
m. Ellen Dorr (1925–)
see: *von Fürstenberg-Herdringen* XXI, 3, page 713

3. Cäcilia, Baroness von Fürstenberg-Herdringen (1928–) (twin)
m. Friedrich Hubert, Baron von Pfetten-Arnbach (1924–)
see: *von Pfetten-Arnbach* XXI, page 783

4. Margarete, Baroness von Fürstenberg-Herdringen (1928–1960) (twin)
m. Marinus, Count Saurma von und zu der Jeltsch (1924–)
see: *Saurma von und zu der Jeltsch* XXI, page 800

XXI. von Fürstenberg-Herdringen 1 continued

5. Maria Luise, Baroness von Fürstenberg-Herdringen (1937–)
m. Marquard, Baron von Pfetten-Arnbach (1926–)
see: *von Pfetten-Arnbach* XXI, page 784

6. Christiane, Baroness von Fürstenberg-Herdringen (1943–)
m. Rolf Becker (1936–)
see: *Becker* XXI, page 653

7. Verena, Baroness von Fürstenberg-Herdringen
December 29, 1947, Herdringen —

XXI. von Fürstenberg-Herdringen 2, from page 712

* **Engelbert-Eberhard**, Baron von Fürstenberg-Herdringen, eldest son of Count Wenemar.
March 5, 1924, Herdringen —
m. October 16, 1958, Schnellenberg Castle, Sauerland, Germany
Irene Ruge, daughter of Rudolf Ruge and of his wife, Irene Vogler.
September 4, 1929, Verden/Aller —

Issue: 1. Wenemar, Baron von Fürstenberg-Herdringen (twin)
May 20, 1960, Neheim-Hüsten —

2. Dagmar, Baroness von Fürstenberg-Herdringen (twin)
May 20, 1960, Neheim-Hüsten —

XXI. von Fürstenberg-Herdringen 3, from page 712

* **Sylvester,** Baron von Fürstenberg-Herdringen, second son of Count Wenemar.
December 13, 1925, Herdringen —
m. April 4, 1958, Meschede, Sauerland, Germany
Ellen Dorr, daughter of Maximilian Dorr and of his wife, Paula Ebers.
October 21, 1925, Münster —

Issue: 1. Donatus, Baron von Fürstenberg-Herdringen
August 8, 1959, Neheim-Hüsten —

XXI. von Fürstenberg-Herdringen 3 continued

2. Gottfried, Baron von Fürstenberg-Herdringen
   October 27, 1960, Neheim-Hüsten —

3. Patricia, Baroness von Fürstenberg-Herdringen
   June 22, 1962, Neheim-Hüsten —

XXI. VON GANS 1, from page 707

Paul von Gans
July 11, 1866, Frankfurt-am-Main — April 18, 1915, Garmisch-Partenkirchen
m. May 18, 1896, Konstanz
* **Ellinka,** Baroness von Fabrice, daughter of Baron Maximilian von Fabrice and of his wife, Countess Ilma Almásy von Szadány und Török-Szent-Miklós.
May 30, 1875, Marseilles, France — August 19, 1938, Munich
(She m. 2: Haupt, Count von Pappenheim – see: *von Pappenheim* XXI, page 781.)

Issue: see: *von Gans*, Addendum, page 1056

XXI. GAUL 1, from page 653

Hans Gaul
April 7, 1941, Greifswall —
m. July 19, 1968, Wesel
* **Beatrix Decker-Eldena,** daughter of Hans Decker-Eldena and of his wife, Huberta von Trotha.
April 3, 1946, Hamburg —

Issue:

XXI. VON GOËSS 1, from page 795

Ernst-Friedrich, Count von Goëss
March 12, 1932, Klagenfurt, Austria —
m. October 12, 1961, Dyck
* **Gabrielle,** Altgräfin zu Salm-Reifferscheidt, Krautheim und Dyck, daughter of Fürst and Altgraf Franz Josef zu Salm-Reifferscheidt, Krautheim und Dyck and of his wife, Princess Cäcilie zu Salm-Salm.
November 9, 1941, Bonn —

XXI. von Goëss 1 continued

Issue: 1. Svea, Countess von Goëss
August 16, 1962, Klagenfurt —

2. Philippa, Countess von Goëss
July 8, 1964, Klagenfurt —

3. Moritz, Count von Goëss
June 5, 1966, Klagenfurt —

XXI. GODER 1, from page 266

Dieter Goder
March 15, 1938, Hamburg —
m. August 14, 1964, Otterndorf-Hamburg —
* **Inka,** Baroness von Saalfeld, daughter of Baron Hans von Saalfeld and of his wife, Elisabeth Faust.
July 7, 1939, Munich —

Issue: 1. Janka Goder
July 3, 1967, Leverkusen —

XXI. VON GRABMAYR 1, from page 849

Leinhard von Grabmayr
December 16, 1924, —
m. October 31, 1961,
* **Elisabeth,** Countess Matz von Spiegelfeld, daughter of Count Sigismund Matz von Spiegelfeld and of his wife, Countess Marie von Lodron-Loterano.
October 7, 1931, Innsbruck —

Issue: 1. Christoph von Grabmayr
June 6, 1962, Bregenz —

XXI. GREUNER

1, from page 932

Johann Georg (Hans) Greuner
May 16, 1930, Berlin —
m. April 13, 1962 (civil), Nieder-Roden, and May 15, 1962 (religious), Kronberg, Taunus
* **Huberta von Wuthenau-Hohenthurm,** daughter of Fedor von Wuthenau-Hohenthurm and of his wife, Countess Helga von Perponcher-Sedlnitzky.
May 16, 1933, Koten, Anholt —

Issue: 1. Hans Philipp Greuner, November 22, 1963 —

2. Nadine Greuner, January 6, 1965 —

XXI. VON GROLL

1, from page 935

Rüdiger von Groll
February 27, 1937, Mainz —
m. April 26, 1968, Munich
* **Gabriele,** Countess zu Ysenburg-Philippseich, daughter of Count Ludwig zu Ysenburg-Philippseich and of his wife, Mariangela Aloisi.
August 30, 1939, Berlin —

Issue: 1. Constantin von Groll, January 12, 1969, Kiel —

XXI. VON GUDENUS

1, from page 777

Ernst, Baron von Gudenus
March 26, 1916, Madrid, Spain —
m. August 18, 1953, Graz, Austria
* **Sophie,** Countess von Nostitz-Rieneck, daughter of Count Friedrich von Nostitz-Rieneck and of his wife, Princess Sophie von Hohenberg.
June 4, 1929, Vienna —

Issue: 1. Sophie, Baroness von Gudenus, June 6, 1954, Graz —

2. Marie-Zdenka, Baroness von Gudenus, August 20, 1955, Graz —

3. Erwein, Baron von Gudenus, August 30, 1958, Thannhausen —

XXI. von Gudenus 1 continued

4. Ferdinand, Baron von Gudenus
July 27, 1960, Thannhausen —

XXI. GUTTMANN 1, from page 639

Karl-Heinz Guttmann
March 13, 1911, Mingstimehlin, Nr. Schlossberg, East Prussia —
m. May 24, 1957, Lahr, Baden
* **Marie Antoinette,** Princess of Anhalt-Dessau, daughter of Prince Joachim Ernst, last reigning Duke of Anhalt-Dessau, and of his second wife, Editha (Edda) Marwitz.
July 14, 1930, Ballenstedt Castle —

Issue:

XXI. VON HALEM 1, from page 686

Gustav Adolf von Halem
November 4, 1899, Bremen —
m. 1: April 24, 1929, Bassenheim. Divorced: April 14, 1939, Berlin
Adelheid von Waldthausen, daughter of Julius von Waldthausen and of his wife, Eleanore Böcking.
March 29, 1901, Vienna —
(She m. 2: September 15, 1939, Gersfeld, Count Herbert zu Schallenberg-Krassl.)
m. 2: June 15, 1939, Berlin
* **Viktoria Margarethe,** Baroness von Dörnberg, daughter of Baron Hans-Karl von Dörnberg and of his wife, Countess Maria Viktoria von Hohenau.
April 24, 1915, Münster —

Issue of first marriage: Not descendants of King George I

1. Johann von Halem
April 8, 1932, Frankfurt-am-Main —

2. Gustav Adolf (Gusdolf) von Halem
July 31, 1935, Berlin —

XXI. von Halem 1 continued

Issue of second marriage: A descendant of King George I
3. Viktor (Vicco) von Halem (1940–)
m. Gabriele Renner (1942–)
see: *von Halem* XXI, 2, below

XXI. von Halem 2, from above

Viktor (Vicco) von Halem, son of Gustav Adolf von Halem.
March 26, 1940, Berlin —
m. July 25, 1964, Herrsching, Bavaria
Gabriele Renner, daughter of
May 15, 1942, Berlin —

Issue: 1. Christian-Manuel von Halem
December 28, 1966, Berlin —

XXI. HANSEN 1, from page 931

Hellmut Hansen
July 14, 1909, Rendesberg — May 1, 1945, Stolpe River, near Kyritz, Poland, killed in action in World War II
m. September 16, 1937, Berlin
* **Carla von Wuthenau-Hohenthurm,** daughter of Carl Adam von Wuthenau-Hohenthurm and of his wife, Countess Gisela von Lüttichau.
March 23, 1915, Dessau —
(She m. 2: Hans-Joachim von Wallenrodt – see: *von Wallenrodt* XXI, page 900.)

Issue: 1. Astrid Hansen
May 13, 1938, Gross Paschleben —

XXI. HARTIG 1, from page 387

Wolfgang, Count Hartig
August 13, 1922, Melk-an-der-Donau (Danube) —
m. September 6, 1947, Vienna
* **Maria Desideria,** Countess von Habsburg-Lorraine, daughter of Archduke Leo-Karl of Austria and of his wife, Marie von Tuillieres, Comtesse Montjoye-Vaufrey et de la Roche.
August 3, 1923, Lissa, near Posen —

XXI. Hartig 1 continued

Issue: 1. Karl Johann, Count Hartig
June 8, 1949, Vienna —

2. Andreas, Count Hartig
February 6, 1952, Vienna —

XXI. HARTUNG 1, from page 828

Hugo Herbert Hartung

July 3, 1908, Sterkade — December 31, 1945, in a concentration camp somewhere in Russia
m. December 12, 1936, Saabor

* **Hermine,** Princess of Schönaich-Carolath, daughter of Prince Johann Georg of Schönaich-Carolath and of his wife, Princess Hermine Reuss zu Greiz, later the Empress Hermine, second wife of Kaiser Wilhelm II.

May 9, 1910, Saabor —

No Issue.

XXI. HAUPTMANN 1, from page 812

Benvenuto Hauptmann

—

m. August 1, 1928, Dwasieden Castle, near Sassnitz. Annulled: November 13, 1928, Berlin

* **Elisabeth**, Princess of Schaumburg-Lippe, daughter of Prince Georg of Schaumburg-Lippe and of his wife, Princess Marie of Saxe-Altenburg.

May 31, 1909, Bückeburg —

(She m. 2: Johann, Baron Herring von Frankensdorff – see: *von Frankensdorff* XXI, page 710.)

No Issue.

XXI. VON HEDEMANN 1, from page 207

Harald von Hedemann

September 22, 1887, Cologne — June 12, 1951, Hankhausen-Rastede
m. November 24, 1927, Rastede, Oldenburg

* **Sophie Charlotte,** Duchess of Oldenburg, daughter of Grand Duke Friedrich August of Oldenburg and of his first wife, Princess Elisabeth of Prussia.

XXI. von Hedemann 1 continued

February 2, 1879, Oldenburg — March 29, 1964, Westertede, Oldenburg
(She m. 1: and divorced: Eitel Friedrich, Prince of Prussia – see: *Prussia (Hohenzollern)* II j–1, page 58.)

No Issue.

XXI. HEFEL 1, from page 376

Ernst Hefel
November 25, 1888, Schruns, Vorarlberg —
m. April 9, 1947 (civil), and April 10, 1947 (religious), Hall
* **Mathilde,** Archduchess of Austria, daughter of Archduke Franz Salvator of Austria and of his wife, Archduchess Marie Valerie of Austria.
August 9, 1906, Ischl —

No Issue.

XXI. VON HELLER 1, from page 279

Eduard von Heller
March 21, 1877, Cairo, Egypt —
m. November 10, 1925, Zürich, Switzerland, and November 1, 1925, Coburg, Germany
* **Klementine,** Princess of Saxe-Coburg and Gotha, daughter of Prince August Leopold of Saxe-Coburg and Gotha and of his wife, Archduchess Karoline of Austria.
March 23, 1897, Pola —

Issue: 1. Marie-Amelie von Heller (1926–)
m. Carlos Nicolis, Conte di Robilant e Cereaglio (1927–)
see: *di Robilant e Cereaglio* XVIII, page 598

2. Helene von Heller
July , 1928, Lausanne — December , 1931, Cairo

3. Alexander von Heller
July 22, 1938, Lausanne — February 5, 1969, Lausanne

XXI. HENCKEL VON DONNERSMARCK 1, from page 108

Karl Joseph, Count von Henckel, Baron von Donnersmarck
November 7, 1928, Romolkwitz —
m. April 10, 1958, Luxemburg

* **Marie Adelaide,** Princess of Luxemburg, Princess of Nassau-Weilburg, Princess of Bourbon-Parma, daughter of Grand Duchess Charlotte of Luxemburg and of her husband, Prince Felix of Bourbon-Parma.
May 21, 1924, Berg Castle —

Issue: 1. Andreas (Andrew), Count von Henckel, Baron von Donnersmarck
February 21, 1959, Berg Castle —

2. Marie-Felix, Countess von Henckel, Baroness von Donnersmarck
March 2, 1960, Berg Castle —

3. Heinrich, Count von Henckel, Baron von Donnersmarck
November 13, 1961, Luxemburg —

XXI. HESS 1, from page 82

Werner Hess
September 20, 1907, Baden-Baden —
m. March 25, 1950, Baden-Baden

* **Maria Aldegunde,** Princess of Hohenzollern-Sigmaringen, daughter of Fürst Friedrich Viktor zu Hohenzollern-Sigmaringen and of his wife, Princess Margarethe of Saxony.
February 19, 1921, Sigmaringen —
(She m. 1: and divorced: Konstantin, Prince of Bavaria - see: *Bavaria* (*Wittelsbach*) XIV h–1, page 475.)

Issue: 1. Monica Hess
July 8, 1953, Baden-Baden —

2. Angelica Hess
October 18, 1954, Baden-Baden —

XXI. VON HEYL ZU HERRNSHEIM

1, from page 691

Arnulf, Baron von Heyl zu Herrnsheim

—

m.

* **Cordula,** Baroness von Dungern, daughter of Baron Camill von Dungern and of his wife, Mechtilde Semper.

August 18, 1941, Berlin-Grunewald —

Issue:

XXI. HILZ

1, from page 486

Egid Hilz

June 24, 1932, Lindau —

m. May 24, 1960, Munich

* **Alexandra,** Princess of Hohenlohe-Oehringen, daughter of Prince August, 7th Fürst zu Hohenlohe-Oehringen, and of his wife, Valerie von Carstanjen.

March 11, 1931, Berlin —

Issue: 1. Gabriele Hilz

February 20, 1963, Karlsruhe —

2. Christian-Kraft Hilz

April 23, 1966, Stuttgart —

XXI. VON HOENNING-O'CARROLL

1, from page 473

Zdenko, Baron von Hoenning-O'Carroll

August 6, 1906, Sünching —

m. 1: May 16, 1934, Krimic

Margarete (Margit), Princess Lobkowicz, daughter of Prince Jaroslav, 11th Fürst Lobkowicz, and of his wife, Comtesse Marie de Beaufort-Spontin.

July 4, 1913, Zamecek-Pilsen, Poland — February 13, 1946,

m. 2: June 2, 1948, Leutstetten Castle, Bavaria

* **Aldegunde,** Princess of Bavaria, daughter of Prince Ludwig of Bavaria and of his wife, Princess Isabella of Croy.

June 9, 1917, Nymphenburg Castle —

XXI. von Hoenning-O'Carroll 1 continued

Issue of first marriage: Not descendants of King George I
11 children

Issue of second marriage:

12. Marie Gabrielle, Baroness von Hoenning-O'Carroll
May 18, 1949, Sünching —

13. Franz, Baron von Hoenning-O'Carroll
September 26, 1950, Sünching —

14. Hildegard, Baroness von Hoenning-O'Carroll
March 29, 1952, Sünching —

15. Josef, Baron von Hoenning-O'Carroll
March 28, 1953, Sünching —

16. Dorothea, Baroness von Hoenning-O'Carroll
May 26, 1956, Sünching —

XXI. VON UND ZU HOENSBROECH 1, from page 378

Reinhart, Count von und zu Hoensbroech
October 15, 1926, Kellenberg —
m. May 14, 1959 (civil), Koslar, and June 9, 1959 (religious), Wallsee
* **Immaculata,** Archduchess of Austria, daughter of Archduke Theodor Salvator of Austria and of his wife, Countess Maria Theresa von Waldburg und Zeil.
December 7, 1933, Wallsee Castle —

Issue: 1. Alexandra, Countess von und zu Hoensbroech
March 19, 1960, Kellenberg —

2. Bronco, Count von und zu Hoensbroech
April 23, 1961, Kellenberg —

3. Consuelo, Count von und zu Hoensbroech
May 30, 1962, Kellenberg —

4. Donata, Countess von und zu Hoensbroech
August 23, 1963, Kellenberg —

XXI. von und zu Hoensbroech 1 continued

5. Elena, Countess von und zu Hoensbroech
May 1, 1965, Kellenberg —

6. Florian, Count von und zu Hoensbroech
March 1, 1969, Kellenberg —

XXI. VON HOHENTHAL 1, from page 171

Alfred, Count von Hohenthal
December 5, 1805, — November 16, 1860,
m. October 3, 1846,
* **Marie,** Princess of Schleswig-Holstein-Sonderburg-Glücksburg, daughter of Duke Wilhelm of Schleswig-Holstein-Sonderburg-Glücksburg and of his wife, Princess Luise of Hesse-Cassel.
October 23, 1810, — May 11, 1869, Dresden
(She m. 1: Friedrich von Lasperg – see: *von Lasperg* XXI, page 741.)

No Issue.

XXI. von Hohenthal 2, from page 655

Botho, Count von Hohenthal
July 9, 1926, Wurzen —
m. October 14, 1952, Rheda
* **Gustava,** Princess zu Bentheim und Tecklenburg, daughter of Prince Adolf, 5th Fürst zu Bentheim und Tecklenburg, and of his wife, Amelie of Schönburg-Waldenburg.
October 21, 1929, Rheda —

Issue: 1. Carl, Count von Hohenthal
November 13, 1955, Gütersloh —

2. Tatjana, Countess von Hohenthal
August 19, 1958, Bonn —

XXI. VON HOLZHAUSEN 1, from page 372

Hans Ulrich, Baron von Holzhausen
September 1, 1929, Windischgarten, Austria —
m. August 29, 1959, Mondsee, Austria
* **Maria Magdalena,** Archduchess of Austria, daughter of Archduke Anton of Austria and of his wife, Princess Ileana of Romania.
October 2, 1939, Sonnberg Castle —

Issue: 1. Johannes, Baron von Holzhausen
July 29, 1960, Salzburg —

2. Georg, Baron von Holzhausen
February 16, 1962, Salzburg —

3. Alexandra, Baroness von Holzhausen
January 22, 1963, Salzburg —

XXI. HOPFINGER 1, from page 371

Joseph Hopfinger
April 14, 1905, Boryslaw, Poland —
m. September 17, 1939, Ouchy, Switzerland. Divorced: July 25, 1950, San Antonio, Texas
* **Assunta,** Archduchess of Austria, daughter of Archduke Leopold Salvator of Austria and of his wife, Princess Blanka of Bourbon, Princess of Castile.
August 10, 1902, Vienna —

Issue: 2 daughters – no details available.

XXI. HORST 1, from page 763

Hans Günther Horst
October 23, 1913, Oldenburg —
m. December 29, 1956, Tegernsee, Bavaria
* **Pauline,** Princess zu Löwenstein-Wertheim-Freudenberg, daughter of Prince Udo, 6th Fürst zu Löwenstein-Wertheim-Freudenberg, and of his wife, Countess Margarete zu Castell-Castell.
June 9, 1928, Heidelberg —

Issue: 1. Peter Michael Horst, August 19, 1957, Munich —

2. Monika-Daniela Horst, March 6, 1963, Munich —

XXI. VON HOYOS-SPRINZENSTEIN 1, from page 923

Friedrich, Count von Hoyos-Sprinzenstein
November 17, 1876, Washington, D.C., USA — December 9, 1951, Werenweg, Germany
m. August 12, 1919, Dresden
* **Wilhelmine von Wuthenau-Hohenthurm,** daughter of Count Carl Adam von Wuthenau-Hohenthurm and of his first wife, Countess Maria Antonia Chotek von Chotkowa und Wognin.
July 30, 1895, Dresden —

Issue: 1. Marie Antoinette, Countess von Hoyos (1920–)
m. Wilhelm Karl, Prince of Prussia, Count Lingen (1919–)
see: *Prussia* (*Hohenzollern*) II k–2, page 59

2. Franziska, Countess von Hoyos (1921–)
m. Nikolaus, Prince zu Bentheim und Tecklenburg (1925–)
see: *zu Bentheim und Tecklenburg* XXI, page 656

3. Ines, Countess von Hoyos (1924–)
m. Karl Wilhelm Schilling (1912–)
see: *Schilling* XXI, page 823

XXI. HUG 1, from page 71

Rudolf Hug
October 21, 1885, Hammerschmeide —
m. May 13, 1932, Freiburg im Breisgau
* **Marie Therese,** Princess of Prussia, daughter of Prince Friedrich Wilhelm of Prussia and of his wife, Princess Agathe of Hohenlohe-Schillingsfürst.
May 2, 1911, Berlin —

Issue: 1. Friedrich Wilhelm Hug (twin)
October 13, 1932, Freiburg im Breisgau —

2. Alois Hug (twin)
October 13, 1932, Freiburg — October 14, 1932, Freiburg

3. Joachim Hug
December 31, 1933, Freiburg —

XXI. Hug 1 continued

4. Charlotte Hug (1935–)
m. Erich Brehm (1930–)
see: *Brehm* XXI, page 671

5. Oda Marie Hug (1937–)
m. Dr. Hans Hermann Piltz (1930–)
see: *Piltz* XXI, page 785

6. Rudolf-Siegismut Hug
October 7, 1939, Tübingen —

7. Siegila Hug
September 26, 1941, Tübingen —

8. Luitgart Luise Hug (1943–)
m. Klaus Beckenbauer (1939–)
see: *Beckenbauer* XXI, page 652

9. Rudmarth Wolfdietrich Hug
October 7, 1945, Tübingen —

10. Angela Griseldis Hug
July 4, 1951, Stuttgart —

11. Rudolf Philipp Hug
June 22, 1957, Stuttgart —

XXI. VON HÜGEL 1, from page 228

Paul, Baron von Hügel. Created Count von Hügel on June 13, 1879.
April 13, 1835, Eschenau — April 13, 1897, Rienthal, near Graz
m. October 24, 1963, Vienna
* **Amelie,** Princess of Teck, daughter of Duke Alexander of Württemberg and of his morganatic wife, Countess Claudine de Rhedey von Kis-Rhede, created Countess von Hohenstein and Princess of Teck.
November 12, 1838, —July 20, 1893, Graz

Issue: 1. Paul Julius, Count von Hügel (1872–1912)
m. and divorced: Anna Homolatsch (–)
see: *von Hügel* XXI, 2, page 728

XXI. von Hügel 2, from page 727

* **Paul Julius,** Count von Hügel, son of Baron/Count Paul.
September 30, 1872, Rienthal, near Graz — March 20, 1912, Steinamanger
m. . Divorced: May 19, 1911,
Anna Homolatsch, daughter of
—

Issue: 1. Huberta, Countess von Hügel
October 8, 1897, Rienthal Castle — December 22, 1912, Bad Boll

2. Ferdinand, Count von Hügel
March 11, 1901, Rienthal Castle —

XXI. HUMBERT 1, from page 171

Rudolf Humbert
— October 29, 1954, Noer Castle
m. September 7, 1921, Oberhof, Thuringia
* **Carmelita Luise,** Countess von Noer, daughter of Prince/Count Friedrich Christian von Noer and of his wife, Carmelita Eisenblat.
April 22, 1871, Noer — May 9, 1948, Noer
(She m. and divorced: Ernst Ludwig, Count zu Rantzau - see: *zu Rantzau* XXI, page 788.)

No Issue.

XXI. HÜYN 1, from page 794

Johannes, Count Hüyn
July 3, 1930, Warsaw —
m. September 11, 1959, Alfter
* **Rosemary**, Altgräfin zu Salm-Reifferscheidt, Krautheim und Dyck, daughter of Fürst and Altgraf Franz Josef zu Salm-Reifferscheidt, Krautheim und Dyck and of his wife, Princess Cäcilie zu Salm-Salm.
February 24, 1937, Alfter —

XXI. Hüyn 1 continued

Issue: 1. Johannes, Count Hüyn
July 28, 1960, Tokyo, Japan —

2. Marie Christine, Countess Hüyn
November 27, 1961, Tokyo —

3. Franz Ferdinand, Count Hüyn
March 16, 1964, Bonn —

4. Assunta, Countess Hüyn
April 30, 1965, Bonn —

XXI. JOOST 1, from page 133

Herbert Joost
April 30, 1908, Hamburg —
m. May 26, 1959, Munich
* **Eleonore,** Princess von Hanau, Countess of Schaumburg, daughter of 6th Fürst Heinrich von Hanau und Horowitz, Count von Schaumburg, and of his wife, Countess Maria Theresa Fugger auf Babenhausen.
May 14, 1925, Horowitz —
(She m. 1: and divorced: Bela Spanyi – see: *Spanyi* XXI, page 848.)

No Issue.

XXI. JOST 1, from page 485

Hans Jost
—
m. , 1946, New York City
* **Erika,** Princess of Hohenlohe-Oehringen, daughter of Prince Friedrich of Hohenlohe-Oehringen and of his wife, Countess Marie von Hatzfeldt.
December 1, 1893, Sommerberg —
(She m. 1: and divorced: Eberhard von Ammon – see: *von Ammon* XXI, page 633.)

No Issue.

XXI. KAISER

1, from page 733

Walther Kaiser, son of Guido Kaiser, brother of Frau Albrecht von Klöss (page 734).
October 15, 1918, Mährisch-Schönburg —
m. April 20, 1949, Engelstein
* **Marie von Klöss,** daughter of Alfons von Klöss and of his wife, Archduchess Eleanora of Austria.
May 7, 1925, Baden, near Vienna —

Issue: 1. Martin Kaiser
April 20, 1950, Zwettl —

2. Guido Kaiser
March 23, 1951, Engelstein —

3. Marius Kaiser
April 7, 1952, Engelstein —

4. Claudia Kaiser
October 7, 1954, Engelstein —

5. Christian Kaiser
October 2, 1957, Engelstein —

XXI. KALAU VOM HOFE

1, from page 815

Christoph Kalau vom Hofe
September 16, 1931, Schwiersee —
m. May 7, 1956, Kronberg, Taunus
* **Dagmar,** Princess of Schaumburg-Lippe, daughter of Prince Heinrich of Schaumburg-Lippe and of his wife, Countess Marie-Erika von Hardenburg.
February 18, 1934, Berlin —

Issue: 1. Alexander Kalau vom Hofe
March 13, 1957, Bilbao, Spain —

2. Caroline Kalau vom Hofe
August 23, 1962, Bilbao —

3. Fabian Kalau vom Hofe
December 16, 1964, Madrid —

XXI. KAMIL 1, from page 427

Hassan Sayed Kamil

November 14, 1918, Langenthal, near Berne, Switzerland —

m. February 10, 1955, Hinterzarte, Schwarzwald

* **Helene,** Duchess of Mecklenburg, daughter of Duke Georg of Mecklenburg, born Count von Carlow, and of his first wife, Irina Mikhailovna Raievskya.

November 15, 1924, St. Leonards-on-Sea, Sussex, England — July 7, 1962, Ibenburgen, Westphalia, as a result of a plane crash

Issue: 1. Sheila Kamil, July 26, 1958, Chur, Switzerland —

XXI. KAUTZ 1, from page 505

Rudolf Adolf Kautz

August 24, 1930, —

m. September 11, 1956,

* **Maria Lovisa,** Countess Bernadotte, daughter of Count Lennart Bernadotte, born Prince of Sweden, and of his wife, Karin Nissvandt.

November 6, 1935, Stockholm, Sweden —

Issue: 1. Henrik Adolf Kautz, July 16, 1957, Konstanz —

2. Karin Kautz, October 13, 1958, Konstanz —

3. Madeleine Kautz, August 23, 1961, Konstanz —

XXI. KEMPKENS 1, from page 788

Ewald Kempkens

December 25, 1915, Uberlingen —

m. October 23, 1948, Krefeld

* **Hermine Elisabeth,** Baroness von Quernheim, daughter of Baron Felix von Quernheim and of his wife, Countess Hermine von Hagenburg.

June 16, 1923, Rostock —

Issue: 1. Franz Kempkens, July 1, 1949 —

2. Felix Kempkens, November 13, 1953 —

XXI. KIPPENBERG 1, from page 270

Burkhard Kippenberg
August 8, 1927, Sökking, near Starnberg, Bavaria —
m. August 8, 1967, Sökking
★ **Feodora,** Princess of Saxe-Meiningen, daughter of Prince Bernhard of Saxe-Meiningen and of his first wife, Margot Grössler.
May 27, 1932, Pitselstettin Castle, near Klagenfurt, Austria —

Issue: 1. Walter Johannes Kippenberg
January 27, 1968, Sökking —

XXI. KISS 1, from page 392

Ernst Kiss

m. , 1959, Regensburg
★ **Kinga,** Archduchess of Austria, daughter of Archduke Joseph of Austria and of his wife, Princess Anna of Saxony.
August 27, 1938, Budapest, Hungary —

Issue: 1. Mátyás Kiss
December 24, 1963, Regensburg —

XXI. VON KLITZING 1, from page 908

Werner von Klitzing
August 3, 1934, Hanover —
m. September 7, 1964, Neuwied
★ **Osterlind,** Princess of Wied, daughter of Hereditary Prince Hermann of Wied and of his wife, Countess Marie Antonia zu Stolberg-Wernigerode.
April 8, 1939, Stuttgart —

Issue: 1. Sophie von Klitzing
September 13, 1965, Frankfurt-am-Main —

2. Franziska von Klitzing
November 30, 1966, Frankfurt-am-Main —

XXI. VON KLÖSS 1, from page 385

Alfons von Klöss

June 9, 1880, Trieste — August 24/25, 1953, Vienna

m. January 9, 1913, Zywiec Castle, Poland

* **Eleanora,** Archduchess of Austria, daughter of Archduke Karl Stephan of Austria and of his wife, Archduchess Maria Theresa of Austria.

November 28, 1886, Pola —

Issue: 1. Albrecht von Klöss (1913–)
m. Erika Kaiser (1920–)
see: *von Klöss* XXI, 2, page 734

2. Karl von Klöss
February 15, 1915, Vienna — September 5, 1939, Kotanie, Poland

3. Rainer von Klöss (1916–)
m. Cornelia Schoute (1920–)
see: *von Klöss* XXI, 3, page 734

4. Ernst von Klöss (1919–)
m. Rixta Hartig (1925–)
see: *von Klöss* XXI, 4, page 734

5. Alfons von Klöss (1920–)
m. Theresia, Countess von Coreth zu Coredo (1923–)
see: *von Klöss* XXI, 5, page 735

6. Friedrich von Klöss
February 13, 1922, Zywiec, Poland — February , 1943, Stalingrad, Russia, killed in action in World War II

7. Marie von Klöss (1925–)
m. Walther Kaiser (1918–)
see: *Kaiser* XXI, page 730

8. Stephan von Klöss (1933–)
m. Ingrid Morocutti (1936–)
see: *von Klöss* XXI, 5, page 735

XXI. von Klöss 2, from page 733

* **Albrecht von Klöss,** eldest son of Alfons.
October 13, 1913, Pola —
m. September 4, 1942, Baden, near Vienna
Erika Kaiser, daughter of Guido Kaiser and of his wife, Emilia Eschler.
October 13, 1920, Baden, near Vienna —

Issue: 1. Karl Stephan von Klöss
October 4, 1943, Baden —

2. Maria Elisabeth von Klöss
December 3, 1944, Baden —

3. Barbara Eleanora von Klöss
June 5, 1946, Baden —

XXI. von Klöss 3, from page 733

* **Rainer von Klöss,** third son of Alfons.
October 12, 1916, Baden —
m. January 17, 1944, Pfaffstätten
Cornelia Schoute, daughter of Cornelius Schoute and of his wife, Auguste Lebensatt.
January 15, 1920, Warmerveer, The Netherlands —

Issue: 1. Elisabeth von Klöss
February 26, 1945, Engelstein —

2. Georg von Klöss
September 5, 1954, Naden —

XXI. von Klöss 4, from page 733

* **Ernst von Klöss,** fourth son of Alfons.
January 1, 1919, Baden —
m. July 11, 1953, Wiener Neustadt
Rixta Hartig, daughter of Julius Eugen Hartig and of his wife, Inka Vissering.
April 27, 1925, —

XXI. von Klöss 4 continued

Issue: 1. Florian von Klöss
March 12, 1954, Vienna —

2. Thomas von Klöss
December 29, 1956, Vienna —

3. Nikolaus von Klöss
September 24, 1957, Vienna —

4. Andrea von Klöss
December 24, 1958, Vienna —

XXI. von Klöss 5, from page 733

* **Alfons von Klöss,** fifth son of Alfons.
May 3, 1920, Pola, Austria —
m. July 12, 1947, Engelstein
Theresia, Countess von Coreth zu Coredo, daughter of Count Max von Coreth zu Coredo and of his wife, Marie Alexandra Menghin von Brezburg.
March 12, 1923, Kittsee —

Issue: 1. Andreas von Klöss
May 5, 1948, Vienna —

2. Johannes von Klöss
November 21, 1949, Graz —

3. Alfons von Klöss
September 19, 1953, Graz —

XXI. von Klöss 6, from page 733

* **Stephan von Klöss,** seventh son of Alfons.
November 23, 1933, Baden, near Vienna —
m. September 3, 1955, Baden
Ingrid Morocutti, daughter of Wolfgang Morocutti and of his wife, Gertrud Binder.
May 24, 1936, Klagenfurt, Austria —

XXI. von Klöss 6 continued

Issue: 1. Michaela von Klöss
June 3, 1956, Baden —

2. Marina von Klöss
January 28, 1958, Baden —

3. Christoph von Klöss
February 18, 1959, Baden —

4. Marcus von Klöss
June 12, 1960, Baden —

XXI. ZU KÖNIGSEGG-AULENDORF 1, from page 886

Johannes, Count zu Königsegg-Aulendorf
April 13, 1925, Königsesswald —
m. September 27, 1955, Munich
* **Stefanie,** Baroness Waldbott von Bassenheim, daughter of Baron Friedrich Waldbott von Bassenheim and of his wife, Archduchess Maria Alice of Austria.
November 19, 1929, Satoralja-Ujhely, Hungary —

Issue: 1. Isabelle, Countess zu Königsegg-Aulendorf
July 23, 1956, Munich —

2. Maximilian, Count zu Königsegg-Aulendorf
June 16, 1958, Munich —

3. Markus, Count zu Königsegg-Aulendorf
May 16, 1963, Munich —

XXI. KONOPATH 1, from page 755

Hanno Konopath
February 24, 1882, —
m. February 24, 1927, Berlin. Divorced: October 2, 1936,
* **Marie Adelheid,** Princess zur Lippe, daughter of Prince Rudolf zur Lippe and of his wife, Princess Luise von Ardeck.
August 30, 1895, Drogelwitz —

XXI. Konopath 1 continued

(She m. 1: and divorced: Heinrich XXXII, Prince Reuss zu Köstritz – see: *Reuss* IX e–2, page 341.)
(She m. 2: and divorced: Heinrich XXXV, Prince Reuss zu Köstritz – see: *Reuss* IX g–1, page 342.)

No Issue.

XXI. VON KOTTULINSKY 1, from page 372

Jaroslav (Rus), Count von Kottulinsky
January 3, 1917, Graz, Austria —January 11, 1959, Rio de Janeiro, Brazil, killed in an air crash
m. December 7, 1957, Vienna
* **Maria Ileana,** Archduchess of Austria, daughter of Archduke Anton of Austria and of his wife, Princess Ileana of Romania.
December 18, 1933, Mödling, Austria —January 11, 1959, Rio de Janeiro, Brazil, killed in an air crash

Issue: 1. Maria Ileana, Countess von Kottulinsky
August 25, 1958, Klagenfurt —
(Guardians: Count Leopold-Zeno von Goëss and his wife, formerly the Countess Theodora von Kottulinsky.)

XXI. VON KOTTWITZ-ERDÖDY 1, from page 377

Alexander, Baron von Kottwitz-Erdödy
September 24, 1943, Göttingen —
m. May 10, 1969, Persenbeug Castle, Austria
* **Maria Alberta,** Archduchess of Austria, daughter of Archduke Hubert Salvator of Austria and of his wife, Princess Rosemary zu Salm-Salm.
June 1, 1944, Persenbeug Castle —

Issue:

XXI. VON KRIPP ZU PRUNBERG UND KRIPPACH 1, from page 861

Martin, Baron von Kripp zu Prunberg und Krippach
December 25, 1924, Krippach —
m. September 8, 1958, Hall, Tyrol, Austria
* **Magdalena,** Countess zu Stolberg-Stolberg, daughter of Count Bernhard zu Stolberg-Stolberg and of his wife, Archduchess Hedwig of Austria.
December 19, 1930, Hall —

Issue: 1. Paul-Bernhard, Baron von Kripp zu Prunberg und Krippach
April 24, 1959, Merano, Italy (twin) —

2. Marie Agnes, Baroness von Kripp zu Prunberg und Krippach
April 24, 1959, Merano, Italy (twin) —

3. Jacob, Baron von Kripp zu Prunberg und Krippach
September 10, 1960, Hall —

4. Sigmund, Baron von Kripp zu Prunberg und Krippach
June 6, 1962, Merano —

5. Franz, Baron von Kripp zu Prunberg und Krippach
February 2, 1964, Merano —

XXI. KUHN 1, from page 142

Alfons Kuhn
December 10, 1924, Bad Salzeflen —
m. September 30, 1957, Herleshausen. Divorced: November , 1961,
* **Johanna,** Princess of Hesse(-Philippsthal-Barchfeld), daughter of Prince Wilhelm, Landgrave of Hesse(-Philippsthal-Barchfeld) and of his wife, Princess Marianne of Prussia.
November 22, 1937, Augustenau Castle —
(She m. 2: Bruno Rieck – see: *Rieck* XXI, page 790.)

Issue: 1. Vera Maria Kuhn
January 21, 1959, Hersfeld —

XXI. KÜHNE-WANZLEBEN 1, from page 691

Eggbrecht Kühne-Wanzleben
July 2, 1935, Kloxin —
m. August 14, 1964, Berneuchen
* **Dorette,** Baroness von Dungern, daughter of Baron Camill von Dungern and of his wife, Mechtilde Semper.
March 29, 1939, Berlin-Grunewald —

Issue: 1. Serena Kühne-Wanzleben
January 14, 1966, Hanover —

2. Melanie Kühne-Wanzleben
—

XXI. KÜNIGL ZU EHRENBURG 1, from page 336

Erich Künigl, Count zu Ehrenburg, Baron von Warth
June 20, 1880, Ehrenburg — December 3, 1930, Bruneck, Italy
m. May 14, 1903, Greiz
* **Emma,** Princess Reuss zu Greiz, daughter of Prince Heinrich XXII Reuss zu Greiz and of his wife, Princess Ida of Schaumburg-Lippe.
January 17, 1881, Greiz — December 6, 1961, Ehrenburg

Issue: 1. Marie-Hermine Künigl, Countess zu Ehrenburg, Baroness von Warth (1904–)
m. Otto Daublebky, Baron von Sterneck zu Ehrenstein (1902–1942)
see: *von Sterneck zu Ehrenstein* XXI, page 854

2. Karl Heinrich Künigl, Count zu Ehrenburg, Baron von Warth (1905–)
m. Ilsa Liane, Countess zu Platen-Hallermund (1908–)
see: *Künigl zu Ehrenburg* XXI, 2, page 740

XXI. Künigl zu Ehrenburg 2, from page 739

★ **Karl Heinrich Künigl,** Count zu Ehrenburg, Baron von Warth, only son of Count Erich.
April 17, 1905, Ehrenburg —
m. December 10, 1931, Greiz

Ilsa Liane, Countess zu Platen-Hallermund, daughter of Count Julius zu Platen-Hallermund and of his wife, Hedwig von Erlin.
March 26, 1908, Berlin-Wilmersdorf —
(She m. 1: May 13, 1930, Eberhard Mohnike who died October 4, 1930.)

Issue: 1. Marie Elizabeth Künigl, Countess zu Ehrenburg, Baroness von Warth (1932)
m. Gilbert Durst (1912–)
see: *Durst* XXI, page 692

2. Erica Künigl, Countess zu Ehrenburg, Baroness von Warth (1935–)
m. Leopold Künigl, Count zu Ehrenburg, Baron von Warth (1927–)
see: *Künigl zu Ehrenburg* XXI, 3, below

3. Margarethe Künigl, Countess zu Ehrenburg, Baroness von Warth (1939–) (twin)
m. Jürgen Teckemeyer (1937–)
see: *Teckemeyer* XXI, page 868

4. Christiane Künigl, Countess zu Ehrenburg, Baroness von Warth (1939–) (twin)
m. Dr. Ulrich Nörtemann (1933–)
see: *Nörtemann* XXI, page 776

5. Erich Künigl, Count zu Ehrenburg, Baron von Warth
December 17, 1942, Meran —

XXI. Künigl zu Ehrenburg 3, from above

Leopold Künigl, Count zu Ehrenburg, Baron von Warth
February 9, 1927, Innsbruck —
m. April 23, 1955, Trins, near Steinach am Brersner, Austria

★ **Erica Künigl,** Countess zu Ehrenburg, Baroness von Warth, daughter of Count Karl Heinrich Künigl zu Ehrenburg, Baron von Warth, and of his wife, Countess Ilse Liane zu Platen-Hallermund.

XXI. Künigl zu Ehrenburg 3 continued

January 24, 1935, Brunico, Italy —

Issue: 1. Christian Künigl, Count zu Ehrenburg, Baron von Warth
September 15, 1955, Innsbruck —

2. Markus Künigl, Count zu Ehrenburg, Baron von Warth
July 25, 1957, Innsbruck —

3. Alexandra Künigl, Countess zu Ehrenburg, Baroness von Warth
July 3, 1962, Innsbruck —

4. Thomas Künigl, Count zu Ehrenburg, Baron von Warth
June 9, 1965, Salzburg —

XXI. KUNZ 1, from page 701

Walter Kunz
September 14, 1932, Vienna —
m. May 9, 1964,
⋆ **Uta Helene,** Countess von Enzenberg zum Freyen und Jöchelsthurn, daughter of Count Karl Eugen von Enzenberg zum Freyen und Jöchelsthurn and of his wife, Carola Ossenbeck.
January 7, 1934, Gera —

Issue: 1. Imma Kunz
March 2, 1965, —

XXI. VON LASPERG 1, from page 171

Friedrich von Lasperg
December 1, 1796, — May 9, 1843,
m. May 19, 1837,
⋆ **Marie,** Princess of Schleswig-Holstein-Sonderburg-Glücksburg, daughter of Duke Wilhelm of Schleswig-Holstein-Sonderburg-Glücksburg and of his wife, Princess Luise of Hesse-Cassel.
October 23, 1810, — May 11, 1869, Dresden
(She m. 2: Alfred, Count von Hohenthal – see: *von Hohenthal* XXI, page 724.)

No Issue.

XXI. VON LEDEBUR-WICHELN

1, from page 379

Mario, Count von Ledebur-Wicheln
July 28, 1931, Samaden —
m. July 20, 1959, Unterach
* **Valerie,** Princess von Altenburg, daughter of Archduke Clemens of Austria and of his wife, Comtesse Elisabeth Rességuier de Miremont, created Princess von Altenburg.
January 16, 1931, Vienna —

Issue: 1. Maria Josepha, Countess von Ledebur-Wicheln
January 25, 1962, Munich —

2. Maria Clementine, Countess von Ledebur-Wicheln
January 25, 1963, Munich —

3. Heinrich, Count von Ledebur-Wicheln
July 29, 1964, Munich —

4. Anna Maria, Countess von Ledebur-Wicheln
September 29, 1965, Munich —

XXI. von Ledebur-Wicheln

2, from page 914

Hubertus, Count von Ledebur-Wicheln
September 2, 1901, Ledeny, Slovakia — February 5, 1945, Oplotnica, Yugoslavia, murdered by partisans
m. May 5, 1938 (civil) and July 29, 1940 (religious), Vienna
* **Olga,** Princess Windisch-Graetz, daughter of Prince Hugo Windisch-Graetz and of his wife, Princess Christine von Auersperg-Breunner.
March 5, 1893, Gonobitz —
(She m. 1: and divorced: Dr. Andreas Picard, Baron von Morsey – see: *Picard* (*von Morsey*) XXI, page 785.)

No Issue.

XXI. LEININGEN 1, from page 647

Ernst, 4th Fürst zu Leiningen, son of Fürst Karl who was a half-brother of Queen Victoria of Great Britain.

November 9, 1830, Osborne House, Isle of Wight — April 5, 1904, Amorbach, Germany
m. September 11, 1858, Karlsruhe

* **Marie,** Princess of Baden, daughter of Grand Duke Karl Leopold of Baden and of his wife, Princess Sophie of Sweden.

November 20, 1834, Karlsruhe — November 21, 1899, Waldleiningen

Issue: 1. Alberta, Princess of Leiningen
December 24, 1863, Osborne House — August 30, 1901, Waldleiningen Castle

2. Emich, 5th Fürst zu Leiningen (1866–1939)
m. Feodore, Princess of Hohenlohe-Langenburg (1866–1932)
see: *Leiningen* XXI, 2, below

XXI. Leiningen 2, from above and page 480

* **Emich,** 5th Fürst zu Leiningen, only son of Fürst Ernst.

January 18, 1866, Osborne House, Isle of Wight — July 18, 1939, Schlossau, Germany
m. July 12, 1894, Langenburg

* **Feodore,** Princess of Hohenlohe-Langenburg, daughter of Prince Hermann, 6th Fürst zu Hohenlohe-Langenburg, and of his wife, Princess Leopoldine of Baden.

July 23, 1866, Langenburg — November 1, 1932, Waldleiningen

Issue: 1. Viktoria, Princess of Leiningen (1895–)
m. and divorced: Maximilian, Count zu Solms-Rödelheim und Assenheim (1898–)
see: *zu Solms-Rödelheim und Assenheim* XXI, page 842

2. Emrich Ernst, Prince of Leiningen
December 29, 1896, — March 21, 1918, , killed in action in World War I

3. Karl, 6th Fürst zu Leiningen (1898–1946)
m. Mariya Kirillovna, Princess/Grand Duchess of Russia (1907–1951)
see: *Leiningen* XXI, 3, page 744

XXI. Leiningen

2 continued

4. Hermann, Prince of Leiningen (1901–   )
   m. Irina, Countess von Schönborn-Wiesentheid (1895–   )
   see: *Leiningen* XXI, 7, page 746

5. Hesso, Prince of Leiningen (1903–1967)
   m. Marie-Luise, Countess von Nesselrode (1905–   )
   see: *Leiningen* XXI, 8, page 747

XXI. Leiningen

3, from pages 743, 304

* **Karl,** 6th Fürst zu Leiningen, eldest son of Prince Karl, 5th Fürst.
February 13, 1898, Strasbourg — August 2, 1946, Mordvinien, Russia, in a concentration camp
m. November 24, 1925, Coburg

* **Mariya Kirillovna,** Princess/Grand Duchess of Russia, daughter of Grand Duke Kirill Vladimirovich of Russia and of his wife, Princess Victoria Melita of Great Britain and Ireland, Princess of Edinburgh.
February 2, 1907, Coburg — October 25, 1951, Madrid, Spain

Issue: 1. Emich, 7th Fürst zu Leiningen (1926–   )
   m. Eilika, Duchess of Oldenburg (1928–   )
   see: *Leiningen* XXI, 4, page 745

2. Karl, Prince of Leiningen (1928–   )
   m. and divorced: Marie Louise, Princess of Bulgaria (1933–   )
   see: *Leiningen* XXI, 5, page 745

3. Kira, Princess of Leiningen (1930–   )
   m. Andrew, Prince of Yugoslavia (1929–   )
   see: *Yugoslavia* (*Karageorgevich*) XX, page 630

4. Margarita, Princess of Leiningen (1932–   )
   m. Friedrich Wilhelm, Fürst zu Hohenzollern-Sigmaringen (1924–   )
   see: *Hohenzollern-Sigmaringen* II hh–1, page 83

XXI. Leiningen 3 continued

5. Mechtilde, Princess of Leiningen (1936–)
m. Karl-Anton Bauscher (1931–)
see: *Bauscher* XXI, page 652

6. Friedrich, Prince of Leiningen (1938–)
m. and divorced: Karin-Evelyn Göss (1942–)
see: *Leiningen* XXI, 6, page 746

7. Peter Viktor, Prince of Leiningen
December 23, 1942, Würzburg —January 12, 1943, Würzburg

XXI. Leiningen 4, from pages 744, 209

* **Emich,** 7th Fürst zu Leiningen, eldest son of Prince Karl, 6th Fürst.
October 18, 1926, Coburg —
m. August 10, 1950, Rastede
* **Eilika,** Duchess of Oldenburg, daughter of Hereditary Grand Duke Nikolaus of Oldenburg and of his wife, Princess Helene zu Waldeck und Pyrmont.
February 2, 1928, Lensahn —

Issue: 1. Melita, Princess of Leiningen
June 10, 1951, Amorbach —

2. Karl Emich, Hereditary Prince of Leiningen
June 12, 1952, Amorbach —

3. Andreas, Prince of Leiningen
November 27, 1955, Amorbach —

4. Stephanie Margarita, Princess of Leiningen
October 1, 1958, Amorbach —

XXI. Leiningen 5, from pages 744, 284

* **Karl,** Prince of Leiningen, second son of Prince Karl, 6th Fürst.
January 2, 1928, Coburg —

XXI. Leiningen 5 continued

m. February 14, 1957 (civil), Amorbach, and February 20, 1957 (religious), Cannes, France. Divorced: December 4, 1968, Frankfurt-am-Main

* **Marie Louise,** Princess of Bulgaria, daughter of King Boris III of Bulgaria and of his wife, Princess Giovanna of Savoy.

January 13, 1933, Sofia, Bulgaria —

(She m. 2: Bronislaw T. Chrobok – see: *Chrobok* XXII, page 943.)

Issue: 1. Karl Boris, Prince of Leiningen
April 17, 1960, Toronto, Ontario, Canada —

2. Hermann, Prince of Leiningen
April 16, 1963, Toronto, Ontario —

XXI. Leiningen 6, from page 745

* **Friedrich,** Prince of Leiningen, third son of Prince Karl, 6th Fürst.

June 18, 1938, Würzburg —

m. July 9, 1960, Würzburg. Divorced: July 4, 1962,

Karin-Evelyn Göss, daughter of

May 27, 1942, Würzburg —

No Issue.

XXI. Leiningen 7, from page 744

* **Hermann,** Prince of Leiningen, second son of 5th Fürst Emich.

January 4, 1901, Amorbach — March 29, 1971, Amorbach

m. December 20, 1938 (civil), Bayrischzell, and December 21, 1938 (religious), Munich

Irina, Countess von Schönborn-Wiesentheid, daughter of Count Klemens von Schönborn-Wiesentheid and of his wife, Baroness Maria-Rosario von Welczek.

July 17, 1895, Laland —

(She m. 1: September 25, 1918 and divorced: March 2, 1938, Munich, Count Philipp von Berckheim, who died November 13, 1945, Mannheim.)

No Issue.

XXI. Leiningen 8, from page 746

* **Hesso,** Prince of Leiningen, third son of 5th Fürst Emich.
July 23, 1903, Amorbach — June 19, 1967, Munich
m. July 11, 1933 (civil), and July 12, 1933 (religious), Amorbach
Marie-Luise, Countess von Nesselrode, daughter of Count Franz von Nesselrode and of his wife, Maria-Rita von Wiese.
July 31, 1905, Honnef —

Issue by adoption (on February 2, 1953):
1. Wolfgang Karl Schormann who became Prince Franz Hesso of Leiningen
March 10, 1944, Pernitz, Austria —

XXI. VON LEVETZOW 1, from page 793

Karl, Baron von Levetzow
June 16, 1918, Krakau, Bohemia — November 5, 1964, Salzburg
m. September 4, 1961, Wolfegg
* **Marie Karoline,** Countess Saint-Julien-Wallsee, daughter of Count Eduard Saint-Julien-Wallsee and of his wife, Countess Ottilie von Enzenberg zum Freyen und Jöchelsthurn.
June 21, 1923, Wolfegg —

Issue: 1. Marie Therese, Baroness von Levetzow
June 4, 1962, Salzburg —

XXI. LIEBES 1, from page 54

Peter Liebes
January 28, 1926, Munich — May 5, 1967, Bonn
m. March 24, 1960, Bonn
* **Christa,** Princess of Prussia, daughter of Prince Wilhelm of Prussia and of his wife, Dorothea von Salviati.
October 31, 1936, Bonn —

No Issue.

THE HOUSE OF LIECHTENSTEIN

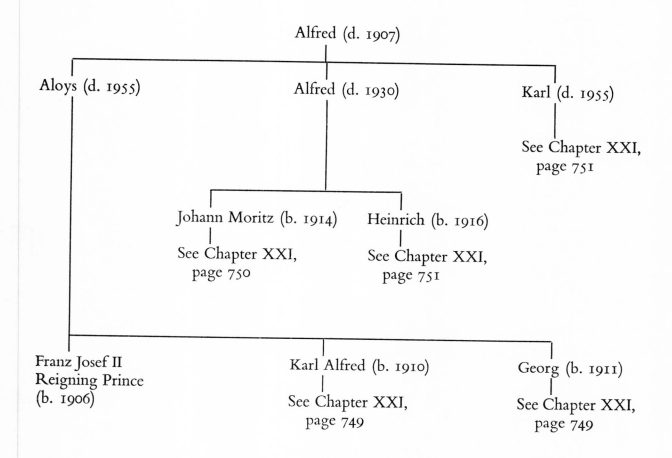

- Alfred (d. 1907)
  - Aloys (d. 1955)
    - Franz Josef II Reigning Prince (b. 1906)
    - Karl Alfred (b. 1910)
      - See Chapter XXI, page 749
    - Georg (b. 1911)
      - See Chapter XXI, page 749
  - Alfred (d. 1930)
    - Johann Moritz (b. 1914)
      - See Chapter XXI, page 750
    - Heinrich (b. 1916)
      - See Chapter XXI, page 751
  - Karl (d. 1955)
    - See Chapter XXI, page 751

XXI. LIECHTENSTEIN 1, from page 376

Karl Alfred, Prince of Liechtenstein, second son of Prince Aloys.
August 16, 1910, Frauenthal, Styria, Austria —
m. February 17, 1949, Persenbeug Castle, Austria

* **Agnes,** Archduchess of Austria, daughter of Archduke Hubert Salvator of Austria and of his wife, Princess Rosemary zu Salm-Salm.
December 14, 1928, Persenbeug Castle —

Issue: 1. Dominik, Prince of Liechtenstein
June 20, 1950, Vienna —

2. Andreas, Prince of Liechtenstein
February 25, 1952, Vienna —

3. Gregor, Prince of Liechtenstein
April 18, 1954, Vienna —

4. Alexandra, Princess of Liechtenstein
December 25, 1955, Vienna —

5. Maria, Princess of Liechtenstein
August 6, 1960, Vienna —

6. Brigitta, Princess of Liechtenstein
April 13, 1967, Vienna —

XXI. Liechtenstein 2, from page 244

Georg, Prince of Liechtenstein, third son of Prince Aloys.
November 11, 1911, Gross-Ullersdorf —
m. September 23, 1948, Altshausen Castle

* **Maria Christina,** Duchess of Württemberg, daughter of Duke Philipp of Württemberg and of his wife, Archduchess Rosa of Austria.
September 2, 1924, Tübingen —

Issue: 1. Margarita, Princess of Liechtenstein
May 1, 1950, Vienna —

2. Maria Assunta, Princess of Liechtenstein
April 28, 1952, Vienna —

XXI. Liechtenstein 2 continued

3. Isabelle, Princess of Liechtenstein
May 17, 1954, Vienna —

4. Christoph, Prince of Liechtenstein
January 15, 1958, Vienna —

5. Marie Helene, Princess of Liechtenstein
September 8, 1960, Vienna —

XXI. Liechtenstein 3, from page 873

Johann Moritz, Prince of Liechtenstein, eldest son of Prince Alfred.
August 6, 1914, Waldstein, near Peggau —
m. November 1, 1944, Burgweintung, near Regensburg
* **Clothilde,** Princess of Thurn und Taxis, daughter of Prince Karl August of Thurn und Taxis and of his wife, Princess Maria Anna of Braganca, Infanta of Portugal.
November 30, 1922, Regensburg —

Issue: 1. Diemut Margarete, Princess of Liechtenstein (twin)
April 1, 1949, Vienna —

2. Gundakar Albert, Prince of Liechtenstein (twin)
April 1, 1949, Vienna —

3. Alfred, Prince of Liechtenstein
September 17, 1951, Vienna —

4. Adelgunde, Princess of Liechtenstein
August 10, 1953, Vienna —

5. Karl Emmeran, Prince of Liechtenstein
July 1, 1955, Regensburg —

6. Maria Eleanore, Princess of Liechtenstein
November 14, 1958, Vienna —

XXI. Liechtenstein 4, from page 361

Heinrich, Prince of Leichtenstein, second son of Prince Alfred.
August 5, 1916, Graz —
m. September 12, 1949, Lignières, France
* **Elisabeth Charlotte,** Archduchess of Austria, daughter of Emperor Karl I of Austria and of his wife, Princess Zita of Bourbon-Parma.
May 31, 1922, El Pardo, near Madrid, Spain (posthumous) —

Issue: 1. Vincenz, Prince of Liechtenstein
July 30, 1950, Graz, Austria —

2. Michael, Prince of Liechtenstein
October 10, 1951, Graz —

3. Charlotte, Princess of Liechtenstein
July 3, 1953, Graz —

4. Christof, Prince of Liechtenstein
April 11, 1956, Graz —

5. Karl, Prince of Liechtenstein
August 31, 1957, Graz —

XXI. Liechtenstein 5, from page 237

Karl, Prince of Liechtenstein, sixth son of Prince Alfred, uncle of Prince Johann Moritz of Liechtenstein (see: 3) and Prince Heinrich (see: 4).
September 16, 1878, Frauenthal — June 20, 1955, Frauenthal
m. April 5, 1921, Tegernsee, Bavaria
* **Elisabeth,** Princess von Urach, Countess of Württemberg, daughter of Duke Wilhelm of Württemberg and of his first wife, Duchess Amelie in Bavaria.
August 23, 1894, Liechtenstein Castle —

Issue: 1. Wilhelm, Prince of Liechtenstein (1922–)
m. Emma von Gutmannsthal-Benvenuti (1926–)
see: *Liechtenstein (von Hohenau)* XXI, 6, page 752

2. Maria Josepha, Princess of Liechtenstein
July 6, 1923, Hollenegg —

XXI. Liechtenstein

5 continued

3. Franziska, Princess of Liechtenstein (1930–)
m. Rochus, Count von Spee (1925–)
see: *von Spee* XXI, page 848

4. Wolfgang, Prince of Liechtenstein
December 25, 1934, Graz —

XXI. Liechtenstein (von Hohenau)

6, from page 751

* **Wilhelm,** Count von Hohenau, born Prince of Liechtenstein, eldest son of Prince Aloys. He renounced his title and rights as a Prince of Liechtenstein and took the title of Count von Hohenau on July 11, 1950.
May 29, 1922, Frauenthal —
m. August 21, 1950, Kitzbühel, Austria
Emma von Gutmannsthal-Benvenuti, daughter of Felix von Gutmannsthal-Benvenuti and of his wife, Hermine Krum.
May 14, 1926, Klagenfurt —

Issue: 1. Felix, Count von Hohenau
May 22, 1951, Graz —

2. Benedikt, Count von Hohenau
January 22, 1953, Vienna —

3. Maria Theresia, Countess von Hohenau
December 30, 1953, Graz —

4. Stefan, Count von Hohenau
June 11, 1957, Graz —

XXI. VON LILL-RASTERN

1, from page 870

Erwin von Lill-Rastern (or: Lill-Rastern von Lilienbach)
June 16, 1905, Vienna —
m. January 19, 1937, Konstanz
* **Maria Rosario,** Countess von Thun und Hohenstein, daughter of Count Konstantin von Thun und Hohenstein and of his wife, Baroness Therese von Stotzingen.
December 27, 1914, Innsbruck —

XXI. von Lill-Rastern 1 continued

Issue: 1. Johannes von Lill-Rastern
March 31, 1945, Krumbach, Bavaria —

2. Matthäus von Lill-Rastern
January 16, 1947, Krumbach —

3. Rainer von Lill-Rastern
June 9, 1948, Göppingen —

4. Lorenz von Lill-Rastern
March 29, 1950, Göppingen —

XXI. VON LIMBURG-STIRUM 1, from page 458

Evrard, Count von Limburg-Stirum
October 31, 1927, Haldenburg, Brabant, Belgium —
m. January 17, 1957, Dreux, France
★ **Hélène,** Princess of France, daughter of Prince Henri, Comte de Paris, and of his wife, Princess Isabella of Orleans e Braganca.
September 17, 1934, Woluwe St. Pierre —

Issue: 1. Catharine, Countess von Limburg-Stirum
October 21, 1957, Salisbury, Southern Rhodesia —

2. Thierry, Count von Limburg-Stirum
July 24, 1959, Lisbon, Portugal —

3. Louis, Count von Limburg-Stirum
June 10, 1962, Brussels —

4. Bruno, Count von Limburg-Stirum
February 20, 1966, Haldenburg —

XXI. ZUR LIPPE-DETMOLD

1, from page 651

Waldemar, Prince zur Lippe-Detmold, second son of Fürst Leopold II.
April 18, 1824, Detmold — March 20, 1895, Detmold
m. November 9, 1858, Karlsruhe

* **Sophie,** Princess of Baden, daughter of Prince Wilhelm, Margrave of Baden, and of his wife, Duchess Elisabeth of Württemberg.
August 7, 1834, Karlsruhe — April 6, 1904, Karlsruhe

No Issue.

XXI. ZUR LIPPE-BIESTERFELD

1, from page 424

Julius Ernst, Prince zur Lippe-Biesterfeld, son of Prince Ernst.
September 2, 1873, Obercassel — September 15, 1952, Obercassel
m. August 11, 1914, Neustrelitz

* **Marie,** Duchess of Mecklenburg-Strelitz, daughter of Grand Duke Adolf Friedrich of Mecklenburg-Strelitz and of his wife, Princess Elisabeth of Anhalt-Dessau.
May 8, 1878, Neustrelitz — October 14, 1948, Obercassel
(She m. 1: and divorced: Georges, Count Jamatel – see: *Jamatel* XVIII, page 567.)

Issue: 1. Elisabeth, Princess zur Lippe-Biesterfeld (1916–1968)
m. Ernst August, Prince zu Solms-Braunfels (1892–)
see: *zu Solms-Braunfels* XXI, page 841

2. Ernst August, Prince zur Lippe-Biesterfeld (1917–)
m. Christa von Arnim auf Kitzscher und Otterwisch (1923–)
see: *zur Lippe-Biesterfeld* XXI, 2, below

XXI. zur Lippe-Biesterfeld

2, from above

* **Ernst August,** Prince zur Lippe-Biesterfeld, only son of Prince Julius Ernst.
April 1, 1917, Dresden-Blasewitz —
m. March 3, 1948, Obercassel

Christa von Arnim auf Kitscher und Otterwisch, daughter of Curt von Arnim auf Kitzscher und Otterwisch and of his wife, Stephanie von Stechow.
July 2, 1923, Leipzig —

XXI. zur Lippe-Biesterfeld 2 continued

Issue: 1. Friedrich Wilhelm, Prince zur Lippe-Biesterfeld
September 7, 1947, Neuwied —

2. Marie Stephanie, Princess zur Lippe-Biesterfeld
August 26, 1949, Beuel —

3. Ernst August, Prince zur Lippe-Biesterfeld
December 24, 1952, Bonn —

4. Marie Christine, Princess zur Lippe-Biesterfeld
December 13, 1959, Bonn —

XXI. zur Lippe-Biesterfeld 3, from page 140

Rudolf, Prince zur Lippe-Biesterfeld, eighth son of Fürst Julius.
April 27, 1856, Neudorf — June 21, 1931, Drogelwitz
m. November 2, 1889, Dresden
* **Luise,** Princess von Ardeck, daughter of Prince Wilhelm of Hesse-Philippsthal-Barchfeld and of his wife, Princess Marie von Hanau, Countess von Schaumburg, created Princess von Ardeck.
December 12, 1868, Langenselbold — November 21, 1959, Wiesbaden

Issue: 1. Friedrich Wilhelm, Prince zur Lippe-Biesterfeld (1890–1938)
m. Godela von Oven (1906–)
see: *zur Lippe-Biesterfeld* XXI, 4, page 756

2. Ernst Julius, Prince zur Lippe-Biesterfeld
January 20, 1892, Berlin — August 28, 1914, Villiers-les-Guise, near Quentin, France, killed in action in World War I

3. Marie Adelheid, Princess zur Lippe-Biesterfeld (1895–)
m. 1: and divorced: Heinrich XXXII, Prince Reuss zu Köstritz (1878–1935)
see: *Reuss* IX e–2, page 341
m. 2: and divorced: Heinrich XXXV, Prince Reuss zu Köstritz (1887–1936)
see: *Reuss* IX g–1, page 342
m. 3: and divorced: Hanno Konopath (–)
see: *Konopath* XXI, page 736

XXI. zur Lippe-Biesterfeld 4, from page 755

* **Friedrich Wilhelm,** Prince zur Lippe-Biesterfeld, son of Prince Rudolf.
November 27, 1890, Berlin — October 24, 1938, Berlin
m. July 1, 1932, Breslau
Godela von Oven, daughter of Eberhard von Oven and of his wife, Maria Wittkop.
December 17, 1906, Glogau —

Issue: 1. Rudolf, Prince zur Lippe-Biesterfeld
January 8, 1937, Berlin —

XXI. ZUR LIPPE-WEISSENFELD 1, from page 834

Ferdinand, Prince zur Lippe-Weissenfeld, son of Prince Clemens.
July 16, 1903, Dresden — September 26, 1939, Lublin, killed in action in World War II
m. September 5, 1928, Guteborn
* **Dorothea,** Princess of Schönburg-Waldenburg, daughter of Prince Ulrich of Schönburg-Waldenburg and of his wife, Princess Pauline zu Löwenstein-Wertheim-Freudenberg.
October 3, 1905, Guteborn —

Issue: 1. Franz, Prince zur Lippe-Weissenfeld
October 14, 1929, Dresden —

2. Margarete, Princess zur Lippe-Weissenfeld
April 28, 1932, Dresden —

XXI. zur Lippe-Weissenfeld 2, from page 779

Christian, Prince zur Lippe-Weissenfeld, second son of Prince Clemens.
August 12, 1907, Doberkitz —
m. October 17, 1935, Bayerhof Castle
* **Pauline,** Countess zu Ortenburg, daughter of Count Friedrich zu Ortenburg and of his wife, Princess Ilka zu Löwenstein-Wertheim-Freudenberg.
December 3, 1913, Bayerhof Castle —

Issue: 1. Clemens, Prince zur Lippe-Weissenfeld
September 16, 1937, Dresden —
(m. January 9, 1965, Schweinfurt, Heidi Fery.
1. Jan Hendrik, Prince zur Lippe-Weissenfeld, born August 26, 1970, New York City.)

XXI. zur Lippe-Weissenfeld 2 continued

2. Friedrich, Prince zur Lippe-Weissenfeld
March 18, 1939, Dresden —

3. Elisabeth, Princess zur Lippe-Weissenfeld (1940–)
m. Prosper Friedrich, Count zu Castell-Castell (1922–)
see: *zu Castell-Castell* XXI, page 676

4. Ferdinand, Prince zur Lippe-Weissenfeld
November 14, 1942, Bautzen —
(m. June 10, 1970, Munich, Karolina von Freibitzsch, born November 29, 1941, Kürbitz, daughter of Joachim von Freibitzsch and of his wife, Ilse.)

5. Christian, Prince zur Lippe-Weissenfeld
October 18, 1945, Teichnitz —

XXI. VON LOË 1, from page 795

Felix, Baron von Loë
September 1, 1896, Wissen, near Weeze — July 25, 1944, Schwaneburg, Latvia, died of wounds received in action in World War II
m. September 8, 1925, Anholt, Westphalia
* **Isabelle,** Princess zu Salm-Salm, daughter of Prince Emanuel zu Salm-Salm and of his wife, Archduchess Maria Christina of Austria.
February 13, 1903, Potsdam —

Issue: 1. Fritz, Count von Loë (1926–)
m. Inez, Baroness von Böselager (1935–)
see: *von Loë* XXI, 2, page 758

2. Christine, Baroness von Loë (1927–)
m. Johannes, Prince zu Löwenstein-Wertheim-Rosenberg (1919–)
see: *zu Löwenstein-Wertheim-Rosenberg* XXI, page 764

3. Wessel, Baron von Loë (1928–)
m. Sophie, Countess zu Waldburg-Zeil (1932–)
see: *von Loë* XXI, 3, page 758

4. Elisabeth, Baroness von Loë (1930–)
m. Philipp, Baron Wambolt und Umstadt (1918–)
see: *Wambolt und Umstadt* XXI, page 901

XXI. von Loë 1 continued

5. Paula, Baroness von Loë
March 1, 1931, Wissen — September 25, 1950, Köln, died of infantile paralysis

6. Franz, Baron von Loë
October 24, 1936, Wissen —

7. Maria, Baroness von Loë
June 3, 1939, Wissen —

XXI. von Loë 2, from page 757

* **Fritz,** Count von Loë, eldest son of Baron Felix.
June 8, 1926, Wissen —
m. October 2, 1957, Höllinghafen

Inez, Baroness von Böselager, daughter of Baron Maximilian von Böselager and of his wife, Baroness Erica von Fürstenberg.
February 6, 1935, Hanover-Münden —

Issue: 1. Raphael, Baron von Loë
August 30, 1958, Wissen —

2. Wessel, Baron von Loë
October 10, 1959, Wissen —

3. Winfried, Baroness von Loë
July 29, 1961, Wissen —

4. Paula, Baroness von Loë
May 17, 1962, Wissen —

5. Augustinus, Baron von Loë
June 12, 1966, Wissen —

XXI. von Loë 3, from pages 757, 890

* **Wessel,** Baron von Loë, second son of Baron Felix.
August 8, 1928, Wissen —
m. May 5, 1957, Syrgenstein Castle, near Wangen

* **Sophie,** Countess von Waldburg-Zeil, daughter of Count Georg von Waldburg-Zeil and of his wife, Archduchess Elisabeth of Austria.
December 5, 1932, Innsbruck —

XXI. von Loë 3 continued

Issue: 1. Georg, Baron von Loë
April 18, 1958, Adendorf —

2. Felix, Baron von Loë
August 30, 1960, Bonn —

3. Philipp, Baron von Loë
October 11, 1961, Bonn —

4. Maria Annunciata, Baroness von Loë
February 15, 1963, Bonn —

5. Agnes, Baroness von Loë
April 25, 1966, Bad Godesberg —

6. Sophie, Baroness von Loë
May 31, 1969, Bonn —

XXI. VON LOËN 1, from page 638

Johannes-Michael, Baron von Loën
September 6, 1902, Dessau —
m. September 27, 1926, Berlin-Schöneberg. Divorced: April 18, 1935, Berlin
* **Marie Auguste,** Princess of Anhalt-Dessau, daughter of Duke Eduard of Anhalt-Dessau and of his wife, Princess Luise of Saxe-Altenburg.
June 10, 1898, Ballenstedt Castle —
(She m. 1: Joachim, Prince of Prussia – see: *Prussia* (*Hohenzollern*) II 0–1, page 62.–)

No Issue.

XXI. VON LÓNYAY DE NAGY-LÓNYA UND VÁSÁROS-NAMÉNY
1, from page 286

Elémer, Count (after 1917, Prince) von Lónyay de Nagy-Lónya und Vásáros-Namény
August 24, 1863, Bodrog-Olaszi, Hungary — July 20, 1946, Budapest
m. March 22, 1900, Miramar
* **Stephanie,** Princess of Belgium, daughter of King Leopold II of the Belgians and of his wife, Archduchess Henrietta of Austria.
May 21, 1864, Laekan Castle — August 23, 1945, Pannonhalma, Hungary
(She m. 1: Crown Prince Rudolf of Austria – see: *Austria* X b–1, page 354.)

No Issue.

THE HOUSE OF LÖWENSTEIN

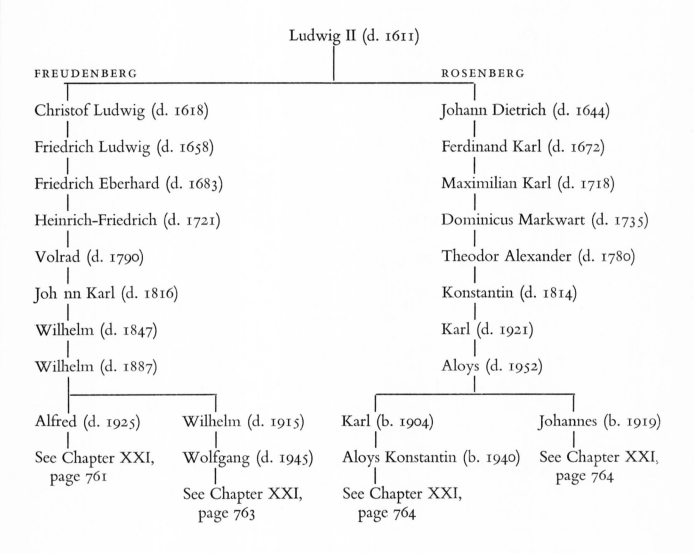

Ludwig II (d. 1611)

FREUDENBERG

- Christof Ludwig (d. 1618)
- Friedrich Ludwig (d. 1658)
- Friedrich Eberhard (d. 1683)
- Heinrich-Friedrich (d. 1721)
- Volrad (d. 1790)
- Joh nn Karl (d. 1816)
- Wilhelm (d. 1847)
- Wilhelm (d. 1887)
  - Alfred (d. 1925)
    - See Chapter XXI, page 761
  - Wilhelm (d. 1915)
    - Wolfgang (d. 1945)
      - See Chapter XXI, page 763

ROSENBERG

- Johann Dietrich (d. 1644)
- Ferdinand Karl (d. 1672)
- Maximilian Karl (d. 1718)
- Dominicus Markwart (d. 1735)
- Theodor Alexander (d. 1780)
- Konstantin (d. 1814)
- Karl (d. 1921)
- Aloys (d. 1952)
  - Karl (b. 1904)
    - Aloys Konstantin (b. 1940)
      - See Chapter XXI, page 764
  - Johannes (b. 1919)
    - See Chapter XXI, page 764

XXI. ZU LÖWENSTEIN-WERTHEIM-FREUDENBERG 1, from page 138

Alfred, 5th Fürst zu Löwenstein-Wertheim-Freudenberg
October 19, 1855, Siebleben, near Gotha — April 20, 1925, Langenzell
m. February 9, 1880, Frankfurt-am-Main
* **Pauline,** Countess von Reichenbach-Lessonitz, daughter of Count Wilhelm von Reichenbach-Lessonitz and of his wife, Baroness Amelie Göler von Ravensburg.
May 6, 1858, Frankfurt-am-Main — October 21, 1927, Langenzell

Issue: 1. Olga, Princess zu Löwenstein-Wertheim-Freudenberg (1880–1961)
m. 1: and divorced: Heinrich, Prince of Schönburg-Waldenburg (1863–1945)
see: *von Schönburg-Waldenburg* XXI, page 832
m. 2: and divorced: Wolfgang, Prince zu Löwenstein-Wertheim-Freudenberg (1890–1945)
see: *zu Löwenstein-Wertheim-Freudenberg* XXI, 4, page 763

2. Pauline, Princess zu Löwenstein-Wertheim-Freudenberg (1881–1945)
m. Ulrich, Prince of Schönburg-Waldenburg (1869–1939)
see: *von Schönburg-Waldenburg* XXI, page 834

3. Amelie, Princess zu Löwenstein-Wertheim-Freudenberg (1883–)
m. Otto, Count zu Castell-Castell (1868–1939)
see: *zu Castell-Castell* XXI, page 673

4. Madeleine, Princess zu Löwenstein-Wertheim-Freudenburg (1885–)
m. Richard, 4th Fürst zu Sayn-Wittgenstein-Berleburg (1882–1945)
see: *zu Sayn-Wittgenstein-Berleburg* XXI, page 802

5. Ilka, Princess zu Löwenstein-Wertheim-Freudenberg (1887–1971)
m. Friedrich, Count zu Ortenburg (1871–1940)
see: *zu Ortenburg* XXI, page 779

XXI. zu Löwenstein-Wertheim-Freudenberg   1 continued

6. Elisabeth, Princess zu Löwenstein-Wertheim-Freudenberg (1890–1953)
m. 1: and divorced: Otto-Konstantin, Prince zu Sayn-Wittgenstein-Berleburg (1878–1955)
see: *zu Sayn-Wittgenstein-Berleburg* XXI, 6, page 806
m. 2: Richard Merton (1881–1960)
see: *Merton* XXI, page 771

7. Udo, 6th Fürst zu Löwenstein-Wertheim-Freudenberg (1896–)
m. Margarete, Countess zu Castell-Castell (1899–)
see: *zu Löwenstein-Wertheim-Freudenberg* XXI, 2, below

XXI. zu Löwenstein-Wertheim-Freudenberg   2, from above

* **Udo,** 6th Fürst zu Löwenstein-Wertheim-Freudenberg, only son of Fürst Alfred.
September 8, 1896, Langenzell —
m. May 3, 1922, Castell

Margarete, Countess zu Castell-Castell, daughter of Count Friedrich Karl, Fürst zu Castell-Castell and of his wife, Countess Gertrud zu Stolberg-Wernigerode.
October 27, 1899, Castell —

Issue: 1. Ameli, Princess zu Löwenstein-Wertheim-Freudenberg (1923–)
m. Anton Günther, Duke of Oldenburg (1923–)
see: *Oldenburg* V bb–6, page 210

2. Alfred, Hereditary Prince zu Löwenstein-Wertheim-Freudenberg (1924–)
m. Ruth Erika von Buggenhagen (1922–)
see: *zu Löwenstein-Wertheim-Freudenberg* XXI, 3, page 763

3. Gertrud, Princess zu Löwenstein-Wertheim-Freudenberg (1926–)
m. Peter, Duke of Oldenburg (1926–)
see: *Oldenburg* V cc–1, page 210

XXI. zu Löwenstein-Wertheim-Freudenberg 2 continued

4. Pauline, Princess zu Löwenstein-Wertheim-Freudenberg (1928–)
m. Hans Günther Horst (1913–)
see: *Horst* XXI, page 725

XXI. zu Löwenstein-Wertheim-Freudenberg 3, from page 762

* **Alfred,** Hereditary Prince zu Löwenstein-Wertheim-Freudenberg, only son of Fürst Udo.
September 19, 1924, Triefenstein Castle —
m. September 9, 1950, Kreuzwertheim
Ruth Erika von Buggenhagen, daughter of Hans Detlof von Buggenhagen and of his wife, Baroness Ruth von Rosenberg.
June 25, 1922, Buggenhagen —

Issue: 1. Ludwig, Prince zu Löwenstein-Wertheim-Freudenberg
May 24, 1951, Kreuzwertheim —

2. Ameli, Princess zu Löwenstein-Wertheim-Freudenberg
February 20, 1953, Kreuzwertheim —

3. Dorothea, Princess zu Löwenstein-Wertheim-Freudenberg
October 30, 1955, Kreuzwertheim —

4. Udo, Prince zu Löwenstein-Wertheim-Freudenberg
June 17, 1957, Kreuzwertheim —

5. Ruth, Princess zu Löwenstein-Wertheim-Freudenberg
December 30, 1959, Kreuzwertheim —

XXI. zu Löwenstein-Wertheim-Freudenberg 4, from page 761

Wolfgang, Prince zu Löwenstein-Wertheim-Freudenberg, son of 4th Fürst Wilhelm.
November 25, 1890, Drehnow — July 8/9, 1945, Pulawy, Poland
m. 1: October 22, 1920, Frankfurt-am-Main. Divorced: February 8, 1938, Berlin
* **Olga,** Princess zu Löwenstein-Wertheim-Freudenberg, daughter of 5th Fürst Alfred zu Löwenstein-Wertheim-Freudenberg and of his wife, Countess Pauline von Reichenbach-Lessonitz.
October 25, 1880, Bonn —

XXI. zu Löwenstein-Wertheim-Freudenberg 4 continued

(She m. 1; and divorced: Heinrich, Prince of Schönburg-Waldenburg – see: *Schönburg-Waldenburg* XXI, page 832.)

m. 2: November 17, 1938, Lindau im Breisgau

Eugenie von Fortenbach, daughter of Major General Jakob Fortenbach and of his wife, Eugenie Schmidt.

August 14, 1900, Würzburg —

Issue of second marriage: Not descendant of King George

1. Wolfram, Prince zu Löwenstein-Wertheim-Freudenberg
   October 21, 1941, Berlin —

XXI. ZU LÖWENSTEIN-WERTHEIM-ROSENBERG 1, from page 57

Aloys-Konstantin, Hereditary Prince zu Löwenstein-Wertheim-Rosenberg, eldest son of 8th Fürst Karl.

December 16, 1941, Würzburg —

m. November 8, 1965, Erbach

* **Anastasia,** Princess of Prussia, daughter of Prince Hubertus of Prussia and of his second wife, Princess Magdalena Reuss zu Köstritz.

February 14, 1944, Brieg —

Issue: 1. Karl-Friedrich, Prince zu Löwenstein-Wertheim-Rosenberg
   September 30, 1966, Frankfurt-am-Main —

2. Hubertus Maximilian, Prince zu Löwenstein-Wertheim-Rosenberg
   December 18, 1968, Frankfurt-am-Main —

XXI. zu Löwenstein-Wertheim-Rosenberg 2, from page 757

Johannes, Prince zu Löwenstein-Wertheim-Rosenberg, son of Prince Aloys.

July 7, 1919, Kleinheubach —

m. August 30, 1949, Wissen, near Weeze

* **Christine,** Baroness von Loë, daughter of Baron Felix von Loë and of his wife, Princess Isabelle zu Salm-Salm.

July 31, 1927, Wissen —

Issue: 1. Michael, Prince zu Löwenstein-Wertheim-Rosenberg
   December 20, 1950, Wissen —

XXI. zu Löwenstein-Wertheim-Rosenberg 2 continued

2. Karl, Prince zu Löwenstein-Wertheim-Rosenberg
January 1, 1952, Hees, near Weeze —

3. Felix, Prince zu Löwenstein-Wertheim-Rosenberg
February 15, 1954, Hees —

4. Isabelle, Princess zu Löwenstein-Wertheim-Rosenberg
November 2, 1957, Schluifeld —

5. Josephine, Princess zu Löwenstein-Wertheim-Rosenberg
April 29, 1958, Schluifeld —

6. Martin, Prince zu Löwenstein-Wertheim-Rosenberg
April 15, 1961, Schluifeld —

7. Stephan, Prince zu Löwenstein-Wertheim-Rosenberg
October 7, 1968, Ehrenburg, Bavaria —

XXI. VON LUCKNER 1, from page 118

Wilhelm, Count von Luckner, son of Count Ferdinand.
January 29, 1805, — February 19, 1865,
m. 1: October 3, 1836, Dresden. Divorced:
* **Wilhelmine,** Countess von Reichenbach-Lessonitz, daughter of Elector Wilhelm II of Hesse and of his second wife, Emilie Ortlopp, created Countess von Reichenbach-Lessonitz.
December 21, 1816, Cassel — December 28, 1858, Dresden
m. 2: December 21, 1847, Dresden
* **Wilhelmine,** Countess von Reichenbach-Lessonitz, his former wife.
(She m. 2: Karl, Baron von Watzdorf – see: *von Watzdorf* XXI, page 904.)

Issue: see: *von Luckner*, Addendum, page 1064

XXI. VON MAASBERG 1, from page 553

Nikolaus, Baron von Maasberg
November 18, 1913, Marburg —

XXI. von Maasberg 1 continued

m. October 28, 1941, Trento
* **Christiane,** Countess Ceschi a Santa Croce, daughter of Count Giovanni Ceschi a Santa Croce and of his wife, Princess Luise Windisch-Graetz.
July 5, 1914, Haasberg Castle —

Issue: 1. Johann, Baron von Maasberg
July 19, 1942, Wisell, Yugoslavia —

2. Marie Luise, Baroness von Maasberg
April 19, 1944, Wisell —

3. Leo Maximilian, Baron von Maasberg
March 28, 1948, Graz —

4. Marie Edithe, Baroness von Maasberg
October 11, 1954, Kitzbühel, Austria —

XXI. VON MATUSCHKA (Topolczan und Spaetgan) 1, from page 75

Eberhard, Count von Matuschka, Baron von Topolczan und Spaetgan.
November 16, 1870, Bechau Castle, Silesia — March 7, 1920, Breslau
m. October 20, 1897, Albrechtsberg Castle
* **Elisabeth,** Countess von Hohenau, daughter of Count Wilhelm von Hohenau and of his wife, Baroness Laura Saurma von und zu der Jeltsch.
June 15, 1879, Lorzendorf — May 27, 1956, Herdringen Castle

Issue: 1. Hans Eberhard, Count von Matuschka, Baron von Topolczan und Spaetgan (1898–1945)
m. Fedora, Countess von Matuschka, Baroness von Topolczan und Spaetgan (1891–)
see: *von Matuschka* XXI, 2, page 767

2. Maria-Lory, Countess von Matuschka, Baroness von Topolczan und Spaetgan (1900–1962)
m. Karl Anton, Count Saurma von der Jeltsch-Lorzendorf (1898–1941)
see: *Saurma von der Jeltsch-Lorzendorf* XXI, page 801

XXI. von Matuschka — 1 continued

3. Marie Elisabeth, Countess von Matuschka, Baroness von Topolczan und Spaetgan. (1901–1956)
   m. Wenemar, Count von Fürstenberg-Herdringen (1897–)
   see: *von Fürstenberg-Herdringen* XXI, page 712

XXI. von Matuschka — 2, from page 766

* **Hans Eberhard,** Count von Matuschka, Baron von Topolczan und Spaetgen, only son of Count Eberhard.

September 6, 1898, Gross Neukirch — December 27, 1945, Tscherepowetz, Russia, in a prisoner-of-war camp

m. March 18, 1927, Berlin

Fedora, Countess von Matuschka, daughter of Count Franz von Matuschka, Baron von Topolczan und Spaetgen and of his wife, Countess Aloisia von Ballestrem.

June 24, 1891, Berlin —

(She m. 1: May 6, 1913, Berlin; divorced: February 12, 1927, Berlin, Roger, Count von Seherr-Thoss, born March 24, 1880, Dobrau, Silesia.)

Issue: 1. Eberhard, Count von Matuschka, Baron von Topolczan und Spaetgen (1929–)
   m. Veronika Augusta Broel (1937–)
   see: *von Matuschka* XXI, 3, below

XXI. von Matuschka — 3, from above

* **Eberhard,** Count von Matuschka, Baron von Topolczan und Spaetgen, only son of Count Hans Eberhard.

July 25, 1929, Breslau —

m. October 25, 1960, Essen

Veronika Augusta Broel, daughter of Günther Wilhelm Broel and of his wife, Irmgard Margarete Beckert.

February 13, 1937, Crimmitschau, Saxony —

No Issue.

XXI. von Matuschka 4, from page 494

Clemens, Count von Matuschka, Baron von Topolczan und Spaetgen.
July 26, 1928, Pitschen am Bergen, Kr. Striegau —
m. October 16, 1956, Waldenburg
★ **Amelie,** Princess of Hohenlohe-Waldenburg-Schillingsfürst, daughter of Prince Friedrich Karl, 8th Fürst zu Hohenlohe-Waldenburg-Schillingsfürst, and of his wife, Countess Mechtilde of Württemberg, Princess von Urach.
December 11, 1936, Waldenburg —

Issue: 1. Stephanie, Countess von Matuschka, Baroness von Topolczan und Spaetgan
July 21, 1957, Rottweil-an-der-Neckar —

2. Marie Gabrielle (Mariella), Countess von Matuschka, Baroness von Topolczan und Spaetgen
October 4, 1958, Rottweil —

3. Karl Joseph, Count von Matuschka, Baron von Topolczan und Spaetgen
January 11, 1960, Herbolsheim, Baden —

4. Philipp, Count von Matuschka, Baron von Topolczan und Spaetgan
November 10, 1961, Carlow, Ireland —

XXI. MAYER 1, from page 696

Norbert Mayer
November 19, 1906, Vienna —
m. December 17, 1939, Vienna
★ **Josepha,** Countess von Enzenberg zum Freyen und Jöchelsthurn, daughter of Count Rudolf von Enzenberg zum Freyen und Jöchelsthurn and of his wife, Countess Marie zu Hardegg auf Glatz und im Machlande.
January 4, 1913, Schwaz —

Issue: 1. Franz Xaver Mayer
January 11, 1942, Vienna —

2. Marie-Eleonore Mayer
April 22, 1943, Vienna —

XXI. Mayer — 1 continued

3. Clemens Mayer
   April 24, 1946, Innsbruck —

4. Georg Mayer
   February 21, 1949, Linz —

XXI. MEES — 1, from page 71

Heinz Mees
April 16, 1918, Lambrecht, Rheinplatz —
m. August 5, 1948, Erbach
* **Elisabeth,** Princess of Prussia, daughter of Prince Friedrich Wilhelm of Prussia and of his wife, Princess Agathe of Hohenlohe-Schillingsfürst.
February 9, 1919, Rauden — August 24, 1961, Frankfurt-am-Main

No Issue.

XXI. MENZEL — 1, from page 836

Rudolf (Rolf) Menzel
August 10, 1924, Berlin —
m. June 12, 1965, Hamburg
* **Karoline-Eleonore,** Baroness von Schröder, daughter of Baron Manfred von Schröder and of his wife, Countess Eleonore-Renata von Pückler.
September 26, 1940, Athens —

Issue: 1. Robin Rudolf Rüdiger Menzel
   June 29, 1966, Stamford, Connecticut, USA —

2. Johann Mortimer Menzel
   July 16, 1968, Washington, D.C. —

XXI. VON MERAN — 1, from page 663

Rudolf, Count von Meran
December 20, 1917, Innsbruck —
m. November 10, 1951, Wolfsegg Castle
* **Marie Therese,** Countess von Blankenstein, daughter of Count Karl von Blankenstein and of

XXI. von Meran

I continued

his wife, Countess Eugenie von Enzenberg zum Freyen und Jöchelsthurn.
May 31, 1929, Battelau —

Issue: 1. Ladislaya Eleonore, Countess von Meran
October 25, 1952, Buenos Aires, Argentina —

2. Adolf, Count von Meran
October 6, 1953, Buenos Aires —

3. Johann, Count von Meran
January 29, 1955, Veinticino de Mayo, Argentina —

4. Rudolf, Count von Meran
February 1, 1956, Veinticino de Mayo —

5. Andreas, Count von Meran
May 24, 1957, Buenos Aires —

6. Gabrielle, Countess von Meran
November 19, 1958, Buenos Aires —

7. Marianna, Countess von Meran
October 9, 1959, Buenos Aires —

8. Karl, Count von Meran
October 12, 1960, Buenos Aires — October 15, 1960, Buenos Aires

9. Heinrich, Count von Meran
November 14, 1961, Nueve Palmira, Uruguay —

10. Christine, Countess von Meran
June 14, 1963, Buenos Aires —

11. Hemma, Countess von Meran
July 21, 1965, Buenos Aires —

XXI. MERTON 1, from page 762

Richard Merton

December 1, 1881, Frankfurt-am-Main — January 6, 1960, Frankfurt-am-Main
m. March 28, 1930, Frankfurt-am-Main

* **Elisabeth,** Princess zu Löwenstein-Wertheim-Freudenberg, daughter of Prince Alfred, 5th Fürst zu Löwenstein-Wertheim-Freudenberg, and of his wife, Countess Pauline von Reichenbach-Lessonitz.

May 5, 1890, Langenzell — March 9, 1953, Frankfurt-am-Main
(She m. 1: and divorced: Otto-Konstantin, Prince zu Sayn-Wittgenstein-Berleburg – see: *zu Sayn-Wittgenstein-Berleburg* XXI, page 806.)

Issue: 1. Alexandra Merton (1932–)
m. Dr. Ortwin Beck (1915–)
see: *Beck* XXI, page 652

XXI. METTERNICH (or Wolff-Metternich zur Glacht) 1, from page 794

Peter, Count Metternich

March 5, 1929, Göttingen —
m. July 18, 1955 (civil), and July 27, 1955 (religious), Alfter, near Bonn

* **Marie Christine,** Altgrafin zu Salm-Reifferscheidt, Krautheim und Dyck, daughter of Fürst und Altgraf Franz Josef zu Salm-Reifferscheidt, Krautheim und Dyck and of his wife, Princess Cäcilie zu Salm-Salm.

January 4, 1932, Alfter —

Issue: 1. Gina, Countess Metternich
October 18, 1956, Bonn —

2. Helena, Countess Metternich
October 22, 1957, Bonn —

3. Maria Pilar, Countess Metternich
December 21, 1959, Bonn —

XXI. Metternich (Wolff-Metternich zur Glacht) 1 continued

4. Simeon, Count Metternich
April 30, 1965, Cassel —

XXI. VON METTERNICH-WINNEBURG 1, from page 941

Paul, 4th Fürst von Metternich-Winneburg, 11th child of Prince Klemens.
October 14, 1834, Vienna — February 6, 1906, Vienna
m. May 9, 1868, Carlburg

* **Melanie,** Countess von Zichy-Ferraris zu Zich und Vásonykeö, daughter of Count Felix von Zichy-Ferraris zu Zich und Vásonykeö and of his wife, Countess Emilie von Reichenbach-Lessonitz.
August 16, 1843, Carlburg — August 3, 1925, Johannisberg Castle on the Rhine

Issue: 1. Klemens–Wenzel, 5th Fürst von Metternich-Winneburg (1869–1930)
m. Isabel de Silva y Carvajal (1880–)
see: *von Metternich-Winneburg* XXI, 2, below

2. Emilie, Princess von Metternich-Winneburg
February 24, 1873, — January 20, 1884,

3. Pauline, Princess von Metternich-Winneburg (1880–)
m. Maximilian Theodor, Prince of Thurn und Taxis (1876–1939)
see: *Thurn und Taxis* XXI, page 875

XXI. von Metternich-Winneburg 2, from above

* **Klemens-Wenzel,** 5th Fürst von Metternich-Winneburg, only son of Fürst Paul.
February 9, 1869, Vienna — March 13, 1930, Munich
m. October 4, 1905, Madrid

Isabel de Silva y Carvajal, daughter of Alvaro de Silva, 12th Marques de Santa Cruz, Grandee of Spain, and of his wife, Maria Louisa Carvajal, Duques de San Carlos, Condesa de Castillejo, Grandee of Spain.
May 3, 1880, Madrid —
(She m. 2: June , 1931, Wladylas Skrzynski, who died December 26, 1937, Rome.)

XXI. von Metternich-Winneburg 2 continued

Issue: 1. Paul Alfons, 6th Fürst von Metternich-Winneburg (1917–)
m. Tatiana Illarionovna, Princess Vassiltschikova (1915–)
see: *von Metternich-Winneburg* XXI, 3, below

XXI. von Metternich-Winneburg 3, from above

* **Paul Alfons,** 6th Fürst von Metternich-Winneburg, 5th Duke of Portella, Count von Königswart, Grandee of Spain.
May 26, 1917, Vienna —
m. September 6, 1941, Berlin
Tatiana Illarionovna, Princess Vassiltschikova, daughter of Prince Illarion Vassiltschikov and of his wife, Princess Lydia Viasemskya.
January 1, 1915, St. Petersburg, Russia —

No Issue.

XXI. VON MONTGELAS 1, from page 133

Ludwig, Count von Montgelas
December 15, 1907, Munich —
m. October 5, 1933, Horowitz
* **Emmerentiana,** Princess von Hanau, Countess von Schaumburg, daughter of Prince Friedrich von Hanau, Count von Schaumburg, and of his wife, Countess Hildegard Almásy von Zsadány und Török-Szent-Miklós.
April 22, 1913, Munich —

Issue: 1. Maximilian, Count von Montgelas (1934–)
m. Astrid Riedesel, Baroness zu Eisenbach (1940–)
see: *von Montgelas* XXI, 2, page 774

2. Tassilo, Count von Montgelas
April 2, 1937, Pähl, near Weilheim —

3. Elisabeth, Countess von Montgelas
March 24, 1939, Pähl —

XXI. von Montgelas 2, from page 773

* **Maximilian,** Count von Montgelas, only son of Count Ludwig.
July 24, 1934, Munich —
m. August 8, 1963, Munich
Astrid Riedesel, Baroness zu Eisenbach, daughter of Baron Bertram Riedesel zu Eisenbach and of his wife, Anna-Luise Jank.
September 17, 1940, Munich —

Issue: 1. Karoline, Countess von Montgelas
February 25, 1966, Munich —

XXI. VON DER MÜHL 1, from page 371

Johannes von der Mühl
—
m. , 1948,
* **Gabriele,** Countess von Wolfenau, daughter of Archduke Leopold of Austria and of his wife, Alice Coburn.
February 12, 1922, —

Issue:

XXI. MÜLLER 1, from page 266

Hans Wolfgang Müller
August 16, 1907, Magdeburg —
m. March 11, 1969,
* **Maleen,** Baroness von Saalfeld, daughter of Baron Hans von Saalfeld and of his wife, Elisabeth Faust.
May 21, 1937, Munich —
(She m. 1: and divorced: Istvan Babotai – see: *Babotai* XXI, page 646.)

Issue: 1. Enzio Müller
June 27, 1969, Munich —

XXI. MURJAHN 1, from page 988

Gerhard Murjahn

—

m. March 18, 1958,

* **Hortense Evgenievna,** Princess Kotchoubey de Beauharnais, daughter of Prince Evgenii Leontievich Kotchoubey de Beauharnais and of his wife, Helen Geraldine Pearce.

January 2, 1935, Paris —

Issue: 1. Daria Alexandra Murjahn

January 29, 1967, West Berlin —

XXI. VON NEIPPERG 1, from page 224

Alfred, Count von Neipperg

January 26, 1807, — November 16, 1865, Winnendon Castle

m. 1: October 19, 1835,

Guiseppina (Josephine), Contessa di Grisoni, daughter of

— November 17, 1837,

m. 2: March 19, 1840,

* **Marie,** Princess of Württemberg, daughter of King Wilhelm I of Württemberg and of his wife Grand Duchess Ekaterina Pavlovna of Russia.

October 30, 1816, — January 4, 1887, Stuttgart

No Issue.

XXI. NIELSEN 1, from page 23

Michael Nielsen

August 12, 1923, Frankfurt-am-Main —

m. December 5, 1953, Mühlacher, Württemberg

* **Marianne,** Princess of Saxe-Coburg and Gotha, daughter of Hereditary Prince Leopold of Saxe-Coburg and Gotha and of his first wife, Baroness Feodore von der Horst.

April 5, 1933, Hirschberg —

Issue: 1. Margarethe-Birgitte Nielsen

September 30, 1954, Leverkusen —

2. Renate Nielsen

April 2, 1957, Köln —

XXI. VON NIEMANS

1, from page 688

Richard, Baron von Niemans
July 6, 1876, Kreuth — June 1, 1943, Würzburg
m. January 8, 1928, Würzburg
* **Ilka,** Baroness von Dungern, daughter of Baron Otto Wilhelm von Dungern and of his wife, Elise von Schreven.
August 8, 1880, Bayerhof — October 16, 1952, Schwebenreid

No Issue.

XXI. VON NORMAN UND AUDENHOVE (von Kuenburg)

1, from page 698

Christoph von Norman und Audenhove, Count von Kuenburg
November 25, 1936, Salzburg —
m. August 15, 1962, Innsbruck
* **Leonhilde,** Countess von Enzenberg zum Freyen und Jöchelsthurn, only daughter of Count Hubert von Enzenberg zum Freyen und Jöchelsthurn and of his wife, Baroness Leonhilde Klezl von Norberg.
August 10, 1941, Innsbruck —

Issue: 1. Bernhard von Norman und Audenhove, Count von Kuenburg
May 30, 1963, Salzburg —

2. Meinrad von Norman und Audenhove, Count von Kuenburg
March 1, 1965, Salzburg —

3. Eleonore von Norman und Audenhove, Countess von Kuenburg
May 14, 1968, Salzburg —

XXI. NÖRTEMANN

1, from page 740

Dr. Ulrich Nörtemann
October 25, 1933, Dannenberg/Elbe —
m. October 5, 1963, Ehrenburg
* **Christiane Künigl,** Countess zu Ehrenburg, Baroness von Warth, daughter of Karl Heinrich Künigl, Count zu Ehrenburg, and of his wife, Countess Ilse Liane zu Platen-Hallermund.
August 26, 1939, Meran —

Issue: 1. Stefan Nörtemann, April 13, 1965, Munich —

2. Sibylle Nörtemann, April 22, 1967, Munich —

3. Matthias Nörtemann, September 16, 1971, Munich —

XXI. VON NOSTITZ-RIENECK 1, from page 356

Friedrich, Count von Nostitz-Rieneck
November 1, 1893, Prague —
m. September 8, 1920, Tetschen Castle on the Elbe

* **Sophie,** Princess von Hohenberg, daughter of Archduke Franz Ferdinand of Austria and of his morganatic wife, Countess Sophie Chotek von Chotkowa und Wognin, created Duchess von Hohenberg.
July 24, 1901, Konopischt, Hungary —

Issue: 1. Erwein, Count von Nostitz-Rieneck
June 29, 1921, Heinrichsgrün — September 11, 1949, Wysoki, Russia, in a prisoner-of-war camp

2. Franz, Count von Nostitz-Rieneck
February 2, 1923, Vienna — February 23, 1945, Berent, killed in action in World War II

3. Aloys, Count von Nostitz-Rieneck (1925–)
m. Theresia, Countess von Waldburg zu Zeil und Trauchburg (1931–)
see: *von Nostitz-Rieneck* XXI, 2, below

4. Sophie, Countess von Nostitz-Rieneck (1929–)
m. Ernst, Baron von Gudenus (1916–)
see: *von Gudenus* XXI, page 716

XXI. von Nostitz-Rieneck 2, from above

* **Aloys,** Count von Nostitz-Rieneck, third son of Count Friedrich.
August 12, 1925, Vienna —
m. September 12, 1962, Zeil Castle

Theresia, Countess von Waldburg zu Zeil und Trauchburg, daughter of Count Georg, 5th Fürst von Waldburg zu Zeil und Trauchburg, and of his wife, Altgräfin Marie Therese zu Salm-Reifferscheidt-Raitz.
August 8, 1931, Zeil Castle —

Issue: 1. Friedrich, Count von Nostitz-Rieneck
July 19, 1963, Graz —

2. Monika, Countess von Nostitz-Rieneck
April 15, 1965, Graz —

XXI. VON OPPERSDORFF

1, from page 873

Franz Eduard, Count von Oppersdorff
June 19, 1919, Oberglogau, Silesia —
m. June 19, 1955, Haus Castle
* **Maria Theresia,** Princess of Thurn und Taxis, daughter of Prince Franz Joseph, 9th Fürst von Thurn und Taxis, and of his wife, Princess Elisabeth of Braganca, Infanta of Portugal.
September 10, 1925, Taxis Castle —

Issue: 1. Fernanda-Franziska, Countess von Oppersdorff
March 23, 1956, Regensburg —

2. Gabriella-Maria, Countess von Oppersdorff
March 25, 1957, Regensburg —

3. Franz-Joseph, Count von Oppersdorff
March 24, 1958, Regensburg —

4. Margarethe-Luise, Countess von Oppersdorff
November 9, 1959, Regensburg —

5. Michael Friedrich, Count von Oppersdorff
June 18, 1962, Regensburg —

XXI. von Oppersdorff

2, from page 128

Friedrich Karl, Count von Oppersdorff
January 30, 1925, Oberglogau, Silesia —
m. February 28, 1962, Frankfurt-am-Main —
* **Elisabeth,** Princess of Hesse, daughter of Landgrave Philipp of Hesse and of his wife, Princess Mafalda of Savoy.
October 8, 1940, Rome —

Issue: 1. Friedrich Karl, Count von Oppersdorff
December 1, 1962, Frankfurt-am-Main —

2. Alexander Wolfgang, Count von Oppersdorff
August 3, 1965, Frankfurt-am-Main —

XXI. ZU ORTENBURG

1, from page 761

Friedrich, Count zu Ortenburg, son of Count Joseph Karl.
July 23, 1871, Coburg — March 4, 1940, Bayerhof
m. July 26, 1905, Langenzell

* **Ilka,** Princess zu Löwenstein-Wertheim-Freudenberg, daughter of 5th Fürst Alfred zu Löwenstein-Wertheim-Freudenberg and of his wife, Countess Pauline von Reichenbach-Lessonitz.
January 9, 1887, Langenzell — March 31, 1971, Bayerhof

Issue: 1. Alfred Friedrich, Count zu Ortenburg (1906–)
m. Jutta von Lücken (1906–)
see: *zu Ortenburg* XXI, 2, page 780

2. Aribo, Count zu Ortenburg
March 31, 1908, Paris — May 18, 1934, Kiel

3. Amelie, Countess zu Ortenburg (1909–)
m. Heinrich, Burggraf and Count zu Dohna-Schlobitten (1907–1940)
see: *zu Dohna-Schlobitten* XXI, page 685

4. Pauline, Countess zu Ortenburg (1913–)
m. Christian, Prince zur Lippe-Weissenfeld (1907–)
see: *zur Lippe-Weissenfeld* XXI, page 756

5. Udo Wilhelm, Count zu Ortenburg
May 20, 1915, Bayerhof Castle — June 11, 1942, Kharkov, Ukraine, killed in action in World War II

6. Joachim, Count zu Ortenburg
October 10, 1918, Bayerhof Castle — September 1, 1941, on the Dnieper River in Russia, killed in action in World War II

7. Georg, Count zu Ortenburg
February 14, 1922, Bayerhof Castle — January 30, 1944, Apeldoorn, The Netherlands, killed in action in World War II

XXI. zu Ortenburg 2, from page 779

* **Alfred Friedrich,** Count zu Ortenburg, eldest son of Count Friedrich.
May 12, 1906, Berlin —
m. May 28, 1936, Berlin
Jutta von Lücken, daughter of Leopold von Lücken and of his wife, Irmgard von Brünneck.
June 21, 1906, Danzig —

Issue: 1. Botho, Count zu Ortenburg, April 21, 1937, Würzburg —
(m. January 9, 1971, Masendorf, Ilse, Baroness von dem Bussche-Haddenhausen, born April 16, 1943, Masendorf.
1. Anna-Madeleine, Countess zu Ortenburg
October 28, 1971, Lübeck —)

2. Engelbert, Count zu Ortenburg (1939–)
m. Margot Pöllmann (1942–)
see: *zu Ortenburg* XXI, 3, below

3. Ilka, Countess zu Ortenburg
June 29, 1942, Würzburg —
(m. October 9, 1971, Schonungen/Main, * Johan, Duke of Oldenburg, see page 209.)

4. Joachim, Count zu Ortenburg
May 26, 1944, Würzburg —
(m. October 10, 1970, Bodenwerder, Ilsabe von Brünneck, born September 28, 1945, Hamburg.)

5. Yvonne, Countess zu Ortenburg
January 2, 1948, Würzburg —
(m. July 18, 1970, Bayerhof, Ludwig von Breitenbuch, born September 23, 1935,
1. Georg-Ludwig von Breitenbuch
June 19, 1971, Göttingen —)

XXI. zu Ortenburg 3, from above

* **Engelbert,** Count zu Ortenburg, second son of Count Alfred Friedrich.
March 11, 1939, Würzburg —
m. March 6, 1965, Montreal, Canada
Margot Pöllmann, daughter of Georg Pöllmann and of his wife, Theodora Pavity.
August 5, 1942, Berlin —

Issue: 1. Peter Jens, Count zu Ortenburg, March 1, 1970, Pointe Claire, Quebec, Canada —

XXI. VON DER OSTEN 1, from page 54

Dinnies von der Osten
May 21, 1929, Köslin, Pommerania —
m. September 12, 1958, Bonn
* **Felicitas,** Princess of Prussia, daughter of Prince Wilhelm of Prussia and of his wife, Dorothea von Salviati.
June 7, 1934, Bonn —

Issue: 1. Friederike von der Osten
July 14, 1959, Godesberg —

2. Dinnies von der Osten
February 15, 1962, Godesberg —

3. Hubertus von der Osten
May 5, 1964, Reinbach, near Hamburg —

4. Cecilie von der Osten
March 12, 1967, —

XXI. VON PAGENHARDT 1, from page 936

Robert, Baron von Pagenhardt
April 28, 1852, Brunswick — September 16, 1922, Baden-Baden
m. May 15, 1878, Wächtersbach. Divorced: June 9, 1899,
* **Alexandra,** Princess zu Ysenburg und Büdingen in Wächtersbach, daughter of Prince Ferdinand Maximilian III, Fürst zu Ysenburg und Büdingen in Wächtersbach, and of his wife, Princess Auguste von Hanau, Countess von Schaumburg.
December 28, 1855, Wächtersbach — October 24, 1932, Munich
(She m. 1: and divorced: Adalbert, Prince zu Ysenburg und Büdingen in Büdingen – see: *zu Ysenburg und Büdingen in Büdingen* XXI, page 940.)

Issue: see: *von Pagenhardt,* Addendum, page 1067

XXI. VON PAPPENHEIM 1, from page 707

Haupt, Count von Pappenheim, son of Count Klemens.
February 16, 1869, Tölz, Austria — January 26, 1954, Munich
m. January 11, 1916,

XXI. von Pappenheim 1 continued

★ **Ellinka,** Baroness von Fabrice, daughter of Baron Maximilian von Fabrice and of his wife, Countess Ilma Almásy von Zsadány und Török-Szent-Miklós.
May 30, 1875, Marseilles, France — August 19, 1938, Munich
(She m. 1: and divorced: Dr. Paul von Gans – see: *von Gans* XXI, page 714.)

No Issue.

XXI. VON PAWEL-RAMMINGEN 1, from page 27

Alfons, Baron von Pawel-Rammingen
July 27, 1843, Coburg — November 20, 1932,
m. April 24, 1880, Windsor Castle
★ **Friederike,** Princess of Hanover, daughter of King Georg V of Hanover and of his wife, Princess Marie of Saxe-Altenburg.
January 9, 1848, Hanover — October 16, 1926, Biarritz, France

Issue: 1. Viktoria, Baroness von Pawel-Rammingen
March 7, 1881, London — March 27, 1881, London

XXI. PETERSEN 1, from page 787

Jürgen Petersen
September 13, 1913, Hamburg —
m. April 21, 1949, Hamburg
★ **Eleonore-Renata,** Countess von Pückler, daughter of Count Karl Friedrich, 3rd Count von Pückler-Burghauss, and of his wife, Princess Olga Elisabeth of Saxe-Altenburg.
November 25, 1919, Friedland —
(She m. 1: and divorced: Manfred, Baron von Schröder – see: *von Schröder* XXI, page 836.)

Issue: 1. Marcus Petersen
December 6, 1950, Hamburg —

2. Sylvius Petersen
January 12, 1959, Bremen —

XXI. PETZNEK 1, from page 354

Leopold Petznek
June 6, 1881, Bruck — July 27, 1956, Vienna
m. May 4, 1948, Vienna
* **Elisabeth,** Archduchess of Austria, daughter of Crown Prince Rudolf of Austria and of his wife, Princess Stephanie of Belgium.
September 2, 1883, Laxenburg — March 22, 1963, Vienna
(She m. 1: and divorced: Otto, Prince Windisch-Graetz – see: *Windisch-Graetz* XXI, page 918.)

No Issue.

XXI. VON PFETTEN-ARNBACH 1, from page 712

Friedrich Hubert, Baron von Pfetten-Arnbach
July 12, 1921, Peuerbach Castle —
m. January 30, 1951, Herdringen Castle
* **Cäcilia,** Countess von Fürstenberg-Herdringen, daughter of Count Wenemar von Fürstenberg-Herdringen and of his wife, Countess Marie Elisabeth von Matuschka, Baroness von Topolczan und Spaetgan.
April 5, 1928, Herdringen —

Issue: 1. Emanuela, Baroness von Pfetten-Arnbach
June 16, 1952, Peuerbach —

2. Georg Christian, Baron von Pfetten-Arnbach
July 1, 1954, Peuerbach —

3. Stephan Marquard, Baron von Pfetten-Arnbach
November 11, 1956, Peuerbach—

4. Maria Verena, Baroness von Pfetten-Arnbach
March 11, 1958, Peuerbach —

XXI. von Pfetten-Arnbach 2, from page 713

Marquard, Baron von Pfetten-Arnbach
August 17, 1926, Meiningen —
m. April 28, 1961, Herdringen
* **Maria Luise,** Baroness von Fürstenberg-Herdringen, daughter of Count Wenemar von Fürstenberg-Herdringen and of his wife, Countess Marie Elisabeth von Matuschka, Baroness von Topolczan und Spaetgan.
July 4, 1937, Herdringen —

Issue: 1. Marie-Isabelle, Baroness von Pfetten-Arnbach
April 14, 1967, Neheim-Hüsten —

XXI. VON PIATTI 1, from page 387

Manfred, Count and Marquess von Piatti
July 22, 1924, Loosdorf Castle —
m. April 29, 1948, Vienna
* **Mechtildis,** Countess von Habsburg-Lorraine, daughter of Archduke Leo Karl of Austria and of his wife, Marie von Tuillieres, Comtesse Montjoye-Vaufrey et de la Roche, created Countess von Habsburg.
August 14, 1924, Lissa, near Posen —

Issue: 1. Andrea, Countess von Piatti
February 3, 1949, Vienna —

2. Alfons, Count von Piatti
September 13, 1950, Vienna —

3. Michael, Count von Piatti
January 23, 1955, Vienna —

4. Ferdinand, Count von Piatti
March 23, 1962, Vienna —

5. Benedikt, Count von Piatti
March 21, 1966, Vienna —

XXI. PICARD (von Morsey) 1, from page 914

Andreas Picard, Baron von Morsey
July 1, 1888, Hohenbrugg — July 7, 1951, Vienna
m. May 20, 1916, Haasberg. Divorced: May, 1937,
* **Olga,** Princess Windisch-Graetz, daughter of Prince Hugo Windisch-Graetz and of his wife, Princess Christine von Auersperg-Breunner.
March 5, 1893, Gonobitz —
(She m. 2: Hubertus, Count von Ledebur-Wicheln - see: *von Ledebur-Wicheln* XXI, page 742.)

No Issue.

XXI. PILTZ 1, from page 727

Hans Hermann Piltz
September 16, 1930, —
m. July 13, 1963,
* **Oda Marie Hug,** daughter of Rudolf Hug and of his wife, Princess Marie Therese of Prussia.
July 8, 1937, Freiburg im Breisgau —

Issue: 1. Luise Dorothea Piltz
May 25, 1965, Frankfurt-am-Main —

XXI. VON PLESSEN 1, from page 924

Johann, Baron von Plessen-Cronstern
July 10, 1890, Fiume, Italy — September 4, 1961, Friedrichsruh
m. April 18, 1932, Hohenthurm
* **Marie von Wuthenau-Hohenthurm,** daughter of Count Carl Adam von Wuthenau-Hohenthurm and of his first wife, Countess Maria Antonia Chotek von Chotkowa und Wognin.
January 28, 1909, Borna, near Leipzig —

Issue: 1. Helene, Baroness von Plessen (1933-)
m. Emanuel, Count von Sternberg (1927-)
see: *von Sternberg* XXI, page 854

XXI. von Plessen 1 continued

2. Helmold, Baron von Plessen (1935–)
m. Silvia, Baroness von Schröder (1941–)
see: *von Plessen* XXI, 2, below

3. Karl-Peter, Baron von Plessen
March 28, 1938, Rome —

4. Christian, Baron von Plessen
January 29, 1940, Rome — November 26, 1948, Kiel

5. Monika, Baroness von Plessen (1940–)
m. Christian, Prince zu Ysenburg und Büdingen (1943–)
see: *zu Ysenburg und Büdingen* XXI, page 939

XXI. von Plessen 2, from above

* **Helmold,** Baron von Plessen, eldest son of Baron Johann.
March 2, 1935, Berlin —
m. May 26, 1964, Krummensee
Silvia, Baroness von Schröder, daughter of Baron Rudolf von Schröder and of his wife, Vera von Bonin.
September 3, 1941, Bliestorf —

Issue: 1. Johann Christian, Baron von Plessen
April 21, 1965, Kiel —

2. Magnus-Leopold, Baron von Plessen
August 3, 1967, Kiel —

XXI. VON PREYSING-LICHTENEGG-MOOS 1, from page 469

Johann Georg, Count von Preysing-Lichtenegg-Moos
December 17, 1887, Moos, Bavaria — March 17, 1924, Munich
m. February 23, 1919, Wildenwart Castle, Bavaria
* **Gundeline,** Princess of Bavaria, daughter of King Ludwig III of Bavaria and of his wife, Archduchess Maria Theresa of Austria.
August 26, 1891, Munich —

XXI. von Preysing-Lichtenegg-Moos 1 continued

Issue: 1. Maria Theresia, Countess von Preysing-Lichtenegg-Moos (1922–)
m. 1: Ludwig, Count von Arco-Zinneburg (1913–1942)
see: *von Arco-Zinneburg* XXI, page 643
m. 2: Ulrich-Philipp, Count von Arco-Zinneburg (1917–)
see: *von Arco-Zinneburg* XXI, page 643

XXI. VON PÜCKLER-BURGHAUSS 1, from page 273

Karl Friedrich, 3rd Count von Pückler-Burghauss, Baron von Groditz.
October 7, 1886, Breslau — May 13, 1945, Cimelice, Poland
m. May 20, 1913, Reichen, near Namslau
* **Olga Elisabeth,** Princess of Saxe-Altenburg, daughter of Prince Albrecht of Saxe-Altenburg and of his wife, Princess Marie of Prussia.
April 17, 1886, Albrechtsberg Castle — January 13, 1955, Münster

Issue: 1. Ella, Count von Pückler (1914–)
m. Andreas Friedrich von Flotow (1913–)
see: *von Flotow* XXI, page 708

2. Eleonore-Renata, Countess von Pückler (1919–)
m. 1: and divorced: Manfred, Baron von Schröder (1914–)
see: *von Schröder* XXI, page 836
m. 2: Jürgen Petersen (1913–)
see: *Petersen* XXI, page 782

XXI. VON QUADT ZU WYKRADT UND ISNY 1, from page 471

Paul, 4th Fürst von Quadt zu Wykradt und Isny
November 28, 1930, Isny —
m. September 3, 1955, Nymphenburg Castle
* **Charlotte,** Princess of Bavaria, twin daughter of Prince Albrecht of Bavaria and of his wife, Countess Maria (Marita) Draskovich von Trakostjan.
May 30, 1931, Munich —

Issue: 1. Alexander, Hereditary Count von Quadt zu Wykradt und Isny
January 18, 1958, Munich —

XXI. von Quadt zu Wykradt und Isny 1 continued

2. Maria Anna, Countess von Quadt zu Wykradt und Isny
April 8, 1960, Friedrichshafen —

3. Gina, Countess von Quadt zu Wykradt und Isny
December 28, 1962, Friedrichshafen —

4. Bertram, Count von Quadt zu Wykradt und Isny
October 23, 1966, Ravensburg —

XXI. VON QUERNHEIM

1, from page 817

Felix, Baron von Quernheim
April 29, 1891, Vorwerk —
m. May 11, 1920, Ringelsbruch
* **Hermine,** Countess von Hagenburg, daughter of Prince Otto of Schaumburg-Lippe and of his wife, Anna von Koppen, created Countess von Hagenburg.
August 27, 1898, Longeville, near Metz — March 11, 1963, Holterhöfe

Issue: 1. Elimar Otto, Baron von Quernheim
May 12, 1921, Darmstadt —

2. Hermine Elisabeth, Baroness von Quernheim (1923–)
m. Ewald Kempkens (1915–)
see: *Kempkens* XXI, page 731

XXI. ZU RANTZAU

1, from page 171

Ernst Ludwig, Count zu Rantzau
May 29, 1869, Schleswig — November 27, 1930, Schleswig
m. October 14, 1894, Noer. Divorced: February 8, 1916, Berlin
* **Carmelita Luise,** Countess von Noer, daughter of Prince/Count Christian von Noer and of his wife, Carmelita Eisenblat.
April 22, 1871, Noer — May 9, 1948, Noer
(She m. 2: Rudolf Humbert – see: *Humbert* XXI, page 728.)

Issue: 1. Friedrich August, Count zu Rantzau (1895–1945)
m. Ehrengard Martha, Countess von der Schulenberg (1906–)
see: *zu Rantzau* XXI, 2, page 789

XXI. von Rantzau 2, from page 788

* **Friedrich August,** Count zu Rantzau, only son of Count Ernst Ludwig.
October 12, 1895, Kiel — December , 1945, Tkwibuli, Caucasus, in a Russian internment camp
m. June 20, 1944, Neumühle, near Salzwedel
Ehrengard Martha, Countess von der Schulenberg, daughter of Count Albrecht von der Schulenberg and of his wife, Countess Erna von Pelken.
October 23, 1906, Berlin —

No Issue.

XXI. RAUSCH 1, from page 937

Hans Rausch
October 8, 1886, Worms — April 22, 1961, Rheinbach
m. January 9, 1919, Wächtersbach. Divorced: March 1, 1941,
* **Anne,** Princess zu Ysenburg und Büdingen in Wächtersbach, daughter of Prince Friedrich Wilhelm zu Ysenburg und Büdingen in Wächtersbach and of his wife, Countess Anna Dobrzensky von Dobrzenicz.
June 19, 1887, Wächtersbach — September 5, 1954, Marburg

Issue: see: *Rausch*, Addendum, page 1083

XXI. VON RECHBERG UND ROTHENLÖWEN ZU HOHENRECHBERG
1, from page 801

Friedrich-Ernst, Count von Rechberg und Rothenlöwen zu Hohenrechberg.
August 3, 1919, Schräbsdorf Castle, Silesia — April 30, 1965, Regensburg
m. September 10, 1956, Herdringen Castle
* **Rose-Marie,** Countess Saurma von der Jeltsch-Lorzendorf, daughter of Count Karl Anton Saurma von der Jeltsch-Lorzendorf and of his wife, Countess Maria-Lory von Matuschka, Baroness von Topolczan und Spaetgan.
December 4, 1931, Lorzendorf —

Issue: 1. Fiona-Pia, Countess von Rechberg von Rothenlöwen zu Hohenrechberg
March 8, 1958, Munich —

XXI. von Rechberg und Rothenlöwen zu Hohenrechberg 1 continued

2. Max Emanuel, Count von Rechberg und Rothenlöwen zu Hohenrechberg
September 25, 1959, Munich —

XXI. REINHOLD 1, from page 68

Hanns Reinhold
November 20, 1917, Berlin-Charlottenburg —
m. September 12, 1942, Potsdam. Divorced: June 2, 1949, Hamm
* **Luise Viktoria,** Princess of Prussia, daughter of Prince Friedrich Sigismund of Prussia and of his wife, Princess Marie Luise of Schaumburg-Lippe.
August 23, 1917, Klein-Glienicke —

Issue: 1. Manfred Reinhold
February 13, 1943, Frankfurt-am-Main —

XXI. RIECK 1, from page 142

Bruno Rieck
May 19, 1927, Hamburg-Ahrensburg —
m. June 8, 1963, Herleshausen
* **Johanna,** Princess of Hesse(-Philippsthal-Barchfeld), daughter of Prince Wilhelm, Landgrave of Hesse(-Philippsthal-Barchfeld), and of his wife, Princess Marianne of Prussia.
November 22, 1937, Augustenau Castle —
(She m. 1: and divorced: Alfons Kuhn – see: *Kuhn* XXI, page 738.)

Issue: 1. Bruno Armin Rieck
January 9, 1964, Hamburg —

2. Monika Rieck
April 18, 1965, Hamburg —

3. Renata Rieck
February 13, 1968, Hamburg —

XXI. VON RIEDEMANN 1, from page 918

Karl Anton von Riedemann
October 3, 1931, Samaden —
m. May 16, 1961, Trieste
* **Olga,** Princess Windisch-Graetz, daughter of Prince Eduard Windisch-Graetz and of his wife, Princess Alexandra (Alix) zu Ysenburg-Birstein.
October 26, 1934, Graz, Austria —

Issue: 1. Mario von Riedemann
April 7, 1962, Vancouver, British Columbia, Canada —

2. Peter von Riedemann
October 20, 1963, Vancouver —

3. Mark von Riedemann
October 20, 1964, Victoria, British Columbia —

4. Cecilia von Riedemann
November 4, 1965, Victoria —

XXI. VON RINTELEN 1, from page 111

Enno von Rintelen
November 9, 1921, Berlin —
m. May 25, 1965, Wiesbaden
* **Clothilde Elisabeth,** Countess von Merenberg, daughter of Count Georg von Merenberg and of his second wife, Elisabeth Anna Müller Uri.
May 14, 1941, Wiesbaden —

Issue: 1. Alexander von Rintelen
March 23, 1966, Wiesbaden —

XXI. RITTER VON MILLER ZU AICHHOLZ 1, from page 674

Oscar Heinrich Ritter von Miller zu Aichholz
July 7, 1934, Vienna —
m. September 5, 1965, Hochburg, Austria
* **Amelie-Alexandrine,** Countess zu Castell-Castell, daughter of Count Luitpold zu Castell-Castell and of his wife, Princess Alexandrine-Lovisa of Denmark.
May 25, 1938, Berlin —

XXI. Ritter von Miller zu Aichholz 1 continued

Issue: 1. Alexander Ritter von Miller zu Aichholz
August 13, 1966, —

XXI. VON ROTHKIRCH UND TRACH 1, from page 137

Edwin, Count von Rothkirch und Trach
November 1, 1888, Munich —
m. 1: September 16, 1922, Oberurf
* **Albertine,** Countess von Schaumburg, daughter of Prince Philipp von Hanau, Count von Schaumburg, and of his wife, Anne von Trott, created Countess von Schaumburg.
August 23, 1902, Lehrbach — August 29, 1935, Höchst-am-Main
m. 2: October 21, 1959, Frankfurt-am-Main
Hertha von Rath, daughter of
April 2, 1899, Frankfurt-am-Main —
(She m. 1: Felix von Richter-Rettersdorff, who died September 8, 1958.)

Issue of first marriage:
1. Leopold, Count von Rothkirch und Trach (1923–)
m. Gabriele Heintze (1927–)
see: *von Rothkirch und Trach* XXI, 2, below

XXI. von Rothkirch und Trach 2, from above

* **Leopold,** Count von Rothkirch und Trach, only son of Count Edwin.
December 27, 1923, Cassel —
m. January 26, 1950, Schliersee
Gabriele Heintze, daughter of
May 10, 1927, Hanover —

Issue: 1. Leonhard, Count von Rothkirch und Trach
February 28, 1951, Fritzlar —

2. Albertine, Countess von Rothkirch und Trach
February 19, 1954, Fritzlar —

XXI. RUMANN 1, from page 174

Arnold Rumann

—

m. January 7, 1922, Grünholz Castle, Holstein. Divorced: , 1933, Berlin

* **Alexandra Viktoria,** Princess of Schleswig-Holstein-Sonderburg-Glücksburg, daughter of Duke Friedrich Ferdinand of Schleswig-Holstein-Sonderburg-Glücksburg and of his wife, Princess Karoline Mathilde of Schleswig-Holstein-Sonderburg-Augustenburg.

April 21, 1887, Grünholz — April 15, 1957, Lyons, France

(She m. 1: and divorced: August Wilhelm, Prince of Prussia – see: *Prussia* (*Hohenzollern*) II l–1, page 59.)

No Issue.

XXI. SACHS 1, from page 339

Reinhold Sachs

July 28, 1922, Ernstbrunn —

m. January 2, 1959, Ernstbrunn

* **Amadea,** Princess Reuss zu Köstritz, daughter of Prince Heinrich XXXIX Reuss zu Köstritz and of his wife, Countess Antonia zu Castell-Castell.

July 23, 1923, Vienna —

No Issue.

XXI. SAINT-JULIEN-WALLSEE 1, from page 696

Eduard, Count Saint-Julien-Wallsee

March 21, 1895, Hayberg — August 17, 1955, Wolfsegg Castle

m. February 5, 1931, Innsbruck

* **Ottilie (Odile) Marie,** Countess von Enzenberg zum Freyen und Jöchelsthurn, daughter of Count Rudolf Josef von Enzenberg zum Freyen und Jöchelsthurn and of his wife, Countess Auguste Eugenie of Württemberg.

September 16, 1902, Trient —

Issue: 1. Marie Karoline, Countess Saint-Julien-Wallsee (1933–)
m. Karl, Baron von Levetzow (1918–1964)
see: *von Levetzow* XXI, page 747

XXI. Saint-Julien-Wallsee 1 continued

2. Franz de Paul, Count Saint-Julien-Wallsee
December 10, 1933, Wolfsegg —

3. Isabelle, Countess Saint-Julien-Wallsee (1935–)
m. Othmar, Baron von und zu Bodman (1925–)
see: *von und zu Bodman* XXI, page 668

4. Beatrix, Countess Saint-Julien-Wallsee
December 10, 1939, Wolfsegg —

XXI. SALM-REIFFERSCHEIDT, KRAUTHEIM UND DYCK 1, from page 797

Franz Josef, Fürst and Altgraf zu Salm-Reifferscheidt, Krautheim und Dyck, son of Fürst Alfred.
April 7, 1899, Vienna — June 13, 1958, Bonn
m. May 27, 1930, Anholt
* **Cäcilie,** Princess zu Salm-Salm, daughter of Prince Emanuel zu Salm-Salm and of his wife, Archduchess Maria Christina of Austria.
March 8, 1911, Potsdam —

Issue: 1. Marie Christine, Altgräfin zu Salm-Reifferscheidt, Krautheim und Dyck (1932–)
m. Peter, Count Metternich (1929–)
see: *Metternich* XXI, page 771

2. Maria Anna, Altgräfin zu Salm-Reifferscheidt, Krautheim und Dyck (1933–)
m. The Honourable Alexander Campbell Geddes (1911–)
see: *Geddes* XVII, page 520

3. Rosemary, Altgräfin zu Salm-Reifferscheidt, Krautheim und Dyck (1937–)
m. Johannes, Count Hüyn (1930–)
see: *Hüyn* XXI, page 728

4. Isabelle, Altgräfin zu Salm-Reifferscheidt, Krautheim und Dyck (1939–)
m. Franz Albrecht, Duke of Ratibor, Prince of Corvey, Prince of Hohenlohe-Schillingsfürst (1920–)
see: *Hohenlohe-Schillingsfürst* (*Ratibor und Corvey*) XV n–1, page 496

XXI. zu Salm-Reifferscheidt, Krautheim und Dyck 1 continued

5. Gabrielle, Altgräfin zu Salm-Reifferscheidt, Krautheim und Dyck (1941–)
m. Ernst-Friedrich, Count von Goëss (1932–)
see: *von Goëss* XXI, page 714

6. Cäcilie, Altgräfin zu Salm-Reifferscheidt, Krautheim und Dyck
December 14, 1933, Bonn —

7. Georgine, Altgräfin zu Salm-Reifferscheidt, Krautheim und Dyck
November 28, 1947, Bonn — November 22, 1953, Bonn

XXI. ZU SALM-SALM 1, from page 383

Emanuel, Prince zu Salm-Salm, son of Prince Emanuel.
November 30, 1871, Münster — August 19, 1916, Pinsk, Russia, killed in action in World War I
m. May 10, 1902, Vienna
* **Maria Christina,** Archduchess of Austria, daughter of Archduke Friedrich of Austria and of his wife, Princess Isabelle of Croy.
November 17, 1879, Krakow, Poland — August 6, 1962, Anholt

Issue: 1. Isabelle, Princess zu Salm-Salm (1903–)
m. Felix, Count von Loë (1896–1944)
see: *von Loë* XXI, page 757

2. Rosemary, Princess zu Salm-Salm (1904–)
m. Hubert Salvator, Archduke of Austria (1894–)
see: *Austria (Habsburg)* X v–2, page 376

3. Nikolaus, 13th Fürst zu Salm, 8th Fürst zu Salm-Salm, 8th Fürst zu Salm-Kyrburg (1906–)
m. 1: and divorced: Ida, Princess of Wrede (1909–)
m. 2: and divorced: Eleonore von Zitzewitz (1919–)
m. 3: Maria Moret (1930–)
see: *zu Salm-Salm* XXI, 2, page 797

XXI. zu Salm-Salm 2 continued

4. Anna, Princess zu Salm-Salm (twin)
   August 2, 1935, Anholt —

5. Margarethe, Princess zu Salm-Salm (1935–) (twin)
   m. György Solznoki-Scheftsik (1926–1965)
   see: *Solznoki-Scheftsik* XXI, page 847

Issue of second marriage:

6. Ludwig, Prince zu Salm-Salm
   April 15, 1953, Hamburg —

Issue of third marriage:

7. Christian, Prince zu Salm-Salm
   August 25, 1964, Geneva, Switzerland —

XXI. zu Salm-Salm 3, from page 797

* **Karl-Philipp,** Hereditary Prince zu Salm-Salm, second son of Fürst Nikolaus.
May 19, 1933, Anholt —
m. February 4, 1961 (civil), and February 8, 1961 (religious), Munich
Erika von Morgen, daughter of Ernst von Morgen and of his wife,
March 19, 1935, Berlin —

Issue: 1. Emanuel, Prince zu Salm-Salm
   December 6, 1961, Münster —

2. Philipp, Prince zu Salm-Salm
   July 5, 1963, Münster —

3. Felicitas, Princess zu Salm-Salm
   July 1, 1965, Düsseldorf —

XXI. ZU SALM-HORSTMAR

I, from page 674

Philipp Ernst, 4th Fürst und Rheingraf zu Salm-Horstmar, son of 3rd Fürst Otto II.
March 31, 1909, Varlar —
m. July 3, 1937, Hochburg, Austria
* **Marie Therese,** Countess zu Castell-Castell, daughter of Count Otto zu Castell-Castell and of his wife, Princess Amelie zu Löwenstein-Wertheim-Freudenberg.
December 30, 1917, Munich —

Issue: 1. Philipp-Otto, Hereditary Prince zu Salm-Horstmar
June 2, 1938, Münster —

2. Gustav, Prince zu Salm-Horstmar
October 22, 1942, Munich —

3. Johann, Prince zu Salm-Horstmar
July 27, 1949, Münster —

XXI. SANDHOFER

I, from page 372

Friedrich Sandhofer, M.D.
August 1, 1934, Salzburg —
m. August 3, 1964, Mondsee, Austria
* **Elisabeth,** Archduchess of Austria, daughter of Archduke Anton of Austria and of his wife, Princess Ileana of Romania.
January 15, 1942, Sonnberg Castle —

Issue: 1. Anton Dominic Sandhofer
October 26, 1966, Innsbruck —

2. Margareta Elisabeth Sandhofer
September 10, 1968, Innsbruck —

XXI. VON SANDIZELL

I, from page 132

Karl Max, Count von Sandizell
October 4, 1895, Sandizell —
m. January 10, 1922, Salzburg. Divorced: March 5, 1928, Munich

XXI. von Sandizell

1 continued

* **Hildegard,** Princess von Hanau, Countess von Schaumburg, daughter of Prince Friedrich von Hanau und Horowitz, Count von Schaumburg, and of his wife, Countess Hildegard Almásy von Zsadány und Török-Szent-Miklós.

March 12, 1903, Sökking, Bavaria —

(She m. 2: Wulf Diether, Count zu Castell-Rüdenhausen – see: *zu Castell-Rüdenhausen* XXI, page 678.)

Issue: 1. Karl Hochbrand, Count von Sandizell (1924–)
m. Irene M. Rohrer (1937–)
see: *von Sandizell* XXI, 2, below

XXI. von Sandizell

2, from above

* **Karl Hochbrand,** Count von Sandizell, only son of Count Karl Max.

February 9, 1924, Sandizell —

m. July 14, 1957, Düsseldorf

Irene M. Rohrer, daughter of

September 1, 1937, Berlin —

Issue: 1. Nikolaus, Count von Sandizell
January 20, 1959, Düsseldorf —

2. Alexandra, Countess von Sandizell
April 29, 1960, Düsseldorf —

3. Tassilo, Count von Sandizell
April 12, 1963, Düsseldorf —

XXI. SAURMA VON UND ZU DER JELTSCH

1, from page 712

Marinus, Count Saurma von und zu der Jeltsch

March 29, 1924, Suchau, Schleswig —

m. April 29, 1954, Herdringen

* **Margarete,** Baroness von Fürstenberg-Herdringen, daughter of Count Wenemar von Fürstenberg-Herdringen and of his wife, Countess Marie-Elisabeth von Matuschka, Baroness von Topolczan und Spaetgan.

April 5, 1928, Herdringen — April 28, 1960, Plausdorf Castle

m. 2: September 16, 1961, Geneva, Switzerland

Monica Graves, daughter of Alan Percy Graves and of his wife, Countess Marie Luise zu Dohna.

April 27, 1936, Berlin —

XXI. Saurma von und zu der Jeltsch 1 continued

Issue of first marriage:
1. Patrick, Count Saurma von und zu der Jeltsch
August 27, 1956, Herdringen —

Issue of second marriage: Not descendants of King George I
2. Caroline, Countess Saurma von und zu der Jeltsch
July 6, 1962, Marburg —

3. Douglas, Count Saurma von und zu der Jeltsch
September 10, 1966, Marburg —

XXI. SAURMA VON DER JELTSCH-LORZENDORF 1, from page 766

Karl Anton, Count Saurma von der Jeltsch-Lorzendorf
February 15, 1898, Lorzendorf — July 10, 1941, Kharkov, Ukraine, killed in action in World War II
m. January 18, 1927, Breslau
* **Marie-Lory,** Countess von Matuschka, Baroness von Topolczan und Spaetgan, daughter of Count Eberhard von Matuschka, Baron von Topolczan und Spaetgan and of his wife, Countess Elisabeth von Hohenau.
January 31, 1900, Gross-Neukirch — June 21, 1962, Herdringen

Issue: 1. Johannes Arthur, Count Saurma von der Jeltsch-Lorzendorf (1927–)
m. Sybille Roechling (1928–)
see: *Saurma von der Jeltsch-Lorzendorf* XXI, 2, page 802

2. Elisabeth, Countess Saurma von der Jeltsch-Lorzendorf (1929–)
m. Alexander, Baron von Ungelter-Deissenhausen (1920–)
see: *von Ungelter-Deissenhausen* XXI, page 881

3. Rose-Marie, Countess Saurma von der Jeltsch-Lorzendorf (1931–)
m. Friedrich Ernst, Count von Rechberg und Rothenlöwen zu Hohenrechberg (1919–1965)
see: *von Rechberg und Rothenlöwen zu Hohenrechberg* XXI, page 789

XXI. Saurma von der Jeltsch-Lorzendorf 2, from page 801

* **Johannes Arthur,** Count Saurma von der Jeltsch-Lorzendorf, only son of Count Karl Anton.
October 6, 1927, Lorzendorf —
m. April 21, 1956, Heidelberg
Sybille Roechling, daughter of
February 10, 1928, Heidelberg —

Issue: 1. Marie Luisanne, Countess Saurma von der Jeltsch-Lorzendorf
August 11, 1961, Köln —

2. Marie Stephanie, Countess Saurma von der Jeltsch-Lorzendorf
June 7, 1964, Heidelberg —

3. Karl-Anton, Count Saurma von der Jeltsch-Lorzendorf
March 7, 1966, Heidelberg —

XXI. SAVICH 1, from page 144

Michael Savich, M.D.
July 25, 1924, Istanbul, Turkey —
m. June 13, 1952, Lausanne, Switzerland
* **Olga,** Princess of Hesse (-Philippsthal-Barchfeld), daughter of Prince Christian of Hesse (-Philippsthal-Barchfeld) and of his first wife, Elizabeth Reid Rodgers.
December 30, 1921, Paris —

No Issue.

XXI. ZU SAYN-WITTGENSTEIN-BERLEBURG 1, from page 761

Richard, 4th Fürst zu Sayn-Wittgenstein-Berleburg, son of Prince Gustav.
May 27, 1882, Berleburg — April 25, 1925, near Hanau, as a result of a road accident
m. November 21, 1902 (civil), Wiesenbach, and (religious), Langenzell

XXI. zu Sayn-Wittgenstein-Berleburg 1 continued

* **Madeleine,** Princess zu Löwenstein-Wertheim-Freudenberg, daughter of Prince Alfred zu Löwenstein-Wertheim-Freudenberg and of his wife, Countess Pauline von Reichenbach-Lessonitz.

March 8, 1885, Langenzell —

Issue: 1. Gustav Albrecht, 5th Fürst zu Sayn-Wittgenstein-Berleburg (1907–1944)
m. Margareta Fouché (1909–)
see: *zu Sayn-Wittgenstein-Berleburg* XXI, 2, below

2. Christian Heinrich, Prince zu Sayn-Wittgenstein-Berleburg (1908–)
by adoption: Prince zu Sayn-Wittgenstein-Hohenstein
m. 1: and divorced: Beatrix, Countess von Bismarck-Schönhausen (1921–)
m. 2: Dagmar, Princess zu Sayn-Wittgenstein-Hohenstein (1919–)
see: *zu Sayn-Wittgenstein-Hohenstein* XXI, page 804

3. Ludwig Ferdinand, Prince zu Sayn-Wittgenstein-Berluburg (1910–1943)
m. Friederike Juliane, Princess zu Salm-Horstmar (1912–)
see: *zu Sayn-Wittgenstein-Berleburg* XXI, 5, page 806

XXI. zu Sayn-Wittgenstein-Berleburg 2, from above

* **Gustav Albrecht,** 5th Fürst zu Sayn-Wittgenstein-Berleburg, eldest son of Fürst Richard.

February 28, 1907, Berleburg — 1944, somewhere in Russia, missing presumed killed in action in World War II

m. January 26, 1934, Björnlunda, Sweden

Margareta Fouché, daughter of Count Carl Fouché, 6th Duke d'Otrante, and of his wife, Countess Madeleine Douglas.

March 27, 1909, Elghammar, near Björnlunda —

Issue: 1. Richard, 6th Fürst zu Sayn-Wittgenstein-Berleburg (1934–)
m. Benedikte, Princess of Denmark (1944–)
see: *zu Sayn-Wittgenstein-Berleburg* XXI, 3, page 804

XXI. zu Sayn-Wittgenstein-Berleburg

2 continued

2. Madeleine, Princess zu Sayn-Wittgenstein-Berleburg (1936–)
   m. Otto, Hereditary Count zu Solms-Laubach (1926–)
   see: *zu Solms-Laubach* XXI, page 842

3. Robin, Prince zu Sayn-Wittgenstein-Berleburg
   January 29, 1938, Giessen —
   (m. January 29, 1970, New York City, Birgitta av Klercher, born April 1, 1942
   1. Sebastian, Prince zu Sayn-Wittgenstein-Berleburg
      January 30, 1971, New York City —)

4. Tatjana, Princess zu Sayn-Wittgenstein-Berleburg (1940–)
   m. Moritz, Hereditary Prince of Hesse (1926–)
   see: *Hesse* IV d–7, page 128

5. Pia, Princess zu Sayn-Wittgenstein-Berleburg
   December 8, 1942, Giessen —

XXI. zu Sayn-Wittgenstein-Berleburg

3, from pages 803, 182

* **Richard,** 6th Fürst zu Sayn-Wittgenstein-Berleburg, eldest son of Fürst Gustav Albrecht.
October 29, 1934, Giessen —
m. February 3, 1968, Fredensborg Castle, near Copenhagen

* **Benedikte,** Princess of Denmark, daughter of King Frederik IX of Denmark and of his wife, Princess Ingrid of Sweden.
April 29, 1944, Amalienborg Castle, Copenhagen —

Issue: 1. Gustav, Prince zu Sayn-Wittgenstein-Berleburg
   January 12, 1969, Frankfurt-am-Main —

2. Alexandra, Princess zu Sayn-Wittgenstein-Berleburg
   November 20, 1970, Frankfurt-am-Main —

XXI. zu Sayn-Wittgenstein-Berleburg (ZU SAYN-WITTGENSTEIN-HOHENSTEIN)

4, from page 803

* **Christian Heinrich,** 5th Fürst zu Sayn-Wittgenstein-Hohenstein, born Prince zu Sayn-Wittgenstein-Berleburg, adopted in 1927 by the 4th Fürst August zu Sayn-Wittgenstein-Hohenstein, second son of 4th Fürst Richard zu Sayn-Wittgenstein-Berleburg.

XXI. zu Sayn-Wittgenstein-Berleburg (zu Sayn-Wittgenstein-Hohenstein) 4 continued

September 20, 1908, Berleburg —
m. 1: March 28, 1945, Berleburg. Divorced: November 27, 1951, Siegen

Beatrix, Countess von Bismarck-Schönhausen, daughter of Count Nikolaus von Bismarck-Schönhausen and of his wife, Brigitte von Wickstedt-Peterswaldt.
June 20, 1921, Varzin —
(She m. 2: October 11, 1961, Munich, Kai von Mengersen, born September 28, 1926.)
m. 2: November 4, 1960 (civil), Arfeld, and (religious) at Schwarzenau über Berleburg

Dagmar, Princess zu Sayn-Wittgenstein-Hohenstein, daughter of Prince Georg zu Sayn-Wittgenstein-Hohenstein and of his wife, Marie Rühm, Baroness von Freusburg.
November 16, 1919, Eisenach —
(She m. 1: April 24, 1942, Eisenach, divorced: June 15, 1954, Cassel, Hans Karl Zirkel, M.D., born January 20, 1913, Erfurt.)

Issue of first marriage:

1. Loretta, Princess zu Sayn-Wittgenstein-Hohenstein (1946–)
   m. Lanzo, Baron Wambolt von Umstadt (1934–)
   see: *Wambolt von Umstadt* XXI, page 901

2. Johanna, Princess zu Sayn-Wittgenstein-Hohenstein
   October 22, 1948, Wittgenstein —
   (m. September 20, 1970, Langenstein, Count Axel Douglas, born July 22, 1943, Konstanz.)

3. Albrecht, Prince zu Sayn-Wittgenstein-Hohenstein
   March 11, 1950, Wittgenstein — March 2, 1953, Langenreid, as a result of a fall

Issue of second marriage:

4. Madeleine, Princess zu Sayn-Wittgenstein-Hohenstein
   March 17, 1961, Marburg —

5. Bernhart, Hereditary Prince zu Sayn-Wittgenstein-Hohenstein
   November 15, 1962, Marburg —

XXI. zu Sayn-Wittgenstein-Berleburg 5, from page 803

* **Ludwig Ferdinand,** Prince zu Sayn-Wittgenstein-Berleburg, third son of Fürst Richard.
April 4, 1910, Berleburg — November 22, 1943, near Shitomir, Russia, killed in action in World War II
m. August 5, 1935, Varlar
Friederike Juliane, Princess zu Salm-Horstmar, daughter of Fürst Otto zu Salm-Horstmar and of his wife, Countess Rose zu Solms-Baruth.
October 5, 1912, Varlar —

Issue: 1. Marita, Princess zu Sayn-Wittgenstein-Berleburg
August 15, 1936, Osterwick —
(m. January 9, 1971, Belburg, Ulrich, Count Grote)

2. Otto-Ludwig, Prince zu Sayn-Wittgenstein-Berleburg
February 25, 1938, Osterwick —
(m. January 28, 1965, Stuttgart, Baroness von Cramm
1. Stanislaus, Prince zu Sayn-Wittgenstein-Berleburg, September 5, 1965, Stuttgart —
2. Stefanie-Christina, Princess zu Sayn-Wittgenstein-Berleburg, December 25, 1966, Stuttgart —)

3. Johann-Stanislaus, Prince zu Sayn-Wittgenstein-Berleburg
August 9, 1939, Osterwick —

4. Ludwig-Ferdinand, Prince zu Sayn-Wittgenstein-Berleburg
January 25, 1942, Osterwick —

5. Ulrike-Christine, Princess zu Sayn-Wittgenstein-Berleburg
January 21, 1944, Kruden, Altmark —

XXI. zu Sayn-Wittgenstein-Berleburg 6, from page 762

Otto-Konstantin, Prince zu Sayn-Wittgenstein-Berleburg, only son of Prince Franz.
June 11, 1878, Munich — November 16, 1955, Bad Ischl
m. 1: September 25, 1909, Langenzell. Divorced: April 13, 1923, Munich
* **Elisabeth,** Princess zu Löwenstein-Wertheim-Freudenberg, daughter of Prince Alfred, 5th Fürst zu Löwenstein-Wertheim-Freudenberg, and of his wife, Countess Pauline von Reichenbach-Lessonitz.
May 5, 1890, Langenzell — March 9, 1953, Frankfurt-am-Main
(She m. 2: Richard Merton – see: *Merton* XXI, page 762.)

XXI. zu Sayn-Wittgenstein-Berleburg 6 continued

m. 2: June 3, 1929, Munich
Ilse Lampl, daughter of Dr. Rudolf Lampl and of his wife, Anna Schausberger.
August 26, 1901, Linz, Austria —

Issue of first marriage:

1. Franz Wilhelm, Prince zu Sayn-Wittgenstein-Berleburg (1910–)
   m. Gabriele, Princess zu Ysenburg und Büdingen in Wächtersbach (1911–)
   see: *zu Sayn-Wittgenstein-Berleburg* XXI, 7, below

2. August Richard, Prince zu Sayn-Wittgenstein-Berleburg
   December 22, 1913, Munich — December 22, 1939, Berlin, murdered by the Gestapo

3. Casimir-Johannes, Prince zu Sayn-Wittgenstein-Berleburg (1917–)
   m. 1: and divorced: Ingrid Alsen (1915–)
   m. 2: Iris Ryle (1917–)
   see: *zu Sayn-Wittgenstein-Berleburg* XXI, 8, page 808

4. Gottfried, Prince zu Sayn-Wittgenstein-Berleburg
   September 16, 1920, Giessen — November 28, 1941, Rshew, Russia, killed in action in World War II

XXI. zu Sayn-Wittgenstein-Berleburg 7, from above and page 938

* **Franz Wilhelm,** Prince zu Sayn-Wittgenstein-Berleburg, eldest son of Prince Otto-Konstantin.
August 24, 1910, Frankfurt-am-Main —
m. February 21, 1942, Berlin
* **Gabriele,** Princess zu Ysenburg und Büdingen in Wächtersbach, daughter of Hereditary Prince Ferdinand zu Ysenburg und Büdingen in Wächtersbach and of his wife, Countess Margita von Dönhoff.
November 23, 1911, Potsdam —

No Issue.

XXI. zu Sayn-Wittgenstein-Berleburg

8, from page 807

* **Casimir-Johannes,** Prince zu Sayn-Wittgenstein-Berleburg, son of Prince Otto-Konstantin.
January 22, 1917, Frankfurt-am-Main —
m. 1: April 21, 1939, Hamburg. Divorced: October 18, 1949, Hamburg

Ingrid Alsen, daughter of Lucian Alsen and of his wife, Viktoria Lücken.
April 12, 1915, Hamburg —
(She m. 2: December 6, 1950, Hamburg, Wilhelm Ernst, Baron von Cramm, born September 30, 1917, Brüggen.)
m. 2: May 1, 1950, London, England

Iris Ryle, daughter of Edward Hewish Ryle and of his wife, Anne Rhodes Moorhouse.
May 16, 1917, Brüggen —

Issue of first marriage:

1. Christian Peter, Prince zu Sayn-Wittgenstein-Berleburg (1940–)
m. Felizitas, Princess Reuss zu Köstritz (1946–)
see: *zu Sayn-Wittgenstein-Berleburg* XXI, 9, page 809

2. Leonille Elisabeth, Princess zu Sayn-Wittgenstein-Berleburg (1941–)
m. Wolfgang-Ernst, Hereditary Prince zu Ysenburg und Büdingen (1936–)
see: *zu Ysenburg und Büdingen* XXI, page 939

Issue of second marriage:

3. Richard Casimir, Prince zu Sayn-Wittgenstein-Berleburg
March 21, 1952, London —

4. Johannes Karl, Prince zu Sayn-Wittgenstein-Berleburg
September 30, 1953, London —

XXI. zu Sayn-Wittgenstein-Berleburg 9, from pages 808, 346

* **Christian Peter,** Prince zu Sayn-Wittgenstein-Berleburg, eldest son of Prince Casimir-Johannes.
February 5, 1940, Hamburg —
m. July 1, 1967, Roheim
* **Felizitas,** Princess Reuss zu Köstritz, daughter of Prince Heinrich III Reuss zu Köstritz and of his first wife, Baroness Franziska Mayr von Melnhof.
October 26, 1946, Frohnleiten-Mauritzen —

Issue: 1. Carl Constantin, Prince zu Sayn-Wittgenstein-Berleburg
June 2, 1968, Düsseldorf —

XXI. SCHÄFER 1, from page 708

Wilhelm Schäfer
January 20, 1868, Ottrau, Hesse — January 19, 1952, Ludwigshafen
m. May 26, 1917, Hofheim, Taunus
* **Blanche,** Baroness von Fabrice, daughter of Baron Maximilian von Fabrice and of his wife, Countess Ilma Almásy von Zsadány und Török-Szent-Miklós.
April 5, 1880, Göttlieben —
(She m. 1: and divorced: Emanuel, Baron von Bodman – see: *von Bodman* XXI, page 668.)

Issue: 1. Klaus Schäfer (1910–)
m. Roza Honstetter (1920–); see: *Schäfer*, Addendum, page 1071

XXI. SCHAFFGOTSCH GENANNT SEMPERFREI VON UND ZU KYNAST VON GREIFFENSTEIN 1, from page 924

Hans Ulrich, Count Schaffgotsch genannt Semperfrei von und zu Kynast von Greiffenstein, Baron von Trachenberg
July 10, 1927, Koppitz —
m. July 19, 1949, Wolfegg
* **Sidonie von Wuthenau-Hohenthurm,** daughter of Count Carl Adam von Wuthenau-Hohenthurm and of his wife, Countess Marie von Waldburg zu Wolfegg und Waldsee.
December 31, 1923, Hohenthurm —

Issue: 1. Hans Ulrich, Count Schaffgotsch genannt Semperfrei von und zu Kynast von Greiffenstein
April 4, 1950, Regensburg —

XXI. Schaffgotsch genannt Semperfrei von und zu Kynast von Greiffenstein 1 continued

2. Karl-Friedrich, Count Schaffgotsch genannt Semperfrei von und zu Kynast von Greiffenstein
July 4, 1951, Rio de Janeiro, Brazil —

3. Sophie, Countess Schaffgotsch genannt Semperfrei von und zu Kynast von Greiffenstein
July 19, 1952, Rio de Janeiro —

4. Christof-Bernhard, Count Schaffgotsch genannt Semperfrei von und zu Kynast von Greiffenstein
January 21, 1954, Rio de Janeiro —

5. Desirée, Countess Schaffgotsch genannt Semperfrei von und zu Kynast von Greiffenstein
January 31, 1962, Rio de Janeiro —

XXI. VON SCHALBURG 1, from page 212

Jürgen von Schalburg
July 22, 1907, Schildfeld —
m. June 25, 1937, Basedow
* **Alexandra,** Countess von Welsburg, daughter of Count Alexander von Welsburg and of his wife, Countess Luise von Hahn.
December 25, 1910, La Tour, near Vevey, Switzerland —

Issue:

XXI. SCHAUMBURG-LIPPE 1, from page 892

Adolf Georg, Fürst zu Schaumburg-Lippe, son of Fürst Georg.
August 1, 1817, Bückeburg — May 8, 1893, Bückeburg
m. October 25, 1844, Arolsen
* **Hermine,** Princess zu Waldeck und Pyrmont, daughter of Fürst Georg Friedrich zu Waldeck und Pyrmont and of his wife, Princess Emma of Anhalt-Bernberg-Schaumburg-Hoym.
September 29, 1827, Arolsen — February 16, 1910, Bückeburg

XXI. Schaumburg-Lippe 1 continued

Issue: 1. Hermine, Princess of Schaumburg-Lippe (1845–1930)
m. Maximilian, Duke of Württemberg (1828–1888)
see: *Württemberg* VI h–2, page 234

2. Georg, Prince of Schaumburg-Lippe (1846–1911)
m. Marie, Princess of Saxe-Altenburg (1864–1918)
see: *Schaumburg-Lippe* XXI, 2, below

3. Hermann, Prince of Schaumburg-Lippe
May 19, 1848, Bückeburg — December 29, 1918, Bückeburg

4. Emma, Princess of Schaumburg-Lippe
December 16, 1850, Bückeburg — November 25, 1855,

5. Ida, Princess of Schaumburg-Lippe (1852–1891)
m. Heinrich XXII, Prince Reuss zu Greiz (1846–1902)
see: *Reuss* IX b–2, page 335

6. Otto, Prince of Schaumburg-Lippe (1854–1935)
m. Anna von Köppen (1860–1932)
She was created Countess von Hagenburg in 1893.
see: *Schaumburg-Lippe (von Hagenburg)* XXI, 11, page 817

7. Adolf, Prince of Schaumburg-Lippe (1859–1917)
m. Viktoria, Princess of Prussia (1866–1929)
see: *Schaumburg-Lippe* XXI, 11–c, page 818

8. Emma, Princess of Schaumburg-Lippe
July 13, 1865, Bückeburg — September 27, 1868, Bückeburg

XXI. Schaumburg-Lippe 2, from above and page 274

* **Georg,** Prince of Schaumburg-Lippe, eldest son of Fürst Adolf Georg.
October 10, 1846, Bückeburg — April 29, 1911, Bückeburg
m. April 16, 1882, Altenburg

* **Marie,** Princess of Saxe-Altenburg, daughter of Prince Moritz of Saxe-Altenburg and of his wife, Princess Auguste of Saxe-Meiningen.
March 14, 1864, Altenburg — May 3, 1918, Bückeburg

XXI. Schaumburg-Lippe 2 continued

Issue: 1. Adolf, Hereditary Prince of Schaumburg-Lippe (1883–1936)
m. Ellen Elisabeth Bischoff-Korthaus (1894–1936)
see: *Schaumburg-Lippe* XXI, 3, page 813

2. Moritz, Prince of Schaumburg-Lippe
March 11, 1884, Stadthagen — March 10, 1920,

3. Peter, Prince of Schaumburg-Lippe
January 6, 1886, Stadthagen — May 17, 1886, Stadthagen

4. Wolrad, Fürst zu Schaumburg-Lippe (1887–1962)
m. Bathildis, Princess of Schaumburg-Lippe (1903–)
see: *Schaumburg-Lippe* XXI, 4, page 813

5. Stefan, Prince of Schaumburg-Lippe (1891–1965)
m. Ingeborg, Duchess of Oldenburg (1901–)
see: *Schaumburg-Lippe* XXI, 7, page 814

6. Heinrich, Prince of Schaumburg-Lippe (1894–1952)
m. Marie-Erika, Countess von Hardenberg (1903–)
see: *Schaumburg-Lippe* XXI, 8, page 815

7. Friedrich Christian, Prince of Schaumburg-Lippe (1906–)
m. 1: Alexandra, Countess zu Castell-Rüdenhausen (1904–1961)
m. 2: Marie-Luise, Princess of Schleswig-Holstein-Sonderburg-Glücksburg (1908–1969)
m. 3: Helene Mayr (1913–)
see: *Schaumburg-Lippe* XXI, 9, page 815

8. Elisabeth, Princess of Schaumburg-Lippe (1909–1932)
m. 1: and annulled: Dr. Benvenuto Hauptmann (–)
see: *Hauptmann* XXI, page 719
m. 2: Johann, Baron Herring von Frankensdorff (1891–)
see: *von Frankensdorff* XXI, page 710

XXI. Schaumburg-Lippe 3, from page 812

* **Adolf,** Hereditary Prince of Schaumburg-Lippe, eldest son of Fürst Georg.
February 23, 1883, Stadthagen — March 26, 1936, Zompango, Mexico, killed in an air crash
m. January 10, 1920, Berlin

Ellen Elisabeth Bischoff-Korthaus, daughter of
November 6, 1894, Munich — March 26, 1936, Zompango, Mexico, killed in an air crash
(She m. 1: and divorced: Eberwyn, Prince zu Bentheim und Steinfurt – see: *zu Bentheim und Steinfurt* XXI, page 658.)

No Issue.

XXI. Schaumburg-Lippe 4, from pages 812, 821

* **Wolrad,** Prince of Schaumburg-Lippe, fourth son of Fürst Georg.
April 19, 1887, Stadthagen — June 15, 1962, Hanover
m. April 16, 1925, Pfaffstadt Castle, Austria

* **Bathildis,** Princess of Schaumburg-Lippe, daughter of Prince Albrecht of Schaumburg-Lippe and of his wife, Duchess Elsa of Württemberg.
November 11, 1903, Wels, Austria —

Issue: 1. Georg-Wilhelm, Hereditary Prince of Schaumburg-Lippe
January 26, 1926, Hagenburg Castle — April 29, 1945, Nössige, near Meissen, Saxony, killed in action in World War II

2. Philipp-Ernst, Hereditary Prince of Schaumburg-Lippe (1928–)
m. Eva-Benita, Baroness von Tiele-Winckler (1927–)
see: *Schaumburg-Lippe* XXI, 5, page 814

3. Konstantin, Prince of Schaumburg-Lippe (1930–)
m. Sigrid Knape (1929–)
see: *Schaumburg-Lippe* XXI, 6, page 814

4. Viktoria-Luise, Princess of Schaumburg-Lippe (1940–)
m. Karl-Georg, Count von Stackelberg (1913–)
see: *von Stackelberg* XXI, page 850

XXI. Schaumburg-Lippe 5, from page 813

★ **Philipp-Ernst,** Hereditary Prince of Schaumburg-Lippe, second son of Fürst Wolrad.
July 26, 1928, Hagenburg Castle —
m. October 3, 1955, Bückeburg
Eva-Benita, Baroness von Tiele-Winckler, daughter of Baron Werner von Tiele-Winckler and of his wife, Countess Elisabeth von Bassewitz.
November 18, 1927, —

Issue: 1. Georg-Wilhelm, Prince of Schaumburg-Lippe
July 14, 1956, Freiburg-im-Breisgau —

2. Alexander, Prince of Schaumburg-Lippe
December 25, 1958, Düsseldorf —

XXI. Schaumburg-Lippe 6, from page 813

★ **Konstantin,** Prince of Schaumburg-Lippe, third son of Fürst Wolrad.
December 22, 1930, Hagenburg Castle —
m. December 28, 1956, Hanover
Sigrid Knape, daughter of Gerhard Knape and of his wife, Lieselotte Henning.
September 2, 1929, Hirschberg —

Issue: 1. York, Prince of Schaumburg-Lippe
June 4, 1960, Bielefeld —

2. Tatjana Sybille, Princess of Schaumburg-Lippe
November 13, 1962, Bielefeld —

XXI. Schaumburg-Lippe 7, from pages 812, 208

★ **Stefan,** Prince of Schaumburg-Lippe, fifth son of Fürst Georg.
June 21, 1891, Stadthagen — February 10, 1965, Kempfenhausen
m. June 4, 1921, Rastede
★ **Ingeborg,** Duchess of Oldenburg, daughter of Grand Duke Friedrich August of Oldenburg and of his wife, Duchess Elisabeth of Mecklenburg-Schwerin.
July 20, 1901, Oldenburg —

XXI. Schaumburg-Lippe 7 continued

Issue: 1. Marie-Alix, Princess of Schaumburg-Lippe (1923–)
m. Peter, Duke of Schleswig-Holstein-Sonderburg-Glücksburg (1922–)
see: *Schleswig-Holstein-Sonderburg-Glücksburg* V h–4, page 176

2. Georg, Prince of Schaumburg-Lippe (twin)
March 9, 1924, Bückeburg — October 17, 1970, Wolfratshausen, Bavaria

3. A son born and died March 9, 1924, Bückeburg (twin)

XXI. Schaumburg-Lippe 8, from page 812

* **Heinrich,** Prince of Schaumburg-Lippe, sixth son of Fürst Georg.
September 25, 1894, Bückeburg — November 11, 1952, Bückeburg
m. June 10, 1933, Sophienreuth, near Schönwald
Marie-Erika, Countess von Hardenberg, daughter of Count Albrecht von Hardenberg and of his wife, Waltraut von Arnim.
February 10, 1903, Hofgeismar — July 15, 1964, Bückeburg
(She m. 1: December 19, 1924; divorced: September 30, 1927, Berlin, Walter Bronsart von Schellendorff, who died September 12, 1958, Lübeck.)

Issue: 1. Dagmar, Princess of Schaumburg-Lippe (1934–)
m. Christoph Kalau von Hofe (1931–)
see: *Kalau von Hofe* XXI, page 730

XXI. Schaumburg-Lippe 9, from pages 812, 177

* **Friedrich Christian,** Prince of Schaumburg-Lippe, seventh son of Fürst Georg.
January 5, 1906, Bückeburg —
m. 1: September 25, 1927, Seeläsgen
Alexandra, Countess zu Castell-Rüdenhausen, daughter of Count Wolfgang zu Castell-Rüdenhausen and of his wife, Hedwig von Faber.
June 29, 1904, Stein — September 9, 1961, Lehenleiten
m. 2: October 15, 1962, Glücksburg
* **Marie Luise,** Princess of Schleswig-Holstein-Sonderburg-Glücksburg, daughter of Prince Albrecht of Schleswig-Holstein-Sonderburg-Glücksburg and of his wife, Countess Ortrud zu Ysenburg und Büdingen in Meerholz and adopted daughter of Duke Ernest Günther of Schleswig-Holstein-Sonderburg-Augustenburg.

XXI. Schaumburg-Lippe 9 continued

December 8, 1908, Berlin — December 29, 1969, Wiesbaden
(She m. 1: and divorced: Rudolf Karl, Baron von Stengal – see: *von Stengal* XXI, page 851.)
m. 3: January , 1971,
Helene Mayer, daughter of Maximilian Mayr and of his wife, Antonia von Bartloff, former wife of the late Duke Ludwig in Bavaria.
March 12, 1913, Lausanne, Switzerland —

Issue of first marriage:

1. Marie Elisabeth, Princess of Schaumburg-Lippe
   December 19, 1928, Gottingue — December 4, 1945, Nürnburg

2. Albrecht-Wolfgang, Prince of Schaumburg-Lippe (1934–)
   m. 1: and divorced: Catherine Whitenack-Hurt (–)
   m. 2: Heidemarie Günther (–)
   see: *Schaumburg-Lippe* XXI, 10, below

3. Christine, Princess of Schaumburg-Lippe (1936–)
   m. Albrecht, Baron von Süsskind-Schwendi (1937–)
   see: *von Süsskind-Schwendi* XXI, page 867

XXI. Schaumburg-Lippe 10, from above

* **Albrecht-Wolfgang,** Prince of Schaumburg-Lippe, only son of Prince Friedrich Christian.
August 5, 1934, Berlin —
m. 1: January 7, 1961, Divorced: . March 9, 1962, Salzburg
Catherine Whitenack-Hurt, daughter of Irven Whitenack and of his wife, Virginia Catlin.
December 13, 1941, Wilmington, Delaware, USA
m. 2: May 6 (civil) and May 8, 1964, Linz
Heidemarie Günther, daughter of Herbert Günther and of his wife, Hilda Gasperi.
—

Issue of second marriage:

1. Stephan, Prince of Schaumburg-Lippe
   September 10, 1965, Linz —

2. Alexandra, Princess of Schaumburg-Lippe
   January 15, 1967, Linz —

XXI. Schaumburg-Lippe 11, from page 811

* **Otto,** Prince of Schaumburg-Lippe, third son of Fürst Adolf Georg.
September 13, 1854, Bückeburg — August 18, 1935, Cottbus
m. November 28, 1893, Elsen (morganatic)

Anna von Koppen, daughter of Heinrich von Koppen and of his wife, Fanny Rosenkrantz.
February 3, 1860, St. Goarshausen — March 27, 1932, Cabel, Lausitz
(She was created Countess von Hagenburg, November 20, 1893, their children being titled Counts and Countesses von Hagenburg.)

Issue: 1. Wilhelm, Count von Hagenburg (1895–1945)
m. 1: and divorced: Marie Holzfuss (1893–)
m. 2: Wilhelmine Bisch (1898–)
see: *von Hagenburg* XXI, 11-a, below

2. Hermine, Countess von Hagenburg (1898–1963)
m. Felix, Baron von Quernheim (1891–); see: *von Quernheim* XXI, page 788

3. Otto Heinrich, Count von Hagenburg (1901–)
m. Gertrud Carnier (1909–); see: *von Hagenburg* XXI, 11–b, page 818

XXI. Schaumburg-Lippe (von Hagenburg) 11–a, from above

* **Wilhelm,** Count von Hagenburg, eldest son of Prince Otto of Schaumburg-Lippe.
January 15, 1895, Metz — April 19, 1945, Cabel, Lausitz, killed in action in World War II
m. 1: June 1920, Berlin-Steglitz. Divorced: June 15, 1928,

Marie Holzfuss, daughter of
November 11, 1893, Aalen, Württemberg —
(She m. 2: March 16, 1953, Aalen, Herr von Seydlitz-Kurzbach.)
m. 2: November 10, 1928, Darmstadt

Wilhelmine Bisch, daughter of Johann Bisch and of his wife, Elisabeth Lapp.
September 4, 1898, Darmstadt —

Issue of second marriage:

1. Gisela, Countess von Hagenburg, April 15, 1930, Salzkotten —
(m. May 21, 1955, Darmstadt, Heinrich Silbernagel, born October 31, 1925
1. Ralph Silbernagel, November 6, 1955, Darmstadt —
2. Claudia Silbernagel, March 7, 1961, Darmstadt —
3. Ronald Silbernagel, May 2, 1964, Darmstadt—)

XXI. Schaumburg-Lippe (von Hagenburg) 11–b, from page 817

★ **Otto Heinrich,** Count von Hagenburg, second son of Prince Otto of Schaumburg-Lippe.
October 13, 1901, Longeville, near Metz —
m. May 27, 1935, Oberkainsbach
Gertrud Carnier, daughter of Joseph Carnier and of his wife, Else Müller.
November 1, 1909, Seligenstadt —

No Issue.

XXI. Schaumburg-Lippe 11–c, from pages 811, 51

★ **Adolf,** Prince of Schaumburg-Lippe, fourth son of Fürst Adolf Georg.
July 20, 1859, Bückeburg — July 9, 1916, Bonn
m. November 19, 1890, Berlin
★ **Viktoria,** Princess of Prussia, daughter of German Emperor Friedrich III, King of Prussia, and of his wife, Princess Victoria of Great Britain and Ireland.
April 12, 1866, New Palace, Potsdam — November 13, 1929, Bonn
(She m. 2: Aleksandr Aleksandrovich Zoubkov – see: *Zoubkov* XXIII, page 1012.)

No Issue.

XXI. Schaumburg-Lippe 12, from page 641

Wilhelm, Prince of Schaumburg-Lippe, son of Fürst Georg, brother of Fürst Adolf Georg.
December 12, 1834, Bückeburg — April 6, 1906, Nachod
m. May 30, 1862, Dessau
★ **Bathildis,** Princess of Anhalt-Dessau, daughter of Prince Friedrich of Anhalt-Dessau and of his wife, Princess Marie of Hesse-Cassel.
December 29, 1837, Dessau — February 10, 1902, Nachod Castle

Issue: 1. Charlotte, Princess of Schaumburg-Lippe (1864–1946)
m. Wilhelm II, Last King of Württemberg (1848–1921)
see: *Württemberg* VI b–3, page 226

2. Franz, Prince of Schaumburg-Lippe
October 8, 1865, Ratiboritz — September 4, 1881, Ratiboritz

XXI. Schaumburg-Lippe 12 continued

3. Friedrich, Prince of Schaumburg-Lippe (1868–1945)
m. 1: Lovisa, Princess of Denmark (1875–1906)
m. 2: Antoinette, Princess of Anhalt-Dessau (1885–1963)
see: *Schaumburg-Lippe* XXI, 13, below

4. Albrecht, Prince of Schaumburg-Lippe (1869–1942)
m. 1: Elsa, Duchess of Württemberg (1876–1936)
m. 2: Maria Herget (1897–1942)
see: *Schaumburg-Lippe* XXI, 15, page 821

5. Maximilian, Prince of Schaumburg-Lippe (1871–1904)
m. Olga, Duchess of Württemberg (1876–1932)
see: *Schaumburg-Lippe* XXI, 18, page 822

6. Bathildis, Princess of Schaumburg-Lippe (1873–1962)
m. Friedrich, Fürst zu Waldeck und Pyrmont (1865–1946)
see: *zu Waldeck und Pyrmont* XXI, page 894

7. A son born June 26, 1874, died June 27, 1874

8. Adelheid, Princess of Schaumburg-Lippe (1875–1971)
m. and divorced: Ernst II, last Reigning Duke of Saxe-Altenburg (1871-1955)
see: *Saxe-Altenburg* VII, page 275

9. Alexandra, Princess of Schaumburg-Lippe
June 9, 1879, Ratiboritz —

XXI. Schaumburg-Lippe 13, from above and pages 181, 637

★ **Friedrich,** Prince of Schaumburg-Lippe, second son of Prince Wilhelm.
January 30, 1868, Ratiboritz — December 12, 1945, Kudowa
m. 1: May 5, 1896, Copenhagen, Denmark
★ **Lovisa,** Princess of Denmark, daughter of King Frederik VIII of Denmark and of his wife, Princess Lovisa of Sweden and Norway.
February 17, 1875, Copenhagen — April 4, 1906, Ratiboritz
m. 2: May 26, 1909, Dessau
★ **Antoinette,** Princess of Anhalt-Dessau, daughter of Hereditary Prince Leopold of Anhalt-Dessau and of his wife, Princess Elisabeth of Hesse-Cassel.
March 3, 1885, Georgium Castle, near Dessau — April 3, 1963, Dessau, East Germany

XXI. Schaumburg-Lippe 13 continued

Issue of first marriage:

1. Marie-Luise, Princess of Schaumburg-Lippe (1897–1938)
m. Friedrich Sigismund, Prince of Prussia (1891–1927)
see: *Prussia (Hohenzollern)* II r–4, page 67

2. Christian, Prince of Schaumburg-Lippe (1898–)
m. Feodora, Princess of Denmark (1910–)
see: *Schaumburg-Lippe* XXI, 14, below

3. Stephanie, Princess of Schaumburg-Lippe (1899–1925)
m. Viktor Adolf, 5th Fürst zu Bentheim und Steinfurt (1883–1961)
see: *zu Bentheim und Steinfurt* XXI, page 658

Issue of second marriage:

4. Leopold, Prince of Schaumburg-Lippe
February 21, 1910, Nachod Castle —

5. Wilhelm, Prince of Schaumburg-Lippe
August 24, 1912, Ratiboritz — March 4, 1938, Neubrandenburg

XXI. Schaumburg-Lippe 14, from above and page 184

⋆ **Christian,** Prince of Schaumburg-Lippe, eldest son of Prince Friedrich.
February 20, 1898, Oldenburg —
m. September 9, 1937, Fredensborg Castle, Denmark
⋆ **Feodora,** Princess of Denmark, daughter of Prince Harald of Denmark and of his wife, Princess Helene of Schleswig-Holstein-Sonderburg-Glücksburg.
July 3, 1910, Jaegersborghus, Denmark —

Issue: 1. Wilhelm, Prince of Schaumburg-Lippe
August 19, 1939, Jagdschloss Glienicke —
(m. January 17, 1971, Munich, Baroness Ilona Hentschel von Gelgenheimb, born October 17, 1940, Breslau
1. Christian, Prince of Schaumburg-Lippe
September 14, 1971, Munich —)

XXI. Schaumburg-Lippe 14 continued

2. Waldemar, Prince of Schaumburg-Lippe
December 19, 1940, Jagdschloss Glienicke —

3. Marie-Luise, Princess of Schaumburg-Lippe
December 27, 1945, Hagenburg Castle —

4. Harald, Prince of Schaumburg-Lippe
March 27, 1948, Hagenburg Castle —

XXI. Schaumburg-Lippe 15, from pages 819, 234

* **Albrecht,** Prince of Schaumburg-Lippe, third son of Prince Wilhelm.
October 24, 1869, Ratiboritz — December 25, 1942, Linz, Austria
m. 1: May 6, 1897, Stuttgart
* **Elsa,** Duchess of Württemberg, daughter of Duke Eugen of Württemberg and of his wife, Grand Duchess Vera Konstantinovna of Russia.
March 1, 1876, Stuttgart — May 27, 1936, Pfaffstadt
m. 2: June 24, 1939, Braunau-an-der-Inn
Maria Herget, daughter of
July 26, 1897, Prague — December 25, 1942, Linz

Issue of first marriage:

1. Max, Prince of Schaumburg-Lippe (1898–)
m. Helga Claire Lee Roderburg (1911–)
see: *Schaumburg-Lippe* XXI, 16, page 822

2. Franz Joseph, Prince of Schaumburg-Lippe (1899–1963)
m. Maria Theresia Peschel (1912–)
see: *Schaumburg-Lippe* XXI, 17, page 822

3. Alexander, Prince of Schaumburg-Lippe
January 20, 1901, Wels — November 26, 1923, Siedlberg, Austria

4. Bathildis, Princess of Schaumburg-Lippe (1903–)
m. Wolrad, Fürst zu Schaumburg-Lippe (1887–)
see: *Schaumburg-Lippe* XXI, 4, page 813

XXI. Schaumburg-Lippe 16, from page 821

* **Max,** Prince of Schaumburg-Lippe, eldest son of Prince Albrecht.
March 28, 1898, Wels, Austria —
m. May 9, 1933, Bad Homburg
Helga Claire Lee Roderburg, daughter of Carl Hermann Roderburg and of his wife, Claude Lennox Miller.
February 24, 1911, Köln —

No Issue.

XXI. Schaumburg-Lippe 17, from page 821

* **Franz Joseph,** Prince of Schaumburg-Lippe, second son of Prince Albrecht.
September 1, 1899, Wels — July 6, 1963, Cassel
m. January 29, 1959, Munich
Maria Theresia Peschel, daughter of Anton Peschel and of his wife, Josephine Rossmanith.
July 29, 1912, Neutitschein —
(She m. 1: August 20, 1932, Schonau; divorced: June 24, 1942, Erich von Wüllerstorff.)
(She m. 2: July 24, 1943, Kaltwassertal, Kreis Strehlen, Schleswig; divorced: June 24, 1957, Hans-Heinrich von Tschirschky und Boegendorff, born September 19, 1914, Reichwaldau.)

No Issue.

XXI. Schaumburg-Lippe 18, from pages 819, 234

* **Maximilian,** Prince of Schaumburg-Lippe, fourth son of Prince Wilhelm.
March 13, 1871, Ratiboritz — April 1, 1904, Abbazia
m. November 3, 1898, Stuttgart
* **Olga,** Duchess of Württemberg, daughter of Duke Eugen of Württemberg and of his wife, Grand Duchess Vera Konstantinovna of Russia.
March 1, 1876, Stuttgart — October 21, 1932, Ludwigsburg

Issue: 1. Eugen, Prince of Schaumburg-Lippe
August 8, 1899, Ludwigsburg — November 9, 1929, Caterham, England, in an air crash

XXI. Schaumburg-Lippe 18 continued

2. Albrecht, Prince of Schaumburg-Lippe (1900–)
m. Walburgis, Baroness von Hirschberg (1906–)
see: *Schaumburg-Lippe* XXI, 19, below

XXI. Schaumburg-Lippe 19, from above

* **Albrecht,** Prince of Schaumburg-Lippe, second son of Prince Maximilian.
October 17, 1900, Ludwigsburg —
m. September 2, 1930, Partenkirchen

Walburgis, Baroness von Hirschberg, daughter of Baron Karl von Hirschberg and of his wife, Baroness Sophie von Faber.
March 26, 1906, Nürnburg —

No Issue.

XXI. SCHENK 1, from page 844

Gert Schenk
July 2, 1910, Charlottenburg, near Potsdam — August 23, 1960, Charlottenburg
m. November 23, 1942, Glienicke, near Potsdam

* **Feodore,** Countess zu Solms-Baruth, daughter of Count Friedrich, 3rd Fürst zu Solms-Baruth, and of his wife, Princess Adelheid of Schleswig-Holstein-Sonderburg-Glücksburg.
April 5, 1920, Baruth —
(She m. 2: Karl Adolf, Fürst von Auersperg – see: *von Auersperg* XXI, page 645.)

Issue: 1. Christian Schenk
August 18, 1953, Graz —

XXI. SCHILLING 1, from page 726

Carl William Schilling
February 25, 1912, Rye, New York, USA —
m. June 10, 1951, Heiligenberg, Baden, Germany

* **Ines,** Countess von Hoyos, daughter of Count Friedrich von Hoyos-Sprinzenstein and of his wife, Wilhelmine von Wuthenau-Hohenthurm.
July 14, 1924, Niemberg —

XXI. Schilling 1 continued

Issue: 1. Henry Carl Frederick Schilling
April 11, 1952, Stuttgart —

2. Lorraine Maria Josepha Schilling
December 15, 1954, Villingen, Germany —

3. Franziska Paula Maria Anna Schilling
July 26, 1956, Villingen —

XXI. SCHIMERT 1, from page 470

Gustav Christian Schimert, M.D.
November 28, 1910, Budapest, Hungary —
m. December 29, 1959,
* **Editha,** Princess of Bavaria, daughter of Crown Prince Rupprecht of Bavaria and of his wife, Princess Antonia of Luxemburg.
September 16, 1924, Hohenberg Castle —
(She m. 1: Tito Tomasso Brunetti – see: *Brunetti* XVIII, page 551.)

Issue: 1. Andreas Schimert
May 26, 1961, Munich —

2. Christian Schimert
March 18, 1963, —

XXI. VON SCHIMONY-SCHIMONSKY 1, from page 665

Herbert Maria von Schimony-Schimonsky
October 10, 1891, Stoblau — October 25/26, 1945, Breslau, murdered by a housebreaker
m. April 7, 1920, Neustadt-Dosse
* **Wanda,** Countess Blücher von Wahlstatt, daughter of Count Gebhard Blücher von Wahlstatt and of his wife, Princess Wanda Radziwill.
February 24, 1898, Radun — October 25/26, 1945, Breslau, murdered by a housebreaker

Issue: 1. Ernst Heinrich von Schimony-Schimonsky
February 7, 1921, Breslau — September 22, 1941, near Kiev, Russia, missing presumed killed in action in World War II

XXI. von Schimony-Schimonsky 1 continued

2. Johann Christoph von Schimony-Schimonsky (1922–)
m. Hildegard Schuster (1928–)
see: *von Schimony-Schimonsky* XXI, 2, below

XXI. Schimony-Schimonsky 2, from above

* **Johann Christoph von Schimony-Schimonsky,** second son of Herbert Maria.
May 16, 1922, Breslau —
m. February 9, 1957, Los Teques, Venezuela
Hildegard Schuster, daughter of Josef Schuster and of his wife, Theresa Fromm.
September 7, 1928, Fürstenfeldbruck, Bavaria —

Issue: 1. Maria Julieta von Schimony-Schimonsky
March 29, 1969, Caracas, Venezuela —

XXI. VON SCHLOTHEIM 1, from page 911

Ernst Hartmann, Baron von Schlotheim
December 27, 1914, Wiesbaden — October 31, 1952, Wiesbaden
m. December 19, 1939, Berlin
* **Benigna Viktoria,** Princess zu Wied, daughter of Prince Viktor zu Wied and of his wife, Countess Gisela zu Solms-Wildenfels.
July 23, 1918, Oslo, Norway —

Issue: 1. Viktoria Elisabeth, Baroness von Schlotheim
April 11, 1948, Wiesbaden —

2. Christine Marie, Baroness von Schlotheim
July 22, 1950, Wiesbaden —

XXI. SCHMALZ 1, from page 71

Wilhelm Schmalz
March 1, 1901, Reussen near Imsen —
m. November 30, 1936, Tabarz, Thuringia
* **Luise Henriette,** Princess of Prussia, daughter of Prince Friedrich Wilhelm of Prussia and of his wife, Princess Agathe of Hohenlohe-Schillingsfürst.
July 21, 1912, Kamenz —

XXI. Schmalz 1 continued

Issue: 1. Agatha Schmalz
October 23, 1937, Berlin-Zehlendorf —

2. Hubertus Schmalz (1938–)
m. Ulrike Gertrud Feuerborn (1945–)
see: *Schmalz* XXI, 2, below

3. Bernhard Schmalz
May 17, 1941, Tabarz —

4. Friedrich Wilhelm Schmalz (1943–)
m. Sybilla Spring (1947–)
see: *Schmalz* XXI, 3, below

XXI. Schmalz 2, from above

* **Hubertus Schmalz,** eldest son of Wilhelm.
November 13, 1938, Berlin-Zehlendorf —
m. January 19, 1967, Keilmünster, Oberlahn
Ulrike Gertrud Feuerborn, daughter of Hubertus Feuerborn and of his wife, Sigrid von Ortzen.
March 22, 1945, Oberrode, Kreis Fulda —

Issue: 1. Alexandra Schmalz
July 10, 1967, Kiel —

XXI. Schmalz 3, from above

* **Friedrich Schmalz,** third son of Wilhelm
September 19, 1943, Tabarz, Thuringia —
m. April 8, 1967, Geisenheim, Theingau
Sybilla Spring, daughter of Jakob Spring and of his wife, Anna Fuhrmann.
January 28, 1947, Geisenheim —

Issue:

XXI. SCHMIDT 1, from page 422

Robert Schmidt

November 1, 1892, —

m. February 4, 1921, Berlin

* **Charlotte,** Duchess of Mecklenburg-Schwerin, daughter of Duke Wilhelm of Mecklenburg-Schwerin and of his wife, Princess Alexandrine of Prussia.

November 7, 1868, Bellevue Castle, near Berlin — December 20, 1944, Partenkirchen

(She m. 1: Heinrich XVIII, Prince Reuss zu Köstritz – see: *Reuss* IX l–1, page 347.)

No Issue.

XXI. SCHMIDT STEINVORTH 1, from page 267

Hans Hermann Schmidt Steinvorth

June 18, 1942, Hanover —

m. April 4, 1966, Barcelona, Spain

* **Jay,** Baroness von Saalfeld, daughter of Baron Enzio von Saalfeld and of his wife, Rut Viererbe.

June 9, 1938, Munich —

Issue:

XXI. SCHNIRRING 1, from page 22

Max Schnirring

May 20, 1896, Stuttgart — July 7, 1944, Stralsund, killed in action with the Luftwaffe in World War II

m. June 22, 1938, Berlin

* **Caroline Mathilde,** Princess of Saxe-Coburg and Gotha, daughter of Reigning Duke Carl Eduard of Saxe-Coburg and Gotha and of his wife, Princess Viktoria Adelheid of Schleswig-Holstein-Sonderburg-Glücksburg.

June 22, 1912, Callenberg Castle —

(She m. 1: and divorced: Friedrich-Wolfgang, Count zu Castell-Rüdenhausen – see: *zu Castell-Rüdenhausen* XXI, page 677.)

(She m. 3: and divorced: Karl Otto Andree – see: *Andree* XXI, page 634.)

XXI. Schnirring 1 continued

Issue: 1. Calma Schnirring (1938–)
m. Richard D. Berger (1941–); see: *Berger* XXIV, page 1015

2. Dagmar Schnirring (1940–)
m. Heinrich Walz (–); see: *Walz* XXI, page 901

3. Peter Michael Schnirring
January 4, 1943, Grösswuesteritz — February 10, 1966, Munich

XXI. SCHÖNAICH-CAROLATH 1, from page 336

Johann Georg, Prince of Schönaich-Carolath, son of Prince Georg.
September 11, 1873, Saabor — April 6, 1920, Wolfelsgrund
m. January 7, 1907, Greiz
★ **Hermine,** Princess Reuss zu Greiz, daughter of Prince Heinrich XXII Reuss zu Greiz and of his wife, Princess Ida of Schaumburg-Lippe.
December 17, 1887, Greiz — August 7, 1947, Paulinenhof, near Frankfurt-an-der-Oder, in an internment camp
(She m. 2: Wilhelm II of Prussia – see: *Prussia* (*Hohenzollern*) II d–3, page 52.)

Issue: 1. Hans Georg, Prince of Schönaich-Carolath (1907–1943)
m. Sibylle, Baroness von Zedlitz und Leipe (1910–)
see: *Schönaich-Carolath* XXI, 2, page 829

2. Georg Wilhelm, Prince of Schönaich-Carolath
March 16, 1909, Saabor — November 1, 1927, Grünberg

3. Hermine, Princess of Schönaich-Carolath (1910–)
m. Hugo Herbert Hartung (1908–1945)
see: *Hartung* XXI, page 719

4. Ferdinand, Prince of Schönaich-Carolath, Baron Standsehr-aux-Amtitz (1913–)
m. Rose Rauch (1917–)
see: *Schönaich-Carolath* XXI, 3, page 829

5. Henriette, Princess of Schönaich-Carolath (1918–)
m. and divorced: Karl Franz Josef, Prince of Prussia (1916–)
see: *Prussia* (*Hohenzollern*) II o–2, page 63

XXI. Schönaich-Carolath 2, from page 828

* **Hans Georg,** Prince of Schönaich-Carolath, eldest son of Prince Johann Georg.
November 3, 1907, Berlin — August 9, 1943, Mantschina, Russia, killed in action in World War II
m. June 20, 1939, Langseifersdorf, and June 24, 1939, Saabor
Sibylle, Baroness von Zedlitz und Leipe, daughter of Baron Günther von Zedlitz und Leipe and of his wife, Ilse von Lieres und Wilkau.
July 4, 1910, Kuchendorf —

Issue: 1. Marina, Princess of Schönaich-Carolath (1940–)
m. Peter, Baron Wiedersperger von Wiedersperg (–)
see: *Wiedersperger von Wiedersperg* XXI, page 911

2. Georg, Prince of Schönaich-Carolath
January 4, 1943, Mellendorf —

XXI. Schönaich-Carolath 3, from page 828

* **Ferdinand,** Prince of Schönaich-Carolath, second son of Prince Johann Georg.
May 4, 1913, Saabor —
m. 1: November 8, 1938, Berlin
Rose Rauch, daughter of
, 1917, —
m. 2: November 9, 1963, Munich
Margarethe, Baroness von Seeckendorff, daughter of Baron Oskar von Seeckendorff.
January 2, 1908, Tientsin, China —

XXI. Schönaich-Carolath 4, from page 832

Heinrich, Prince of Schönaich-Carolath, second son of Prince Ludwig.
April 24, 1852, Amtitz — June 20, 1920, Amtitz
m. October 4, 1888, Droyssig
* **Margarita,** Princess of Schönburg-Waldenburg, daughter of Prince Hugo of Schönburg-Waldenburg and of his wife, Princess Hermine Reuss zu Greiz.
July 18, 1864, Droyssig — January 21, 1937,

No Issue.

XXI. VON SCHÖNBORN-BUCHHEIM 1, from page 458

Friedrich Karl, Count von Schönborn-Buchheim
March 30, 1938, Schönborn Castle —
m. September 10, 1964, Dreux, France
* **Isabelle,** Princess of France, daughter of Prince Henri, Comte de Paris, and of his wife, Princess Isabella of Orleans e Braganca.
April 8, 1932, Brussels, Belgium —

Issue: 1. Damien, Count von Schönborn-Buchheim
July 17, 1965, Vienna —

2. Vinzenz, Count von Schönborn-Buchheim
October 28, 1966, Vienna —

3. Lorraine, Countess von Schönborn-Buchheim
January 3, 1968, Johannesburg, South Africa —

4. Claire, Countess von Schönborn-Buchheim
October 7, 1969, Paris —

XXI. VON SCHÖNBORN-WIESENTHEID 1, from page 542

Karl, Count von Schönborn-Wiesentheid
October 14, 1916, Würzburg —
m. April 21, 1953 (civil), Sintra, Portugal, and June 14, 1953 (religious), Müge, Portugal
* **Donna Graziella Alvares Pereira di Mello,** daughter of Don Antonia Alvares Pereira di Mello and of his wife, Nobile Olga Nicolis, dei Conti de Robilant e Cereaglio.
December 20, 1929, Pau, France —

Issue: 1. Filipp, Hereditary Count von Schönborn-Wiesentheid
July 24, 1954, Würzburg —

2. Teresa, Countess von Schönborn-Wiesentheid
November 7, 1955, Würzburg —

3. Maria, Countess von Schönborn-Wiesentheid
July 28, 1958, Würzburg —

4. Paul, Count von Schönborn-Wiesentheid
May 15, 1962, Lisbon, Portugal —

XXI. von Schönborn-Wiesentheid 2, from page 873

Rudolf Erwein, Count von Schönborn-Wiesentheid
October 1, 1918, Würzburg —
m. 1: April 18 and 19, 1947, Regensburg. Divorced: September 5, 1968, Munich
* **Helene,** Princess of Thurn und Taxis, daughter of Prince Franz Joseph of Thurn und Taxis and of his wife, Princess Elisabeth of Braganca, Infanta of Portugal.
May 27, 1924, Regensburg —
m. 2: November 20, , Heusenstamm
Katharina, Countess Spanocchi, daughter of Count Lelio Spanocchi.

Issue of first marriage:
1. Albrecht, Count von Schönborn-Wiesentheid
February 20, 1948, Würzburg —

2. Johann, Count von Schönborn-Wiesentheid
July 3, 1949, Würzburg —

3. Gabrielle, Countess von Schönborn-Wiesentheid
October 16, 1950, Würzburg —
(m. July 29, 1969, Keilberg, Alexander, Prince zu Sayn-Wittgenstein-Sayn, b. November 22, 1943
1. Heinrich, Prince zu Sayn-Wittgenstein-Sayn
January 3, 1971, Munich —)

4. Peter, Count von Schönborn-Wiesentheid
November 10, 1954, Regensburg —

XXI. VON SCHÖNBURG-HARTENSTEIN 1, from page 880

Aloys, Hereditary Prince of Schönburg-Hartenstein
August 18, 1916, Goldegg, near St. Pölten, Austria — May 13, 1945, Prague
m. December 30, 1944, Hartenstein
* **Elisabeth von Trotha,** daughter of Major General Thilo von Trotha and of his wife, Princess Ida zu Ysenburg und Büdingen in Wächtersbach.
July 7, 1920, Frankfurt-am-Main —

Issue: 1. Aloys, 6th Fürst von Schönburg-Hartenstein
October 4, 1945, Munich —

XXI. VON SCHÖNBURG-WALDENBURG 1, from page 335

Hugo, Prince of Schönburg-Waldenburg, son of Fürst Otto Friedrich.
August 29, 1822, Waldenburg — June 9, 1896, Wiesbaden

XXI. von Schönburg-Waldenburg 1 continued

m. April 29, 1862, Greiz
* **Hermine,** Princess Reuss zu Greiz, daughter of Prince Heinrich IX Reuss zu Greiz and of his wife, Princess Karoline of Hesse-Homburg.
December 25, 1840, Greiz — January 4, 1890, Droyssig

Issue: 1. Heinrich, Prince of Schönburg-Waldenburg (1863–1945)
m. 1: and divorced: Olga, Princess zu Löwenstein-Wertheim-Freudenberg (1880–1961)
m. 2: Adelheid, Princess zur Lippe (1884–1963)
see: *Schönburg-Waldenburg* XXI, 2, below

2. Margarita, Princess of Schönburg-Waldenburg (1864–1937)
m. Heinrich, Prince of Schönaich-Carolath (1852–1920)
see: *Schönaich-Carolath* XXI, 4, page 829

3. Elisabeth, Princess of Schönburg-Waldenburg
November 8, 1867, Droyssig — , 1943, Dresden

XXI. von Schönburg-Waldenburg 2, from above and page 761

* **Heinrich,** Prince of Schönburg-Waldenburg, only son of Prince Hugo.
June 8, 1863, Droyssig — December 28, 1945, Rheda
m. 1: October 5, 1898, Langenzell. Divorced: August 20, 1920, Leipzig
* **Olga,** Princess zu Löwenstein-Wertheim-Freudenberg, daughter of Prince Alfred zu Löwenstein-Wertheim-Freudenberg and of his wife, Countess Pauline von Reichenbach-Lessonitz.
October 25, 1880, Bonn — July 1, 1961, Heidelberg
m. 2: July 14, 1921, Schwalenburg Castle
Adelheid, Princess zur Lippe-Biesterfeld, daughter of Count Friedrich zur Lippe-Biesterfeld and of his wife, Princess Maria zu Löwenstein-Wertheim-Freudenberg.
October 14, 1884, Darmstadt — March 9, 1963, Frankfurt-am-Main

Issue of first marriage:
1. Hermine, Princess of Schönburg-Waldenburg (1899–)
m. Heinrich XXXVI, Prince Reuss zu Köstritz (1888–1956)
see: *Reuss* IX, j–1, page 346

2. Amelie, Princess of Schönburg-Waldenburg (1902–)
m. Adolf, 5th Fürst zu Bentheim und Tecklenburg (1889–)
see: *zu Bentheim und Tecklenburg* XXI, page 655

XXI. von Schönburg-Waldenburg 2 continued

3. Alfred, Prince of Schönburg-Waldenburg (1905–1941)
m. Marie Eleonore, Princess zu Wied (1909–1956)
see: *von Schönburg-Waldenburg* XXI, 3, below

4. Hugo, Prince of Schönburg-Waldenburg (1910–1942)
m. Waltraut Benedicta von Klüchtner (1918–)
see: *von Schönburg-Waldenburg* XXI, 4, below

Issue of second marriage:

5. Marie, Princess of Schönburg-Waldenburg (1922–)
m. Wolff, Baron von Wolzogen und Neuhaus (1910–)
see: *von Wolzogen und Neuhaus* XXI, page 922

XXI. von Schönburg-Waldenburg 3, from above

* **Alfred,** Prince of Schönburg-Waldenburg, eldest son of Prince Heinrich.
October 30, 1905, Droyssig — March 10, 1941, Zeitz, killed in action in World War II
m. November 16, 1937, Munich

* **Marie Eleonore,** Princess zu Wied, daughter of Prince Wilhelm zu Wied, former King of Albania, and of his wife, Princess Sophie of Schönburg-Waldenburg.
February 19, 1909, Potsdam — September 29, 1956, Romania, in a concentration camp
(She m. 2: Jon Bunea – see: *Bunea* XX, page 626.)

No Issue.

XXI. von Schönburg-Waldenburg 4, from above

* **Hugo,** Prince of Schönburg-Waldenburg, second son of Prince Heinrich
October 15, 1910, Droyssig — January 16, 1942, Knutowa, Russia, killed in action in World War II
m. November 4, 1937, Leipzig

Waltraut Benedicta von Klüchtner, daughter of Wilko von Klüchtner and of his wife, Ottilie Greiner.
July 2, 1918, Sondershausen —
(She m. 2: September 17, 1954, Munich, Jürgen von Goerne, born February 12, 1908, Allenstein.)

XXI. von Schönburg-Waldenburg 4 continued

Issue: 1. Michaela, Princess of Schönburg-Waldenburg (1940–)
m. Alexander, Hereditary Prince of Hohenlohe-Jatsberg (1940–)
see: *Hohenlohe-Jatsberg* XV k–1, page 494

XXI. von Schönburg-Waldenburg 5, from page 761

Ulrich, Prince of Schönburg-Waldenburg, second son of Prince Georg.
August 25, 1869, Hermsdorf — December 1, 1939, Güteborn
m. February 24, 1900, Frankfurt-am-Main
* **Pauline,** Princess zu Löwenstein-Wertheim-Freudenberg, daughter of Prince Alfred zu Löwenstein-Wertheim-Freudenberg and of his wife, Countess Pauline von Reichenbach-Lessonitz.
October 16, 1881, Heidelberg — April 24, 1945, Miltitz, Saxony

Issue: 1. Charlotte, Princess of Schönburg-Waldenburg
February 3, 1901, Langenzell —

2. Wolf, 6th Fürst von Schönburg-Waldenburg (1902–)
m. Luciana, Contessa Bargagli-Stoffi (1921–)
see: *Schönburg-Waldenburg* XXI, 6, below

3. Dorothea, Princess of Schönburg-Waldenburg (1905–)
m. Ferdinand, Prince zur Lippe-Weissenfeld (1903–1939)
see: *zur Lippe-Weissenfeld* XXI, page 756

4. Georg, Prince of Schönburg-Waldenburg (1908–)
m. Pauline, Countess zu Castell-Castell (1906–)
see: *Schönburg-Waldenburg* XXI, 7, page 835

5. Wilhelm, Prince of Schönburg-Waldenburg (1913–1944)
m. Marie Elisabeth, Princess zu Stolberg-Rossla (1921–)
see: *Schönburg-Waldenburg* XXI, 8, page 836

XXI. von Schönburg-Waldenburg 6, from above

* **Wolf,** 6th Fürst von Schönburg-Waldenburg, son of Prince Ulrich.
November 26, 1902, Dresden —
m. October 16, 1944, Asciano, Italy
Luciana, Contessa Bargagli-Stoffi, daughter of Conte Luigi, Marchese Bargagli-Stoffi, and of his wife, Guiseppina (Josephine) Rovatti.

XXI. von Schönburg-Waldenburg 6 continued

January 17, 1921, Bologna, Italy —

NOTE: Prince Wolf, 6th Fürst, was adopted by his uncle, Prince Hermann of Schönburg-Waldenburg, in 1941.

Issue: 1. Grazia, Princess of Schönburg-Waldenburg
March 4, 1946, Asciano, Italy —

2. Alessandra, Princess of Schönburg-Waldenburg
April 18, 1949, Asciano —

3. Anna-Luise, Princess of Schönburg-Waldenburg
November 21, 1952, Asciano —

XXI. von Schönburg-Waldenburg 7, from pages 834, 674

* **Georg,** Prince of Schönburg-Waldenburg, second son of Prince Ulrich.
November 18, 1908, Güteborn —
m. April 30, 1935, Burghausen, and May 4, 1935, Munich

* **Pauline,** Countess zu Castell-Castell, daughter of Count Otto zu Castell-Castell and of his wife, Princess Amelie zu Löwenstein-Wertheim-Freudenberg.
September 5, 1906, Langenzell —

Issue: 1. Anna-Amelie, Princess of Schönburg-Waldenburg (1936–1966) (twin)
m. Franz Salvator, Archduke of Austria (1923–)
see: *Austria (Habsburg)* X w–2, page 378

2. Clementine, Princess of Schönburg-Waldenburg (twin)
January 22, 1936, Frankfurt-am-Main —

3. Stephanie, Princess of Schönburg-Waldenburg (1938–)
m. Ludwig, Count von Waldburg zu Wolfegg und Waldsee (1934–)
see: *von Waldburg zu Wolfegg und Waldsee* XXI, page 888

4. Luise, Princess of Schönburg-Waldenburg (1943–)
m. Andreas, Prince of Hohenlohe-Langenburg (1938–)
see: *Hohenlohe-Langenburg* XV a–5, page 482

XXI. von Schönburg-Waldenburg 8, from pages 834, 865

* **Wilhelm,** Prince of Schönburg-Waldenburg, third son of Prince Ulrich. Adopted in 1942 by Princess Anna Luise of Schwarzburg (born Princess of Schönburg-Waldenburg).
April 3, 1913, Güteborn — June 11, 1944, near Parfouru, Normandy, killed in action in World War II
m. September 27, 1939, Rossla
* **Marie Elisabeth,** Princess zu Stolberg-Rossla, daughter of Prince Christoph Martin, 3rd Fürst zu Stolberg-Rossla and of his wife, Princess Ida Reuss zu Greiz.
October 1, 1921, Rossla —

Issue: 1. Ulrich, Prince of Schönburg-Waldenburg
October 9, 1940, Dresden —

2. Wolf Christoph, Prince of Schönburg-Waldenburg (1943–)
m. Eveline Mente (1944–)
see: *von Schönburg-Waldenburg* XXI, 9, below

XXI. von Schönburg-Waldenburg 9, from above

* **Wolf Christoph,** Prince of Schönburg-Waldenburg, second son of Prince Wilhelm.
April 3, 1943, Dresden —
m. December 6, 1968, Lüneburg
Eveline Mente, daughter of Werner Mente and of his wife, Johanna Kutter.
June 6, 1944, Hindenburg —

Issue: 1. Kai-Philipp, Prince of Schönburg-Waldenburg
April 24, 1969, Hamburg —

XXI. VON SCHRÖDER 1, from page 787

Manfred, Baron von Schröder
November 6, 1914, Hamburg —
m. September 19, 1939, Athens, Greece. Divorced: June 16, 1948, Hamburg
* **Eleonore Renata,** Countess von Pückler, daughter of Count Karl Friedrich, 3rd Count von Pückler-Burghauss, and of his wife, Princess Olga Elisabeth of Saxe-Altenburg.

XXI. von Schröder 1 continued

November 25, 1919, Friedland —
(She m. 2: Jürgen Petersen – see: *Petersen* XXI, page 782.)

Issue: 1. Karoline-Eleonore, Baroness von Schröder (1940–)
m. Rudolf (Rolf) Menzel (1924–)
see: *Menzel* XXI, page 769

2. Rüdiger, Baron von Schröder
March 10, 1943, Bliestorf, Holstein —

XXI. VON SCHWARZBURG 1, from page 637

Günther Sizzo, Fürst von Schwarzburg, Prince of Leutenberg
June 3, 1860, Rudolstadt — March 24, 1926, Gross-Harthau, Saxony
m. January 25, 1897, Dessau
⋆ **Alexandra,** Princess of Anhalt-Dessau, daughter of Duke Friedrich I of Anhalt-Dessau and of his wife, Princess Antoinette of Saxe-Altenburg.
April 4, 1868, Dessau — August 26, 1958, Schwetzingen

Issue: 1. Marie Antoinette, Princess of Schwarzburg (1898–)
m. Friedrich Magnus (V), Count zu Solms-Wildenfels (1886–1945)
see: *zu Solms-Wildenfels* XXI, page 843

2. Friedrich Günther, Fürst zu Schwarzburg (1901–)
m. and divorced: Sophie, Princess of Saxe-Weimar-Eisenach (1911–)
see: *zu Schwarzburg* XXI, 2, below

XXI. zu Schwarzburg 2, from above and page 253

⋆ **Friedrich Günther,** Fürst zu Schwarzburg, only son of Fürst Günther Sizzo.
March 5, 1901, Gross-Harthau —
m. March 7, 1938, Heinrichau. Divorced: November 1, 1938,
⋆ **Sophie,** Princess of Saxe-Weimar-Eisenach, daughter of Grand Duke Wilhelm Ernst of Saxe-Weimar-Eisenach and of his wife, Princess Feodore of Saxe-Meiningen.
March 20, 1911, Weimar —

No Issue.

XXI. ZU SCHWARZBURG-SONDERHAUSEN

1, from page 272

Karl Günther, Fürst zu Schwarzburg-Sonderhausen, son of Fürst Günther Friedrich Karl II.
August 7, 1830, Arnstadt — March 28, 1909, Weisser Hirsch, near Dresden
m. June 12, 1869, Altenburg

★ **Marie,** Princess of Saxe-Altenburg, daughter of Prince Eduard of Saxe-Altenburg and of his second wife, Princess Luise Reuss zu Greiz.
June 28, 1845, Munich — July 5, 1930, Sonderhausen

No Issue.

XXI. SCHWARZE

1, from page 902

Hans-Dieter Schwarze
August 30, 1926, Münster —
m. August 5, 1963, Munich

★ **Karin,** Baroness von Wangenheim, daughter of Baron Götz von Wangenheim and of his wife, Princess Luise-Marie of Saxe-Meiningen.
October 29, 1937, Berlin-Dahlem —

Issue: 1. Daniel Simeon Schwarze
August 26, 1965, Munich —

XXI. SCHWARZENBURG

1, from page 864

Heinrich, Prince of Schwarzenburg
January 29, 1903, Pressburg —
m. November 30, 1946, Kirchdorf

★ **Eleonore,** Countess zu Stolberg-Stolberg, daughter of Count Georg zu Stolberg-Stolberg and of his wife, Princess Regina Reuss zu Köstritz.
August 8, 1920, Micheldorf —

Issue: 1. Elisabeth Regina, Princess of Schwarzenburg
October 1, 1947, Vienna —
(m. May 31, 1970, Rüdiger von Pejoh
1. Anna Eleonore von Pejoh, born May 14, 1971)

By adoption, November 24, 1960:
2. Karl, Hereditary Prince of Schwarzenburg, son of 6th Fürst Karl zu Schwarzenburg
December 10, 1937, Prague, Czechoslovakia —

XXI. Schwarzenburg 2, from page 107

Adolf, 10th Fürst zu Schwarzenburg
August 18, 1890, Frauenberg — February 27, 1950, Bordighera
m. October 29, 1930, Berg Castle, Luxemburg

* **Hilda,** Princess of Luxemburg, daughter of Grand Duke Wilhelm of Luxemburg and of his wife, Infanta Maria Anna of Portugal.
February 15, 1897, Berg Castle —

No Issue.

XXI. ZU SEILERN UND ASPANG 1, from page 558

Friedrich, Count zu Seilern und Aspang
November 15, 1924, Vienna —
m. December 2, 1950, Trieste

* **Christiane,** Baroness Economo di San Serff, daughter of Baron Leonidas Economo di San Serff and of his wife, Princess Wilhelmine Windisch-Graetz.
January 9, 1920, Vienna —

Issue: 1. Johannes Christian, Count zu Seilern und Aspang
October 2, 1951, Trieste —

2. Peter, Count zu Seilern und Aspang
December 31, 1952, Trieste —

3. Franz-Tassilo, Count zu Seilern und Aspang
December 15, 1954, Trieste —

XXI. VON SIMPSON 1, from page 707

Hans Hippolyt von Simpson
March 27, 1885, Nettienen —
m. August 26, 1913, Göttlieben. Divorced: March 15, 1924, Berlin

* **Luigina,** Baroness von Fabrice, daughter of Baron Maximilian von Fabrice and of his wife, Countess Ilma Almásy von Zsadány und Török-Szent-Miklós.
July 30, 1876, Nonnenhorn, Bavaria — April 29, 1958, Augsburg
(She m. 1: Walther Sturtzkopf – see: *Sturtzkopf* XXI, page 867.)
(She m. 2: and divorced: Edgar Böcking – see: *Böcking* XXI, page 667.)
(She m. 4: Dr. Edwin Tietjens – see: *Tietjens* XXI, page 876.)

Issue:

XXI. SOLMS (Solms-Braunfels) 1, from page 337

Hermann, Prince zu Solms-Braunfels, son of Prince Wilhelm.
October 8, 1845, Düsseldorf — August 30, 1900, Braunfels Castle
m. 1: April 30, 1872, Salzburg
Maria, Princess zu Solms-Braunfels, daughter of Prince Karl zu Solms-Braunfels and of his wife, Princess Sophie zu Löwenstein-Wertheim-Rosenberg.
June 26, 1852, Zinkau — July 23, 1882, Königsberg
m. 2: November 17, 1887, Gera
* **Elisabeth,** Princess Reuss zu Schleiz, daughter of Prince Heinrich XIV Reuss zu Schleiz and of his wife, Duchess Agnes of Württemberg.
October 27, 1859, Gera — February 23, 1951, Hungen Castle

Issue of second marriage:

1. Marie Agnes, Princess zu Solms-Braunfels (1888–)
m. Joseph, Count zu Erbach-Fürstenau (1874–)
see: *zu Erbach-Fürstenau* XXI, page 703

2. Helene, Princess zu Solms-Braunfels (1890–)
m. Raimond, Count zu Erbach-Fürstenau (1868–1926)
see: *zu Erbach-Fürstenau* XXI, page 702

3. Ernst August, Prince zu Solms-Braunfels (1892–)
m. Elisabeth, Princess zur Lippe-Biesterfeld (1916–1968)
see: *zu Solms-Braunfels* XXI, 2, below

4. Friedrich Eugen, Prince zu Solms-Braunfels
November 23, 1893, Darmstadt — December 26, 1903, Darmstadt

XXI. Solms (Solms-Braunfels) 2, from above and page 754

* **Ernst August,** Prince zu Solms-Braunfels, eldest son of Prince Hermann.
March 10, 1892, Darmstadt —
m. February 15, 1939, Dresden
* **Elisabeth,** Princess zur Lippe-Biesterfeld, daughter of Prince Julius Ernst zur Lippe-Biesterfeld and of his wife, Duchess Marie of Mecklenburg-Strelitz.
January 23, 1916, Dresden-Blasewitz — July 24, 1968,

XXI. Solms (Solms-Braunfels) 2 continued

Issue: 1. Maria-Angela, Princess zu Solms-Braunfels
August 6, 1940, Gera —
(m. March 8, 1963, Bad Homburg, Werner Zawade, born October 29, 1924)

XXI. SOLMS (ZU SOLMS-RÖDELHEIM UND ASSENHEIM) 1, from page 743

Maximilian, Count zu Solms-Rödelheim und Assenheim, son of Count Franz.
September 24, 1893, Assenheim —
m. 1: February 23, 1922, Amorbach. Divorced: October 1, 1937,
* **Viktoria,** Princess of Leiningen, daughter of Fürst Emich zu Leiningen and of his wife, Princess Feodore of Hohenlohe-Langenburg.
May 12, 1895, Amorbach —
m. 2: October 30, 1937, Riga, Latvia
Freda von Gersdorf, daughter of Georg von Gersdorf and of his wife, Baroness Alexandrine von Rosen.
April 25/May 8, 1901, Daugeln, Latvia —

Issue of first marriage:
1. Markwart, Hereditary Count zu Solms-Rödelheim und Assenheim
June 30, 1925, Assenheim —

Issue of second marriage: Not descendant of King George I
2. Johann Georg, Count zu Solms-Rödelheim und Assenheim
February 1, 1938, Marburg —

XXI. SOLMS (ZU SOLMS-LAUBACH) 1, from page 804

Otto, Hereditary Count zu Solms-Laubach, eldest son of Count Otto II.
August 26, 1926, Laubach —
m. July 29, 1958, Berleburg
* **Madeleine,** Princess zu Sayn-Wittgenstein-Berleburg, daughter of Prince Gustav Albrecht, 5th Fürst zu Sayn-Wittgenstein-Berleburg, and of his wife, Margarita Fouché d'Otrante.
April 22, 1936, Giessen —

XXI. Solms (zu Solms-Laubach) 1 continued

Issue: 1. Tatiana, Countess zu Solms-Laubach (twin)
December 16, 1958, London, England —

2. Ariane, Countess zu Solms-Laubach (twin)
December 16, 1958, London —

3. Anna Margareta, Countess zu Solms-Laubach
June 29, 1960, Berleburg —

4. Christina, Countess zu Solms-Laubach
July 19, 1962, Frankfurt-am-Main —

5. Karl, Count zu Solms-Laubach
December 1, 1963, Laubach —

6. Elisabeth, Countess zu Solms-Laubach (twin)
August 12, 1968, Frankfurt-am-Main —

7. Maria, Countess zu Solms-Laubach (twin)
August 12, 1968, Frankfurt-am-Main —

XXI. SOLMS (ZU SOLMS-WILDENFELS) 1, from page 837

Friedrich Magnus (V), Count zu Solms-Wildenfels, son of Count Friedrich Magnus (IV).
November 1, 1886, Wildenfels — September 6, 1945, Gross-Harthau
m. January 4, 1925, Wildenfels
* **Marie Antoinette,** Princess von Schwarzburg, daughter of Prince Günther Sizzo, Fürst zu Schwarzburg, and of his wife, Princess Alexandra of Anhalt-Dessau.
February 7, 1898, Gross-Harthau —

Issue: 1. Alexandra, Countess zu Solms-Wildenfels
January 1, 1926, Wildenfels —

2. Friedrich Magnus (VI), Count zu Solms-Wildenfels (1927–)
m. and divorced: Katharina Duerst (1923–)
see: *zu Solms-Wildenfels* XXI, 2, page 844

3. Jutta, Countess zu Solms-Wildenfels (1928–)
m. Salim Farid Saad (1922–); see: *Saad* XX, page 627

XXI. Solms (zu Solms-Wildenfels) 1 continued

4. Albrecht Sizzo, Count zu Solms-Wildenfels
May 28, 1929, Wildenfels —

5. Kristin, Countess zu Solms-Wildenfels
May 27, 1938, Wildenfels —

XXI. Solms (zu Solms-Wildenfels) 2, from page 843

* **Friedrich Magnus** (VI), Count zu Solms-Wildenfels, eldest son of Count Friedrich Magnus (V).
January 18, 1927, Wildenfels —
m. February 7, 1948, Esslingen. Divorced:
Katharina Duerst, daughter of Harald Eduard Duerst and of his wife, Käthe Saile-Rathenow.
April 22, 1923, Rathenow —
(She m. 1: and divorced: a man named Rademacher.)

Issue: 1. Friedrich Magnus (VII), Count zu Solms-Wildenfels
March 9, 1950, Esslingen —

XXI. SOLMS (ZU SOLMS-BARUTH) 1, from page 175

Friedrich, 3rd Fürst zu Solms-Baruth, eldest son of Fürst Friedrich.
March 25, 1886, Klitschdorf — September 12, 1951, Windhoek, South West Africa
m. August 1, 1914, Potsdam
* **Adelheid,** Princess of Schleswig-Holstein-Sonderburg-Glücksburg, daughter of Duke Friedrich Ferdinand of Schleswig-Holstein-Sonderburg-Glücksburg and of his wife, Princess Karoline Mathilde of Schleswig-Holstein-Sonderburg-Augustenburg.
October 19, 1889, Grünholz —

Issue: 1. Friederike-Luise, Countess zu Solms-Baruth
October 10, 1916, Baruth —

2. Feodore, Countess zu Solms-Baruth (1920–)
m. 1: Dr. Gert Schenk (1910–); see: *Schenk* XXI, page 823
m. 2: Karl Adolf, 10th Fürst von Auersperg (1915–); see: *von Auersperg* XXI, Addendum, page 1026

XXI. Solms (zu Solms-Baruth)

1 continued

3. Rose, Countess zu Solms-Baruth (1925–)
m. Neville Lewis (1895–)
see: *Lewis* XVII, page 529

4. Friedrich, 4th Fürst zu Solms-Baruth
December 22, 1926, Baruth —
(m. August 17, 1963, South-West Africa, Birgitta, Baroness von Berchem-Königsfeld, born January 9, 1924, Berlin
1. Friedrich, Count zu Solms-Baruth, November 27, 1963, Marienthal —
2. Julian, Count zu Solms-Baruth, August 6, 1965, Marienthal —)

5. Caroline Mathilde, Countess zu Solms-Baruth
April 15, 1929, Klitschdorf —
(m. May 12, 1963, Johann van Steenderen, born June 8, 1905)

XXI. Solms (zu Solms-Baruth)

2, from page 175

Hans, Count zu Solms-Baruth, son of Fürst Friedrich.
April 3, 1893, Klitschdorf —
m. May 27, 1920, Glücksburg Castle
* **Karoline Mathilde,** Princess of Schleswig-Holstein-Sonderburg-Glücksburg, daughter of Duke Friedrich Ferdinand of Schleswig-Holstein-Sonderburg-Glücksburg and of his wife, Princess Karoline Mathilde of Schleswig-Holstein-Sonderburg-Augustenburg.
May 1, 1894, Grünholz —

Issue: 1. Viktoria Luise, Countess zu Solms-Baruth (1921–)
m. 1: and divorced: Friedrich, Prince of Saxe-Coburg and Gotha (1918–)
see: *Saxe-Coburg and Gotha* II k–1, page 25
m. 2: Richard C. Whitten (1910–)
see: *Whitten* XXIV, page 1025

2. Friedrich Hans, Count zu Solms-Baruth (1923–)
m. Oda, Princess zu Stolberg-Wernigerode (1925–)
see: *zu Solms-Baruth* XXI, 3, page 846

3. Hubertus, Count zu Solms-Baruth (1934–)
m. 1: Elisabeth-Charlotte von Kerssenbrock (1935–1968)
m. 2: Gerta Stael (1939–)
see: *zu Solms-Baruth* XXI, 4, page 846

XXI. Solms (zu Solms-Baruth) 3, from page 845

* **Friedrich Hans,** Count zu Solms-Baruth, eldest son of Count Hans.
March 3, 1923, Cassel —
m. January 21, 1950, Werfen, near Salzburg, Austria

Oda, Princess zu Stolberg-Wernigerode, daughter of Prince Botho zu Stolberg-Wernigerode and of his wife, Princess Renate of Schönaich-Carolath.
June 10, 1925, Wernigerode —

Issue: 1. Irina, Countess zu Solms-Baruth
July 25, 1953, Salzburg —

2. Christian-Friedrich, Count zu Solms-Baruth
July 13, 1954, Salzburg —

3. Huberta, Countess zu Solms-Baruth
August 22, 1958, Klagenfurt —

XXI. Solms (zu Solms-Baruth) 4, from page 845

* **Hubertus,** Count zu Solms-Baruth, second son of Count Hans.
December 7, 1934, Berlin —
m. 1: August 12, 1961, Barntrup

Elisabeth-Charlotte von Kerssenbrock, daughter of Ernst-Otto von Kerssenbrock and of his wife, Elisabeth-Charlotte von Klot-Heydenfeld.
December 3, 1935, Barntrup — November 6, 1968, Lemgo
m. 2: December 13, 1969, Salzburg

Gerta Stael, daughter of Fabian Stael and of his wife, Helene von Osten-Sacken.
March 23, 1939, Riga, Latvia —

Issue of first marriage:

1. Ruprecht, Count zu Solms-Baruth
August 5, 1963, Munich —

2. Donata, Countess zu Solms-Baruth
March 23, 1965, Freising —

3. Eilika, Countess zu Solms-Baruth
August 8, 1966, Freising —

XXI. SOLZNOKI-SCHEFTSIK 1, from page 798

György (George) Solznoki-Scheftsik
July 11, 1926, Török-Szent-Miklós, Hungary — April 30, 1965, Paris
m. September 23, 1957, Petersburg, near Bonn, Germany
* **Margarethe,** Princess zu Salm-Salm, daughter of Prince Nikolaus, 13th Fürst zu Salm, 8th Fürst zu Salm-Salm, 8th Fürst zu Salm-Kyrburg, and of his first wife, Princess Ida of Wrede.
August 2, 1935, Anholt —

Issue: 1. Stephan Solznoki-Scheftsik
May 10, 1958, Orleans, France —

2. Portia Solznoki-Scheftsik
January 15, 1960, Orleans —

3. Cecile Solznoki-Scheftsik
July 9, 1961, Orleans —

4. Jean Solznoki-Scheftsik
August 2, 1963, Orleans —

XXI. SOMSSICH DE SÁARD 1, from page 886

Pongrácz, Count Somssich de Sáard
August 12, 1920, Budapest, Hungary —
m. April 23, 1952, Leopoldville, Belgian Congo
* **Isabelle,** Baroness Waldbott von Bassenheim, daughter of Baron Friedrich Waldbott von Bassenheim and of his wife, Archduchess Maria Alice of Austria.
April 20, 1926, Satoralja-Ujhely, Hungary —

Issue: 1. István (Stephen), Count Somssich de Sáard
May 23, 1953, Leopoldville, Congo —

2. Gabor, Count Somssich de Sáard
March 14, 1955, Munich —

3. Christoph, Count Somssich de Sáard
July 26, 1960, Usumbura, Burundi —

XXI. SPANYI 1, from page 133

Bela Spanyi
February 23, 1921, Klagenfurt, Austria —
m. January 15, 1946, Hinterhör. Divorced: February 8, 1954, Steyr
* **Eleonore,** Princess von Hanau, Countess von Schaumburg, daughter of Prince Heinrich, 6th Fürst von Hanau und Horowitz, Count von Schaumburg, and of his wife, Countess Maria Antonia Strachwitz von Gross-Zauche und Cammenitz.
May 14, 1925, Horowitz —
(She m. 2: Herbert Joost – see: *Joost* XXI, page 729.)

Issue: 1. Elisabeth Spanyi
October 28, 1946, Rosenheim —

2. Ellen Spanyi
January 18, 1952, Graz —

XXI. VON SPEE 1, from page 752

Rochus, Count von Spee
October 25, 1925, Borken, Westphalia —
m. May 29, 1965, Hollenegg
* **Franziska,** Princess of Liechtenstein, daughter of Prince Karl of Liechtenstein and of his wife, Princess Elisabeth von Urach, Countess of Württemberg.
June 14, 1930, Hollenegg —

Issue: 1. Isabelle, Countess von Spee
June 10, 1966, Menden —

2. Monika, Countess von Spee
December 25, 1967, Menden —

XXI. VON SPIEGELFELD (MATZ) 1, from page 697

Sigmund, Count Matz von Spiegelfeld
May 29, 1898, Linz, Austria —
m. July 16, 1923, Tratzberg Castle
* **Marie,** Countess von Enzenberg zum Freyen und Jöchelsthurn, daughter of Count Hubert von Enzenberg zum Freyen und Jöchelsthurn and of his wife, Countess Maria von Lodron-Loterano.
August 26, 1900, Schwaz —

XXI. von Spiegelfeld (Matz)

1 continued

Issue: 1. Christoph Matz, Count von Spiegelfeld (1924–)
m. Angelika, Countess von Lodron-Loterano (1923–)
see: *von Spiegelfeld (Matz)* XXI, 2, below

2. Monika Matz, Countess von Spiegelfeld (1927–)
m. 1: Franz, Count Deym von Stritez (1925–1962)
see: *Deym von Stritez* XXI, page 684
m. 2: Albrecht, Count Deym von Stritez (1924–)
see: *Deym von Stritez* XXI, page 684

3. Anna Maria Matz, Countess von Spiegelfeld
July 3, 1928, Tijucas, Brazil —

4. Elisabeth Matz, Countess von Spiegelfeld (1931–)
m. Lienhard von Grabmayr (1924–)
see: *von Grabmayr* XXI, page 715

XXI. von Spiegelfeld (Matz)

2, from above

* **Christoph Matz,** Count von Spiegelfeld, only son of Count Sigmund.
May 28, 1924, Schwaz —
m. May 5, 1955,
Angelika, Countess von Lodron-Loterano, daughter of Count Alberich von Lodron-Loterano and of his wife,
June 3, 1923, Gmund —

Issue: 1. Andreas Matz, Count von Spiegelfeld
June 17, 1956, Schwaz —

2. Margarita Matz, Countess von Spiegelfeld
November 18, 1957, Innsbruck —

3. Stefan Matz, Count von Spiegelfeld,
February 18, 1959, Innsbruck —

XXI. VON STACKELBERG 1, from page 813

Karl Georg, Count von Stackelberg
August 1, 1913, Arensburg, Estonia —
m. 1: August 22, 1940, Berlin. Divorced: 1950
Luise Arnberger, daughter of Nils Arnberger and of his wife, Karin Burmann.
September 9, 1916, —
m. 2: December 4, 1950, Bielefeld. Divorced:
Klara Maria Armster, daughter of Karl Wilhelm Armster and of his wife, Ilse von Camp-Massaunen auf Hebron-Damnitz.
March 7, 1925, Berlin —
m. 3: December 16, 1966, Willing, Bavaria
* **Viktoria Luise,** Princess of Schaumburg-Lippe, daughter of Prince Wolrad, Fürst zu Schaumburg-Lippe and of his wife, Princess Bathildis of Schaumburg-Lippe.
July 31, 1940, Hagenburg Castle —

Issue of third marriage:
1. Arved-André, Count von Stackelberg
June 24, 1967, Munich —

2. Stefan-Matthias, Count von Stackelberg
September 20, 1968, Munich —

XXI. VON STAUFFENBERG (SCHENK) 1, from page 854

Berthold Schenk, Count von Stauffenberg, son of Count Claus von Stauffenberg (who was executed after the attempt on the life of Hitler in July 1944).
July 3, 1934, Bamberg —
m. September 22, 1958, Thurn
* **Mechtild Kunigunde Bentzel,** Countess zu Sternau und Hohenau, daughter of Count Götz-Kraft Bentzel zu Sternau und Hohenau and of his wife, Baroness Irmgard von Sturmfeder-Brandt genannt Flender.
January 27, 1938, Bamberg —

Issue: 1. Claus Philipp Schenk, Count von Stauffenberg, June 1, 1959, Bamberg —

2. Sebastian Schenk, Count von Stauffenberg, December 2, 1961, Roding —

3. Gottfried Schenk, Count von Stauffenberg, October 7, 1964, Roding —

XXI. STEEB

1, from page 855

Hans Georg, Baron Steeb
June 25, 1927, Graz, Austria —
m. August 15, 1959, Liemberg
* **Felicitas Daublebsky,** Baroness von Sterneck zu Ehrenstein, daughter of Baron Otto Daublebsky von Sterneck zu Ehrenstein and of his wife, Countess Marie-Hermine Künigl zu Ehrenburg, Baroness von Warth.
March 27, 1933, Klagenfurt —

Issue: 1. Christian, Baron Steeb, November 2, 1960, Graz —

2. Richard, Baron Steeb, October 31, 1961, Graz —

3. Heinrich, Baron Steeb, January 28, 1963, Graz —

XXI. VON STEIN-LIEBENSTEIN ZU BARCHFELD

1, from page 103

Friedrich, Baron von Stein-Liebenstein zu Barchfeld
February 14, 1777, — December 4, 1849,
m. February 15, 1813,
* **Amelie,** Princess of Nassau-Weilburg, daughter of Prince Karl Christian of Nassau-Weilburg and of his wife, Princess Caroline of Orange-Nassau.
August 7, 1776, Kirchheimbolanden — February 19, 1841, Schaumburg
(She m. 1: Fürst Viktor II of Anhalt-Bernberg-Schaumburg-Hoym – see: *Anhalt-Bernberg-Schaumburg-Hoym* XXI, page 642.)

Issue: 1. Friedrich Gustav, Baron von Stein-Liebenstein zu Barchfeld
December 10, 1813, — June 18, 1875, Eisenach
(m. May 18, 1841, Caroline Schulze, June 16, 1815 — November 5, 1867)

XXI. VON STENGAL

1, from page 177

Rudolf Karl, Baron von Stengal
December 7, 1899, Munich —
m. April 19, 1934, Primkenau. Divorced: August 10, 1955, Munich
* **Marie Luise,** Princess of Schleswig-Holstein-Sonderburg-Glücksburg, daughter of Prince Albrecht of Schleswig-Holstein-Sonderburg-Glücksburg and of his wife, Princess Ortrud zu Ysenburg und Büdingen and adopted daughter of Duke Ernst Günther of Schleswig-Holstein-Sonderburg-Augustenburg.

XXI. von Stengal 1 continued

December 8, 1908, Berlin — December 29, 1969, Wiesbaden
(She m. 2: Friedrich, Prince of Schaumburg-Lippe – see: *Schaumburg-Lippe* XXI, page 815.)

Issue: 1. Hertha Margarete, Baroness von Stengal (1935–)
m. Adolpho de Ceno Clemares (–)
see: *de Ceno Clemares* XVIII, page 552

XXI. ZU STERNAU UND HOHENAU (Bentzel) 1, from page 491

Franz-Erich Bentzel, Count zu Sternau und Hohenau
March 2, 1850, Nürnburg — February 8, 1922, Jägersburg
m. May 28, 1879, Frankfurt-am-Main
⋆ **Jadwiga Friederike,** Princess of Hohenlohe-Oehringen, daughter of Prince Felix of Hohenlohe-Oehringen and of his wife, Princess Alexandrine von Hanau, Countess von Schaumburg.
October 6, 1857, Frankfurt-am-Main — January 29, 1940, Jägersburg Castle

Issue: 1. Hugo Bentzel, Count zu Sternau und Hohenau
March 11, 1881, Au Castle — January 28, 1916,

2. Franz Moritz Bentzel, Count zu Sternau und Hohenau (1882–1945)
m. 1: Elisabeth Rosenow (1890–)
m. 2: Irma Aben (1901–)
see: *zu Sternau und Hohenau* (*Bentzel*) XXI, below

3. Waldemar Bentzel, Count zu Sternau und Hohenau
June 20, 1886, Bamberg — August 16, 1898, Jägersburg

XXI. zu Sternau und Hohenau (Bentzel) 2, from above

⋆ **Franz Moritz Bentzel,** Count zu Sternau und Hohenau, only son of Count Franz-Erich.
April 3, 1882, Linz — October 1, 1945, Munich
m. 1: November 3, 1910, Berlin-Grunewald. Divorced:
Elisabeth Rosenow, daughter of Richard Rosenow and of his wife, Luise Munk.
February 21, 1890, Beelitz, near Potsdam —
m. 2: July 30, 1928, Munich
Irma Aben, daughter of Wilhelm Aben and of his wife, Sophie Burmeister.
November 24, 1901, Wismar, Mecklenburg —

XXI. zu Sternau und Hohenau (Bentzel) 2 continued

Issue: 1. Franz Hubertus Bentzel, Count zu Sternau und Hohenau (1911–)
m. Ingeborg Kornfeld (1916–)
see: *zu Sternau und Hohenau (Benztel)* XXI, 3, below

2. Götz-Kraft Bentzel, Count zu Sternau und Hohenau (1912–1943)
m. Irmgard, Baroness von Sturmfeder-Brandt (1907–)
see: *zu Sternau und Hohenau (Bentzel)* XXI, 4, below

3. Elisabeth Bentzel, Countess zu Sternau und Hohenau (1919–)
m. Heinz Frank (1914–)
see: *Frank* XXI, page 710

4. Erika Bentzel, Countess zu Sternau und Hohenau (1920–)
m. Hans Ehling (1916–)
see: *Ehling* XXI, page 693

XXI. zu Sternau und Hohenau (Bentzel) 3, from above

★ **Franz Hubertus Bentzel,** Count zu Sternau und Hohenau, eldest son of Count Franz Moritz Bentzel.
July 18, 1911, Pasing, near Munich —
m. April 1, 1943, Berlin
Ingeborg Kornfeld, daughter of Wilhelm Kornfeld and of his wife, Charlotte Düsterbeck.
August 1, 1916, Berlin-Staaken —

Issue: 1. Thomas Christian Bentzel, Count zu Sternau und Hohenau
September 11, 1947, Munich —

2. Martin Franz Bentzel, Count zu Sternau und Hohenau
February 17, 1949, Munich —

XXI. zu Sternau und Hohenau (Bentzel) 4, from above

★ **Götz-Kraft Bentzel,** Count zu Sternau und Hohenau, second son of Count Franz Moritz.
August 5, 1913, Mörlach Castle – missing since August 8, 1943, somewhere in Russia, presumed killed in action in World War II

XXI. zu Sternau und Hohenau (Bentzel) 4 continued

m. March 6, 1937, Thurn Castle

Irmgard, Baroness von Sturmfeder-Brandt, daughter of Baron Ludwig von Sturmfeder-Brandt and of his wife, Baroness Elisabeth Norneck von Weinheim.

February 14, 1907, Berlin-Steglitz —

Issue: 1. Mechtild Kunigunde Bentzel, Countess zu Sternau und Hohenau (1938–)
m. Berthold Schenk, Count von Stauffenberg (1934–)
see: *von Stauffenberg (Schenk)* XXI, page 850

2. Johannes Bentzel, Count zu Sternau und Hohenau
July 3, 1939, Bamberg —

XXI. VON STERNBERG 1, from page 785

Emanuel, Count von Sternberg

February 11, 1927, Prague, Czechoslovakia —

m. September 27, 1957, Kiel

* **Helene,** Baroness von Plessen, daughter of Baron Johann von Plessen and of his wife, Marie von Wuthenau-Hohenthurm.

February 8, 1933, Berlin —

Issue: 1. Marianne, Countess von Sternberg
March 4, 1959, Arnsberg, Westphalia —

2. Stephanie, Countess von Sternberg
May 13, 1962, Kiel —

XXI. VON STERNECK ZU EHRENSTEIN (Daublebsky) 1, from page 739

Otto Daublebsky, Count von Sterneck und Ehrenstein

January 13, 1902, Hornstein — October 19, 1942, Newelkorodock, near Smolensk, Russia, killed in action in World War II

m. September 6, 1924, Ehrenburg

* **Marie-Hermine Künigl,** Countess zu Ehrenburg, Baroness von Warth, daughter of Count Karl Heinrich Künigl zu Ehrenburg, Baron von Warth, and of his wife, Countess Ilse Liane zu Platen-Hallermund.

March 7, 1904, Ehrenburg —

XXI. von Sterneck zu Ehrenstein (Daublebsky) 1 continued

Issue: 1. Rosmarie Daublebsky, Countess von Sterneck zu Ehrenstein (1926–)
m. Anton, Count Bolza (1916–)
see: *Bolza* XXI, page 669

2. Walther Daublebsky, Count von Sterneck zu Ehrenstein (1929–)
m. Eva Ortner (1926–)
see: *von Sterneck zu Ehrenstein* XXI, 2, below

3. Erich Daublebsky, Count von Sterneck zu Ehrenstein
December 7, 1931, Klagenfurt —

4. Felicitas Daublebsky, Countess von Sterneck zu Ehrenstein (1933–)
m. Hans Georg, Baron Steeb (1927–)
see: *Steeb* XXI, page 851

XXI. von Sterneck zu Ehrenstein (Daublebsky) 2, from above

* **Walther Daublebsky,** Count von Sterneck zu Ehrenstein, eldest son of Count Otto.
July 20, 1929, Klagenfurt —
m. August 24, 1954, Vienna
Eva Ortner, daughter of
November 5, 1926, Vienna —

No Issue.

XXI. VON STILLFRIED UND RATTONITZ 1, from page 858

Rüdiger, Count von Stillfried und Rattonitz
July 14, 1923, Silbitz, Schleswig —
m. January 26, 1944, Lindau
* **Elisabeth,** Countess zu Stolberg-Wernigerode, daughter of Count Franz Xaver zu Stolberg-Wernigerode and of his wife, Princess Barbara of Bourbon-Sicily.
April 17, 1923, Peterswaldau —

XXI. von Stillfried und Rattonitz 1 continued

Issue: 1. Barbara, Countess von Stillfried und Rattonitz
December 22, 1948, Moos, near Platting, Bavaria — March 29, 1951, Lindau

2. Maria, Countess von Stillfried und Rattonitz
August 13, 1950, Lindau —

XXI. VON STOCKAR-SCHERER-CASTELL 1, from page 708

Walther von Stockar-Scherer-Castell
October 13, 1878, Zürich, Switzerland — November 12, 1938, Castell
m. June 26, 1902, Göttlieben
* **Agnes,** Baroness von Fabrice, daughter of Baron Maximilian von Fabrice and of his wife, Countess Ilma Almásy von Zsadány und Török-Szent-Miklós.
December 28, 1881, Göttlieben — November 5, 1964, Castell

Issue: 1. Maximilian von Stockar-Scherer-Castell (1904–)
m. 1: and divorced: Louise de Meuron (1907–)
m. 2: Veronika Bühler (1919–)
see: *von Stockar-Scherer-Castell*, 2, Addendum, page 1073

2. Walter von Stockar-Scherer-Castell (1906–)
m. 1: and divorced: Renée Dürler (1912–)
m. 2: Georgina Koch de Vigier (1910–)
see: *von Stockar-Scherer-Castell*, 3, Addendum, page 1073

3. Elisabeth von Stockar-Scherer-Castell (1908–)
m. Paul Felber (1889–)
see: *Felber*, Addendum, page 1055

XXI. ZU STOLBERG-WERNIGERODE 1, from page 345

Gisbert, Count zu Stolberg-Wernigerode, second son of Count Ludwig Christian.
May 2, 1942, Radenz —
m. September 10, 1967, Büdingen
* **Feodora,** Princess Reuss zu Köstritz, daughter of Prince Heinrich I Reuss zu Köstritz and of his wife, Duchess Woizlawa Feodora of Mecklenburg-Schwerin.
February 5, 1942, Gera, Austria —

Issue:

XXI. zu Stolberg-Wernigerode 2, from page 439

Franz Xaver, Count zu Stolberg-Wernigerode, son of Count Anton.
July 19, 1894, Peterswaldau — May 4, 1947, Gostynie, Poland
m. May 31, 1922, Munich
* **Barbara,** Princess of Bourbon-Sicily, daughter of Prince Ferdinand of Bourbon-Sicily, Duke of Calabria, and of his wife, Princess Maria of Bavaria.
December 14, 1902, Nymphenburg Castle — January 1, 1927, Peterswaldau

Issue: 1. Elisabeth, Countess zu Stolberg-Wernigerode (1923–)
m. Rüdiger, Count von Stillfried und Rattonitz (1923–)
see: *von Stillfried und Rattonitz* XXI, page 855

2. Maria, Countess zu Stolberg-Wernigerode
May 11, 1924, Peterswaldau —

3. Anton, Count zu Stolberg-Wernigerode
July 4, 1925, Peterswaldau —

4. Sophie, Countess zu Stolberg-Wernigerode
December 12, 1926, Peterswaldau —

XXI. ZU STOLBERG-STOLBERG 1, from page 892

Alfred, Fürst and Count zu Stolberg, son of Prince Joseph.
November 23, 1820, Stolberg —January 24, 1903, Rottleberode
m. June 15, 1848, Arolsen
* **Auguste,** Princess zu Waldeck und Pyrmont, daughter of Prince Georg Friedrich, Fürst zu Waldeck und Pyrmont, and of his wife, Princess Emma of Anhalt-Bernberg-Schaumburg-Hoym.
July 21, 1824, Arolsen — September 4, 1893, Norderney

Issue: 1. Wolffgang, 2nd Fürst and Count zu Stolberg (1849–1903)
m. Irmgard, Countess zu Ysenburg und Büdingen in Meerholz (1868–1918)
see: *zu Stolberg-Stolberg* XXI, 2, below

2. Eberhard Berengar, Prince zu Stolberg-Stolberg
June 5, 1851, — August 20, 1851,

3. Vollrath, Prince zu Stolberg-Stolberg
September 9, 1854, Mannheim — May 18, 1906, Stolberg

4. Heinrich, Prince zu Stolberg-Stolberg
March 6, 1855, Stolberg — December 15, 1935, Stolberg

5. Erika, Princess zu Stolberg-Stolberg (1856–1928)
m. Georg Albrecht, Count zu Erbach-Erbach (1844–1915)
see: *zu Erbach-Erbach* XXI, page 702

6. Albrecht, Prince zu Stolberg-Stolberg
January 16, 1861, Stolberg — July 29, 1903, Eulbach Castle

7. Volkwin, Prince zu Stolberg-Stolberg
September 15, 1865, Stolberg — May 25, 1935, Rottleberode Castle

XXI. zu Stolberg-Stolberg 2, from above

* **Wolffgang,** 2nd Fürst and Count zu Stolberg, eldest son of Fürst Alfred.
April 15, 1849, Stolberg — January 27, 1903, Rottleberode
m. May 19, 1897, Meerholz
Irmgard, Countess zu Ysenburg und Büdingen in Meerholz, daughter of Count Karl zu Ysenburg und Büdingen in Meerholz and of his wife, Princess Agnes zu Ysenburg und Büdingen in Büdingen.

XXI. zu Stolberg-Stolberg

2 continued

July 11, 1868, Meerholz — July 4, 1918, Nordhausen

Issue: 1. Imagina, Princess zu Stolberg-Stolberg
March 22, 1901, Rottleberode —

2. Wolffgang-Heinrich, 3rd Fürst and Count zu Stolberg (1903–)
m. Irma Erfert (1910–)
see: *zu Stolberg-Stolberg* XXI, 3, below

XXI. zu Stolberg-Stolberg

3, from above

* **Wolffgang-Heinrich,** 3rd Fürst and Count zu Stolberg, only son of Fürst Wolffgang.
April 28, 1903, Rottleberode —
m. January 22, 1933, Stolberg
Irma Erfert, daughter of Willy Erfert and of his wife, Martha Carben.
April 28, 1910, Perleberg —

Issue: 1. Sixtina, Princess zu Stolberg-Stolberg (1933–)
m. Georg-Friedrich, Prince zu Waldeck und Pyrmont (1936–)
see: *zu Waldeck und Pyrmont* XXI, page 898

2. Johann Wolffgang, Hereditary Prince zu Stolberg-Stolberg
March 27, 1935, Berlin — September 26, 1964, Postiano, Italy

3. Jost Christian, Hereditary Prince zu Stolberg-Stolberg
July 19, 1940, Stolberg —

4. Sophie Charlotte, Princess zu Stolberg-Stolberg (1943–)
m. Friedrich Wilhelm, Fürst zu Wied (1931–)
see: *zu Wied* (*Runkel*) XXI, page 908

XXI. zu Stolberg-Stolberg 4, from page 375

Bernhard, Count zu Stolberg-Stolberg, son of Count Leopold.
January 20, 1881, Mankato — September 22, 1952, Hall
m. April 24, 1918, Wallsee Castle

* **Hedwig,** Archduchess of Austria, daughter of Archduke Franz Salvator of Austria and of his wife, Archduchess Maria Valerie of Austria.
September 24, 1896, Ischl — October , 1971,

Issue: 1. Marie Elisabeth, Countess zu Stolberg-Stolberg, Mother Maria Bonificia OSB of the Cloistered Order of St. Benedikt at Ban Me Thuot, Viet Nam.
March 21, 1919, Innsbruck —

2. Franz Joseph, Count zu Stolberg-Stolberg (1920–)
m. Marie Elisabeth Christiane, Countess Kinsky von Wchinitz und Tettau (1936–)
see: *zu Stolberg-Stolberg* XXI, 5, page 862

3. Friedrich Leopold, Count zu Stolberg-Stolberg (1921–)
m. Aloysia von Pachmann (1923–)
see: *zu Stolberg-Stolberg* XXI, 6, page 862

4. Bernhard, Count zu Stolberg-Stolberg
August 30, 1922, Stams — October 6, 1953, Innsbruck

5. Therese, Countess zu Stolberg-Stolberg (1923–)
m. Paul Joseph, Count Wolff Metternich zur Glacht (1916–)
see: *Wolff Metternich zur Glacht* XXI, page 921

6. Karl, Count zu Stolberg-Stolberg (1925–)
m. Edina Winkelbauer (1923–)
see: *zu Stolberg-Stolberg* XXI, 7, page 863

7. Ferdinand, Count zu Stolberg-Stolberg (1926–)
m. Jutta, Baroness von Cramm-Badenburg (1938–)
see: *zu Stolberg-Stolberg* XXI, 8, page 863

8. Anna Regina, Countess zu Stolberg-Stolberg (1927–)
m. Jacques de Spirlet (1930–)
see: *de Spirlet* XVIII, page 622

9. Magdalena, Countess zu Stolberg-Stolberg (1930–)
m. Martin, Baron von Kripp zu Prunberg und Krippach (1924–)
see: *von Kripp zu Prunberg und Krippach* XXI, page 738

XXI. zu Stolberg-Stolberg 5, from page 861

* **Franz Joseph,** Count zu Stolberg-Stolberg, eldest son of Count Bernhard.
April 30, 1920, Wallsee Castle —
m. August 5, 1957, Kremsmünster

Elisabeth Christiane, Countess Kinsky von Wchinitz und Tettau, daughter of Count Rudolf Kinsky von Wchinitz und Tettau and of his wife, Baroness Elisabeth Herring von Frankensdorff.
May 16, 1936, Mähren-Kromau —

Issue: 1. Marie-Valerie, Countess zu Stolberg-Stolberg
June 6, 1958, Vienna —

2. Marie-Christine, Countess zu Stolberg-Stolberg
July 20, 1959, Vienna —

3. Marie-Antoinette, Countess zu Stolberg-Stolberg
September 8, 1960, Hall, Tyrol, Austria —

4. Marie-Sophie, Countess zu Stolberg-Stolberg
December 14, 1961, Hall —

XXI. zu Stolberg-Stolberg 6, from page 861

* **Friedrich Ludwig,** Count zu Stolberg-Stolberg, second son of Count Bernhard.
May 23, 1921, Wallsee Castle —
m. March 24, 1948, Werfen, near Salzburg

Aloysia von Pachmann, daughter of Ernst von Pachmann and of his wife, Countess Wilhelmine von Galen.
July 24, 1923, Zell-am-See —

Issue: 1. Christoph, Count zu Stolberg-Stolberg
July 18, 1948, Zermatt, Switzerland —

2. Maria Elisabeth, Countess zu Stolberg-Stolberg
December 19, 1949, Hall —

3. Peter, Count zu Stolberg-Stolberg
February 3, 1951, Hall —

XXI. zu Stolberg-Stolberg 6 continued

4. Johannes, Count zu Stolberg-Stolberg
May 14, 1952, Hall —

5. Markus, Count zu Stolberg-Stolberg
May 19, 1953, Hall —

6. Eleonore, Countess zu Stolberg-Stolberg
June 7, 1959, Innsbruck —

7. Marie Imaculata, Countess zu Stolberg-Stolberg
January 9, 1964, Innsbruck —

XXI. zu Stolberg-Stolberg 7, from page 861

* **Karl,** Count zu Stolberg-Stolberg, third son of Count Bernhard.
June 7, 1925, Reichen, Silesia —
m. August 22, 1951, Maria-Wörth

Edina Winkelbauer, daughter of Dr. Adolf Winkelbauer and of his wife, Countess Edina von Clam und Gallas.
May 25, 1923, Vienna —

Issue: 1. Christian Friedrich, Count zu Stolberg-Stolberg
June 9, 1952, Vienna —

2. Andreas, Count zu Stolberg-Stolberg
October 8, 1954, Klagenfurt —

3. Claudia, Countess zu Stolberg-Stolberg
May 25, 1962, Reichen —

XXI. zu Stolberg-Stolberg 8, from page 861

* **Ferdinand,** Count zu Stolberg-Stolberg, fourth son of Count Bernhard.
December 8, 1926, Reichen, Silesia —
m. April 23, 1966, Badenburg

Jutta, Baroness von Cramm-Badenburg, daughter of Baron Adalbert von Cramm-Badenburg and of his wife,
March 15, 1938, Badenburg —

Issue:

XXI. zu Stolberg-Stolberg 9, from page 338

Georg, Count zu Stolberg-Stolberg, son of Count Hermann.
February 25, 1883, Wertheim — February 25, 1963, Gusterheim, Styria
m. July 12, 1916, Dresden

* **Regina,** Princess Reuss zu Köstritz, daughter of Prince Heinrich XXIV Reuss zu Köstritz and of his wife, Princess Elisabeth Reuss zu Köstritz.
April 4, 1886, Jankendorf —

Issue: 1. Elisabeth, Countess zu Stolberg-Stolberg (1918–)
m. 1: Dr. Walther Eisenbach (1906–1944)
see: *Eisenbach* XXI, page 694
m. 2: Alexander, Baron von Warsberg (1910–)
see: *von Warsberg* XXI, page 902

2. Eleonore, Countess zu Stolberg-Stolberg (1920–)
m. Heinrich, Prince zu Schwarzenburg (1903–)
see: *zu Schwarzenburg* XXI, page 838

3. Maria Andrea, Countess zu Stolberg-Stolberg (twin)
November 24, 1921, Micheldorf —
Sister Walburga of the Order of St. Benedict

4. Marie Christina, Countess zu Stolberg-Stolberg (twin)
November 24, 1921, Micheldorf — June 23, 1948, Mergentheim

5. Hermann, Count zu Stolberg-Stolberg
March 4, 1925, Ernstbrunn — January, 1945, in Russia, missing presumed killed in action in World War II

6. Lukas, Count zu Stolberg-Stolberg (1926–)
m. Lydia Maria Perko Edle von Monshoff (1937–)
see: *zu Stolberg-Stolberg* XXI, 10, below

XXI. zu Stolberg-Stolberg 10, from above

* **Lukas,** Count zu Stolberg-Stolberg, only surviving son of Count Georg.
October 19, 1926, Ernstbrunn —
m. December 28, 1962,

Lydia Maria Perko Edle von Monshoff, daughter of Felix Perko Edler von Monshoff and of his wife, Dorothea Mraovic Edle von Gric.

XXI. zu Stolberg-Stolberg 10 continued

May 24, 1937, Vienna —

Issue: 1. Sophie, Countess zu Stolberg-Stolberg
October 17, 1963, Graz —

2. Regina, Countess zu Stolberg-Stolberg
November 21, 1964, Graz —

3. Georg, Count zu Stolberg-Stolberg
January 15, 1966, Graz —

XXI. ZU STOLBERG-ROSSLA 1, from page 336

Christoph Martin, 3rd Fürst zu Stolberg-Rossla, son of Fürst Botho.
April 1, 1888, Rossla — February 27, 1949, Ortenberg
m. November 7, 1911, Greiz
* **Ida,** Princess Reuss zu Greiz, daughter of Prince Heinrich XXII Reuss zu Greiz and of his wife, Princess Ida of Schaumburg-Lippe.
September 4, 1891, Greiz —

Issue: 1. Karoline-Christine, Princess zu Stolberg-Rossla (1912–)
m. 1: Hans Albert von Boltenstern (1905–1940)
see: *von Boltenstern* XXI, page 669
m. 2: Wilhard, Baron von Eberstein (1894–1964)
see: *von Eberstein* XXI, page 692

2. Heinrich-Botho, Prince of Stolberg-Rossla
December 13, 1914, Potsdam —

3. Johann Martin, 4th Fürst zu Stolberg-Rossla (1917–)
m. Hildegard-Anna Sauerbier (1922–)
see: *zu Stolberg-Rossla* XXI, 2, page 866

4. Marie Elisabeth, Princess zu Stolberg-Rossla (1921–)
m. Wilhelm, Prince of Schönburg-Waldenburg (1913–1944)
see: *Schönburg-Waldenburg* XXI, page 836

XXI. zu Stolberg-Rossla 2, from page 865

* **Johann Martin,** 4th Fürst zu Stolberg-Rossla, second son of Fürst Christoph Martin.
October 6, 1917, Rossla —
m. January 28, 1967,
Hildegard-Anna Sauerbier, daughter of
October 5, 1922, Hanau —

Issue:

XXI. STRACHWITZ VON GROSS-ZAUCHE UND CAMMENITZ
1, from page 709

Hyacinth, Count Strachwitz von Gross-Zauche und Cammenitz
May 2, 1920, Gross-Stein —
m. November 16, 1943, Breslau. Divorced: October 12, 1946, Landshutt
* **Constance,** Countess von Francken-Sierstorpff, daughter of Count Hans-Clemens von Francken-Sierstorpff and of his wife, Princess Elisabeth of Hohenlohe-Oehringen.
July 8, 1923, Zyrowa —
(She m. 2: William D. Denson – see: *Denson* XXIV, page 1016.)

Issue: 1. Ivonne, Countess Strachwitz von Gross-Zauche und Cammenitz
August 8, 1944, Breslau —

XXI. STRANDES 1, from page 931

Adolf Strandes
March 10, 1913, Merzin —
m. January 28, 1950, Tegernsee, Bavaria
* **Ilona von Wuthenau-Hohenthurm,** daughter of Carl Adam von Wuthenau-Hohenthurm and of his wife, Countess Gisela von Lüttichau.
November 14, 1913, Bad Liebenstein —
(She m. 1: and divorced: Hans-Joachim von Wallenrodt – see: *von Wollenrodt* XXI, page 900.)

Issue: 1. Carl-Adolf Strandes
August 23, 1950, Tegernsee —

2. Maria-Ilona Strandes
July 17, 1954, Tegernsee —

XXI. STURTZKOPF 1, from page 707

Walther Sturtzkopf
May 10, 1871, Hanover — October 5, 1898, Konstanz
m. May 24, 1894, Göttlieben
* **Luigina,** Baroness von Fabrice, daughter of Baron Maximilian von Fabrice and of his wife, Countess Ilma Almásy von Zsadány und Török-Szent-Miklós.
July 30, 1876, Nonnenhorn, Bavaria — April 29, 1958, Augsburg
(She m. 2: and divorced: Edgar Böcking – see *Böcking* XXI, page 667.)
(She m. 3: and divorced: Hans Hippolyt von Simpson – see: *von Simpson* XXI, page 839.)
(She m. 4: Dr. Edwin Tietjens – see: *Tietjens* XXI, page 876.)

Issue: 1. Hermine Sturtzkopf (1895–)
m. Georg von Szebeny (1887–); see: *von Szebeny*, Addendum, page 1074

2. Charley Sturtzkopf (1896–)
m. Eugenie Bleifuss (1929–); see: *Sturtzkopf*, Addendum, page 1074

XXI. VON SÜSSKIND-SCHWENDI 1, from page 816

Albrecht, Baron von Süsskind-Schwendi
February 20, 1937, Schweinfurt —
m. September 21, 1958, Lehenleitern, Austria
* **Christine,** Princess of Schaumburg-Lippe, daughter of Prince Friedrich Christian of Schaumburg-Lippe and of his wife, Countess Alexandra zu Castell-Rüdenhausen.
October 16, 1936, Berlin —

Issue: 1. Gabriele, Baroness von Süsskind-Schwendi, November 3, 1959, Heidenheim an der Brenz —

2. Konstantin, Baron von Süsskind-Schwendi, September 5, 1962, Heidenheim —

XXI. VON TAUBENHEIM 1, from page 235

Wilhelm, Count von Taubenheim
April 16, 1805, Stuttgart — January 4, 1894, Stuttgart
m. September 17, 1842, Serach, near Essen
* **Marie,** Countess of Württemberg, daughter of Duke Wilhelm of Württemberg and of his wife, Baroness Wilhelmine von Tunderfeldt-Rhodis.
May 29, 1815, Stuttgart — December 31, 1866, Stuttgart

Issue: 1. Marie, Countess von Taubenheim – a Deaconess at Stuttgart
July 31, 1843, Stuttgart — April 11, 1919,

XXI. von Taubenheim

1 continued

2. Wilhelm, Count von Taubenheim
   April 4, 1845, — , 1887,

3. Olga, Countess von Taubenheim (1850–1925)
   m. August, Baron von Wöllwert-Lauterberg (1845–1908)
   see: *von Wöllwert-Lauterberg* XXI, page 922

4. Sophie, Countess von Taubenheim (1852–1929)
   m. Ernst Baier von Ehrenberg (1855–1920)
   see: *Baier von Ehrenberg* XXI, page 651

XXI. TECKEMEYER

1, from page 740

Jürgen Teckemeyer
July 26, 1937, Duisburg —
m. November 26, 1961,
* **Margarethe Künigl,** Countess zu Ehrenburg, Baroness von Warth, daughter of Count Karl Heinrich Künigl zu Ehrenburg, Baron von Warth, and of his wife, Countess Ilse Liane zu Platen-Hallermund.
August 26, 1939, Meran —

Issue: 1. Eric Teckemeyer
May 25, 1962, Munich —

2. Marion Teckemeyer
May 23, 1964, Munich —

XXI. THEISEN

1, from page 342

Erich Theisen
June 7, 1905, Kastellaun — , 1954, Berlin
m. . Divorced: September 23, 1946, Berlin
* **Marie Luise,** Princess Reuss zu Köstritz, daughter of Prince Heinrich XXXIII Reuss zu Köstritz and of his wife, Princess Viktoria Margarete of Prussia.
January 9, 1915, Cassel —
(She m. 2: and divorced: Dr. Alexander Bodey – see: *Bodey* XXI, page 668.)

Issue: 1. Viktoria Sibylle Theisen
December 31, 1942, Berlin-Charlottenburg —

XXI. VON THUN UND HOHENSTEIN 1, from page 236

Franz, Count von Thun und Hohenstein
July 27, 1826, Choltitz — July 30, 1888, Schwaz
m. June 16, 1877, Innsbruck

* **Auguste Eugenie,** Princess von Urach, Countess of Württemberg, daughter of Count Wilhelm of Württemberg, Duke von Urach, and of his first wife, Princess Theodelinda de Beauharnais.
December 27, 1842, Stuttgart — March 11, 1916, Schwaz
(She m. 1: Parzival Rudolf, Count von Enzenberg zum Freyen und Jöchelsthurn - see: *von Enzenberg zum Freyen und Jöchelsthurn* XXI, page 694.)

Issue: 1. Konstantin, Count von Thun und Hohenstein (1878–1962)
m. Therese, Baroness von Stotzingen (1881–1966)
see: *von Thun und Hohenstein* XXI, 2, below

2. Maria, Countess von Thun und Hohenstein (1879–1958)
m. Cajetan, Conte Forni (1856–1921)
see: *Forni* XVIII, page 561

XXI. von Thun und Hohenstein 2, from above

* **Konstantin,** Count von Thun und Hohenstein, only son of Count Franz.
March 15, 1878, Innsbruck — March 27, 1962, Donzdorf, Württemberg
m. September 29, 1903, Steisslingen

Therese, Baroness von Stotzingen, daughter of Baron Roderich von Stotzingen and of his wife, Countess Karoline von Rechberg und Rothenlöwen zu Hohenrechberg.
— April 18, 1966, Donzdorf

Issue: 1. Johann, Count von Thun und Hohenstein
July 9, 1906, Innsbruck — July 10, 1906, Innsbruck

2. Roderich, Count von Thun und Hohenstein (1908–)
m. Manuela, Countess von Tattenbach (1926–)
see: *von Thun und Hohenstein* XXI, 3, page 870

3. Otmar, Count von Thun und Hohenstein (1910–)
m. Helene Grabmayer von Angerheim (1926–)
see: *von Thun und Hohenstein* XXI, 4, page 870

XXI. von Thun und Hohenstein

2 continued

4. Maria Rosario, Countess von Thun und Hohenstein (1914–)
m. Erwin von Lill-Rastern (1905–)
see: *von Lill-Rastern* XXI, page 752

5. Joseph Bernhard, Count von Thun und Hohenstein (1917–)
m. Oda, Baroness von Fürstenberg (1920–)
see: *von Thun und Hohenstein* XXI, 5, page 871

6. Matteo, Count von Thun und Hohenstein
August 23, 1919, Innsbruck — September 17, 1941, near Werchnij-Rogatschik, Russia, killed in action in World War II

XXI. von Thun und Hohenstein

3, from page 869

* **Roderich,** Count von Thun und Hohenstein, eldest son of Count Konstantin.
January 10, 1908, Innsbruck —
m. October 3, 1955, San Jose, Costa Rica
Manuela, Countess von Tattenbach, daughter of Count Franz von Tattenbach and of his wife, Louisa Eglesyas.
September 24, 1926, Berlin —

No Issue.

XXI. von Thun und Hohenstein

4, from page 869

* **Otmar,** Count von Thun und Hohenstein, second son of Count Konstantin.
October 1, 1910, Innsbruck —
m. August 21, 1951, San Romedio Nonstal
Helene Grabmayer von Angerheim, daughter of Anton Grabmayer von Angerheim and of his wife, Rosa Trafojer.
November 25, 1926, Bozen —

Issue: 1. Matthäus, Count von Thun und Hohenstein
June 17, 1952, Bozen-Greis —

2. Peter, Count von Thun und Hohenstein
February 23, 1955, Innsbruck —

XXI. von Thun und Hohenstein 5, from page 870

***Joseph Bernhard,** Count von Thun und Hohenstein, third son of Count Konstantin.
October 25, 1917, Innsbruck —
m. June 18, 1943, Murnau
Oda, Baroness von Fürstenberg, daughter of Baron Wilderich von Fürstenberg and of his wife, Marie Melhame of the House of Emire von Akura.
December 13, 1920, Herringhausen Castle —

Issue: 1. Monika, Countess von Thun und Hohenstein
April 9, 1944, Herdringen — April 27, 1945, Herdringen

2. Georg (Jörg), Count von Thun und Hohenstein
June 12, 1946, Herdringen —

3. Angelika, Countess von Thun und Hohenstein
July 28, 1947, Herdringen —

4. Konstantin, Count von Thun und Hohenstein
June 13, 1949, Herdringen —

5. Maria Assunta, Countess von Thun und Hohenstein
July 22, 1951, Herdringen —

6. Franziscus von Assisi, Count von Thun und Hohenstein
December 5, 1952, Hüsten, Westphalia —

7. Johanna, Countess von Thun und Hohenstein
December 29, 1957, Neheim-Hüsten —

XXI. THURN UND TAXIS 1, from page 390

Albrecht, 8th Fürst von Thurn und Taxis, son of Hereditary Prince Maximilian.
May 8, 1867, Regensburg — January 22, 1952, Regensburg
m. July 15, 1890, Budapest, Hungary
***Margarete,** Archduchess of Austria, daughter of Archduke Joseph of Austria and of his wife, Princess Clothilde of Saxe-Coburg and Gotha.
July 6, 1870, Alcsut, Hungary — May 2, 1955, Regensburg

XXI. Thurn und Taxis

1 continued

Issue: 1. Franz Joseph, 9th Fürst von Thurn und Taxis (1893–1971)
m. Elisabeth, Princess of Braganca, Infanta of Portugal (1894–)
see: *Thurn und Taxis* XXI, 2, below

2. Karl August, 10th Fürst von Thurn und Taxis (1898–)
m. Maria Anna, Princess of Braganca, Infanta of Portugal (1899–1971)
see: *Thurn und Taxis* XXI, 3, page 873

3. Ludwig Philipp, Prince of Thurn und Taxis (1901–1933)
m. Elisabeth, Princess of Luxemburg (1901–1950)
see: *Thurn und Taxis* XXI, 4, page 874

4. Max Emanuel, Prince of Thurn und Taxis
March 1, 1902, Regensburg —

5. Elisabeth Helene, Princess of Thurn und Taxis (1903–)
m. Friedrich Christian, Prince of Saxony, Margraf von Meissen (1893–1968)
see: *Saxony* VII dd–1, page 289

6. Raphael Rainer, Prince of Thurn und Taxis (1906–)
m. Margarete, Princess of Thurn und Taxis (1913–)
see: *Thurn und Taxis* XXI, 5, page 874

7. Philipp Ernst, Prince of Thurn und Taxis (1908–1964)
m. Eulalia, Princess of Thurn und Taxis (1908–)
see: *Thurn und Taxis* XXI, 6, page 874

XXI. Thurn und Taxis

2, from above

* **Franz Joseph,** 9th Fürst von Thurn und Taxis, eldest son of Fürst Albrecht.
December 21, 1893, Regensburg — July 13, 1971, Regensburg
m. November 23, 1920, Bronnbach Castle

Elisabeth, Princess of Braganca, Infanta of Portugal, daughter of Duke Miguel of Braganca, Infante of Portugal and of his second wife, Princess Therese zu Löwenstein-Wertheim-Rosenberg.
November 19, 1894, Kleinheubach —

XXI. Thurn und Taxis 2 continued

Issue: 1. Gabriel, Hereditary Prince of Thurn und Taxis
October 16, 1922, Haus Castle — December 17, 1942, Stalingrad, Russia, killed in action in World War II

2. Helene, Princess of Thurn und Taxis (1924–)
m. Rudolf Erwein, Count von Schönborn-Wiesentheid (1918–)
see: *von Schönborn-Wiesentheid* XXI, page 831

3. Maria Theresia, Princess of Thurn und Taxis (1925–)
m. Eduard, Count von Oppersdorff (1919–)
see: *von Oppersdorff* XXI, page 778

4. Maria Ferdinande, Princess of Thurn und Taxis (1927–)
m. and annulled: Franz Joseph, Prince of Hohenzollern-Sigmaringen (1926–)
see: *Hohenzollern-Sigmaringen* II gg–1, page 84

XXI. Thurn und Taxis 3, from page 872

* **Karl August,** 10th Fürst von Thurn und Taxis, second son of 8th Fürst Albrecht.
July 23, 1898, Garatshausen Castle —
m. August 18, 1921, Taxis Castle
Maria Anna, Princess of Braganca, Infanta of Portugal, daughter of Duke Miguel of Braganca, Infante of Portugal, and of his second wife, Princess Therese zu Löwenstein-Wertheim-Rosenberg.
September 3, 1899, Fischhorn Castle — July , 1971,

Issue: 1. Clothilde, Princess of Thurn und Taxis (1922–)
m. Johann Moritz, Prince of Liechtenstein (1914–)
see: *Liechtenstein* XXI, page 750

2. Mafalda, Princess of Thurn und Taxis (1924–)
m. Franz von Assisi, Prince of Thurn und Taxis (1915–)
see: *Thurn und Taxis* XXI, 9, page 876

3. Johannes Baptista, Hereditary Prince of Thurn und Taxis
June 5, 1926, Höfling Castle, near Regensburg —

XXI. Thurn und Taxis 4, from pages 872, 107

* **Ludwig Philipp,** Prince of Thurn und Taxis, third son of Fürst Albrecht.
February 2, 1901, Regensburg — April 22, 1933, Niederaichbach Castle
m. November 14, 1922, Hohenberg Castle, near Lenggries, Bavaria

* **Elisabeth,** Princess of Luxemburg, Princess of Nassau-Weilburg, daughter of Grand Duke Wilhelm of Luxemburg, Prince of Nassau-Weilburg, and of his wife, Princess Maria Anna of Braganca, Infanta of Portugal.
March 7, 1901, Luxemburg — August 2, 1950, Hohenberg Castle

Issue: 1. Anselm, Prince of Thurn und Taxis
April 14, 1924, Jagdhaus Tiergarten, near Regensburg — February 25, 1944, near Solotaia-Balka, Russia, killed in action in World War II

2. Iniga, Princess of Thurn und Taxis (1925–)
m. Eberhard, Count of Württemberg, Fürst von Urach (1907–)
see: *Württemberg* VI m–1, page 240

XXI. Thurn und Taxis 5, from pages 872, 875

* **Raphael Rainer,** Prince of Thurn und Taxis, fifth son of 8th Fürst Albrecht.
May 30, 1906, Regensburg —
m. May 24, 1932, Regensburg

* **Margarete (Rita),** Princess of Thurn und Taxis, daughter of Prince Maximilian Theodor of Thurn und Taxis and of his wife, Princess Pauline Metternich-Winneburg.
October 19, 1913, Berlin —

Issue: 1. Max Emmanuel, Prince of Thurn und Taxis
September 7, 1935, Bullachburg Castle —

XXI. Thurn und Taxis 6, from page 872

* **Philipp Ernst,** Prince of Thurn und Taxis, sixth son of 8th Fürst Albrecht.
May 7, 1908, Prüffening Castle — July 23, 1964, Hohenberg Castle
m. September 8, 1929, Taxis Castle

XXI. Thurn und Taxis 6 continued

Eulalia (Illa), Princess of Thurn und Taxis, daughter of Prince Friedrich of Thurn und Taxis and of his wife, Princess Eleonore de Ligne.
December 21, 1908, Biskupitz —

Issue: 1. Albrecht Friedrich, Prince of Thurn und Taxis (1930–)
m. Alexandra, Baroness von der Ropp (1932–)
see: *Thurn und Taxis* XXI, 7, below

2. Margarete Eleonore, Princess of Thurn und Taxis
December 1, 1933, Hohenberg Castle —

3. Antonia, Princess of Thurn und Taxis
January 28, 1936, Hohenberg Castle —

XXI. Thurn und Taxis 7, from above

* **Albrecht Friedrich,** Prince of Thurn und Taxis, eldest son of Prince Philipp Ernst.
July 5, 1930, Prüffening Castle —
m. July 28, 1962 (civil), Sushaupt, and July 30, 1962 (religious), Bukenstein
Alexandra, Baroness von der Ropp, daughter of Baron Schweter von der Ropp and of his wife, Ursule von Boetticher.
October 31, 1932, Königsberg —

No Issue.

XXI. Thurn und Taxis 8, from page 772

Maximilian Theodor, Prince of Thurn und Taxis, son of Prince Theodor.
March 8, 1876, Mentone — October 3, 1939, Plass Castle, near Pilsen
m. February 5, 1906, Vienna
* **Pauline,** Princess von Metternich-Winneburg, daughter of Fürst Paul von Metternich-Winneburg and of his wife, Countess Melanie von Zichy-Ferraris zu Zich und Vásonykeö.
January 6, 1880, Pressburg — May 19, 1960, Füssen

Issue: 1. Margarete (Rita), Princess of Thurn und Taxis (1913–)
m. Raphael Rainer, Prince of Thurn und Taxis (1906–)
see: *Thurn und Taxis* XXI, 5, page 874

XXI. Thurn und Taxis 9, from page 873

Franz von Assisi, Prince von Thurn und Taxis, fourth son of Prince Erich.
April 15, 1915, Lissa Castle —
m. 1: May 27, 1950, Vienna (marriage not recognized). Divorced: March 27, 1952, Vienna, and by the church November 2, 1963
Beatrix Estella de Gamas, daughter of Miguel Angel de Gamas and of his wife Elena Mascias.
—
(She m. 2: Carlos Aristimuno.)
m. 2: December 22, 1961 (civil), and January 16, 1964, Andechs, Bavaria
* **Mafalda,** Princess von Thurn und Taxis, daughter of Prince Karl August von Thurn und Taxis and of his wife, Infanta Maria Anna of Portugal.
March 6, 1924, Regensburg —

Issue: 1. Daria, Princess von Thurn und Taxis
March 6, 1962, Munich —

XXI. TIETJENS 1, from page 707

Edwin Tietjens
March 20, 1894, St. Petersburg — May 22, 1944, Buckow, near Berlin
m. September 14, 1926, Riga, Latvia
* **Luigina,** Baroness von Fabrice, daughter of Baron Maximilian von Fabrice and of his wife, Countess Ilma Almásy von Zsadány und Török-Szent-Miklós.
July 30, 1876, Nonnenhorn — April 29, 1958, Augsburg
(She m. 1: Walther Sturtzkopf – see: *Sturtzkopf* XXI, page 867.)
(She m. 2: and divorced: Edgar Böcking – see: *Böcking* XXI, page 667.)
(She m. 3: and divorced: Hans Hippolyt von Simpson – see: *von Simpson* XXI, page 839.)

No Issue.

XXI. TÖRRING-JETTENBACH 1, from page 197

Karl Theodor, Count zu Törring-Jettenbach, son of Count Hans Veit.
September 22, 1900, Winhöring Castle — May 14, 1967, Munich
m. January 10, 1934, Munich
* **Elisabeth,** Princess of Greece and Denmark, daughter of Prince Nicholas of Greece and Denmark and of his wife, Grand Duchess Elena Vladimirovna of Russia.
May 24, 1904, Tatoi, Greece — January 11, 1955, Munich

XXI. Törring-Jettenbach **1 continued**

Issue: 1. Hans Veit, Count zu Törring-Jettenbach (1935–)
m. Henriette, Princess of Hohenlohe-Bartenstein (1938–)
see: *Törring-Jettenbach* XXI, 2, below

2. Helene, Countess zu Törring-Jettenbach (1937–)
m. Ferdinand, Archduke of Austria (1918–)
see: *Austria* (*Habsburg*) X 1–2, page 365

XXI. Törring-Jettenbach **2, from above**

* **Hans Veit,** Count zu Törring-Jettenbach, son of Count Karl Theodor.
January 11, 1935, Winhöring Castle —
m. April 20, 1964, Bartenstein Castle
Henriette, Princess of Hohenlohe-Bartenstein, daughter of Prince Karl, 8th Fürst zu Hohenlohe-Bartenstein, and of his wife, Baroness Klara von Meyern-Hohenberg.
August 23, 1938, Bartenstein Castle —

Issue: 1. Clarissa, Countess zu Törring-Jettenbach
March 31, 1965, Munich —

2. Ignacz, Count zu Törring-Jettenbach
March 30, 1966, Munich —

3. Karl Theodor, Count zu Törring-Jettenbach
February 17, 1969, Munich —

XXI. Törring-Jettenbach **3, from page 885**

Hans-Heribert, Count zu Törring-Jettenbach, son of Count Hans Veit.
December 25, 1903, Winhöring —
m. 1: October 9 and 10, 1938. Marriage annulled: November 3, 1947.
Viktoria Lindpaintner, daughter of Paul Lindpaintner and of his wife, Marie Wegemann.
February 13, 1918, Frankfurt-am-Main —
m. 2: December 10, 1947, Winhöring
* **Marie Immakulata,** Baroness Waldbott von Bassenheim, daughter of Baron Friedrich Waldbott von Bassenheim and of his wife, Archduchess Maria Alice of Austria.
July 27, 1921, Harmshutta, Hungary —

XXI. Törring-Jettenbach 3 continued

Issue: 1. Alice, Countess zu Törring-Jettenbach
June 5, 1949, Munich —

2. Marie-Jose, Countess zu Törring-Jettenbach
October 27, 1950, Munich —

3. Hans-Kaspar, Count zu Törring-Jettenbach
July 22, 1953, Munich —

4. Maximilian-Gaudenz, Count zu Törring-Jettenbach
January 29, 1955, Munich —

5. Sophie, Countess zu Törring-Jettenbach
March 26, 1957, Munich —

XXI. TREUSCH VON BUTTLAR-BRANDENFELS 1, from page 137

Hans Treusch, Baron von Buttlar-Brandenfels
May 5, 1885, Berlin — July 27, 1946, Oberurf
m. 1: May 30, 1918, . Divorced: March 15, 1927,
Marie Louise Schrey, daughter of
—
m. 2: June 2, 1927, Oberurf
* **Marie Luise (Marielier),** Countess von Schaumburg, daughter of Prince Philipp von Hanau, Count of Schaumburg, and of his wife, Anne von Trott, created Countess von Schaumburg.
December 17, 1903, Lehrbach —

Issue: 1. Marielier (Lily) Treusch, Baroness von Buttlar-Brandenfels (1928–)
m. Leopold Beierl (1915–)
see: *Beierl* XXI, page 662

2. Marianne Treusch, Baroness von Buttlar-Brandenfels (1930–)
m. Herbert Weygand (1936–)
see: *Weygand* XXI, page 905

XXI. Treusch von Buttlar-Brandenfels 1 continued

3. Hans Treusch, Baron von Buttlar-Brandenfels (1933–)
m. Inge Parpart (1931–)
see: *Treusch von Buttlar-Brandenfels* XXI, 2, below

XXI. Treusch von Buttlar-Brandenfels 2, from above

★ **Hans Treusch,** Baron von Buttlar-Brandenfels, only son of Baron Hans.
February 23, 1933, Treysa —
m. January 21, 1959, Cassel
Inge Parpart, daughter of Alfred Parpart and of his wife, Hildegarde Hochsprung.
September 6, 1931, Köslin, Pomerania —

Issue: 1. Hans Bernhard Treusch, Baron von Buttlar-Brandenfels
October 12, 1961, Marburg —

XXI. VON TROTHA 1, from page 937

Thilo von Trotha
July 27, 1882, Callenberg — December 14, 1969, Skopau
m. April 14, 1916, Wächtersbach
★ **Ida,** Princess zu Ysenburg und Büdingen in Wächtersbach, daughter of Prince Friedrich zu Ysenburg und Büdingen in Wächtersbach and of his wife, Countess Anna Dobrzensky von Dobrzenicz.
August 9, 1885, Wächtersbach — October 18, 1964, Stuttgart

Issue: 1. Huberta von Trotha (1917–)
m. 1: and divorced: Albert Heino, Baron von Beust (1911–)
see: *von Beust* XXI, page 662
m. 2: and divorced: Angus, Count von Douglas (1913–)
see: *von Douglas* XXI, page 687
m. 3: Hans Becker-Eldena (1916–)
see: *Becker-Eldena* XXI, page 653

2. Alexandra von Trotha (1919–)
m. and divorced: Alexander von Brandenstein (1909–)
see: *von Brandenstein* XXI, page 670

XXI. von Trotha — 1 continued

3. Elisabeth von Trotha (1920–)
   m. Aloys, Hereditary Prince of Schönburg-Hartenstein (1916–1945)
   see: *Schönburg-Hartenstein* XXI, page 831

4. Irene Eleanore von Trotha
   February 28, 1922, Skopau —

5. Wolf-Ulrich von Trotha
   October 28, 1923, Skopau — June 26, 1944, Arezzo, Austria, killed in action in World War II

6. Hans Christian von Trotha (twin)
   October 4, 1926, Skopau — June 26, 1944, Arezzo, Austria, killed in action in World War II on the same day as his brother, Wolf-Ulrich

7. Thilo von Trotha (1926–1966) (twin)
   m. Alexandra, Princess of Hohenlohe-Langenburg (1935–)
   see: *von Trotha* XXI, 2, below

XXI. von Trotha — 2, from above

* **Thilo von Trotha,** youngest son of Thilo.
October 4, 1926, Skopau — June 26, 1966, Pfaffenhofen, near Munich, killed in a road accident
m. July 18, 1959, Hösskirch

Alexandra, Princess of Hohenlohe-Langenburg, daughter of Prince Karl Erwein of Hohenlohe-Langenburg and of his wife, Countess Viktoria Czernin von und zu Chudenitz.
July 19, 1935, Dresden —

Issue: 1. Thilo von Trotha
   April 26, 1960, Gottmadingen, near Konstanz —

2. Irene-Eleanore von Trotha
   May 28, 1962, Saulgau, Württemberg —

XXI. von Trotha 2 continued

3. Hans-Ulrich von Trotha
July 19, 1965, Stuttgart —

XXI. VON TWICKEL 1, from page 681

Johann, Baron von Twickel
July 25, 1940, Berlin —
m. May 6, 1968, Munich
⋆ **Viktoria Benigna,** Princess Biron von Curland, daughter of Prince Biron Karl von Curland and of his wife, Princess Herzelaide of Prussia.
July 2, 1939, Gross Wartenberg —

Issue: 1. Nikolaus, Baron von Twickel
April 1, 1969, Munich —

XXI. VON UNGELTER-DEISSENHAUSEN 1, from page 801

Alexander, Baron von Ungelter-Deissenhausen
September 14, 1920, Berlin —
m. September 10, 1956, Herdringen Castle
⋆ **Elisabeth,** Countess Saurma von der Jeltsch-Lorzendorf, daughter of Count Karl Anton Saurma von der Jeltsch-Lorzendorf and of his wife, Countess Marie-Lory von Matuschka, Baroness von Topolczan und Spaetgan.
July 4, 1929, Lorzendorf —

Issue: 1. Marie-Alexandrine, Baroness von Ungelter-Deissenhausen
January 29, 1957, Munich —

2. Maria Regina, Baroness von Ungelter-Deissenhausen
August 14, 1958, Munich —

3. Maria Johanna, Baroness von Ungelter-Deissenhausen
May 11, 1965, Kösching Castle —

XXI. VETTER VON DER LILIE 1, from page 695

Rudolf, Count Vetter von der Lilie
September 18, 1860, Laibach — March 2, 1932, Innsbruck
m. October 29, 1891, Graz
* **Theodolinde,** Countess von Enzenberg zum Freyen und Jöchelsthurn, daughter of Count Parzival Rudolf von Enzenberg zum Freyen und Jöchelsthurn and of his wife, Countess Auguste Eugenie of Württemberg.
October 3, 1866, Schwaz — July 8, 1951, Innsbruck

Issue: 1. Auguste, Countess Vetter von der Lilie
August 14, 1892, Bregenz — December 14, 1956, Innsbruck

2. Rudolf, Count Vetter von der Lilie (1898–) (twin)
m. Dorothea Wenzel, Baroness von Sternbach (1899–)
see: *Vetter von der Lilie* XXI, 2, below

3. Bohuslav, Count Vetter von der Lilie (twin)
July 24, 1898, Innsbruck — April 8, 1918, Hall, Tyrol

XXI. Vetter von der Lilie 2, from above

* **Rudolf,** Count Vetter von der Lilie, eldest son of Count Rudolf.
July 24, 1898, Innsbruck —
m. November 5, 1924, Innsbruck
Dorothea Wenzel, Baroness von Sternbach, daughter of
December 23, 1899, Linz —

Issue: 1. Felix Georg, Count Vetter von der Lilie (1928–)
m. Elisabeth, Baroness von Fürstenberg (1938–)
see: *Vetter von der Lilie* XXI, 3, below

2. Maria Antonia, Countess Vetter von der Lilie (1932–)
m. Erasmus, Baron von Fürstenberg (1936–)
see: *von Fürstenberg* XXI, page 711

XXI. Vetter von der Lilie 3, from above

* **Felix Georg,** Count Vetter von der Lilie, only son of Count Rudolf.
March 6, 1928, Innsbruck —
m. April 2, 1964 (civil), Innsbruck, and April 29, 1964 (religious), Weihenstephan

XXI. Vetter von der Lilie 3 continued

Elisabeth, Baroness von Fürstenberg, daughter of
February 12, 1938, Landshüt —

Issue: 1. Georg, Count Vetter von der Lilie
March 15, 1965, Innsbruck —

XXI. VON VINCKE 1, from page 125

Friedrich, Baron von Vincke
July 24, 1867, Zeesen — December 31, 1925, Wiesbaden
m. September 3, 1898, Frankfurt-am-Main. Divorced: May 24, 1923, Frankfurt-am-Main
* **Sibylle,** Princess of Hesse-Cassel, daughter of Prince Friedrich Wilhelm, Landgrave of Hesse-Cassel and of his wife, Princess Anne of Prussia.
June 3, 1877, Panker Castle, Holstein — February 11, 1953, Wiesbaden

Issue: 1. Itel-Jobst, Baron von Vincke (1899–)
m. Martha Hoeppe-Menée (1909–)
see: *von Vincke* XXI, 2, below

2. Alfram-Dietrich, Baron von Vincke (1903–1966)
m. Gurli Marie Nielsen (1912–)
see: *von Vincke* XXI, 3, page 884

XXI. von Vincke 2, from above

Itel-Jobst, Baron von Vincke, eldest son of Baron Friedrich.
June 20, 1899, Frankfurt-am-Main —
m. May 14, 1929, Wiesbaden
Martha Hoeppe-Menée, daughter of Alfred Hoeppe-Menée and of his wife,
November 16, 1909, Thionville, Germany (now in France) —

No Issue.

XXI. von Vincke 3, from page 883

* **Alfram-Dietrich,** Baron von Vincke, second son of Baron Friedrich.
May 18, 1903, Frankfurt-am-Main — March 30, 1966, Wiesbaden
m. December 7, 1935, Zingst
Gurli Marie Nielsen, daughter of
March 14, 1912, Copenhagen, Denmark —

No Issue.

XXI. VLANGALI-HANDJERI 1, from page 170

Michael, Prince Vlangali-Handjeri
, 1833, Riga, Latvia — July 27, 1911, Manerbe
m. 1: October 24, 1865, London
* **Luise Karoline,** Princess von Noer, daughter of Prince Friedrich von Noer and of his wife, Countess Henriette Danneskiold-Samsoe.
July 29, 1836, Schleswig — September 25, 1866, Manerbe
m. 2: , 1871, London, England
Ida Ramsay, daughter of
, 1858, — December 13, 1913, Manerbe

Issue of first marriage:
1. Karl, Prince Vlangali-Handjeri (1866–1933) (twin)
m. Luise Amelie, Princess von Noer (1873–1955)
see: *Vlangali-Handjeri* XXI, 2, below

2. Alexander, Prince Vlangali-Handjeri (twin)
July 28, 1866, Manerbe — January 4, 1867, Manerbe

XXI. Vlangali-Handjeri 2, from above and page 170

* **Karl,** Prince Vlangali-Handjeri, only son of Prince Michael.
July 28, 1866, Manerbe — November 1, 1933, Manerbe
m. November 26, 1899, London, England
* **Luise Amelie,** Princess von Noer, daughter of Prince Friedrich Christian von Noer, Count von Noer, and of his wife, Carmelita Eisenblat.
November 1, 1873, Noer — June 2, 1955, Kiel

Issue: 1. Karoline Mathilde, Princess Vlangali-Handjeri (1900–)
m. Dr. Louis Laur (1904–1957)
see: *Laur* XVIII, page 568

XXI. VOGELBACHER 1, from page 1083

Heinrich Vogelbacher
December 11, 1922, Heidelberg —
m. July 21, 1946, Romrod
* **Helga Rausch,** daughter of Hans Rausch and of his wife, Princess Anne zu Ysenburg und Büdingen in Wächtersbach.
July 31, 1921, Frankfurt-am-Main —

Issue: 1. Dieter Vogelbacher
November 11, 1946, Romrod —

2. Peter Vogelbacher
April 12, 1958, Romrod —

XXI. WACKERLE-FÜHRICH 1, from page 701

Karl Heinz Wackerle-Führich
December 17, 1934, Innsbruck —
m. July 15, 1961, Schwaz
* **Dietlind Gabrielle,** Countess von Enzenberg zum Freyen und Jöchelsthurn, daughter of Count Karl von Enzenberg zum Freyen und Jöchelsthurn and of his wife, Carola Ossenbeck.
December 24, 1939, St. Pölten, near Vienna —

Issue: 1. Gabriele Wackerle-Führich, April 22, 1962, Innsbruck —

2. Bernhard Wackerle-Führich, April 24, 1963, Innsbruck —

3. Hubert Wackerle-Führich, November 14, 1965, Innsbruck —

XXI. WALDBOTT VON BASSENHEIM 1, from page 384

Friedrich, Baron Waldbott von Bassenheim
September 17, 1889, Tolcsva, Hungary — December 16, 1959, Seefeld, Bavaria
m. May 8, 1920, Lucerne, Switzerland
* **Maria Alice,** Archduchess of Austria, daughter of Archduke Friedrich of Austria and of his wife, Princess Isabella of Croy.
January 15, 1893, Pressburg — July 1, 1962, Halbthurn

Issue: 1. Marie Immakulata, Baroness Waldbott von Bassenheim (1921–)
m. Hans-Heribert, Count zu Törring-Jettenbach (1903–)
see: *zu Törring-Jettenbach* XXI, page 877

XXI. Waldbott von Bassenheim — 1 continued

2. Anton, Baron Waldbott von Bassenheim (1922–)
   m. Thea Schonpflug (1938–)
   see: *Waldbott von Bassenheim* XXI, 2, below

3. Paul, Baron Waldbott von Bassenheim (1924–)
   m. Marie Therese, Countess von Wikkenburg-Capellini genannt Stechelini (1929–)
   see: *Waldbott von Bassenheim* XXI, 3, page 887

4. Isabelle, Baroness Waldbott von Bassenheim (1926–)
   m. Pongrácz, Count Somssich de Sáard (1920–)
   see: *Somssich de Sáard* XXI, page 847

5. Stefanie, Baroness Waldbott von Bassenheim (1929–)
   m. Johannes, Count zu Königsegg-Aulendorf (1925–)
   see: *zu Königsegg-Aulendorf* XXI, page 736

6. Josef, Baron Waldbott von Bassenheim
   January 26, 1933, Satoralja-Ujhely, Hungary —

XXI. Waldbott von Bassenheim — 2, from above

* **Anton,** Baron Waldbott von Bassenheim, eldest son of Baron Friedrich.
August 24, 1922, Regecz-Hutta, Hungary —
m. May 9, 1960, Vienna

Thea Schonpflug, daughter of
January 13, 1938, Podersdorf —

Issue: 1. Christian, Baron Waldbott von Bassenheim
   April 19, 1961, Vienna —

2. Christine, Baroness Waldbott von Bassenheim
   August 6, 1963, Eisenstadt —

3. Peter, Baron Waldbott von Bassenheim (twin)
   January 24, 1966, Eisenstadt —

4. Alice, Baroness Waldbott von Bassenheim (twin)
   January 24, 1966, Eisenstadt —

XXI. Waldbott von Bassenheim 3, from page 886

* **Paul,** Baron Waldbott von Bassenheim, second son of Baron Friedrich.
February 9, 1914, —
m. June 16, 1958, Wolfegg Castle
Marie Therese, Countess von Wikkenburg-Capellini genannt Stechelini, daughter of
August 17, 1929, Gmunden, Austria —

No Issue.

XXI. VON WALDBURG ZU WOLFEGG UND WALDSEE 1, from page 82

Heinrich, Count von Waldburg zu Wolfegg und Waldsee, son of Count Maximilian.
September 16, 1911, Wolfegg —
m. January 4, 1942, Sigmaringen
* **Maria Antonia,** Princess of Hohenzollern-Sigmaringen, daughter of Fürst Friedrich Viktor of Hohenzollern-Sigmaringen and of his wife, Princess Margarethe of Saxony.
February 19, 1921, Sigmaringen —

Issue: 1. Sidonia, Countess von Waldburg zu Wolfegg und Waldsee
December 4, 1942, Freiburg-im-Breisgau —

2. Sophie, Countess von Waldburg zu Wolfegg und Waldsee
July 9, 1946, Krauchenwies —

3. Friedrich, Count von Waldburg zu Wolfegg und Waldsee
May 21, 1948, Wolfegg —

4. Josef, Count von Waldburg zu Wolfegg und Waldsee
December 15, 1950, Heinrichsburg —

5. Margarete, Countess von Waldburg zu Wolfegg und Waldsee
February 26, 1953, Heinrichsburg —

6. Anne, Countess von Waldburg zu Wolfegg und Waldsee
August 20, 1954, Heinrichsburg —

7. Hubert, Count von Waldburg zu Wolfegg und Waldsee
June 25, 1956, Heinrichsburg —

XXI. von Waldburg zu Wolfegg und Waldsee 1 continued

8. Maria Theresa, Countess von Waldburg zu Wolfegg und Waldsee
January 8, 1958, Heinrichsburg —

9. Jakobe, Count von Waldburg zu Wolfegg und Waldsee
July 20, 1960, Heinrichsburg —

10. Ludmila, Countess von Waldburg zu Wolfegg and Waldsee
July 29, 1964, Biberach-an-der-Riss —

XXI. von Waldburg zu Wolfegg und Waldsee 2, from page 835

Ludwig, Count von Waldburg zu Wolfegg und Waldsee, eldest son of Count Hubert.
June 15, 1934, Pähl, near Weilheim —
m. August 17, 1960 (civil), and September 7, 1960 (religious), Uberackern
* **Stephanie,** Princess of Schönburg-Waldenburg, daughter of Prince Georg of Schönburg-Waldenburg and of his wife, Countess Pauline zu Castell-Castell.
September 22, 1938, Gusow —

Issue: 1. Elisabeth, Countess von Waldburg zu Wolfegg und Waldsee
June 7, 1962, Möckmühl —

2. Hubertus, Count von Waldburg zu Wolfegg und Waldsee
May 15, 1964, Möckmühl —

XXI. VON WALDBURG ZU ZEIL UND TRAUCHBURG 1, from page 471

Georg, Fürst von Waldburg zu Zeil und Trauchburg, son of Count Erich August, 6th Fürst.
June 5, 1923, Würzburg —
m. October 23, 1957, Nymphenburg Castle, Munich
* **Gabriele,** Princess of Bavaria, daughter of Prince Albrecht of Bavaria and of his wife, Countess Maria Draskovich von Trakostjan.
May 30, 1931, Munich —

Issue: 1. Walburga, Countess von Waldburg zu Zeil und Trauchburg
September 21, 1958, Ravensburg —

XXI. von Waldburg zu Zeil und Trauchburg 1 continued

2. Gabriele, Countess von Waldburg zu Zeil und Trauchburg
   November 22, 1959, Ravensburg —

3. Monika, Countess von Waldburg zu Zeil und Trauchburg
   March 22, 1961, Ravensburg —

4. Erich, Hereditary Count von Waldburg zu Zeil und Trauchburg
   November 21, 1962, Ravensburg —

5. Adelheid, Countess von Waldburg zu Zeil und Trauchburg
   November 28, 1964, Ravensburg —

6. Elisabeth, Countess von Waldburg zu Zeil und Trauchburg
   July 30, 1966, Ravensburg —

XXI. von Waldburg zu Zeil und Trauchburg 2, from page 473

Konstantin, Count von Waldburg zu Zeil und Trauchburg, second son of Fürst Georg.
March 15, 1909, Zeil Castle —
m. August 14, 1951, Nymphenburg Castle, Munich

* **Eleonore,** Princess of Bavaria, daughter of Prince Franz of Bavaria and of his wife, Princess Isabella of Croy.
September 11, 1918, Nymphenburg —

Issue: 1. Erich, Count von Waldburg zu Zeil und Trauchburg
   September 25, 1952, Glashütte, near Wengen —

2. Elisabeth, Countess von Waldburg zu Zeil und Trauchburg
   January 6, 1954, Glashütte —

3. Georg, Count von Waldburg zu Zeil und Trauchburg
   May 1, 1955, Munich —

4. Eleonore, Countess von Waldburg zu Zeil und Trauchburg
   February 22, 1957, Munich —

5. Konstantin, Count von Waldburg zu Zeil und Trauchburg
   July 30, 1958, Munich —

6. Maria Theresia, Countess von Waldburg zu Zeil und Trauchburg
   January 19, 1960, Munich —

XXI. VON WALDBURG-ZEIL 1, from page 375

Georg, Count von Waldburg-Zeil, son of Count Clemens.
January 7, 1878, Hohenems — October 26, 1955, Syrgenstein Castle
m. 1: September 19, 1912, Niederwallsee
* **Elisabeth,** Archduchess of Austria, daughter of Archduke Franz Salvator of Austria and of his wife, Archduchess Marie Valerie of Austria.
January 27, 1892, Vienna — January 29, 1930, Syrgenstein Castle
m. 2: December 29, 1931, Bad Ischl
* **Gertrud,** Archduchess of Austria, daughter of Archduke Franz Salvator of Austria and of his wife, Archduchess Marie Valerie of Austria.
November 19, 1900, Wallsee Castle — December 20, 1942, Ravensburg

Issue of first marriage:

1. Marie Valerie, Countess von Waldburg-Zeil (1913–)
m. Georg, Archduke of Austria (1905–)
see: *Austria (Habsburg)* X p–1, page 368

2. Elisabeth, Countess von Waldburg-Zeil
February 23, 1917, Wallsee —

3. Franz Josef, Count von Waldburg-Zeil (1927–)
m. Priscilla, Countess von Schönborn-Wiesentheid (1934–)
see: *von Waldburg-Zeil* XXI, 2, below

4. Sophie, Countess von Waldburg-Zeil (1932–)
m. Wessel, Baron von Loë (1928–)
see: *von Loë* XXI, page 758

5. Josef, Count von Waldburg-Zeil (1934–)
m. Maria Benedikta, Baroness von Redwitz (1937–)
see: *von Waldburg-Zeil* XXI, 3, page 891

XXI. von Waldburg-Zeil 2, from above

* **Franz Josef,** Count von Waldburg-Zeil, son of Count Georg.
March 7, 1927, Chur —
m. June 21, 1956, Pommersfelden
Priscilla, Countess von Schönborn-Wiesentheid, daughter of Count Klemens von Schönborn-Wiesentheid and of his wife, Countess Maria Dorothea von Pappenheim.

XXI. von Waldburg-Zeil 2 continued

February 5, 1934, Munich —

Issue: 1. Maria Rosario, Countess von Waldburg-Zeil
April 2, 1957, Hohenems —

2. Karoline, Countess von Waldburg-Zeil
December 15, 1958, Hohenems —

3. Elisabeth, Countess von Waldburg-Zeil
January 28, 1960, Hohenems —

4. Franz-Clemens, Count von Waldburg-Zeil
March 5, 1962, Hohenems —

5. Stephan-Georg, Count von Waldburg-Zeil
August 3, 1963, Hohenems —

XXI. von Waldburg-Zeil 3, from page 890

* **Josef,** Count von Waldburg-Zeil, second son of Count Georg.
April 12, 1934, Syrgenstein Castle —
m. May 21, 1960, Bergen, near Neuburg/Danube
Maria Benedikta, Baroness von Redwitz, daughter of Baron Alfons von Redwitz of the House of Küps and of his wife, Countess Helga von Moy de Sons.
April 12, 1937, Wertheim-am-Main —

Issue: 1. Vitus Franziskus, Count von Waldburg-Zeil
March 17, 1961, Munich —

2. Marie-Christine, Countess von Waldburg-Zeil
July 2, 1962, Ravensburg —

3. Aloys, Count von Waldburg-Zeil
June 23, 1963, Ravensburg —

4. Maria, Countess von Waldburg-Zeil
August 29, 1964, Ravensburg —

XXI. ZU WALDECK UND PYRMONT

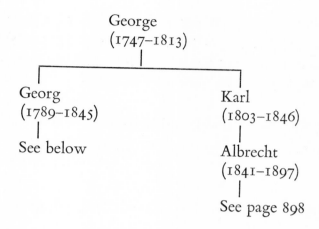

George
(1747–1813)

Georg
(1789–1845)
See below

Karl
(1803–1846)

Albrecht
(1841–1897)
See page 898

1, from page 643

Georg, Fürst zu Waldeck und Pyrmont, son of Fürst Georg.
September 20, 1789, Weil, near Basel, Switzerland — May 15, 1845, Arolsen
m. June 26, 1823,

* **Emma,** Princess of Anhalt-Bernberg-Schaumburg-Hoym, daughter of Fürst Viktor II of Anhalt-Bernberg-Schaumburg-Hoym and of his wife, Princess Amelie of Nassau-Weilburg.
May 20, 1802, Schaumburg Castle — August 1, 1858, Pyrmont

Issue: 1. Auguste, Princess zu Waldeck und Pyrmont (1824–1893)
m. Alfred, Prince and Count zu Stolberg (1820–1903)
see: *zu Stolberg-Stolberg* XXI, page 859

2. Josef, Prince zu Waldeck und Pyrmont
November 24, 1825, — December 27, 1829,

3. Hermine, Princess zu Waldeck und Pyrmont (1827–1910)
m. Adolf Georg, Fürst zu Schaumburg-Lippe (1817–1893)
see: *Schaumburg-Lippe* XXI, page 810

XXI. zu Waldeck und Pyrmont 1 continued

4. Georg Viktor, Fürst zu Waldeck und Pyrmont (1831–1893)
   m. 1: Helene, Princess of Nassau-Weilburg (1831–1888)
   m. 2: Luise, Princess of Schleswig-Holstein-Sonderburg-Glücksburg (1858–1936)
   see: *zu Waldeck und Pyrmont* XXI, 2, below

5. Wolrad, Prince zu Waldeck und Pyrmont
   January 24, 1833, — January 20, 1867,

XXI. zu Waldeck und Pyrmont 2, from above and pages 105, 172

* **Georg Viktor,** Fürst zu Waldeck und Pyrmont, second son of Fürst Georg Friedrich.
January 14, 1831, Arolsen — May 12, 1893, Marienbad
m. 1: September 26, 1853, Wiesbaden
* **Helene,** Princess of Nassau-Weilburg, daughter of Duke Wilhelm of Nassau-Weilburg and of his wife, Princess Pauline of Württemberg.
August 12, 1831, Wiesbaden — October 27, 1888, Bad Pyrmont
m. 2: April 29, 1891, Luisenlund
* **Luise,** Princess of Schleswig-Holstein-Sonderburg-Glücksburg, daughter of Duke Friedrich of Schleswig-Holstein-Sonderburg-Glücksburg and of his wife, Princess Adelheid of Schaumburg-Lippe.
January 6, 1858, Kiel — July 2, 1936, Marburg-an-der-Lahn

Issue of first marriage:

1. Sophie, Princess zu Waldeck und Pyrmont
   July 24, 1854, Arolsen — August 5, 1869, Arolsen

2. Pauline, Princess zu Waldeck und Pyrmont (1855–1925)
   m. Alexis, 4th Fürst zu Bentheim und Steinfurt (1845–1919)
   see: *zu Bentheim und Steinfurt* XXI, page 656

3. Marie, Princess zu Waldeck und Pyrmont (1857–1877)
   m. Wilhelm II, King of Württemberg (1848–1921)
   see: *Württemberg* VI b–3, page 226

4. Emma, Princess zu Waldeck und Pyrmont (1858–1934)
   m. Willem III, King of the Netherlands (1817–1890)
   see: *The Netherlands* (*Orange-Nassau*) III a–5, page 97

XXI. zu Waldeck und Pyrmont 2 continued

5. Helene, Princess zu Waldeck und Pyrmont (1861–1922)
m. Leopold, Prince of Great Britain and Ireland, Duke of Albany (1857–1884)
see: *Great Britain* (*Saxe-Coburg and Gotha*) I j–1, page 21

6. Friedrich, Fürst zu Waldeck und Pyrmont (1865–1946)
m. Bathildis, Princess of Schaumburg-Lippe (1873–1962)
see: *zu Waldeck und Pyrmont* XXI, 3, below

7. Elisabeth, Princess zu Waldeck und Pyrmont (1873–1967)
m. Alexander, 2nd Fürst zu Erbach-Schönberg (1872–1944)
see: *zu Erbach-Schönberg* XXI, page 704

Issue of second marriage:

8. Wolrad Friedrich, Prince zu Waldeck und Pyrmont
June 26, 1892, Arolsen — October 14, 1914, Moors Lede, near Lille, France, killed in action in World War I

XXI. zu Waldeck und Pyrmont 3, from above and page 819

* **Friedrich,** Last Reigning Prince (Fürst) zu Waldeck und Pyrmont, eldest son of Fürst Georg Viktor. Abdicated November 13, 1918.
January 20, 1865, Arolsen — May 26, 1946, Arolsen
m. August 9, 1895, Nachod

* **Bathildis,** Princess of Schaumburg-Lippe, daughter of Prince Wilhelm of Schaumburg-Lippe and of his wife, Princess Bathildis of Anhalt-Dessau.
May 21, 1873, Ratibortiz — April 6, 1962, Arolsen

Issue: 1. Josias, Hereditary Prince zu Waldeck und Pyrmont (1896–1967)
m. Altburg, Duchess of Oldenburg (1903–)
see: *zu Waldeck und Pyrmont* XXI, 4, page 895

2. Maximilian, Prince zu Waldeck und Pyrmont (1898–)
m. Gustava, Countess zu Platen-Hallermund (1899–)
see: *zu Waldeck und Pyrmont* XXI, 5, page 896

XXI. zu Waldeck und Pyrmont 3 continued

3. Helene, Princess zu Waldeck und Pyrmont (1899–1948)
m. Nikolaus, Hereditary Grand Duke of Oldenburg (1897–1970)
see: *Oldenburg* V bb–5, page 208

4. Georg, Prince zu Waldeck und Pyrmont (1902–)
m. Ingeborg, Countess zu Platen-Hallermund (1902–)
see: *zu Waldeck und Pyrmont* XXI, 8, page 897

XXI. zu Waldeck und Pyrmont 4, from pages 894, 208

* **Josias,** Hereditary Prince zu Waldeck und Pyrmont, eldest son of Fürst Friedrich.
May 13, 1896, Arolsen — November 30, 1967, Schaumburg, near Diez
m. August 25, 1922, Rastede, Oldenburg

* **Altburg,** Duchess of Oldenburg, daughter of Grand Duke Friedrich August of Oldenburg and of his wife, Duchess Elisabeth of Mecklenburg-Schwerin.
May 19, 1903, Oldenburg —

Issue: 1. Margarethe, Princess zu Waldeck und Pyrmont (1923–)
m. Franz August, Count zu Erbach-Erbach und von Warthenbergh (1925–)
see: *zu Erbach-Erbach und von Warthenbergh* XXI, page 702

2. Alexandra, Princess zu Waldeck und Pyrmont (1924–)
m. Botho, Prince zu Bentheim und Steinfurt (1924–)
see: *zu Bentheim und Steinfurt* XXI, page 661

3. Ingrid, Princess zu Waldeck und Pyrmont
September 2, 1931, Munich —

4. Wittekind, Prince zu Waldeck und Pyrmont
March 9, 1936, Arolsen —

5. Guda, Princess zu Waldeck und Pyrmont (1939–)
m. 1: and divorced: Friedrich Wilhelm, Fürst zu Wied (1931–)
see: *Wied* (*Runkel*) XXI, page 908
(She m. 2: May 4, 1968, Dr. Horst Dierkes, born February 21, 1939, Hanover.)

XXI. zu Waldeck und Pyrmont 5, from page 894

★ **Maximilian,** Prince zu Waldeck und Pyrmont, second son of Fürst Friedrich.
September 13, 1898, Arolsen —
m. September 12, 1929, Kiel

Gustava, Countess zu Platen-Hallermund, daughter of Count Karl zu Platen-Hallermund and of his wife, Elfriede von Köppen.
December 7, 1899, Segeberg —

Issue: 1. Marie-Luise, Princess zu Waldeck und Pyrmont (1930–)
m. Albrecht, 3rd Fürst zu Castell-Castell (1925–)
see: *zu Castell-Castell* XXI, page 673

2. Friedrich-Karl, Prince zu Waldeck und Pyrmont (1933–)
m. Ingeborg von Biela (1932–)
see: *zu Waldeck und Pyrmont* XXI, 6, below

3. Georg-Viktor, Prince zu Waldeck und Pyrmont (1936–)
m. Margarete von Klitzing (1938–)
see: *zu Waldeck und Pyrmont* XXI, 7, page 897

4. Helene, Princess zu Waldeck und Pyrmont
October 27, 1943, Schwerin —

XXI. zu Waldeck und Pyrmont 6, from above

★ **Friedrich-Karl,** Prince zu Waldeck und Pyrmont, eldest son of Prince Maximilian.
August 21, 1933, Kiel —
m. January 26, 1959, Berlin

Ingeborg von Biela, daughter of Wolf von Biela and of his wife, Adelheid Schneider.
July 2, 1933, Kiel —

Issue: 1. Karoline, Princess zu Waldeck und Pyrmont
January 8, 1960, Hanover —

2. Donata, Princess zu Waldeck und Pyrmont
February 2, 1961, Hanover —

3. Juliane, Princess zu Waldeck und Pyrmont
June 25, 1962, Hanover —

XXI. zu Waldeck und Pyrmont 7, from page 896

* **Georg-Viktor,** Prince zu Waldeck und Pyrmont, second son of Prince Maximilian.
June 11, 1936, Schwerin —
m. February 6, 1963, Hanover

Margarete von Klitzing, daughter of
February 7, 1938, Fürstenwalde —

Issue: 1. Friederike, Princess zu Waldeck und Pyrmont
December 28, 1963, Arolsen —

2. Barbara, Princess zu Waldeck und Pyrmont
March 15, 1965, Cassel

3. Christian-Ludwig, Prince zu Waldeck und Pyrmont
May 16, 1967, Arnsberg —

XXI. zu Waldeck und Pyrmont 8, from page 895

* **Georg,** Prince zu Waldeck und Pyrmont, third son of Fürst Friedrich.
March 10, 1902, Arolsen —
m. January 20, 1932, Kiel

Ingeborg, Countess zu Platen-Hallermund, daughter of Count Karl zu Platen-Hallermund and of his wife, Elfriede von Köppen.
February 27, 1902, Schleswig —

Issue: 1. Josias, Prince zu Waldeck und Pyrmont
November 23, 1935, Hanover —

2. Georg-Friedrich, Prince zu Waldeck und Pyrmont (1936–)
m. Sixtina, Princess zu Stolberg-Stolberg (1933–)
see: *zu Waldeck und Pyrmont* XXI, 9, page 898

3. Rixa, Princess zu Waldeck und Pyrmont
July 14, 1939, Brunswick —

4. Volkwin, Prince zu Waldeck und Pyrmont (1940–)
m. Orlinda, Baroness von Gablenz (1938–)
see: *zu Waldeck und Pyrmont* XXI, 10, page 898

5. Christian, Prince zu Waldeck und Pyrmont
January 5, 1945, Arolsen —
(m. June 5, 1971, Sybille Pieper)

XXI. zu Waldeck und Pyrmont 9, from pages 897, 860

⋆ **Georg-Friedrich,** Prince zu Waldeck und Pyrmont, second son of Prince Georg.
November 22, 1936, Hanover —
m. August 30, 1961,
⋆ **Sixtina,** Princess zu Stolberg-Stolberg, daughter of Prince Wolffgang-Heinrich, 3rd Fürst zu Stolberg and of his wife, Irma Erfert.
November 4, 1933, Stolberg —

Issue: 1. Henriette, Princess zu Waldeck und Pyrmont
April 6, 1963, Ludwigsburg —

2. Marie Isabell, Princess zu Waldeck und Pyrmont
August 29, 1965, Arolsen —

3. Philipp Heinrich, Prince zu Waldeck und Pyrmont
April 12, 1968, Flensburg —

XXI. zu Waldeck und Pyrmont 10, from page 897

⋆ **Volkwin,** Prince zu Waldeck und Pyrmont, third son of Prince Georg.
September 20, 1940, Brunswick —
m. March 2, 1968, Bad Driburg
Orlinda, Baroness von Gablenz, daughter of Baron Eccard von Gablenz and of his wife, Orlanda von Caprivi.
August 11, 1938, Bielefeld —

Issue: 1. Friedrich Anton, Prince zu Waldeck und Pyrmont
July 4, 1969, Arolsen —

XXI. zu Waldeck und Pyrmont 11, from page 492

Albrecht, Prince zu Waldeck und Pyrmont, eldest son of Prince Karl and nephew of Fürst Georg Friedrich.
December 11, 1841, Cleve — January 11, 1897, Tiergarten
m. 1: June 2, 1864,
Dorothea Gage, daughter of Richard Gage and of his wife,
(She was created Countess von Rhoden.)
January 30, 1834, — December 12, 1883,
m. 2: May 8, 1886, Bamberg
⋆ **Luise,** Princess of Hohenlohe-Oehringen, daughter of Prince Felix of Hohenlohe-Oehringen and of his wife, Princess Alexandrine von Hanau, Countess von Schaumburg.

XXI. zu Waldeck und Pyrmont 11 continued

January 26, 1867, Heidelberg — July 23, 1945, Gauting
(She m. 2: and separated: George Granville Hope-Johnstone – see: *Hope-Johnstone*, XVIII, page 524.)

Issue of second marriage:
1. Georg Friedrich, Prince zu Waldeck und Pyrmont
March 15, 1887, — March 29, 1888, Plappeville, near Metz

2. Karl Alexander, Prince zu Waldeck und Pyrmont
September 15, 1891, Tiergarten — October 28, 1910, Dresden

XXI. VON WALDERDORFF 1, from page 675

Franz, Count von Walderdorff
November 20, 1930, Hauzenstein —
m. August 18, 1962, Copenhagen, Denmark
* **Christa,** Countess zu Castell-Castell, daughter of Count Gustav zu Castell-Castell and of his wife, Baroness Vibeke von Lotzbeck.
May 19, 1939, Kolberg —

Issue: 1. Carl-Gustav, Count von Walderdorff
July 6, 1963, São Paulo, Brazil —

2. Francisca Anne, Countess von Walderdorff
March 8, 1965, São Paulo, Brazil —

XXI. VON WALDSTÄTTEN 1, from page 1006

Herbert, Baron von Waldstätten
January 1, 1913, Vienna —
m. 1: April 27, 1940, Rome. Divorced: July 2, 1946,
* **Irina Nikolaievna,** Princess Orlova, daughter of Prince Nikolai Vladimirovich Orlov and of his wife, Princess Nadezhda Petrovna of Russia.
March 17, 1918, Koreiz, Crimea —
(She m. 2: Dr. Anthony Adama Zylstra – see: *Zylstra* XXI, page 941.)

XXI. von Waldstätten

1 continued

m. 2: December 28, 1947, Mayerhofen
Eva Ikoldy-Szabo de Iklod, daughter of
July 7, 1918, Budapest —

Issue of first marriage:
1. Elisabeth (Maya), Baroness von Waldstätten
February 7, 1944, Budapest —

XXI. VON WALDSTEIN-WARTENBERG

1, from page 377

Clemens, Count von Waldstein-Wartenberg
December 8, 1936, Vienna —
m. September 3, 1969, Persenbeug Castle
* **Josepha,** Archduchess of Austria, daughter of Archduke Hubert Salvator of Austria and of his wife, Princess Rosemary zu Salm-Salm.
September 2, 1937, Persenbeug Castle —

Issue:

XXI. VON WALLENRODT

1, from page 931

Hans-Joachim von Wallenrodt
August 27, 1914, Hanover —
m. 1: September 16, 1937, Berlin. Divorced: November 16, 1948, Munich
* **Ilona von Wuthenau-Hohenthurm,** daughter of Carl Adam von Wuthenau-Hohenthurm and of his wife, Councess Gisela von Lüttichau.
November 14, 1913, Bad Lichtenstein —
(She m. 2: Adolf Strandes – see: *Strandes* XXI, page 866.)
m. 2: April 14, 1950, Tegernsee, Bavaria
* **Carla von Wuthenau-Hohenthurm,** daughter of Carl Adam von Wuthenau-Hohenthurm and of his wife, Countess Gisela von Lüttichau.
March 23, 1915, Dessau —
(She m. 1: Hellmut Hansen – see: *Hansen* XXI, page 718.)

Issue: see: *von Wallenrodt,* Addendum, page 1078

XXI. WALZ 1, from page 828

Heinrich Walz

—

m. February 26, 1964, Forchheim

* **Dagmar Schnirring,** daughter of Captain Max Schnirring and of his wife, Princess Caroline-Mathilde of Saxe-Coburg and Gotha.

November 22, 1940, Grosswüsteritz —

Issue: 1. Maria-Valeska Walz

August 14, 1965, Munich —

2. Larissa Walz

September 16, 1967, Bamburg —

XXI. WAMBOLT VON UMSTADT 1, from page 805

Lanzo, Baron Wambolt von Umstadt

July 2, 1934, Heidelberg —

m. September , 1966, Berleberg

* **Loretta,** Princess zu Sayn-Wittgenstein-Hohenstein, daughter of Fürst Christian Heinrich zu Sayn-Wittgenstein-Hohenstein and of his wife, Countess Beatrix von Bismarck-Schönhausen.

June 6, 1942, Wittgenstein —

Issue:

XXI. WAMBOLT VON UMSTADT 1, from page 757

Philipp, Baron Wambolt von Umstadt

August 15, 1918, Frischau, Czechoslovakia —

m. September 22, 1954, Wissen

* **Elisabeth,** Baroness von Loë, daughter of Baron Felix von Loë and of his wife, Princess Isabelle zu Salm-Salm.

March 15, 1930, Wissen —

Issue:

XXI. VON WANGENHEIM

1, from page 269

Götz, Baron Wangenheim
January 18, 1895, Berlin — October 5, 1941, Chernyetroyskoye, Russia, killed in action in World War II
m. October 25, 1936, Detmold
* **Luise,** Princess of Saxe-Meiningen, daughter of Prince Friedrich of Saxe-Meiningen and of his wife, Princess Adelheid zur Lippe.
March 13, 1899, Köln —

Issue: 1. Karin, Baroness von Wangenheim (1937–)
m. Hans-Dieter Schwarze (1926–)
see: *Schwarze* XXI, page 838

2. Ernst Friedrich, Baron von Wangenheim (1941–)
m. Christa Margarete Binninger (1941–)
see: *von Wangenheim* XXI, 2, below

XXI. von Wangenheim

2, from above

* **Ernst Friedrich,** Baron von Wangenheim, only son of Baron Götz.
April 14, 1941, Detmold —
m. July 4, 1963, Bad Homburg
Christa Margarete Binninger, daughter of
March 20, 1931, Frankfurt-am-Main —

Issue: 1. Verena Regina, Baroness von Wangenheim
November 20, 1966, Bad Homburg —

XXI. VON WARSBERG

1, from page 864

Alexander, Baron von Warsberg
November 3, 1910, Salzburg —
m. August 12, 1951, Pöls, Styria, Austria
* **Elisabeth,** Countess zu Stolberg-Stolberg, daughter of Count Georg zu Stolberg-Stolberg and of his wife, Princess Regina Reuss zu Köstritz.
June 2, 1918, Vienna —
(She m. 1: Dr. Walther Eisenbach – see: *Eisenbach* XXI, page 694.)

Issue: 1. Johannes, Baron von Warsberg
December 28, 1952, Heidelberg —

XXI. von Warsberg 1 continued

2. Markus, Baron von Warsberg
   February 18, 1954, Heidelberg —

3. Katharina, Baroness von Warsberg
   April 25, 1956, Heidelberg —

4. Stephan, Baron von Warsberg
   August 15, 1961, Heidelberg —

XXI. VON WASHINGTON 1, from page 206

Maximilian, Baron von Washington
August 2, 1829, Nötzing — July 3, 1903, Graz, Austria
m. August 15, 1855, Rastede
* **Friederike,** Duchess of Oldenburg, daughter of Grand Duke August of Oldenburg and of his first wife, Princess Adelheid of Anhalt-Bernberg-Schaumburg-Hoym.
June 8, 1820, Oldenburg — March 20, 1891, Pöls, Austria

Issue: 1. Georg, Baron von Washington (1856–1930)
m. Gisela, Countess Welser von Welserheimb (1857–1913)
see: *von Washington* XXI, 2, below

2. Stephan, Baron von Washington
   June 17, 1858, Pöls — September 10, 1899, Palermo, Italy

XXI. von Washington 2, from above

* **Georg,** Baron von Washington, son of Baron Maximilian.
July 31, 1856, Pöls — December 22, 1930, Pöls
m. March 27, 1883, Pöls
Gisela, Countess Welser von Welserheimb, daughter of Count Vincenz Welser von Welserheimb and of his wife, Countess Charlotte von Normann-Ehrenfels.
August 25, 1857, Pöls — July 1, 1913, Pöls

No Issue.

XXI. VON WATZDORFF

1, from page 118

Karl, Baron von Watzdorff
March 9, 1807, Dresden — December 5, 1846, Dresden
m. December 21, 1847, Dresden
* **Wilhelmine,** Countess von Reichenbach-Lessonitz, daughter of Elector Wilhelm II of Hesse and of his second and morganatic wife, Emilie Ortlopp, created Countess von Reichenbach (1812) and Countess von Lessonitz (1824).
December 21, 1816, Cassel — December 25, 1858, Dresden
(She m. 1: and divorced: Wilhelm, Count von Luckner – see: *von Luckner* XXI, page 765.)
(She m. 3: her first husband – see: *von Luckner* XXI, page 765.)

Issue: see: *von Watzdorff*, Addendum, page 1079

XXI. von Watzdorff

2, from page 941

Konrad, Baron von Watzdorff, son of Baron Karl.
August 22, 1844, Dresden — May 28, 1922, Somloszöllös, Hungary
m. January 12, 1870, Calburg
* **Emilie,** Countess zu Zichy-Ferraris zu Zich und Vásonykeö, daughter of Count Felix zu Zichy-Ferraris zu Zich und Vásonykeö and of his wife, Countess Emilie von Reichenbach-Lessonitz.
July 1, 1847, Guns — July 6, 1935, Somloszöllös, Hungary

Issue: see: *von Watzdorff*, Addendum, page 1079

XXI. VON WEDEL-JARLSBERG

1, from page 346

Alfred, Count von Wedel-Jarlsberg
February 22, 1895, Berlin —
m. 1: May 15, 1927, . Divorced: 1933
Viktoria, Baroness von Dobeneck, daughter of
—
m. 2: June 23, 1936, . Divorced: 1948
Alice Bronsch, daughter of
—
m. 3: October 10, 1950, Prillwitz Castle
* **Karoline,** Princess Reuss zu Köstritz, daughter of Prince Heinrich XXXVI Reuss zu Köstritz and of his wife, Princess Hermine of Schönburg-Waldenburg.
May 7, 1923, Leipzig —

XXI. von Wedel-Jarlsberg 1 continued

Issue: of third marriage

1. Christian, Count von Wedel-Jarlsberg
   July 24, 1951, Frankfurt-am-Main —

XXI. WEYGAND 1, from page 878

Herbert Weygand
January 8, 1936, Frankfurt-am-Main —
m. October 30, 1960, Oberurf

* **Marianne Treusch,** Baroness von Buttlar-Brandenfels, daughter of Baron Hans Treusch von Buttlar-Brandenfels and of his wife, Countess Marie Luise (Marielier) von Schaumburg.
May 9, 1930, Treysa —

Issue:

1. Michael von Buttlar
   February 28, 1956, Hamburg —

2. Thomas von Buttlar
   December 8, 1958, Traunstein —

3. Christiane Weygand (twin)
   April 12, 1963, Treysa —

4. Mathias Weygand (twin)
   April 12, 1963, Treysa —

XXI. WIED

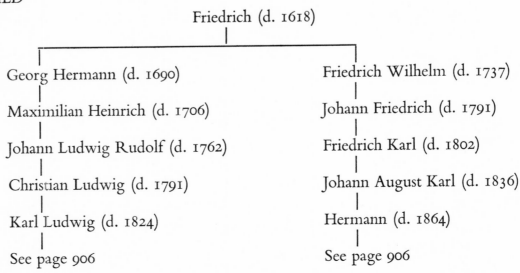

Friedrich (d. 1618)

Georg Hermann (d. 1690)
|
Maximilian Heinrich (d. 1706)
|
Johann Ludwig Rudolf (d. 1762)
|
Christian Ludwig (d. 1791)
|
Karl Ludwig (d. 1824)
|
See page 906

Friedrich Wilhelm (d. 1737)
|
Johann Friedrich (d. 1791)
|
Friedrich Karl (d. 1802)
|
Johann August Karl (d. 1836)
|
Hermann (d. 1864)
|
See page 906

XXI. Wied (Runkel) 1 from page 102

Karl Ludwig, Fürst zu Wied-Runkel, son of Fürst Christian Ludwig.
September 9, 1763, Dierdorf — March 9, 1824, Dierdorf
m. September 4, 1787, Kirchheimbolanden
* **Karoline,** Princess of Nassau-Weilburg, daughter of Prince Karl Christian of Nassau-Weilburg and of his wife, Princess Caroline of Orange-Nassau.
February 14, 1770, Kirchheimbolanden — July 8, 1828, Wiesbaden

No Issue.

XXI. Wied (Runkel) 2, from page 105

Herman, 4th Fürst zu Wied, son of Fürst Johann August Karl.
May 22, 1814, Neuwied — March 5, 1864,
m. June 20, 1842, Biebrich
* **Marie,** Princess of Nassau-Weilburg, daughter of Prince Wilhelm of Nassau-Weilburg and of his first wife, Princess Luise of Saxe-Altenburg.
January 29, 1825, Biebrich — March 24, 1902, Neuwied

Issue: 1. Elisabeth (Carmen Sylva), Princess of Wied (1853–1916)
m. Carol I, First King of Romania (1839–1914)
see: *Romania* (*Hohenzollern-Sigmaringen*) II jj–1, page 87

2. Wilhelm, 5th Fürst zu Wied (1845–1907)
m. Marie, Princess of the Netherlands (1841–1901)
see: *Wied* (*Runkel*) XXI, 3, below

3. Otto, Prince of Wied
November 22, 1850, — February 18, 1862, Neuwied

XXI. Wied (Runkel) 3, from above and page 101

* **Wilhelm,** 5th Fürst zu Wied, eldest son of Fürst Hermann.
August 22, 1845, Neuwied — October 22, 1907, Neuwied
m. July 18, 1871, Wassanaer
* **Marie,** Princess of the Netherlands, daughter of Prince Fredrik of the Netherlands and of his wife, Princess Luise of Prussia.
July 5, 1841, Pauw Haus — June 22, 1910, Neuwied

XXI. Wied (Runkel) 3 continued

Issue: 1. Friedrich, 6th Fürst zu Wied (1872–1945)
m. Pauline, Princess of Württemberg (1877–1965)
see: *Wied (Runkel)* XXI, 4, below

2. Alexander, Prince of Wied
May 28, 1874, Neuwied — January 15, 1877, Neuwied

3. Wilhelm, First King of Albania, born Prince of Wied (1876–1945)
m. Sophie, Princess of Schönburg-Waldenburg (1855–1936)
see: *Wied (Runkel) Albania* XXI, 11, page 910

4. Viktor, Prince of Wied (1877–1946)
m. Gisela, Countess zu Solms-Wildenfels (1891–)
see: *Wied (Runkel)* XXI, 12, page 911

5. Luise, Princess of Wied
October 24, 1880, Neuwied —

6. Elisabeth, Princess of Wied
January 28, 1883, Neuwied — November 14, 1938, Neuwied

XXI. Wied (Runkel) 4, from above and page 226

* **Friedrich,** 6th Fürst zu Wied, eldest son of Fürst Wilhelm.
June 27, 1872, Neuwied — June 18, 1945, Neuwied
m. October 29, 1890, Stuttgart
* **Pauline,** Princess of Württemberg, daughter of King Wilhelm II of Württemberg and of his wife, Princess Marie zu Waldeck und Pyrmont.
December 19, 1877, Stuttgart — May 7, 1965, Ludwigsburg

Issue: 1. Hermann, Hereditary Prince of Wied (1899–1941)
m. Maria Antonia, Countess zu Stolberg-Wernigerode (1909–)
see: *Wied (Runkel)* XXI, 5, page 908

2. Dietrich, Prince of Wied (1901–)
m. Julie, Countess Grote (1902–)
see: *Wied (Runkel)* XXI, 8, page 909

XXI. Wied (Runkel) 5, from page 907

* **Hermann,** Hereditary Prince of Wied, eldest son of Fürst Friedrich.
August 18, 1899, Potsdam — November 5, 1941, Rezeszow (Reichshof), Poland, killed in action in World War II
m. April 29, 1930, Neuwied

Maria Antonia, Countess zu Solms-Wernigerode, daughter of Count Carl zu Solms-Wernigerode and of his wife, Hilde von Witzleben.
February 6, 1909, Varpalota, Hungary —
(She m. 2: August 31, 1943, Strahwalde, near Herrnhut, Edmund Franz von Gordon.)

Issue: 1. Friedrich Wilhelm, 7th Fürst zu Wied (1931–)
m. 1: and divorced: Guda, Princess zu Waldeck und Pyrmont (1939–)
m. 2: Sophie Charlotte, Princess zu Stolberg-Stolberg (1943–)
see: *Wied (Runkel)* XXI, 6, below

2. Metfried, Prince of Wied (1935–)
m. Felicitas, Baroness von der Pahlen (1938–)
see: *Wied (Runkel)* XXI, 7, page 909

3. Osterlind, Princess of Wied (1939–)
m. Werner von Klitzing (1934–)
see: *von Klitzing* XXI, page 732

XXI. Wied (Runkel) 6, from above and pages 860, 895

* **Friedrich Wilhelm,** 7th Fürst zu Wied, eldest son of Hereditary Prince Hermann.
June 2, 1931, Stuttgart —
m. 1: August 31, 1958 (civil), and September 9, 1958 (religious), Arolsen. Divorced: January , 1962, Koblenz

* **Guda,** Princess zu Waldeck und Pyrmont, daughter of Hereditary Prince Josias zu Waldeck und Pyrmont and of his wife, Duchess Altburg of Oldenburg.
August 22, 1939, Arolsen —
(She m. 2: March 4, 1968, Dr. Horst Dierkes, born April 21, 1939.)
m. 2: July 15, 1967, Runkel

* **Sophie Charlotte,** Princess zu Stolberg-Stolberg, daughter of Prince Wolffgang-Heinrich, 3rd Fürst and Count zu Stolberg, and of his wife, Irma Erfert.
October 4, 1943, Nordhausen —

XXI. Wied (Runkel) 6 continued

Issue of first marriage:
1. Alexander, Hereditary Prince of Wied
September 29, 1960, Neuwied —

2. Carl, Prince of Wied
October 27, 1961, Neuwied —

Issue of second marriage:
3. Christina Elisabeth, Princess of Wied
June 9, 1970, Neuwied —

XXI. Wied (Runkel) 7, from page 908

* **Metfried,** Prince of Wied, second son of Hereditary Prince Hermann.
April 25, 1935, Stuttgart —
m. February 14, 1968, Neuwied
Felicitas, Baroness von der Pahlen, daughter of Baron Hans-Georg von der Pahlen and of his wife, Irmgard von Mitzloff.
December 31, 1948, Linnig, Jülich —

Issue: 1. Friedrich Christian, Prince of Wied
August 5, 1968, Waldbröhl —

XXI. Wied (Runkel) 8, from page 907

* **Dietrich,** Prince of Wied, second son of Fürst Friedrich.
October 30, 1901, Potsdam —
m. July 8, 1928, Berlin
Julie, Countess Grote, daughter of Count Otto Grote and of his wife, Alice von Bergen.
October 9, 1902, Berlin —

Issue: 1. Maximilian, Prince of Wied
May 30, 1929, Stuttgart —

2. Ulrich, Prince of Wied (1931–)
m. Ilke Ferdinande Fischer (1936–)
see: *Wied* (*Runkel*) XXI, 9, page 910

3. Wilhelm, Prince of Wied
August 24, 1936, Stuttgart — April 24, 1937, Stuttgart

XXI. Wied (Runkel)

8 continued

4. Ludwig, Prince of Wied (1938–)
m. Helga Gmeinert (1940–)
see: *Wied (Runkel)* XXI, 10, below

XXI. Wied (Runkel)

9, from page 909

* **Ulrich,** Prince of Wied, second son of Prince Dietrich.
June 12, 1931, Hanover —
m. December 2, 1968, Munich
Ilke Ferdinande Fischer, daughter of Gottfried Fischer and of his wife, Maria Mühlenbien.
December 9, 1936, Bonn —

Issue:

XXI. Wied (Runkel)

10, from above

* **Ludwig,** Prince of Wied, fourth son of Prince Dietrich.
August 27, 1938, Stuttgart —
m. May 31, 1966, Munich
Helga Gmeinert, daughter of Hans Gmeinert and of his wife, Anneliese Kopsch.
May 7, 1940, Sorav, Niederlavsitz —

Issue: 1. Edzard, Prince of Wied
January 16, 1968, Munich —

XXI. WIED (RUNKEL) ALBANIA

11, from page 907

* **Wilhelm,** Prince of Wied, elected King of Albania February 6, 1914, deposed September 1914; third son of Fürst Wilhelm.
March 26, 1876, Neuwied — April 18, 1945, Sinaia, Romania
m. November 30, 1906, Waldenburg
Sophie, Princess of Schönburg-Waldenburg, daughter of Hereditary Prince Viktor of Schönburg-Waldenburg and of his wife, Princess Lucie zu Sayn-Wittgenstein-Berleburg.
May 21, 1885, Potsdam — February 3, 1936, Fantanele Castle, Romania

XXI. Wied (Runkel) 11 continued

Issue: 1. Marie Eleonore, Princess of Wied (1909–1956)
m. 1: Alfred, Prince of Schönburg-Waldenburg (1905–1941)
see: *Schönburg-Waldenburg* XXI, page 833
m. 2: Jon Bunea (1899–)
see: *Bunea* XX, page 626

2. Karl Viktor, Crown Prince of Albania, Prince of Wied
May 19, 1913, Potsdam —
(m. September 8, 1966, New York City, Eileen Johnston, b. Chester, England, 1922)

XXI. Wied (Runkel) 12, from page 907

* **Viktor,** Prince of Wied, fourth son of Fürst Wilhelm.
December 7, 1877, Neuwied — March 1, 1946, Moosburg
m. June 6, 1912, Wildenfels

Gisela, Countess zu Solms-Wildenfels, daughter of Count Friedrich zu Solms-Wildenfels and of his wife, Countess Anne von Bentinck.
December 30, 1891, Wildenfels —

Issue: 1. Marie Elisabeth, Princess of Wied
March 14, 1913, Oslo, Norway —

2. Benigna-Viktoria, Princess of Wied (1918–)
m. Ernst-Hartmann, Baron von Schlotheim (1914–)
see: *von Schlotheim* XXI, page 825

XXI. WIEDERSPERGER VON WIEDERSPERG 1, from page 829

Peter, Baron Wiedersperger von Wiedersperg
February 12, 1943, Iglau —
m. October 28, 1967, Karlstadt/Main

* **Marina,** Princess of Schönaich-Carolath, daughter of Prince Hans Georg of Schönaich-Carolath and of his wife, Baroness Sibylle von Zedlitz und Leipe.
May 8, 1940, Berlin —

Issue: 1. Marietta, Baroness Wiedersperger von Wiedersperg
June 9, 1968, Landshut —

XXI. WILLIM

1, from page 233

Melchior Willim, M.D.
August 25, 1855, — October 29, 1910,
m. May 1, 1880, Karlsruhe
* **Pauline,** Duchess of Württemberg, daughter of Duke Eugen of Württemberg and of his wife, Princess Mathilde of Schaumburg-Lippe.
April 11, 1854, Düsseldorf — April 23/24, 1914,
(She renounced her rights as a member of the Royal House of Württemberg on May 1, 1880, and assumed the surname of 'von Kirbach.)

No Issue.

XXI. WINDISCH-GRAETZ

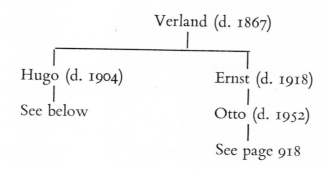

Verland (d. 1867)
- Hugo (d. 1904)
  - See below
- Ernst (d. 1918)
  - Otto (d. 1952)
    - See page 918

1, from pages 415, 397

Hugo, Prince Windisch-Graetz, eldest son of Fürst Veriand.
May 26, 1823, Vienna — November 26, 1904, Haasberg Castle
m. 1: October 20, 1849, Ludwigslust
* **Luise,** Duchess of Mecklenburg-Schwerin, daughter of Duke Paul Friedrich of Mecklenburg-Schwerin and of his wife, Princess Alexandrine of Prussia.
May 17, 1824, Schwerin — March 9, 1859, Venedig
m. 2: October 9, 1867, Teplitz
* **Matylda,** Princess Radziwill, daughter of Prince William Radziwill and of his second wife, Countess Mathilde von Clary und Aldringen.
October 16, 1836, Berlin — January 5, 1918, Vienna

Issue of first marriage:

1. Alexandrine, Princess Windisch-Graetz
   August 29, 1850, Como — July 12, 1933, Gonobitz

XXI. Windisch-Graetz — 1 continued

2. Olga, Princess Windisch-Graetz (1853–1934)
m. Andrea (Andrew), Conte Mocenigo (1850–1878)
see: *Mocenigo* XVIII, page 579

3. Hugo, Prince Windisch-Graetz (1854–1920)
m. Christine, Princess von Auersperg-Breunner (1866–1962)
see: *Windisch-Graetz* XXI, 2, below

4. Marie, Princess Windisch-Graetz (1856–1929)
m. Paul Friedrich, Duke of Mecklenburg-Schwerin (1852–1925)
see: *Mecklenburg-Schwerin* XII c–1, page 420

Issue of second marriage:

5. Ernst, Prince Windisch-Graetz
September 4, 1872, Gonobitz — February 1, 1897, Ajaccio

6. Aloisia, Princess Windisch-Graetz
June 25, 1874, — January 10, 1888, Vienna

7. Elisabeth, Princess Windisch-Graetz
July 24, 1876, — December 21, 1886, Vienna

XXI. Windisch-Graetz — 2, from above

* **Hugo,** Prince Windisch-Graetz, eldest son of Prince Hugo.
November 17, 1854, Florence — May 15, 1920, Haasberg Castle
m. May 16, 1885, Vienna

Christine, Princess von Auersperg, daughter of Fürst Vincenz von Auersperg and of his wife, Countess Wilhelmine von Colloredo-Mannsfeld.
February 26, 1866, Vienna — July 12, 1962, Trieste

Issue: 1. Luise, Princess Windisch-Graetz (1886–)
m. Giovanni, Count Ceschi a Santa Croce (1871–1936)
see: *Ceschi a Santa Croce* XVIII, page 553

XXI. Windisch-Graetz

2 continued

2. Hugo, Prince Windisch-Graetz (1887–1959)
   m. Leontine, Princess von Fürstenberg (1892–)
   see: *Windisch-Graetz* XXI, 3, page 915

3. Elisabeth, Princess Windisch-Graetz (1889–)
   m. Leone Rosa (1884–)
   see: *Rosa* XVIII, page 599

4. Alfred, Prince Windisch-Graetz (1890–)
   m. Isabelle, Princess of Hohenlohe-Langenburg (1891–)
   see: *Windisch-Graetz* XXI, 6, page 916

5. Eduard, Prince Windisch-Graetz (1891–)
   m. Alexandra (Alix), Princess zu Ysenburg-Birstein (1899–1945)
   see: *Windisch-Graetz* XXI, 8, page 917

6. Olga, Princess Windisch-Graetz (1893–)
   m. 1: and divorced: Andreas Picard, Baron von Morsey (1888–1951)
   see: *Picard (von Morsey)* XXI, page 785
   m. 2: Hubertus, Count von Ledebur-Wicheln (1901-1945)
   see: *von Ledebur-Wicheln* XXI, page 742

7. Wilhelmine, Princess Windisch-Graetz (1895–)
   m. Leonidas, Baron Economo di San Serff (1874–1952)
   see: *Economo di San Serff* XVIII, page 558

8. Franz, Prince Windisch-Graetz (1896–)
   m. Desirée von Wagner-Latour Edle von Thurmburg (1907–)
   see: *Windisch-Graetz* XXI, 9, page 918

9. Gabriele, Princess Windisch-Graetz (1898–)
   m. Johann, Prince of Hohenlohe-Schillingsfürst, Prince of Ratibor und Corvey (1882–1948)
   see: *Hohenlohe-Schillingsfürst (Ratibor und Corvey)* XV 0–1, page 496

XXI. Windisch-Graetz — 2 continued

10. Gottlieb, Prince Windisch-Graetz
August 15, 1899, Gonobitz — May 13, 1945, Trieste, died of wounds received in battle

11. Maria Antoinette, Princess Windisch-Graetz (1911–)
m. Girolamo, Conte di Bosdari (1907–)
see: *Bosdari* XVIII, page 548

XXI. Windisch-Graetz — 3, from page 914

* **Hugo,** Prince Windisch-Graetz, eldest son of Prince Hugo.
July 30, 1887, Haasberg Castle — May 26, 1959, Trieste
m. November 26, 1912, Donaueschingen
Leontine, Princess von Fürstenberg, daughter of Fürst Maximilian von Fürstenberg and of his wife, Countess Irma von Schönborn-Buchheim.
June 16, 1892, Lana —

Issue: 1. Irma, Princess Windisch-Graetz (1913–)
m. Franz, Fürst von Weikersheim (1904–)
see: *von Weikersheim* XV a–5–a, page 483

2. Hugo, Prince Windisch-Graetz
September 1, 1914, Donaueschingen — August 8, 1942, near Rome, killed in action in World War II

3. Maximilian, Prince Windisch-Graetz (1914–)
m. Donna Maria Luisa Serra di Carafa (1921–)
see: *Windisch-Graetz* XXI, 4, below

4. Friedrich, Prince Windisch-Graetz (1917–)
m. Dorothea, Princess of Hesse (1934–)
see: *Windisch-Graetz* XXI, 5, page 916

XXI. Windisch-Graetz — 4, from above

* **Maximilian,** Prince Windisch-Graetz, son of Prince Hugo.
September 1, 1914, Donaueschingen —
m. November 11, 1946, Cortino d'Ampezzo, Italy
Donna Maria Luisa Serra di Carafa, daughter of Principe Gianbattista Serra di Barafa and of his wife, Countess Maria Grazia Carafa d'Andria.

XXI. Windisch-Graetz

4 continued

July 20, 1921, Vienna —

Issue: 1. Irma, Princess Windisch-Graetz
July 7, 1951, Trieste —

2. Maximiliana, Princess Windisch-Graetz
November 16, 1952, Trieste —

3. Mariano-Hugo, Prince Windisch-Graetz
July 27, 1955, Trieste —

4. Manfredo, Prince Windisch-Graetz
April 1, 1963, Trieste —

XXI. Windisch-Graetz

5, from pages 915, 129

* **Friedrich,** Prince Windisch-Graetz, third son of Prince Hugo.
July 7, 1917, Heiligenberg —
m. April 1, 1959, Munich
* **Dorothea,** Princess of Hesse, daughter of Prince Christoph of Hesse and of his wife, Princess Sophia of Greece and Denmark.
July 24, 1934, Panker Castle, Holstein —

Issue: 1. Marina, Princess Windisch-Graetz
December 3, 1960, Milan —

2. Clarissa, Princess Windisch-Graetz
August 7, 1966, Erba, Como —

XXI. Windisch-Graetz

6, from page 914

* **Alfred,** Prince Windisch-Graetz, second son of Prince Hugo.
March 12, 1890, Gonobitz —
m. May 29, 1929, Vienna
Isabelle, Princess of Hohenlohe-Langenburg, daughter of Prince Gottfried of Hohenlohe-Langenburg and of his wife, Countess Anne von Schönborn-Buchheim.
May 30, 1891, Rothenhaus —

Issue: 1. Christiane, Princess Windisch-Graetz
March 10, 1920, Rothenhaus —

XXI. Windisch-Graetz 6 continued

2. Gottfried, Prince Windisch-Graetz
April 5, 1927, Vienna —

3. Veriand, Prince Windisch-Graetz (1929–)
m. Caroline Knoft (1939–)
see: *Windisch-Graetz* XXI, 7, below

XXI. Windisch-Graetz 7, from above

* **Veriand,** Prince Windisch-Graetz, second son of Prince Alfred.
December 29, 1929, Dresden —
m. October 21, 1961, London, England
Caroline Knoft, daughter of
October 28, 1939, London —

Issue: 1. Konstantin, Prince Windisch-Graetz
July 9, 1962, New York City —

2. Franz Karl, Prince Windisch-Graetz
August 23, 1964, Würzburg —

XXI. Windisch-Graetz 8, from page 914

* **Eduard,** Prince Windisch-Graetz, third son of Prince Hugo.
July 15, 1891, Gonobitz —
m. June 14, 1923, Birstein
Alexandra, Princess zu Ysenburg-Birstein, daughter of Prince Franz Joseph zu Ysenburg-Birstein and of his wife, Princess Friederike zu Solms-Braunfels.
December 21, 1899, Birstein — December 22, 1945, Barcola, near Trieste

Issue: 1. Friederike Marie, Princess Windisch-Graetz (1924–)
m. Cecil Thomas Weston-Baker (1919–)
see: *Weston-Baker* XVII, page 535

2. Leontine, Princess Windisch-Graetz (1925–)
m. Robert Anthony Henley (1921–)
see: *Henley* XVII, page 522

XXI. Windisch-Graetz 8 continued

3. Wilhelmine, Princess Windisch-Graetz (1930–)
m. Gottfried, Count von Degenfeld-Schönburg (1925–)
see: *von Degenfeld-Schönburg* XXI, page 683

4. Olga, Princess Windisch-Graetz (1934–)
m. Karl Anton von Riedemann (1931–)
see: *von Riedemann* XXI, page 791

XXI. Windisch-Graetz 9, from page 914

* **Franz,** Prince Windisch-Graetz, fourth son of Prince Hugo.
November 4, 1896, Gonobitz —
m. May 5, 1937, Vienna
Desirée von Wagner-Latour Edle von Thurmburg, daughter of
August 15, 1907, Stanislau —

No Issue.

XXI. Windisch-Graetz 10, from page 354

Otto, Prince Windisch-Graetz, son of Prince Ernst.
October 7, 1873, Graz — December 25, 1952, Lugano, Switzerland
m. January 23, 1902, Vienna. Divorced: March 26, 1924, Vienna
* **Elisabeth,** Archduchess of Austria, daughter of Crown Prince Rudolf of Austria and of his wife, Princess Stephanie of Belgium.
September 2, 1883, Laxenburg — March 22, 1963, Vienna
(She m. 2: Leopold Petznek – see: *Petznek* XXI, page 783.)

Issue: 1. Franz Josef, Prince Windisch-Graetz (1904–)
m. Ghislaine, Countess von Arschot-Schoonhoven (1912–)
see: *Windisch-Graetz* XXI, 11, page 919

2. Ernst Veriand, Prince Windisch-Graetz (1905–1952)
m. 1: and divorced: Ellen Skinner (1906–)
m. 2: Eva, Baroness von Isbary (1921–)
see: *Windisch-Graetz* XXI, 12, page 919

XXI. Windisch-Graetz 10 continued

3. Rudolf, Prince Windisch-Graetz
February 4, 1907, Ploshwitz — June 14, 1930, Vienna, killed in a motorcycle accident

4. Stephanie, Princess Windisch-Graetz (1909–)
m. 1: Peter, Count d'Alcantara di Querrieu (1907–1944)
see: *d'Alcantara di Querrieu* XVIII, page 538
m. 2: Karl Axel Björklund (1906–)
see: *Björklund* XIX, page 614

XXI. Windisch-Graetz 11, from page 918

* **Franz Josef,** Prince Windisch-Graetz, eldest son of Prince Otto.
March 22, 1904, Prague, Czechoslovakia —
m. January 3, 1934, Brussels
Ghislaine, Countess von Arschot-Schoonhoven, daughter of Count Wilhelm von Arschot-Schoonhoven and of his wife, Eva Nuber Zarouki.
March 10, 1912, Brussels —

Issue: 1. Stephanie, Princess Windisch-Graetz
January 17, 1939, Brussels —

2. Wilhelm, Prince Windisch-Graetz
November 19, 1950, Nairobi, Kenya —

XXI. Windisch-Graetz 12, from page 918

* **Ernst Veriand,** Prince Windisch-Graetz, second son of Prince Otto.
April 21, 1905, Prague — December 21, 1952, Vienna
m. October 17, 1927, Vienna. Annulled by the Church in 1940.
Ellen Skinner, daughter of Henry Skinner and of his wife, Mary Overmüller.
April 6, 1906, Scheibbs, Austria —
m. 2: May 11, 1947, Schwarzenbach, near Pilach, Austria
Eva, Baroness von Isbary, daughter of Baron Lothair von Isbary and of his wife, Baroness Aloysia Klepsch-Kloth von Rhoden.
April 5, 1921, Vienna —

XXI. Windisch-Graetz 12 continued

Issue of first marriage:

1. Otto, Prince Windisch-Graetz (1928–)
m. Johanna, Countess von Wimpffen (1936–)
see: *Windisch-Graetz* XXI, 13, below

2. Stephanie, Princess Windisch-Graetz (1933–)
m. Joseph Christoforetti (1919–)
see: *Christoforetti* XXI, page 679

Issue of second marriage:

3. Eleonore, Princess Windisch-Graetz, August 25, 1947, Vienna —
(m. March 21, 1968, Friedrich Johann, Count zu Hardegg auf Glatz)

4. Elisabeth, Princess Windisch-Graetz, October 24, 1951, Vienna —

XXI. Windisch-Graetz 13, from above

★ **Otto,** Prince Windisch-Graetz, only son of Prince Ernst Veriand.
December 5, 1928, Vienna —
m. 1: April 27, 1957, Vienna. Divorced: 1969, Vienna
Johanna, Countess von Wimpffen, daughter of Count Franz von Wimpffen and of his wife, Katharine Schiffer.
May 26, 1936, Budapest —
m. 2: December 22, 1969, Vienna
Maria Magdalena Gamper, daughter of Hans Gamper and of his wife, Sophie Ladurner.
November 7, 1932, Meran —

Issue of first marriage:

1. Henriette Raphaela, Princess Windisch-Graetz, January 31, 1958, Salzburg —

2. Desirée, Princess Windisch-Graetz, January 1, 1959, Salzburg —

3. Philipp, Prince Windisch-Graetz, October 22, 1960, Salzburg —

4. Ernst, Prince Windisch-Graetz, September 25, 1962, Vienna —

5. Dominique, Prince Windisch-Graetz, April 22, 1966, Vienna —

Issue of second marriage:

6. Johannes, Prince Windisch-Graetz, February 7, 1971, Vienna —

XXI. WINKHAUS 1, from page 659

Wolfgang Paul Winkhaus
May 11, 1929, Münster —
m. May 23, 1964, Burgsteinfurt
* **Charlotte,** Princess zu Bentheim und Steinfurt, daughter of Prince Viktor Adolf, 5th Fürst zu Bentheim und Steinfurt, and of his second wife, Princess Helene zu Solms-Hohensolms-Lich.
July 3, 1936, Münster —

Issue: 1. Sophie Charlotte Winkhaus
March 13, 1965, Münster —

2. Christine Irene Winkhaus (twin)
June 6, 1966, Münster —

3. Juliana Margarete Winkhaus (twin)
June 6, 1966, Münster —

XXI. WOLFF METTERNICH ZUR GLACHT 1, from page 861

Paul Joseph, Count Wolff Metternich zur Glacht
June 4, 1916, Strasburg —
m. August 7, 1945, Hall, Tyrol, Austria
* **Therese,** Countess zu Stolberg-Stolberg, daughter of Count Bernhard zu Stolberg-Stolberg and of his wife, Archduchess Hedwig of Austria.
October 11, 1923, Linsen —

Issue: 1. Michael Donatus, Count Wolff Metternich zur Glacht
May 1, 1946, Heppingen —

2. Franz Josef, Count Wolff Metternich zur Glacht
October 7, 1947, Heppingen —

3. Paul Christoph, Count Wolff Metternich zur Glacht
April 14, 1952, Heppingen —

4. Margarita, Countess Wolff Metternich zur Glacht
March 29, 1956, Heppingen —

5. Valerie, Countess Wolff Metternich zur Glacht
June 26, 1960, Heppingen —

XXI. VON WOLLWERT-LAUTERBURG

1, from page 868

August, Baron von Wollwert-Lauterburg
December 29, 1843, Esslingen — August 12, 1908, Stuttgart
m. September 17, 1872, Stuttgart
★ **Olga,** Countess von Taubenheim, daughter of Count Wilhelm von Taubenheim and of his wife, Countess Marie of Würtemberg.
September 15, 1850, Stuttgart — May 16, 1925, Stuttgart

Issue: 1. Olga, Baroness von Wollwert-Lauterburg
February 4, 1874, — April 6, 1894, Stuttgart

XXI. VON WOLZOGEN UND NEUHAUS

1, from page 833

Wolff, Baron von Wolzogen und Neuhaus
June 5, 1910, Berlin-Halensee —
m. September 19 and 20, 1944, Droyssig
★ **Marie,** Princess of Schönburg-Waldenburg, daughter of Prince Heinrich of Schönburg-Waldenburg and of his second wife, Princess Adelheid zur Lippe.
March 29, 1922, Droyssig —

Issue: 1. Wolf-Heinrich, Baron von Wolzogen und Neuhaus
August 28, 1947, Büdingen —

2. Hans-Christoph, Baron von Wolzogen und Neuhaus
August 25, 1948, Büdingen —

XXI. VON WUTHENAU-HOHENTHURM

1, from page 236

Maximilian Adam, Count von Wuthenau-Hohenthurm
June 23, 1834, Dresden — March 20, 1912, Leipzig
m. April 25, 1857, St. Julien, near Geneva, Switzerland
★ **Pauline,** Countess of Württemberg, daughter of Count Alexander of Württemberg and of his wife, Countess Helene Festitics von Tolna.
August 8, 1836, Hietzing, near Vienna — October 6, 1911, Hohenthurm

Issue: 1. Max Adam Traugott von Wuthenau-Hohenthurm
May 1, 1859, Pirna, Saxony — May 18, 1859, Pirna

2. Wilma von Wuthenau-Hohenthurm (1861–1931)
m. Carl Hans Fedor von Wuthenau-Hohenthurm (1850–1915)
see: *von Wuthenau-Hohenthurm* XXI, 13, page 930

XXI. von Wuthenau-Hohenthurm 1 continued

3. Carl Adam, Count von Wuthenau-Hohenthurm (1863–1946)
   m. 1: Maria Antonia, Countess Chotek von Chotkowa und Wognin (1874–1930)
   m. 2: Dorothea Wolff (1899–)
   see: *von Wuthenau-Hohenthurm* XXI, 2, below

XXI. von Wuthenau-Hohenthurm 2, from above

* **Carl Adam,** Count von Wuthenau-Hohenthurm, second son of Count Maximilian Adam.
June 26, 1863, Dresden — November 13, 1946, Halle
m. 1: September 27, 1893, Gross-Priesen, Bohemia

Maria Antonia, Countess Chotek von Chotkowa und Wognin, daughter of Count Bohuslaw Chotek von Chotkowa und Wognin and of his wife, Countess Wilhelmine Kinsky von Wchinitz und Tettau (whose sister, Countess Sophie, was married to Archduke Franz Ferdinand of Austria and was assassinated at Sarajevo in 1914).
May 12, 1874, Adlerkostelitz — June 13, 1930, Hohenthurm
m. 2: February 18, 1937, Berlin

Dorothea Wolff, daughter of Major Franz Wolff and of his wife, Margarethe Heinnicke.
February 5, 1899, Schleswig —

Issue of first marriage:

1. Wilhelmine von Wuthenau-Hohenthurm (1895–)
   m. Friedrich, Count von Hoyos-Sprinzenstein (1876–1951)
   see: *von Hoyos-Sprinzenstein* XXI, page 726)

2. Carl Adam, Count von Wuthenau-Hohenthurm (1896–)
   m. Marie, Countess von Waldburg zu Wolfegg und Waldsee (1902–)
   see: *von Wuthenau-Hohenthurm* XXI, 3, page 924

3. Friedrich von Wuthenau-Hohenthurm (1897–)
   m. 1: Anna, Countess von Nostitz-Rieneck (1905–1934)
   m. 2: Franziska Ziegler (–)
   see: *von Wuthenau-Hohenthurm* XXI, 4, page 925

XXI. von Wuthenau-Hohenthurm 2 continued

4. Alexander von Wuthenau-Hohenthurm (1900–)
m. 1: Rachelle di Catinelli Edle von Obradich-Bevilaqua (1900–1945)
m. 2: Beatrix Pietsch Edle von Sidonienburg (1919–)
see: *von Wuthenau-Hohenthurm* XXI, 10, page 927

5. Franz Ferdinand von Wuthenau-Hohenthurm (1901–1966)
m. Elinor Bromberg (1911–)
see: *von Wuthenau-Hohenthurm* XXI, 11, page 928

6. Marie von Wuthenau-Hohenthurm (1909–)
m. Johann, Baron von Plessen-Cronstern (1890–1961)
see: *von Plessen* XXI, page 785

XXI. von Wuthenau-Hohenthurm 3, from page 923

* **Carl Adam,** Count von Wuthenau-Hohenthurm, eldest son of Count Carl Adam.
November 15, 1896, Dresden —
m. February 23, 1922, Wolfegg
Marie, Countess von Waldburg zu Wolfegg und Waldsee, daughter of Fürst Maximilian von Waldburg zu Wolfegg und Waldsee and of his wife, Princess Sidonia Lobkowicz.
September 17, 1902, Waldsee —

Issue: 1. Walburga von Wuthenau-Hohenthurm
February 6, 1923, Hohenthurm —

2. Sidonie von Wuthenau-Hohenthurm (1923–)
m. Hans Ulrich, Count Schaffgotsch genannt Semperfrei von und zu Kynast und Greiffenstein, Baron von Trachenberg (1927–)
see: *Schaffgotsch genannt Semperfrei von und zu Kynast und Greiffenstein* XXI, page 809

3. Wilhelmine von Wuthenau-Hohenthurm
February 3, 1925, Wolfegg —

4. Maximilian von Wuthenau-Hohenthurm
December 10, 1927, Hohenthurm —

XXI. von Wuthenau-Hohenthurm 3 continued

5. Albrecht von Wuthenau-Hohenthurm
December 19, 1939, Munich —

XXI. von Wuthenau-Hohenthurm 4, from page 923

* **Friedrich von Wuthenau-Hohenthurm,** second son of Count Carl Adam.
October 19, 1897, Dresden —
m. 1: June 5, 1928, Plan
Anna, Countess von Nostitz-Rieneck, daughter of Count Josef von Nostitz-Rieneck and of his wife, Princess Roza Lobkowicz.
August 23, 1905, Horkal — February 10, 1934, Halle
m. 2: February 19, 1936, Würzburg
Franziska Ziegler, daughter of Karl Ziegler and of his wife, Anna Kraus.
—

Issue of first marriage:

1. Josef von Wuthenau-Hohenthurm (1929–)
m. Ursula Nutsch (1928–)
see: *von Wuthenau-Hohenthurm* XXI, 5, page 926

2. Antonius von Wuthenau-Hohenthurm (1930–) (twin)
m. Ingrid Ritscher (1938–)
see: *von Wuthenau-Hohenthurm* XXI, 6, page 926

3. Johannes von Wuthenau-Hohenthurm (twin)
July 11, 1930, Plan —

4. Nikolaus von Wuthenau-Hohenthurm (1931–)
m. Dorothea Kós (1937–)
see: *von Wuthenau-Hohenthurm* XXI, 7, page 926

Issue of second marriage:

5. Karl-Friedrich von Wuthenau-Hohenthurm (1936–)
m. Marie-Luise Schöllhorn (1934–)
see: *von Wuthenau-Hohenthurm* XXI, 8, page 927

6. Michael von Wuthenau-Hohenthurm (1938–)
m. Ursula Schwörer (1941–)
see: *von Wuthenau-Hohenthurm* XXI, 9, page 927

XXI. von Wuthenau-Hohenthurm 5, from page 925

* **Josef von Wuthenau-Hohenthurm,** eldest son of Friedrich.
April 28, 1929, Hohenthurm —
m. July 16, 1962, Kehl/Rhine
Ursula Nutsch, daughter of Paul Nutsch and of his wife, Elsa Kirchhofer.
June 20, 1938, Kehl —

Issue: 1. Friedrich Karl von Wuthenau-Hohenthurm
October 1, 1965, Kehl —

XXI. von Wuthenau-Hohenthurm 6, from page 925

* **Antonius von Wuthenau-Hohenthurm,** second son of Friedrich.
July 11, 1930, Plan —
m. February 26, 1962, Bad Waldsee
Ingrid Ritscher, daughter of Eberhard Ritscher and of his wife, Auguste Gros.
April 7, 1938, Bad Waldsee —

Issue: 1. Katharina von Wuthenau-Hohenthurm
January 31, 1963, Munich —

2. Monika von Wuthenau-Hohenthurm
April 15, 1964, Bad Waldsee —

XXI. von Wuthenau-Hohenthurm 7, from page 925

* **Nikolaus von Wuthenau-Hohenthurm,** fourth son of Friedrich.
November 24, 1931, Halle —
m. June 6, 1964, Vineland, Ontario, Canada
Dorothea Kós, daughter of Hubert Kós and of his wife, Mary Sheeham.
May 9, 1937, Budapest, Hungary —

Issue: 1. Hubertus von Wuthenau-Hohenthurm
July 16, 1966, Toronto, Ontario, Canada —

2. Michael von Wuthenau-Hohenthurm
March 19, 1968, Toronto —

XXI. von Wuthenau-Hohenthurm 8, from page 925

* **Karl-Friedrich von Wuthenau-Hohenthurm,** fifth son of Friedrich.
December 11, 1936, Halle —
m. May 19, 1959, Bad Waldsee
Marie-Luise Schöllhorn, daughter of Friedrich Schöllhorn and of his wife, Margarete Jeske.
August 23, 1934, Bad Waldsee —

Issue: 1. Marie-Christine von Wuthenau-Hohenthurm
May 5, 1960, Bad Waldsee —

2. Alexander von Wuthenau-Hohenthurm
January 21, 1965, Bad Waldsee —

3. Elisabeth von Wuthenau-Hohenthurm
November 7, 1967, Westkirchen —

XXI. von Wuthenau-Hohenthurm 9, from page 925

* **Michael von Wuthenau-Hohenthurm,** sixth son of Friedrich.
November 8, 1938, Halle —
m. August 28, 1965, Karlsruhe
Ursula Schwörer, daughter of Hans Schwörer and of his wife, Brunhilde Kesper.
April 28, 1941, Tauberbischofsheim —

Issue: 1. Beatrice von Wuthenau-Hohenthurm
January 9, 1967, Karlsruhe —

2. Nikolaus von Wuthenau-Hohenthurm
August 12, 1968, Karlsruhe —

XXI. von Wuthenau-Hohenthurm 10, from page 924

* **Alexander von Wuthenau-Hohenthurm,** third son of Count Carl Adam.
January 8, 1900, Dresden —
m. 1: October 30, 1935, St. Louis, Missouri, USA
Rachelle di Catinelli Edle von Obradich-Bevilaqua, daughter of Arthur di Catinelli Edler von Obradich-Bevilaqua and of his wife, Anna Luppio de Tihovac.
October 2, 1900, Fiume, Italy — June 2, 1945, Taxco de Alarcon, Mexico

XXI. von Wuthenau-Hohenthurm 10 continued

m. 2: January 5, 1948, Cuernavaca, Mexico
Beatrix Pietsch Edle von Sidonienburg, daughter of Walter Pietsch Edler von Sidonienburg and of his wife, Anna di Catinelli Edle von Obradich-Bevilaqua.
November 18, 1919, Vienna —

Issue of first marriage:
1. Maria de la Luz von Wuthenau-Hohenthurm
May 22, 1937, Halle —

2. Isabel von Wuthenau-Hohenthurm
March 7, 1939, Taxco de Alarcon, Mexico —

3. Franzesca-Fernanda von Wuthenau-Hohenthurm (1940–)
m. Antonio Saldivar y Fernandez de Valle (1933–)
see: *Saldivar* XVIII, page 601

4. Alexander von Wuthenau-Hohenthurm
June 14, 1942, Taxco de Alarcon, Mexico —

Issue of second marriage:
5. Guadalupe von Wuthenau-Hohenthurm
August 22, 1948, Taxco de Alarcon —

6. Antonio von Wuthenau-Hohenthurm
June 11, 1950, Taxco de Alarcon —

7. Beatrice von Wuthenau-Hohenthurm
November 4, 1952, Taxco de Alarcon —

XXI. von Wuthenau-Hohenthurm 11, from page 924

* **Franz Ferdinand von Wuthenau-Hohenthurm,** fourth son of Count Carl Adam.
August 18, 1901, Kassebaude, near Dresden — April 3, 1966, San Isidro, Argentina
m. August 27, 1930, Dresden
Elinor Bromberg, daughter of Erwin Bromberg and of his wife, Emily Höfler.

XXI. von Wuthenau-Hohenthurm 11 continued

June 27, 1911, São Paulo, Brazil —

Issue: 1. Marie Antoinette von Wuthenau-Hohenthurm (1932–)
m. Alvise, Conte Sagramoso (1924–)
see: *Sagramoso* XVIII, page 601

2. Franz Ferdinand von Wuthenau-Hohenthurm (1936–)
m. Cristina de Bary (1941–)
see: *von Wuthenau-Hohenthurm* XXI, 12, below

3. Marie Elisabeth (Elisalex) von Wuthenau-Hohenthurm (1945–)
m. Alberto Bosch (1934–)
see: *Bosch* XXIV, page 1015

4. Maria Paula (Paulette) von Wuthenau-Hohenthurm
July 15, 1948, Buenos Aires, Argentina —

XXI. von Wuthenau-Hohenthurm 12, from above

* **Franz Ferdinand von Wuthenau-Hohenthurm,** only son of Franz Ferdinand.
May 1, 1936, Buenos Aires —
m. September 28, 1962, Buenos Aires
Cristina de Bary, daughter of Enrique de Bary and of his wife, Hildda ap Iwan.
January 26, 1941, Buenos Aires —

Issue: 1. Celedonio von Wuthenau-Hohenthurm
October 20, 1963, Buenos Aires —

2. Candelaria von Wuthenau-Hohenthurm
June 12, 1965, Buenos Aires —

XXI. von Wuthenau-Hohenthurm 13, from page 922

Carl Hans Fedor von Wuthenau-Hohenthurm

December 14, 1950, Gross-Paschleben — April 4, 1915, Schwenzin, Mecklenburg

m. September 28, 1880, Hohenthurm

* **Wilma von Wuthenau-Hohenthurm,** daughter of Count Maximilian von Wuthenau-Hohenthurm and of his wife, Countess Pauline of Württemberg.

January 12, 1861, Dresden — May 7, 1931, Geuz, Austria

Issue: 1. Carl Adam von Wuthenau-Hohenthurm (1882–1950)
m. Gisela, Countess von Lüttichau (1876–1963)
see: *von Wuthenau-Hohenthurm* XXI, 14, below

2. Maximilian von Wuthenau-Hohenthurm
January 26, 1884, Niemberg — August 10, 1947, in a prisoner-of-war camp at Kamyshin on the Volga, Russia

3. Wilma von Wuthenau-Hohenthurm
January 11, 1886, Niemberg — January , 1945, missing since the Russians invaded the town of Kraschnitz, where she was last known to be living

4. Wilhelm von Wuthenau-Hohenthurm (1888–)
m. Maria Ingeborg Zanders (1907–)
see: *von Wuthenau-Hohenthurm* XXI, 15, page 931

5. Fedor von Wuthenau-Hohenthurm (1889–1940)
m. Helga, Countess von Perponcher-Sedlnitzky (1900
see: *von Wuthenau-Hohenthurm* XXI, 16, page 932

6. Gisela von Wuthenau-Hohenthurm (1893–1937)
m. Dominik Pescatore (1879–)
see: *Pescatore* XVIII, page 593

XXI. von Wuthenau-Hohenthurm 14, from above

* **Carl Adam von Wuthenau-Hohenthurm,** eldest son of Carl Hans Fedor.

June 21, 1882, Niemberg — September 2, 1950, Ilten

m. March 27, 1912, Munich

XXI. von Wuthenau-Hohenthurm 14 continued

Gisela, Countess von Lüttichau, daughter of Count Bernhard von Lüttichau and of his wife, Ida von Selchow.

September 3, 1876, Berlin — May 15, 1963, Tegernsee, Bavaria

(She m. 1: May 3, 1899, Berlin, Fredy, Count von Perponcher-Sedlnitzky, who died August 11, 1917, at Babelsberg, near Potsdam. They were divorced: June 26, 1909. Their daughter, Helga, married Carl Adam von Wuthenau-Hohenthurm's brother, Fedor.)

Issue: 1. Ilona von Wuthenau-Hohenthurm (1913–)
m. 1: and divorced: Hans-Joachim von Wallenrodt (1914–)
see: *von Wallenrodt* XXI, page 900
m. 2: Adolf Strandes (1913–)
see: *Strandes* XXI, page 866

2. Carla von Wuthenau-Hohenthurm (1915–)
m. 1: Hellmut Hansen (1909–1945)
see: *Hansen* XXI, page 718
m. 2: Hans-Joachim von Wallenrodt (1914–)
see: *von Wallenrodt* XXI, page 900

3. Carl Adam von Wuthenau-Hohenthurm
January 17, 1917, Gross-Paschleben — May 20, 1941, Rethymnon, Crete, killed in action in World War II

4. Traugott-Helo von Wuthenau-Hohenthurm
April 24, 1919, Gross-Paschleben — June 24, 1944, somewhere in Russia, missing and presumed killed in action in World War II

XXI. von Wuthenau-Hohenthurm 15, from page 930

* **Wilhelm von Wuthenau-Hohenthurm,** third son of Carl Hans Fedor.
June 14, 1888, Niemberg —
m. November 28, 1936, Berlin

Maria Ingeborg Zanders, daughter of Hans Zanders and of his wife, Olga Peltzer.
February 24, 1907, Bergisch Gladbach, Rhineland —

XXI. von Wuthenau-Hohenthurm

15 continued

Issue: 1. Hans Adam von Wuthenau-Hohenthurm
September 14, 1938, Vienna — August 19, 1941, Velden at Worthersee, Austria, where he was reported missing,

2. Peter von Wuthenau-Hohenthurm
September 12, 1940, Vienna —

XXI. von Wuthenau-Hohenthurm

16, from page 930

* **Fedor von Wuthenau-Hohenthurm,** fourth son of Carl Hans Fedor.
October 5, 1889, Geuz, Austria — August 2, 1940, Gross Paschleben
m. March 16, 1929, Gross Paschleben
Helga, Countess von Perponcher-Sedlnitzky, daughter of Count Fredy von Perponcher-Sedlnitzky and of his wife, Countess Gisela von Lüttichau.
March 27, 1900, Berlin —
(Since 1946 she has gone by the title of Countess von Perponcher.)

Issue: 1. Gisela von Wuthenau-Hohenthurm (since 1946, Countess von Perponcher) (1929–)
m. Richard Ernest Dubé (–)
see: *Dubé* XXIV, page 1017

2. Huberta von Wuthenau-Hohenthurm (since 1946, Countess von Perponcher) (1933–)
m. Johann-Georg Greuner (1930–)
see: *Greuner* XXI, page 716

XXI. WUTHOLEN

1, from page 384

Ferdinand Wutholen
—
m.
* **Charlotte (Sarolta),** Princess of Hungary, Princess of Habsburg-Lorraine, daughter of Archduke Albrecht of Austria by his second wife, Katalin Bocskay de Felsö-Banya, who assumed the surname of Habsburg-Lorraine.
May 3, 1940, Budapest, Hungary —

Issue:

THE HOUSE OF YSENBURG

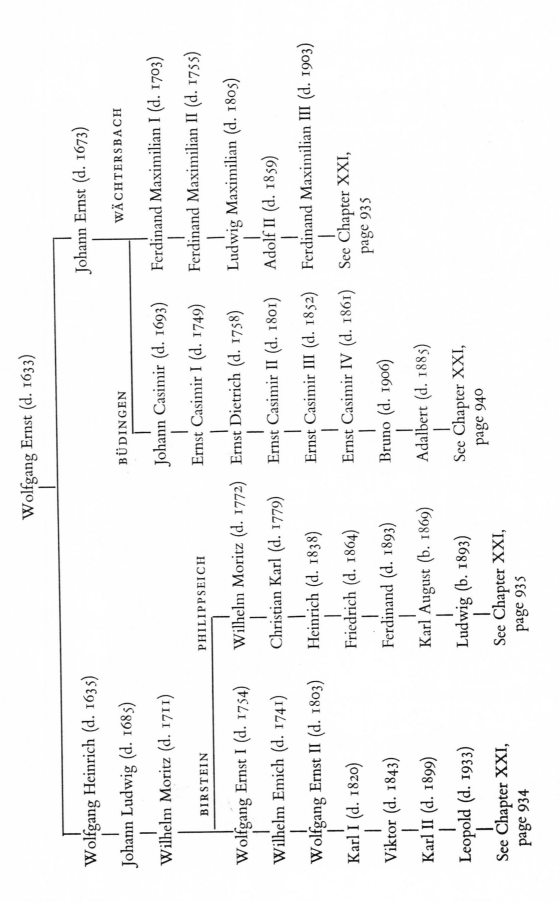

Wolfgang Ernst (d. 1633)

- Wolfgang Heinrich (d. 1635)
  - Johann Ludwig (d. 1685)
    - Wilhelm Moritz (d. 1711)
      - BIRSTEIN
        - Wolfgang Ernst I (d. 1754)
        - Wilhelm Emich (d. 1741)
        - Wolfgang Ernst II (d. 1803)
        - Karl I (d. 1820)
        - Viktor (d. 1843)
        - Karl II (d. 1899)
        - Leopold (d. 1933)
        - See Chapter XXI, page 934
      - PHILIPPSEICH
        - Wilhelm Moritz (d. 1772)
        - Christian Karl (d. 1779)
        - Heinrich (d. 1838)
        - Friedrich (d. 1864)
        - Ferdinand (d. 1893)
        - Karl August (b. 1869)
        - Ludwig (b. 1893)
        - See Chapter XXI, page 935
- Johann Ernst (d. 1673)
  - BÜDINGEN
    - Johann Casimir (d. 1693)
    - Ernst Casimir I (d. 1749)
    - Ernst Dietrich (d. 1758)
    - Ernst Casimir II (d. 1801)
    - Ernst Casimir III (d. 1852)
    - Ernst Casimir IV (d. 1861)
    - Bruno (d. 1906)
    - Adalbert (d. 1885)
    - See Chapter XXI, page 940
  - WÄCHTERSBACH
    - Ferdinand Maximilian I (d. 1703)
    - Ferdinand Maximilian II (d. 1755)
    - Ludwig Maximilian (d. 1805)
    - Adolf II (d. 1859)
    - Ferdinand Maximilian III (d. 1903)
    - See Chapter XXI, page 935

XXI. ZU YSENBURG UND BIRSTEIN 1, from page 258

Leopold, Prince zu Ysenburg und Birstein
March 10, 1866, Offenbach — January 30, 1933, Munich
m. 1: April 22, 1902, Heidelberg
* **Olga,** Princess of Saxe-Weimar-Eisenach, daughter of Prince Hermann of Saxe-Weimar-Eisenach and of his wife, Princess Auguste of Württemberg.
September 8, 1869, Stuttgart — January 12, 1924, Berchtesgaden
m. 2: December 12, 1924, Berchtesgaden
Marie, Countess Eckbrecht von Dürckheim-Montmartin, daughter of Count Ernst Eckbrecht von Dürckheim-Montmartin and of his wife, Countess Vincenzia Spangen von Uyternesse.
October 27, 1880, Munich — December 14, 1937, Bad Homburg

Issue of first marriage:
1. Wilhelm Karl, Prince zu Ysenburg und Birstein (1903–1956)
m. Helene, Countess von Korff genannt Schmising-Kerssenbrock (1900–)
see: *zu Ysenburg und Birstein* XXI, 2, below

XXI. zu Ysenburg und Birstein 2, from above

* **Wilhelm Karl,** Prince zu Ysenburg und Birstein, only son of Leopold.
January 16, 1903, Darmstadt — November 23, 1956, Mülheim/Ruhr
m. April 12, 1930 (civil), Bonn, and April 30, 1930 (religious), Wiesbaden
Helene, Countess von Korff genannt Schmising-Kerssenbrock, daughter of Count Alfred von Korff genannt Schmising-Kerssenbrock and of his wife, Baroness Helene von Hilgers.
April 6, 1900, Darmstadt —

No Issue.

XXI. ZU YSENBURG UND BÜDINGEN IN PHILIPPSEICH 1, from page 139

Ferdinand, Count zu Ysenburg und Büdingen in Philippseich
October 15, 1841, Meerholz — January 5, 1920, Philippseich
m. October 11, 1886, Oberurf

XXI. zu Ysenburg und Büdingen in Philippseich 1 continued

* **Elisabeth,** Princess von Ardeck, daughter of Prince Wilhelm of Hesse-Philippsthal-Barchfeld and of his wife, Princess Marie von Hanau, Countess von Schaumburg, created Princess von Ardeck in 1876.
June 8, 1864, Cassel — March 4, 1919, Ahrweiler

Issue: 1. Marie Berthe, Countess zu Ysenburg und Büdingen in Philippseich
April 29, 1890, Philippseich — February 17, 1964, Langenselbach

2. Irmgard, Countess zu Ysenburg und Büdingen in Philippseich
March 17, 1894, Philippseich — July 11, 1921, Bad Homburg

3. Elisabeth, Countess zu Ysenburg und Büdingen in Philippseich
August 4, 1897, Philippseich — October 17, 1917, Langen

XXI. ZU YSENBURG-PHILIPPSEICH 1, from page 539

Ludwig, Count von Ysenburg-Philippseich
July 23, 1893, Hohenschwangau —
m. March 31, 1937, Pisignano, Italy
* **Mariangela Aloisi,** daughter of Dr. Domenico Aloisi and of his wife, Princess Marie zu Ysenburg und Büdingen in Wächtersbach.
July 4, 1911, Pisignano —

Issue: 1. Christian, Count von Ysenburg-Philippseich
July 29, 1938, Berlin —

2. Gabriele, Countess von Ysenburg-Philippseich (1939–)
m. Rüdiger von Groll (1937–)
see: *von Groll* XXI, page 716

3. Elizabeth, Countess von Ysenburg-Philippseich (1941–)
m. Ernst, Prince Biron von Curland (1940–)
see: *von Curland* XXI, page 682

XXI. ZU YSENBURG UND BÜDINGEN IN WÄCHTERSBACH 1, from page 119

Ferdinand Maximilian III, Prince zu Ysenburg und Büdingen in Wächtersbach
October 24, 1824, Wächtersbach — June 5, 1903,

XXI. zu Ysenburg und Büdingen in Wächtersbach 1 continued

m. July 17, 1849, Wilhelmshohe

* **Auguste,** Princess von Hanau, daughter of Elector Friedrich Wilhelm I of Hesse and of his morganatic wife, Gertrud von Falkenstein, Princess von Hanau, Countess von Schaumburg.

September 21, 1829, — September 18, 1887,

Issue: 1. Friedrich Wilhelm, Fürst zu Ysenburg und Büdingen in Wächtersbach (1850–1933)
m. Anna, Countess Dobrzensky von Dobrzenicz (1852–1913)
see: *zu Ysenburg und Büdingen in Wächtersbach* XXI, 2, below

2. Alexandra, Princess zu Ysenburg und Büdingen in Wächtersbach (1855–1932)
m. 1: and divorced: Adalbert, Prince zu Ysenburg und Büdingen in Büdingen (1839–1885)
see: *zu Ysenburg und Büdingen in Büdingen* XXI, page 940
m. 2: and divorced: Robert, Baron von Pagenhardt (1852–1922)
see: *von Pagenhardt* XXI, page 781

3. Gerta, Princess zu Ysenburg und Büdingen in Wächtersbach (1863–1945)
m. Wilhelm, Prince of Saxe-Weimar-Eisenach (1853–1924)
see: *Saxe-Weimar-Eisenach* VII e–2, page 258

XXI. zu Ysenburg und Büdingen in Wächtersbach 2, from above

* **Friedrich Wilhelm,** 2nd Fürst zu Ysenburg und Büdingen in Wächtersbach, only son of Prince Ferdinand Maximilian III.

June 17, 1850, Wächtersbach — April 20, 1933, Wächtersbach

m. September 16, 1879, Wächtersbach

Anna, Countess Dobrzensky von Dobrzenicz, daughter of Lieutenant Field Marshal Count Prokop Dobrzensky von Dobrzenicz and of his wife, Countess Elisabeth von Harbuval.

February 25, 1852, Prague — September 21, 1913, Nauheim

Issue: 1. Friedrich Maximilian, Hereditary Prince zu Ysenburg und Büdingen in Wächtersbach (1880–1927)
m. Margarete (Margita), Countess von Donhoff (1876–1954)
see: *zu Ysenburg und Büdingen in Wächtersbach* XXI, 3, page 937

XXI. zu Ysenburg und Büdingen in Wächtersbach 2 continued

2. Maria, Princess zu Ysenburg und Büdingen in Wächtersbach (1881–1958)
   m. Domenico Aloisi, M.D. (1867–1945)
   see: *Aloisi* XVIII, page 539

3. Elisabeth, Princess zu Ysenburg und Büdingen in Wächtersbach (1883–)
   m. Edouard, Comte Desrousseaux, Duc de Vandières (1866–1935)
   see: *Desrousseaux de Vandières* XVIII, page 556

4. Ida, Princess zu Ysenburg und Büdingen in Wächtersbach (1885–1964)
   m. Major General Thilo von Trotha (1882–1969)
   see: *von Trotha* XXI, page 879

5. Therese, Princess zu Ysenburg und Büdingen in Wächtersbach (1887–) (twin)
   m. Franz, Count Ceschi a Santa Croce (1872–1952)
   see: *Ceschi a Santa Croce* XVIII, page 553

6. Anne, Princess zu Ysenburg und Büdingen in Wächtersbach (1887–1954) (twin)
   m. and divorced: Hans Rausch (1886–)
   see: *Rausch* XXI, page 789

XXI. zu Ysenburg und Büdingen in Wächtersbach 3, from page 936

* **Friedrich Maximilian,** Hereditary Prince zu Ysenburg und Büdingen in Wächtersbach, only son of Fürst Friedrich Wilhelm.

June 25, 1880, Wächtersbach — March 11, 1927, Berlin

m. December 19, 1903, Freiburg-im-Breisgau

Margarete (Margita), Countess von Donhoff, daughter of Count Otto von Donhoff and of his wife, Countess Maria von Schlippenbach.

April 19, 1876, Beseritz — September 22, 1954, Wächtersbach

XXI. zu Ysenburg und Büdingen in Wächtersbach 3 continued

Issue: 1. Otto Friedrich, 7th Fürst zu Ysenburg und Büdingen (1904–). Adopted by Karl Gustav, 6th Fürst zu Ysenburg und Büdingen.
m. Felizitas, Princess Reuss zu Köstritz (1912–)
see: *zu Ysenburg und Büdingen* XXI, 4, below

2. Gabriele Georgine, Princess zu Ysenburg und Büdingen in Wächtersbach (1911–)
m. Franz Wilhelm, Prince zu Sayn-Wittgenstein-Berleburg (1910–)
see: *zu Sayn-Wittgenstein-Berleburg* XXI, page 807

XXI. zu Ysenburg und Büdingen 4, from above and page 344

* **Otto Friedrich,** 7th Fürst zu Ysenburg und Büdingen, only son of Hereditary Prince Friedrich Maximilian and adopted son of Prince Karl Gustav, 6th Fürst zu Ysenburg und Büdingen.
September 16, 1904, Halberstadt —
m. September 3, 1935, Stonsdorf Castle
* **Felizitas,** Princess Reuss zu Köstritz, daughter of Prince Heinrich XXXIV Reuss zu Köstritz and of his wife, Princess Sophie Renate Reuss zu Köstritz.
July 5, 1912, Oels, Silesia —

Issue: 1. Wolfgang Ernst, Hereditary Prince zu Ysenburg und Büdingen (1936–)
m. Leonille Elisabeth, Princess zu Sayn-Wittgenstein-Berleburg (1941–)
see: *zu Ysenburg und Büdingen* XXI, 5, page 939

2. Alexandra, Princess zu Ysenburg und Büdingen (1937–)
m. Welf Heinrich, Prince of Hanover, Great Britain and Ireland (1923–)
see: *Hanover* (*Guelph*) I n–1, page 31

3. Ferdinand Heinrich, Prince zu Ysenburg und Büdingen
October 19, 1940, Frankfurt-am-Main —

XXI. zu Ysenburg und Büdingen 4 continued

4. Christian Albrecht, Prince zu Ysenburg und Büdingen (1943–)
m. Monika, Baroness von Plessen (1940–)
see: *zu Ysenburg und Büdingen* XXI, 6, below

5. Sylvester, Prince zu Ysenburg und Büdingen
December 31, 1949, Gelnhausen —

XXI. zu Ysenburg und Büdingen 5, from pages 938, 808

* **Wolfgang Ernst,** Hereditary Prince zu Ysenburg und Büdingen, eldest son of Prince Otto Friedrich, 7th Fürst.
June 20, 1936, Frankfurt-am-Main —
m. January 27, 1967, Rabertshausen
* **Leonille Elisabeth,** Princess zu Sayn-Wittgenstein-Berleburg, daughter of Prince Casimir Johannes zu Sayn-Wittgenstein-Berleburg and of his wife, Ingrid Alsen.
July 6, 1941, Hamburg —

Issue: 1. Casimir Alexander, Prince zu Ysenburg und Büdingen
December 30, 1967, Frankfurt-am-Main —

2. Ferdinand Maximilian, Prince zu Ysenburg und Büdingen
July 28, 1969, Frankfurt-am-Main —

XXI. zu Ysenburg und Büdingen 6, from above and page 786

* **Christian Albrecht,** Prince zu Ysenburg und Büdingen, third son of Prince Otto Friedrich, 7th Fürst.
January 3, 1943, Frankfurt-am-Main —
m. February 17, 1966, Büdingen
* **Monika,** Baroness von Plessen, daughter of Baron Johann Ludwig von Plessen-Cronstern and of his wife, Maria Immaculata von Wuthenau-Hohenthurm.
January 29, 1940, Rome —

Issue: 1. Margita, Princess zu Ysenburg und Büdingen
November 7, 1966, Frankfurt-am-Main —

2. Johann-Albrecht, Prince zu Ysenburg und Büdingen
July 10, 1968, Frankfurt-am-Main —

XXI. ZU YSENBURG UND BÜDINGEN IN BÜDINGEN

1, from page 936

Adalbert, Prince zu Ysenburg und Büdingen in Büdingen
February 17, 1839, Büdingen — August 29, 1885, Kennenburg, near Esslingen
m. November 18, 1875, Wächtersbach. Divorced: April 28, 1877, by Decree of Grand Duke Ludwig IV of Hesse and the Rhine

* **Alexandra,** Princess zu Ysenburg und Büdingen in Wächtersbach, daughter of Fürst Ferdinand Maximilian III zu Ysenburg und Büdingen in Wächtersbach and of his wife, Princess Auguste von Hanau, Countess von Schaumburg.
December 28, 1855, Wächtersbach — October 24, 1932, Munich
(She m. 2: and divorced: Robert, Baron von Pagenhardt – see: *von Pagenhardt* XXI, page 781.)

No Issue.

XXI. ZU YSENBURG IN MEERHOLZ

1, from page 335

Friedrich, Count zu Ysenburg in Meerholz
August 10, 1847, Meerholz — March 29, 1889, Meerholz
m. July 20, 1875, Greiz

* **Marie,** Princess Reuss zu Greiz, daughter of Prince Heinrich XX Reuss zu Greiz and of his wife, Princess Karoline of Hesse-Homburg.
March 19, 1855, Greiz — December 31, 1909,

No Issue.

XXI. VON ZICHY-FERRARIS ZU ZICH UND VÁSONYKEÖ

1, from page 118

Felix, Count von Zichy-Ferraris zu Zich und Vásonykeö
November 20, 1810, — September 8, 1885,
m. March 10, 1839,

* **Emilie,** Countess von Reichenbach-Lessonitz, daughter of Elector Wilhelm II of Hesse and of his second, morganatic, wife, Emilie Ortlopp, created Countess von Reichenbach (1821) and Countess von Lessonitz (1824).
June 8, 1820, Cassel — January 30, 1891, Budapest, Hungary

XXI. von Zichy-Ferraris zu Zich und Vásonykeö 1 continued

Issue: 1. Viktor, Count von Zichy-Ferraris zu Zich und Vásonykeö
July 1, 1842, Budapest—May 28, 1880, Budapest

2. Melanie, Countess von Zichy-Ferraris zu Zich und Vásonykeö (1843–1925)
m. Paul, 4th Fürst von Metternich-Winneburg (1834–1906)
see: *von Metternich-Winneburg* XXI, page 772

3. Ludwig, Count von Zichy-Ferraris zu Zich und Vásonykeö
August 11, 1844, —May 29, 1899, Vienna

4. Karoline, Countess von Zichy-Ferraris zu Zich und Vásonykeö (1845–1871)
m. Gyula, Count Széchényi von Sárvár-Felsövidék (1829–1921)
see: *Széchényi von Sárvár-Felsövidék*, Addendum, page 1035

5. Emilie, Countess von Zichy-Ferraris zu Zich und Vásonykeö (1847–1935)
m. Konrad, Count von Watzdorff (1844–1922)
see: *von Watzdorff* XXI, page 904

6. Emanuel, Count von Zichy-Ferraris zu Zich und Vásonykeö
February 19, 1852, —June 2, 1914, Vienna

XXI. ZYLSTRA 1, from page 1006

Anthony Adama Zylstra, M.D.
January 9, 1902, Izendijke, The Netherlands —
m. January 8, 1960,
* **Irina Nikolaievna,** Princess Orlova, daughter of Prince Nikolai Vladimirovich Orlov and of his wife, Princess Nadeshda Petrovna of Russia.
March 17, 1918, Koreiz, Crimea —
(She m. 1: and divorced: Herbert, Baron von Waldstätten – see: *von Waldstätten* XXI, page 899.)

No Issue.

XXII

THE FAMILIES OF POLAND

XXII. BNINSKI

1, from page 947

Raphael, Count Bninski
February 17, 1918, Dobrzya, Poland — October 13, 1943, Warsaw
m. December 8, 1942, Balice
* **Izabela,** Princess Czartoryska, daughter of Prince Olgierd Czartoryski and of his wife, Archduchess Mechtild of Austria.
August 8, 1917, Sielec, Poland —

Issue: 1. Karol (Charles), Count Bninski (posthumous)
November 17, 1943, Poznan, Poland —

XXII. BOLDIREFF

1, from page 967

Wlodzimierz Boldireff, son of Oleg.
—
m. November 27, 1966, Montreal, Quebec, Canada
* **Maria-Roza,** Princess Swiatopelk-Czetwertynska, daughter of Prince Stanislaw Swiatopelk-Czetwertynski and of his wife, Baroness Ewa (Eva) Buxhoveden.
September 9, 1937, Warsaw —

XXII. CHROBOK

1, from page 284

Bronislaw T. Chrobok
August 27, 1933, Katowice, Poland —
m. November 16, 1969, Toronto, Ontario, Canada
* **Marie Louise,** Princess of Bulgaria, daughter of King Boris III of Bulgaria and of his wife, Princess Giovanna of Savoy.
January 13, 1933, Sofia, Bulgaria —
(She m. 1: and divorced: Karl, Prince of Leiningen – see: *Leiningen* XXI, page 745.)

Issue: 1. Alexandra-Nadejda Chrobok, September 14, 1970, Toronto —

2. Pawel (Paul) Chrobok, May 3, 1972, Toronto —

XXII. CIENSKI

1, from page 954

Tadeusz (Thaddeus) Cienski
August 7, 1934, Lwow, Poland —

XXII. Cienski 1 continued

m. January 5, 1963, Johannesburg, South Africa

★ **Anna Maria,** Countess Mycielska, daughter of Count Kasimierz (Casimir) Mycielski and of his wife, Countess Roza Potocka.

Issue: 1. Jan Cienski
August 10, 1965, Johannesburg —

2. Mikolaj (Nicholas) Cienski
July 12, 1966, Johannesburg —

XXII. CZARTORYSKI

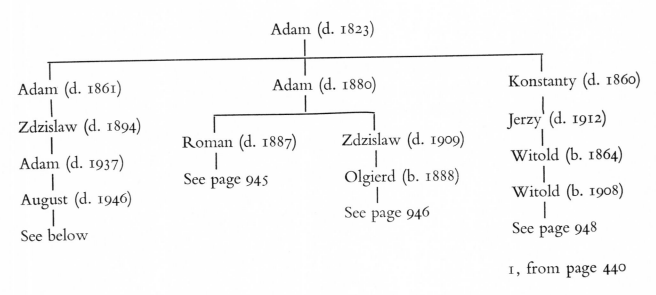

- Adam (d. 1823)
  - Adam (d. 1861)
    - Zdzislaw (d. 1894)
      - Adam (d. 1937)
        - August (d. 1946)
          - See below
  - Adam (d. 1880)
    - Roman (d. 1887)
      - See page 945
    - Zdzislaw (d. 1909)
      - Olgierd (b. 1888)
        - See page 946
  - Konstanty (d. 1860)
    - Jerzy (d. 1912)
      - Witold (b. 1864)
        - Witold (b. 1908)
          - See page 948

1, from page 440

August, Prince Czartoryski, son of Prince Adam.
October 20, 1907, Warsaw — July 1, 1946, Seville, Spain
m. August 12, 1937 (civil), and August 16, 1937 (religious), Ouchy, Switzerland

★ **Dolores,** Princess of Bourbon-Sicily, Infanta of Spain, daughter of Prince Carlos of Bourbon-Sicily, Infante of Spain, and of his wife, Princess Isabelle of France.
November 15, 1909, Madrid —
(She m. 2: Carlos Chias – see: *Chias* XVIII, page 555.)

Issue: 1. Adam, Prince Czartoryski
January 2, 1940, Seville —

2. Luis Pedro (Ludwik Peter), Prince Czartoryski
March 13, 1945, Seville — May 3, 1946,

XXII. Czartoryski 2, from page 396

Adam, Prince Czartoryski, son of Prince Konstanty (Constantine).
June 24, 1804, Warsaw — December 19, 1880, Rokosowo
m. 1: December 12, 1832, Schmiedeberg
* **Wanda,** Princess Radziwill, daughter of Prince Antoni Henryk Radziwill and of his wife, Princess Luise of Prussia.
January 29, 1813, Berlin — September 16, 1845, Ruhberg near Schmiedeberg
m. 2: February 16, 1848, Kornik
Elzbieta, Countess Dzialynska, daughter of Count Titus Dzialynski and of his wife, Countess Cölestine Saryusz von Zamoysc-Zamoyska.
August 16, 1826, Posen, Poland — August 21, 1891, Rokosowo

Issue of first marriage:

1. Angelica, Princess Czartoryska
March 12, 1837, — September 26, 1869, Rokosowo

2. Roman, Prince Czartoryski (1839–1887)
m. Florentine, Countess Dzieduszycki (1844–)
see: *Czartoryski* XXII, 3, below

3. Adam, Prince Czartoryski
January 2, 1845, Berlin — March 7, 1912, Posen

Issue of second marriage: Not descendants of King George I

4. Sigismund, Prince Czartoryski
September 29, 1853, Posen — December 24, 1920, Rokosowo

5. Helena, Princess Czartoryska (1855–1936)
m. Stanislas, Count Plater-Zyberk (1850–1936)

6. Zdzislaw (Ladislas), Prince Czartoryski (1858–1909)
m. Maria Prawdzic-Zaleska (1853–1942)
see: *Czartoryski* XXII, 4, page 946

XXII. Czartoryski 3, from above

* **Roman,** Prince Czartoryski, eldest son of Adam.
November 23, 1839, Berlin — February 18, 1887, Jablonow, Poland
m. December 6, 1873, Lemberg

XXII. Czartoryski 3 continued

Florentina, Countess Dzieduszycka, daughter of Count Titus Dzieduszycki and of his wife, Countess Elzbieta (Elizabeth) Dzieduszycka.

May 28, 1844, Lemberg — , Jablonow

(She m. 2: May 29, 1892, Kopyczyne, divorced: 1897, Antoni Wolniewicz.)

(She m. 3: December 26, 1902, Jablonow, divorced: Ludwik Cienski.)

No Issue.

XXII. Czartoryski 4, from page 945

NOTE: This family do not descend from George I but, as the son married a descendant, the line is given.

Zdzislaw, Prince Czartoryski, son of Prince Adam by his second wife.

January 4, 1858, Posen — January 25, 1909, Sielec

m. February 17, 1884, Vienna

Maria Prawdzic-Zaleska, daughter of Aleksander Prawdzic-Zaleski and of his wife, Martina Grabianska.

November 15, 1853, Ostakowce — October 29, 1942, Krakow

Issue: 1. Elzbieta, Princess Czartoryska (1888–)
m. Jan, Count Szoldrski (1881–1939)

2. Olgierd, Prince Czartoryski (1888–)
m. * Mechtildis, Archduchess of Austria (1891–1966)
see: *Czartoryski* XXII, 5, below

XXII. Czartoryski 5, from above and page 385

Olgierd, Prince Czartoryski, son of Prince Zdzislaw.

October 25, 1888, Sielec —

m. January 11, 1913, Zywiez Castle, Poland

*** Mechtildis,** Archduchess of Austria, daughter of Archduke Karl Stefan of Austria and of his wife, Archduchess Maria Theresia of Austria.

October 11, 1891, Pola — February 6, 1966, Rio de Janeiro, Brazil

Issue: 1. Konstanty (Constantine), Prince Czartoryski (1913–)
m. Karolina, Countess Plater-Zyberk (1917–)
see: *Czartoryski* XXII, 6, page 947

XXII. Czartoryski

5 continued

2. Cäcilia, Princess Czartoryska (1915–)
m. Jerzy (George), Count Rostworowski (1911–)
see: *Rostworowski* XXII, page 961

3. Izabela, Princess Czartoryska (1917–)
m. Raphael, Count Bninski (1918–1943)
see: *Bninski* XXII, page 943

4. Aleksander, Prince Czartoryski
October 21, 1919, Sielec —

XXII. Czartoryski

6, from page 946

* **Konstanty,** Prince Czartoryski, son of Olgierd.
December 9, 1913, Sielec —
m. December 21, 1941, Rio de Janeiro, Brazil
Karolina, Countess Plater-Zyberk, daughter of Count Henryk Plater-Zyberk and of his wife, Countess Elzbieta Plater-Zyberk.
December 8, 1917, Swojatycze —

Issue: 1. Karol (Charles), Prince Czartoryski (1942–)
m. Alice Ternynck (1940–)
see: *Czartoryski* XXII, 7, below

2. Krzysztof (Christopher), Prince Czartoryski
August 26, 1944, Rio de Janeiro —

XXII. Czartoryski

7, from above

* **Karol,** Prince Czartoryski, eldest son of Prince Konstanty.
December 19, 1942, Rio de Janeiro —
m. August 28, 1964, Montreal, Quebec, Canada
Alice Ternynck, daughter of Rene Ternynck and of his wife, Henriette Leroy.
June 5, 1940, Paris —

Issue: 1. Maria Elena, Princess Czartoryska
September 16, 1965, São Paulo, Brazil —

XXII. Czartoryski 8, from page 399

Witold, Prince Czartoryski, son of Prince Sigismund, grandson of Adam.
February 8, 1908, Pelkinie — July 17, 1945, St. Gilgen, Switzerland
m. January 1, 1937,
* **Elzbieta,** Princess Radziwill, daughter of Prince Antoni Albrecht Radziwill and of his wife, Dorothy Parker-Deacon.
January 21, 1917, London —
(She m. 2: Jan Tomaszewski – see: *Tomaszewski* XXII, page 969.)

Issue: 1. Krystyna (Christina), Princess Czartoryska (1938–)
m. Jan Gromnicki (1929–)
see: *Gromnicki* XXII, page 949

2. Albrecht, Prince Czartoryski (1939–)
m. Patrizia, Contessa di Collalto (1937–)
see: *Czartoryski* XXII, 9, below

XXII. Czartoryski 9, from above

* **Albrecht,** Prince Czartoryski, only son of Prince Witold.
November 23, 1939, Vienna —
m. July 5, 1963, Paris
Patrizia, Contessa di Collalto, daughter of Conte Orlando di Collalto and of his wife, Marzia Fabbricotti of the House of the Counts Fabbricotti.
May 8, 1937, Rome —

Issue: 1. Aleksander, Prince Czartoryski
October 20, 1962, Paris —

2. Olivia, Princess Czartoryska
November 15, 1967, Paris —

XXII. DORIA-DERNALOWICZ 1, from page 950

Tadeusz (Thaddeus) Doria-Dernalowicz
January 29, 1916, Repki — April 5, 1959, Cracow
m. November 4, 1943, Repki
* **Anna,** Princess Lubomirska, daughter of Prince Hubert Lubomirski and of his wife, Princess Teresa Radziwill.
May 6, 1916, Volodarka, Poland —

Issue: 1. Jolanda Doria-Dernalowicz
June 1, 1944, Repki —

XXII. GROMNICKI 1, from page 948

Jan Gromnicki
April 29, 1929, Lachowice, Poland —
m. May 26, 1962, Montgé
* **Krystyna,** Princess Czartoryska, daughter of Prince Witold Czartoryski and of his wife, Princess Elzbieta Radziwill.
February 2, 1938, Warsaw —

Issue: 1. Witold Gromnicki
November 27, 1962, Paris —

2. Ewa-Maria Gromnicki
April 30, 1964, Paris —

3. Jerzy (George) Gromnicki
, 1968, Paris —

XXII. Gromnicki 2, from page 957

Jerzy (George) Gromnicki
April 23, 1930, Lachowice, Poland —
m. November 28, 1959, Montrésor, France
* **Elzbieta,** Countess Potocka, daughter of Count Roman Potocki and of his wife, Princess Anna Swiatopelk-Czetwertynska.
February 30, 1930, Derazne, Poland —

Issue: 1. Krystyna Gromnicki
May 12, 1961, Paris —

XXII. KRASINSKI 1, from page 951

Jan, Count Krasinski

—

m.

* **Wanda,** Princess Lubomirska, daughter of Prince Hubert Lubomirski and of his wife, Princess Teresa Radziwill.

June 13, 1923, Nice, France —

(She m. 1: and annulled: Leszek Pawlikowski – see: *Pawlikowski* XXII, page 954.)

(She m. 3: Jozef Rucinski – see: *Rucinski* XXII, page 962.)

Issue: 1. Krysztof, Count Krasinski
June 14, 1948, London, England —

2. Dominik, Count Krasinski
August 12, 1949, London —

XXII. LUBOMIRSKI 1, from page 399

Hubert, Prince Lubomirski, second son of Prince Stanislaw.

November 15, 1875, Rovno — September 21, 1939, Rovno, killed in action in World War II

m. October 5, 1911, Nieswicz

* **Teresa,** Princess Radziwill, daughter of Prince Jerzy Radziwill and of his wife, Countess Roza Branicka.

December 29, 1889, Berlin —

Issue: 1. Jan, Prince Lubomirski (1913–)
m. Gabriela, Countess Przezdziecka (1917–)
see: *Lubomirski* XXII, 2, page 951

2. Hubert, Prince Lubomirski (1914–) (twin)
m. 1: and divorced: Anna Krzyzanowska (–)
m. 2: Greta Calvi (–)
see: *Lubomirski* XXII, 3, page 951

3. Stanislaw, Prince Lubomirski (1914–) (twin)
m. Halina Krajewska (1925–)
see: *Lubomirski* XXII, 4, page 952

4. Anna, Princess Lubomirska (1916–)
m. Tadeusz Doria-Dernalowicz (1916–1959)
see: *Doria-Dernalowicz* XXII, page 949

XXII. Lubomirski

1 continued

5. Zdzislaw, Prince Lubomirski
March 10, 1917, Kiev, Ukraine —

6. Henryk, Prince Lubomirski (1919–)
m. Adela Malachowska (1921–)
see: *Lubomirski* XXII, 5, page 952

7. Wanda, Princess Lubomirska (1923–)
m. 1: and annulled: Leszek Pawlikowski (–)
see: *Pawlikowski* XXII, page 954
m. 2: Jan, Count Krasinski (–)
see: *Krasinski* XXII, page 950
m. 3: Jozef Rucinski (1907–)
see: *Rucinski* XXII, page 962

XXII. Lubomirski

2, from page 950

★ **Jan,** Prince Lubomirski, eldest son of Prince Hubert.
April 29, 1913, Warsaw —
m. October 28, 1942, Warsaw
Gabriela, Countess Przezdziecka, daughter of Count Konstanty Przezdziecki and of his wife, Princess Sophia Lubomirska.
March 14, 1917, Kiev —

No Issue.

XXII. Lubomirski

3, from page 950

★ **Hubert,** Prince Lubomirski, second son of Prince Hubert.
July 10, 1914, Volodarka, Poland —
m. 1: July 12, 1947, Warsaw. Divorced:
Anna Krzyzanowska, daughter of
—

m. 2:
Greta Calvi, daughter of
—

XXII. Lubomirski

3 continued

Issue of second marriage:

1. Irena, Princess Lubomirska
   July 15, 1953, Dretyn, Poland —

2. Ryszard (Richard), Prince Lubomirski
   August 3, 1954, Dretyn —

XXII. Lubomirski

4, from page 950

* **Stanislaw,** Prince Lubomirski, third son of Prince Hubert.
July 10, 1914, Volodarka —
m. January 1, 1949, Czersk, Poland
Halina Krajewska, daughter of
May 10, 1925, Czersk —

Issue: 1. Tadeusz, Prince Lubomirski
   October 20, 1950, Buczyna Dretyn, Poland —

2. Teresa, Princess Lubomirska
   February 10, 1953, Dretyn —

3. Krzysztof, Prince Lubomirski
   January 20, 1959, Trzebielino, Poland —

XXII. Lubomirski

5, from page 951

* **Henryk,** Prince Lubomirski, fifth son of Prince Hubert.
September 2, 1919, Viareggio, Italy —
m. September 18, 1946, London
Adela Malachowska, daughter of Antoni Malachowski and of his wife,
, 1921, —

No Issue.

XXII. VON MAUBERG 1, from page 957

Wenceslaus von Mauberg
July 27, 1931, Warsaw —
m. November 3, 1956, Gliwice, Poland
* **Helena,** Countess Potocka, daughter of Count Roman Potocki and of his wife, Princess Anna Swiatopelk-Czetwertynska.
May 18, 1934, Warsaw —

Issue: 1. Anna von Mauberg
June 3, 1957, Chorzow, Poland —

2. Katarzyna (Catherine) von Mauberg
July 4, 1958, Zabrze —

3. Andrzej (Andrew) von Mauberg
September 5, 1962, Gliwice —

XXII. MILEWSKI 1, from page 406

Jan Milewski, Ph.D.
November 20, 1937, Warsaw —
m. December 12, 1967, Warsaw
* **Krystyna,** Princess Radziwill, daughter of Prince Edmond Radziwill and of his wife, Princess Izabela Radziwill.
June 12, 1937, Ilyka, Poland —

Issue:

XXII. MORAWSKI 1, from page 971

Maciej (Matthias) Morawski
—
m. , 1968,
* **Jadwiga (Hedwig) Zeromska,** daughter of Wlodzimierz (Vladimir) Zeromski and of his wife, Princess Elzbieta Radziwill.
December 17, 1934, —

Issue:

XXII. MYCIELSKI 1, from page 959

Kasimierz, Count Mycielski
January 11, 1904, Przeworsk —
m. January 25, 1939, Cracow
* **Roza,** Countess Potocka, daughter of Count Franciszek Potocki and of his wife, Princess Malgorzata (Margaret) Radziwill.
April 16, 1907, Cracow —

Issue: 1. Maciej (Matthias), Count Mycielski
March 1, 1940, Paris —

2. Anna Maria, Countess Mycielska (1942–)
m. Tadeusz Cienski (1934–)
see: *Cienski* XXII, page 943

XXII. D'ORNANO 1, from page 958

Hubert, Count d'Ornano
March 31, 1926, Melgiew, Poland —
m. July 6, 1963, Deauville, France
* **Izabela,** Countess Potocka, daughter of Count Jozef Potocki and of his wife, Princess Krystyna Radziwill.
July 16, 1937, Warsaw —

Issue: 1. Filip (Philip), Count d'Ornano
December 30, 1964, Paris —

XXII. PAWLIKOWSKI 1, from page 951

Leszek Pawlikowski
—
m. September , 1944, Warsaw. Annulled:
* **Wanda,** Princess Lubomirska, daughter of Prince Hubert Lubomirski and of his wife, Princess Teresa Radziwill.
June 13, 1923, Nice, France —
(She m. 2: Jan, Count Krasinski – see: *Krasinski* XXII, page 950.)
(She m. 3: Jozef Rucinski – see: *Rucinski* XXII, page 962.)

No Issue.

XXII. PLATER-ZYBERK 1, from page 965

Jan (John), Count Plater-Zyberk
February 2, 1908, Horodziec, Poland —
m. October 15, 1935, Warsaw
* **Roza,** Princess Swiatopelk-Czetwertynska, daughter of Prince Ludwik Swiatopelk-Czetwertynski and of his wife, Princess Roza Radziwill.
April 1, 1914, Zoludek, Poland —

Issue: 1. Victor, Count Plater-Zyberk (1936–)
m. Elisabeth Therese Marie Thaôn d'Arnold (1942–)
see: *Plater-Zyberk* XXII, 2, below

2. Krzysztof (Christopher), Count Plater-Zyberk (1938–)
m. Elzbieta (Elizabeth) Markowska (1945–)
see: *Plater-Zyberk* XXII, 3, below

3. Ludwik, Count Plater-Zyberk
October 5, 1942, Thonon, France —

4. Krystyna (Christina), Countess Plater-Zyberk
April 11, 1947, Lausanne, Switzerland —

XXII. Plater-Zyberk 2, from above

* **Victor,** Count Plater-Zyberk, eldest son of Count Jan.
June 27, 1936, Horodziec —
m. October 18, 1969, Utelle, France
Elisabeth Therese Marie Thaôn d'Arnold, daughter of Michel Paul Thaôn d'Arnold and of his wife, Ana Elisa Eremia.
August 15, 1942, Thonon —

Issue:

XXII. Plater-Zyberk 3, from above

* **Krzysztof,** Count Plater-Zyberk, second son of Count Jan.
March 29, 1938, Zoludek —
m. May 14, 1966, Lausanne, Switzerland
Elzbieta Markowska, daughter of Zdzislaw Markowski and of his wife, Patricia Shevan.
January 26, 1945, Monterey, California, USA —

XXII. Plater-Zyberk 3 continued

Issue: 1. Izabela-Aleksandra, Countess Plater-Zyberk
October 8, 1967, Montreux, Switzerland —

2. Roman-Jacques, Count Plater-Zyberk
August 7, 1969, Lausanne, Switzerland —

XXII. POTOCKI 1, from page 398

Jozef, Count Potocki, brother of Count Roman (see: *Potocki* XXII, 6, page 958).
September 8, 1862, Lemberg (Lwow) — August 25, 1922, Montrésor, France
m. April 28, 1892, Berlin
★ **Helena,** Princess Radziwill, daughter of Prince Antoni Radziwill and of his wife, Maria Dorothea di Castellane.
February 14, 1874, Berlin — December 12, 1958, Madrid

Issue: 1. Roman, Count Potocki (1893–)
m. Anna, Princess Swiatopelk-Czetwertynska (1902–)
see: *Potocki* XXII, 2, below

2. Jozef, Count Potocki (1895–1968)
m. Krystyna, Princess Radziwill (1908–)
see: *Potocki* XXII, 4, page 957

XXII. Potocki 2, from above

★ **Roman,** Count Potocki, eldest son of Count Jozef.
June 3, 1893, Warsaw —
m. January 29, 1929, Warsaw
Anna, Princess Swiatopelk-Czetwertynska, daughter of Prince Severin Swiatopelk-Czetwertynski and of his wife, Countess Sofia Przezdziecka.
December 6, 1902, Suchowolja —

Issue: 1. Maria, Countess Potocka (1929–)
m. Stanislaw, Count Rey (1923–)
see: *Rey* XXII, page 961

2. Roman, Count Potocki
September 7, 1930, Derazne, Poland —

XXII. Potocki 2 continued

3. Elzbieta, Countess Potocka (1933–)
m. Jerzy (George) Gromnicki (1930–)
see: *Gromnicki* XXII, page 949

4. Helena, Countess Potocka (1934–)
m. Wenceslaus von Mauberg (1931–)
see: *von Mauberg* XXII, page 953

5. Marek (Mark), Count Potocki (1938–)
m. Charlotte Hernod (1946–)
see: *Potocki* XXII, 3, below

XXII. Potocki 3, from above

★ **Marek,** Count Potocki, only son of Count Roman.
August 21, 1938, Warsaw —
m. April 19, 1969, Paris
Charlotte Hernod, daughter of Lennart Hernod and of his wife, Sonia Jonsson.
, 1946, —

Issue:

XXII. Potocki 4, from pages 956, 406

★ **Jozef,** Count Potocki, second son of Count Jozef.
April 8, 1895, Szepetowka, Poland — September 12, 1968, Lausanne, Switzerland
m. October 8, 1930, Warsaw
★ **Krystyna,** Princess Radziwill, daughter of Prince Janusz Radziwill and of his wife, Princess Anna Lubomirska.
November 15, 1908, Warsaw —

Issue: 1. Anna, Countess Potocka
August 19, 1931, Warsaw —

2. Dorota, Countess Potocka (1934–)
m. Don Luis Arias (–1970)
see: *Arias* XVIII, page 543

XXII. Potocki 4 continued

3. Izabela, Countess Potocka (1937–)
m. Hubert, Count d'Ornano (1926–)
see: *d'Ornano* XXII, page 954

4. Piotr (Peter), Count Potocki (1940–)
m. Teresa Bejar (–)
see: *Potocki* XXII, 5, below

XXII. Potocki 5, from above

★ **Piotr,** Count Potocki, only son of Count Jozef.
October 13, 1940, Lisbon, Portugal —
m. April 27, 1969, Seville, Spain
Teresa Bejar, daughter of The Duke of Bejar and of his wife,

XXII. Potocki 6, from page 398

Roman, Count Potocki, brother of Count Jozef (see: *Potocki* XXII, 1, page 956).
December 16, 1852, Lancut — September 24, 1915, Lancut
m. June 6, 1885, Berlin
★ **Elzbieta,** Princess Radziwill, daughter of Prince Antoni Radziwill and of his wife, Maria Dorothea di Castellane.
November, 1, 1861, Berlin — May 13, 1950, Lausanne, Switzerland
(He m. 1: November 21, 1882, Warsaw, Countess Izabela Potocka, who died March 21, 1883, Vienna.)

Issue: 1. Alfred, Count Potocki (1886–1958)
m. Izabela (Isa) Narkiewicz-Jodko (1916–)
see: *Potocki* XXII, 6, below

2. Jerzy, Count Potocki (1889–1961)
m. Susanita Yturregui (1899–)
see: *Potocki* XXII, 7, page 959

XXII. Potocki 6, from above

★ **Alfred,** Count Potocki, eldest son of Count Roman.
June 14, 1886, Lancut — March 30, 1958, Geneva, Switzerland
m. March 24, 1956, Monte Carlo

XXII. Potocki

6 continued

Izabela (Isa) Narkiewicz-Jodko, daughter of Zygmut (Sigismund) Narkiewicz-Jodko and of his wife, Stanislawa Jordan-Walewska.
April 16, 1916, Lausanne —
(She m. 1: January 4, 1936, Albert Sidney, banker, who died May 6, 1948, New York City.)

No Issue.

XXII. Potocki

7, from page 958

* **Jerzy (George),** Count Potocki, second son of Count Roman.
January 21, 1889, Vienna — September 20, 1961, Geneva
m. June 28, 1931, Paris
Susanita Yturregui, daughter of Juan Manoel Yturregui and of his wife, Susanna Orbegossoy-Moncada.
October 8, 1899, Lima, Peru —

Issue: 1. Stanislaw, Count Potocki
April 28, 1932, Paris —

XXII. Potocki

8, from page 403

Franciszek (Francis), Count Potocki
February 14, 1877, Peczara — October 16, 1949, Cracow
m. July 16, 1903, Olyka
* **Malgorzata (Margaret),** Princess Radziwill, daughter of Prince Ferdynand Radziwill and of his wife, Princess Pelagia Sapieha.
December 16, 1875, Berlin — July 17, 1962, Cracow

Issue: 1. Ignace, Count Potocki (1904–1937)
m. Jadwiga Dembinska (1908–)
see: *Potocki* XXII, 9, page 960

2. Roza, Countess Potocka (1907–)
m. Kasimierz, Count Mycielski (1904–)
see: *Mycielski* XXII, page 954

3. Pelagia, Countess Potocka
October 16, 1909, Cracow —

XXII. Potocki 8 continued

4. Konstanty, Count Potocki (1910–)
m. Anna, Countess Rey (1925–)
see: *Potocki* XXII, 10, below

XXII. Potocki 9, from page 959

★ **Ignace,** Count Potocki, son of Count Franciszek.
March 24, 1904, Cracow — November 11, 1937, Rudka
m. November 17, 1931, Warsaw
Jadwiga Dembinska, daughter of Stephan Dembinski and of his wife, Princess Maria Swiatopelk-Czetwertynska.
July 31, 1908, Szyszcyce, Poland —
(She m. 2: Anton, Count von Oppersdorff.)

Issue: 1. Elzbieta, Countess Potocka (1932–)
m. Michal, Prince Radziwill (1907–)
see: *Radziwill* XI h–2, page 404

2. Joanna, Countess Potocka (1933–)
m. Marc Aebi (1928–)
see: *Aebi* XXI, page 633

3. Tomasz, Count Potocki
October 29, 1936, Rudka —

XXII. Potocki 10, from above

★ **Konstanty (Constantine),** Count Potocki, son of Count Franciszek.
June 9, 1910, Ischl, Austria —
m. May 31, 1952, Montrésor, France
Anna, Countess Rey, daughter of Count Stanislaw Rey and of his wife, Countess Jadwiga Branicka.
August 8, 1925, Milanow, Poland —

Issue: 1. Jan, Count Potocki
May 29, 1953, Johannesburg, South Africa —

2. Sofia, Countess Potocka
August 9, 1954, Johannesburg —

XXII. REY 1, from page 956

Stanislaw, Count Rey
August 5, 1923, Sieciechowice, Poland —
m. August 29, 1950, Montmelian, France
* **Maria,** Countess Potocka, daughter of Count Roman Potocki and of his wife, Princess Anna Swiatopelk-Czetwertynska.
October 22, 1929, Warsaw —

Issue: 1. Jan, Count Rey
July 5, 1951, Tours, France —

2. Konstanty, Count Rey
March 11, 1953, Tours —

3. Helena, Countess Rey
November 9, 1954, Tours —

4. Izabela, Countess Rey
July 25, 1960, Tours —

XXII. ROSTWOROWSKI 1, from page 966

Stephan, Count Rostworowski, son of Count Karl Rostworowski and of his wife, Teresa Fudakowska.
May 3, 1907, Cracow —
m. December 30, 1950, Paihle, Belgium
* **Maria-Elzbieta,** Princess Swiatopelk-Czetwertynska, daughter of Prince Ludwik Swiatopelk-Czetwertynski and of his wife, Princess Roza Radziwill.
March 21, 1920, Zakopane, Poland —
(She m. 1: and divorced: Stephan Zantara – see: *Zantara* XXII, page 970.)

No Issue.

XXII. Rostworowski 2, from page 947

Jerzy (George), Count Rostworowski
September 13, 1911, Warsaw —
m. June 25, 1947, London, England

XXII. Rostworowski 2 continued

* **Cäcilia,** Princess Czartoryska, daughter of Prince Olgierd Czartoryski and of his wife, Archduchess Mechtildis of Austria.

April 9, 1915, Sielec, Poland —

Issue: 1. Izabela Maria Teresa, Countess Rostworowska
March 30, 1948, London —

2. Karol Stefan, Count Rostworowski
May 27, 1950, Rio de Janeiro, Brazil —

3. Jerzy Olgierd, Count Rostworowski
February 12, 1953, Rio de Janeiro —

4. Margarida Maria, Countess Rostworowska
December 20, 1956, São Paulo, Brazil —

XXII. RUCINSKI 1, from page 951

Jozef Rucinski

August 13, 1907, Kiev, Ukraine —
m. December 24, 1965, San Francisco, California, USA

* **Wanda,** Princess Lubomirska, daughter of Prince Hubert Lubomirski and of his wife, Princess Teresa Radziwill.

June 13, 1923, Nice, France —
(She m. 1: and annulled: Leszek Pawlikowski – see: *Pawlikowski* XXII, page 954.)
(She m. 2: Jan, Count Krasinski – see: *Krasinski* XXII, page 950.)

No Issue.

XXII. RZYSZCZEWSKI 1, from page 397

Michal, Count Rzyszczewski

December 17, 1840, — September 9, 1881,
m. January 28, 1874,

* **Eufemia,** Princess Radziwill, daughter of Prince Wilhelm Radziwill and of his wife, Countess Mathilde von Clary und Aldringen.

October 1, 1850, Berlin — November 29, 1877, Krzycho, Poland

XXII. Rzyszczewski — 1 continued

Issue: 1. Leon, Count Rzyszczewski
October 15, 1874, Rome — April , 1954, Cracow, Poland

2. Antoni, Count Rzyszczewski (1876–1954)
m. Ernestine Dentler (–)
see: *Rzyszczewski* XXII, 2, below

3. Ewa (Eva), Countess Rzyszczewska
December 24, 1876, Krzycho, Poland — January 24, 1965, London

4. Eufemia, Countess Rzyszczewska
November 29, 1877, Krzycho — November 24, 1954, London

XXII. Rzyszczewski — 2, from above

* **Antoni,** Count Rzyszczewski, son of Count Michal.
January 9, 1876, Dresden — June 17, 1954, Rome
m.
Ernestine Dentler, daughter of
—

Issue: 1. Octavia, Countess Rzyszczewska (1907–)
m. Ettore (Hector) Manzolini, Conte di Campoleone (1879–)
see: *Manzolini* XVIII, page 577

XXII. SARYUSZ VON ZAMOYSC-ZAMOYSKI — 1, from page 440

Jan de Kanty, Count Saryusz von Zamoysc-Zamoyski
August 17, 1900, Cracow, Poland — September 28, 1961, Monte Carlo
m. March 9, 1929, Madrid
* **Isabella,** Princess of Bourbon-Sicily, Infanta of Spain, daughter of Prince Carlos of Bourbon-Sicily, Infante of Spain, and of his wife, Dona Maria de las Mercedes de Borbon y Habsburgo, Infanta of Spain.
October 10, 1904, Madrid —

Issue: 1. Carlos (Karol), Count Saryusz von Zamoysc-Zamoyski (1930–)
m. Esperanza Rey Luque (–)
see: *Saryusz von Zamoysc-Zamoyski* XXII, 2, page 964

XXII. Saryusz von Zamoysc-Zamoyski 1 continued

2. Maria Cristina, Countess Saryusz von Zamoysc-Zamoyska
September 2, 1932, Budapest — December 6, 1959, Madrid

3. Jose (Jozef), Count Saryusz von Zamoysc-Zamoyski
June 25, 1935, Paris —

4. Maria Teresa, Countess Saryusz von Zamoysc-Zamoyska
A Nun in the Carmelite Cloister in Spain.
April 18, 1938, Presburg —

XXII. Saryusz von Zamoysc-Zamoyski 2, from page 963

* **Carlos,** Count Saryusz von Zamoysc-Zamoyski, eldest son of Count Jan de Kanty.
October 28, 1930, Budapest, Hungary —
m. December 18, 1956, Madrid
Esperanza Rey Luque, daughter of
—

Issue: 1. Maria de Rocio, Countess Saryusz von Zamoysc-Zamoyska
January 1, 1958, Madrid —

XXII. SKORZEWSKI 1, from page 404

Zygmund (Sigismund), Count Skorzewski
May 3, 1894, Czerniejew, Poland —
m. June 15, 1927, Chevreuse, France
* **Leontyna,** Princess Radziwill, daughter of Prince Michal Radziwill and of his wife, Mariya de Bernardaky.
September 26, 1904, St. Petersburg, Russia —

Issue: 1. Maria, Countess Skorzewska (1928–)
m. Paul Moretti (1908–); see: *Moretti* XVIII, page 582

2. Jadwiga, Countess Skorzewska (1930–)
m. Jean-Claude Roussel (1923–); see: *Roussel* XVIII, page 600

3. Leon, Count Skorzewski (1933–)
m. Ulrique Schnabel (1944–); see: *Skorzewski* XXII, 2, page 965

XXII. Skorzewski

2, from page 964

* **Leon,** Count Skorzewski, only son of Count Zygmund.
March 13, 1933, Czerniejew, Poland —
m. May 2, 1968, Lucerne, Switzerland

Ulrique Schnabel, daughter of Wilhelm Hermann Schnabel and of his wife, Marlene Bertele.
July 4, 1944, —

Issue:

XXII. SWIATOPELK-CZETWERTYNSKI

1, from page 398

Ludwik, Prince Swiatopelk-Czetwertynski
January 12, 1877, Milanow — May 3, 1941, Auschwitz concentration camp
m. January 27, 1906, Rome

* **Roza (Rose),** Princess Radziwill, daughter of Prince Jerzy (George) Radziwill and of his wife, Countess Maria Roza Branicka.
November 26, 1884, Berlin — December 1, 1949, St. Fontaine, Belgium

Issue: 1. Jerzy, Prince Swiatopelk-Czetwertynski (1907–)
m. Roza, Countess Zoltowska (1909–)
see: *Swiatopelk-Czetwertynski* XXII, 2, page 966

2. Stanislaw, Prince Swiatopelk-Czetwertynski (1910–)
m. Ewa, Baroness Buxhoeveden (1911–)
see: *Swiatopelk-Czetwertynski* XXII, 3, page 966

3. Andrzej (Andrew), Prince Swiatopelk-Czetwertynski (1911–1939)
m. Roza Dembinska (–1939)
see: *Swiatopelk-Czetwertynski* XXII, 7, page 968

4. Roza, Princess Swiatopelk-Czetwertynska (1914–)
m. Jan, Count Plater-Zyberk (1908–)
see: *Plater-Zyberk* XXII, page 955

XXII. Swiatopelk-Czetwertynski 1 continued

5. Maria-Elzbieta, Princess Swiatopelk-Czetwertynska (1920–)
m. 1: and annulled: Stefan Zantara (–)
see: *Zantara* XXII, page 970
m. 2: Stephan, Count Rostworowski (1907–)
see: *Rostworowski* XXII, page 961

XXII. Swiatopelk-Czetwertynski 2, from page 965

* **Jerzy,** Prince Swiatopelk-Czetwertynski, eldest son of Prince Ludwik.
February 19, 1907, Warsaw —
m. June 22, 1936, Czacz
Roza, Countess Zoltowska, daughter of Count Stanislaw Zoltowski and of his wife, Countess Ludowika Ostrowska.
November 11, 1909, Czacz —

Issue: 1. Michal, Prince Swiatopelk-Czetwertynski
November 20, 1935, Warsaw —

2. Maria, Princess Swiatopelk-Czetwertynska
November 22, 1939, Czacz — February 15, 1941,

3. Anna, Princess Swiatopelk-Czetwertynska
February 17, 1947, Brussels —

4. Stanislaw, Prince Swiatopelk-Czetwertynski
November 17, 1949, St. Fontaine, Belgium —

5. Maria-Anna, Princess Swiatopelk-Czetwertynska
March 3, 1954, Brussels —

XXII. Swiatopelk-Czetwertynski 3, from page 965

* **Stanislaw,** Prince Swiatopelk-Czetwertynski, second son of Prince Ludwik.
March 7, 1910, Warsaw —
m. October 24, 1933, Warsaw
Ewa (Eva), Baroness Buxhoeveden, daughter of Baron Albrecht Buxhoeveden and of his wife, Izabela Dzialowska.
June, 27, 1911, Lublin —

XXII. Swiatopelk-Czetwertynski 3 continued

Issue: 1. Izabela, Princess Swiatopelk-Czetwertynska (1934–)
m. Philippe du Bois d'Aische (1930–)
see: *du Bois d'Aische* XVIII, page 545

2. Ludwik, Prince Swiatopelk-Czetwertynski (1935–)
m. Katarina Klingenstierna (1939–)
see: *Swiatopelk-Czetwertynski* XXII, 4, below

3. Maria-Roza, Princess Swiatopelk-Czetwertynska (1937–)
m. Wlodzimierz Boldireff (–)
see: *Boldireff* XXII, page 943

4. Albrecht-Stanislaw, Prince Swiatopelk-Czetwertynski (1940–)
m. Elisabeth Thoullier (–)
see: *Swiatopelk-Czetwertynski* XXII, 5, page 968

5. Severin, Prince Swiatopelk-Czetwertynski (1941–)
m. Denise Elie (–)
see: *Swiatopelk-Czetwertynski* XXII, 6, page 968

6. Andrzej (Andrew), Prince Swiatopelk-Czetwertynski
February 13, 1944, Konstancin, Poland —

7. Jan, Prince Swiatopelk-Czetwertynski
January 7, 1948, Gdynia, Poland —

8. Aniela (Angela), Princess Swiatopelk-Czetwertynska
July 12, 1950, Anin, Poland —

9. Dorota (Dorothy), Princess Swiatopelk-Czetwertynska
March 13, 1952, Anin —

XXII. Swiatopelk-Czetwertynski 4, from above

* **Ludwik,** Prince Swiatopelk-Czetwertynski, eldest son of Prince Stanislaw. Adopted in 1955 by Mlle. Berthe de Lolieux de la Roce.
September 14, 1935, Lipiczno, Poland —
m. December 28, 1962, Stockholm, Sweden

Katarina Klingenstierna, daughter of Carl Klingenstierna, one-time Belgian Ambassador to Sweden, and of his wife,
October 10, 1939, Nordköping, Sweden —

XXII. Swiatopelk-Czetwertynski 4 continued

Issue: 1. Wlodzimierz (Vladimir), Prince Swiatopelk-Czetwertynski
July 6, 1963, Frankfurt-am-Main, Germany —

2. Ewa (Eva), Princess Swiatopelk-Czetwertynska
July 23, 1965, Stockholm, Sweden —

XXII. Swiatopelk-Czetwertynski 5, from page 967

* **Albrecht-Stanislaw,** Prince Swiatopelk-Czetwertynski, second son of Prince Stanislaw.
February 3, 1940, Warsaw —
m.
Elisabeth Thoullier, daughter of
—

Issue: 1. A daughter – no details available

XXII. Swiatopelk-Czetwertynski 6, from page 967

* **Severin,** Prince Swiatopelk-Czetwertynski, third son of Prince Stanislaw.
December 14, 1941, Warsaw —
m. December 20, 1969, Montreal, Quebec, Canada
Denise Elie, daughter of
—

Issue:

XXII. Swiatopelk-Czetwertynski 7, from page 965

* **Andrzej (Andrew),** Prince Swiatopelk-Czetwertynski, third son of Prince Ludwik.
September 16, 1911, Zoludek — between September 18 and 23, 1939, near Grodno in the Skidel Forest, shot by the Russians
m.
Roza Dembinska, daughter of Stephan Dembinski and of his wife, Princess Maria Swiatopelk-Czetwertynska.
— between September 18 and 23, 1939, near Grodno in the Skidel Forest, shot by the Russians

No Issue.

XXII. TOMASZEWSKI

1, from page 399

Jan Tomaszewski
January 27, 1903, Bremen —
m. February 15, 1947, Lisbon, Portugal
* **Elzbieta,** Princess Radziwill, daughter of Prince Antoni Albrecht Radziwill and of his wife, Dorothy Parker-Deacon
November 21, 1917, London —
(She m. 1: Witold, Prince Czartoryski – see: *Czartoryski* XXII, page 948.)

Issue: 1. Jerzy (George) Tomaszewski
December 16, 1947, Funchal, Madeira —

2. Mikolaj (Nicholas) Tomaszewski
December 16, 1953, Lisbon, Portugal —

3. Aleksander Tomaszewski
November 9, 1957, Lisbon — November 12, 1957, Lisbon

XXII. TYSZKIEWICZ

1, from page 399

Alfred, Count Tyszkiewicz
October , 1882, Brize — May 16, 1930, Verneuil, France
m. May 21, 1916, Bialocerkiew, Poland
* **Elzbieta,** Princess Radziwill, daughter of Prince Jerzy (George) Radziwill and of his wife, Countess Maria Roza Branicka.
March 6, 1894, Warsaw —
(She m. 2: Wlodzimierz (Vladimir) Zeromski – see: *Zeromski* XXII, page 971.)

Issue: 1. Jan, Count Tyszkiewicz, Reverend Father Marie Jean, a Trappist Monk
November 24, 1917, Bialocerkiew, Poland —

XXII. Tyszkiewicz

2, from page 1000

Stefan, Count Tyszkiewicz
November 24, 1894, Warsaw —
m. July 18, 1917, Yalta, Crimea, Russia
* **Elena Georgeievna,** Princess Romanovskya de Beauharnais, Duchess of Leuchtenberg, daughter of Prince Georgii Maksimilianovich Romanovsky de Beauharnais, Duke of Leuchtenberg, and of his wife, Princess Anastasia Petrovich-Niegosh of Montenegro.

XXII. Tyszkiewicz 2 continued

January 15, 1892, Nice, France —

Issue: 1. Nataliya, Countess Tyszkiewicz
January 18, 1921, Warsaw —

XXII. Tyszkiewicz 3, from page 410

Wladyslaw (Ladislas), Count Tyszkiewicz
August 2, 1903, Czerwonydwor, Poland — February 6, 1956, Lodz
m. August 2, 1918, Balice
* **Eleanore,** Princess Radziwill, daughter of Prince Jerome Radziwill and of his wife, Archduchess Renata Maria of Austria.
August 2, 1918, Balice —
(She m. 2: Roger de Froidcourt – see: *Froidcourt* XVIII, page 562.)

No Issue.

XXII. ZANTARA 1, from page 966

Stefan Zantara
, 1914, Warsaw —
m. September 3, 1943, Grenoble, France. Marriage annulled: October 23, 1950, Lyon
* **Maria-Elzbieta,** Princess Swiatopelk-Czetwertynska, daughter of Prince Ludwik Swiatopelk-Czetwertynski and of his wife, Princess Roza Radziwill.
March 21, 1920, Zakopane, Poland —
(She m. 2: Stephan, Count Rostworowski – see: *Rostworowski* XXII, page 961.)

Issue: 1. Teresa Zantara
October 5, 1945, Newbury, Berkshire, England —

2. Andrzej (Andrew) Zantara
December 30, 1946, Newbury —

XXII. ZEROMSKI 1, from page 399

Wlodzimierz (Vladimir) Zeromski
February 16, 1877, — September 20, 1956, Verneuil, France
m. September 5, 1933, Warsaw
★ **Elzbieta,** Princess Radziwill, daughter of Prince Jerzy (George) Radziwill and of his wife, Countess Maria Roza Branicka.
March 6, 1894, Warsaw —
(She m. 1: Alfred, Count Tyszkiewicz – see: *Tyszkiewicz* XXII, page 969.)

Issue: 1. Jadwiga (Hedwig) Zeromska (1934–)
m. Maciej (Matthias) Morawski (–)
see: *Morawski* XXII, page 953

XXIII

THE FAMILIES OF RUSSIA

XXIII. BAGRATION-MOUKHRANSKY 1, from page 476

Irakli (Heraclius) Georgeievich, Prince Bagration-Moukhransky of Georgia.
March 21, 1909, Tiflis, Georgia, Russia —
m. 1: June 20, 1940,
Maria Antonia Pasquini of the House of the Counts Pasquini di Costafiorita, daughter of

April 26, 1911, — February 22, 1944,
m. 2: August 29, 1946, San Sebastian, Spain
* **Dona Maria de las Mercedes de Baviera y de Borbon,** Infanta of Spain, daughter of Prince Ferdinand Maria de Baviera, Infante of Spain, and of his first wife, Dona Maria Theresia de Borbon y Habsburgo, Infanta of Spain.
October 3, 1911, Madrid —

Issue of first marriage: Not descendants of King George I – eleven children

Issue of second marriage: Descendants of King George I
1. Maria de la Paz, Princess Bagration-Moukhranskya (1947–)
m. Don José Luis Blanco de Briones (–)
see: *Blanco de Briones* XVIII, page 545

2. Bagrat, Prince Bagration-Moukhransky
June 12, 1949, Madrid —

XXIII. Bagration-Moukhransky 2, from page 315

Konstantin Aleksandrovich, Prince Bagration-Moukhransky
March 2, 1889, Tiflis, Russia — May 19, 1915, Jaroslav, near Lemberg (Lwow), killed in action in World War I
m. August 24, 1911, Tiflis
* **Tatyana Konstantinovna,** Princess of Russia, daughter of Grand Duke Konstantin Konstantinovich of Russia and of his wife, Princess Elisabeth (Elizabeta Mavrikievna) of Saxe-Altenburg
January 11/23, 1890, St. Petersburg —
(She m. 2: Aleksandr Vassilievich Korochenzov – see: *Korochenzov* XXIII, page 987.)

XXIII. Bagration-Moukhransky 2 continued

(She entered the Russian Orthodox Cloistered Order of Olberg on the Mount of Olives, Jerusalem, in 1946 and is now the Abbess Tamara.)

Issue: 1. Theimouraz Konstantinovich, Prince Bagration-Moukhransky (1912–)
m. 1: Ekaterina Ratchitch (1919–1946)
m. 2: Irina Sergeievna Czernisheva-Besobrasova (1925–)
see: *Bagration-Moukhransky* XXIII, 3, below

2. Nataliya Konstantinovna, Princess Bagration-Moukhranskya (1914–)
m. Charles Hepburn Johnston (1912–)
see: *Johnston* XVII, page 526

XXIII. Bagration-Moukhransky 3, from above

* **Theimouraz Konstantinovich,** Prince Bagration-Moukhransky, only son of Prince Konstantin Aleksandrovich.
August 12, 1912, Pavlovsk, Russia —
m. 1: October 27, 1940, Topcider, near Belgrade, Yugoslavia
Ekaterina (Catherine) Ratchitch, daughter of Stefan Ratchitch and of his wife, Pava Pachitch.
July 4, 1919, London — December 20, 1946, Neuilly, France
m. 2: November 27, 1949, New York City
Irina Sergeievna Czernisheva-Besobrasova, daughter of Sergei Aleksandrovich Czernishev-Besobrasov.
September 26, 1925, Neuilly-sur-Seine, France —

No Issue.

XXIII. BARIATINSKY 1, from page 299

Aleksandr Vladimirovich, Prince Bariatinsky
May 22, 1870, — March 6, 1910, Florence, Italy
m. October 18, 1901, Biarritz, France
* **Ekaterina Aleksandrovna,** Princess Yourievskya, daughter of the Emperor Aleksandr II and of his second and morganatic wife, Princess Ekaterina Mikhailovna Dolgorukya, created Princess Yourievskya.
September 9, 1878, St. Petersburg — December 22, 1959, North Hayling, England

XXIII. Bariatinsky 1 continued

(She m. 2: and divorced: Sergei Platonovich, Prince Obolensky-Neledinsky-Meletzky – see: *Obolensky-Neledinsky-Meletzky* XXIII, page 1005.)

Issue: 1: Andrei Aleksandrovich, Prince Bariatinsky (1902–193)
m. Helene (– –)
see: *Bariatinsky* XXIII, 2, below

2. Aleksandr Aleksandrovich, Prince Bariatinsky
March 24, 1905, Pau, France —
On June 21, 1949, he became a United States citizen as Alexander Barry.

XXIII. Bariatinsky 2, from above

★ **Andrei Aleksandrovich,** Prince Bariatinsky, eldest son of Prince Aleksandr Vladimirovich.
August 2, 1902, Paris —
m. , 1926, Paris
Helene
—

Issue: 1. Elena Ekaterina Andreievna, Princess Bariatinskya
November , 1927, Paris —

XXIII. CHAVCHAVADZE 1, from page 323

Pavel (Paul) Aleksandrovich, Prince Chavchavadze
June 27, 1899, St. Petersburg, Russia —
m. September 3, 1922, London, England
★ **Nina Georgeievna,** Princess of Russia, daughter of Grand Duke Georgii Mikhailovich of Russia and of his wife, Princess Maria of Greece and Denmark.
June 7, 1901, Mikhailovskoye, near Peterhof, Russia —

Issue: 1. David Pavlovich, (Prince) Chavchavadze (1924–)
m. 1: and divorced: Helen McLanahan Husted (1933–)
m. 2: Judith Clippinger (1929–)
see: *Chavchavadze* XXIII, 2, page 976

XXIII. Chavchavadze 2, from page 975

NOTE: Since the members of the Chavchavadze family are citizens of the United States, neither their title nor the old Russian form of names or their patronimics are used. The Russian equivalent and title have been given in brackets.

* **David (Pavlovich), (Prince) Chavchavadze,** only son of Pavel.
May 20, 1924, London —
m. 1: September 13, 1952, Washington, D.C. Divorced: June , 1959,
Helen McLanahan Husted, daughter of Ellery Husted and of his wife,
February 1, 1933, New York City —
m. 2: December 28, 1959, Cincinnati, Ohio
Judith Clippinger, daughter of John Henry Clippinger and of his wife, Jane Becker.
March 25, 1929, Cincinnati —

Issue of first marriage:

1. Maria (Mariya Davidovna), (Princess) Chavchavadze
August 28, 1953, Washington, D.C. —

2. Alexandra (Aleksandra Davidovna), (Princess) Chavchavadze
December 24, 1954, West Berlin —

Issue of second marriage:

3. Catherine (Ekaterina Davidovna), (Princess) Chavchavadze
December 29, 1960, Washington, D.C. —

4. Michael (Mikhail Davidovich), (Prince) Chavchavadze
August 1, 1966, Washington, D.C. —

XXIII. CHEREMETEV 1, from page 1008

Vladimir Alekseievich Cheremetev
May 6/18, 1847, Moscow — February 17/March 1, 1893, St. Petersburg
m. January 7/19, 1879, St. Petersburg
* **Elena Grigorievna,** Countess Strogonova, daughter of Count Grigorii Aleksandrovich Strogonov and of his wife, Grand Duchess Mariya Nikolaievna of Russia.

XXIII. Cheremetev

1 continued

January 29/February 11, 1861, St. Petersburg — January 29/February 12, 1908, Tsarskoye-Selo
(She m. 2: General Grigorii Nikitich Milashevich – see: *Milashevich* XXIII, page 1002.)

Issue: 1. Sergei Vladimirovich Cheremetev (1880–1968)
m. 1: Aleksandra Aleksandrovna, Countess Cheremeteva (1886–1942)
m. 1: Stella Webber (1880–)
see: *Cheremetev* XXIII, 2, below

2. Sofia Vladimirovna Cheremeteva (1883–1956)
m. Dimitrii Vladimirovich von Daehn (1874–1937)
see: *von/de Daehn* XXIII, page 979

XXIII. Cheremetev

2, from above

* **Sergei Vladimirovich Cheremetev,** Colonel in the Russian Imperial Army, only son of Vladimir Alekseievich.
January 5/17, 1880, St. Petersburg — March 17, 1968, Rome
m. 1: January 24, 1907, St. Petersburg. Divorced:
Aleksandra Aleksandrovna, Countess Cheremeteva, daughter of Count Aleksandr Cheremetev and of his wife,
August 2/14, 1886, Ulianka, Russia — , 1942, near Paris
m. 2: February 7, 1939, Paris
Stella Webber, daughter of Charles Webber and of his wife,
February 1, 1880, Chicago, Illinois, USA —

Issue of first marriage:
1. Nikita Sergeievich Cheremetev (1908–)
m. Ekaterina Vandoro (1915–)
see: *Cheremetev* XXIII, 3, below

XXIII. Cheremetev

3, from above

* **Nikita Sergeievich Cheremetev,** only son of Sergei Vladimirovich.
February 27, 1908, St. Petersburg —
m. November 3, 1935,
Ekaterina Vandoro, daughter of Lucas Vandoro and of his wife,
November 24, 1915, Yalta, Crimea —

XXIII. Cheremetev 3 continued

Issue: 1. Mariya Nikitievna Cheremeteva (1937–)
m. Brandon Grove Jnr. (1929–)
see: *Grove* XXIV, page 1018

2. Vladimir Nikitich Cheremetev
June 29, 1938, Piraeus, Greece —

3. Sergei Nikitich Cheremetev
October 11, 1943, Athens, Greece —

4. Aleksandr Nikitich Cheremetev
October 14, 1949, Limassol, Cyprus —

XXIII. Cheremetev 4, from page 1012

Nikolai Dimitriievich, Count Cheremetev
October 28, 1904, Moscow —
m. June 19, 1938, Rome
* **Irina Felixovna,** Princess Yousoupova, Countess Soumarakova-Elston, daughter of Prince Felix Felixovich Yousoupov, Count Soumarakov-Elston, and of his wife, Princess Irina Aleksandrovna of Russia.
March 21, 1915, St. Petersburg —

Issue: 1. Kseniya Nikolaievna, Countess Cheremeteva (1942–)
m. Elia Sfiris (1932–)
see: *Sfiris* XX, page 628

XXIII. Cheremetev (Cheremetieff) 5, from page 1010

Petr (Peter) Sergeievich, Count Cheremetieff, son of Count Sergei Oscarovich.
September 13, 1931, Port Lyantey, Morocco —
m. November 9, 1961, Paris
* **Marie Eugenie,** Countess de Witt, daughter of Count Serge de Witt and of his wife, Princess Marie Clothilde Bonaparte.
August 29, 1939, Boulogne-sur-Seine —

No Issue.

XXIII. VON/DE DAEHN 1, from page 977

Dimitrii Vladimirovich von Daehn, son of Vladimir von Daehn, Minister Secretary for Finland, and of his wife, Princess Nina Swiatopelk-Mirska. After settling in Rome the family preferred 'de Daehn'.

September 6/18, 1874, Lagodekhi, Caucasus, Russia — September 4, 1937, Rome
m. February 3/16, 1902, Tiflis, Georgia

* **Sofia Vladimirovna Cheremeteva,** daughter of Vladimir Alekseievich Cheremetev and of his wife, Countess Elena Grigorievna Strogonova.

November 10/22, 1883, St. Petersburg — December , 1956, Rome

No Issue.

XXIII. DEMIDOV 1, from page 546

Anatole Demidov, First Prince di San Donato

April 5, 1813, St. Petersburg — April 29, 1870, St. Petersburg
m. November 1, 1840, Florence

* **Mathilde,** Princess Bonaparte, daughter of Prince Jérôme Bonaparte, King of Westphalia, and of his wife, Princess Catherine of Württemberg.

May 27, 1820, Trieste — January 2, 1904, Paris
(She m. 2: December 1873, Claudius Popelin, November 2, 1825 — May 17, 1892.)

No Issue.

XXIII. ELTCHANINOV (Eltchaninoff) 1, from page 1007

Nikolai Vladimirovich Eltchaninov

February 18, 1906, — March , 1952, Paris
m. January 15, 1930, Paris

* **Tatiana Ivanovna von Ploen,** daughter of Ivan von Ploen and of his wife, Countess Ekaterina Konstantinovna von Zarnekau.

November 13, 1908, Moscow — June 9, 1960, Brussels

Issue: 1. Mariya (Marie) Nikolaievna Eltchaninova
December 13, 1931, Paris —

2. Nikolai Nikolaievich Eltchaninov (1934–)
m. and divorced: Kira Borisovna Gandourina (1935–)
see: *Eltchaninov* XXIII, 2, page 980

XXIII. Eltchaninov 2, from page 979

★ **Nikolai Nikolaievich Eltchaninov,** only son of Nikolai Vladimirovich.
May 29, 1934, Paris —
m. July 7, 1957, Paris. Divorced: October 29, 1965, Montpellier, France
Kira (Kyra) Borisovna Gandourina, daughter of Boris Antonovich Gandourine and of his wife, Nataliya Borisovna Zhukovskya.
October 10, 1935, Paris —

Issue: 1. Ariane Nikolaievna Eltchaninova
May 12, 1958, Paris —

2. Isabelle Anne Nikolaievna Eltchaninova
April 30, 1959, Paris —

NOTE: The family prefer to use 'Eltchaninoff' as residents and citizens of France.

XXIII. FLEVITSKY 1, from page 307

Georgii Flevitsky
, 1904, St. Petersburg — May 11, 1960, New York City
m. November 20, 1956, New York City
★ **Aleksandra Alekseievna,** Countess Belevskya-Zhukovskya, daughter of Count Aleksei Alekseievich Belevsky-Zhukovsky and of his first wife, Princess Mariya Petrovna Troubetskoya.
March 4, 1899, Moscow —
(She m. 1: Henry Lepp – see: *Lepp* XXIII, page 990.)

No Issue.

XXIII. GALITZINE 1, from page 426

Boris Dimitrievich, Prince Galitzine
February 6, 1891, Gatchina, Russia — June 6, 1919, Tsarizine, killed in the Russian Civil War
m. November 14, 1916, Tiflis, Georgia
★ **Mariya (Marie),** Countess von Carlow, daughter of Duke Georg Alexander of Mecklenburg-Strelitz and of his wife, Nataliya Feodorovna Vanlyarskya, created Countess von Carlow.
November 1, 1893, Oranienbaum, Russia —

XXIII. Galitzine 1 continued

(She m. 2: Vladimir Petrovich, Count Kleinmichel – see: *Kleinmichel* XXI, page 986.)

Issue: 1. Dimitrii Borisovich, Prince Galitzine
November 16, 1917, Kislovodsk, Russia — October 26, 1944, Hartogenborg, The Netherlands, killed in action in World War II

2. Nataliya Borisovna, Princess Galitzine (1920–)
m. and divorced: Nigel Hesseltine (1916–)
see: *Hesseltine* XVII, page 523

XXIII. Galitzine 2, from pages 426, 34

Vladimir Emmanuelovich, Prince Galitzine
June 5, 1884, St. Petersburg —July 13, 1954, London, England
m. 1: February 10, 1913, St. Petersburg
* **Ekaterina (Catherine),** Countess von Carlow, daughter of Duke Georg Alexander of Mecklenburg-Strelitz and of his wife, Nataliya Feodorovna Vanlyarskya, created Countess von Carlow.
July 25, 1891, Oranienbaum — October 8, 1940, London, killed during a bombing raid in World War II
m. 2: August 12, 1945, London
* **Mabel Iris FitzGeorge,** daughter of George FitzGeorge and of his wife, Rosa Frederika Baring.
September 23, 1886, London —
(She m. 1: Robert Shekelton Balfour – see: *FitzGeorge-Balfour* XVII, page 519.)

Issue of first marriage:
1. Nikolai Vladimirovich, Prince Galitzine (1913–)
m. 1: and divorced: Elizabeth Beatrice Branch (1924–)
m. 2: Anita Frisch (1933–)
see: *Galitzine* XXIII, 3, page 982

2. Georgii Vladimirovich, Prince Galitzine (1916–)
m. 1: and divorced: Anne Marie, Baroness von Slatin (1916–)
m. 2: Jean Dawney (1925–)
see: *Galitzine* XXIII, 4, page 982

XXIII. Galitzine 2 continued

3. Emanuel Vladimirovich, Prince Galitzine (1918–)
m. Gwendoline Rhodes (1920–)
see: *Galitzine* XXIII, 5, page 983

XXIII. Galitzine 3, from page 981

★ **Nikolai Vladimirovich,** Prince Galitzine, eldest son of Prince Vladimir Emanuelovich.
December 20, 1913, Tsarskoye-Selo, Russia —
m. 1: December 11, 1946, London. Divorced: 1955, London
Elizabeth Beatrice Branch, daughter of Colonel Cyril Branch of Horsham, Sussex, England, and of his wife,
October 26, 1924, Lancaster, England —
m. 2: May 4, 1956, Montreal, Quebec, Canada
Anita Frisch, daughter of Dr. Harald Frisch and of his wife,
December 22, 1933, Riga, Latvia —

Issue of first marriage:
1. Andrei (Andrew) Nikolaievich, Prince Galitzine
June 22, 1949, London —

Issue of second marriage:
2. Aleksandr (Alexander) Nikolaievich, Prince Galitzine
February 6, 1957, Montreal, Quebec —

3. Petr (Peter) Nikolaievich, Prince Galitzine
November 26, 1958, Montreal —

4. Marina Nikolaievna, Princess Galitzine
January 13, 1962, Ottawa —

XXIII. Galitzine 4, from page 981

★ **Georgii (George) Vladimirovich,** Prince Galitzine, second son of Prince Vladimir Emmanuelovich.
April 20, 1916, Tiflis, Georgia —
m. 1: September 11, 1943, London. Divorced: 1954,

XXIII. Galitzine 4 continued

Anne Marie, Baroness von Slatin, daughter of Major General Sir Rudolf Slatin Pasha, Baron von Slatin, and of his wife,
November 12, 1916, Vienna —
m. 2: May 5, 1963, Rome
Jean Dawney, daughter of Frederick Dawney and of his wife,
March 22, 1925, Brighton, England —

Issue of first marriage:
1. Caroline Georgeievna, Princess Galitzine
June 14, 1944, London —

2. Aleksandr (Alexander) Georgeievich, Prince Galitzine
September 6, 1945, London —

3. Georgii (George) Georgeievich, Prince Galitzine
December 3, 1946, London —

Issue of second marriage:
4. Ekaterina (Catherine) Georgeievna, Princess Galitzine
September 20, 1964, London —

XXIII. Galitzine 5, from page 982

* **Emanuel Vladimirovich,** Prince Galitzine, third son of Prince Vladimir Emmanuelovich.
May 28, 1918, Kislovodsk, Caucasus, Russia —
m. February 23, 1943, London
Gwendoline Rhodes, daughter of Captain Stanley Rhodes of Donaghdee, County Down, Ireland, and of his wife,
July 4, 1920, Shipley, England —

Issue: 1. Nikolai (Nicholas) Emanuelovich, Prince Galitzine
October 19, 1944, Belfast, Northern Ireland —

2. Mikhail (Michael) Emanuelovich, Prince Galitzine
January 25, 1949, Bombay, India —

3. Emanuel Emanuelovich, Prince Galitzine
March 11, 1951, Montevideo, Uruguay —

XXIII. Galitzine 6, from page 319

Aleksandr Nikolaievich, Prince Galitzine
October 13, 1885, St. Petersburg —
m. February 4, 1927, Cap d'Antibes, France
* **Marina Petrovna,** Princess of Russia, daughter of Grand Duke Petr Nikolaievich of Russia and of his wife, Princess Militza Nikolaievna Petrovich-Niegosh of Montenegro.
February 28/March 11, 1892, Nice, France —

No Issue.

XXIII. GAYDEBUROV 1, from page 998

Oleg Evgenievich Gaydeburov
February 27, 1922, Athens, Greece —
m. June 15, 1952, Sea Cliff, New York
* **Olga Konstantinovna de Beauharnais,** Duchess of Leuchtenberg, daughter of Duke Konstantin Georgeievich de Beauharnais, Duke of Leuchtenberg, and of his wife, Daria Alekseievna, Princess Obolenskya.
April 25, 1932, Seeon Castle, Bavaria —

Issue: 1. Georgii Olegiievich Gaydeburov
March 30, 1953, Manhasset, N.Y. —

2. Nina Olegiievna Gaydeburova
April 29, 1956, Manhasset, N.Y. —

XXIII. GRABBÉ 1, from page 998

Dimitrii Georgeievich, Count Grabbé. As a US citizen the title has been dropped.
July 23, 1927, Belgrade, Yugoslavia —
m. July 12, 1950, Montreal, Quebec, Canada
* **Kseniya Konstantinovna de Beauharnais,** Duchess of Leuchtenberg, daughter of Konstantin Georgeievich de Beauharnais, Duke of Leuchtenberg, and of his wife, Princess Daria Alekseievna Obolenskya.
May 20, 1930, Traunstein, Bavaria —

XXIII. Grabbé 1 continued

Issue: 1. Mikhail (Michael) Dimitrievich Grabbé
March 7, 1951, Sea Cliff, N.Y. —

2. Nina Dimitrievna Grabbé
October 17, 1952, New York City —

3. Paul Dimitrievich Grabbé
March 7, 1956, Sea Cliff —

4. Aleksei Dimitrievich Grabbé
March , 1960, Sea Cliff —

5. Kseniya Dimitrievna Grabbé
February 16, 1963, Sea Cliff —

6. Olga Dimitrievna Grabbé (twin)
July 7, 1965, Sea Cliff —

7. Mariya Dimitrievna Grabbé (twin)
July 7, 1965, Sea Cliff —

XXIII. GRAVENITZ 1, from page 999

Waldemar, Baron von Gravenitz, Captain in the Russian Imperial Navy.
October 30/November 12, 1872, Vernoyo, Russia — April 24, 1916, Helsinki, Finland
m. , 1911,
* **Daria Evgeniievna,** Countess de Beauharnais, daughter of Duke Evgenii Maksimilianovich de Beauharnais of Leuchtenberg and of his wife, Daria Konstantinovna Opotchinina, created Countess de Beauharnais.
March 7/19, 1870, St. Petersburg — last heard of in Russia in the 1930s
(She m. 1: and divorced: Leon Mikhailovich, Prince Kotchoubey – see: *Kotchoubey de Beauharnais* XXIII, page 987.)
(She m. 3: Marchesi – an Italian – no further information available.)
(She m. 4: a Spaniard – no further information available.)

No Issue.

XXIII. IANOUCHEVSKY 1, from page 307

Vladimir Aleksandrovich Ianouchevsky
June 9, 1897, St. Petersburg —
m. October 28, 1959, New York City
* **Mariya Alekseievna,** Countess Belevskya-Zhukovskya, daughter of Count Aleksei Alekseievich Belevsky-Zhukovsky and of his first wife, Princess Mariya Petrovna Troubetskoya.
October 26, 1901, Moscow —
(She m. 1: Vladimir Sergeievich Sverbeev – see: *Sverbeev* XXIII, page 1009.)

No Issue.

XXIII. KARANFILOV 1, from page 997

Konstantin Grigorievich Karanfilov
January 11, 1905, Sebastopol, Crimea —
m. February 25, 1933, Toulon, France
* **Tamara Georgeievna de Beauharnais,** Duchess of Leuchtenberg, daughter of Georgii Nikolaievich de Beauharnais, Duke of Leuchtenberg, and of his wife, Princess Olga Nikolaievna Repnina.
December 1/14, 1901, St. Petersburg —

Issue: 1. Tatiana Konstantinovna Karanfilova (1934–)
m. Sergei Vsevolozhsky (1926–)
see: *Vsevolozhsky* XXIII, page 1010

2. Marina Konstantinovna Karanfilova
December 1, 1937, Toulon — February 2, 1950, Toulon

3. Nataliya Konstantinovna Karanfilova
October 28, 1942, Toulon —

XXIII. KLEINMICHEL 1, from page 426

Vladimir Petrovich, Count Kleinmichel
January 29, 1901, Rischkowoursk, Russia —
m. June 14, 1929, London
* **Mariya (Marie),** Countess von Carlow, daughter of Duke Georg Alexander of Mecklenburg-Strelitz and of his morganatic wife, Nataliya Feodorovna Vanlyarskya, Countess von Carlow.
November 1, 1893, Oranienbaum, Russia —

XXIII. Kleinmichel 1 continued

(She m. 1: Boris Dimitrievich, Prince Galitzine – see: *Galitzine* XXIII, page 980.)

Issue: 1. Sophia Vladimirovna, Countess Kleinmichel (1930–)
m. Philip Goodman (1931–)
see: *Goodman* XVII, page 521

XXIII. KOROCHENZOV 1, from page 315

Aleksandr Vassilievich Korochenzov
August 17, 1877, — February 6, 1922, Lausanne, Switzerland
m. November 9, 1921, Geneva, Switzerland
* **Tatyana Konstantinovna,** Princess of Russia, daughter of Grand Duke Konstantin Konstantinovich of Russia and of his wife, Princess Elisabeth of Saxe-Altenburg.
January 11, 1890, St. Petersburg —
(She is now Abbess Tamara of the Russian Orthodox Cloistered Order of Olberg on the Mount of Olives, Jerusalem.)
(She m. 1: Konstantin Aleksandrovich, Prince Bagration-Moukhransky – see: *Bagration-Moukhransky* XXIII, page 973.)

No Issue.

XXIII. KOTCHOUBEY DE BEAUHARNAIS 1, from page 999

Leon Mikhailovich, Prince Kotchoubey
June 11/23, 1862, — May 9, 1927, Paris
m. September 7, 1893, Baden-Baden. Divorced:
* **Daria Evgeniievna,** Countess de Beauharnais, daughter of Duke Evgenii Maksimilianovich of Leuchtenberg and of his wife, Daria Konstantinovna Opotchinina, created Countess de Beauharnais.
March 7/19, 1870, St. Petersburg — last heard of in Russia in the 1930s
(She m. 2: Waldemar, Baron von Gravenitz – see: *Gravenitz* XXIII, page 985.)
(She m. 3: Marchesi – an Italian – no further information available.)
(She m. 4: a Spaniard – no further information available.)

XXIII. Kotchoubey de Beauharnais — I continued

Issue: 1. Evgenii Leontievich, Prince Kotchoubey de Beauharnais (1894–1951)
m. Helen Geraldine Pearce (1898–)
see: *Kotchoubey de Beauharnais* XXIII, 2, below

2. Nataliya Leontievna, Princess Kotchoubey, Sister Sophia O.S.B.
October 18, 1899, Wiesbaden, Germany —

XXIII. Kotchoubey de Beauharnais — 2, from above

★ **Evgenii Leontievich,** Prince Kotchoubey de Beauharnais, son of Prince Leon Mikhailovich Kotchoubey.
July 24, 1894, Peterhof, Russia — November 6, 1951, Paris
m. August 30, 1917, Victoria, British Columbia, Canada
Helen Geraldine Pearce, daughter of
July 23, 1898, Redhouse, South Africa —

Issue: 1. Diana Evgenia Evgeniievna, Princess Kotchoubey de Beauharnais (1918–)
m. 1: and divorced: Georges Snopko (1894–)
see: *Snopko* XVIII, page 605
m. 2: Georges Bataille (–)
see: *Bataille* XVIII, page 543

2. Nataliya Aleksandra Leontievna, Princess Kotchoubey de Beauharnais (1923–)
m. André Laguerre (–)
see: *Laguerre* XVIII, page 569

3. Elena Josephine Evgeniievna, Princess Kotchoubey de Beauharnais (1928–)
m. Pierre Pellegrino (–)
see: *Pellegrino* XVIII, page 592

4. Hortense Stephanie Evgeniievna, Princess Kotchoubey de Beauharnais (1935–)
m. Gerhard Murjahn (–)
see: *Murjahn* XXI, page 775

XXIII. KULIKOVSKY 1, from page 300

Nikolai Aleksandrovich Kulikovsky
November 11, 1882, Evstratovka, Ukraine — August 10, 1958, Cooksville, Ontario
m. November 1, 1916, Red Cross Hospital Chapel, Kiev
* **Olga Aleksandrovna,** Grand Duchess of Russia, daughter of Emperor Aleksandr III of All the Russias and of his wife, Princess Dagmar (Mariya Feodorovna) of Denmark.
June 1/13, 1882, Peterhof Palace, Russia — November 24, 1960, Toronto, Ontario, Canada
(She m. 1: and marriage annulled: Petr Aleksandrovich, Duke and Prince of Oldenburg – see: *Oldenburg* V hh–2, page 216.)

Issue: 1. Tikhon Nikolaievich Kulikovsky (1917–)
m. 1: and divorced: Agnete Petersen (1920–)
m. 2: Livia Sebesteyn (1925–)
see: *Kulikovsky* XXIII, 2, below

2. Gouri Nikolaievich Kulikovsky (1919–)
m. and divorced: Ruth Schwartz (1921–)
see: *Kulikovsky* XXIII, 3, page 990

XXIII. Kulikovsky 2, from above

* **Tikhon Nikolaievich Kulikovsky,** son of Nikolai Aleksandrovich.
August 12/25, 1917, Villa Ai-Todor, Crimea, near Yalta —
m. 1: , 1942, Copenhagen. Divorced: 1955, Brampton, Ontario
Agnete Petersen, daughter of Carl Petersen and of his wife,
May 17, 1920, Ballerup, Denmark —
m. 2: September 21, 1959, Toronto, Ontario
Livia Sebesteyn, daughter of Alador Sebesteyn and of his wife,
December 7, 1925, Budapest, Hungary —
(She m. 1: and divorced: Dr. E. de Alador.)

Issue: 1. Olga Tikonovna Kulikovskya
July 9, 1964, Toronto, Ontario, Canada —

XXIII. Kulikovsky 3, from page 989

* **Gouri Nikolaievich Kulikovsky,** second son of Nikolai Aleksandrovich.
April 2/23, 1919, Novo-Minskaya, Caucasus, Russia —
m. 1: October 5, 1940, Copenhagen. Divorced: 1956, Brampton, Ontario
Ruth Schwartz, daughter of
February 6, 1921, Copenhagen —

Issue: 1. Kseniya Gourievna Kulikovskya
June 29, 1941, Ballerup, Denmark —
m. 1: Ralph Jones (-)
see: *Jones* XXIV, page 1019
m. 2: unknown
(She has a daughter named Vivian by her second marriage.)

2. Leonid Gourievich Kulikovsky
May 2, 1943, Ballerup —

3. Aleksandr Gourievich Kulikovsky
November 29, 1948, Toronto, Ontario —

XXIII. LEPP 1, from page 307

Henry Lepp
, 1896, Aleksandrovsk, Russia — May , 1955, Dordogne, France
m. September 9, 1925, Berlin
* **Aleksandra Alekseievna,** Countess Belevskya-Zhukovskya, daughter of Count Aleksei Alekseievich Belevsky-Zhukovsky and of his first wife, Princess Mariya Petrovna Troubetskoya.
March 4, 1899, Moscow —
(She m. 2: Georgii Flevitsky - see: *Flevitsky* XXIII, page 980.)

No Issue.

XXIII. LEUCHTENBERG (de Beauharnais) 1, from page 296

Maximilian de Beauharnais, 3rd Duke of Leuchtenberg, Fürst von Eichstätt, second son of Eugene de Beauharnais, 1st Duke of Leuchtenberg, Fürst von Eichstätt, and of his wife, Princess Auguste of Bavaria.

October 2, 1817, Munich — October 20/November 1, 1852, St. Petersburg

m. July 2/14, 1839, St. Petersburg

* **Mariya Nikolaievna,** Grand Duchess of Russia, daughter of Emperor Nikolai I and of his wife, Princess Charlotte (Aleksandra Feodorovna) of Prussia.

August 6/18, 1819, Pavlovsk — February 9/21, 1876, St. Petersburg

(She m. 2: Grigorii Aleksandrovich, Count Strogonov – see: *Strogonov* XXIII, page 1008.)

Issue: 1. Aleksandra Maksimilianovna, Duchess of Leuchtenberg, Princess Romanovskya
March 28/April 9, 1840, St. Petersburg —July 31/August 12, 1843, St. Petersburg

2. Mariya Maksimilianovna, Duchess of Leuchtenberg, Princess Romanovskya (1841–1914)
m. Wilhelm, Prince of Baden (1829–1897)
see: *Baden (Zähringen)* XXI, page 648

3. Nikolai Maksimilianovich, 4th Duke of Leuchtenberg, Prince Romanovsky, Fürst von Eichstätt (1843–1891)
m. Nadezhda Sergeievna Annenkova (1839–1891)
see: *Leuchtenberg (de Beauharnais)* XXIII, 2, page 992

4. Evgeniya Maksimilianovna, Duchess of Leuchtenberg, Princess Romanovskya (1845–1925)
m. Alexander, Duke and Prince of Oldenburg (1844–1932)
see: *Oldenburg* V hh–1, page 215

5. Evgenii Maksimilianovich, 5th Duke of Leuchtenberg, Prince Romanovsky (1847–1901)
m. 1: Daria Konstantinovna Opotchinina (1845–1870)
m. 2: Zinaida Dimitrievna Skobeleva (–1899)
see: *Leuchtenberg (de Beauharnais)* XXIII, 10, page 998

XXIII. Leuchtenberg (de Beauharnais) 1 continued

6. Sergei Maksimilianovich, Duke of Leuchtenberg, Prince Romanovsky
December 8/20, 1849, St. Petersburg — October 12/24, 1877, Youan-Chuflik, Bulgaria, killed in action in the Russo-Turkish War

7. Georgii Maksimilianovich, 6th Duke of Leuchtenberg, Prince Romanovsky (1852–1912)
m. 1: Therese, Duchess of Oldenburg (1852–1883)
m. 2: and divorced: Anastasia Nikolaievna, Princess Petrovich-Niegosh of Montenegro (1868–1935)
see: *Leuchtenberg (de Beauharnais)* XXIII, 11, page 999

XXIII. Leuchtenberg (de Beauharnais) 2, from page 991

* **Nikolai Maksimilianovich,** 4th Duke of Leuchtenberg, Prince Romanovsky, Fürst von Eichstätt, eldest son of Maximilian de Beauharnais, 3rd Duke of Leuchtenberg.
July 23/August 4, 1843, Sergeievskoye, Dasha, Russia — January 6, 1891, Paris
m. October , 1868, , morganatic

Nadezhda Sergeievna Annenkova, daughter of Sergei Petrovich Annenkov and of his wife, Ekaterina Dimitrievna Shidlovskya.
July 17, 1840, — May 25/June 6, 1891, St. Petersburg
(She m. 1: Vladimir Nikolaievich Akinfov whom she divorced July 22/August 3, 1867.)

Issue: 1. Nikolai Nikolaievich, Prince Romanovsky de Beauharnais, created Duke of Leuchtenberg in 1890 (1868–1928)
m. Mariya Nikolaievna, Countess Grabbé (1869–1948)
see: *Leuchtenberg (de Beauharnais)* XXIII, 3, page 993

2. Georgii Nikolaievich, Prince Romanovsky de Beauharnais, created Duke of Leuchtenberg in 1890 (1872–1929)
m. Olga Nikolaievna, Princess Repnina (1872–1953)
see: *Leuchtenberg (de Beauharnais)* XXIII, 7, page 996

XXIII. Leuchtenberg (de Beauharnais) 3, from page 992

★ **Nikolai Nikolaievich,** Prince Romanovsky de Beauharnais, created Duke of Leuchtenberg on November 11/23, 1890, at Gatchina by the Emperor Aleksandr III Aleksandrovich.

October 17, 1868, Genoa, Italy — March 2, 1928, Ruth, Vaucluse, France

m. April 24/May 6, 1894, St. Petersburg

Mariya Nikolaievna, Countess Grabbé, daughter of Count Nikolai Pavlovich Grabbé and of his wife, Countess Aleksandra Feodorovna Orlova-Denisova.

November 11/23, 1869, Tsarskoye-Selo — October 24, 1948, Orange, Vaucluse, France

Issue: 1. Aleksandra Nikolaievna, Duchess of Leuchtenberg, titles herself Princess de Beauharnais (1895–)

m. 1: and divorced: Levan, Prince Melikov (1893–1928)

see: *Melikov* XXIII, page 1001

m. 2: Nikolai Ivanovich Terestchenko (1897–1926)

see: *Terestchenko* XXIII, page 1009

2. Nikolai Nikolaievich, Duke of Leuchtenberg (1896–1937)

m. 1: Olga Nikolaievna Fomina (1898–1921)

m. 2: Elisabeth Müller-Himmler (1906–)

see: *Leuchtenberg (de Beauharnais)* XXIII, 4, page 994

3. Nadezhda Nikolaievna, Duchess of Leuchtenberg (1898–1962)

m. Aleksandr Mogilevsky (1885–1953)

see: *Mogilevsky* XXIII, page 1002

4. Maksimilian Nikolaievich, Duke of Leuchtenberg

March 26/April 8, 1900, St. Petersburg — December 28, 1905, Seeon, Bavaria

5. Sergei Nikolaievich, Duke of Leuchtenberg (1903–)

m. 1: and divorced: Anna Aleksandrovna Naumova (1900–)

m. 2: and divorced: Kira Nikolaievna Wolkova (1915–)

m. 3: Olga Sergeievna Wickberg (1926–)

see: *Leuchtenberg (de Beauharnais)* XXIII, 6, page 995

XXIII. Leuchtenberg (de Beauharnais) 3 continued

6. Mikhail Nikolaievich, Duke of Leuchtenberg
February 17/March 2, 1905, St. Petersburg — February 9, 1928, Orange, Vaucluse, France

7. Mariya Nikolaievna, Duchess of Leuchtenberg (1907–)
m. Nikolai, Count Mengden-Altenwoga (1899–)
see: *Mengden-Altenwoga* XXIII, page 1002

XXIII. Leuchtenberg (de Beauharnais) 4, from page 993

* **Nikolai Nikolaievich,** Duke of Leuchtenberg, eldest son of Duke Nikolai Nikolaievich.
July 29/August 8, 1896, Gori, Government of Novgorod, Russia — May 5, 1937, Munich, Germany
m. 1: September 8, 1919, Novotcherskask, Russia
Olga Nikolaievna Fomina, daughter of Nikolai Pavlovich Fomine and of his wife,
July 29, 1898, St. Petersburg — September 2, 1921, Constantinople
m. 2: November 3, 1928, Munich
Elisabeth Müller-Himmler, daughter of
July 31, 1906, Tutzing, Bavaria —
(She m. 2: December 28, 1938, Munich, Conrad Warmund Fink, D.Phil., born July 7, 1900, Munich.)

Issue of second marriage:

1. Evgeniya Nikolaievna, Duchess of Leuchtenberg (1929–)
m. Martin von Bruch (1911–)
see: *von Bruch* XXI, page 671

2. Nikolai Nikolaievich, Duke of Leuchtenberg (1933–)
m. Anne Christine Bügge (1936–)
see: *Leuchtenberg (de Beauharnais)* XXIII, 5, page 995

XXIII. Leuchtenberg (de Beauharnais) 5, from page 994

* **Nikolai Nikolaievich,** Duke of Leuchtenberg, only son of Duke Nikolai Nikolaievich.
October 12, 1933, Munich —
m. August 24, 1962, Oberkirchen
Anne Christine Bügge, daughter of
December 17, 1936, Stettin —

Issue: 1. Nikolai Nikolaievich, Duke of Leuchtenberg
January 20, 1963, Bonn —

2. Konstantin Nikolaievich, Duke of Leuchtenberg
June 25, 1965, Hargelar —

XXIII. Leuchtenberg (de Beauharnais) 6, from page 993

* **Sergei Nikolaievich,** Duke of Leuchtenberg, third son of Duke Nikolai Nikolaievich. As a United States citizen he uses the name of Serge de Beauharnais von Leuchtenberg.
June 24/July 7, 1903, St. Petersburg —
m. 2: October 29, 1925, Nice, France. Divorced: December 16, 1938, Leipzig
Anna Aleksandrovna Naumova, daughter of Aleksandr Nikolaievich Naumov and of his wife, Anna Konstantinovna Utschkova.
March 15, 1900, Pharos, Crimea —
m. 2: March 8, 1939 (civil), Leipzig, Germany, and April 17, 1939 (religious), Vevey, Switzerland. Divorced: 1942, Berlin
Kira Nikolaievna Wolkova, daughter of Nikolai Wolkov and of his wife, Anna Vassilieva.
January 16, 1915, St. Petersburg —
m. 3: July 23, 1945, Munich
Olga Sergeievna Wickberg, daughter of Sergei Nikolaievich Wickberg and of his wife, Nina Axelevna Wickberg.
November 15, 1926, Zgurowka, near Poltava, Russia —

Issue of first marriage:
1. Maria Magdalena Sergeievna, Duchess of Leuchtenberg (1926–   )
m. Joseph de Pasquale (1919–   )
see: *de Pasquale* XXIV, page 1022

XXIII. Leuchtenberg (de Beauharnais) 6 continued

2. Anna Sergeievna, Duchess of Leuchtenberg (1928–)
m. Robert Bayard Stout (1931–)
see: *Stout* XXIV, page 1024

3. Olga Sergeievna, Duchess of Leuchtenberg (1931–)
m. Ronald Gerald Newburgh (1926–)
see: *Newburgh* XXIV, page 1021

4. Nataliya Sergeievna, Duchess of Leuchtenberg
February 28, 1934, Colombes, near Paris —

Issue of third marriage:

5. Serge de Beauharnais von Leuchtenberg
November 27, 1955, Monterey, California, USA —

6. Elizabeth de Beauharnais von Leuchtenberg
September 25, 1957, Monterey —

XXIII. Leuchtenberg (de Beauharnais) 7, from page 992

* **Georgii Nikolaievich,** Prince Romanovsky de Beauharnais, second son of Duke Nikolai Maksimilianovich. Created Duke of Leuchtenberg at Gatchina on November 11/23, 1890, by the Emperor Aleksandr III Aleksandrovich.

December 10, 1872, Rome — August 9, 1929, Seeon Castle, Bavaria
m. April 23/May 5, 1895, St. Petersburg

Olga Nikolaievna, Princess Repnina, daughter of Prince Nikolai Vassilievich Repnin and of his wife, Princess Sofia Dimitrievna Wolkonskya.

August 9/21, 1872, Jagotin, Government of Poltava, Russia — April 27, 1953, Seeon Castle, Bavaria

Issue: 1. Elena Georgeievna, Duchess of Leuchtenberg (1896–)
m. Arkadj Konstantinovich Ougritchitch-Trebinsky (–)
see: *Ougritchitch-Trebinsky* XXIII, page 1006

2. Dimitrii Georgeievich, Duke of Leuchtenberg (1898–)
m. Ekaterina Konstantinovna Arapova (1900–)
see: *Leuchtenberg (de Beauharnais)* XXIII, 8, page 997

XXIII. Leuchtenberg (de Beauharnais) 7 continued

3. Nataliya Georgeievna, Duchess of Leuchtenberg (1900–)
m. Vladimir Feodorovich, Baron Meller-Zakomelsky (1894–1962)
see: *Meller-Zakomelsky* XXIII, page 1001

4. Tamara Georgeievna, Duchess of Leuchtenberg (1901–)
m. Konstantin Grigorievich Karanfilov (1905–)
see: *Karanfilov* XXIII, page 986

5. Andrei Georgeievich, Duke of Leuchtenberg
June 26/July 9, 1903, St. Petersburg — , 1919, Narva, Estonia, killed in the Russian Civil War

6. Konstantin Georgeievich, Duke of Leuchtenberg (1905–)
m. Daria Alekseievna, Princess Obolenskya (1903–)
see: *Leuchtenberg (de Beauharnais)* XXIII, 9, page 998

XXIII. Leuchtenberg (de Beauharnais) 8, from page 996

* **Dimitrii Georgeievich,** Duke of Leuchtenberg, eldest son of Duke Georgii Nikolaievich.
April 18/30, 1898, St. Petersburg —
m. May 13, 1921, Rome

Ekaterina Konstantinovna Arapova, daughter of Aleksandr Viktorovich Arapov and of his wife, Anna Aleksandrovna Pantschulidseva.
January 4/16, 1900, Simbirsk —
(She m. 1: February 16, 1919, Boris Aleksandrovich, Prince Chavchavadze, who died of typhus on December 19, 1919, in General Wrangel's White Army.)

Issue: 1. Elena Dimitrievna, Duchess of Leuchtenberg
May 30, 1922, Munich —

2. Georgii Dimitrievich, Duke of Leuchtenberg (a Lieutenant in the Canadian Army)
January 11, 1927, Munich — January 27, 1963, St. Sauveur, Quebec, Canada

XXIII. Leuchtenberg (de Beauharnais) 9, from page 997

★ **Konstantin Georgeievich,** Duke of Leuchtenberg, third son of Duke Georgii Nikolaievich.
May 6/19, 1905, St. Petersburg —
m. September 20, 1929, Seeon Castle, Bavaria
Daria Alekseievna, Princess Obolenskya, daughter of Prince Aleksei Dimitrievich Obolensky and of his wife, Princess Elizabeta Nikolaievna Saltykova.
July 12, 1903, Kaluga, near Moscow —

Issue: 1. Kseniya (Xenia) Konstantinovna, Duchess of Leuchtenberg (1930–)
m. Dimitrii Georgeievich, Count Grabbé (1927–)
see: *Grabbé* XXIII, page 984

2. Olga Konstantinovna, Duchess of Leuchtenberg (1932–)
m. Oleg Evgeniievich Gaydeburov (1922–)
see: *Gaydeburov* XXIII, page 984

XXIII. Leuchtenberg (de Beauharnais) 10, from page 991

★ **Evgenii Maksimilianovich,** 5th Duke of Leuchtenberg, Prince Romanovsky, second son of Duke Maximilian de Beauharnais of Leuchtenberg.
January 27/February 8, 1847, St. Petersburg — August 18/31, 1901, St. Petersburg
m. 1: January 8/20, 1869, Florence, Italy (morganatic)
Daria Konstantinovna Opotchinina, daughter of Konstantin Feodorovich Opotchinin and of his wife, Vera Ivanovna Skobeleva.
March 7/19, 1845, St. Petersburg — March 7/19, 1870, St. Petersburg
(She was created Countess de Beauharnais on January 8/20, 1869, by Imperial Ukase of the Emperor Aleksandr II Nikolaievich.)
m. 2: July 2/14, 1878, Peterhof
Zinaida Dimitrievna Skobeleva, daughter of General Dimitrii Ivanovich Skobelev and of his wife, Olga Nikolaievna Poltavtzeva.
— June 16/28, 1899, St. Petersburg
(She was created Countess de Beauharnais on August 16/28, 1889, by Imperial Ukase of the Emperor Aleksandr III Aleksandrovich.)

XXIII. Leuchtenberg (de Beauharnais) 10 continued

Issue of first marriage:

1. Daria Evgeniievna, Countess de Beauharnais (1870–)
   m. 1: and divorced: Leon Mikhailovich, Prince Kotchoubey (1862–1927)
   see: *Kotchoubey de Beauharnais* XXIII, page 987
   m. 2: Waldemar, Baron von Gravenitz (1872–1916)
   see: *von Gravenitz* XXIII, page 985
   m. 3: Marchesi – an Italian – no further information available
   m. 4: a Spaniard – no further information available
   (She returned to Russia in the 1930s and was never heard from again.)

XXIII. Leuchtenberg (de Beauharnais) 11, from pages 992, 214

* **Georgii Maksimilianovich,** 6th Duke of Leuchtenberg, Prince Romanovsky, fourth son of Maximilian de Beauharnais, Duke of Leuchtenberg, Fürst von Eichstätt.
February 17/29, 1852, St. Petersburg — May 3, 1912, Paris
m. 1: May 12, 1879, Stuttgart

* **Therese,** Duchess of Oldenburg, daughter of Duke Peter of Oldenburg and of his wife, Princess Therese of Nassau-Weilburg.
March 18/30, 1852, St. Petersburg — April 7/19, 1883,
m. 2: August 16/28, 1889, Peterhof, Russia. Divorced: November 15, 1906, by the Holy Synod of the Russian Orthodox Church

Anastasia Nikolaievna, Princess Petrovich-Niegosh of Montenegro, daughter of King Nicolas I of Montenegro and of his wife, Milena Vukotic.
December 23, 1867/January 1, 1868, Cetinje — November 15, 1935, Cap d'Antibes, France
(She m. 2: Nikolai Nikolaievich, Grand Duke of Russia – see: *Russia* VIII p–2, page 318.)

Issue of first marriage:

1. Aleksandr Georgeievich, 7th Duke of Leuchtenberg, Prince Romanovsky (1881–1942)
   m. Nadezhda Nikolaievna Caralli (1883–)
   see: *Leuchtenberg (de Beauharnais)* XXIII, 12, page 1000

XXIII. Leuchtenberg (de Beauharnais) 11 continued

Issue of second marriage:

2. Sergei Georgeievich, 8th Duke of Leuchtenberg, Prince Romanovsky
   July 4/16, 1890, Peterhof —

3. Elena Georgeievna, Duchess of Leuchtenberg, Princess Romanovskya (1892–)
   m. Stefan, Count Tyszkiewicz (1894–)
   see: *Tyszkiewicz* XXII, page 969

XXIII. Leuchtenberg (de Beauharnais) 12, from page 999

* **Aleksandr Georgeievich,** 7th Duke of Leuchtenberg, Prince Romanovsky, eldest son of Duke Georgii Maksimilianovich.
November 1/13, 1881, St. Petersburg — September 26, 1942, Salis-de-Béarn, France
m. April 9/22, 1917, St. Petersburg
Nadezhda Nikolaievna Caralli, daughter of Nikolai Caralli and of his wife,
July 2/14, 1883, St. Petersburg —
(She m. 1: a man named Schleiffer.)
(She m. 2: a man named Ignatiev from whom she was divorced by the Russian Holy Synod on October 9/22, 1916.)

No Issue.

XXIII. LORIS-MELIKOV (Loris-Melikoff) 1, from page 111

Mikhail Tarielovich, Count Loris-Melikov
June 8/16, 1900, Tsarskoye-Selo, Russia —
m. November 14, 1923, Wiesbaden, Germany
* **Olga,** Countess von Merenberg, daughter of Count Georg von Merenberg and of his first wife, Princess Olga Aleksandrovna Yourievskya.
October 3, 1898, Wiesbaden —

Issue: 1. Aleksandr Mikhailovich, Count Loris-Melikov (1926–)
   m. Micheline Prunier (1932–)
   see: *Loris-Melikov* XXIII, 2, page 1001

XXIII. Loris-Melikov (Loris-Melikoff) 2, from page 1000

★ **Aleksandr Mikhailovich,** Count Loris-Melikov, only son of Count Mikhail Tarielovich.
May 26, 1926, Paris —
m. September 27, 1958, 'La Houssière', Liège, Belgium
Micheline Prunier, daughter of
June 21, 1932, Liège, Belgium —

Issue: 1. Ann Elisabeth, Countess Loris-Melikoff
July 23, 1959, Basel, Switzerland —

2. Dominique, Countess Loris-Melikoff
March , 1961, Basel —

3. Nathalie, Countess Loris-Melikoff
December 28, 1963, Basel —

4. Michael, Count Loris-Melikoff
December 18, 1964, Basel —

XXIII. MELIKOV 1, from page 993

Levan, Prince Melikov
February 15, 1893, —January 26, 1928, New York City
m. September 25, 1916, St. Petersburg
★ **Aleksandra Nikolaievna,** Duchess of Leuchtenberg, daughter of Duke Nikolai Nikolaievich de Beauharnais of Leuchtenberg, Prince Romanovsky, and of his wife, Countess Mariya Nikolaievna Grabbé.
March 1/13, 1895, St. Petersburg —
(She m. 2: Nikolai Ivanovich Terestchenko - see: *Terestchenko* XXIII, page 1009.)

No Issue.

XXIII. MELLER-ZAKOMELSKY 1, from page 997

Vladimir Feodorovich, Baron Meller-Zakomelsky
July 21, 1894, Koltyshevka, Russia —June 5, 1962, Fontana, California
m. October 15, 1924, Seeon Castle, Bavaria
★ **Nataliya Georgeievna,** Duchess of Leuchtenberg, daughter of Georgii Nikolaievich, Duke of Leuchtenberg, and of his wife, Princess Olga Nikolaievna Repnina.

XXIII. Meller-Zakomelsky 1 continued

May 16/28, 1900, St. Petersburg —

No Issue.

XXIII. MENGDEN-ALTENWOGA 1, from page 994

Nikolai, Count Mengden-Altenwoga
April 1/13, 1899, St. Petersburg —
m. May 19, 1929, Paris
* **Mariya Nikolaievna,** Duchess of Leuchtenberg, Princess Romanovskya, daughter of Duke Nikolai Nikolaievich of Leuchtenberg, Prince Romanovsky de Beauharnais, and of his wife, Countess Mariya Nikolaievna Grabbé.
May 21/June 3, 1907, St. Petersburg —

No Issue.

XXIII. MILASHEVICH 1, from page 1008

Grigorii Nikitich Milashevich, General
— , 1918, Sebastopol, Crimea, assassinated during the Revolution
m. , 1896, St. Petersburg
* **Elena Grigorievna,** Countess Strogonova, daughter of Count Grigorii Aleksandrovich Strogonov and of his wife, Grand Duchess Mariya Nikolaievna of Russia.
January 29/February 10, 1861, St. Petersburg — January 29/February 11, 1908, Tsarskoye-Selo
(She m. 1: Vladimir Alekseievich Cheremetev - see: *Cheremetev* XXIII, page 976.)

No Issue.

XXIII. MOGILEVSKY 1, from page 993

Aleksandr Mogilevsky
January 27, 1885, Odessa, Ukraine — March , 1953, Tokyo, Japan
m. , 1929,
* **Nadezhda Nikolaievna de Beauharnais,** Duchess of Leuchtenberg, daughter of Nikolai Nikolaievich, Prince Romanovsky, Duke of Leuchtenberg, and of his wife, Countess Mariya Nikolaievna Grabbé.

XXIII. Mogilevsky 1 continued

July 27/August 8, 1898, Gori, Government of Novgorod, Russia —
December 2, 1962, Salinas, California, USA

Issue: 1. Mikhail Aleksandrovich Mogilevsky (1929–)
m. Joan Russell (1931–)
see: *Mogilevsky* XXIII, 2, below

XXIII. Mogilevsky 2, from above

* **Mikhail Aleksandrovich Mogilevsky,** only son of Aleksandr.
September 24, 1929, Bandung, Java —
m. June 30, 1953, Winslow, Maine, USA
Joan Russell, daughter of Clyde Russell and of his wife,
January 15, 1931, Waterville, Maine, USA —

Issue: 1. Michelle de Beauharnais Mogilevsky
January 29, 1956, Spokane, Washington, USA —

2. Anton de Beauharnais Mogilevsky
February 14, 1960, Ithaca, New York —

3. André Jon de Beauharnais Mogilevsky
August 1, 1962, Waterville, Maine —

XXIII. MOJAISKY (Mozhaisky) 1, from page 308

Nikolai Mojaisky
June 17, 1928, Paris —
m. November 17, 1949, Paris. Divorced: January , 1956, Paris
* **Elena Sergeievna,** Countess Belevskya-Zhukovskya, daughter of Count Sergei Alekseievich Belevsky-Zhukovsky and of his wife, Nina Botkina.
August 31, 1929, Paris —
(She m. 2: Kirill Mikhailovich, Count Nieroth – see: *Nieroth* XXIII, page 1004.)

Issue: 1. Aleksei (Alexis) Nikolaievich Mojaisky
December 20, 1951, Paris —

XXIII. MORDVINOV (Mordvinoff) 1, from page 610

Aleksandr, Count Mordvinov
December 20, 1887, St. Petersburg — February 13, 1950, Paris
m. September 25, 1911, Paris
* **Marie Claire Vérola,** daughter of Paul Vérola and of his wife, Countess Alexandra von Ostenburg.
May 9, 1886, Nice, France — April 26, 1943, Paris

Issue: 1. Marie Madeleine, Countess Mordvinoff
January 17, 1913, Paris —

XXIII. NARISHKIN 1, from page 216

Leo Vassilievich Narishkin
December , 1876, — April 4, 1931, Juan les Pins, France
m. October 17, 1908,
* **Aleksandra Konstantinovna,** Countess von Zarnekau, daughter of Duke Konstantin of Oldenburg and of his wife, Agrippina Djaparidze, created Countess von Zarnekau.
May 10, 1883, Koutais, Caucasus, Russia — May 28, 1957, Paris
(She m. 1: and divorced: Prince Yourievsky – see: *Yourievsky* VIII k–1, page 311.)

No Issue.

XXIII. NIEROTH 1, from page 308

Kirill Mikhailovich, Count Nieroth
April 14, 1930, Paris —
m. July 16, 1956, Paris
* **Elena Sergeievna,** Countess Belevskya-Zhukovskya, daughter of Count Sergei Alekseievich Belevsky-Zhukovsky and of his wife, Nina Sergeievna Botkina.
August 31, 1929, Paris —
(She m. 1: and divorced: Nikolai Mojaisky – see: *Mojaisky* XXIII, page 1003.)

XXIII. Nieroth

1 continued

Issue: 1. Petr Kirillovich, Count Nieroth
June 17, 1957, Neuilly-sur-Seine, France —

2. Elisabeth Kirillovna, Countess Nieroth
February 2, 1966, Houston, Texas, USA —

XXIII. OBOLENSKY-NELEDINSKY-MELETZKY

1, from page 299

Sergei Platonovich, Prince Obolensky-Neledinsky-Meletzky, son of Prince Platon. He became a United States citizen on September 24, 1931, at which time he took the name of Serge Obolensky.
October 3, 1890, Tsarskoye-Selo, Russia —
m. 1: October 9, 1916, Yalta, Crimea. Divorced: June 22, 1924, London
* **Ekaterina Aleksandrovna,** Princess Yourievskya, daughter of Emperor Aleksandr II and of his second and morganatic wife, Princess Ekaterina Mikhailovna Dolgorukya.
September 9, 1878, St. Petersburg — December 22, 1959, North Hayling, England
(She m. 1: Aleksandr Vladimirovich, Prince Bariatinsky – see: *Bariatinsky* XXIII, page 974.)
m. 2: July 24, 1924. Divorced: December 7, 1932,
Alice Astor, daughter of Colonel John Jacob Astor who died in the *Titanic*, and of his wife, Ava, who later married Charles Lister, 4th Baron Riddlesdale.
— , 1956,
(She m. 2: and divorced: Raimund von Hoffmannsthal, son of the Austrian poet, Hugo von Hoffmannsthal.)
(She m. 3: and divorced: Philip Harding.)
(She m. 4: and divorced: David Bouverie.)
m. 3: June , 1971, Arlington, Virginia
Marilyn Fraser Wall, daughter of
, 1927, —
(This was her second marriage.)

Issue of second marriage: Not descendants of King George I
1. Ivan Obolensky of New York City, married to and divorced from Clare McGinnis.

2. Sylvia Obolensky, married to John Henshef van der Ueersch.

XXIII. ORLOV

1, from page 319

Nikolai Vladimirovich, Prince Orlov
March 12, 1896, St. Petersburg — May 30, 1961, New York City
m. April 10, 1917, Haraks, Crimea. Divorced: 1940,

⋆ **Nadezhda Petrovna,** Princess of Russia, daughter of Grand Duke Petr Nikolaievich of Russia and of his wife, Princess Militza Nikolaievna Petrovich-Niegosh of Montenegro.
March 3, 1898, Dulber, Crimea —

Issue: 1. Irina Nikolaievna, Princess Orlova (1918–)
m. 1: and divorced: Herbert, Baron von Waldstätten (1913–)
see: *von Waldstätten* XXI, page 899
m. 2: Dr. Anthony Adama Zylstra (–)
see: *Zylstra* XXI, page 941

2. Kseniya (Xenia) Nikolaievna, Princess Orlova (1921–1963)
m. 1: and divorced: Paul de Montaignac (–)
see: *de Montaignac* XVIII, page 580
m. 2: Jean Albert, Baron d'Almont (1909–)
see: *d'Almont* XVIII, page 539

XXIII. OUGRITCHITCH-TREBINSKY

1, from page 996

Arkadj Konstantinovich Ougritchitch-Trebinksy
April 22, 1897, Poltava —
m. June 6, 1920, Agram, Yugoslavia

⋆ **Elena Georgeievna de Beauharnais,** Duchess of Leuchtenberg, daughter of Georgii Nikolaievich de Beauharnais, Duke of Leuchtenberg, and of his wife, Princess Olga Nikolaievna Repnina.
June 2/14, 1896, St. Petersburg —

Issue: 1. Nina Arkadjevna Ougritchitch-Trebinskya (1925–)
m. Robert Wythe Cannaday Jnr. (1924–)
see: *Cannaday* XXIV, page 1016

XXIII. PEREVOSTCHIKOV 1, from page 307

Petr Dimitrievich Perevostchikov

—

m. January , 1917, Moscow

★ **Elizabeta Alekseievna,** Countess Belevskya-Zhukovskya, daughter of Count Aleksei Belevsky-Zhukovsky and of his first wife, Princess Mariya Petrovna Troubetskoya.

September 8, 1896, Moscow —

(She m. 2: Arthur Lourié – see: *Lourié* XVIII, page 572.)

Issue: 1. Mariya Petrovna Perevostchikova (1917–)

m. and divorced: Lucien Teissier (–)

see: *Teissier* XVIII, page 607

2. Dimitrii Petrovich Perevostchikov (1919–1960)

m. and divorced: Marina Ourousova (–)

see: *Perevostchikov* XXIII, 2, below

XXIII. Perevostchikov 2, from above

★ **Dimitrii Petrovich Perevostchikov,** only son of Petr Dimitrievich.

June 24, 1919, Rapallo, Italy — August 23, 1960, Paris

m. , 1944, Paris. Divorced: 1947, Paris

Marina Ourousova, daughter of

—

No Issue.

XXIII. VON PLOEN 1, from page 217

Ivan von Ploen

, 1878, — , 1955, Paris

m. 1907, Moscow

★ **Ekaterina Konstantinovna,** Countess von Zarnekau, daughter of Duke Konstantin of Oldenburg and of his wife, Agrippina Djaparidze.

September 16, 1884, Koutais, Caucasus, Russia — December 24, 1962, Paris

Issue: 1. Tatiana Ivanovna von Ploen (1908–1960)

m. Nikolai Vladimirovich Eltchaninov (1906–1952)

see: *Eltchaninov* XXIII, page 979

XXIII. POUTIATINE 1, from page 309

Sergei Mikhailovich, Prince Poutiatine
December 7, 1893, St. Petersburg — February 26, 1966, Charleston, South Carolina, USA
m. September 6/19, 1917, Pavlovsk, Russia. Divorced: 1924, Paris

* **Mariya Pavlovna,** Grand Duchess of Russia, daughter of Grand Duke Pavel (Paul) Aleksandrovich of Russia and of his first wife, Princess Alexandra of Greece and Denmark.
April 6, 1890, St. Petersburg — December 13, 1958, Mainau Castle, Lake Konstanz, Switzerland
(She m. 1: and divorced: Wilhelm, Prince of Sweden – see: *Sweden* (*Bernadotte*) XVI e–1, page 504.)

Issue: 1. Roman Sergeievich, Prince Poutiatine
July 17, 1918, St. Petersburg — May , 1919, Bucharest, Romania, died of typhoid fever

XXIII. STROGONOV 1, from page 296

Grigorii Aleksandrovich, Count Strogonov
June 18, 1824, — March 1/13, 1879,
m. November 4/16, 1856, St. Petersburg

* **Mariya Nikolaievna,** Grand Duchess of Russia, daughter of Emperor Nikolai I Pavlovich of All the Russias and of his wife, Princess Charlotte (Aleksandra Feodorovna) of Prussia.
August 6/18, 1819, Pavlovsk — February 9/21, 1876, St. Petersburg
(She m. 1: Maximilian de Beauharnais, 3rd Duke of Leuchtenberg, Fürst von Eichstätt – see: *Leuchtenberg* (*de Beauharnais*) XXIII, page 991.)

Issue: 1. Elena Grigorievna, Countess Strogonova (1861–1908)
m. 1: Vladimir Alekseievich Cheremetev (1847–1893)
see: *Cheremetev* XXIII, page 976
m. 2: General Grigorii Nikitich Milashevich (–1918)
see: *Milashevich* XXIII, page 1002

XXIII. SVERBEEV 1, from page 307

Vladimir Sergeievich Sverbeev
November 11, 1890, Yalta, Crimea — January 3, 1951, Paris
m. September 17, 1922, Berlin
* **Mariya Alekseievna,** Countess Belevskya-Zhukovskya, daughter of Count Aleksei Alekseievich Belevsky-Zhukovsky and of his first wife, Princess Mariya Petrovna Troubetskoya.
October 26, 1901, Moscow —
(She m. 2: Vladimir Aleksandrovich Ianouchevsky – see: *Ianouchevsky* XXIII, page 986.)

Issue: 1. Elizabeta Vladimirovna Sverbeeva (1923–)
m. 1: and divorced: Aleksandr Georgeievich Tarsaidze (1901–)
see: *Tarsaidze* XXIII, below
m. 2: Charles Byron-Patrikiades (1919–)
see: *Byron-Patrikiades* XX, page 626

XXIII. TARSAIDZE 1, from above

Aleksandr Georgeievich Tarsaidze
June 22, 1901, Tiflis, Georgia —
m. November 9, 1947, New York City. Divorced: January , 1953, New York City
* **Elizabeta Vladimirovna Sverbeeva,** daughter of Vladimir Sergeievich Sverbeev and of his wife, Countess Mariya Alekseievna Belevskya-Zhukovskya.
August 28, 1923, Berlin —
(She m. 2: Charles Byron-Patrikiades – see: *Byron-Patrikiades* XX, page 626.)

No Issue.

XXIII. TERESTCHENKO 1, from page 993

Nikolai Ivanovich Terestchenko
, 1887, — October 15, 1926, Paris
m. , 1923,
* **Aleksandra Nikolaievna,** Duchess of Leuchtenberg, daughter of Nikolai Nikolaievich de Beauharnais, Duke of Leuchtenberg, and of his wife, Countess Mariya Nikolaievna Grabbé.

XXIII. Terestchenko 1 continued

March 1/13, 1895, St. Petersburg —
(She m. 1: and divorced: Levan, Prince Melikov – see: *Melikov* XXIII, page 1001.)

No Issue.

XXIII. VSEVOLOZHSKY 1, from page 986

Sergei Vsevolozhsky
September 9, 1926, Paris —
m. February 16, 1958, Paris
* **Tatiana Konstantinovna Karanfilova,** daughter of Konstantin Grigorievich Karanfilov and of his wife, Princess Tamara Georgeievna de Beauharnais, Duchess of Leuchtenberg.
August 10, 1934, Toulon, France —

Issue: 1. Sergei Sergeievich Vsevolozhsky
January 3, 1959, Paris —

2. Andrei Sergeievich Vsevolozhsky
October 21, 1962, Aix-en-Provence, France —

XXIII. DE WITT 1, from page 547

Sergei, Count de Witt
December 30, 1891, Moscow —
m. October 17, 1938, London, England
* **Marie Clothilde,** Princess Bonaparte, daughter of Prince Napoléon Victor Bonaparte and of his wife, Princess Clementine of Belgium.
March 20, 1912, Brussels, Belgium —

Issue: 1. Marie Eugenie, Countess de Witt (1939–)
m. Petr (Peter), Count Cheremetieff (1931–)
see: *Cheremetev (Cheremetieff)* XXIII, page 978

2. Helene, Countess de Witt (1941–)
m. Henri, Comte de Lau d'Allemans (1927–)
see: *de Lau d'Allemans* XVIII, page 568

XXIII. de Witt 1 continued

3. Napoléon Serge, Count de Witt
   November 2, 1942, Sousse, Tunisia — November 4, 1942, Sousse

4. Yolande, Countess de Witt
   January 9, 1943, Sousse — July 6, 1945,

5. Vera, Countess de Witt (1945–)
   m. Godefroy, Marquis de Commarque (1939–)
   see: *de Commarque* XVIII, page 556

6. Beaudouin, Count de Witt
   January 24, 1947, Sousse, Tunisia —
   (m. Mlle de Rocca-Serra)

7. Isabelle, Countess de Witt
   January 26, 1949, Dordogne, France —

8. Jean Jérôme, Count de Witt
   April 12, 1950, Dordogne —

9. Vladimir, Count de Witt
   January 27, 1952, Dordogne —

10. Anne, Countess de Witt
    September 28, 1953, Dordogne —

XXIII. YOUSOUPOV 1, from page 323

Felix Felixovich, Prince Yousoupov, Count Soumarokov-Elston, only surviving son of Prince Felix.

March 11/23, 1887, St. Petersburg — September 27, 1967, Paris
m. February 9/22, 1914, St. Petersburg

* **Irina Aleksandrovna,** Princess of Russia, daughter of Grand Duke Aleksandr Mikhailovich of Russia, and of his wife, Grand Duchess Kseniya (Xenia) Aleksandrovna of Russia.

XXIII. Yousoupov 1 continued

July 3/15, 1895, St. Petersburg — February 26, 1970, Paris

Issue: 1. Irina Felixovna, Princess Yousoupov, Countess Soumarokova-Elston (1915–)
m. Nikolai Dimitriievich, Count Cheremetev (1904–)
see: *Cheremetev* XXIII, page 978

XXIII. ZOUBKOV 1, from page 51

Alexsandr Alexsandrovich Zoubkov, son of Aleksandr Anatolovich.
September 25, 1900, Icanovo, near Odessa, Ukraine — January 26, 1936, Berlin
m. November 9, 1927, Bonn

* **Viktoria,** Princess of Prussia, daughter of Friedrich III, German Emperor, King of Prussia, and of his wife, Princess Victoria, the Princess Royal of Great Britain and Ireland.
April 12, 1866, New Palace, Potsdam — November 13, 1929, Bonn
(She m. 1: Adolf, Prince of Schaumburg-Lippe – see: *Schaumburg-Lippe* XXI, page 818.)

No Issue.

XXIV

THE FAMILIES OF NORTH AND SOUTH AMERICA

XXIV. ANCRUM 1, from page 325

Calhoun Ancrum

April 28, 1915, , Philippine Islands —

m. June 17, 1945, London, England. Divorced: September 14, 1954, Massachusetts

* **Kseniya (Xenia) Andreievna,** Princess Romanova, daughter of Prince Andrei Aleksandrovich of Russia and of his first wife, Donna Elisabeth Ruffo (Duchess Elizabeta Fabrizievna Sasso-Ruffo).

March 10, 1919, Paris —

(She m. 2: Dr. Geoffrey Tooth – see: *Tooth*, page 534.)

No Issue.

XXIV. ARCELUS 1, from page 559

Victor Arcelus

February 20, 1935, Montevideo, Uruguay —

m. September 16, 1969, New York City

* **Donna Fiammetta Farace,** daughter of Nobile Ruggero, Marquis di Villaforesta, and of his wife, Princess Ekaterina Ivanovna of Russia.

February 19, 1940, Budapest, Hungary —

Issue:

XXIV. BEADLESTON 1, from page 330

William L. Beadleston

July 31, 1938, Long Branch, New Jersey —

m. January 8, 1967, Woodside, California

* **Marina Vassilievna,** Princess Romanova, daughter of Prince Vassili Aleksandrovich of Russia and of his wife, Princess Nataliya Aleksandrovna Galitzine.

May 22, 1940, San Francisco, California —

Issue: 1. Tatiana Beadleston

May 18, 1968, New York City —

2. Alexandra Beadleston

May 19, 1970, New York City —

XXIV. BERGER 1, from page 828

Richard Darrell Berger

February 14, 1941, Fremont, Ohio —

m. July 5, 1961, Fremont, Ohio

* **Calma Schnirring,** daughter of Max Schnirring and of his wife, Princess Caroline Mathilde of Saxe-Coburg and Gotha.

November 18, 1938, Valparaiso, Chile —

Issue: 1. Sascha Berger, September 22, 1961, Coburg, Germany —

2. Richard Berger, July 7, 1962, Fremont, Ohio —

3. Victor Berger, September 28, 1964, Groton, Massachusetts —

4. Samuel Clinton Berger, May 28, 1965, Fort Knox, Kentucky —

5. Wesley Berger, October 11, 1967, —

6. David Berger, September 25, 1968, —

XXIV. BOSCH 1, from page 929

Alberto Bosch

August 7, 1934, Buenos Aires, Argentina —

m. December 15, 1962, Buenos Aires

* **Marie Elisabeth (Elisalex) von Wuthenau-Hohenthurm,** daughter of Franz Ferdinand von Wuthenau-Hohenthurm and of his wife, Elinor Bromberg.

September 2, 1945, Buenos Aires —

Issue: 1. Bernadette Bosch
October 21, 1963, Buenos Aires —

2. Juan Alberto Bosch
December 30, 1964, Buenos Aires —

3. Francico Fernando Bosch
February 24, 1966, Buenos Aires —

XXIV. BRYAN

1, from page 156

Michael Kelly Bryan

, 1910, Memphis, Tennessee —

m. May 5, 1957, Pound Ridge, N.Y. Divorced: 1958,

* **Iris,** Lady Mountbatten, daughter of Prince Alexander of Battenberg, First Marquess of Carisbrooke, and of his wife, Lady Irene Denison.

January 13, 1920, London —

(She m. 1: and divorced: Hamilton Keyes O'Malley – see: *O'Malley* XVII, page 531.)

(She m. 3: and divorced: William Kemp – see: *Kemp* XXIV, page 1020.)

Issue: 1. Robin Alexander Bryan
December 20, 1957, New York City —

XXIV. CANNADAY

1, from page 1006

Robert Wythe Cannaday Jnr.

May 4, 1924, Spring Valley, Virginia —

m. November 18, 1950, New York City

* **Nina Arkadjevna Ougritchitch-Trebinskya,** daughter of Arkadj Konstantinovich Ougritchitch-Trebinsky and of his wife, Elena Georgeievna de Beauharnais, Duchess of Leuchtenberg.

January 15, 1925, Paris, France —

Issue: 1. Robert Wythe Cannaday III
December 23, 1953, Washington, D.C. —

2. Helene Nina Cannaday
August 20, 1960, Saigon, South Vietnam —

XXIV. DENSON

1, from page 709

William D. Denson

May 31, 1913, Birmingham, Alabama —

m. December 31, 1949, Mountain Laces, New Jersey

* **Constance,** Countess von Francken-Sierstorpff, daughter ot Count Hans-Clemens von Francken-Sierstorpff and of his wife, Princess Elisabeth (Lily) of Hohenlohe-Oehringen.

July 8, 1923, Zyrowa —

XXIV. Denson 1 continued

(She m. 1: and divorced: Hyacinth, Count Strachwitz von Gross-Zauche und Cammenitz - see: *Strachwitz von Gross-Zauche und Cammenitz* XXI, page 866.)

Issue: 1. **William Denson**
October 8, 1950, Bethesda, Maryland —

2. **Olivia Denson**
October 25, 1952, Bethesda —

XXIV. DUBÉ 1, from page 932

Richard Ernst Dubé

—

m. December 5, 1964, Westwood, New Jersey

★ **Gisela von Wuthenau-Hohenthurm,** daughter of Fedor von Wuthenau-Hohenthurm and of his wife, Countess Helga von Perponcher-Sedlnitzky.
December 30, 1929, Gross-Parschleben —

Issue:

XXIV. DE ELIA 1, from page 110

Don Maximo de Elia
, Buenos Aires, Argentina — , 1929, St. Jean de Luz, France

m. , 1913,

★ **Alexandrine,** Countess von Merenberg, daughter of Prince Nikolaus of Nassau-Weilburg and of his morganatic wife, Nataliya Aleksandrovna Pushkina, created Countess von Merenberg.
December 14, 1869, Wiesbaden — September 29, 1950, Buenos Aires

No Issue.

XXIV. EREÑÚ 1, from page 588

Don Juan Ereñú y Ferreira
January 27, 1908, Rosario de Santa Fé, Argentina — January 6, 1969, Palma de Mallorca.

★ **Dona Blanca Maria de las Nieves Orlandis y Habsburgo,** daughter of Don Ramon Orlandis y Villalonga and of his wife, Archduchess Maria Antonia of Austria.

XXIV. Ereñú

1 continued

September 7, 1926, Palma de Mallorca — December 18, 1969, Palma de Mallorca

Issue: 1. Don Joaquin Alfonso Ereñú y Orlandis
June 25, 1949, Buenos Aires —

2. Don Maria Antonia Ereñú y Orlandis
June 13, 1950, Buenos Aires —

3. Don Carlos Alberto Ereñú y Orlandis
September 8, 1951, Buenos Aires —

4. Dona Cristina Eugenia Ereñú y Orlandis
January 7, 1958, Buenos Aires —

5. Don Eugenio Ereñú y Orlandis
May 20, 1959, Buenos Aires —

XXIV. GROVE

1, from page 978

Brandon H. Grove
April 8, 1929, Chicago, Illinois —
m. November 1, 1959, London, England
* **Mary Nikitievna Cheremeteva,** daughter of Nikita Sergeievich Cheremetev and of his wife, Ekaterina Vandoro.
February 7, 1937, Athens, Greece —

Issue: 1. John Grove
March 4, 1963, Washington, D.C. —

2. Catherine Grove
March 21, 1964, New Delhi, India —

3. Paul Cheremetev Grove
May 17, 1965, Washington, D.C. —

XXIV. GRUNDLAND 1, from page 559

Alberto Grundland
July 12, 1931, Montevideo, Uruguay —
m. March 25, 1966, Montevideo
* **Donna Nicoletta Farace,** daughter of Nobile Ruggero, Marquis di Villaforesta, and of his wife, Princess Ekaterina Ivanovna of Russia.
July 23, 1938, Rome —

Issue: 1. Eduardo Alberto Grundland
January 15, 1967, Montevideo —

2. Alexandra Gabriella Grundland
September 17, 1971, Montevideo —

XXIV. HARRIS 1, from page 54

Clyde Kenneth Harris
April 18, 1918, Maud, Oklahoma — March 2, 1958, Amarillo, Texas
m. June 17, 1949, Burg Hohenzollern, Bavaria
* **Cecilie,** Princess of Prussia, daughter of Crown Prince Friedrich Wilhelm of Prussia and of his wife, Duchess Cecilie of Mecklenburg-Schwerin.
September 5, 1917, Cecilienhof Castle, Potsdam —

Issue: 1. Kira Harris
October 20, 1954, Amarillo, Texas —

XXIV. JONES 1, from page 990

Ralph Jones
—
m. January , 1960, Toronto, Ontario. Divorced:
* **Kseniya (Xenia) Gourievna Kulikovskya,** daughter of Gouri Nikolaievich Kulikovsky and of his wife, Ruth Schwartz.
June 29, 1941, Ballerup, Denmark —
(She m. 2: in Copenhagen and has a daughter – Vivian.)

Issue: 1. Paul Jones
November , 1960, Ottawa, Canada —

XXIV. JUD

1, from page 323

Herman Jud

February 14, 1911, Hicksville, Long Island, N.Y. —

m. August 10, 1946, Glen Cove, Long Island, N.Y.

* **Kseniya Georgeievna,** Princess of Russia, daughter of Grand Duke Georgii Mikhailovich of Russia and of his wife, Princess Maria of Greece and Denmark.

August 8/22, 1903, Mikhailovskoye, near Peterhof, Russia — September 17, 1965, Glen Cove, Long Island, N.Y.

(She m. 1: and divorced: William Bateman Leeds – see: *Leeds* XXIV, below.)

No Issue.

XXIV. KEMP

1, from page 156

William Kemp

, 1921, —

m. December 17, 1965, Toronto, Ontario, Canada. Divorced: 1966, Toronto

* **Iris,** Lady Mountbatten, daughter of Prince Alexander of Battenberg, First Marquess of Carisbrook, and of his wife, Lady Irene Denison.

January 13, 1920, London —

(She m. 1: and divorced: Hamilton Keyes O'Malley – see: *O'Malley* XVII, page 531.)

(She m. 2: and divorced: Michael Kelly Bryan – see: *Bryan* XXIV, page 1016.)

No Issue.

XXIV. LEEDS

1, from page 323

William Bateman Leeds, Junior, son of William B. Leeds.

September 19, 1902, New York City —

m. 1: October 9, 1921, Paris. Divorced: March 19, 1930, New York City

* **Kseniya (Xenia) Georgeievna,** Princess of Russia, daughter of Grand Duke Georgii Mikailovich of Russia and of his wife, Princess Maria of Greece and Denmark.

August 9, 1903, Mikhailovskoye, near Peterhof, Russia — September 17, 1965, Glen Cove, Long Island, N.Y.

XXIV. Leeds 1 continued

(She m. 2: Herman Jud – see: *Jud* XXIV, page 1020.)
m. 2: May 23, 1936, Miami, Florida
Olive Hamilton, daughter of
September 24, 1908, Duquesne, Pennsylvania —

Issue of first marriage:
1. Nancy Leeds (1925–)
m. Edward Judson Wynkoop (1917–)
see: *Wynkoop* XXIV, page 1025

XXIV. LOCKETT DE LOAYZA 1, from page 471

Juan Bradstock Edgart Lockett de Loayza
March 30, 1912, Lima, Peru —
m. February 12, 1949, Lima
* **Hilda,** Princess of Bavaria, daughter of Crown Prince Rupprecht of Bavaria and of his second wife, Princess Antonia of Luxemburg.
May 24, 1926, Berchtesgaden —

Issue: 1. Christopher Lockett von Wittelsbach
April 9, 1950, Lima —

2. Bradstock Lockett von Wittelsbach
May 3, 1953, Lima —

3. Alexander Lockett von Wittelsbach
April 11, 1958, Rosswies, Germany —

4. Marie Isabel Lockett von Wittelsbach
July 5, 1960, Rosswies —

XXIV. NEWBURGH 1, from page 996

Ronald Gerald Newburgh
February 21, 1926, Boston —
m. June 25, 1957, Brookline, Massachusetts
* **Olga Sergeievna de Beauharnais,** Duchess of Leuchtenberg, daughter of Sergei Nikolaievich de Beauharnais, Duke of Leuchtenberg, and of his wife, Anna Aleksandrovna Naumova.
June 25, 1931, Bois-Colombes, near Paris —

XXIV. Newburgh

1 continued

Issue: 1. George Alexander de Beauharnais Newburgh
January 24, 1958, Boston —

2. Stephanie Anne de Beauharnais Newburgh
January 21, 1960, Boston —

XXIV. OXENBURG

1, from page 631

Howard Oxenburg

, 1920, —

m. May 11, 1960, , Florida. Divorced: 1966,

* **Elisabeth,** Princess of Yugoslavia, daughter of Prince Paul of Yugoslavia and of his wife, Princess Olga of Greece and Denmark.

April 7, 1936, Belgrade, Yugoslavia —

(She m. 2: Neil Balfour – see: *Balfour* XVII, page 515.)

Issue: 1. Catherine Oxenburg
September 22, 1961, New York City —

2. Christina Oxenburg
December 7, 1962, New York City —

XXIV. DE PASQUALE

1, from page 995

Joseph de Pasquale

October 14, 1919, Philadelphia, Pennsylvania —

m. August 7, 1949, Lennox, Massachusetts

* **Maria Magdalene Sergeievna de Beauharnais,** Duchess of Leuchtenberg, daughter of Sergei Nikolaievich de Beauharnais, Duke of Leuchtenberg, and of his first wife, Anna Aleksandrovna Naumova.

September 1, 1926, Nice, France —

Issue: 1. Marie Alexandra de Pasquale
August 6, 1950, Pittsfield, Massachusetts —

2. Elisabeth de Pasquale
January 16, 1952, Boston —

3. Joseph Serge de Pasquale
July 3, 1956, Pittsfield —

XXIV. de Pasquale 1 continued

4. Charles Nicholas de Pasquale
December 19, 1957, Boston —

XXIV. PATTERSON 1, from page 58

Kirby Williams Patterson
July 24, 1907, Springfield, Missouri —
m. September 26, 1946, Springfield. Divorced: 1962, Washington, D.C.
* **Viktoria Marina,** Princess of Prussia, Countess Lingen, daughter of Prince Adalbert of Prussia, Count Lingen, and of his wife, Princess Adelheid of Saxe-Meiningen, Duchess of Saxony.
September 11, 1917, Kiel —

Issue: 1. Marina-Adelaide Patterson (twin)
August 21, 1948, Springfield, Missouri —

2. Berengar-Orin Patterson (twin)
August 21, 1948, Springfield —

3. Dohna-Maria Patterson
August 7, 1954, Springfield —

XXIV. SAINT 1, from page 464

Harry Saint
—
m.
* **Dona Gerarda de Orleans-Borbon y Parodi Delfino,** daughter of Don Alvaro, Infante de Orleans y Borbon, and of his wife, Carla Parodi di Delfino.
August 25, 1939, Rome —

Issue: 1. Carla Saint
May 22, 1967, New York City —

2. Marco Saint
March 20, 1969, New York City —

XXIV. SOTOMAYOR-LUNA

1, from page 439

Manoel Sotomayor-Luna, one-time Vice-President of Ecuador.
November 27, 1884, Quito, Ecuador — October 16, 1949, Guayaquil, Ecuador.
m. March 3, 1948, Rome
* **Marie Christine,** Princess of Bourbon-Sicily, daughter of Prince Ferdinand of Bourbon-Sicily, Duke of Calabria and of his wife, Princess Maria of Bavaria.
May 4, 1899, Madrid —

No Issue.

XXIV. STOUT

1, from page 996

Robert Bayard Stout
April 24, 1931, —
m. December 15, 1954, Boston
* **Anna Sergeievna de Beauharnais,** Duchess of Leuchtenberg, daughter of Sergei Nikolaievich de Beauharnais von Leuchtenberg, formerly Duke of Leuchtenberg, and of his first wife, Anna Aleksandrovna Naumova.
February 2, 1928, Nice, France —

Issue: 1. Eugene de Beauharnais Stout
April 12, 1957, Long Island, N.Y. —

XXIV. SUCRE

1, from page 371

Luis Perez Sucre
— , 195 , Porte Alegre, Brazil
m. , 1912, Montevideo, Uruguay
* **Maria Antonia,** Archduchess of Austria, daughter of Archduke Leopold Salvator of Austria and of his wife, Princess Blanka of Castile, Princess of Bourbon.
July 13, 1899, Agram —
(She m. 1: Ramon Orlandis y Villalonga – see: *Orlandis* XVIII, page 588.)

No Issue.

XXIV. WHITTEN 1, from page 845

Richard C. B. Whitten

May 9, 1910, Indianapolis, Indiana —

m. November 16, 1947, Steinwald

★ **Viktoria Luise,** Countess zu Solms-Baruth, daughter of Count Hans zu Solms-Baruth and of his wife, Princess Caroline of Schleswig-Holstein-Sonderburg-Glücksburg.

March 31, 1921, Cassel —

(She m. 1: and divorced: Friedrich Josias, Prince of Saxe-Coburg and Gotha – see: *Saxe-Coburg and Gotha* I k–1, page 25.)

Issue: 1. Victoria Whitten

August 23, 1948, Wayland, Missouri —

XXIV. WILSON 1, from page 310

John C. Wilson

, 1899, — October , 1961, New York City

m. 1937,

★ **Nataliya Pavlovna,** Princess Paleya, daughter of Grand Duke Pavel Aleksandrovich of Russia and of his second wife, Olga Valerianovna Karnovitch, created Princess Paleya.

November 22/December 5, 1905, Paris —

(She m. 1: and divorced: Lucien Lelong – see: *Lelong* XVIII, page 569.)

No Issue.

XXIV. WYNKOOP 1, from page 1020

Edward Judson Wynkoop

May 23, 1917, Syracuse, N.Y. —

m. December 22, 1945, Glen Cove, Long Island

★ **Nancy Leeds,** daughter of William Bateman Leeds, and of his first wife, Princess Kseniya (Xenia) Georgeievna of Russia.

February 4, 1925, New York City —

Issue: 1. Alexandra Wynkoop

March 30, 1959, Stamford, Connecticut —

ADDENDUM

The names in this Addendum are all included in the indexes

XVIII. DEBIÈVRE from page 1031

Guy Debièvre
July 21, 1931, Lille, France —
m. April 26, 1960,
* **Marie Caroline,** Countess Lexa von Aehrenthal, daughter of Count Johann Lexa von Aehrenthal and of his wife, Countess Ernestine von Harrach zu Rohrau und Thannhausen.
December 24, 1935, Prague, Czechoslovakia —

Issue: 1. Francoise Debièvre
November 16, 1960, Chatoux, France —

2. Jean-Luc Debièvre
January 23, 1962, Haubourdin, France —

XXI. VON AUERSPERG 1, from page 845

Karl Adolf, 10th Fürst von Auersperg, son of Count Adolf.
March 13, 1915, Goldegg —
m. 1: February 3, 1937, Vienna
Margit, Countess Batthyány von Német-Ujvár, daughter of Count Ladislaus Batthyány von Német-Ujvár and of his wife, Countess Marie Therese von Coreth zu Coredo und Starkenberg.
April 18, 1914, Köpscény, Hungary — January 22, 1959, in a road accident near Paysandú, Uruguay
m. 2: October 6, 1961, Vienna
* **Feodore,** Countess zu Solms-Baruth, daughter of Count Friedrich, 3rd Fürst zu Solms-Baruth, and of his wife, Princess Adelheid of Schleswig-Holstein-Sonderburg-Glücksburg.
April 5, 1920, Baruth —
(She m. 1: Dr. Gert Schenk – see: *Schenk* XXI, page 823.)
NOTE: There were four children of the first marriage, not descendants of George I: Adolf, Ferdinand, Gabrielle, and Johanna.

Issue of second marriage:
5. Karoline Mathilde, Countess von Auersperg, May 24, 1962, Montevideo, Uruguay —

6. Alexander, Count von Auersperg, September 8, 1963, Montevideo —

7. Margarita, Countess von Auersperg, February 2, 1966, Montevideo —

8. Mercedes, Countess von Auersperg, August 10, 1968, Montevideo —

XXI. VON KESSELSTATT 1, from page 1035

Eugen, Count von Kesselstatt
June 10, 1870, Gleichenberg — November 10, 1933, Grundlsee, Austria
m. April 20, 1892, Abbazia
* **Margareta,** Countess Széchényi von Sárvár-Felsövidék, daughter of Count Gyula Széchényi von Sárvár-Felsövidék and of his wife, Countess Karoline von Zichy-Ferraris zu Zich und Vásony-keö.
May 27, 1866, Marczali, Hungary — February 17, 1915, Kesselstatt

Issue: 1. Caroline, Countess von Kesselstatt (1893–)
m. Joseph, Count von Spee (1876–1941) - see: *von Spee* XXI, 1, page 1032

2. Franz de Paul, Count von Kesselstatt (1894–1938)
m. Gabrielle, Princess of Liechtenstein (1905–) - see: *von Kesselstatt* XXI, 2, below

3. Elisabeth, Countess von Kesselstatt, June 1, 1896, Kesselstatt —

4. Franziska, Countess von Kesselstatt (1898–1949)
m. Hanns Günther von Obernitz (1899–1944) - see: *von Obernitz* XXI, page 1040

5. Marguerite Andrea, Countess von Kesselstatt, March 24, 1900, Kesselstatt —

6. Johannes, Count von Kesselstatt (1902–1963)
m. 1: Ferdinanda-Johanna, Countess von Hahn (1902–1944)
m. 2: Alexandra Elisabeth, Countess von Schmettow (1914–) - see: *von Kesselstatt* XXI, 4, page 1028

7. Georg, Count von Kesselstatt (1905–)
m. Adelma, Baroness Vay de Vaja (1932–) - see: *von Kesselstatt* XXI, 6, page 1030

XXI. von Kesselstatt 2, from above

* **Franz de Paul,** Count von Kesselstatt, eldest son of Count Eugen.
July 17, 1894, Grundlsee — September 2, 1938, Darmstadt
m. June 23, 1925, Vienna
Gabrielle, Princess of Liechtenstein, daughter of Prince Eduard of Liechtenstein and of his wife, Countess Olga von Pückler und Limpurg.
May 2, 1905, Vienna —
(She m. 2: October 10, 1951, Föhren Castle, near Trier, Harrison Day Blair, born November 18, 1901, Sterling, Colorado.

XXI. von Kesselstatt — 2 continued

Issue: 1. Franz Eugen, Count von Kesselstatt (1926–)
m. Louisette von Laveran-Stieber von Hinzberg (1926–)
see: *von Kesselstatt* XXI, 3, below

2. Johannes, Count von Kesselstatt
May 21, 1927, Kesselstatt —

XXI. von Kesselstatt — 3, from above

* **Franz Eugen,** Count von Kesselstatt, only son of Count Franz de Paula.
May 1, 1926, Kesselstatt —
m. October 27, 1953, St. Peter-Freienstein
Louisette von Laveran-Stieber von Hinzberg, daughter of
January 12, 1926, St. Peter-Freienstein —

Issue: 1. Gabrielle, Count von Kesselstatt, November 1, 1954, Trier —

2. Rudolf, Count von Kesselstatt, January 31, 1956, Trier —

3. Georg, Count von Kesselstatt, January 26, 1957, Trier —

4. Clemens, Count von Kesselstatt, June 7, 1959, Trier —

5. Franz, Count von Kesselstatt, May 26, 1961, Trier —

6. Theresa, Countess von Kesselstatt, February 28, 1964, Trier —

XXI. von Kesselstatt — 4, from page 1027

* **Johannes,** Count von Kesselstatt, second son of Count Eugen.
April 16, 1902, Grundlsee — January 9, 1963, Berenbach, Germany
m. 1: January 3, 1929, Kesselstatt
Ferdinanda-Johanna, Countess von Hahn, daughter of Count Ferdinand.
July 1, 1902, Arenfels — April 22, 1944, Logenburg, Germany
m. 2: June 28, 1945, Logenburg
Alexandra, Countess von Schmettow, daughter of Count Lazarus.
June 28, 1914, Potsdam —

XXI. von Kesselstatt 4 continued

Issue of first marriage:

1. Ferdinand, Count von Kesselstatt (1930–)
   m. Hella White (1937–)
   see: *von Kesselstatt* XXI, 5, below

2. Alice-Eugenia, Countess von Kesselstatt (1932–)
   m. Rolf Alfred Wirtz (1939–)
   see: *Wirtz* XXI, page 1040

3. Eugen, Count von Kesselstatt
   February 23, 1935, Bad Godesberg — April 22, 1944, Logenburg. (He died the same day as his mother.)

4. Franz-Edmund, Count von Kesselstatt
   April 6, 1936, Bad Godesberg — April 22, 1944, Logenburg. (He died the same day as his mother and his brother.)

XXI. von Kesselstatt 5, from above

* **Ferdinand,** Count von Kesselstatt, eldest son of Count Johannes.
December 16, 1930, Bonn —
m. August 2, 1958, Kiedrich
Hella White, daughter of Rudolf White and of his wife,
August 22, 1937, Eltville (State unknown), USA —

Issue:

1. Aiga Alice, Countess von Kesselstatt
   March 7, 1959, Wiesbaden —

2. Maximilian, Count von Kesselstatt
   July 14, 1961, Wiesbaden —

3. Johannes, Count von Kesselstatt
   February 9, 1964, Wiesbaden —

4. Isabella, Countess von Kesselstatt
   August 2, 1965, Eltville —

XXI. von Kesselstatt 6, from page 1027

* **Georg,** Count von Kesselstatt, third son of Count Eugen.
June 5, 1905, Kesselstatt —
m. November 5, 1955, Buenos Aires, Argentina
Adelma, Baroness Vay de Vaja, daughter of Baron Ladislas Vay de Vaja and of his wife,
May 11, 1932, Debreczen, Hungary —

No Issue.

XXI. LEXA VON AEHRENTHAL 1, from page 1036

Aloys, Count Lexa von Aehrenthal
September 27, 1854, Gross-Skal — February 17, 1912, Vienna
m. July 22, 1902, Vienna
* **Pauline,** Countess Széchényi von Sárvár-Felsövidék, daughter of Count Gyula Széchényi von Sárvár-Felsövidék and of his wife, Countess Karoline Zichy-Ferraris zu Zich und Vásonykeö.
November 25, 1871, Vienna — August 14, 1945, Doxan, Czechoslovakia

Issue: 1. Caroline, Countess Lexa von Aehrenthal
September 13, 1904, St. Petersburg, Russia —

2. Johann, Count Lexa von Aehrenthal (1905–)
m. Ernestine, Countess von Harrach zu Rohrau und Thannhausen (1903–)
see: *Lexa von Aehrenthal* XXI, 2, below

3. Elisabeth, Countess Lexa von Aehrenthal (1909–)
m. Josef, Count von Thun und Hohenstein (1907–)
see: *von Thun und Hohenstein* XXI, page 1039

XXI. Lexa von Aehrenthal 2, from above

* **Johann,** Count Lexa von Aehrenthal, eldest son of Count Aloys.
August 9, 1905, Tsarskoye-Selo, Russia —
m. November 7, 1932, Vienna
Ernestine, Countess von Harrach zu Rohrau und Thannhausen, daughter of Count Otto von Harrach zu Rohrau und Thannhausen and of his wife, Princess Karoline zu Oettingen-Oettingen und Oettingen-Wallerstein.
August 11, 1903, Rohrau —

XXI. Lexa von Aehrenthal 2 continued

Issue: 1. Johann Aloys, Count Lexa von Aehrenthal (1933–)
m. Alice, Baroness von Warsberg (1936–)
see: *Lexa von Aehrenthal* XXI, 3, below

2. Marie Caroline, Countess Lexa von Aehrenthal (1935–)
m. Guy Debièvre (1931–)
see: *Debièvre* XVIII, page 1026

3. Marie Pauline, Countess Lexa von Aehrenthal
February 17, 1941, Prague, Czechoslovakia —

XXI. Lexa von Aehrenthal 3, from above

* **Johann Aloys,** Count Lexa von Aehrenthal, only son of Count Johann.
November 28, 1933, Prague —
m. August 4, 1963, Pörtschach
Alice, Baroness von Warsberg, daughter of Baron Oscar von Warsberg and of his wife,
July 7, 1936, Zagrab —

Issue:

XXI. LOBKOWICZ from page 1038

Ottokar, Fürst von Lobkowicz
January 28, 1922, Prague —
m. October 7, 1954, Grundlsee
* **Susanna Marie,** Countess Széchényi von Sárvár-Felsövidék, daughter of Count János Széchényi von Sárvár-Felsövidék and of his wife, Countess Juliane Széchényi von Sárvár-Felsövidék.
December 10, 1932, Vienna —

Issue: 1. Georg, Prince Lobkowicz (twin)
April 23, 1956, Zürich, Switzerland —

2. Anton, Prince Lobkowicz (twin)
April 23, 1956, Zürich, Switzerland —

3. Elisabeth, Princess Lobkowicz
April 3, 1959, Bad Ausee, Austria —

XXI. SEMSEY DE SEMSE from page 1037

Tomas, Count Semsey de Semse
November 28, 1926, Rome —
m. July 31, 1957, Buenos Aires, Argentina
* **Gabrielle,** Countess Széchényi von Sárvár-Felsövidék, daughter of Count Endre Széchényi von Sárvár-Felsövidék and of his wife, Countess Ella Somssich de Sáard.
July 18, 1936, Budapest, Hungary —

Issue: 1. Julia, Countess Semsey de Semse
April 19, 1964, Buenos Aires, Argentina —

2. Andras, Count Semsey de Semse
December 10, 1966, Buenos Aires, Argentina —

XXI. VON SPEE 1, from page 1027

Joseph, Count von Spee
April 18, 1876, Düsseldorf — November 10, 1941, Bonn
m. January 14, 1920, Heckenmünster
* **Caroline,** Countess von Kesselstatt, daughter of Count Eugen von Kesselstatt and of his wife, Countess Margareta Széchényi von Sárvár-Felsövidék.
July 17, 1893, Grundlsee —

Issue: 1. Joseph Eugen, Count von Spee (1920–1945)
m. Edith von Kleinmayr (1925–)
see: *von Spee* XXI, 2, page 1033

2. Antonia, Countess von Spee (1922–)
m. Egon, Baron von Wendt (1917–)
see: *von Wendt* XXI, page 1039

3. Franz Wilhelm, Count von Spee (1923–)
m. 1: Anna Maria, Countess Henckel, Baroness von Donnersmarck (1928–1954)
m. 2: Marie Charlotte, Baroness von Mylius (1929–)
see: *von Spee* XXI, 3, page 1033

4. Maximilian, Count von Spee (1924–)
m. Marie-Elisabeth, Countess von Ballestrom (1933–)
see: *von Spee* XXI, 4, page 1034

XXI. von Spee 1 continued

5. Degenhardt-Wilderich, Count von Spee (1926–)
m. Brigitta, Countess von Westphalen zu Fürstenberg (1925–)
see: *von Spee* XXI, 5, page 1034

6. Georg, Count von Spee (1929–)
m. Maria Zitz, Baroness von Pereira-Arnstein (1928–)
see: *von Spee* XXI, 6, page 1035

XXI. von Spee 2, from page 1032

* **Joseph Eugen,** Count von Spee, eldest son of Count Joseph.
October 19, 1920, Schleiden — February 17, 1945, Leeuwarden, The Netherlands
m. September 16, 1943, Klagenfurt, Austria
Edith von Kleinmayr, daughter of
February 28, 1925, Klagenfurt —

No Issue.

XXI. von Spee 3, from page 1032

* **Franz Wilhelm,** Count von Spee, second son of Count Joseph.
March 14, 1923, Schleiden —
m. 1: August 6, 1953, Stepperg
Anna Maria, Countess Henckel, Baroness von Donnersmarck, daughter of Count Georg Henckel, Baron von Donnersmarck, and of his wife, Countess Sophie von Waldburg zu Wolfegg und Waldsee.
December 14, 1928, Grambschutz — November 12, 1954, Burg Maubach
m. 2: June 4, 1956, Kirchberg
Marie Charlotte, Baroness von Mylius, daughter of
February 9, 1929, Kophof —

Issue of first marriage:
1. Pia, Countess von Spee
July 17, 1954, Burg Maubach —

Issue of second marriage:
2. Brigida, Countess von Spee
May 28, 1957, Burg Maubach —

XXI. von Spee 3 continued

3. Mariano, Count von Spee
July 23, 1958, Burg Maubach —

4. Johannes, Count von Spee
January 4, 1960, Burg Maubach —

5. Wilderich, Count von Spee
April 16, 1964, Burg Maubach —

6. Peter, Count von Spee
November 13, 1966, Burg Maubach —

XXI. von Spee 4, from page 1032

* **Maximilian,** Count von Spee, third son of Count Joseph.
August 28, 1924, Schleiden —
m. December 28, 1955, Düren
Marie-Elisabeth, Countess von Ballestrom, daughter of Count Franz Georg.
March 17, 1933, Breslau —

Issue: 1. Jan Seger, Count von Spee
December 15, 1956, Bremen —

2. Per-Degenhardt, Count von Spee
October 24, 1958, Emden —

3. Juliane-Hedwig, Count von Spee
March 11, 1960, Emden —

4. Monika Antonia, Countess von Spee
August 28, 1963, Emden —

5. Franz Hilarius, Count von Spee
January 15, 1965, Emden —

XXI. von Spee 5, from page 1033

* **Degenhardt-Wilderich,** Count von Spee, fourth son of Count Joseph.
November 1, 1926, Schleiden —

XXI. von Spee 5 continued

m. July 3, 1956, Fürstenberg
Brigitta, Countess von Westphalen zu Fürstenberg, daughter of Count Friedrich von Westphalen zu Fürstenberg and of his wife,
September 26, 1925, Fürstenberg —

No Issue.

XXI. von Spee 6, from page 1033

***Georg,** Count von Spee, fifth son of Count Joseph.
March 10, 1929, Schleiden —
m. February 11, 1966, Düsseldorf
Maria Zita, Baroness von Pereira-Arnstein, daughter of Baron Ferdinand.
November 12, 1928, Rotterdam, The Netherlands —

Issue:

XXI. SZÉCHÉNYI VON SÁRVÁR-FELSÖVIDÉK 1, from page 941

Gyula, Count Széchényi von Sárvár-Felsövidék
November 11, 1829, Vienna — January 13, 1921, Budapest, Hungary
m. July 6, 1863, Oroszvár, Hungary
* **Karoline,** Countess von Zichy-Ferraris zu Zich und Vásonykeö, daughter of Count Felix von Zichy-Ferraris zu Zich und Vásonykeö and of his wife, Countess Emilie von Reichenbach-Lessonitz.
October 13, 1845, Guns — December 25, 1871, Vienna

Issue: 1. Andor Pál, Count Széchényi von Sárvár-Felsövidék (1864–1943)
m. 1: Andrea, Countess Csekonics von Zsombolya und Janova (1870–1913)
m. 2: Maria, Baroness Szegedy-Ensch von Mezö-Szeged (1897–)
see: *Széchényi von Sárvár-Felsövidék* XXI, 2, page 1036

2. Margareta, Countess Széchényi von Sárvár-Felsövidék (1866–1915)
m. Eugen, Count von Kesselstatt (1870–1933)
see: *von Kesselstatt,* XXI, 1, page 1027

XXI. Széchényi von Sárvár-Felsövidék 1 continued

3. Karoline, Countess Széchényi von Sárvár-Felsövidék (1869–1932)
m. Simon, Count von Wimpffen (1867–1925)
see: *von Wimpffen* XXI, page 1040

4. Pauline, Countess Széchényi von Sárvár-Felsövidék (1871–1945)
m. Aloys, Count Lexa von Aehrenthal (1954–1912)
see: *Lexa von Aehrenthal* XXI, 1, page 1030

XXI. Széchényi von Sárvár-Felsövidék 2, from page 1035

* **Andor Pál,** Count Széchényi von Sárvár-Felsövidék, eldest son of Count Gyula.
June 13, 1864, Oroszvár, Hungary — April 13, 1943, Marczali, Hungary
m. 1: October 13, 1894, Zsombolya, Hungary
Andrea, Countess Csekonics von Zsombolya und Janova, daughter of Count Andreas.
December 27, 1870, Budapest — June 20, 1913, Vienna
m. 2: March 25, 1925, Marczali, Hungary
Maria, Baroness Szegedy-Ensch von Mezö-Szeged, daughter of Baron Alexander.
April 21, 1897, Inke, Hungary —

Issue of first marriage:

1. Joseph, Count Széchényi von Sárvár-Felsövidék (1897–)
m. Hedwig Mórgo-Mórgowska (1919–)
see: *Széchényi von Sárvár-Felsövidék* XXI, 3, page 1037

2. Juliana, Countess Széchényi von Sárvár-Felsövidék (1900–)
m. Janos, Count Széchényi von Sárvár-Felsövidék (1897–)
see: *Széchényi von Sárvár-Felsövidék* XXI, 5, page 1037

3. Endre, Count Széchényi von Sárvár-Felsövidék (1902–)
m. Ella, Countess Somssich de Sáard (1907–)
see: *Széchényi von Sárvár-Felsövidék* XXI, 4, page 1037

XXI. Széchényi von Sárvár-Felsövidék 3, from page 1036

★ **Joseph,** Count Széchényi von Sárvár-Felsövidék, eldest son of Count Andor Pál.
February 26, 1897, Marczali, Hungary —
m. June 2, 1945, Lublin, Poland
Hedwig Mórgo-Mórgowska, daughter of Florian Mórgo-Mórgowski.
February 17, 1919, Zdoldonow, Poland —

Issue: 1. Maria Andrea, Countess Széchényi von Sárvár-Felsövidék
July 20, 1946, Lublin, Poland —

2. Beata Andrea, Countess Széchényi von Sárvár-Felsövidék
March 14, 1948, Lublin —

3. Joseph, Count Széchényi von Sárvár-Felsövidék
February 15, 1958, Innsbruck, Austria —

XXI. Széchényi von Sárvár-Felsövidék 4, from page 1036

★ **Endre,** Count Széchényi von Sárvár-Felsövidék, second son of Count Andor Pál.
April 29, 1902, Marczali, Hungary —
m. June 2, 1932, Budapest
Ella, Countess Somssich de Sáard, daughter of Count Anton Somssich de Sáard.
January 12, 1907, Ormand, Hungary —

Issue: 1. Gabrielle, Countess Széchényi von Sárvár-Felsövidék (1936–)
m. Tomas, Count Semsey de Semse (1926–)
see: *Semsey de Semse* XXI, page 1032

XXI. Széchényi von Sárvár-Felsövidék 5, from page 1036

János, Count Széchényi von Sárvár-Felsövidék
August 7, 1897, Linz, Austria —
m. January 15, 1931, Budapest, Hungary
★ **Juliana,** Countess Széchényi von Sárvár-Felsövidék, daughter of Count Andor Pál Széchényi von Sárvár-Felsövidék and of his wife, Countess Andrea Csekonics von Zsombolya und Janova.
December 6, 1900, Marczali, Hungary —

XXI. Széchényi von Sárvár-Felsövidék 5 continued

Issue: 1. Andrea Maria, Countess Széchényi von Sárvár-Felsövidék (1931–)
m. Michael Somerville-Winters (1926–)
see: *Somerville-Winters* XXIV, page 1041

2. Susanna Maria, Countess Széchényi von Sárvár-Felsövidék (1932–)
m. Ottokar, Fürst von Lobkowicz (1922–)
see: *von Lobkowicz* XXI, page 1031

3. Janos-Peter, Count Széchényi von Sárvár-Felsövidék (1934–)
m. Adrienne Anders (1941–)
see: *Széchényi von Sárvár-Felsövidék* XXI, 6, below

4. Maria Alice, Countess Széchényi von Sárvár-Felsövidék
July 29, 1938, Budapest —

5. István (Stephen), Count Széchényi von Sárvár-Felsövidék (1941–)
m. Ursula Kneght (1937–)
see: *Széchényi von Sárvár-Felsövidék* XXI, 7, page 1039

XXI. Széchényi von Sárvár-Felsövidék 6, from above

* **Janos-Peter,** Count Széchényi von Sárvár-Felsövidék, eldest son of Count János.
July 31, 1934, Vienna —
m. October 10, 1959, Absam, Austria
Adrienne Anders, daughter of Karl Anders and of his wife,
October 7, 1941, Budapest, Hungary —

Issue: 1. Judith, Countess Széchényi von Sárvár-Felsövidék
November 27, 1961, Zürich, Switzerland —

2. Ferdinand, Count Széchényi von Sárvár-Felsövidék
January 20, 1962, Vienna —

3. Denes-Philipp, Count Széchényi von Sárvár-Felsövidék
May 7, 1963, Baden, near Vienna —

XXI. Széchényi von Sárvár-Felsövidék 7, from page 1038

⋆ **István,** Count Széchényi von Sárvár-Felsövidék, third son of Count János.
September 25, 1941, Szombathely, Hungary —
m. April 6, 1966, St. Galen, Switzerland
Ursula Kneght, daughter of Johann Kneght and of his wife,
July 23, 1937, St. Galen —

Issue:

XXI. VON THUN UND HOHENSTEIN from page 1030

Josef, Count von Thun und Hohenstein
December 31, 1907, Prague, Czechoslovakia —
m. January 3, 1943, Prague
⋆ **Elisabeth,** Countess Lexa von Aehrenthal, daughter of Count Aloys Lexa von Aehrenthal and of his wife, Countess Pauline Széchényi von Sárvár-Felsövidék.
August 9, 1908, Hietzing, Austria —

No Issue.

XXI. VON WENDT from page 1032

Egon, Baron von Wendt
October 16, 1917, Hermeskeil —
m. May 20, 1943, Bengen/Rhine
⋆ **Antonia,** Countess von Spee, daughter of Count Joseph von Spee and of his wife, Countess Caroline von Kesselstatt.
February 14, 1922, Schleiden —

Issue: 1. Franz Egon, Baron von Wendt
March 6, 1944, Burg Maubach —

2. Maximilian, Baron von Wendt
March 17, 1945, Schellenstein —

3. Clemens, Baron von Wendt
August 14, 1946, Schellenstein —

4. Marie Agnes, Baroness von Wendt
September 25, 1948, Schellenstein —

XXI. von Wendt

continued

5. Karl, Baron von Wendt
May 10, 1951, Wuppertal-Elberfeld —

XXI. VON WIMPFFEN

from page 1036

Simon, Count von Wimpffen
August 21, 1867, Böslau, Austria — April 11, 1925, Vienna
m. May 30, 1890,
* **Karoline,** Countess Széchényi von Sárvár-Felsövidék, daughter of Count Gyula Széchényi von Sárvár-Felsövidék and of his wife, Countess Karoline von Zichy-Ferraris zu Zich und Vásonykeö.
March 8, 1869, — April 27, 1932, Pechtoldsdorf, Austria

No Issue.

XXI. WIRTZ

from page 1029

Rolf Alfred Wirtz
April 25, 1939, Cologne, Germany —
m. April 25, 1966, Mettlach
* **Alice-Eugenia,** Countess von Kesselstatt, daughter of Count Johannes von Kesselstatt and of his wife, Countess Ferdinanda-Johanna von Hahn.
May 4, 1932, Bad Godesberg —

Issue:

XXI. VON OBERNITZ

from page 1027

Hanns Günther von Obernitz
May 5, 1899, Düsseldorf, Germany — January 14, 1944, Bromberg
m. November 15, 1935, Nürnberg
* **Franziska,** Countess von Kesselstatt, daughter of Count Eugen von Kesselstatt and of his wife, Countess Margareta Széchényi von Sárvár-Felsövidék.
October 3, 1898, Grundlsee — August 21, 1949, Königswinter

No Issue.

XXIV. SOMERVILLE-WINTERS from page 1038

Michael Somerville-Winters
June 17, 1926, Shanghai, China —
m. December 23, 1955, Austin, Texas, USA
* **Andrea Maria,** Countess Széchényi von Sárvár-Felsövidék, daughter of Count János Széchényi von Sárvár-Felsövidék and of his wife, Countess Juliana Széchényi von Sárvár-Felsövidék.
November 3, 1931, Vienna —

Issue: 1. Anne Somerville-Winters
February 20, 1957, Port Arthur, Texas —

2. Elizabeth Somerville-Winters
April 17, 1958, Port Arthur, Texas —

3. Adrienne Somerville-Winters
November 6, 1959, Port Arthur, Texas —

4. Andrew Somerville-Winters
April 6, 1961, Parkersburg, West Virginia —

5. Brian Somerville-Winters
September 4, 1963, Wilmington, Delaware —

VI. VON SCHENCK 1, from page 226

Dedo von Schenck
February 11, 1853, Mansfeld Castle — April 28, 1918, Wiesbaden
m. October 2, 1884, Berlin
* **Helene von Wardenberg,** daughter of Prince Friedrich of Württemberg and of his morganatic wife, Marie Bethge.
April 18, 1865, Berlin — September 25, 1938, Potsdam

Issue: 1. Albrecht von Schenck
September 20, 1885, — June 10, 1888, Göttingen

2. Eberhard von Schenck (1887–)
m. Irmgard Ecker (1895–)
see: *von Schenck,* 2, below

3. Freda von Schenck (1890–1946)
m. 1: and divorced: Kurt, Baron von Reibnitz (1877–1937)
see: *von Reibnitz,* page 1085
m. 2: Werner, Count von der Schulenburg (1886–1945)
see: *von der Schulenburg,* page 1071

4. Dedo von Schenck
July 23, 1892, — August 15, 1892, Berlin

VI. von Schenck 2, from above

* **Eberhard von Schenck,** second son of Dedo von Schenck.
November 15, 1887, Berlin —
m. September 14, 1918, Hamburg
Irmgard Ecker, daughter of
July 1, 1895, Hamburg —

Issue: 1. Dedo von Schenck (1922–)
m. Maria Margarethe Sander (1922–)
see: *von Schenck,* 3, page 1043

2. Albrecht von Schenck
November 25, 1923, Berlin — December 25, 1941, Neuruppin

VI. von Schenck 3, from page 1042

* **Dedo von Schenck,** son of Eberhard von Schenck.
March 29, 1922, Berlin —
m. April 19, 1944, Berlin
Maria Margarethe Sander, daughter of Heinz Sander and of his wife,
August 3, 1922, Hamburg —

Issue: 1. Ulrike von Schenck
January 12, 1949, Hamburg —

2. Kersten von Schenck
November 10, 1951, Hamburg —

VI. VON KEUDELL 1, from page 247

Robert von Keudell
February 27, 1824, Königsberg — April 26, 1903, Königsberg
m. September 15, 1883, Coburg
* **Alexandra von Grünhof,** daughter of Duke Ernst of Württemberg and of his morganatic wife, Natalie Eischborn.
August 10, 1861, Wiesbaden — April 13, 1933, Hohenlübbichow

Issue: 1. Walter von Keudell (1884–)
m. Johanna von Kyaw (1890–)
see: *von Keudell*, 2, below

2. Otto von Keudell (1887–)
m. 1: Maria Momm (1895–1945)
m. 2: Edelgarde von Stülpnagel (1912–)
see: *von Keudell*, 4, page 1045

3. Hedwig von Keudell (1891–)
m. Karl von der Trenck (1881–1963)
see: *von der Trenck*, page 1076

VI. von Keudell 2, from above

* **Walter von Keudell,** eldest son of Robert.
July 17, 1884, Castellamare, Italy —
m. February 6, 1912, Dresden
Johanna von Kyaw, daughter of Kurt von Kyaw and of his wife,
January 5, 1890, Dresden —

VI. von Keudell 2 continued

Issue: 1. Leopold Robert von Keudell
April 3, 1913, Frankfurt-an-der-Oder — 1941 or 1942 in Russia, last heard of in action in World War II

2. Irmgard von Keudell (1914–)
m. 1: Horst von Wallenberg (1915–1940)
see: *von Wallenberg*, page 1077
m. 2: Georg von Reden-Lütcken (1913–)
see: *von Reden-Lütcken*, page 1070

3. Veronika von Keudell (1916–)
m. Ludwig Hübner (1907–)
see: *Hübner*, page 1062

4. Dietrich von Keudell (1918–1951)
m. Luise von Below (1922–)
see: *von Keudell*, 3, below

VI. von Keudell 3, from above

* **Dietrich von Keudell,** son of Walter.
September 21, 1918, Berlin — May 18, 1951, Kahlesand-on-the-Elbe
m. May 22, 1943, Lugowen
Luise von Below, daughter of Paul von Below and of his wife,
July 13, 1922, Lugowen —

Issue: 1. Jutta von Keudell
October 17, 1944, Königsberg —

2. Luise von Keudell
March 10, 1947, Lüneburg —

3. Karin von Keudell
August 26, 1948, Lüneburg —

4. Leopold von Keudell
July 16, 1950, Freiburg —

VI. von Keudell 4, from page 1043

★ **Otto von Keudell,** second son of Robert.
February 28, 1887, Rome —
m. 1: August 14, 1920, Wiesbaden
Maria Momm, daughter of Wilhelm Momm and of his wife,
July 15, 1895, Ottweiler — April 17, 1945,
m. 2: September 5, 1947, Niederaudorf
Edelgarde von Stülpnagel, daughter of Joachim von Stülpnagel and of his wife,
April 26, 1912, Charlottenburg —

Issue of first marriage:

1. Robert von Keudell
May 29, 1921, Koblenz — February 16, 1942, killed in action in World War II

2. Wilhelm von Keudell (1922–)
m. Ragnhild Geissendörffer (1941–)
see: *von Keudell*, 5, page 1046

3. Otto von Keudell
May 16, 1924, Berlin — June 26, 1942, killed in action in World War II

4. Walter von Keudell
May 25, 1926, Berlin —

5. Maria von Keudell
August 31, 1930, Berlin —

6. Alexander von Keudell (1933–)
m. Sabine Langen (1943–)
see: *von Keudell*, 6, page 1046

7. Ernst von Keudell (1937–)
m. Edelgard Giesbert (1942–)
see: *von Keudell*, 7, page 1046

Issue of second marriage:

8. Theodor von Keudell
June 15, 1949, Ludwigsburg —

9. Christoph von Keudell
December 5, 1954, Stuttgart —

VI. von Keudell 5, from page 1045

* **Wilhelm von Keudell,** second son of Otto.
July 2, 1922, Lichterfelden —
m. April , 1966, Frankfurt-am-Main
Ragnhild Geissendörffer, daughter of
April 7, 1941, —

Issue:

VI. von Keudell 6, from page 1045

* **Alexander von Keudell,** fifth son of Otto.
December 17, 1933, Berlin —
m. October 22, 1965, Düsseldorf
Sabine Langen, daughter of
January 8, 1943, —

Issue:

VI. von Keudell 7, from page 1045

* **Ernst von Keudell,** sixth son of Otto.
February 2, 1937, Berlin —
m. May , 1965, Mömbris
Edelgard Giesbert, daughter of
October 14, 1942, —

Issue: 1. Annette von Keudell
June 8, 1966, Munich —

VI. VON ARPEAU UND GALLATIN from page 247

Karl, Count von Arpeau und Gallatin
March 20, 1802, Trelny — May 12, 1877, St. Prex
m. July 3, 1830, Ulm
* **Alexandrine,** Countess von Urach, daughter of Duke Karl Heinrich of Württemberg and of his morganatic wife, Karoline Alexei.
December 19, 1803, — August 22, 1884, Baden-Baden

No Issue.

VI. VON HOHENLOHE-KIRCHBERG from page 247

Karl-Ludwig, Fürst von Hohenlohe-Kirchberg
November 2, 1780, — December 16, 1861,
m. May 26, 1821,
* **Marie,** Countess von Urach, daughter of Duke Karl Heinrich of Württemberg and of his morganatic wife, Karoline Alexei.
December 17, 1802, Berlin — January 28, 1882, Kirchberg

No Issue.

XV. VON BRAUNECK (Hohenlohe-Oehringen) from page 483

* **Friedrich,** Prince of Hohenlohe-Oehringen, eldest son of Fürst August. Renounced rights to the succession August 22, 1842.
August 12, 1812, Oehringen — December 10, 1892, Oehringen
m. March 28, 1844, Kochendorf (morganatic)
Mathilde von Breuning, daughter of Johann Karl von Breuning and of his wife,
November 10, 1821, — January 12, 1896, Stuttgart
(She was created Baroness von Brauneck by the King of Württemberg.)

Issue (assumed the title von Brauneck):
1. Kraft August, Baron von Brauneck
December 27, 1844, Ingelfingen — September 11, 1871, Ottlitz

2. Alexander, Baron von Brauneck
January 2, 1846, Ingelfingen — July 30, 1849,

XV. SCHWARZBURG-SONDERHAUSEN from page 483

Günther Friedrich Karl III, Fürst von Schwarzburg-Sonderhausen
September 24, 1801, Sonderhausen — September 15, 1889, Sonderhausen
m. May 29, 1835,
* **Friederike,** Princess of Hohenlohe-Oehringen, daughter of Prince August of Hohenlohe-Oehringen and of his wife, Duchess Luise of Württemberg.
July 3, 1814, Oehringen — June 3, 1888, Salzburg

Issue: 1. Marie, Princess von Schwarzburg-Sonderhausen
June 14, 1837, Sonder — April 21, 1921, Reichenhall

2. Günther Friedrich Karl, Prince von Schwarzburg-Sonderhausen
April 13, 1839, — November 25, 1871,

XV. VON FRANKENBERG UND LUDWIGSDORFF 1, from page 484

Friedrich Ludwig, Count von Frankenberg und Ludwigsdorff
February 5, 1835, Breslau — December 31, 1897, Slawentzitz
m. June 24, 1872, Slawentzitz
* **Luise,** Princess of Hohenlohe-Oehringen, daughter of Fürst Hugo zu Hohenlohe-Oehringen and of his wife, Princess Pauline von Fürstenberg.
July 14, 1851, Slawentzitz — February 18, 1920, Slawentzitz

Issue: 1. Margarethe, Countess von Frankenberg und Ludwigsdorff
April 17, 1873, Berlin — April 1, 1886, Berlin

2. Konrad, Count von Frankenberg und Ludwigsdorff (1877–1937)
m. Alice Friedmann (1879–1927)
see: *von Frankenberg und Ludwigsdorff*, 2, below

3. Luise, Countess von Frankenberg und Ludwigsdorff (1879–1941)
m. Friedrich, Count von Westphalen zu Fürstenberg (1872–1932)
see: *von Westphalen zu Fürstenberg*, page 1081

XV. von Frankenberg und Ludwigsdorff 2, from above

* **Konrad,** Count von Frankenberg und Ludwigsdorff, only son of Count Friedrich Ludwig.
May 3, 1877, Slawentzitz — June 5, 1937, Berlin
m. May 28, 1907, London
Alice Friedmann, daughter of
July 22, 1879, Berlin — January 30, 1927, Berlin

No Issue.

XXI. VON AICHELBURG from page 1057

Othmar, Count von Aichelburg
September 27, 1901, Jistebnitz —
m. August 23, 1922, Munich. Divorced:
* **Marie von Gans,** daughter of Paul von Gans and of his wife, Baroness Ellinka von Fabrice.
October 31, 1905, Schmölz —
(She m. 2: and divorced: Wilhelm Borgnis – see: *Borgnis*, page 1052.)
(She m. 3: Otto, Baron von Leithner – see: *von Leithner*, page 1063.)

Issue: 1. Elisabeth, Countess von Aichelburg (1923–)
m. and divorced: George Pollak (1909–)
see: *Pollak*, page 1070

XXI. ANDERS from page 1065

Herbert Anders
July 4, 1919, Hussinitz —
m.
* **Marie-Luise Marckwort,** daughter of Karl Marckwort and of his wife, Pauline von Dawans.
February 27, 1922, Gardessen —

Issue: 1. Gabriele Anders
December 15, 1945, —

2. Dorie Anders
December 16, 1947, —

XXI. ARENDT from page 1058

Egon Arendt
August 18, 1889, Wormditt — November 14, 1964, Fürstenfeldbruck
m. January 10, 1924, Dittfurt
* **Gertrud,** Baroness von Gise, daughter of Baron Reinhard von Gise and of his wife, Baroness Friederike von Dungern.
March 21, 1890, Dittfurt —

No Issue.

XXI. BIERLEIN from page 1071

Ernst Bierlein
February 26, 1920, Munich —
m. February 21, 1945, Munich. Divorced:
* **Ellinka**, Countess von Einsiedel, daughter of Count Adolkar von Einsiedel and of his wife, Margot von Gans.
July 26, 1922, Würmegg —
(She m. 2: Walter Rupprecht – see: *Rupprecht*, page 1071.)

Issue: 1. Peter Bierlein
December 3, 1945, Munich —

2. Marie Bierlein
December 10, 1954, Munich —

XXI. VON BISCHOFFSHAUSEN from page 1056

Werner, Baron von Bischoffshausen
September 23, 1894, Bollensdorf —
m. January 3, 1917, Berne, Switzerland. Divorced:
* **Margot von Gans,** daughter of Paul von Gans and of his wife, Baroness Ellinka von Fabrice.
July 11, 1899, Boulogne, France —
(She m. 2: and divorced: Adolkar, Count von Einsiedel – see: *von Einsiedel*, page 1054.)
(She m. 3: Harold Rydon – see: *Rydon*, page 1084.)

Issue: 1. Claus-Henning, Baron von Bischoffshausen
June 5, 1919, Herrenhaus Schmölz — April 23, 1942, Brjansk, Russia, killed in action in World War II

XXI. VON BLIXEN-FINECKE 1, from page 664

Carl, Baron von Blixen-Finecke and * **Auguste,** Princess of Hesse-Cassel.

Issue: 1. Vilhelm Carl, Baron von Blixen-Finecke
May 29, 1857, — January 31, 1909, Copenhagen, Denmark

2. Vilhelm, Baron von Blixen-Finecke (1863–1942)
m. Bertha Castenskiold (1868–1951)
see: *von Blixen-Finecke*, 2, page 1051

XXI. von Blixen-Finecke 2, from page 1050

* **Vilhelm,** Baron von Blixen-Finecke, son of Baron Carl.
June 21, 1863, Copenhagen —July 7, 1942, Hesselagergaard, Denmark
m. November 9, 1888, Copenhagen
Bertha Castenskiold, daughter of Carl Vilhelm Castenskiold and of his wife,
July 29, 1868, Borreby, Denmark — February 11, 1951, Hesselagergaard

Issue: 1. Carl August, Baron von Blixen-Finecke (1889–1954)
m. Brita Ekström (1893–   )
see: *von Blixen-Finecke*, 3, below

XXI. von Blixen-Finecke 3, from above

* **Carl August,** Baron von Blixen-Finecke, only son of Baron Vilhelm.
September 20, 1889, Copenhagen — December 5, 1954, Hesselagergaard
m. May 10, 1917,
Brita Ekström, daughter of Hugo Ekström and of his wife,
October 6, 1893, Landskrona, Denmark —

Issue: 1. Anna Elisabeth, Baroness von Blixen-Finecke (1918–   )
m. Thorbjörn Möller (1897–   )
see: *Möller*, page 1086

2. Gustav Frederik, Baron von Blixen-Finecke (1920–1966)
m. 1: Charlotte Scavenius (1930–1954)
m. 2: Carin von Rosen (1933–   )

XXI. von Blixen-Finecke 4, from above

* **Gustav Frederik,** Baron von Blixen-Finecke, only son of Baron Carl August.
September 1, 1920, Sevedö — April 30, 1966, Caracas, Venezuela
m. 1: September 1, 1951, Klintholm
Charlotte Scavenius, daughter of
June 18, 1930, Klintholm — May 13, 1954,
m. 2: March 3, 1960, Nyeri, Kenya
Carin von Rosen, daughter of Eric von Rosen and of his wife,
March 31, 1933,   —

Issue of first marriage:
1. Axel, Baron von Blixen-Finecke
May 15, 1952, Nyborg —

Issue of second marriage:
2. Brita Madelein, Baroness von Blixen-Finecke
February 8, 1961, Nyeri —

XXI. BORGNIS from page 1057

Wilhelm Borgnis
September 17, 1890, Frankfurt-am-Main —
m. October 6, 1927, Munich. Divorced:

* **Marie von Gans,** daughter of Paul von Gans and of his wife, Baroness Ellinka von Fabrice.
October 31, 1905, Schmölz —
(She m. 1: and divorced: Othmar, Count von Aichelburg – see: *von Aichelburg*, page 1049.)
(She m. 3: Otto, Baron von Leithner – see: *von Leithner*, page 1063.)

No Issue.

XVIII. VON BÜRKEL from page 566

Ludwig von Bürkel
July 5, 1877, Munich — June 11, 1946, Benediktbeuron
m. November 22, 1943, Kochel

* **Ilka Halm-Nicolai,** daughter of Carlo Halm-Nicolai and of his wife, Baroness Ilma von Fabrice.
November 2, 1902, Florence, Italy — April 14, 1965, Baden, Switzerland

No Issue.

XXI. VON DAWANS 1, from page 1079

Georg Ludwig von Dawans
August 30, 1860, Pforzheim — February 4, 1912, Strassburg
m. April 1, 1891, Alt-Franken, near Dresden

* **Armgard,** Baroness von Watzdorff, daughter of Baron Wilhelm von Watzdorff and of his wife, Laura von Witzleben.
May 3, 1867, Dresden — January 16, 1945, Bofsheim

Issue: 1. Pauline von Dawans (1892–1952)
m. Karl Marckwort (1919–)
see: *Marckwort*, page 1065

2. Amelie von Dawans
October 22, 1893, Erfurt — December 22, 1893, Erfurt

XXI. von Dawans — 1 continued

3. Margot von Dawans
October 7, 1897, Erfurt — December 7, 1959, Karlsruhe

4. Sigismund-Helmut von Dawans (1899–1944)
m. 1: and divorced: Ingeborg Hane (1902–)
m. 2: Ilse Schneider (1911–)
see: *von Dawans*, 2, below

XXI. von Dawans — 2, from above

* **Sigismund-Helmut von Dawans,** only son of Georg Ludwig.
September 23, 1899, Erfurt — June 10, 1944, Caen, France, in action in World War II
m. 1: April 6, 1923, Blankensee. Divorced:
Ingeborg Hane, daughter of Walter Hane and of his wife,
May 10, 1902, Hamburg —
m. 2: August 1, 1931, Konstanz
Ilse Schneider, daughter of Karl Friedrich Schneider and of his wife,
June 25, 1911, Konstanz —

Issue of first marriage:

1. Horst von Dawans (1924–)
m. Annemarie Schaub (1922–)
see: *von Dawans*, 3, page 1054

2. Ingrid von Dawans (1932–)
m. Hans-Gerd Wasum (1931–)
see: *Wasum*, page 1078

3. Christel von Dawans (1934–)
m. Götz von Winterfeld (1928–)
see: *von Winterfeld*, page 1082

4. Achim von Dawans (1935–)
m. Sylvia Johannsen (1939–)
see: *von Dawans*, 4, page 1054

5. Hans-Dieter von Dawans
April 13, 1939, Königsberg —

XXI. von Gans 3, from page 1057

* **Anthony von Gans,** eldest son of Joszi von Gans.
October 31, 1940, Melbourne, Australia —
m. October 1, 1966, Düsseldorf
Brigitte Kompach, daughter of
October 16, 1941, Rydultau —

Issue:

XXI. VON GISE from page 688

Reinhard, Baron von Gise
November 30, 1854, Munich — November 7, 1913, Königsgut
m. January 17, 1884, Bayerhof
* **Friederike,** Baroness von Dungern, daughter of Baron Hermann von Dungern and of his wife, Baroness Wilhelmine von Dungern.
June 17, 1862, Frankfurt-am-Main — November 21, 1925, Obertheres

Issue: 1. Johann Nepomuk, Baron von Gise (1887–1946)
m. Lilla Fuchs (1896–)
see: *von Gise*, 2, page 1059

2. Ernst, Baron von Gise (1888–1945)
m. Ilsemaria Lechler (1907–)
see: *von Gise*, 3, page 1059

3. Gertrud, Baroness von Gise (1890–)
m. Egon Arendt (1889–1964)
see: *Arendt*, page 1049

4. Guntram, Baron von Gise (1892–1919)
m. Else Mörs (1890–)
see: *von Gise*, 4, page 1059

5. Margarita, Baroness von Gise (1893–)
m. Erich Neumann (1876–1952)
see: *Neumann*, page 1067

6. Zeno, Baron von Gise (1896–)
m. 1: and divorced: Käthe Sprecher (1898–)
m. 2: Liselotte Hansen (1916–)
see: *von Gise*, 6, page 1060

XXI. von Gise 2, from page 1058

* **Johann Nepomuk,** Baron von Gise, eldest son of Baron Reinhard.
February 3, 1887, Schweinfurt — September 24, 1946, Regensburg
m. February 26, 1916, Jena
Lilla Fuchs, daughter of
January 25, 1896, Darmstadt —

Issue: 1. Gunhild, Baroness von Gise
March 31, 1917, Jena —

2. Rüdiger, Baron von Gise
March 25, 1921, Dittfurt — March 4, 1944, Greece, killed in action in World War II

XXI. von Gise 3, from page 1058

* **Ernst,** Baron von Gise, second son of Baron Reinhard.
July 17, 1888, Schweinfurt — May , 1945, missing in Russia in action in World War II
m. February 25, 1930, Stuttgart
Ilsemaria Lechler, daughter of Reinhold Lechler and of his wife,
March 12, 1907, Cassel —

Issue: 1. Verena, Baroness von Gise (1931–)
m. Helmut Müller (1925–)
see: *Müller*, page 1066

2. Jutta, Baroness von Gise (1934–)
m. Walter Köppe (1928–)
see: *Köppe*, page 1063

3. Ingrid, Baroness von Gise (1935–)
m. Max Hagenauer (1929–)
see: *Hagenauer*, page 1061

XXI. von Gise 4, from page 1058

***Guntram,** Baron von Gise, third son of Baron Reinhard.
February 5, 1892, Dittfurt — July 30, 1919, Frankfurt-an-der-Oder
m. July 30, 1919,
Else Mörs, daughter of
May 25, 1890, Frankfurt-an-der-Oder —

XXI. von Gise — 4 continued

Issue: 1. Harro, Baron von Gise (1920–)
m. 1: Josefine Thiel (1927–1956)
m. 2: Elfriede Altenfelder (1922–)
see: *von Gise*, 5, below

XXI. von Gise — 5, from above

★ **Harro,** Baron von Gise, only son of Baron Guntram.
June 3, 1920, Frankfurt-an-der-Oder (posthumous) —
m. 1: August 22, 1946,
Josefine Thiel, daughter of
August 22, 1927, Neuvogelsiefen — October 16, 1956,
m. 2: October 15, 1961,
Elfriede Altenfelder, daughter of
May 19, 1922, —

Issue of first marriage:
1. Harro, Baron von Gise
January 8, 1948, Obertheres —

2. Hilde, Baroness von Gise
January 26, 1951, Obertheres —

Issue of second marriage:
3. Gertraud, Baroness von Gise
July 18, 1962, Schweinfurt —

XXI. von Gise — 6, from page 1058

★ **Zeno,** Baron von Gise, fourth son of Baron Reinhard.
January 18, 1896, Dittfurt —
m. 1: January 10, 1928, Dittfurt. Divorced:
Käthe Sprecher, daughter of
August 25, 1898, Berlin —
m. 2: December 23, 1944, Hamburg
Liselotte Hansen, daughter of Karl Hansen and of his wife
December 6, 1916, Altona, near Hamburg —

Issue of second marriage:
1. Ute, Baroness von Gise
September 9, 1946, Hamburg —

XXI. HAGENAUER from page 1059

Max Hagenauer
July 14, 1929, Straubing —
m. August 28, 1959,
* **Ingrid,** Baroness von Gise, daughter of Baron Ernst von Gise and of his wife, Ilsemaria Lechler.
June 14, 1935, Immenstadt —

Issue: 1. Ulrike Hagenauer
June 15, 1960, Immenstadt —

2. Sabine Hagenauer
October 11, 1964, Immenstadt —

XXI. HEGNER from page 1073

Anton Hegner
February 22, 1926, —
m. January 21, 1958,
* **Barbara von Stockar-Scherer-Castell,** daughter of Maximilian von Stockar-Scherer-Castell and of his first wife, Louise de Meuron.
August 27, 1933, Arnsoldingen, near Berne, Switzerland —

Issue: 1. Isabelle Hegner
November 16, 1960, Buenos Aires, Argentina —

2. Livia Hegner
April 15, 1963, Zürich, Switzerland —

3. Wolfgang Hegner
June 4, 1964, New York City —

XXI. HOLTHAUS from page 1062

Erich Holthaus
August 20, 1891, Düren —
m. October 15, 1921, Königsfeld
* **Erika Kollmann,** daughter of Kurt Kollmann and of his wife, Baroness Dora von Dungern,
June 15, 1896, Bayerhof Castle —

No Issue.

XXI. HÜBNER from page 1044

Ludwig Hübner
June 6, 1907, Darmstadt —
m. August 1, 1961, Mainz
***Veronika von Keudell,** daughter of Robert von Keudell and of his wife, Alexandra von Grünhof.
February 21, 1916, Berlin —

No Issue.

XXI. JUNGWIRTH from page 1055

Herbert Jungwirth
July 13, 1939, Gmunden —
m. August 15, 1962, Salzburg
* **Doria-Elisabeth Frank,** daughter of Heinz Frank and of his wife, Countess Elisabeth Bentzel zu Sternau und Hohenau.
September 3, 1940, Munich —

Issue: 1. Andreas Jungwirth
December 9, 1962, Pöcking —

2. Thomas Jungwirth
October 13, 1965, Mittersill —

XXI. KOLLMANN from page 688

Kurt Kollmann
November 7, 1868, Woycin, Poland —
m. September 14, 1893,
* **Dora,** Baroness von Dungern, daughter of Baron Hermann von Dungern and of his wife, Baroness Wilhelmine von Dungern.
May 20, 1871, Bayerhof Castle — October 24, 1930, Fürstenfeldbruck

Issue: 1. Erika Kollmann (1896–)
m. Erich Kolthaus (1891–)
see: *Kolthaus*, page 1061

2. Siegfried Kollmann
May 28, 1898, Wiesbaden — October 31, 1914, Messin, France, killed in action in World War I

XXI. KÄHNY from page 1076

Fritz Kähny
August 3, 1913, Baden —
m. July 20, 1946, Hilsbach
* **Waltraut von der Trenck**, daughter of Karl von der Trenck and of his wife, Hedwig von Keudell.
July 21, 1923, Königsberg —

Issue: 1. Karl Heinz Kähny
December 4, 1947, Heidelberg —

2. Friedrich Wilhelm Kähny
March 28, 1949, Sulzfeld —

3. Christoph von Kähny
December 18, 1952, Sulzfeld —

4. Bernhard Kähny
July 10, 1956, Karlsruhe —

5. Rose Kähny
November 11, 1961, Sulzfeld —

XXI. KÖPPE from page 1059

Walter Köppe
May 14, 1928, Sonthofen —
m. May 7, 1957,
* **Jutta,** Baroness von Gise, daughter of Baron Ernst von Gise and of his wife, Ilsemaria Lechler.
July 21, 1934, Immenstadt —

No Issue.

XXI. VON LEITHNER from page 1057

Otto, Baron von Leithner
January 1, 1902, Vienna —
m. July 5, 1910, Mexico City
* **Marie von Gans,** daughter of Paul von Gans and of his wife, Baroness Ellinka von Fabrice.
October 31, 1905, Schmölz —
(She m. 1: and divorced: Othmar, Count von Aichelburg – see: *von Aichelburg*, page 1049.)
(She m. 2: and divorced: Wilhelm Borgnis – see: *Borgnis*, page 1052.)

No Issue.

XXI. VON LILGENAU from page 1070

Wolf-Christian, Baron von Lilgenau
December 15, 1925, Schüsselburg —
m. September 3, 1961. Divorced:
* **Wilhelmine,** Baroness Ritter von Záhony, daughter of Baron Johann Ritter von Záhony and of his wife, Countess Marie Welser von Welserheimb.
September 3, 1925, Graz —

No Issue.

XXI. VON LUCKNER 1, from page 765

Wilhelm, Count von Luckner and * **Wilhelmine,** Countess von Reichenbach-Lessonitz.

Issue: 1. Nicolaus Alfred, Count von Luckner
January 1, 1838, — November , 1864,
(m. June 11, 1862, Elisabeth Hock. No Issue)

2. Nicolaus Rudolf, Count von Luckner (1849–1902)
m. Mathilde Zinck (1853–1934)
see: *von Luckner*, 2, below

XXI. Von Luckner 2, from above

* **Nicolaus Rudolf,** Count von Luckner, son of Count Wilhelm.
June 2, 1849, Dresden — April 12, 1902, Alt-Franken
m. September 25, 1886, Alt-Franken
Mathilde Zinck, daughter of
August 6, 1853, Munich — December 18, 1934, Alt-Franken

Issue: 1. Nicolaus Felix, Count von Luckner (1884–)
m. Andrea Gallay (1884–)
see: *von Luckner*, 3, page 1065

XXI. von Luckner 3, from page 1064

Nicolaus Felix, Count von Luckner, only son of Count Nicolaus Rudolf.
April 3, 1884, Dresden —
m. August 29, 1918, Geneva, Switzerland
Andrea Gallay, daughter of
February 3, 1884, Paris —

No Issue.

XXI. MARCKWORT from page 1052

Karl Marckwort
August 16, 1888, Lamme, near Brunswick — January 24, 1944, Stettin
m. January 29, 1919, Hildesheim
* **Pauline von Dawans,** daughter of Georg Ludwig von Dawans and of his wife, Baroness Armgard von Watzdorff.
January 29, 1892, Mannheim — July 29, 1952, Leutershausen

Issue: 1. Marie-Luise Marckwort (1922–)
m. Herbert Anders (1919–)
see: *Anders,* page 1049

2. Kasimir Marckwort
—

XXI. MARKUS from page 1074

Gábor Markus
June 8, 1921, Budapest, Hungary —
October 7, 1953,
* **Gina von Szebeny,** daughter of Georg von Szebeny and of his wife, Hermine Sturtzkopf.
March 24, 1926, Budapest — February 4, 1962, Buffalo, New York

No Issue.

XXI. McCULLOUGH from page 1057

Denys McCullough
April 10, 1927, Stockport, England —
m. November 22, 1950, Melbourne, Australia
* **Bianca von Gans,** daughter of Joszi von Gans and of his second wife, Baroness Melitta von Riedel.
April 28, 1928, Munich —

Issue: 1. Keith McCullough
May 19, 1953, Brisbane, Australia —

2. Anthony McCullough
July 21, 1956, Melbourne —

XXI. VON MONSHOFF from page 1075

Carl Friedrich Perko Edler von Monshoff
May 14, 1938, —
m. September 14, 1962,
* **Benedicta Szmrecsanyi de Szmrecsan,** daughter of Béla Szmrecsanyi de Szmrecsan and of his wife, Countess Maria Emma Welser von Welserheimb.
September 26, 1938, Budapest —

Issue:

XXI. MÜLLER from page 1059

Helmut Müller
July 10, 1925, Kempten —
m. July 20, 1961,
* **Verena,** Baroness von Gise, daughter of Baron Ernst von Gise and of his wife, Ilsemaria Lechler.
June 7, 1931, Immenstadt —

Issue: 1. Florian Müller
September 18, 1962, Immenstadt —

XXI. NEUMANN 1, from page 1058

Erich Neumann
December 13, 1876, Stumm — December 7, 1952, Probsteierhagen, near Kiel
m. March 26, 1935, Königsberg
***Margarita,** Baroness von Gise, daughter of Baron Reinhard von Gise and of his wife, Baroness Friederike von Dungern.
October 24, 1893, Dittfurt —

Issue: 1. Hans-Jürgen Neumann (1936–)
m. Marianne Höske (1939–)
see: *Neumann*, 2, below

2. Sieglinde Neumann
October 17, 1938, —

XXI. Neumann 2, from above

* **Hans-Jürgen Neumann,** only son of Erich.
January 10, 1936, Kiel —
m. October 14, 1960,
Marianne Höske, daughter of
January 13, 1939, —

Issue: 1. Christiane Neumann
October 27, 1961, —

XXI. VON PAGENHARDT 1, from page 781

Robert, Baron von Pagenhardt and * **Alexandra,** Princess zu Ysenburg und Büdingen in Wächtersbach.

Issue: 1. Auguste, Baroness von Pagenhardt
March 4, 1879, Diedenhofen — October 20, 1941, Berchtesgaden

2. Ferdinand, Baron von Pagenhardt (1881–1960)
m. 1: and divorced: Marthe de la Roche-Burchard (1886–1932)
m. 2: Maria Margaretha von Salis-Soglio-Maienfeld (1899–)
see: *von Pagenhardt*, 2, page 1068

3. Friedrich Wilhelm, Baron von Pagenhardt
December 29, 1882, — August 15, 1907,

XXI. von Pagenhardt — 1 continued

4. Maximilian, Baron von Pagenhardt (1884–1943)
   m. Marie Adams (1896–)
   see: *von Pagenhardt*, 3, below

5. Kraft, Baron von Pagenhardt (1889–1957)
   m. Marion Schmidt-Stawitz (1901–)
   see: *von Pagenhardt*, 5, page 1069

6. Anna, Baroness von Pagenhardt (1890–)
   m. Christian Gustaf Fielfe-Fairwil (1883–)
   see: *Fielfe-Fairwil*, page 1055

XXI. von Pagenhardt — 2, from page 1067

* **Ferdinand,** Baron von Pagenhardt, eldest son of Baron Robert.
March 11, 1881, Wiesbaden — June 13, 1960, Kreuzlingen
m. 1: March 31, 1908, Basel, Switzerland. Divorced:
Marthe de la Roche-Burchard, daughter of
September 7, 1886, Basel — January 3, 1932, Basel
m. 2: March 13, 1934, Ponte im Engadin
Maria Margaretha von Salis-Soglio-Maienfeld, daughter of
January 1, 1899, Basel —

No Issue.

XXI. von Pagenhardt — 3, from above

* **Maximilian,** Baron von Pagenhardt, third son of Baron Robert.
June 20, 1884, Stuttgart — September 25, 1943, Washington, D.C.
m. May 25, 1918, St. Louis, Missouri
Marie Adams, daughter of Arthur Adams, and of his wife,
November 27, 1896, —

Issue: 1. Maximilian, Baron von Pagenhardt (1923–)
   m. 1: and divorced: Hope Allen (1923–)
   m. 2: and divorced: Sylvia Hommel (–)
   m. 3: Heidi Schweizer (–)
   see: *von Pagenhardt*, 4, page 1069

XXI. von Pagenhardt 4, from page 1068

* **Maximilian,** Baron von Pagenhardt, only son of Baron Maximilian.
August 21, 1923, St. Louis, Missouri —
m. 1: April 11, 1946. Divorced:
Hope Allen, daughter of Thomas Allen and of his wife,
November 11, 1923, —
m. 2: January 8, 1958. Divorced:
Sylvia Hommel, daughter of Carl Hommel and of his wife, —
m. 3: July 25, 1962,
Heidi Schweizer, daughter of Hans Schweizer and of his wife,
—

Issue of first marriage:
1. Alexandra, Baroness von Pagenhardt
August 30, 1951, Palo Alto, California —

2. Tania, Baroness von Pagenhardt
April 27, 1953, Palo Alto —

XXI. von Pagenhardt 5, from page 1068

* **Kraft,** Baron von Pagenhardt, fifth son of Baron Robert.
February 13, 1889, Stuttgart — March 10, 1957, Frankfurt-am-Main
m. August 2, 1921, Frankfurt-am-Main
Marion Schmidt-Stawitz, daughter of
April 5, 1901, Frankfurt-am-Main —

No Issue.

XVIII. PESCATORE from page 593

Bonaventura Pescatore, son of Dominik.
November 3, 1921, Munich —
m. May 3, 1921,
Traute Christel Plep, daughter of Rudolf Plep and of his wife,
June 10, 1921, Königsberg —

Issue: 1. Rüdiger Pescatore
July 25, 1953, Munich —

2. Dominik Pescatore
April 22, 1955, Munich —

3. Birgit Pescatore
December 7, 1956, Munich —

XXI. POLLAK from page 1049

George Pollak
September 22, 1909, Vienna —
m. February 22, 1947, Paris. Divorced:
* **Elisabeth, Countess von Aichelburg,** daughter of Count Othmar von Aichelburg and of his wife, Marie von Gans.
August 10, 1923, Seeshaupt —

Issue: 1. Robert Pollak
February 28, 1948, Paris —

XXI. VON REDEN-LÜTCKEN from page 1044

Georg von Reden-Lütcken
January 29, 1913, Reden —
m. January 25, 1947, Urestorf
* **Irmgard von Keudell,** daughter of Walter von Keudell and of his wife, Johanna von Kyaw.
November 1, 1914, Dresden —
(She m. 1: Horst von Wallenberg – see: *von Wallenberg*, page 1077.)

Issue: 1. Georg Wilhelm von Reden-Lütcken
November 14, 1948, Hamburg —

2. Johanna von Reden-Lütcken
April 21, 1950, Hamburg —

XXI. RITTER VON ZÁHONY from page 1080

Johann, Baron Ritter von Záhony
December 11, 1898, Lilbenwald — February 26, 1937, Graz
m. July 8, 1924, Graz
* **Marie,** Countess Welser von Welserheimb, daughter of Count Otto Welser von Welserheimb and of his wife, Countess Wilhelmine von Watzdorff.
September 12, 1903, Pola —

Issue: 1. Wilhelmine, Baroness Ritter von Záhony (1925–)
m. and divorced: Wolf-Christian, Baron von Lilgenau (1925–)
see: *von Lilgenau*, page 1064

2. Carl Wilhelm, Baron Ritter von Záhony
May 29, 1927, Graz —

3. Hans Friedrich, Baron Ritter von Záhony
April 2, 1933, Graz — November 14, 1959, Graz

XXI. RUPPRECHT from page 1054

Walter Rupprecht
February 26, 1924, Basel, Switzerland —
m. September 2, 1957, Muensing
* **Ellinka,** Countess von Einsiedel, daughter of Count Adolkar von Einsiedel and of his wife, Margot von Gans.
July 26, 1922, Würmegg —
(She m. 1: and divorced: Ernst Bierlein – see: *Bierlein*, page 1050.)

Issue: 1. Karl Alexander Rupprecht
October 29, 1962, Malaga, Spain —

XXI. SCHÄFER from page 809

* **Klaus Schäfer**
November 16, 1910, Basel, Switzerland —
m.
Roza Honstetter, daughter of
June 1, 1920, Ludwigshafen —

Issue: 1. Klaus Schäfer
May 25, 1940, Immenstadt —

2. Hans-Georg Schäfer
December 30, 1945, Überlingen —

3. Hermann Schäfer
April 9, 1950, Überlingen —

XXI. VON DER SCHULENBURG 1, from page 1042

Werner, Count von der Schulenburg
October 31, 1886, Hehlen — February 5, 1945, Hameln
m. February 29, 1916, Munich
* **Freda von Schenck,** daughter of Dedo von Schenck and of his wife, Helene von Wardenberg.
March 21, 1890, Berlin — March 2, 1946, Berlin-Zehlendorf
(She m. 1: and divorced: Kurt, Baron von Reibnitz – see: *von Reibnitz*, page 1085.)

Issue: 1. Johannes-Heinrich, Count von der Schulenburg (1916–)
m. Inge Guht (1920–)
see: *von der Schulenburg*, page 1072

XXI. von der Schulenburg 2, from page 1071

* **Johannes-Heinrich,** Count von der Schulenburg, son of Count Werner.
December 20, 1916, Berlin —
m. November 1, 1946, Bad Pyrmont
Inge Guht, daughter of Friedrich Guht and of his wife,
July 27, 1920, Hanover —

Issue: 1. Friedrich Werner, Count von der Schulenburg
August 30, 1947, Hehlen —

2. Marie-Christine, Countess von der Schulenburg
September 2, 1949, Hehlen —

3. Ingeborg, Countess von der Schulenburg
November 3, 1951, Hehlen —

4. Christian-Günther, Count von der Schulenburg
November 23, 1954, Hehlen —

5. Gabriele, Countess von der Schulenburg
June 10, 1961, Göttingen —

XXI. SIEGRIST from page 1055

Karl Siegrist
October 2, 1933, Lucerne, Switzerland —
m. October 7, 1962, Sempach
* **Julia Felber,** daughter of Paul Felber and of his wife, Elisabeth von Stockar-Scherer-Castell.
October 11, 1935, Zürich, Switzerland —

Issue: 1. Elisabeth Siegrist
September 23, 1963, Lucerne —

2. Karl Siegrist
October 7, 1964, Lucerne —

3. Kathrin Siegrist
November 28, 1966, Lucerne —

XXI. VON STOCKAR-SCHERER-CASTELL 2, from page 856

* **Maximilian von Stockar-Scherer-Castell,** eldest son of Walther.
July 11, 1904, —
m. 1: January 4, 1927, Berne, Switzerland. Divorced:
Louise de Meuron, daughter of Frédéric de Meuron and of his wife,
June 1, 1907, Berne —
m. 2: February 8, 1961,
Veronika Bühler, daughter of Hans Bühler and of his wife,
May 24, 1919, Winterthur —

Issue of first marriage:
1. Sibylle von Stockar-Scherer-Castell (1930–)
m. and divorced: Max Froelicher (1923–)
see: *Froelicher*, page 1056

2. Barbara von Stockar-Scherer-Castell (1933–)
m. Anton Hegner (1926–)
see: *Hegner*, page 1061

XXI. von Stockar-Scherer-Castell 3, from page 856

* **Walther von Stockar-Scherer-Castell,** second son of Walther.
September 2, 1906, Castell Castle —
m. 1: January 5, 1933, New York City. Divorced:
Renée Dürler, daughter of Alfred Dürler and of his wife,
December 9, 1912, Zürich, Switzerland —
m. 2: February 11, 1941, Derendingen
Georgine Koch de Vigier, daughter of Ernst Koch de Vigier and of his wife,
July 8, 1910, Derendingen —

Issue of first marriage:
1. Marc Antoine von Stockar-Scherer-Castell (1935–)
m. Monika Bruman (1936—)
see: *von Stockar-Scherer-Castell*, 4, page 1074

Issue of second marriage:
2. Urs Caspar von Stockar-Scherer-Castell
July 17, 1942, Zürich —

3. Monika Goldi von Stockar-Scherer-Castell
August 8, 1944, Zürich —

XXI. von Stockar-Scherer-Castell 4, from page 1073

* **Marc Antoine von Stockar-Scherer-Castell,** eldest son of Walther.
January 17, 1935, Zürich —
m. December 11, 1958, Zürich
Monika Bruman, daughter of Franz Bruman and of his wife,
November 3, 1936, Zürich —

Issue: 1. Daniel Marc von Stockar-Scherer-Castell
September 4, 1961, Zürich —

2. Thomas Caspar von Stockar-Scherer-Castell
January 10, 1964, Zürich —

XXI. STURTZKOPF from page 867

* **Charley Sturtzkopf,** only son of Walther.
May 10, 1896, Berlin —
m. September 6, 1948, Munich
Eugenie Bleifuss, daughter of
August 29, 1929, Munich—

Issue: 1. Robert Sturtzkopf
February 17, 1951, Munich—

XXI. VON SZEBENY 1, from page 867

Georg von Szebeny
November 7, 1887, Budapest —
m. June 5, 1920, Schwerin
* **Hermine Sturtzkopf,** daughter of Walther Sturtzkopf and of his wife, Baroness Luigina von Fabrice.
March 10, 1895, Berlin —

Issue: 1. Dénes von Szebeny (1921–)
m. 1: and divorced: Emily Leidenfrost (1919–)
m. 2: Irmgard Gericke (1931–)
see: *von Szebeny*, 2, page 1075

2. Gina von Szebeny (1926–)
m. Gábor Markus (1921–1962)
see: *Markus*, page 1065

XXI. von Szebeny 2, from page 1074

* **Dénes von Szebeny,** only son of Georg.
April 27, 1921, Budapest —
m. 1: August 29, 1942, Budapest. Divorced:
Emily Leidenfrost, daughter of
November 7, 1919, —
m. 2: July 13, 1960, Mannheim
Irmgard Gericke, daughter of
February 14, 1931, Berlin —

Issue of first marriage:
1. Denise von Szebeny. September 4, 1943, Budapest —

Issue of second marriage:
2. Gábor von Szebeny. September 26, 1963, 'Mannheim —

XXI. SZMRECSANYI DE SZMRECSAN from page 1081

Béla Szmrecsanyi de Szmrecsan
November 8, 1904, Innsbruck —
m. September 26, 1937, Graz
* **Maria Emma,** Countess Welser von Welserheimb, daughter of Count Otto Welser von Welserheimb and of his wife, Countess Wilhelmine von Watzdorff.
January 11, 1906, Pola —

Issue: 1. Benedicta Szmrecsanyi de Szmrecsan (1938–)
m. Carl Friedrich Perko Edler von Monshoff (1938–)
see: *von Monshoff*, page 1066

2. Fruzsina Szmrecsanyi de Szmrecsan
April 8, 1940, Budapest —

3. Bertalan Szmrecsanyi de Szmrecsan
November 3, 1942, Budapest —

XXI. THIEL from page 1076

Walter Thiel
March 11, 1923, Königsberg —
m. September 17, 1955, Offenbach
* **Erika von der Trenck,** daughter of Karl von der Trenck and of his wife, Hedwig von Keudell.
March 25, 1925, Königsberg —

No Issue.

XXI. VON DER TRENCK

1, from page 1043

Karl von der Trenck
October 3, 1881, Berlin — July 1, 1963, Bad Rappenau
m. July 17, 1918, Königsberg
* **Hedwig von Keudell,** daughter of Robert von Keudell and of his wife, Alexandra von Grünhof.
April 13, 1891, Berlin —

Issue: 1. Wilhelm von der Trenck (1919–)
m. Thea Springmann (1917–)
see: *von der Trenck*, 2, below

2. Helmut von der Trenck (1921–)
m. Elisabeth Heipmann (1927–)
see: *von der Trenck*, 3, page 1077

3. Waltraut von der Trenck (1923–)
m. Fritz Kähny (1913–)
see: *Kähny*, page 1063

4. Erika von der Trenck (1925–)
m. Walter Thiel (1923–)
see: *Thiel*, page 1075

5. Ilse von der Trenck (1930–)
m. Wolfram Vogel (1926–)
see: *Vogel*, page 1077

XXI. von der Trenck

2, from above

* **Wilhelm von der Trenck,** eldest son of Karl von der Trenck.
November 10, 1919, Königsberg —
m. May 20, 1947, Dunau, near Hanover
Thea Springmann, daughter of Theodor Springmann and of his wife,
May 20, 1917, —

Issue: 1. Karl Theodor von der Trenck
September 20, 1948, Heidelberg —

2. Britta von der Trenck
July 17, 1950, Herborn —

3. Oda von der Trenck
May 18, 1959, Hamburg —

XXI. von der Trenck 3, from page 1076

★ **Helmut von der Trenck,** second son of Karl.
July 18, 1921, Königsberg —
m. September 12, 1953, Sulzfeld
Elisabeth Heipmann, daughter of Heinrich Heipmann and of his wife,
May 20, 1927, Grundensee —

Issue: 1. Anneliese von der Trenck
October 1, 1954, Lübeck —

2. Karl Friedrich von der Trenck
August 29, 1956, Lübeck —

3. Stefan von der Trenck
March 19, 1959, Lübeck —

4. Ulrike von der Trenck
August 26, 1962, Lüneburg —

XXI. VOGEL from page 1076

Wolfram Vogel
February 24, 1926, Dortmund —
m. April 12, 1962, Sulzfeld
★ **Ilse von der Trenck,** daughter of Karl von der Trenck and of his wife, Hedwig von Keudell.
March 31, 1930, Königsberg —

Issue: 1. Martin Vogel
January 19, 1963, Bad Segeberg —

2. Klaus Vogel
January 12, 1964, Itzehoe —

XXI. VON WALLENBERG from page 1044

Horst von Wallenberg
October 13, 1915, Oderwitz — May 27, 1940, St. Vincent, France, killed in action in World War II
m. March 24, 1940, Hohenlübbichow
★ **Irmgard von Keudell,** daughter of Walter von Keudell and of his wife, Johanna von Kyaw.
November 1, 1914, Dresden —
(She m. 1: Georg von Reden-Lütcken – see: *von Reden-Lütcken*, page 1070.)

No Issue.

XXI. VON WALLENRODT from page 900

Hans-Joachim von Wallenrodt and * **Ilona von Wuthenau-Hohenthurm.**

Issue: 1. Manfred Traugott von Wallenrodt (1938–)
m. Karin Stoltenberg (1940–)
see: *von Wallenrodt*, 2, below

2. Hans-Joachim Traugott von Wallenrodt (1943–)
m. Monika Ignatzy (1944–)
see: *von Wallenrodt*, 3, below

XXI. von Wallenrodt 2, from above

* **Manfred Traugott von Wallenrodt,** eldest son of Hans-Joachim.
November 2, 1938, Dresden —
m. December 15, 1966, Bochum
Karin Stoltenberg, daughter of
February 21, 1940, Bochum —

Issue:

XXI. von Wallenrodt 3, from above

* **Hans-Joachim Traugott von Wallenrodt,** second son of Hans-Joachim.
January 21, 1943, Geuz Castle —
m. October 6, 1964, Bad Wiessee
Monika Ignatzy, daughter of
October 2, 1944, Welper —

Issue: 1. Jacqueline von Wallenrodt
October 23, 1965, Kempten —

XXI. WASUM from page 1053

Hans-Gerd Wasum
May 16, 1931, Bacharach —
m. April 3, 1956,
* **Ingrid von Dawans,** daughter of Sigismund-Helmut von Dawans and of his second wife, Ilse Schneider.
July 17, 1932, Konstanz —

No Issue.

XXI. VON WATZDORFF from page 904

Karl, Baron von Watzdorff and ***Wilhelmine,** Countess von Reichenbach-Lessonitz.

Issue: 1. Wilhelm Emil, Baron von Watzdorff (1842–1915)
m. Laura von Witzleben (1842–1915)
see: *von Watzdorff*, 2, below

2. Konrad, Baron von Watzdorff (1844–1922)
m. Emilie, Countess von Zichy-Ferraris zu Zich und Vásonykeö (1847–1935)
see: *von Watzdorff*, page 904, and 3, below

XXI. von Watzdorff 2, from above

* **Wilhelm Emil,** Baron von Watzdorff, eldest son of Baron Karl.
April 13, 1842, — January 11, 1915, Dresden
m. June 11, 1866, Dresden
Laura von Witzleben, daughter of Jobst Rudolf von Witzleben and of his wife,
August 15, 1842, Dresden — March 13, 1915, Dresden

Issue: 1. Armgard, Baroness von Watzdorff (1867–1945)
m. Georg Ludwig von Dawans (1860–1912)
see: *von Dawans*, page 1052

XXI. von Watzdorff 3, from above and page 904

* **Konrad,** Baron von Watzdorff and * **Emilie,** Countess von Zichy-Ferraris zu Zich und Vásonykeö.

Issue: 1. Ludwig Konrad, Baron von Watzdorff (1871–1952)
m. Theresia, Countess Festetics von Tolna (1877–1940)
see: *von Watzdorff*, 4, page 1080

2. Alfred, Baron von Watzdorff
October 28, 1872, — May 28, 1927, Graz

3. Wilhelmine, Baroness von Watzdorff (1877–1958)
m. Otto, Count Welser von Welserheimb (1871–1945)
see: *Welser von Welserheimb*, page 1080

4. Karl, Baron von Watzdorff
February 16, 1879, Graz — November 19, 1934, Somloszöllös, Hungary

XXI. von Watzdorff

4, from page 1079

* **Ludwig Konrad,** Baron von Watzdorff, eldest son of Baron Konrad.
February 3, 1871, Pressburg — February 5, 1952, Szombathely, Hungary
m. October 30, 1899, Graz
Theresia, Countess Festetics von Tolna, daughter of Count Emmerich Festetics von Tolna and of his wife,
October 5, 1877, Vienna — January 16, 1940,

Issue: 1. Konrad, Baron von Watzdorff
November 1, 1900, Graz — , 1944, Budapest

2. Emanuel, Baron von Watzdorff
March 12, 1904, Graz — July , 1946, Graz

XXI. WEISS

from page 1057

Hanno Weiss
August 1, 1926, Vienna —
m. April 26, 1952, Vienna
* **Isabel von Gans,** daughter of Joszi von Gans and of his second wife, Baroness Melitta von Riedel.
January 10, 1932, Frankfurt-am-Main —

Issue: 1. Carina-Bianca Weiss
January 10, 1956, Vienna —

XXI. WELSER VON WELSERHEIMB

from page 1079

Otto, Count Welser von Welserheimb
December 5, 1871, Berlin — April 23, 1945, Graz
m. May 28, 1901, Graz
* **Wilhelmine,** Baroness von Watzdorff, daughter of Baron Konrad von Watzdorff and of his wife, Countess Emilie von Zichy-Ferraris zu Zich und Vásonykeö.
June 20, 1877, Graz — June 2, 1958, Graz

Issue: 1. Zeno, Count Welser von Welserheimb (1902–)
m. Sophia, Countess Széchényi von Sárvár-Felsövidék (1911–)
see: *Welser von Welserheimb,* page 1081

2. Marie, Countess Welser von Welserheimb (1903–)
m. Johann, Baron Ritter von Záhony (1898–1937)
see: *Ritter von Záhony,* page 1070

XXI. Welser von Welserheimb 1 continued

3. Maria Emma, Countess Welser von Welserheimb (1906–)
m. Béla Szmrecsanyi de Szmrecsan (1904–)
see: *Szmrecsanyi de Szmrecsan*, page 1075

4. Hildegard, Countess Welser von Welserheimb
December 14, 1909, Pola —

5. Leopold, Count Welser von Welserheimb
March 24, 1911, Pola —

XXI. Welser von Welserheimb 2, from page 1080

* **Zeno,** Count Welser von Welserheimb, eldest son of Count Otto.
September 21, 1902, Pola —
m. March 12, 1934, Somogy-Tarnocza, Hungary
Sophia, Countess Széchényi von Sárvár-Felsövidék, daughter of Count Friedrich Széchényi von Sárvár-Felsövidék and of his wife, Baroness Karoline von Schloissnig.
January 9, 1911, Somogy-Tarnocza, Hungary —

Issue: 1. Otto, Count Welser von Welserheimb
June 1, 1935, Kaspovar, Hungary —

2. Carla, Countess Welser von Welserheimb
March 5, 1936, Kaspovar —

3. Leopold, Count Welser von Welserheimb
January 6, 1939, Tab —

4. Josef, Count Welser von Welserheimb
August 15, 1942, Tab —

5. Marie, Countess Welser von Welserheimb
September 22, 1947, Reitenau —

XXI. VON WESTPHALEN zu FÜRSTENBERG from page 1048

Friedrich, Count von Westphalen zu Fürstenberg
February 21, 1872, Laër — May 2, 1932, Berlin
m. July 24, 1901, Tillowitz
* **Luise,** Count von Frankenberg und Ludwigsdorff, daughter of Count Friedrich Ludwig von Frankenberg und Ludwigsdorff and of his wife,
August 23, 1879, Tillowitz — October 13, 1941, Berlin

XXI. Westphalen zu Fürstenberg — 1 continued

Issue: 1. Friedrich Franz, Count von Westphalen zu Fürstenberg (1902–)
m. 1: and divorced: Vera FitzGerald (1905–)
m. 2: Margrit Philippi (1921–)
see: *von Westphalen zu Fürstenberg*, 2, below

2. Margarethe, Countess von Westphalen zu Fürstenberg
October 9, 1913, Potsdam —

XXI. von Westphalen zu Fürstenberg — 2, from above

* **Friedrich Franz,** Count von Westphalen zu Fürstenberg, only son of Count Friedrich.
May 18, 1902, Potsdam —
m. 1: August 21, 1933, London, England. Divorced:
Vera FitzGerald, daughter of
November 21, 1905, Birmingham, England —
m. 2: May 12, 1958, Frankfurt-am-Main
Margrit Philippi, daughter of Richard Philippi and of his wife,
May 25, 1921, Frankfurt-am-Main —

No Issue.

XXI. VON WINTERFELD — from page 1053

Götz von Winterfeld
February 1, 1928, Marburg —
m. April 9, 1960,
* **Christel von Dawans,** daughter of Sigismund-Helmut von Dawans and of his wife, Ilse Schneider.
July 21, 1934, Berlin —

Issue: 1. Claus-Heinrich von Winterfeld
February 23, 1961, Marburg —

2. Christoph von Winterfeld
January 29, 1964, Bremen —

XXI. VON ESMARCH from page 706

Johann Friedrich von Esmarch and * **Henriette,** Princess of Schleswig-Holstein-Sonderburg-Augustenburg.

Issue: 1. A son born and died December 25, 1872, Kiel.

2. Karl Friedrich von Esmarch (1874–1929)
m. Emma Awiszus (1873–1929)
see: *von Esmarch*, 2, below

3. Heinrich von Esmarch
January 20, 1877, Kiel — January 24, 1877, Kiel

XXI. von Esmarch 2, from above

* **Karl-Friedrich von Esmarch (Carlfried),** son of Johann Friedrich.
July 1, 1874, Kiel — January 15, 1929, Boostedt, near Neu-Münster, killed with his wife in an accident
m. September 15, 1898, London, England
Emma Awiszus, daughter of
March 5, 1873, Danzig — January 15, 1929, Boostedt, killed with her husband in an accident

No Issue.

XXI. RAUSCH 1, from page 789

Hans Rausch and * **Anne,** Princess zu Ysenburg and Büdingen in Wächtersbach.

Issue: 1. Helga Rausch (1921–)
m. Heinrich Vogelbacher (1922–)
see: *Vogelbacher*, page 885

2. Annemarie Rausch (1922—)
m. Emil Grigo (1908–)
see: *Grigo*, page 1085

3. Huberta Rausch (1924–)
m. Wilhelm Heiss (1920–)
see: *Heiss*, page 1085

4. Ferdinand Rausch (1927–)
m. Dagmar Leitner (1928–)
see: *Rausch*, 2, page 1084

XXI. Rausch 2, from page 1083

★ **Ferdinand Rausch,** son of Hans.
March 30, 1927, Frankfurt-am-Main —
m. December 29, 1951, Romrod
Dagmar Leitner, daughter of
May 5, 1928, Neu-Danzig —

Issue: 1. Marion Rausch
March 17, 1953, —

2. Regina Rausch
September 4, 1955, —

XXI. RYDON from page 1056

Harold Rydon
November 2, 1890, London —
m. April 16, 1947, Arusha, Tanganyika
★ **Margot von Gans,** daughter of Paul von Gans and of his wife, Baroness Ellinka von Fabrice.
July 11, 1899, Boulogne, France —
(She m. 1: and divorced: Werner, Baron von Bischoffshausen —
see: *von Bischoffshausen*, page 1050.)
(She m. 2: and divorced: Adolkar, Count von Einsiedel —
see: *von Einsiedel*, page 1054.)

No Issue.

XXI. TRUCHSESS VON WETZHAUSEN from page 688

Kurt, Baron Truchsess von Wetzhausen
November 14, 1889, Ansbach — March 18, 1919, Wetzhausen
m. April 7, 1908, Munich —
★ **Isabelle,** Baroness von Dungern, daughter of Baron Hermann von Dungern and of his wife, Baroness Wilhelmine von Dungern.
June 23, 1863, — , 1936, Wetzhausen
(She m. 1: Alfred, Baron Wolffskeel von Reichenberg – see: *Wolffskeel von Reichenberg*, page 1085.)

No Issue.

XXI. WOLFFSKEEL VON REICHENBERG from page 688

Alfred, Baron Wolffskeel von Reichenberg
October 5, 1851, — November 21, 1896, Reichenberg
m. July 15, 1886,
* **Isabelle,** Baroness von Dungern, daughter of Baron Hermann von Dungern and of his wife, Baroness Wilhelmine von Dungern.
June 23, 1863, — , 1936, Wetzhausen
(She m. 2: Kurt, Baron Truchsess von Wetzhausen – see: *Truchsess von Wetzhausen*, p. 1084.)

No Issue.

XXI. HEISS from page 1083

Wilhelm Heiss
February 11, 1920, Salzwedel —
m. December 26, 1950, Romrod
* **Huberta Rausch,** daughter of Hans Rausch and of his wife, Princess Anne zu Ysenburg und Büdingen in Wächtersbach.
May 29, 1924, Frankfurt-am-Main —

No Issue.

XXI. GRIGO from page 1083

Emil Grigo
September 10, 1908, Skoppen, East Prussia —
m. October 10, 1959, Zell
* **Annemaria Rausch,** daughter of Hans Rausch and of his wife, Princess Anne zu Ysenburg und Büdingen in Wächtersbach.
September 2, 1922, Frankfurt-am-Main —

No Issue.

XXI. VON REIBNITZ from page 1042

Kurt, Baron von Reibnitz
November 12, 1877, Kiel — June 26, 1937, Königsberg
m. June 28, 1910, Potsdam. Divorced:
Freda von Schenck, daughter of Dedo von Schenck and of his wife, Helene von Wardenberg.
March 21, 1890, Berlin — March 2, 1946, Berlin-Zehlendorf
(She m. 2: Werner, Count von der Schulenburg – see: *von der Schulenburg*, page 1071.)

No Issue.

XXI. MÖLLER from page 1051

Thorbjörn Möller
October 22, 1897, Mittweida —
m. November 23, 1946,
* **Anna,** Baroness von Blixen-Finecke, daughter of Baron Carl August von Blixen-Finecke and of his wife, Brita Ekström.
July 18, 1918, Copenhagen —

Issue: 1. Agnes Möller
May 8, 1947, Copenhagen —

2. Carl Gustaf Möller
January 29, 1949, Copenhagen —